Social History of Crime, Policing and Punishment

The International Library of Criminology, Criminal Justice and Penology

Series Editors: Gerald Mars and David Nelken

Titles in the Series:

Social History of Crime, Policing and Punishment

Edited by

Robert P. Weiss

State University of New York

Ashgate

DARTMOUTH

Aldershot • Brookfield USA • Singapore • Sydney

Published by
Dartmouth Publishing Company Limited
Ashgate Publishing Limited
Gower House
Croft Road
Aldershot
Hants GU11 3HR
England

Ashgate Publishing Company
Old Post Road
Brookfield
Vermont 05036
USA

British Library Cataloguing in Publication Data
Social history of crime, policing and punishment. – (The
    international library of criminology, criminal justice and
    penology)
    1. Crime – Social aspects – History 2. Police – History
    3. Punishment – Social aspects – History
    I. Weiss, Robert P.
    364'.09

Library of Congress Catalog Card Number: 99-72665

ISBN 1 84014 453 X

Printed in Great Britain by Galliards, Great Yarmouth

for David

Contents

PART III   POLICING AND PROSECUTION

PART IV   SOCIAL HISTORIES OF PUNISHMENT

Acknowledgements

The editor and publishers wish to thank the following for permission to use copyright material.

American Sociological Association for the essay: E.M. Beck and Stewart E. Tolnay (1990), 'The Killing Fields of The Deep South: The Market for Cotton and the Lynching of Blacks, 1882–1930', *American Sociological Review*, **55**, pp. 526–39.

Cambridge University Press for the essays: Anton Blok (1972), 'The Peasant and the Brigand: Social Banditry Reconsidered', *Comparative Studies in Society and History*, **14**, pp. 494–503; Eric Hobsbawm (1972), 'Social Bandits: Reply', *Comparative Studies in Society and History*, **14**, pp. 503–505; Steven Hahn (1982), 'Hunting, Fishing, and Foraging: Common Rights and Class Relations in the Postbellum South', *Radical History Review*, **26**, pp. 37–64. Copyright © 1982 MARHO. Reproduced by permission from Cambridge University Press; Robert P. Weiss (1986), 'Private Detective Agencies and Labour Discipline in the United States, 1855–1946', *Historical Journal*, **29**, pp. 87–107; Linda Chisholm (1986), 'The Pedagogy of Porter: The Origins of the Reformatory in the Cape Colony, 1882–1910', *Journal of African History*, **27**, pp. 481–95.

Carnegie–Mellon University Press for the essays: William A. Muraskin (1976), 'The Social-Control Theory in American History: A Critique', *Journal of Social History*, **11**, pp. 559–69; J.M. Beattie (1975), 'The Criminality of Women in Eighteenth-Century England', *Journal of Social History*, **8**, pp. 80–116; Wilbur R. Miller (1975), 'Police Authority in London and New York City 1830–1870', *Journal of Social History*, **8**, pp. 81–101; Patricia O'Brien (1978), 'Crime and Punishment as Historical Problem', *Journal of Social History*, **11**, pp. 508–20. Copyright © 1978 Peter N. Stern; John A. Conley (1981), 'Prisons, Production, and Profit: Reconsidering the Importance of Prison Industries', *Journal of Social History*, **14**, pp. 257–75; Gilles Vandal (1997), 'Property Offenses, Social Tension and Racial Antagonism in Post-Civil War Rural Louisiana', *Journal of Social History*, Fall, pp. 127–53; Gerda W. Ray (1995), 'From Cossack to Trooper: Manliness, Police Reform, and the State', *Journal of Social History*, **28**, pp. 565–86.

Global Options for the essays: Peter Linebaugh (1976), 'Karl Marx, the Theft of Wood and Working Class Composition: A Contribution to the Current Debate', *Crime and Social Justice*, **6**, pp. 5–16; Adrian Howe (1990), 'Prologue to a History of Women's Imprisonment: In Search of a Feminist Perspective', *Social Justice*, **17**, pp. 5–22.

The Journal of Interdisciplinary History for the essay: Ricardo D. Salvatore (1992), 'Criminology, Prison Reform, and the Buenos Aires Working Class', *Journal of Interdisciplinary History*, **XXIII**, pp. 279–99, with permission of the editors of the *Journal of Interdisciplinary History* and the MIT Press, Cambridge, Massachusetts. Copyright © 1993 by the Massachusetts Institute of Technology and the editors of the *Journal of Interdisciplinary History*.

Series Preface

The International Library of Criminology, Criminal Justice and Penology, represents an important publishing initiative to bring together the most significant journal essays in contemporary criminology, criminal justice and penology. The series makes available to researchers, teachers and students an extensive range of essays which are indispensable for obtaining an overview of the latest theories and findings in this fast changing subject.

This series consists of volumes dealing with criminological schools and theories as well as with approaches to particular areas of crime, criminal justice and penology. Each volume is edited by a recognised authority who has selected twenty or so of the best journal articles in the field of their special competence and provided an informative introduction giving a summary of the field and the relevance of the articles chosen. The original pagination is retained for ease of reference.

The difficulties of keeping on top of the steadily growing literature in criminology are complicated by the many disciplines from which its theories and findings are drawn (sociology, law, sociology of law, psychology, psychiatry, philosophy and economics are the most obvious). The development of new specialisms with their own journals (policing, victimology, mediation) as well as the debates between rival schools of thought (feminist criminology, left realism, critical criminology, abolitionism etc.) make necessary overviews that offer syntheses of the state of the art. These problems are addressed by the INTERNATIONAL LIBRARY in making available for research and teaching the key essays from specialist journals.

GERALD MARS
Professor in Applied Anthropology, University of Bradford
School of Management

DAVID NELKEN
Distinguished Research Professor, Cardiff Law Schoool,
University of Wales, Cardiff

Introduction

What is Criminal Justice Social History?

In the introductory essay to his reader, *Rethinking Social History*, Adrian Wilson (1993:9) defines the diverse genre of 'social history' as having three central characteristics, which I paraphrase here. First, social history focuses on the 'history of the people', defined in the largest body of research as the lives and struggles of industrial workers, peasants, the urban poor and women. Second, its methodology employs social scientific concepts to examine social statistics, legal texts and other governmental records. Thus, the epistemology of social history has been within the positivist and empiricist traditions. More recently, greater emphasis has been given to consciousness and symbolic meaning, and cultural documents are sought that might help reveal subjective states of 'subaltern' actors, such as letters, diaries, songs and verse.[1] Third, social historians have the objective of constructing an interdisciplinary or 'total history' that incorporates all the pertinent social sciences. Social historical analyses have emphasized process more than structure, social change over equilibrium, and social conflict and class struggle over consensus.

The roots of social history extend back to the mid-nineteenth century English historiography, when pioneers, such as Arnold Toynbee, challenged the mainstream 'state historiography' of politics and elites with histories of the people. There are also individual works of great merit that date from the first third of the twentieth century. But *criminal justice* social history as a distinct subfield dates from the 'new social history' movement that emerged from the intellectual, political and social turmoil of the 1960s. British Marxist E.P. Thompson's *Whigs and Hunters* (1975), which argued that the death penalty statutes of the Black Act of 1723 served to consolidate property interests in the early formation of capitalism, helped launch social history deep into the territory of crime and the criminal law. Contemporary social developments helped generate widespread interest in critical legal studies, although criminal justice was being put to quite another purpose in late capitalism – chiefly, to mop up the social detritus of 'post-industrial' capitalism. Beginning in the mid-1970s, conservative politicians attacked the welfare state, intensified the war on drugs, passed harsher criminal sentencing legislation, and the courts gave police greater discretion. Imprisonment rates consequently skyrocketed. In this hothouse, revisionist interpretations of the origin and development of the police, prisons, courts, parole and probation flourished. Interpreted generally as instruments of ruling class domination, different versions of this new social history mainstream were more or less economistic and functionalist, while others gave greater autonomy to race and gender as causal factors in social domination. But the partisan state was universal in the literature.

This volume samples some of the best monographs in this literature, grouping contributions chronologically into essays that best illustrate:

1. the early theoretical debates, particularly over the political meaning of criminal action;
2. examples of crime as resistance, protest, and survival;

3. new forms of policing the class structure; and
4. the role of punishment in labour discipline and 'social control' in general.

With the waning in recent decades of Marxist-inspired research, criminal justice history is taking a 'linguistic turn' (see Adrian Howe, Chapter 25). Postmodernists reject macro-sociological or 'global' (Carlen, 1994:134) and 'totalizing' histories, and its most radical adherents deny objective reality and material causality – more or less the heart, if not the soul, of past social history. Yet, in this void, postmodernists have failed to provide a clear or coherent research alternative for the study of criminal justice.

The Early Debates

Revisionist history took as one of its first targets the 'asylum' movement of the American Revolutionary and Jacksonian periods, inverting the humanitarian reform interpretation of the origin of penitentiaries, mental hospitals, poorhouses and orphanages and other 'welfare' institutions. William A. Muraskin's 1976 review essay for the *Journal of Social History*, reproduced as Chapter 1 of this volume, compares and contrasts two important early works in this literature: David Rothman's 1971 *Discovery of the Asylum*, a 'traditional revisionist history' and Anthony Platt's *The Child Savers: The Invention of Delinquency* (1969), a study employing the 'social control' hypothesis. Muraskin's critique of these two seminal works reveals many of the strengths and weaknesses of the early social control perspective. Where Rothman assumed social consensus and saw humanitarian ideas creating the 'well-ordered asylum', social control theorists posited conscious class interest in controlling subordinate groups as the motive force in institutional development. Using labelling theory, Platt refocuses historical inquiry from delinquent behaviours to the motives of law-makers and 'reformers'. The 'real' interests behind the creation of delinquency – revealed through an analysis of the class backgrounds of various reformers – were not humanitarian but those of class control, an explanation that Muraskin finds 'simplistic, moralistic, and reductionist'. Other critiques (Donajgrodski, 1977; Jones, 1983; Mayer, 1985) challenged the social control perspective for its lack of conceptual rigour and clarity. But the concept is tenacious and, in one form or another, the sociology of crime, law, deviance and punishment still makes extensive use of it (see Melossi, 1990; Platt, 1994; Ulmer, 1998).

Eric Hobsbawm (1959; 1969) was a pioneer of the 'new' social historical interpretation of crime as social protest and resistance to the new social relations of capitalism. In *Primitive Rebels* (1959) and *Bandits* (1969), he claimed that banditry is a universal form of peasant protest. Appearing throughout the world relatively unchanged over four centuries, banditry reached its peak during the advent of capitalism, when peasants and landless labourers were displaced by the new market economy. Fellow peasants view bandits in their communities not as simple criminals but as 'noble robbers', 'primitive resistance fighters' and 'terror-bringing avengers'. While banditry represented a form of social protest against oppression, bandits are only primitive liberation fighters insofar as they lacked political organizational capacity, a coherent alternative political ideology and a revolutionary strategy. Hence, according to Hobsbawm, bandits are 'prepolitical' phenomena, they are reformist rather than revolutionary and are replaced in time with more sophisticated forms of social protest, including various rural secret societies, millenarian peasant movements, pre-industrial urban mobs, labour sects, and early revolutionary labour organizations.

Hobsbawm's work soon drew criticism from Anton Blok. In his 1972 critique (Chapter 2), Blok maintains that Hobsbawm exaggerates the degree of class conflict. 'Rather than actual champions of the poor and the weak', Blok argues, 'bandits quite often terrorized those from whose very ranks they managed to rise, and thus helped to suppress them' (p.17). This is not simply an empirical dispute. Logically, bandits who expect to last a long time must have connections with established power-holders who protect them and for whom, as the *quid pro quo*, bandits act as retainers. In this way, bandits obstruct national peasant mobilization directly by intimidation and indirectly by providing channels for upward mobility. Similarly to *mafia*-like gangs, they undermine class solidarity. Banditry appeared in societies with weak central state apparatuses, Blok observes, where protection from more powerful persons or groups necessarily gave bandits respect as protectors, and through whom peasants could experience power vicariously. Blok argues that this charisma contributed to the *myth* of banditry – what peasants *wished* they were about – rather than its *reality*.[2] Hobsbawm, in his reply to Blok in Chapter 3 of this volume, observes that he and Blok differ more on interpretation than facts, and that the myth and reality of banditry cannot be easily disentangled.

A particularly seminal year in social history scholarship was 1975, and one of its most iconoclastic and influential endeavours was the volume edited by Douglas Hay et al. (1975), *Albion's Fatal Tree: Crime and Society in Eighteenth-Century England*. While Hobsbawm's bandits might have been antisocial, eighteenth-century English smugglers, poachers, wreckers and coastal plunderers appeared to constitute collective resistance to the state's redefinition of 'use-rights in common or woods, perquisites in industry, as thefts or offenses' (1975:13). Smuggling and wrecking, in particular, tended toward crowd activities, which sometimes involved entire villages. Villagers did not regard these 'social crimes' as genuinely criminal because, in pre-capitalist times, they were a legitimate part of local economies. The rural poor – principally labourers, farmers and miners – supplemented their meagre incomes with poached game, wood, fruit and the contents of wrecked ships. With the development of commercial capitalism, however, access to such goods as a customary 'use-right' came to be redefined, by the state, as theft. *Albion's Fatal Tree*, like Karl Marx's study of laws prohibiting firewood-gathering in the forests of the Rhineland (Marx, 1842; see also Linebaugh in Chapter 6 and Ditton in Chapter 7 of this volume), help document the way in which criminal law acted as a principal instrument in the creation of private property by redefining the exercise of common rights as crimes. *Albion's Fatal Tree* helped debunk the prevailing interpretation of eighteenth-century England as a stable and consensual society. Combining labelling theory with revisionist history, the volume became popular reading among radical criminologists as well as historians, helping widen one of the most fruitful avenues of criminological research – labour discipline. Labour historians have a long and rich historical account of private and state police intervention in strikes, walkouts and shop-floor sabotage, but social historians pushed research beyond the struggles of the industrial proletariat to include, as class struggle, theft and even idleness by the rural poor.[3]

John H. Langbein's 1983 *Past and Present* critique (Chapter 4), 'Albion's Fatal Flaws', attacks the main thesis of Douglas Hay's 'Property, Authority and the Criminal Law', the lead essay in *Albion's Fatal Tree*. Hay's chapter attempts to account for the well known criminal justice paradox that, while the number of capital offences increased dramatically during the eighteenth century, the actual number of executions declined. Hay's explanation was that acts of discretion showed the law in both its functions, as coercion and as benevolence. Law can only serve as ruling class ideology if it possesses at least partial autonomy. Langbein counter-argues that criminal law and procedure genuinely served the interests of the common people and seeks to demonstrate this through a review of the historical sources, an examination of offences and offenders (which he found quite conventional), prosecution (records which reveal the poverty of typical offenders and victims) and prosecutorial and judicial discretion (the extent of which Hay exaggerated). What little discretion that was exercised in eighteenth-century criminal justice was good-faith and non-conspiratorial. Langbein asserts that, in any case, the criminal justice system was no more central to the ruling order than was the garbage collection system.

Appearing in a journal noted for its own revisionist historiography, Langbein's sardonic polemic suggests how divisive was the issue regarding the political significance of law and the role of criminals in class rule. Many Marxists and other left-wing thinkers expressed doubts as well (Hirst, 1972; Mugford, 1974; Ignatieff, 1981; Philips, 1983), usually dismissing criminals as *lumpenproletariat* with great reactionary potential. A defence from one of the *Albion* contributors came quickly, and a well researched and detailed rebuttal is presented by Peter Linebaugh in Chapter 5. His *New York University Law Review* essay contrasts, in his words, 'a legal view of social relations with a social view of legal issues'. Linebaugh argues that Langbein's attack misinterprets Hay's essay by substituting Hay's class analysis with an elite, ahistorical interpretation hopelessly wedded to functionalism. Linebaugh rebuts, in turn, each point in Langbein's critique: from the death penalty paradox through an empirical and conceptual analysis of offences, offenders, prosecutions, juries and the sources of law. He concludes by reaffirming the centrality of criminal law in governing eighteenth-century England – that it indeed had an importance much like that of trash collection. Both were central concerns to authorities. More accurately, criminal justice functioned like the flush toilet, to change Langbein's analogy to a metaphor and turn the notion on its head.

Social Histories of Crime

In an earlier essay (Chapter 6), Peter Linebaugh develops the discussion which Marx presented in the *Rheinische Zeitung* regarding the debates over the law on theft of wood passed by the Prussian government in 1843. Linebaugh concluded that this petty theft was not merely *lumpen* pathology, nor original accumulation, but *resistance* to the wage relation by 'direct appropriation of wealth'.

Linebaugh's 1976 theft of wood essay appeared in *Crime and Social Justice*, **6**,[4] and it quickly became an important stimulus to the 'new' criminology's demystification of legal history. Jason Ditton's essay (Chapter 7) develops the argument that legal rights protected private property as 'capital' by criminalizing customary rights. But acts of resistance are not always what they seem. As Ditton's analysis of the wage-theft structure argues, pilferage and other wage-thefts might actually increase the power of *employers*. When used as 'controlled larceny', such 'invisible wages' can become a crucial form of domination – a means of discipline that is cheaper than paying higher wages and that also maintains the pecuniary desire of workers. But, criminal behaviour as protest and insurgency is the *leitmotif* of the studies by Hahn, Smith, and Vandal in Part II of this volume. They provide compelling examples of the effect of class power on changing definitions of crime in the US South after the Civil War. Their analyses also suggest the material significance of this crime, its cultural meanings and political potentialities.

Steven Hahn's essay, 'Hunting, Fishing, and Foraging: Common Rights and Class Relations in the Postbellum South' (Chapter 8), appeared in a special issue of the *Radical History Review* devoted to power, property, and crime[5] and is an important contribution to the study of the criminalization of customary rights in southern US history. The postbellum planters and various entrepreneurs had great difficulty creating a reliable wage labour force among freedmen. Many blacks even shunned the 'ownership' variants of plantation work, sharecropping and tenant farming. Those who tried to cobble together an economic life outside of wage labour and debt peonage by hunting, fishing, subsistence farming and petty theft instead faced the prospect of imprisonment terms for violating the Black Codes, vagrancy statutes and trespassing laws which were enforced with most vigour during the harvest seasons. Alternatively, they could be sent to the penitentiary for game and livestock theft. Freedmen's resistance to the imposition of capitalist labour relations struck at the heart of property rights, according to Hahn. As we will see in Part IV of this volume, the period of southern history from Reconstruction through Jim Crow presents many salient and poignant examples of criminal justice marshalled in the service of labour market discipline and backed by the threat of penal slavery.

While the chapters in Part II of this volume by Linebaugh, Ditton, and Hahn address theft as resistance and survival, Albert C. Smith's classic essay (Chapter 9) 'reveals the relationships among race, class, and violent property crime' (p. 166) in the New South. The seasonal pattern of arson, the kinds of property destroyed and the race of suspects and victims in two postbellum Black Belt Georgia counties suggest arson as violent interracial protest: '... arson generally constituted a means by which the poor and the propertyless could strike out against those who dominated a racist and economically exploitive society' Smith argues (p. 192). In Chapter 10, 'Property Offenses, Social Tension and Racial Antagonism in Post-Civil War Rural Louisiana', Gilles Vandal argues that petty theft, grand larceny, burglary and robbery in postbellum rural Louisiana represented 'an alternative mode of industry' (p. 216). Frequently committing crimes in outlaw bands, robbers created a climate of fear in rural Louisiana. Coupled with inefficient and corrupt legal authorities, vigilance committees proliferated as supplements to legally sworn authorities, and often lynched with the latter's compliance. We learn more about vigilantism in Chapter 24, where Beck and Tolnay discuss lynching frequency and cotton price fluctuation.

Part II concludes with two chapters on the history of criminality and punishment of women – subjects still not well developed today. Not surprisingly, debate surrounds the very significance of women in criminal justice. J.M. Beattie (Chapter 11) and Malcolm M. Feeley and Deborah L. Little (Chapter 12) present opposing views on the question of how central women were to crime, and thus of what significance they would be to criminal justice social history. Beattie's study of eighteenth-century female crime found that women committed fewer crimes of property or violence and attributed this to socialization and their 'relationship to the wider community'. Paternalistic controls gave rural women greater economic security, albeit at an obvious cost. Urban women, by contrast, were more criminal than their rural counterparts, with patterns and levels of crime similar to men. Feeley and Little found a *high* rate of felony indictments of women in much of the eighteenth century, followed by a sharp decline of women's criminal cases in English and some American courts through the following century.

This decline coincides with the shift in women's economic roles during industrialism and the rise of informal and more private forms of social control of women, including Victorian ideology and sexual controls. As their economic position changed during industrialization, labour market factors explain *fewer* features of women's reality. Broadening the concept of social control beyond formal criminal justice also better accommodates gender, ethnicity and race in understanding deviance and its control. Class struggle, however, is still a fruitful research direction. Resistance to wage production and capital's battle for factory discipline were prominent subjects for research on the history of punishment (see Part IV of this volume).

Policing and Prosecution

Providing another angle with which to view the relation between law and society, Michael Hindus in Chapter 13 compares the pattern of prosecutions from 1767 to 1878 in two societies of enormous contrast: South Carolina, which was aristocratic, predominantly black and slave, and Massachusetts, a democratic, heterogeneous and industrializing society. While Massachusetts developed formal legal authority, with a predictable and rational legal system that supported the capitalist economy, the slaveholding aristocracy of South Carolina relied on 'a host of informal and extralegal arrangements' (p. 334). One of the most influential studies in comparative institutional development was Wilbur R. Miller's groundbreaking comparison of police authority in London and New York (Chapter 14). Police in both cities were charged with combating strikes, riots, and daily breaches of the 'public order', especially prostitution, gambling, and alcohol abuse. The contrast rests with the approach: whereas the English Bobby's authority was impersonal and subject to bureaucratic restrictions on discretionary power, the New York cops possessed personal authority based on unregulated discretion.

While, by the mid-nineteenth century, the metropolitan police were busy trying to maintain social discipline necessary for capitalist development, private policing agencies (deputized or with *de facto* state power) in the United States were involved in labour discipline at the factory gate and shop floor. Chapter 15 on the Pinkerton's private detective agency recounts the for-hire provision of armed guards, labour spies, *agents provocateurs* and strikebreakers recruited from the surplus population. When private detectives proved insufficient to break strikes and enforce lockouts, or when their very participation precipitated greater conflict, the National Guard and state militias were called on to restore order. Pennsylvania tried to remedy the evils of 'Pinkertonism' by issuing police commissions to the Coal and Iron Police, but when this strategy failed to quell violence, the Pennsylvania Legislature responded with the creation of the first State Police in 1905. The 'age of industrial violence', as the first two decades of the twentieth century in the USA was called, led other industrial states to create state police agencies of their own. In Chapter 16, Gerda Ray focuses on the efforts at legitimizing New York's State Police. Created in 1917, the new police faced formidable opposition by trade unions as strikebreaking 'Cossacks'. Proponents attempted to legitimate the new police by invoking 'elite definitions of masculine authority', Ray (p. 380) argues, in an extension of theorizing on gender, class and state.

Social Histories of Punishment

The problem of voluntarism and determinism in the early debates on the meaning of crime besets penal analysis too. The Rusche and Kirchheimer (1968) thesis and other materialist accounts have been criticized as favouring the functional prerequisites of the capitalist system over the complexity of politics and ideology. In a strategy to avoid the twin traps of instrumentalism and economism, Michel Foucault's (1979) analysis goes beyond class exploitation and broadens the concept of power. But critics such as Patricia O'Brien argue that Foucault replaces economic determinism with a 'new functionalism': Foucault's theory is not 'fully social' and fails to adequately explain structural transformation. In Chapter 17 O'Brien proposes family, ideology, and a broader conception of class as institutions that mediate between criminal justice and larger social phenomena. Theoretical hybrids combining insights from Foucault and Rusche and Kirchheimer guided analyses for several new social history research directions beyond eighteenth-century England. In Continental Europe, there is O'Brien's (1982) own study of nineteenth-century France; Pieter Spierenburg's (1987) comparative study of Amsterdam and the Auburn system, and Ruth Pike's (1983) study of Spain. In the USA, studies of the northern penitentiary and southern convict lease (Chapters 22 and 23) made use of theoretical integrations combining Foucault's 'technology of power' and labour market structures.

Many social histories of penal confinement and other disciplinary projects in Third World nations employ Rusche and Kirchheimer's labour exploitation thesis; others try to modify it by incorporating surplus populations and 'problem populations' (Spitzer, 1975). In Chapter 18, Linda Chishom's 'The Pedagogy of Porter' analyses the origin of the South African reformatory. Coinciding with the emergence of industrial capitalism in the last quarter of the nineteenth century, the Porter Reformatory trained and disciplined a juvenile convict labour force for merchant capital and commercial agriculture. In Chapter 19 Ricardo D. Salvatore analyses the effect of the great influx of European immigrants at the turn of the twentieth century on Argentine prison reform, and recounts efforts to turn the penitentiary into an instrument of their social control and labour discipline. During the nineteenth century, Latin American prisons aimed to control the growing urban surplus population swelling with outcasts from break-up of the *haciendas*. Combining Spitzer's 'problem populations' hypotheses with Joseph Gusfield's concept of 'moral passage', Martha Huggins (Chapter 20) examines the social control of the nineteenth-century Pernambuco poor in their transition from slavery to free labour. But these studies are just a beginning. Much more research on Third World nations is needed, as well as accounts of the role of criminal justice in their socially painful and politically tumultuous transformations to 'free market' development.

In Chapter 21 John A. Conley examines Oklahoma's adoption of the Auburn model of prison factory production in 1909, two years after achieving statehood. Although initially enjoying strong political and economic backing for a penal regime centred on production and profit, support vanished once its industries became competitive with private interests. By the time of the Great Depression, the 'contract system' had expired everywhere but in the southern border states. The northern USA and some European prisons continued to model their regimes on the factory, but as a deterrent and a discipline and thus an augmentation of 'market coercion'. The penal system in the postbellum South, by contrast, resembled the plantation and complemented that region's overtly coercive labour system.

The dramatic transformation of southern criminal justice after the Civil War would seem to be well explained by the Rusche and Kirchheimer thesis, with penal servitude filling gaps in the new labour market. The Civil War also appears to provide researchers with clear and abrupt lines of social structural demarcation: facing unprecedented black criminality, empty treasuries, and without prison structures, penal objectives for postbellum state administrators were unabashedly fiscal and economic. Fearful of the sudden black mobility, and suffering a chronic labour shortage not ameliorated by European immigration, freedmen were viewed by the state authorities as both a threat and a resource, according to Christopher Adamson in Chapter 22. 'Economic modernization of the South depended on the mobilization of cheap convict labor', Adamson (p. 500) asserts. Marxists might ask, however, since when did capitalism *require* forced labour? This line of argument raises the larger question, how *new* was the New South? Did bourgeois mercantile and industrial capitalism sprout quickly and certainly from the ashes of slavery, as the earlier critical historians such as C. Vann Woodward (1951) claimed in *Origins of the New South*? Or, as the 1970s revisionists led by Jonathan Wiener (1978; 1979) and Gavin Wright (1986) argue, was the postbellum South an economically stagnant, technologically backward legacy of slavery? In this interpretation, the penal system was merely an extension of the slave system and an integral part of the South's larger system of juridico-legal coercion of direct producers, articulating with bonded labour of debt peonage and sharecropping. The functional importance of criminal justice, and the effects of the convict lease on wages and markets, is at the centre of the 'continuity' debate.[6]

In Chapter 23 Martha Myers and James Massey's examination of postbellum punishment in Georgia supports the labour exploitation thesis and the argument for discontinuity. The 'demand for free labor and the demand for convict labor do not necessarily stand in opposition to one another', they conclude (p. 524). Jim Crow and convict leasing served both industrial and agricultural capital; they did so not as containment of surplus labourers, but directly in the accumulation of capital by reinforcing free labour. Another Rusche and Kirchheimer hypothesis predicts that, in periods of labour scarcity, corporal and capital punishment will decline as a waste of resources. This might be true with state punishment, but much of southern justice was informal and extralegal. E.M. Beck and Stewart Tolnay's study of lynching in the Deep South from 1882 to 1930 (Chapter 24) reveals its relationship to cotton market fluctuation. Black lynchings increased with economic distress, as white labourers were threatened by cheap black competition. This is congruent with the Adamson thesis concerning threats and resources, and bears on the objection of 'popular justice' arguments that vigilantism was a substitute for the rule of law. During economic crises, Beck and Tolnay argue, the interests of the southern ruling class and white labourers converged in racial violence, as authorities looked the other way during mob violence.[7]

This volume concludes with an essay by Adrian Howe (Chapter 25) who searches for a social history of imprisonment in Australia that is both feminist and socialist. Her survey of works from various revisionist perspectives finds many shortcomings. Among the more promising concepts with which to build a non-patriarchal perspective is Foucault's 'carceral network', involving a diffusion of 'disciplinary power' throughout society. An 'autonomous' social history of women's penality is part of a new frontier for criminal justice social history, the successful exploration of which will require new navigational aids, if not a total reorientation.

New Directions?

The main currents of social history have been channelled by conflicting interpretations of Marx (Gouldner, 1973:427), based on the so-called 'early' and 'late' Marx.[8] Young Marx, the humanist, is a hermeneutist, searching for acts of a class-conscious volition and instrumental manipulations of the state. Marx the scientist, on the other hand, directs attention to political, ideological, and economic structures of 'relative autonomy', with the state reproducing the capitalist class 'as a whole' and then only 'in the last instance' (Poulantzas, 1973). Thus far, social historians have failed to devise a dialectical reconciliation of these contrasting images of society and the nature of human action. 'Critical', 'materialist' and 'structuralist' versions of criminal justice social history have all fallen short of an adequate social history, especially for women.[9] But will postmodernism be the answer? It is fitting that we end with a quote from someone who was at the centre of the earliest theoretical controversies – Eric Hobsbawm. He warns of the profound relativism and particularity of 'identity history', which threatens more than history as an academic enterprise. 'A history which is designed *only* for Jews (or African Americans, or Greeks, or women, or proletarians, or homosexuals) cannot be good history, though it may be comforting history to those who practice it' (Hobsbawm, 1997:277). Given the global situation today, Hobsbawm concludes, this is not only bad history, 'it is dangerous history'.

Whatever its future prospects, social history has been one of the most fruitful theoretical and methodological approaches to the study of crime and its control.

Notes

1   V.A.C. Gatrell's *The Hanging Tree: Execution and The English People 1770–1868* (1994) is a history of people from 'below' the scaffold, so to speak. Gatrell reconstructs the perceptions and emotional experience of hanging, from the executioner to the crowds who watched. On a study of the perceptions and values of the governing elite, see Wiener (1990).

2   The Blok–Hobsbawm exchange sparked a long controversy (see *Latin American Research Review*, **25**, 1990 and **26**, 1991 and especially Joseph, 1990) over whether common crimes, most frequently committed against those of the same class stratum, are reactionary or progressive in their implications. This debate gained more than academic significance with the rise in crime and widespread civil protest of the 1960s and 1970s and the 'political prisoner' movement. Ordinary crime (or 'street crime'), including robbery and even rape, was romanticized by some of the New Left intellectuals and radical criminologists as having political meaning or significance. This interpretation certainly informed the political prisoner movement in the USA. Common street crimes were associated with civil disobedience, rioting, and acts of governmental sabotage as 'political crimes' but categorized as 'ordinary' by power-holders. For social science, conceptual clarity was clearly called for. Steven Spitzer (1975) introduced a typology of 'problem populations' that distinguished 'social junk' from 'social dynamite'. A few years later, criminologist Richard Quinney (1980:65) initiated a comprehensive radical theory of criminal causation in which he proposed a typology to help explain crimes committed by persons occupying different levels of the social structure, and differentiating reactionary from progressive criminal action. Generated by class struggle in the development of capitalism, crimes were grouped as to whether they were committed by corporations and state officials in the course of 'domination' and 'repression', or whether they were committed as acts of 'accommodation' or 'resistance' to the conditions of capitalism.

3   As Foucault observed in *Madness and Civilization* (1971: 56–7): '... idleness is rebellion – the

worst of them all, in a sense: it waits for nature to be generous as in the innocence of Eden ...' For research into the development of vagrancy laws, see Chambliss (1964) and Oshinsky (1996).

4   *Crime and Social Justice* is now *Social Justice: A Journal of Crime, Conflict and World Order*. Issue no. 6 was the first to be published after its merger with *Issues in Criminology* (Fall–Winter 1976), the latter having lost its institutional base in the politically motivated closing of Berkeley's School of Criminology during the Ronald Reagan governorship.

5   Begun in 1973 as a *Newsletter* of the Mid-Atlantic Radical Historians' Organization (MARHO), and housed at the History Department at John Jay College of New York, *Radical History Review* provided an early alternative to the mainstream journals *American Historical Review* and *American Journal of History*, as well to orthodox Marxist journals favouring structuralism.

6   Edward L. Ayers (1984) resolves this controversy through a compromise in which convict leasing represents change and continuity, serving as a bridge or link from slavery to capitalist relations. Alex Lichtenstein (1996) also rejects the argument that forced labour and capitalism were incompatible.

7   If the law were so easily manipulated and transparently racist, Christopher Waldrep (1998: 1–3) objects, why was extralegal punishment usually a first resort? Waldrep argues that partial autonomy interpretations of the law such as Douglas Hay's underestimate the attitudes of ordinary people who, in the South, did not trust law to control African Americans. Tolnay and Beck (1994) argue that popular justice and conflict theories are contrary explanations of the lynching–execution relationship. In their conflict theory, lynchings supplemented executions; they were not an alternative, as popular justice advocates maintain.

8   See the E.P. Thompson (1978)–Perry Anderson (1980) debates within the larger domain of social history.

9   Anthony Platt (1994), another early theoretical combatant, proffers a compromise of integration and linkages – a synthesis of the old and the new. Some of poststructuralism's integrative potential is exemplified in Michael Dutton's *Policing and Punishment in China* (1993).

References

Anderson, Perry (1980), *Arguments Within English Marxism*, London: New Left Books.

Ayers, Edward L. (1984), *Vengeance and Justice: Crime and Punishment in the Nineteenth Century American South*, New York: Oxford.

Carlen, Pat (1994), 'Gender, Class, Racism, and Criminal Justice: Against Global and Gender-Centric Theories, For Poststructuralist Perspectives', in George S. Bridges and Martha A. Myers (eds), *Inequality, Crime, and Social Control*, Boulder, Col.: Westview Press, pp. 134–75.

Chambliss, William (1964), 'A Sociological Analysis of the Law of Vagrancy', *Social Problems*, **XII**, pp. 67–77.

Donajgrodski, A.P. (ed.) (1977), *Introduction to Social Control in Nineteenth Century Britain*, Totowa, NJ: Rowman and Littlefield.

Dutton, Michael (1992), *Policing and Punishment in China – From Patriarchy to 'The People'*, Melbourne: Cambridge University Press.

Foucault, Michel (1971), *Madness and Civilization*, New York: Vintage.

Foucault, Michel (1979), *Discipline and Punish: The Birth of the Prison*, New York: Pantheon.

Gatrell, V.A.C. (1994), *The Hanging Tree: Execution and The English People 1770–1868*, Oxford: Oxford University Press.

Gouldner, Alvin W. (1973), *For Sociology*, New York: Basic Books.

Hay, Douglas, Linebaugh, Peter, Rule, John G., Thompson, E.P. and Winslow, Cal (1975), *Albion's Fatal Tree: Crime and Society in Eighteenth-Century England*, New York: Pantheon Books.

Hindus, Michael (1980), *Prison and Plantation: Crime, Justice, and Authority in Massachusetts and South Carolina, 1867–1878*, Chapel Hill: University of North Carolina Press.

Hirst, Paul Q. (1972), 'Marx and Engels on Crime, Law and Morality', *Economy and Society*, **1** (1), February, pp. 28–56.

Hobsbawm, Eric (1959), *Primitive Rebels*, New York: W.W. Norton.

Hobsbawm, Eric (1969), *Bandits*, New York: Delacorte.

Hobsbawm, Eric (1997), *On History*, New York: The New Press.

Ignatieff, Michael (1981), 'State, Civil Society and Total Institutions: A Critique of Recent Social Histories of Punishment', in M. Tonry and N. Morris (eds), *Crime and Justice: An Annual Review of Research*, vol. 3, Chicago: University of Chicago Press, pp. 153–91.

Jones, Gareth Steadman (1983), 'Class Expression Versus Social Control? A Critique of Recent Trends in the Social History of "Leisure"', in S. Cohen and A. Scull (eds), *Social Control and the State*, Oxford: Basil Blackwell.

Joseph, Gilbert M. (1990), 'On the Trail of Latin American Bandits', *Latin American Research Review*, **25** (3), pp. 7–53.

Lichtenstein, Alex (1996), *Twice the Work of Free Labor: The Political Economy of Convict Labor in the New South*, New York: Verso.

Linebaugh, Peter (1992), *The London Hanged: Crime and Civil Society in the Eighteenth Century*, Cambridge: Cambridge University Press.

Marx, Karl (1842), 'Proceedings of the Sixth Rhine Province Assembly. Third Article. Debates on the Law of the Theft of Wood', in Karl Marx and Frederick Engels, *Collected Works*, vol. 1, New York: International Publishers, 1975.

Mayer, John A. (1985), 'Notes Towards a Working Definition of Social Control in Historical Analysis', in S. Cohen and A. Scull (eds), *Social Control and the State*, Oxford: Basil Blackwell.

Melossi, Dario (1990), *The State of Social Control*, New York: St Martins Press.

Mugford, Stephen K. (1974), 'Marxism and Criminology: A Comment on the Symposium Review on "the New Criminology"', *The Sociological Quarterly*, **15**, Autumn, pp. 591–6.

Myers, Martha (1998), *Race, Labor, and Punishment in the New South*, Columbus: Ohio State University Press.

O'Brien, Patricia (1982), *The Promise of Punishment: Prisons in Nineteenth Century France*, Princeton, NJ: Princeton University Press.

Oshinsky, David M. (1996), *'Worse Than Slavery': Parchman Farm and the Ordeal of Jim Crow Justice*, New York: The Free Press.

Philips, David (1983), 'A Just Measure of Crime, Authority, Hunters and Blue Locusts: The 'Revisionist' Social History of Crime and the Law in Britain, 1780–1850', in S. Cohen and A. Scull (eds), *Social Control and the State*, Oxford: Basil Blackwell, pp. 5–74.

Pike, Ruth (1983), *Penal Servitude in Early Modern Spain*, Madison, Wis.: University of Wisconsin Press.

Platt, Anthony (1969), *The Child Savers: The Invention of Delinquency*, Chicago: University of Chicago Press.

Platt, Anthony (1994), 'Rethinking and Unthinking "Social Control"', in George S. Bridges and Martha A. Myers (eds), *Inequality, Crime, and Social Control*, Boulder, Col.: Westview Press, pp. 72–9.

Poulantzas, Nicos (1973), *Political Power and Social Classes*, New York: Verso.

Quinney, Richard (1980), *Class, State and Crime*, New York: Longman.

Rothman, David (1971), *The Discovery of the Asylum*, Boston, Mass.: Little, Brown.

Rusche, Georg and Kirchheimer, Otto (1968), *Punishment and Social Structure*, New York: Russell & Russell.

Spierenburg, Pieter (1987), 'From Amsterdam to Auburn: An Explanation for the Use of the Prison in 17th Century Holland and 19th Century America', *Journal of Social History*, Spring, pp. 439–61.

Spitzer, Steven (1975), 'Toward a Marxian Theory of Deviance', *Social Problems*, **22**, pp. 638–51.

Thompson, E.P. (1975), *Whigs and Hunters: The Origin of the Black Act*, New York: Pantheon.

Thompson, E.P. (1978), *The Poverty of Theory*, London: Verso.

Tolnay, Stewart E. and Beck, E.M. (1994), 'Lethal Social Control in the South: Lynchings and Executions Between 1880 and 1930', in George S. Bridges and Martha A. Myers (eds), *Inequality, Crime, and Social Control*, Boulder, Col.: Westview Press, pp. 176–94.

Ulmer, Jeffery T. (1998), *Sociology of Crime, Law and Deviance*, vol. 1, Stamford, Conn.: JAL Press Inc.

Waldrep, Christopher (1998), *Roots of Disorder: Race and Criminal Justice in the American South, 1817–80*, Urbana and Chicago: University of Illinois Press.

Wiener, Jonathan M. (1978), *Social Origins of the New South: Alabama, 1860–1880*, Baton Rouge: LSU Press.

Wiener, Jonathan M. (1979), 'Class Structure and Economic Development in the American South, 1869–1955', *American Historical Review*, **LXXXXIV** (4), October, pp. 970–92.

Wiener, Martin J. (1990), *Reconstructing the Criminal: Culture, Law and Policy in England, 1830–1914*, Cambridge: Cambridge University Press.

Wilson, Adrian (1993), *Rethinking Social History: English Society 1570–1920 and its Interpretation*, Manchester: Manchester University Press.

Woodman, Harold (1977), 'Sequel to Slavery: The New History Views the Postbellum South', *Journal of Southern History*, **XLIII** (4), 523–54.

Woodward, C. Vann (1951), *Origins of the New South, 1877–1913*, Baton Rouge: LSU Press.

Wright, Gavin (1986), *New South, Old South: Revolutions in the Southern Economy Since the Civil War*, New York: Basic Books.

Part I
What is Criminal Justice Social History?

[1]

THE SOCIAL-CONTROL THEORY IN AMERICAN HISTORY:
A CRITIQUE

Discovery of the Asylum. By David Rothman (Boston: 1971. xi-xx + 376 pp. $12.50).
The Child Savers: The Invention of Delinquency. By Anthony Platt (Chicago: 1969. 230 pp. $2.45).

The social-control thesis in American history initially promised to have a liberating effect on traditional scholarship. Where others accepted axioms, social-control adherents asked provocative questions. Yet the social-control thesis also suffers from flaws serious enough to make one question its long-range credibility. In this essay we shall first identify the positive qualities of the social-control thesis by pitting it against one of the best examples of traditional "revisionist" history. Then, using one of the thesis' major statements as a focus, we shall critically examine the social-control argument itself to determine its strengths and weaknesses.

The compelling need for the iconoclasm of the social-control historians becomes clear if we examine some of the best orthodox scholarship of recent years. Among traditional revisionist histories, David Rothman's *Discovery of the Asylum*, Sam Bass Warner's *Private City*[1] and *Urban Wilderness*,[2] and David B. Davis' "Some Themes of Counter-Subversion: An Analysis of Anti-Masonic, Anti-Catholic, and Anti-Mormon Literature"[3] are exciting, fresh, and replete with insights, yet severely flawed. The central problem with these works is that they posit as their subject an imaginary, homogeneous group labeled "the Americans." Davis describes the Americans' desire for national unity and security:

> Though *most Americans* took pride in their material progress, they also expressed a yearning for reassurance and security, for unity in some cause transcending individual self-interest . . . *many Americans* felt a compelling need to articulate their loyalties, to prove their faith . . . . *Most Americans* . . . appeared willing to tolerate diversity and even eccentricity, but when they saw themselves excluded . . . they imagined a "mystic power" conspiring to enslave them (pp. 209-11). (Italics added.)

The results of "the Americans' " fear of change and lack of identity are the anti-Masonic, anti-Catholic and anti-Mormon movements. For Rothman the problem of the early nineteenth century is that

> *Many Americans* . . . judged their society with eighteenth-century criteria in mind. As a result, *they* defined as corrupting the fluidity and mobility that *they* saw. Thinking that an orderly society had to be a fixed one, . . . *[they* had to find a way to have a cohesive yet fluid society]. The pessimism and fear underlying this outlook point to

> the difficulties *Americans* had in fitting their perception . . . into an eighteenth-century definition of a well-ordered community . . . . Yet for all the desperation in this image, *Americans shared* an incredible optimism (pp. 69-71). (Italics added.)

Warner emphasizes social divisions within the population but his discussion treats these divisions as surface phenomena which do not penetrate the basic national unity. *Urban Wilderness* is about

> the responsibility [which] rests . . . with successive generations of *Americans* who, by *their* unwillingness to move beyond the confines of private landownership, have produced today's disordered, inhumane, and restricted city (p. 15). As city dwellers, *we* [Americans] have remained what we were as farmers: a nation of small proprietors, jealously protecting our individual property rights as if they were the cornerstone of our civil liberties (pp. 27-38). (Italics added.)

Private City, Warner's book on Philadelphia, shows the divisive power of "privatism" over the American people: "Under the American tradition, the first purpose of the citizen is the private search for wealth; the goal of a city is to be a community of private money makers" (p. x). Warner deviates from Davis and Rothman in that he is aware of the existence of an urban elite, a group different from and superior to the rest of the population. However, for Warner, the elite is not dissimilar from the majority of people, only better. The elite is the group whose intervention in public affairs is *ipso facto* of benefit to the common man. This elite threatens the majority only by the possible (or actual) withdrawal of its skills, foresight, humanitarianism, and *noblesse oblige* from public life. When the elite takes part in public affairs, they are "Grade-A" Americans whose labors are not only in harmony with, but are also the most efficient vehicle for, the achievement of the public good.[4]

Emphasis upon "the Americans" as a distinct entity is consistent with, and to some extent based upon, the work of other prominent scholars, among them Marvin Meyers, Winthrop Jordan, and Rowland Berthoff. These historians not only postulate a basically unified national group, but like Rothman, Davis, and Warner, emphasize identity crises and other socio-psychological difficulties as a way of explaining the past.

All one has to do to bring down this sophisticated intellectual construct of the American past is to ask: Who are "the Americans"? In whose interest is it to restore old values and disintegrated hierarchies; to build internal improvements; to eliminate skilled competition; to restrict immigration; and to refuse to spend government funds on public needs? Were all Americans panicked by the decline of deference, place, status, and order, or were some afraid and others not? If all were afraid of change, were they afraid of the same aspects of change – did the artisan fear the decline of deference and the merchant-capitalist the rise of skilled immigrant competition?

The social-control historians have asked, "Who are 'the Americans'?" and have refused to accept facile answers. Their answers to this simple question have undermined the basic assumption of American consensus which eminent, traditional historians have taken for granted. Unlike orthodox scholars, social controlists have developed a model of society in which group conflict, not harmony and unity, is the basic feature. Where Davis, Warner, Rothman, and others find a consensus of interests underlying sometimes violent surface struggles, the social-control theorists see abiding, unalterable divisions.[5] If divisions and conflict are basic to society, then popular historical phrases such as "society wants," "the people thought," "Americans feared," have no meaning. They are labels for a nonexistent social group.

Since social-control historians see conflict as basic and believe history shows that groups are not equal in their resources and power, they postulate the existence of ruling and subordinate groups. In this unequal environment, those with power, status, and wealth will fight to use their assets to maintain themselves. They will try to control their subordinates by manipulation or brute force. The social-control historians have been especially interested in the past use of nonviolent means for controlling the population — especially the use of apparently "progressive," "humanitarian" reforms.

How social-control theory specifically alters the traditional approach becomes clear if we analyze Rothman's *Discovery of the Asylum* using a social-control perspective. From the social-control point of view, Rothman's magnum opus is a book standing on its head. It accurately portrays the major events and general features of Jacksonian society, but the main social groups are insufficiently differentiated and are therefore distorted almost beyond recognition.

Rothman maintains that the general American problem was how to approach the postcolonial world with its economic, social, cultural, and political instability when Americans had been accustomed to a stable, ordered world and found the new situation deviant and threatening. To Rothman the period was one in which the desire and need for "social order" was paramount. But by "social order" he means the attempt of the *general public* to contain, cure, and prevent specific problems (crime, insanity, and pauperism), and thereby to build a model of what the good society should look like. Rothman's Americans are Marvin Meyers' "venturesome conservatives," primarily engaged in reforming *themselves* symbolically. While Rothman attempts to anchor his discussion in social and economic realities, he actually presents a highly idealistic intellectual history of the period. He ritualistically appeals to material and social conditions as "first cause," but his work is primarily a history of ideas.

To a proponent of social-control theory, the first question to ask is: "Who are the reformers and of what are they specifically afraid?" Certainly, the reformers are not "the people." They are a small group of highly educated, middle- (or upper-) income individuals. While they may be both exceptionally idealistic and intellectual, and thereby a unique group, they are similar to the general upper-middle class in most of their social and economic characteristics. The decline of order, status, deference, and morality that Rothman posits has special meaning for this class since it was and is the natural beneficiary of a more stable situation. Its anxiety is not a general American malaise, but a specific class uneasiness. (This is not to deny that the working classes are also disturbed and unhappy, but their unhappiness stems not from the decline of a colonial or federalist rigidity but from the threats to the revolutionary heritage and to their position as respected artisans.[6] They fear different changes and need different remedies than the "discovery" of the asylum, prison, and poorhouse.) The apparent idealism and humanitarianism motivating the reformers, so the argument would go, come not from the power of a general world view grown outmoded, but from contemporary self-interest made into self-serving ideology.

To a social-control historian rereading the evidence, Rothman's book describes an elite with conflicting goals. To some extent it is fearful of the loss of past privileges and power, but to a greater extent, it wants to control the population, not in the interest of past rights, but in the interest of future ones. The desire of Rothman's reformers for teaching asylum inmates hard work, discipline, obedience, and self-control supports the idea that the elite wants to change preindustrial workers into docile industrial ones. As Rothman himself says:

> Medical superintendents (of the asylums) . . . had very special qualities in mind when they spoke about the family. The routine that they would create in the asylum would b, ar no resemblance to a casual, indulgent, and negligent household that failed to discipline its members or to inculcate a respect for order and authority . . . . They took their inspiration from the colonial period, believing they were restoring traditional virtues. But *to a surprising degree,* the result was more in tune with their own era. Regularity, order, and punctuality brought the asylum routine closer to the factory than the village (p. 153).[7] (Italics added.)

Where Rothman is surprised, the social-control historian is not.

If we turn *Discovery of the Asylum* on its head, many of the book's problems are solved. Rothman's reformers are initially portrayed as a highly humanitarian, concerned group. To make the interpretation work, Rothman must argue that their views represent those held by the general public, including an emphasis on environmentalism (social causation) rather than moralism (individual responsibility) in understanding deviance. Their experiments in reform are undone only because the internal contradictions of the well-intended reformers are played out and the general public slowly loses interest, refusing to continue adequately to finance their projects.

There is something rather unconvincing about this interpretation. The exact relationship between the desires of reformers and the general public is asserted, not argued. It is hard to believe that any large group of people (the so-called "Americans" or even the middle-class solely) ever accepted an environmentalist interpretation of deviance. Such a "humane" interpretation has not gained mass acceptance even in twentieth-century America, among the middle class, despite its supposed intellectual dominance. It could hardly have been popularly accepted in the 1840s.[8] Moralism, with its emphasis on personal responsibility and guilt, has always been the basic attitude of the bourgeoisie though portions of the environmentalist argument have been accepted from time to time. In his discussion of *The Cholera Years,*[9] Charles Rosenberg has argued persuasively that a degree of environmental awareness was quite compatible with the most blatant class-shaped moralism.

By seeing the reformers as the most idealistic and ideological portion of the middle class (the rest were unashamedly concerned with self-protection and the maintenance of privilege), the social-control viewpoint can make a more convincing case for continuity over time than can Rothman's theoretical argument about the importance of discontinuity, of changing ideas — from environmentalism to moralism — in the history of public institutions. Rothman himself admits that his theory of reform might obscure some uglier attitudes:

> Once begun, the decline from rehabilitation to custodianship took on a self-reinforcing quality . . . . Convenience had always been part of the reason for the asylum's popularity. The institutional program had a pragmatic quality; the penitentiary and

the almshouse were workable substitutes for stocks and edicts of banishment. Nevertheless, in the first formulation of the asylum idea, the prospect of improvement, both of the individual and the society, was far more significant, and the institutions' organization reflected this priority. The abundant evidence of the close fit between the reform and the actual appearance and arrangements of the institutions testified convincingly to the founder's sense of priorities (pp. 239-49).[10]

However, the earlier chapters, dealing with the origin of the asylum, provide much evidence of both nonidealistic support for reformers by the middle class and significant custodian and guard brutality, both of which give little encouragement to a thesis emphasizing reformer idealism. In response to these embarrassments, Rothman insists that the vindictiveness of correctional personnel was not proof of nonreformist middle-class influence, but rather the "close fit" between ideal and practice.[11]

A social-control historian, reinterpreting Rothman's evidence, would claim that his picture is severely distorted, highlighting the elite's view of Jacksonian society but labeling it the "American" view. Rothman's emphasis on the most humane and idealistic spokesmen for the upper-class position lauds their more utopian reforms, but neglects to deal with their basic aim — to stabilize society in their own class interest. From a social-control perspective the utopian aspects of the reforms lapsed because the majority of the elite was not concerned with the apparent idealism of the reforms but rather with the social control of dangerous elements. Where Rothman sees a basic discontinuity in "public" attitudes toward the uses of the asylum, critics would see a fundamental unity. The elite ultimately realized that protection of its class interest required a less grandiose restructuring of society, and it is only in this respect that old social theory had any importance to reformers and their clients — time made it obvious that total control was not necessary to maintain their privilege. Most social-control theorists would also insist that the idealistic aspects of the reformers' programs were to a larger or smaller extent propaganda designed to put a decent face on what they were doing. Reformer ideology was a front for class interest.

When one compares Rothman's interpretation with that of a social-control historian, it is hard to deny that Rothman comes off second best. The book is an intellectual tour de force, more stimulating than convincing. At the end of the book, Rothman himself comes much closer to a social-control theory of American history when he discusses the destruction of the ideals of the founding fathers. Here, the issues of control of the dangerous classes (especially the immigrants), and social divisions in society finally become prominent, but they come too late. A social-control point of view expressed earlier would have enlivened and clarified his discussion of the Jacksonian reform movement. The social-control approach, brought to bear upon *Discovery of the Asylum*, shows itself to be a liberating intellectual tool.

While the bold strokes of the social-control interpretation are liberating to traditional historical analysis, its major drawbacks are its underdeveloped and crude conceptualizations. If an undiluted social-control perspective becomes the new orthodoxy, we could end up with a less sophisticated, more simplistic notion of historical causation than we have presently. This misfortune has already begun in many colleges across the country. The social-control interpretation reflects and supports the alienation and cynicism that characterize the 1970s and as a result holds widespread appeal. Some of the best social-control interpretations of American history are those by Clifford Griffin, Francis Fox Piven and Richard Cloward,[12] Raymond Mohl, Michael B. Katz, and Anthony Platt. Since, of these, Platt's work is the most sophisticated and complex, analysis of it will provide clarification of the basic dangers and weaknesses inherent in adopting social control as *the* new model for American history.

Anthony Platt's *The Child Savers: The Invention of Delinquency* is perhaps the best study employing the social-control hypothesis. The book "attempts to locate the social basis of humanitarian ideals and to reconcile the intentions of the child savers with the institutions that they helped to create" (p. 4). Platt spends a great deal of time discussing the different theories of crime and delinquency put forth by American criminologists and writers over a hundred-year period; his discussion is clear, concise, and illuminating. He gives the reader a strong feeling of the complex intellectual currents, from Utilitarianism to Social Darwinism, that have affected the image held by the middle class of crime and criminals. He points out that the greatest weakness in our understanding of the history and sociology of crime is that investigators study the lawbreakers rather than the lawmakers. By the use of labeling theory, he is able to show persuasively the decisive role of the lawmakers in shaping our perceptions of crime. The fact that only two people may be present during the commission of a crime, the "criminal" and the "victim," is deceptive, since the one who defines the act as criminal and can enforce that definition is the crucial participant.

In his treatment of the evolution of the concept of juvenile delinquency and the steps leading to creation of the juvenile-court system and the segregation of younger from older offenders, Platt argues that "humanitarianism" played only a small role. Rather, there were three social roots in the creation of the concept of juvenile delinquency as a separate crime category: (a) the desire of the American middle class to control the children of the dangerous classes, (b) the professional strivings of those involved in prison institutions who wished to raise their status from that of mere custodians and keepers of criminals, and (c) the desire of middle-class women to enter careers and make their lives more meaningful while simultaneously legitimizing their strivings by keeping to fields (children, family, morality) traditionally associated with women. Among those major influences, Platt sees little or no room for altruism as it is normally conceived.

Platt's vision of the importance of profession-formation as an influence on the discovery of juvenile delinquency and its optimistic ideas about the reformability of the young criminal draw upon, and are reinforced by, Roy Lubove's powerful debunking of humanitarianism in the development of social work, *The Professional Altruist.*[13] Platt's emphasis on the role of women, restive in their middle-class idleness and desirous of gaining a place in the sun, is supported by Christopher Lasch's study of late nineteenth- and early twentieth-century America, *The New Radicalism in America.*[14] Platt's overall concept of class self-interest behind the movement is in harmony with social-control interpretation as it has been developed in American studies generally. Platt clearly states that thesis when he reviews the attitude of the radical nineteenth-century governor of Illinois, John Altgeld. He states, approvingly, "What Altgeld was intimating [by his statements] was that the whole machinery of the criminal law was *politically* designed to intimidate and control the poor" (p. 126).

Platt's book is a persuasive counterbalance to the literature that sees the history of American attitudes toward crime as growing steadily in humanitarianism and progress. After reading it, one would be hard put to argue the older, more idealistic view. In this respect, it is an excellent example of the positive power and usefulness of the social-control interpretation. However, the book suffers from major flaws built into the social-control theory.

Platt sets out to investigate the social roots of humanitarianism; to let the reader understand the "real" motives behind the ideology of humanitarianism. He intends to let the reader comprehend the reformers so that he can truly see why they acted as they did, especially why so much evil and harm came out of apparently laudable desires.

Despite the brilliance of much of his presentation, he fails in this overall goal. He does not adequately explain the relationship of altruism to social and class position, nor does he enable us to understand clearly the motivation and attitudes of the lawmakers. Rather, despite many insights, he gives us an overly simplistic, moralistic, and reductionist interpretation of the material. He often asks the wrong questions and as a result, comes up with irrelevant answers.

It is noteworthy that when one reads or discusses the book, the paramount importance of the social-control thesis is clear. However, when one goes back over the work, page by page, one finds that the concept is only implicitly stated and therefore never cogently argued. The actual presentation is much more limited, emphasizing the status and career concerns of middle-class women and correctional personnel. Both groups have, according to Platt, powerful ulterior motives for their humanitarianism. Altruism is only a rationale for their self-seeking. This argument may be convincing but it is, nevertheless, irrelevant to the social-control concept which posits class self-interest and class control as the real goals of reform movements. Both women and crime workers are groups within the middle class but they are not *the* middle class. No analysis restricted to the examination of these two groups could prove Altgeld or Platt right "that the whole machinery of the criminal law was *politically* designed to intimidate and control the poor" in the interests of the rich and well-born.

If we look at Platt's argument concerning the self-interest of middle-class women and correctional personnel, we find that the case he does present, while stimulating, is far from satisfactory. His argument is reductionist: he reduces the ideology and claims of women and prison guards to specific, limited self-advancement. Technically one could argue that his material is a needed supplement to balance other, more truly idealistic, portraits of their roles. But Platt does not argue this position. He is out to demonstrate the social roots of humanitarianism, and, once found, he reduces idealism to those roots; at the very least this is the impression the reader gets (p. 4).

This interpretation is just not convincing. The reduction of ideas to knee-jerk socioeconomic conditioning is persuasive neither from a liberal academic perspective nor from a Marxist one. The growth and development of ideas and their interaction with class interest is a complex phenomenon. It involves not only immediate self-interest, consciously or unconsciously perceived, but long-term developmental trends, of a material and nonmaterial form.[15] Granted, "pure" idealism or "pure" humanitarianism do not exist, but while the material and social world places definite limitations on the power of ideas, socioeconomic factors determine boundaries or outer limits, not specific responses. Once the economic limitations and pressures are known, one can, and indeed must, deal with ideas as real, powerful influences.

Humanitarianism was a real force in the nineteenth and twentieth centuries. It was not simply propaganda or "false consciousness" manipulated by the middle class to deceive others, though that is the way it is treated by social-control historians. One can and should discuss the social roots of humanitarianism, placing it within the context of the middle-class world view, and examining its role in justifying and rationalizing a new social and economic order. One must recognize the extent to which humanitarianism was part of middle-class ideology, and that it strengthened the bourgeoisie's own faith (as well as that of other classes) in its claim to represent the public good and the progressive movement of history.

Such social roots go far beyond the fear of disorder, the desire for careers, and the hope for professional status that Platt emphasizes. Not only are they more significant but they are infinitely more complex than he is willing to admit, or is conceptually able to handle. If we are to understand what the reformers wanted and believed we must understand the dynamics of middle-class ideology. As Arnold Hauser, the Marxist art critic, states, ideology is not a simple affair:

> What most sharply distinguishes a propagandistic from an ideological presentation and interpretation of the facts is ... that its falsification and manipulation of the truth is always conscious and intentional. Ideology, on the other hand, is mere deception – in essence self-deception – never simply lies and deceit. It obscures truth in order not so much to mislead others as to maintain and increase the self-confidence of those who express and benefit from such deception (p. 134).

The role of ideology, its part in self-deception and creating "false consciousness" plus its interaction with material interests and with cultural traditions and other bodies of thought, is too complex and important to be reduced to simplistic, direct socioeconomic interests. While Platt is a minor offender compared to his fellows, most social-control historians tend to reduce middle-class ideology to the concept of propaganda: conscious manipulation and lies.

It is anything but that. Indeed, much of what reformers claimed as humanitarianism was indeed just that. Because certain reforms are in the long-range interest of the middle class, because they help rationalize and stabilize the social structure, to make the lower classes less unhappy or turbulent, does not prove they are not humanitarian. It only proves that "ideas" do not float in space but have roots in material or class interests. As Hobsbawm has pointed out concerning the French revolutionary bourgeoisie at the birth of the modern era, the fact that the middle class wanted to believe that it stood for progress and human betterment, that like all rising classes it projected its self-interest as the world's interest, does not make it untrue. At the time, they were right.[16]

Platt and others are unable to cope with the complex mixture of real and false, actual and perceived benefits in middle-class reform. Since many of the major reforms of the nineteenth century were later aborted, it is easy for Platt to dismiss them all as initially conceived in self-interest. The price of failure is to have malevolence read backwards into history. Platt assumes that the reformers knew or should have known what real reforms were necessary and that they chose the wrong ones. The element of moralizing and casting blame is powerful in social-control books. Platt goes so far as to insist that reformers were responsible not only for their own ideas but for what other, less responsible men might do with those ideas: "Since progressive educators failed to confront the full implications of their assumptions about the educational process in a democracy, they must be held partly responsible for the misuse that others made of their ideas. Penal reformers exploited the rhetoric of the new education to give respectability and legitimacy to programs of agricultural and industrial training in reformatories" (p. 59). Heaven help the social-control historians like Anthony Platt if they are to be held responsible for every anti-intellectual militant who uses their theories to justify his actions! But if Platt's teleological technique catches on, we can be sure that someday a commentator will discuss the Machiavellian middle-class purposes behind the social-control theory of history.

All of which brings us to another problem with the kind of reductionism found in Platt. He investigates the social roots of ideas in order to debunk them, rather than to focus upon the interplay between ideas and socioeconomic conditions. Yet, how can an idealist like Platt dismiss the possibility of idealism? How can an outraged moralist deny the legitimacy of moralism? The irony of social-control theorists is that they think of themselves as materialists and realists but are inspired by idealism and emotionalism. As Hauser perceptively observes: "The study of ideology implies its application to its own assertions. Deliberating upon ideology inevitably leads to the recognition that the critics of ideologies themselves think ideologically. Such criticism is only valid if it is also aware of the limits of its own point of view" (p. 136).

The complexity of criticizing nineteenth-century reformers never occurs to Platt. How would he explain himself and the other middle-class academic social-control historians? Do they have social and class roots, too? Would "exposing them" and the self-interest that is built into their situation totally discredit their position? Certainly not, but all ideology (be it radical, liberal, or conservative) includes truth, self-deception, and distortion, complexly interwoven, and cutting the Gordian knot is no substitute for analysis.

An example of how Platt's viewpoint, and the social-control theory generally, fail, is his use of the term "pseudo-science" when reviewing changing nineteenth-century theories of behavior: "American penologists supported this derogatory image of criminals and enthusiastically welcomed pseudo-scientific proposals for their containment" (p. 24). The term "pseudo-scientific" assumes that in a given period people had a choice between true and false science and some purposefully picked the latter. Unfortunately, Platt's distinction does not hold, as anyone who has read Thomas Kuhn's *Structure of Scientific Revolutions*[17] would immediately recognize. George Rosen, in "Disease, Debility, and Death," a study of medicine in the nineteenth century, has pointed out that given the then-current state of scientific knowledge, many extremely erroneous theories were not only perfectly "scientific" but as persuasive as the "correct" interpretations which were also formulated at the time.[18]

We are not suggesting that one cannot make judgments, nor point out the political, social, or economic influences that might make one rival scientific theory more attractive than another, but the judgments must be fair and not do violence to history. Even if we granted the usefulness of the word "pseudo-science," we would still need to face the problem of how self-interested middle-class reformers and criminologists accepted those views. The implication of the

social-control argument is that they consciously chose false scientific explanations in order to better control the dangerous masses, an argument which
confuses ideology with propaganda and a class world view with cynical manipulation. Since they accepted the scientific explanations they   believed were true,
but the nature and acceptability of which were strongly influenced by class
interest, the situation is more complex and ambiguous. It requires a much more
sophisticated level of analysis than imputing "pseudo-ness" and conscious
manipulation to the situation.

In the final analysis, the social-control historians have asked the right questions and revealed part of the truth. But their conceptual scheme, imputing
conscious manipulation of ideas for purposes of social control, is too primitive
and simplistic to be adequate. They have raised the questions of class divisions,
power differentials, ideology, and the relationship between ideals and socioeconomic realities, but they have been carried away with moralism, outraged
indignation, and their desire to make their research immediately useful for
current reform movements. What we need is a calm, sophisticated analysis that
examines the actual workings of a class society and uses conceptual tools that
are adequate for the job.

At the beginning of this article we presented a social-control-style critique of
Rothman's *Discovery of the Asylum.* We found that Rothman's interpretation
was unacceptable. But as we have seen from Platt's work, the social-control
revision is not a totally adequate alternative. The attitude of the Jacksonian
middle class and elite to reform, to the prison, asylum, and poorhouse is more
complex than the social-control interpretation can handle. Christopher Lasch has
recently opened the door to a new perspective that combines the insights of
both liberal and Marxist scholarship. Lasch attempts to explain the reform
phenomenon as part of the complex mental and intellectual ideas generated by
the ascension of the middle class:

> The rise of egalitarianism in western Europe and the United States seems to have
> been associated with a heightened awareness of deviancy and of social differences of
> all kinds, and with a growing uneasiness in the face of those differences – a certain
> intolerance even, which expressed itself in a determination to compel or persuade all
> members of society to conform to a single standard of citizenship . . . . The humani-
> tarian reformers of the nineteenth century not only reflected the changing sensibility
> of the period – this growing consciousness of differences of all kinds – they played a
> central part in the process whereby this consciousness came to be embodied in
> various forms of institutionalized segregation.[19]

Lasch is also concerned with escaping from parochial discussions that continually find the causes of events in specific American situations. Many of the most
important changes in American history were simultaneously happening in
Europe. Exclusive reference to American events cannot explain international
occurrences, a mistake made by both liberal and social-control scholars. Lasch
does not have all the answers, but he has started the process of transcending the
categories and conflicts that separate liberal from radical historians. It is only by
asking new and more sophisticated questions about American society, classes,
power, and ideology that we can improve our understanding of the past.

Queens College, City University of New York   William A. Muraskin

REVIEW ESSAY   569

FOOTNOTES

1. (Philadelphia, 1968).

2. (New York, 1972).

3. *Mississippi Valley Historical Review* 47 (1960): 205-24.

4. Warner, *Private City*, passim, pp. 79-98.

5. See John Horton's article on "order and conflict" theories of society and Richard Quinney's article on the social reality of crime in R. Serge Denisoff and Charles H. McCaghy, eds., *Deviance, Conflict and Criminality* (New York, 1973).

6. See Michael Feldley's "Urbanization as a Cause of Violence: Philadelphia as a Test Case," in Allen F. Davis and Mark H. Haller, eds., *The People of Philadelphia* (Philadelphia, 1973), pp. 53-71.

7. Also see p. 146 for the similarity between the work ethic in the mental asylum and the penitentiary.

8. See Roy Lubove, *Professional Altruist* (New York, 1971).

9. (Chicago, 1962).

10. See also p. 89, where the author recognizes the possibility that critics will notice that reformer idealism may be irrelevant.

11. See Rothman, *Asylum*, pp. 101-2, 105, and note 42 on p. 333 for some unconvincing attempts to make the power of nonreformist influences disappear.

12. I have dealt at great length with the Piven and Cloward work and their use of the social-control concept in an article entitled, "Regulating the Poor: The Problem With Social Control," which will appear in the November issue of *Contemporary Sociology*.

13. Lubove's book is not a social-control work though it contains many of the views developed by that interpretive school. Lubove's attitudes toward social workers are more complex and ambiguous than those which social-control historians have about reformers.

14. (New York, 1965).

15. See Maynard Solomon's *Marxism and Art* (New York, 1974), for example.

16. Eric Hobsbawm, *The Age of Revolution, 1789-1848* (New York, 1962), pp. 74-100.

17. (Chicago, 1970).

18. In H.J. Dyos and M. Wolff, eds., *The Victorian City* (London, 1973).

19. *The World of Nations* (New York, 1974), pp. 16-17. Also, see p. 316 for his rejection of the "fear of disorder" concept that both Rothman and social-control historians accept.

[2]

The Peasant and the Brigand: Social Banditry Reconsidered

ANTON BLOK

University of Amsterdam

About a decade ago, Hobsbawm presented an interesting argument on a markedly little known subject for which he coined the term 'social banditry' (1959: 1–29). The author is a British social historian and an expert on social protest movements. He claims that social banditry is a universal and virtually unchanging phenomenon which embodies a rather primitive form of organized social protest of peasants against oppression. Social bandits are robbers of a special kind, for they are not considered as simple criminals by public opinion. They are persons whom the State regards as outlaws, but who remain within the bounds of the moral order of the peasant community. Peasants see them as heroes, as champions, and as avengers, since they right wrongs when they defy the landlords or the representatives of the State. Yet their programme, if indeed social bandits have any, does not go beyond the restoration of the traditional order which leaves exploitation of the poor and oppression of the weak within certain limits. Social bandits are thus reformers rather than revolutionaries, though they may prove a valuable asset for those who seek to overthrow an established regime. By themselves, social bandits lack organizational capacity, and modern forms of political mobilization tend to render them obsolete. The phenomenon belongs largely to the past, if only to the very recent past. The golden age of brigandage coincided with the advent of capitalism when the impact of the market dislocated large sectors of the peasantry.

In *Bandits*** Hobsbawm elaborates some of the main themes he surveyed in *Primitive Rebels* (1959). Like its predecessor, this study is an essay on the uniformities of social brigandage. The author maintains that these uniformities should not be seen as a consequence of cultural diffusion, but as reflections of similar situations within peasant societies: 'Social banditry is universally found, wherever societies are based on agriculture (including pastoral economies), and consist largely of peasants and landless labourers ruled, oppressed and exploited by someone else—lords, towns, governments, lawyers, or even banks' (1969: 15). Hobsbawm starts out from

* E. J. Hobsbawm, London: Weidenfeld & Nicolson, 1969, 128 pp.

494

generalizations and then proceeds to provide evidence for them from various parts of the world. For example, in discussing the recruitment of bandits, he states the categories that are likely to supply outlaws, indicates the causal nexus, and closes with examples. Writes Hobsbawm:

The characteristic bandit unit in a highland area is likely to consist of young herdsmen, landless labourers and ex-soldiers and unlikely to contain married men with children or artisans. Such formulae do not exhaust the question, but they do cover a surprisingly large part of the field. For instance, of the south Italian band leaders in the 1860s, those for whom we have occupational descriptions include twenty-eight 'shepherds', 'cow-herds', 'ex-servicemen', 'landless labourers', and 'field guards' (or combinations of these occupations) and only five others (*Bandits*, 1969: 28).

In this way the author deals with several aspects of social banditry and distinguishes three main types of bandits: the noble robber, the primitive resistance fighter, and the terror-bringing avenger. Whatever the differences among them, they have in common the fact that they voice popular discontent.

The approach leaves little room for a more comprehensive analysis over time of particular bandits or bands—accounts which are badly needed, as I hope to demonstrate presently. Where Hobsbawm embarks upon an extended case, the result cannot be else than sketchy (1969: 96–108). We should therefore read this study as the author asks us to in his Preface: as a postscript in essay form to *Primitive Rebels*. In this realm, *Bandits* seems an appreciable book, well written and elegantly edited, furnished with 62 illustrations most of which are quite fascinating.[1] The reader is offered a necessarily selective panorama on no less than 90 different bandits, who form the raw material to illustrate the author's ideas on brigandage at large.

Yet it is precisely because the interpretations do not extend very much beyond those already contained in *Primitive Rebels* that the reader who is somewhat familiar with the subject will be slightly disappointed. Anxious to find additional evidence for his hypotheses, the author avoids discussing the many cases contradicting them. If, as Popper said, theories are nets cast to catch what we call 'the world'—to rationalize, to explain, and to master it—Hobsbawm does not seem particularly concerned to make the mesh ever finer and finer. It could hardly be otherwise, for he tells us that he entertains the hope that the new data will not conflict with his original model as sketched out in *Primitive Rebels*. And he adds: 'Still, the wider the generalization, the more likely it is that individual pecularities are

---

[1] Unfortunately, some illustrations bear subscripts which are not altogether comprehensible (e.g. p. 26), while several others fail to illustrate any part of the actual text. It can neither go unnoticed that it is out of key in a study on bandits to mis-spell repeatedly the Italian word *banditi*, especially in phrases like 'Italy, the classic country of the *banditti*' (p. 19), and 'Italy, whose *banditti* were long the most famous in literature and art, and which probably possesses more local monographs than any other country' (p. 121).

496 ANTON BLOK

neglected' (1969: 11). One might wonder about the type of generalization that permits the neglect of particular cases, the more so since there were several questions in the first book which required thorough reconsideration.

It is my contention that there is much more to brigandage than just the fact that it may voice popular protest. Though Hobsbawm mentions several other aspects of banditry, his model fails to account for these complexities, and even obscures them, because he insists on the interpretation of new data in terms of his original model. This review attempts to explore the model of the social bandit as a special type of peasant protest and rebellion. I shall argue that the element of class conflict as embodied in certain forms of banditry has received undue emphasis. Rather than actual champions of the poor and the weak, bandits quite often terrorized those from whose very ranks they managed to rise, and thus helped to suppress them. The often ambiguous position of bandits may be understood when we appreciate the significance of the various links that tie the peasant community to the larger society. Likewise, the distinction between direct and constructed reference groups may help to explain why peasants and romanticists (including some of us) indulge in an idealized picture of the rural bandit as an avenger of social injustice, in spite of the obvious evidence to the contrary. The present discussion may contribute to a more adequate understanding of peasant mobilization and peasant movements. If we agree on political mobilization as a process through which people seek to acquire more control over the social conditions that shape their lives, it may be argued that bandits do not seem the appropriate agents to transform any organizational capacity among peasants into a politically effective force. Rather than promoting the articulation of peasant interests within a national context, bandits tend to obstruct or to deviate concerted peasant action. They may do so directly by means of physical violence and intimidation. In fact, we know that bandits have fulfilled pivotal roles in the demobilization of peasants. Indirectly, brigandage may impede large-scale peasant mobilization since it provides channels to move up in the social hierarchy, and thus tends to weaken class solidarity. In this paper, therefore, I shall focus on the interdependencies between lords, peasants, and bandits. The vignettes are mainly based on Sicilian material since my fieldwork experience has been restricted to this area.

To appreciate the importance and ubiquity of the social bandit, we should recognize which categories Hobsbawm excludes from this type. They involve all urban robbers, the urban equivalent of the peasant bandit as much as members of the so-called 'underworld'; rural desperadoes who are not peasants, e.g. the bandit gentry; raiders who form a community of their own, such as the Bedouin; *mafia*-like gangs; the landlord's bandits; and the classic blood-vengeance bandits (1969: 13–14). This narrows to a considerable extent the universe of social brigandage.[2] There are even further provisos, since not all categories necessarily exclude one another. Particular bandits may, either simultaneously or in the course of their careers, express popular discontent as well as the power of the landlord or the State (1959: 13). Furthermore, we know of outlaws and bandits who were glorified or, at least accepted, in their native districts while feared as raiders far outside of these areas. For example, the nineteenth-century Indian *Thuggee* (Thugs), who specialized in ritually strangling and robbing travellers, lived as ordinary peasants in their native areas where they were protected by local rulers with whom they shared the booty, but operated well over a hundred miles from their homes (MacKenzie, 1967: 64–6). As Barrington Moore has aptly said with respect to nineteenth-century China: 'It is necessary to be aware of romanticizing the robber as a friend of the poor, just as much as of accepting the official image. Characteristically the local inhabitants would bargain with the bandits in order to be left in peace. Quite often local gentry leaders were on cordial terms with bandits' (1968: 214).[3]

Hobsbawm is aware of these varieties and complexities, but he does not attempt to account for them. h.s prime interest is social protest: 'Though in practice social banditry cann̄c. always be clearly separated from other kinds of banditry, this does not affect the fundamental analysis of the social bandit as a special type of peasant protest and rebellion' (1969: 33). However, when it is recognized that 'the crucial fact about the bandit's position is its ambiguity . . . the more successful he is as a bandit, the more he is *both* a representative and champion of the poor *and* a part of the system of the rich' (1969: 76), we may question the heuristic value of his model of the social bandit with respect to brigandage at large. As Hobsbawm admits elsewhere, few bandits lived up to the role of popular hero. Yet, 'such is the need for heroes and champions, that if there are no real ones, unsuitable candidates are pressed into service. In real life most Robin Hoods were far from noble' (1969: 34). For instance, Schinderhannes, a famous bandit chief who operated in Rhineland in the late 1790s, 'was in no sense a social bandit but found it advantageous for his public relations to advertise that he robbed only Jews . . .' (1959: 20).

The point I want to make is not that 'social banditry' cannot be a useful sociological concept. This it certainly is, though in a much different way than Hobsbawm suggests. In a sense, all bandits are 'social' in so far as they, like all human beings, are linked to other people by various ties. We

---

[2] We should remember that unsuccessful bandits are less likely to be recorded, for they do not live long enough to get widely known, let alone to reach the annals of history. Hobsbawm does not make clear whether or not this category belongs to his universe, since he does not mention it at all.

[3] See also Eberhard (1965: 100–6). The same pattern has been described by the Flemish writer Hugo Claus in his play *Het Lied van de Moordenaar* (*The Ballad of the Murderer*). Amsterdam/Antwerp: Bezige Bij, 1957. The play deals with a band operating in west Flanders at the end of the eighteenth century.

H

498   ANTON BLOK

cannot understand the behaviour of bandits without reference to other groups, classes, or networks with which bandits form specific configurations of interdependent individuals.[4] What seems wrong with Hobsbawm's perception of brigandage is that it pays too much attention to the peasants and the bandits themselves. Before looking at them, it is necessary to look at the larger society in which peasant communities are contained. Without taking into account these higher levels, which include the landed gentry and the formal authorities, brigandage cannot be fully understood as indeed many particular characteristics of peasant communities are dependent upon or a reflex of the impact of the outside world. Given the specific conditions of outlawry, bandits have to rely very strongly on other people. It is important to appreciate that all outlaws and robbers require protection in order to operate as bandits and to survive at all. If they lack protection, they remain lonely wolves to be quickly dispatched, and those who hunt them down may be either the landlord's retainers, the police, or the peasants. Our task is therefore first to discover the people on whom the bandit relies.

Protection of bandits may range from a close though narrow circle of kinsmen and affiliated friends to powerful politicians, including those who hold formal office as well as grass-roots politicians. Protection thus involves the presence of a power domain. Of all categories, the peasants are weakest. In fact, this is the main reason why they are peasants (cf. Wolf, 1966: 1–11; Landsberger, 1969: 1–8). It may hence be argued that unless bandits find political protection, their reign will be short. This yields the following hypothesis, which may be tested against data bearing on all kinds of robbery: *The more successful a man is as a bandit, the more extensive the protection granted him.* The second variable may be difficult to quantify, though mere numbers and social positions of protectors may prove helpful beginnings. The first variable can be expressed in terms of the period of action: less than three years, like Schinderhannes in Rhineland and Corrientes in Andalusia, or more, like the Sicilians Grisafi (1904–17) and Giuliano (1943–50). Another measure of success involves the bandit's actions and the extent to which these operations are organized. Rinaldi, Rocco, and Capraro, who controlled large areas of western and central Sicily in the early 1870s, provide an example. Their mounted and well-armed bands synchronized their actions and fought regular battles with the police and the army.[5] Grisafi's domain was a mountainous corner in southwestern Sicily

4 For the concept of configuration, see Elias (1970).
5 Cf. D'Alessandro (1959: 97). This important study is regretfully not utilized by Hobsbawm. It might have induced him to revise some of the ideas on *mafia* as expressed in *Primitive Rebels*, especially the notion that *mafiosi* can be understood in terms of social rebels. In the book here under review, Hobsbawm refers to the Sicilian *mafia* as those 'unofficial political systems and networks, which are still very poorly understood and known' (p. 33). The reader should know, however, that over the past ten years several studies on *mafia* have been published, some of which are quite instructive e.g., Pantaleone (1966) and Romano (1966).

over which he ruled absolutely, interfering in every kind of affair, even the most intimate, making his will felt in every field, including the electoral field, and levying tolls and taxes, blackmailing and committing crimes of bloodshed without stint. Some 30 murders were put down to him, besides an unending series of crimes. . . . Grisafi relied on a network of assistance that had grown wide, thick and strong in the course of time . . . [involving] 357 persons in all, of whom 90 were in his hometown alone (Mori, 1933: 130–4).

The more banditry is politically oriented and evolves into what Italian scholars have called *brigantaggio politico*,[6] the more likely it is that it will assume 'anti-social' features when we take this term in the sense as understood by Hobsbawm, that is, anti-peasant. A surprisingly large number of the bandits mentioned by Hobsbawm were anti-peasant during most of their careers, which they typically initiated by righting personal wrongs. Sooner or later they were either killed or drawn into and constrained by the power domains of the established regional elites. Bandits thus represented the other side of a barely suppressed class war, especially those whose reign was long. Giuliano, who shot down peaceful Communist demonstrators upon orders of high-ranking politicians, is incidentally mentioned by Hobsbawm as an example of a bandit whose long career was due to 'a very great deal of political protection' (1969: 46 n.). Pantaleone, who is more explicit on this incident, observes:

This was the most sensational of Giuliano's crimes, but not of course the only one. In the months between the Portella shooting [May 1, 1947] and the April elections the following year, his gang concentrated its attacks on party members, trade unions and left-wing party headquarters, completely terrorizing the villagers in the provinces of Palermo and Trapani which were the usual setting for his activities (1966: 133).[7]

A similar orientation holds good for Giuliano's contemporary, Liggio, still today one of the most violent outlaws in western Sicily. The zone of terror which he established in the island region during the aftermath of the second world war was primarily aimed at the demobilization of the peasants who had just begun to organize themselves in order to attain agrarian reform.[8]

The Marxists have consistently argued that peasants require outside leadership in order to change their conditions.[9] Bandits are not instrumental in turning peasant anarchy and rebellion (e.g. *jacqueries*) into sustained and concerted action on a wider scale. This is not, as Hobsbawm (1959: 5, 26) maintains, because their ambitions are modest and because they lack organization and ideology, but rather because their first loyalty is *not* to the peasants. When bandits assume retainership (either part time or full time) they serve to prevent and suppress peasant mobilization in at least

[6] During the nineteenth and twentieth centuries, Sicilian brigandage provided alternately an *instrumentum regni* and a staff of the large landowners to suppress the peasants. See Romano (1952: 279–86).   [7] For a case study on Giuliano's career, see Maxwell (1957).
[8] The atmosphere in which Liggio operated is described in Dolci (1963: 25–50). See also Pantaleone (1966: 113–22). Liggio is still active today. He is regarded as being involved in the kidnapping and murder of the Palermitan journalist, de Mauro, in September 1970. For the concepts of terror and zone of terror, see Walter (1969: 5–7).
[9] See the observations in Wolf (1966: 92; 1969: 294); Moore (1968: 479); and Landsberger (1969: 57).

two ways: first, by putting down collective peasant action through terror; second, by carving out avenues of upward mobility which, like many other vertical bonds in peasant societies, tend to weaken class tensions. Though bandits are thus essentially conservative, politically speaking, there are none the less specific circumstances under which they may become effective in destroying an established regime. This is most likely to happen when they can rely on a promising, rival power which questions the existing power structure. The armed bands who had helped Garibaldi to unsettle Bourbon government in Sicily in 1860 are an example of the strategic role which bandits may fulfil in major upheavals. Even then, however, bandits may provide embarrassments since they may simply dissolve, change their allegiance upon the occasion, or fail to understand the situation in a wider context.[10]

Though Hobsbawm describes the myths and legends about bandits, his two studies fail to penetrate them. Even when we admit that it is the urban middle class rather than the ordinary peasantry who idealize the bandit, we may well ask to whom or what the peasants refer when they glorify the bandit. Here we may follow Elizabeth Bott, who draws a distinction between direct and constructed reference groups. The former are groups in which the referent is an actual group: either membership or non-membership groups whose norms have been internalized by the individual. The latter concern groups in which the referent is a concept or social category rather than an actual group: 'The amount of construction and projection of norms into constructed reference groups is relatively high' (1964: 167–8).

The 'social bandit' as conceptualized and described by Hobsbawm is such a construct, stereotype, or figment of human imagination. Though such constructs may not correspond to actual conditions, they are psychologically real, since they represent fundamental aspirations of people, in this case of the peasants. Successful bandits stand out as men who evolved from poverty to relative wealth, and who acquired power. To use a standard Sicilian expression, they are men who *make themselves respected*. The notion of honour as expressed in a person's successful control over resources by means of physical force is characteristic of Medieval European and contemporary Mediterranean societies. This concern with honour and the specific meaning attached to it are related to the relatively low level of State formation in these societies. In the absence of stable central control over the means of violence, people could not rely for protection on State institutions. With respect to sheer physical survival, they were largely de-

---

[10] See Mack Smith (1950) and Eberhard's discussion of the various stages of banditry in Medieval China (1965: 101–2). Similar complexities are described for early nineteenth-century Banten in north-western Java (Sartono, 1966: 109–27). The heterogeneity of the *déclassé* and floating population of which bandits make part raises specific organizational problems in revolutionary movements. The role of external power holders who challenge the power that constrains the peasants is discussed by Wolf (1969: 290–1).

pendent on their own, or on the protection of more powerful persons.[11] Successful bandits inspire fear and respect. Hence the fascination they radiate, especially among those who are in no sense respected—the peasants, from whose ranks they usually emerge.

The element of social protest is expressed in the myth, which thus builds up around the bandit. This process, or at least part of it, is pictured very skilfully and with great subtlety in Francesco Rosi's film *Salvatore Giuliano* (1962) in which we see surprisingly little of the bandit himself. Indeed the very physical absence of outlaws from the ordinary day-to-day life facilitates the formation of myths and legends in which the bandit appears as a man fighting the rich to succour the poor. We idealize all the more easily those things and people with whom we are least acquainted, or whom we rarely actually see, and we tend to ignore information that is detrimental to a beloved image.[12] Actual bandit life is often unpleasant and grim. It involves prolonged residence in humid caves and long toilsome marches as well as much and brutal action against numerous poor and helpless victims (e.g., Pereira de Queiroz, 1968: 112–22). Physical discomfort might be one reason why bandits seek to come to terms with their protectors in a more definite way, that is, when they assume the role of retainer. Many notorious delinquents and bandit leaders, like di Miceli and Scordato in mid-nineteenth-century Palermo, were given special charge of public security (Mack Smith, 1968: 419). In Sicily this and similar avenues to 'respectability' are institutionalized in the *mafia*, on which brigandage largely depends. We must expect to find similar mechanisms in Sardinia, Spain, Mexico and the Philippines.[13] Like the bandit's real life, these conversions in which bandits turn into retainers and help to reinforce oppression of the peasantry do not provide attractive ingredients for myths and ballads.

Actual brigandage expresses man's pursuit of honour and power.[14] This holds true for the bandit as much as his protector, who manipulates

[11] Cf. Bloch (1961: 145–62); Schneider (1971); and Elias (1971). Of particular interest is an article of the late Dutch historian Niermeyer (1959) dealing with the semantic shifts of the term '*honor*' in Medieval European societies.

[12] 'Since human beings have an infinite capacity for self-conceit, reality can only be reached by exposing their illusions'. This is, according to Alexander Parker, how the early seventeenth-century writer Francisco de Quevedo focuses on the problem of the delinquent in his novel *La vida del Buscón*, the masterpiece of the picaresque genre. See Parker (1967: 56–74).

[13] In Bourbon Spain, bandits could obtain pardon from the king and pass into royal service (Pitt-Rivers 1961: 180). See also Brenan (1962:156). For data on Mexico, see Friedrich (1962, 1965). Van den Muyzenberg's article deals with the Huks in Central Luzon (1971). The new development of brigandage in Sardinia in the 1960s is too easily dismissed by Hobsbawm (1969: 76). He fails to recognize the part played by shepherds and outlaws in kidnapping and extortion and to note the rapid and violent ascent of both rural and urban bourgeois in recent years. (Anna H. Eyken, personal communication; cf. Brigaglia, 1971: 299–314.) The Sardinian case demonstrates that banditry, in spite of improved communications, is by no means as *passé* as Hobsbawm maintains.

[14] Parker (1967: 135) points to the emphasis in the picaresque novel on self-assertion, the longing for 'respectability', and 'the will to power' as salient attributes of the delinquent. This orientation of bandits and *mafiosi* as well as the measure of political protection granted them is elaborated in a forthcoming publication (Blok, 1972).

502   ANTON BLOK

him in order to extend his power domains. The myth of the bandit (Hobsbawm's social bandit) represents a craving for a different society, a more human world in which people are justly dealt with and in which there is no suffering. These myths require our attention. It has been argued that they are the institutionalized expression of a dormant protest element which, under certain conditions, may 'gather force and break through the culturally accepted patterns which kept it within its institutionalized bounds' (Wertheim, 1964: 32). Hobsbawm's comparative treatment of banditry over-emphasizes the element of social protest and obscures the significance of the links which bandits maintain with established power-holders. In future research on the subject, the relative importance of both dimensions of banditry must be accounted for.

REFERENCES

Bloch, Marc (1961), *Feudal Society*. Chicago: The University of Chicago Press.

Blok, Anton (1972), 'The Mafia of a Sicilian Village (1860–1960): An Anthropological Study of Political Middlemen'. Ph.D. Dissertation, University of Amsterdam.

Bott, Elizabeth (1964), *Family and Social Network*. London: Tavistock.

Brenan, Gerald (1962), *The Spanish Labyrinth: An Account of the Social and Political Background of the Spanish Civil War*. Cambridge: Cambridge University Press.

Brigaglia, Manlio (1971), *Sardegna Perchè Banditi*. Milano: Edizioni Leader.

D'Alessandro, Enzo (1959), *Brigantaggio e Mafia in Sicilia*. Messina/Florence: D'Anna.

Dolci, Danilo (1963), *Waste: An Eye-witness Report on Some Aspects of Waste in Western Sicily*. London: Macgibbon & Kee.

Eberhard, Wolfram (1965), *Conquerors and Rulers: Social Forces in Medieval China*. Leyden: Brill.

Elias, Norbert (1970), *Was ist Soziologie?* München: Juventa Verlag.

—— (1971), 'The Genesis of Sport as a Sociological Problem', in Eric Dunning, ed., *The Sociology of Sport: A Selection of Readings* (New Sociology Library, No. 2). London: Frank Cass & Co.

Friedrich, Paul (1962), 'Assumptions Underlying Tarascan Political Homicide', *Psychiatry*, 25, 2: 315–27.

—— (1965), 'A Mexican Cacicazgo', *Ethnology*, 4, 2: 190–209.

Hobsbawm, E. J. (1959), *Primitive Rebels: Studies in Archaic Forms of Social Movement in the Nineteenth and Twentieth Centuries*. Manchester: University Press.

Landsberger, Henry A., ed. (1969), *Latin American Peasant Movements*. Ithaca/London: Cornell University Press.

MacKenzie, Norman, ed. (1967), *Secret Societies*. London: Aldus Books

Maxwell, Gavin (1957), *God Protect Me From My Friends*. London: Longmans.

Mack Smith, Denis (1950), 'The Peasants' Revolt in Sicily in 1860', in, *Studi in Onore di Gino Luzzatto* (vol. 3: 210–40). Milano: Giuffrè

—— (1968) *A History of Sicily* (2 vols). London: Chatto & Windus.

Moore, Barrington, Jr. (1968), *Social Origins of Dictatorship and Democracy. Lord and Peasant in the Making of the Modern World*. Boston: Beacon Press.

Mori, Cesare (1933), *The Last Struggle With the Mafia*. London: Putnam.

Niermeyer, J. F. (1959), 'De Semantiek van *Honor* en de Oorsprong van het Heerlijk Gezag', in, *Dancwerc*. Opstellen Aangeboden aan Prof. Dr. D.Th. Enklaar ter Gelegenheid van zijn 60ste Verjaardag. Groningen: J. B. Wolters.

Pantaleone, Michele (1966), *Mafia and Politics*. London: Chatto & Windus.

Parker, Alexander A. (1967), *Literature and the Delinquent: The Picaresque Novel in Spain and Europe 1599–1753*. Edinburgh: University of Edinburgh Press.

Pereira de Queiroz, Maria Isaura (1968), *Os Cangaceiros: Les Bandits d'Honneur Brésiliens*. Paris: Julliard (Collection Archives No. 34).

Pitt-Rivers, J. A. (1961), *The People of the Sierra*. Chicago: University of Chicago Press.

Romano, S. F. (1952), 'Sul Brigantaggio e Sulla Mafia', in S. F. Romano, *Momenti del Risorgimento in Sicilia*. Messina/Firenze: D'Anna.

—— (1966) *Storia Della Mafia*. Milano: Feltrinelli.

Sartono Kartodirdjo (1966). 'The Peasants' Revolt of Banten in 1888: Its Conditions, Course, and Sequel. A Case Study of Social Movements in Indonesia'. Ph.D. Dissertation, University of Amsterdam.

Schneider, Jane (1971), 'Of Vigilance and Virgins: Honor, Shame and Access to Resources in Mediterranean Societies', *Ethnology*, 10, 1: 1–24.

Van den Muyzenberg, Otto D. (1971), 'Politieke Mobilisering en Geweld in Centraal Luzon (Philippijnen)', *Sociologische Gids*, 18, 2: 48–60.

Walter, Victor Eugene (1969), *Terror and Resistance: A Study of Political Violence*. New York: Oxford University Press.

Wertheim, W. F. (1964), *East–West parallels*. The Hague: Van Hoeve.

Wolf, Eric R. (1966), *Peasants*. Englewood Cliffs: Prentice-Hall

—— (1969), *Peasant Wars of the Twentieth Century*. New York: Harper & Row.

[3]

Social Bandits: Reply

ERIC HOBSBAWM

University of London

The concept of social banditry, which forms the basis of a chapter in my
Primitive Rebels (1959) and of *Bandits* (1969), has been often referred to
but has received comparatively little critical analysis from students familiar
with the phenomena of banditry. Mr. Blok's critique of it is therefore most
welcome. What seems to be at issue are not so much facts as interpretations.
Most of the points made by Blok have also been made in the works criticized, notably in Hobsbawm (1969). Thus the difficulty of distinguishing
between different types of bandits, the personal motivations of bandits, the
problem of their protectors and supporters, the function of banditry as a
channel of upward social mobility, and various other such matters are discussed by me. There is little substantial disagreement about the facts.

As to interpretation, the major difference seems to be that Mr. Blok
denies that there is a type of banditry which can be regarded as a very elementary form of social protest. Consequently he believes that the 'myth'
of the social bandit, which he appears to accept as having widespread
existence, represents not what (some) bandits do, but merely what peasants

would wish them—or someone—to be doing. My view is that the myth cannot be entirely divorced from the reality of banditry.

Here again, there is no disagreement about the facts. I do not claim that the bandit is necessarily or even typically a conscious social protester. On the contrary (Hobsbawm, 1969: 19) I state

As individuals they are not so much political or social rebels, let alone revolutionaries, as peasants who refuse to submit, and in doing so stand out from their fellows, or even more simply men who find themselves excluded from the usual career of their kind and therefore forced into outlawry and 'crime'. *En masse* they are little more than symptoms of crisis and tension in their society. . . . Banditry itself is therefore not a programme for peasant society, but a form of self-help to escape it in particular circumstances.

What turns them into expressions of peasant discontent is that they 'have no ideas other than those of the peasantry . . . of which they form a part'. What can turn them into champions of peasant discontent is the role which peasant society ascribes to them (and to which, for various reasons suggested, they may tend to conform), together with the arms and independence which enable them to play it. However, I insist—it is the key to Hobsbawm, 1969, chapter 6—that

the crucial fact about the bandit's social situation is its ambiguity. He is an outsider and rebel, a poor man who refuses to accept the normal rules of poverty. . . . This draws him close to the poor: he is one of them. It sets him in opposition to the hierarchy of power, wealth and influence: he is not one of them. . . . At the same time the bandit is, inevitably, drawn into the web of wealth and power, because, unlike other peasants, he acquires wealth and exerts power. He is 'one of us' who is constantly in the process of becoming associated with 'them' (p. 76).

This means that the 'pure' Robin Hood is inevitably rare (a) because to avoid or reject the temptations of power and wealth requires a degree of political consciousness which is rarely to be found among such men, and (b) because to do so implies the rejection of most of that support and protection from the local power-structure, which is so helpful to the bandit who wishes to pursue a successful career. Does he exist at all?

The strongest evidence for his existence lies in the sharp distinction which rural public opinion makes between bandits who do and those who do not play the role of Robin Hood, or between those who are believed to play it and those who do not. Such distinctions can be traced in conversation, in song and story, and probably in vocabulary (Hobsbawm, 1969: 41). There are 'good' bandits and 'bad' bandits, not to mention those about whom public opinion is indifferent. In the Argentine Chaco the late 'Maté Cosido' was a 'good' bandit. In the opinion of an informant (October 1968), a former policeman who had spent much of his career vainly pursuing him, he was moderate in the use of killing and violence, helped widows and never robbed good Argentines, not even Argentine banks, but only 'los cobradores de la Bunge y de la Clayton', i.e., the symbols of foreign business. The late Velasquez did not enjoy this reputation.

The value of such testimony is not fundamentally affected by the fact that in the mind of this informant a real bandit has plainly come to acquire the characteristics of the mythical stereotype as well; in this instance of one remarkably similar to Jesse James, a man who operated in a comparable socio-economic environment. The myth-making or otherwise distorting capacities of the human memory are well-known, and not confined to bandits. The significance of such information is, that it shows (a) the selectivity of the bandit myth (some bandits are 'good' whereas others are not), (b) the bandit myth (high moral status, 'good' actions) actually formulated by the policeman who fought the bandit, and therefore also (c) the myth of the 'good' bandit as compatible with a close and critical acquaintance with the actual behaviour of the 'hero'. It seems simplest to assume that that there is some relation between a bandit's real behaviour and his subsequent myth. There is, of course, also some evidence that certain bandits have genuinely attempted to play the Robin Hood role.*

However, one point in Mr. Blok's critique is well taken. My discussion fails to distinguish clearly between the versions of the 'myth' which are held about bandits who are personally known to those who hold it, and versions held by those at a more or less great distance in time and place from them; between what is said about the active bandit *now* and about the remembered bandit; about the local or remote bandit. These distinctions have not so far been adequately investigated to my knowledge. I see no reason to believe that such a study would eliminate all living examples of Robin Hoods.

The other major divergence is a matter of definition. My work has not been concerned with banditry as such, but 'only with some kinds of robbers, namely those who are *not* regarded as simple criminals by public opinion' (Hobsbawm, 1969: 13), or more exactly with that variant of robbery which represents an element of social protest. It is not open to the criticism of 'over-emphasizing' or under-emphasizing this element, since its object is not to quantify it in relation to other kinds of banditry, but to analyse the complex nature of this type of protest and the social role of the men cast to represent it.

Beyond this the differences between myself and Mr. Blok, in so far as they exist, appear to be matters of judgement about which argument is difficult. I am, however, grateful to him for drawing my attention to D'Alessandro, *Brigantaggio e mafia* (1959), which I did not know. It may be worth adding that various foreign editions of Hobsbawm (1959) and the forthcoming British reprint have noted, or will note, some literature on the relevant topics that has appeared since first publication.

* I cannot resist quoting the case of a somewhat more political peasant activist in Bihar (India), sentenced to jail for attacking landlords and joining the Communist Party (CPI) thereafter, who was the despair of his comrades in the late 1960s, since he insisted on distributing the money collected for the Party to the peasants, as he had been in the habit of doing in his pre-marxist days. (Personal information.)

[4]

ALBION'S FATAL FLAWS*

DOUGLAS HAY'S ESSAY, "PROPERTY, AUTHORITY AND THE CRIMINAL
Law", which sounds the opening shot for the collection titled *Albion's
Fatal Tree*, has attracted a huge following, especially outside specialist
legal history circles.[1] Hay's main thesis is that some of the most
characteristic features of eighteenth-century English criminal procedure for cases of serious crime require to be understood as "a
ruling-class conspiracy" against the lower orders.[2] In the present
article I shall show that when tested against detailed evidence of the
work of the felony courts, Hay's thesis appears fundamentally mistaken. (I shall not be discussing the other essays in the *Albion* volume.)

Although the Hay essay has several strands, in its most important
dimension it purports to explain a celebrated peculiarity of the criminal justice system of the eighteenth century, namely the large number
of offences punishable by death. The list of nominally capital offences
grew throughout the century;[3] various authors reckon it at upwards
of 200 by the early nineteenth century, although that figure is bloated
in ways that I shall discuss later. In the actual administration of the
criminal law, however, capital punishment had been on the wane
since the sixteenth century, in the sense that a declining proportion
of persons convicted of felony were executed. The puzzle is, why did
the "penal death rate"[4] decline while the legislature was threatening
ever more capital punishment?

The conventional account of this paradox is Radzinowicz's.[5] I have
always found it fundamentally persuasive. I still do, and I shall return
to it at the end of this article. Hay offers quite a different explanation.
The widening gap between the expanding threats of death on one

* An earlier version of this paper was presented to the October 1981 meeting of the
American Society for Legal History. Suggestions and references from John Beattie,
J. S. Cockburn, G. R. Elton, Owen Fiss, George Fletcher, Lawrence Friedman,
Charles Gray, Thomas Green, Douglas Hay, R. H. Helmholz, Dennis Hutchinson,
Gareth Jones, P. J. R. King, Mark Kishlansky, David Langum, Norval Morris,
Richard Posner, A. W. B. Simpson, Lawrence Stone and John Styles are gratefully
acknowledged.

[1] Douglas Hay, "Property, Authority and the Criminal Law", in Douglas Hay,
Peter Linebaugh, John G. Rule, E. P. Thompson and Cal Winslow, *Albion's Fatal
Tree: Crime and Society in Eighteenth-Century England* (London, 1975), pp. 17-63.

[2] *Ibid.*, p. 52

[3] For various counts, see Leon Radzinowicz, *A History of English Criminal Law and
its Administration from 1750*, 4 vols. (London, 1948-68), i, pp. 3-4; but see p. 118
below.

[4] The famous phrase of J. C. Jeaffreson, *Middlesex County Records*, 4 vols. (London,
1886-92), iii, p. xvii.

[5] Discussed on pp. 115-16 below.

hand and relatively infrequent imposition of the death penalty on the other hand enhanced the discretion of the elite to decide whom to execute and whom to spare. It was "a ruling-class conspiracy" to use the criminal law in order to extract deference from the lower orders. Hay detects this self-serving discretion throughout the main phases of the criminal process — prosecution, trial, sentencing and executive clemency.[6]

Hay does not seriously claim to have identified a conspiracy in the conventional sense of the term, that is, an agreement to promote unlawful or wicked ends. Rather, he says, the plot was one in which "the common assumptions of the conspirators lay so deep that they were never questioned, and rarely made explicit".[7] This way of speaking directs attention away from the mechanism of class concert, which the essay hardly clarifies, and towards the supposed object, emphasized incessantly, of class domination and oppression ("the law . . . allowed the rulers of England to make the courts a selective instrument of class justice . . .").[8]

I think that a critic interested in broad questions of Marxist historical method might take a stern view of so ambiguous a notion of conspiracy, but that is not my mission. Still less do I wish to bring the general tenets of Marxist theory into question. It is true that I am criticizing a Marxist work, and that my own predilections are non-Marxist, but my critique would be largely unaffected if I were to assume that Marx and his followers have correctly characterized the main movements in Western social and political history. Even the most dedicated Marxist would concede that there is a variety of subjects on which Marxist historical method does not throw much light — the history of climatic changes, the invention of the flush toilet, or what have you. In this article I shall be saying that the aspects of eighteenth-century English criminal procedure emphasized in the Hay essay belong on that list of subjects. The criminal law and its procedures existed to serve and protect the interests of the people who suffered as victims of crime, people who were overwhelmingly non-élite.

I
SOURCES

I shall develop this view by drawing on data from a group of 171 cases conducted at four sessions of the Old Bailey during the years

[6] *Prosecution*: "it was in the hands of the gentleman who went to law to evoke gratitude as well as fear in the maintenance of deference" (Hay, "Property, Authority and the Criminal Law", p. 41). *Trial*: "The nature of the criminal trial gave enormous discretion to men of property . . . [in addition to] the prosecutor" (*ibid.*, p. 42). *Sentencing*: character evidence from "employers, respectable farmers and neighbouring gentlemen" might "induce the judge to pass a lesser sentence, or recommend a pardon" (*ibid.*, p. 42). *Clemency*: the pardon process "epitomizes the discretionary element of the law . . ." (*ibid.*, p. 43).
[7] *Ibid.*, p. 52
[8] *Ibid.*, p. 48.

from 1754 to 1756. The data comes from a study being published elsewhere, which is devoted to reconstructing and establishing the reliability of a pair of sources that supply narrative accounts of what was happening at these criminal trials.[9] One source is a set of judge's notes — that is, courtroom minutes of evidence and jury instructions — taken down by Sir Dudley Ryder, chief justice of King's Bench, who sat at the Old Bailey for these four sessions and actually presided over the trial of 44 of the 171 cases. Like his brethren on the common law bench, Ryder served intermittently as a trial judge at the Old Bailey. His notes are exceptionally detailed by comparison with others that survive for the period, for the simple reason that Ryder knew shorthand. As a youth he had mastered one of the standard shorthand systems of the day. His Old Bailey notes, as well as a diary of his assize notes that Hay used in his essay[10] and that I shall also draw upon, have been transcribed into typescript by a cipher expert.

The four Old Bailey sessions at which Ryder sat during his brief judicial career were also the subject of a series of contemporary pamphlet reports, now called the Old Bailey Sessions Papers.[11] The pamphlets were prepared for a lay readership and sold on the streets of London immediately after the trials. I have written about their origins and characteristics in an article published a few years ago.[12] The pamphlets continue to be the main source for the detail of the criminal trials that I shall be discussing for the Ryder years. The Ryder notes both confirm the reliability of what the pamphlets report and add detail, especially legal detail, that the pamphlets bleached out.

In emphasizing a two-year period from mid-century I run the usual risk of sampling error, and I shall be unable to correct adequately for developments later in the century. (The Hay essay also relies heavily but not entirely on mid-century sources.) The main objection to basing a critique of Hay's essay on Old Bailey sources is that London was uniquely urban, whereas Hay's essay blends provincial and London sources. To be sure, we do see less sheep-stealing and more shop-lifting in London than we would find in Lancashire. Fortu-

---

[9] John H. Langbein, "Shaping the Eighteenth-Century Criminal Trial: A View from the Ryder Sources", *Univ. of Chicago Law Rev.*, l (1983). The Ryder Old Bailey Notes appear as Document no. 14 of the transcribed notebooks. The manuscript and a copy of the typescript are deposited in Lincoln's Inn. The manuscript diary (hereafter Ryder Assize Diary) is transcribed as Document no. 19(f), volume 1129 of the Harrowby Manuscripts, Sandon Hall. Copies of both typescripts have also been deposited at the University of Chicago Law School Library.

[10] Hay, "Property, Authority and the Criminal Law", pp. 28-9.

[11] During the Ryder years the pamphlets were published in London eight times a year, usually in two parts, and bear the title *The Proceedings on the King's Commissions of the Peace, Oyer and Terminer, and Gaol Delivery for the City of London; and also the Gaol Delivery for the County of Middlesex, Held at Justice-Hall in the Old-Bailey* (hereafter *Old Bailey Sessions Papers*).

[12] John H. Langbein, "The Criminal Trial before the Lawyers", *Univ. of Chicago Law Rev.*, xlv (1978), pp. 263, 267-72. For further discussion, see Langbein, "Shaping the Eighteenth-Century Criminal Trial".

nately, when such issues arise in this paper, I shall be able to refer to the findings for provincial Essex contained in a splendid paper by P. J. R. King.[13] It should also be observed that English criminal procedure was very much a national system. Although a few details of Old Bailey practice were peculiar,[14] the fundamental principles applied equally in the metropolis and in the provinces. However much the clientele differed, the procedural institutions were shared. So were the royal judges who sat in turns at the Old Bailey and rode the assize circuits. In 1755, for example, Dudley Ryder presided on the Northern Circuit in March, at the Old Bailey in April, on the Home Circuit in August, and back at the Old Bailey in October.

II
OFFENCES AND OFFENDERS

Prosecutions for felony in the eighteenth century were for offences that had been felony for centuries before. The law that the courts had occasion to enforce in the eighteenth century was not for the most part the law that the contemporary legislature was enacting. An itemization of the offences in my sample for 1754-6, representing four months' worth of all the cases of serious crime prosecuted in the metropolis, will provide a convenient illustration of the actual business in the court of capital jurisdiction. (See Table.)

The prosaic nature of these offences will come as a surprise to readers who have taken seriously Hay's preoccupation with such legislation as that against food riots and work-place insurrections.[15] In my data we do not see offences that exemplify the advance of pre-industrial capitalism. Virtually all of the offences had been felonious back into the middle ages, a point Hay has lately acknowledged in another context in an article in this journal.[16] Most of the offences

[13] P. J. R. King, "Decision-Makers and Decision-Making in the 18th Century Criminal Law: The Social Groups Involved in the Punishment of Property Offenders and the Criteria on Which Their Decisions Were Based" (typescript, March 1981). King's paper, still unpublished, was presented to a conference at the University of Kent, Canterbury, in April 1981.

[14] For example, (1) the Old Bailey sat eight times a year, provincial assizes twice; (2) the Old Bailey had a permanent judge, the Recorder of London, as well as rotating common law judges like Ryder; the recorder pronounced sentence and conveyed recommendations for clemency to the monarch on behalf of the court; (3) the pre-trial process that culminated in trial before the Old Bailey was more systematic, on account of the work of the quasi-official "court justice" (J.P.) for Middlesex and the institution of "the sitting Alderman" in the City.

[15] See Hay, "Property, Authority and the Criminal Law", pp. 20-1: "the class that controlled Parliament was using the criminal sanction to enforce two of the radical redefinitions of property which gentlemen were making in their own interests during the eighteenth century".

[16] Douglas Hay, "War, Dearth and Theft in the Eighteenth Century: The Record of the English Courts", *Past and Present*, no. 95 (May 1982), p. 146: "In spite of the flood of new capital statutes that followed the Restoration, most capital prosecutions continued to be made under Tudor legislation. In the years considered here, 1742 to
(cont. on p. 100)

were only nominally capital, as benefit of clergy pertained and reduced the sanction from death to transportation.[17]

TABLE

OFFENCES PROSECUTED AT DUDLEY RYDER'S FOUR OLD BAILEY
SESSIONS 1754-1756*

Homicide	3
Burglary, breaking and entering	7
Highway robbery	4
Livestock theft	6
Pocket-picking	13
Shop-lifting	20
Theft from lodgings, inns, pubs	15
Domestic theft	10
Theft from work-places or employers	13
Other theft, 40s. or over	15
Other theft, under 40s.	53
Receiving stolen goods	13
Forging a will	1
Aiding a gaol-break	1
Assault and robbery	2
Perjury and abuse of legal process	3

* Notes and sources: Offences prosecuted October 1754, April and October 1755,
and April 1756, the four sessions at which Dudley Ryder was among the trial commissioners. Offences are categorized in the Table in lay terms; each has been tabulated
as originally charged, although juries returned lesser offences or acquitted outright in
many. When a case involves multiple charges, only the most serious has been tabulated,
in order to avoid double counting. In eight cases involving multiple defendants the
court tried separate indictments for receiving stolen goods simultaneously with the
related larceny cases, which accounts for the discrepancy between 171 trials and 179
offences. Ryder Old Bailey Notes, pp. 1-62; *Old Bailey Sessions Papers* (Oct. 1754,
Apr., Oct. 1755, Apr. 1756). See nn. 9, 11 above.

It is very hard to find figures worthy of romance, even social romance, among the shop-lifters, pickpockets, pilfering housemaids
and dishonest apprentices who populated the Old Bailey dock. To be
sure, most of them were poor, as criminals tend to be. Anatole France
made the most of that in a famous utterance. "The law [of France]",
he said, "in its majestic equality, forbids the rich as well as the poor
to sleep under bridges, to beg in the streets, and to steal bread".[18]
Actually, to the extent that our sources let us see anything about the
economic circumstances of the persons accused, we can say that the
culprits tried at the Old Bailey are seldom destitute. Some plead
hunger or say they are unemployed, but in the main we see employed
persons who have yielded to temptation rather than necessity. To

(n. 16 cont.)
1802, at least 95 per cent of the 450 capital charges tried at Staffordshire assizes were
based on statutes enacted before 1742". (The main Tudor legislation that Hay has in
mind supplied statutory basis for offences that had been common law felonies from
medieval times. Developments in benefit of clergy, discussed on p. 117 below, precipitated much of the Tudor legislation.)

[17] Discussed on p. 117 below.

[18] Anatole France, *Le lys rouge* (Paris, 1894), quoted in John Bartlett, *Familiar
Quotations*, 15th edn. (Boston, 1980), p. 655.

turn these little crooks into class warriors one must wear rose-coloured glasses of the deepest hue.

III
PROSECUTION

If the criminals were often poor, their victims (whom we see serving as private prosecutors in the Old Bailey trials) were not much better off — a point that is played down in Hay's essay.[19] In the Old Bailey cases we often cross a class line when we move from the offender to his victim, but not a class gulf. The victim is usually more propertied than the person who victimized him, although often only slightly. I have not hit upon a way of quantifying this, in part because information about the social status of the victim is so haphazard in the Old Bailey sources but I think that anyone who studies a volume of the Old Bailey Sessions Papers will conclude that the victims seldom eome from the propertied élite. They are typically small shopkeepers, artisans, lodging-house keepers, innkeepers and so forth. Included on the list of victim-prosecutors for the first dozen cases in the October 1754 sessions, for example, are a loom maker, a brass founder, a wine merchant, and a pewterer, each prosecuting pilfering employees; a baker's servant and a journeyman tailor prosecuting thieving prostitutes; a lodging-house keeper and a former room-mate prosecuting for the theft of furniture and domestic goods from lodgings; and a calico printer who had been mugged on the street. Only one — a major who prosecuted a stablehand for horse-stealing — fits Hay's image with any ease.

King's data corroborates the Old Bailey sources in a helpful way. He has worked with Essex quarter sessions records, mostly recognizances in which descriptions of the victims appear fairly regularly. I stress, as King does, that there are important differences between cases triable at quarter sessions on the one hand and at assizes or the Old Bailey on the other hand; in particular, the felonies tried at quarter sessions were non-capital, that is, petty larceny. Nevertheless, it is very telling that King's tabulations of the occupational status of prosecutors for the period 1760-1800 show that "Around 90% of these prosecutors came from three groups — the farmers, the tradesmen and artisans, and the labourers".[20] King further points to the works of Brewer and Styles and of David Philips, both published

---

[19] Hay, "Property, Authority and the Criminal Law", p. 37: "The poor suffer from theft as well as the rich, and in eighteenth-century England probably far more poor men lost goods to thieves, if only because the rich were few and their property more secure".

[20] King, "Decision-Makers and Decision-Making in the 18th Century Criminal Law", p. 9

after the Hay essay, which reach similar conclusions.[21] Prosecution was not a preserve of the ruling class.

Indeed, one of the main themes in the history of the administration of the criminal law in the second half of the eighteenth century was the effort to encourage prosecutorial activity by the lower orders. In one sense this is a development that traces back to the 1690s, when parliament began to enact the statutes that offered rewards for successful prosecution of certain heinous felonies, including highway robbery, burglary, housebreaking and horse-stealing.[22] In the 1750s the campaign waged by Henry Fielding to obtain a subsidy for expenses for poor prosecutors and witnesses came to fruition in legislation of 1752 and 1754,[23] and we know from Dudley Ryder's assize diary that the statutes were being put to use. He tells us that it had become the convention to award five shillings per day in expenses, and in one case he reports that he refused an award to an innkeeper who seemed too prosperous.[24]

In disputing Hay's version of the prosecutorial process — that "it was in the hands of the gentleman who went to law to evoke gratitude as well as fear in the maintenance of deference" — I have been arguing that gentlemen prosecutors were few and far between. I want also to take modest exception to the notion that since prosecution was private, a potential prosecutor had the discretion to threaten it in self-serving ways. In fact, various factors worked to circumscribe the prosecutor's discretion.

The most endemic aspect of what one might call prosecutorial discretion is the phenomenon of non-reporting of crime. We are all familiar with the recent discussion about whether increases in reported instances of rape reflect increased incidence of the offence, or lessened aversion to reporting it. When we deal with grand larceny, which in all its forms was the predominant eighteenth-century felony, we can be sure that a victim who chose to forgive an offender by not reporting the crime could seldom be stopped. But this was hardly a

---

[21] *Ibid.*, pp. 3, 12, citing John Brewer and John Styles, *An Ungovernable People: The English and their Law in the Seventeenth and Eighteenth Centuries* (London, 1980), Introduction, pp. 18-19; David Philips, *Crime and Authority in Victorian England: The Black Country, 1835-1860* (London, 1977), pp. 123-9.

[22] See the convenient summary in Patrick Colquhoun, *A Treatise on the Police of the Metropolis*, 7th edn. (London, 1806), pp. 390-2.

[23] 25 George II, c. 36, s. 11 (1752); 27 George II, c. 3, s. 3 (1754). Hay has remarked upon these and subsequent acts in his recent article, "War, Dearth and Theft in the Eighteenth Century", pp. 147-8, but without attempt to reconcile the earlier essay.

[24] Ryder Assize Diary, pp. 7, 13. Beattie reports that his "examination of about ten years in the Surrey and Sussex assizes between the 1750s and 1780s reveals a range of awards from about a pound (though one or two were as little as fifteen shillings) to as much as ten pounds. A very large number were between one and two pounds, though most were probably between two and three pounds": John M. Beattie, "Judicial Records and the Measurement of Crime in Eighteenth-Century England", in L. A. Knafla (ed.), *Crime and Criminal Justice in Europe and Canada* (Waterloo, Ont., 1980), pp. 127, 130.

peculiarity of eighteenth-century English social structure. It is true in today's Anglo-American legal systems and, indeed, in contemporary socialist legal systems. The victim of the property crime has a practical monopoly over disclosure of the offence. Every criminal justice system must depend upon the self-interest of owners for the enforcement of the laws protecting property.

Despite the nominally private character of prosecution in English law, there were forces at work that limited prosecutorial discretion. In homicide, of course, the coroner system largely eliminated it, because the coroner investigated every suspicious death. There was no equally comprehensive approach to larceny. As a matter of statutory design, the pre-trial binding-over system administered by the justices of the peace purported to limit prosecutorial discretion by requiring the J.P. to bind over to trial "all such . . . as do declare anything material to prove the . . . Felony . . .".[25] Yet this scheme assumed, in the language of the statute, a victim willing to "bring" the accusation to the attention of the J.P. There is good reason to think that many potential prosecutors did not bring charges. In his famous essay of 1751, Henry Fielding, who was campaigning to increase the levels of prosecution, stresses that potential prosecutors were either too forgiving or else too necessitous to take the time and incur the expense and nuisance of prosecuting.[26] Among his complaints Fielding did not find room for the abuse that Hay treats as central: affluent victims supposedly manipulating the prosecutorial power in a self-serving manner.

There were aspects of the pre-trial system that limited the discretion of a victim in not reporting to the J.P. Whenever the victim needed the J.P. to help him recover stolen goods — for example, by issuing search or arrest warrants, or by granting immunity from prosecution in order to obtain accomplice disclosures — the J.P. had notice and was able to bind over. These pre-trial investigative steps are frequently evidenced in the Old Bailey cases in my sample, although of course I have no way of identifying the dark figure of unreported events.

When the J.P. did bind over, it was usually on pain of a hefty fine for the prosecutor's non-appearance. Such recognizances survive for most of the Old Bailey trials of the mid-1750s; typically the penal sum they impose is twenty pounds. In the London Record Office papers for the April 1754 sessions there is a pitiful deposition from a shopkeeper, Moses Smith, who had been "bound [over] to prosecute and give Evidence" against an accused for feloniously stealing a handkerchief out of Smith's shop. Smith explains "that he was

[25] 2 & 3 Philip & Mary, c. 10 (1555).
[26] Henry Fielding, *An Enquiry into the Causes of the Late Increase of Robbers* (London, 1751), p. 106.

taken ill about a fortnight before the [trial, with] a violent Fever
which continued for several weeks". Smith sent two of his sureties
to the lord mayor's clerk to report the problem; the clerk replied that
Smith should have his wife attend the trial in his place. "But", the
deposition continues, "the said Smith being then so dangerously ill
and keeping no Servant [n]or having any person to attend his Shop
but his Wife, . . . she could not leave her husband at that time without subjecting him to great Danger". The document concludes with
a recital that Smith "did not neglect attending the Sessions with any
design to let the [accused] escape any punishment which might have
been inflicted on him had he been prosecuted . . .".[27] This picture
of a wretched little shopkeeper and his wife, too poor to be able to
hire someone to relieve them on the day of the trial, and now terrified
of the fine for non-prosecution, contrasts strongly with the notion of
unbounded prosecutorial discretion.

Finally, I should advert to another dimension of prosecutorial discretion, which concerns the decision not of whether to prosecute, but
on what charge. Ordinary grand larceny was subject to benefit of
clergy, meaning in practice that first-time offenders would be transported rather than executed. However, many (perhaps most) property offences could be characterized as something more than ordinary
grand larceny. A variety of statutes dealing with thefts from the person, from dwelling houses and shops, and on the highway, withdrew
benefit of clergy when these larcenies involved goods above particular
amounts. The issue that I do not yet understand is how prosecutors
arrived at the decision of whether to invoke these special statutes
when the facts permitted. In some of the Old Bailey cases it is clear
that the indictment itself down-values the goods, or neglects to charge
an aggravating circumstance — for example, that the offence was
committed in a dwelling house or a shop. In other cases when such
matters are charged, or fully charged, we see juries down-valuing the
goods or refusing to find the aggravating circumstance, in order to
make the offence clergyable and spare the culprit from the capital
sanction. The patterns of indictment down-charging seem sufficiently
recurrent that we may doubt whether there was much room for prosecutorial caprice. I suspect that the J.P.s and the clerks of assize and
their Old Bailey counterparts had an important hand in advising prosecutors how to charge,[28] and that they were guided primarily by their
sense of what verdicts juries were customarily prepared to return in
various circumstances.

[27] Corporation of London Record Office, Sessions Papers, April 1754 Sessions, loose
document, unnumbered, commencing "Moses Smith of Aldersgate . . .".
[28] In the case of Thomas Rolf, discussed on pp. 111-12 below, the prosecutrix
testified that she thought the money stolen from her amounted to more than eight
shillings, but she valued the sum at five shillings on the advice of the court justice,
John Fielding, who told her "Do it rather under than over": Ryder Old Bailey Notes,
p. 30.

I concede, although the actual evidence for it is thin, that élite victims must have been treated with greater courtesy, and allowed greater prosecutorial discretion, than victims like Moses Smith who came from lower social orders. Hay points to a single case, evidenced in the diary of a Lancashire squire, in which both the accused thief and the squire-prosecutor behave as though the prosecutor retains a power of non-prosecution, even though the prosecutor had used the J.P.s of Liverpool to obtain a search warrant and to conduct a pre-trial examination of the accused.[29] If we assume that this was not an aberration, it shows us only that the prosecutorial system was not an engine of egalitarianism. Of course, the prosecutorial system of so stratified a society will be sensitive to the patterns of deference that otherwise pervade the society. What I resist is the idea that such practices justify treating the prosecutorial system as having been constructed for the purpose of furthering the class interests of the élite. It is one thing to avoid conflict with the privileged orders, another thing to promote class aims.

The whole of the criminal justice system, especially the prosecutorial system, was primarily designed to protect the people, overwhelmingly non-élite, who suffered from crime. One can argue, as I am prepared to, that it was a great error on the part of the English to attempt to perpetuate a system of private prosecution and private policing from a medieval setting, where it may have made sense, to the changed circumstances of a more urban and impersonal eighteenth-century society. That was part of a set of constitutional convictions that contemporaries held deeply, even though in retrospect their concern looks to have been misplaced. Within the confines of a system that lacked professional prosecution, steps were taken to make the system serve the interests of the non-élite prosecutors who predominated. They were aided and afforced by the J.P.s, and in some cases subsidized and rewarded for prosecutorial efforts. Accordingly, I would venture to predict that when we finally obtain a satisfactory history of the prosecutorial system of the eighteenth century, self-serving gentlemen will be seen to have played an inconsequential role.

IV

JURIES

Whereas Hay has exaggerated the extent of prosecutorial discretion, he has underemphasized the importance of jury discretion. I had occasion above to refer to the role of juries in down-valuing goods or returning what we today call a "lesser included offence". I shall

---

[29] Hay, "Property, Authority and the Criminal Law", p. 41 n. 2, citing *Blundell's Diary and Letter Book, 1702-1728*, ed. M. Blundell (Liverpool, 1952), pp. 109-11.

follow John Beattie in calling both phenomena by the label of "partial verdict". Acquittals and partial verdicts receive short shrift in Hay's essay. I shall dwell on them because I think that his theory of ruling-class conspiracy is impossible to reconcile with the reality of jury discretion.

Beattie has computed for the period 1736-53 that about 10 per cent of the bills submitted to the Surrey grand jury in urban cases of capital crime were dismissed.[30] I am concerned with the second jury, the trial or petty jury. Beattie has computed that the petty juries acquitted in a third of the capital cases in which the Surrey grand juries had indicted; in another 30 per cent the petty juries returned partial verdicts.[31] My figures for the Old Bailey are in accord. The 171 cases produced 203 accused, of whom 84 were acquitted. I have not tabulated the frequency with which juries down-valued or convicted of lesser offences for the whole of my sample; in the October 1754 sessions, for which I do have the figures, of 31 guilty verdicts 14 involved these two types of partial verdict.

Both the acquittals and the partial verdicts follow patterns that are principled and predictable. When our sources give us narrative accounts of the trials we see that acquittals are usually returned in cases in which the evidence falls short of the standard of proof that was understood to be appropriate in criminal cases. Virtually all cases in which there was only a single accusing witness resulted in acquittal, as did cases in which the identification of the accused was put in any serious doubt.

The partial verdicts are especially interesting, because they were in truth sentencing decisions. They usually had the effect of reducing the sentence from death to transportation; in the relatively few cases in which the goods were valued below a shilling, the effect was to reduce the sentence from transportation to whipping. The striking aspect of the partial verdict practice in the cases in my sample is its regularity, hence predictability. In all cases of highway robbery and livestock theft in which juries convicted, they convicted capitally. They returned capital verdicts in most cases of burglary. Otherwise, juries applied what should be called a strong presumption against capital verdicts, a presumption that would be overcome when the circumstances were especially audacious. Old Bailey juries were harsh on professional or gang criminals, which is scarcely surprising in the setting of London's amateurish law enforcement. Capital verdicts for shop-lifting and for theft from a dwelling house usually occurred in cases with gang overtones, often involving multiple offences and requiring the evidence of an accomplice-turned-crown-witness.

[30] John M. Beattie, "Crime and the Courts in Surrey, 1736-1753", in J. S. Cockburn (ed.), *Crime in England, 1550-1800* (Princeton, 1977), pp. 155, 163.
[31] *Ibid.*, p. 176.

If I were going to organize a ruling-class conspiracy to use the criminal law to terrorize the lower orders, I would not interpose autonomous bodies of non-conspirators like the petty juries. If, on the other hand, I were going to reckon the jurors among my conspirators, I would be troubled that they were so predictably humane by the standards of the day.

I find Hay's account of the jury baffling. He wants to make the jurors co-conspirators. He says: "All men of property knew that judges, justices [of the peace] and juries had to be drawn from their own ranks".[32] This is not a considered statement, because it assimilates men of great wealth and station to the same "ranks" as those who satisfied the ten-pound-a-year minimum juror qualification.[33] In the Reverend Martin Madan's *Thoughts on Executive Justice*, a source several times cited' by Hay, the author worries that petty jurors at assizes are receiving inadequate instruction from the judge, "as they usually consist of low and ignorant country people!".[34] In his paper on the enforcement of the game laws, Hay points out that the farmers and tradesmen who were the typical jurors had interests different from those of the propertied élite.[35] From an Elizabethan sample Samaha has reported finding "ordinary people in the town — petty tradesmen such as alehouse keepers and occasionally even day labourers" sitting on trial juries at Colchester assizes, and he concludes: "To send a suspect to the gallows . . . required the concurrence of every segment in the community, since they were all represented at various stages of the criminal process . . .".[36] It hardly seems tenable for Hay to align petty jurors with the English social élite.

Hay is also on weak ground when he conjectures: "A panel of the poor would not convict a labourer who stole wood from a lord's park, a sheep from a farmer's fold, or corn from a merchant's yard". Although Hay is careful to say that he does not think that the juries of

[32] Hay, "Property, Authority and the Criminal Law", p. 38.

[33] The act of 4 & 5 William & Mary, c. 24, s. 15 (1692) fixed the juror qualification at ten pounds a year for England, six pounds for Wales; ss. 18-19 set the sum for talesman at five pounds for England and three for Wales. For the city of London the act of 3 George II, c. 25, ss. 19-20 (1730) imposed a hundred-pound qualification. An act of 4 George II, c. 7, s. 3 (1731) qualified for jury service in Middlesex men possessed of leaseholds of fifty pounds per year, apparently in recognition of the prevalence of leasehold conveyancing. These acts are treated as governing in the 1766 edition of Giles Duncomb, *Trials per Pais: or, The Law of England Concerning Juries by Nisi Prius*, 8th edn. (London, 1766), pp. 110, 162-4.

[34] Martin Madan, *Thoughts on Executive Justice, with Respect to the Criminal Laws, Particularly on the Circuits*, 2nd edn. (London, 1785), p. 148. In his recent "War, Dearth and Theft in the Eighteenth Century", p. 154 and n. 100, Hay states the point somewhat more softly, saying that "at quarter sessions and assizes trial jurors were drawn from a much higher social class than most of those indicted for theft".

[35] Douglas Hay, "Poaching and the Game Laws on Cannrock Chase", in Hay *et al.*, *Albion's Fatal Tree*, pp. 189, 211.

[36] Joel B. Samaha, "Hanging for Felony: The Rule of Law in Elizabethan Colchester", *Hist. Jl.*, xxi (1978), pp. 763, 781-2.

the day "convicted against the evidence", he speculates that "a more democratic jury might not have convicted at all".[37] I doubt whether the English poor of the eighteenth century generally condoned the theft of livestock and victuals, and Hay does not produce evidence that they did. Empirical study of twentieth-century juries in the United States — juries long since democratized and freed of property qualifications — squarely contradicts the notion that they are hostile to the law of larceny.[38]

We may come close to understanding how Hay went astray if we reflect upon a passage such as this, in which Hay takes it for granted that the criminal law lacked the adherence of the lower orders. To be sure, there were corners of the criminal law that did not command universal regard. The source of Hay's undoing, I suspect, is that the only part of the substantive criminal law with which he was deeply acquainted when he wrote his essay was the uniquely class-based and arbitrary game law. There certainly was popular dissatisfaction with the game law (and not confined to the poor),[39] but to extrapolate from that bizarre scheme (most of it misdemeanour) to the whole of the law of felony would be a grievous error, just as it would be folly in our own day to equate public attitudes towards marijuana offences and, say, automobile theft. When Hay speaks indifferently of stealing wood from a lord's park and sheep from a farmer's fold, he is making that sort of error. The property crimes that were of major conse- quence in the workload of eighteenth-century criminal courts — in particular the theft of livestock, shop goods, and personal and house- hold belongings — were those about whose blameworthiness there was a moral consensus that knew no class lines. That is why men of the non-élite could predominate (as prosecutors and jurors) in con- victing persons who committed property crimes.

V

JUDGES

The royal judges who presided at assize and Old Bailey trials for felony were certainly élite figures. The trial judge had a variety of means of influencing the verdict of the jury, especially through his powers to comment on the evidence and to instruct the jurors on the

[37] Hay, "Property, Authority and the Criminal Law", pp. 38-9.
[38] Harry Kalven Jr. and Hans Zeisel, *The American Jury* (Boston, 1966), pp. 76-7.
[39] It would be a mistake to think that hostility to the game laws followed any line between élite and non-élite. Blackstone, for example, who thought the game laws "of so questionable a nature", implied derisively that the "false grammar" of one of the statutes reflected on those who promoted the cause: William Blackstone, *Commentaries on the Laws of England*, 4 vols. (Oxford, 1765-9), iv, pp. 174-5. See also P. B. Munsche, *Gentlemen and Poachers: The English Game Laws, 1671-1831* (Cambridge, 1981); P. B. Munsche, "The Game Laws in Wiltshire, 1750-1800", in Cockburn (ed.), *Crime in England*, pp. 210-28.

law.[40] The limits on judicial influence must, however, be understood. Since there was as yet virtually no diversion of felony cases away from trial by jury, all those open-and-shut cases went to jury trial that would today be processed in short-form procedures such as plea bargaining or trial "by the bench" (that is, by judges sitting without juries).[41] Accordingly, most cases that went to jury trial in the eighteenth century involved evidence so overwhelming that conviction was a certainty, there was no room for influence. Further, when jurors deferred to judges, it was because jurors understood that judges spoke from wisdom and experience about matters of legal principle. If the jurors had suspected the judges of abusing their authority in order to promote élite interests, jurors would not have been so ready to follow the judges' lead. The history of bitter judge/jury antagonism in the seditious libel cases later in the century should stand as warning enough against the notion that judges could command jury verdicts by fiat.[42] When the sources for the Old Bailey cases permit us to see what the judges were saying to the juries, it seems largely dictated by the state of the facts or the law.

Hay's boldest theme concerns the supposed discretion of the judges in post-verdict proceedings, that is, in sentencing and clemency matters. In the modern world we are accustomed to judges having a broad, explicit discretion to fix sentences, but that was a nineteenth-century development. In the eighteenth century the English judge had no direct power to choose between death and transportation for felony convicts.[43] The jury, however, did — through the power that it exercised so vigorously of returning a partial verdict that reduced a non-clergyable offence to a clergyable one. Hay is correct to stress that the trial judge had considerable influence over the process by which convicts might receive executive clemency after sentencing. The pardon process is best understood as an adjunct to the sentencing system, compensating for the lack of direct judicial discretion. The secretaries of state and the monarch regularly deferred to the judges on pardon matters.[44]

[40] Langbein, "Criminal Trial before the Lawyers", pp. 284-300.
[41] See John H. Langbein, "Understanding the Short History of Plea Bargaining", *Law and Society Rev.*, xiii (1979), p. 261.
[42] See Thomas A. Green, *The Jury, Seditious Libel, and the Criminal Law* (forthcoming William Andrews Clark Memorial Lib. ser., Univ. of California at Los Angeles).
[43] The statute of 4 George I, c. 11 (1717) that had made transportation the regular sanction for clergyable offences did preserve to the judge the option to impose the lesser sanction of branding, and there are a couple of cases in which that happens in the Dudley Ryder sources under discussion. I should say that I do not understand what conventions may have been prevailing in respect of that seldom-used option. I suspect that a larger sample would show that a disproportionate number of these cases involved married women or gainfully employed fathers — cases in which transportation would have worked hardship on the family (and, perhaps, on the ratepayers as well).
[44] When the trial judges initiated pardon requests, the monarch granted them routinely. Chief Baron Macdonald described the long-established practice to a parlia-

(cont. on p. 110)

"Roughly half of those condemned to death during the eighteenth century did not go to the gallows", Hay writes, "but were transported to the colonies or imprisoned".[45] Data published in 1772 by Theodore Stephen Janssen, who had served as mayor of London in 1755, discloses that for the 23 mayoral years 1749-71 some 443 capital convicts were reprieved (or died in gaol) out of a total of 1,121 sentenced to death at the Old Bailey. Of these 443 who escaped execution, 401 were pardoned for transportation. One indication that these pardons were not awarded capriciously, but with a view to considerations of principle, is that pardon rates varied with the gravity of the offence. Of the 81 persons convicted of murder in Janssen's figures, 72 were executed; of 17 for attempted murder, 15 were executed; of 362 for highway robbery, 251 were executed; of 208 for house-breaking, 118 were executed. By contrast, only 6 of the 23 persons convicted of shop-lifting above the clergyable limit were allowed to hang; 22 of 90 for livestock thefts; 27 of 80 for stealing privately (picking pockets); 27 of 63 for stealing from a dwelling house in an amount above the clergyable sum; and neither of the two condemned sodomites.[46]

What factors were motivating the commutations and pardons? Hay notices that "The grounds for mercy were *ostensibly* that the offence was minor, or that the convict was of good character, or that the crime he had committed was not common enough in that county to require

(n. 44 cont.)
mentary committee in 1819: "The judges send what are called 'circuit letters' to the secretary of state, stating the places where prisoners have been convicted, their offences, and in general the favourable circumstances that have appeared, that would make a case proper to be recommended to His Majesty, for his pardon; and I do not remember any case in which such pardon was refused when recommended": *Report from the Select Committee Appointed to Consider of So Much of the Criminal Law as Relates to Capital Punishment in Felonies*, Parliamentary Papers (1819), viii, p. 48. The Recorder of London prepared an equivalent document for each Old Bailey sessions; for an example from one of the four sessions at which Dudley Ryder sat, see Public Record Office, London (hereafter P.R.O.), S.P. 36/132/296 (Apr. 1755 sessions). When the convict or a supporter petitioned for clemency, as in the case of Richard Tickner discussed on p. 112 and n. 54 below, the secretaries of state and often the monarch reviewed the merits of the case.

[45] Hay, "Property, Authority and the Criminal Law", p. 43.

[46] Stephen Theodore Janssen, *This Sheet Contains Three Tables, from 1749 to 1771* (London, 1772; Guildhall Lib., London, B'side 27.15). The broadside is reprinted as a foldout appendix in the endpapers of John Howard, *An Account of the Principal Lazarettos in Europe*, 2nd edn. (London, 1791).

It is interesting to note that Janssen emphasizes in this compilation the theme to which John Beattie and now Hay, in his "War, Dearth and Theft in the Eighteenth Century", have been directing recent scholarly attention, namely the seeming connection between rising crime rates and demobilization of the forces following periods of war. Janssen says: "It is worth observing that, as a great many idle Men and Lads are taken into the Sea & Land Service during a war; so we then find the Gangs of Robbers soon broken & that the Business at the Old Bailey gradually diminished to half its duration in time of Peace, nor are half the number of Criminals condemned. For in some Years of war they have not amounted to 20, whereas in Peace they have arisen to 70, 80, and 90. It is farther observable that at the conclusion of a War, through very bad Policy, when we turn adrift so many thousand Men, great numbers fall heedlessly to thieving as soon as their Pockets are empty, and are at once brought to the Gallows".

an exemplary hanging",[47] but Hay thinks that these grounds formed a mere smoke-screen. The judges "were not usually willing to antagonize a body of respectable [local] feeling", he writes. The pardon system was "capricious"; indeed, "the claims of class saved far more men who had been left to hang by the assize judge than did the claims of humanity".[48] In support of this view Hay offers the evidence of a few cases in which élite petitioners referred to the previous good character of the accused and especially to the good repute of his family.

Although my main objection to this line of argument is that it is unrepresentative, I want to say in passing that I would not accept the implication that such factors ought to have been extraneous to what were in effect sentencing decisions. In an age before probation and large-scale penal imprisonment, the existence of family and employment relationships was highly relevant to the decision whether or not to release an offender into the community (or, likewise, whether or not to turn him loose on the inhabitants of Virginia and Maryland by transporting him). Even today, if a convict can get respectable people to support him, sentencing officers are inclined to give weight to that evidence on the ground that it has predictive value on the question of the likelihood of successful resocialization.

Hay's account of the clemency system highlights the peripheral issue of social class and neglects to explore the factors that were of central importance. The Ryder notebooks give us a good window on this question, and the picture we see bears no resemblance to Hay's. Ryder is preoccupied with the merits in clemency questions, and he resists recommendations that involve only élite connections.

In the Old Bailey notebook there is one striking example, the case of Thomas Rolf, convicted of highway robbery at the October 1754 sessions and sentenced to death. The evidence indicated that Rolf, who had been apprehended at the scene, had behaved politely and apologetically to his victim as he robbed her. He told her that destitution led him to his crime. He was unable to find work and his wife was about to deliver their third child.[49] Ryder records in his notes that he urged the jury to convict, since "compassion could not justify finding contrary to truth", but after they heeded this instruction and found him guilty, the jurors "desired I would intercede for him. I said the Recorder [of London] would have an opportunity of representing it fully to His Majesty. [This is a reference to the recorder's regular report to the monarch after each Old Bailey sessions.] And indeed I never in all my life met with a robbery on the highway so clearly proved to be the effect of mere necessity and committed for

[47] Hay, "Property, Authority and the Criminal Law", p. 43 (my italics).
[48] *Ibid.*, pp. 43-4.
[49] *Old Bailey Sessions Papers* (Oct. 1754), Case no. 504, p. 326.

want of necessaries to maintain himself, wife big with child, and two infants".[50] Ryder made this notation with a view towards advising the recorder, and Rolf thereafter received a free pardon,[51] that is one not conditioned on transportation or some other sanction, even though the crown had to pay the prosecutrix the statutory forty-pound reward for apprehending and convicting him.[52]

Ryder's assize diary for the summer 1754 sittings on the Home Circuit contains considerable mention of his practice regarding judicial reprieve, reprieve being the decisive first step towards executive commutation. At Guildford assizes he noted that he let two burglars hang because "It was a very plain and bad case", but he reprieved a horsethief "because the evidence doubtful", a sheepthief "because the evidence not clear", and a pickpocket against whom the evidence amounted in Ryder's view "not quite [to] a clear case".[53]

At the same assizes Ryder resisted élite intervention for clemency in two cases of highway robbery. Richard Gilbert "was recommended to reprieve by Creswick and Andrews his master, being but 20 years old, but being for highway [robbery, and Gilbert having been convicted of two offences committed the same day, I] did not reprieve him". In the case of Richard Tickner, Ryder refused to reprieve although requested to do so by Arthur Onslow the Speaker of the House of Commons, Richard Onslow the lord lieutenant of Surrey, and Henry Talbot the high sheriff of Surrey. Arthur Onslow went to the king; Ryder's opinion was sought, and he records it thus: since "there was no reason to doubt [that Tickner had committed the crime] and there were no circumstances of alleviation, I could not take on myself to say he was an object of mercy . . .".[54] The king let him

---

[50] Ryder Old Bailey Notes, pp. 21-2.
[51] *Old Bailey Sessions Papers* (Jan. 1755), p. 80.
[52] P.R.O., T.53/45, Money Book, p. 353.
[53] Ryder Assize Diary, pp. 17-18.
[54] *Ibid.* Both Onslow's letter and Ryder's reply survive in the State Papers. Onslow wrote that Tickner, condemned "for a Robbery on the highway of some few shillings", was "a young Man of a very honest Family with us, and for the saving of whose life I am so much importuned, that I cannot avoid troubling your Lordship [the secretary of state] with an humble request for your assistance in obtaining a reprieve for him, in order to his transportation for any time, be the length of it what it will": P.R.O., S.P. 36/128/67 (3 Sept. 1754). Ryder's reply recites that a copy of Onslow's letter had been transmitted to him. Ryder reports on the evidence that had been adduced at Tickner's trial, remarking that the victim testified that Tickner "came up to him, presented a Pistol to his Breast & demanded his Money with a Curse, which on the Second like demand he delivered him to the amount of 14 Shillings". Ryder also reports that three pistols were found on Tickner when he was taken, and that he initially refused to identify himself. He concludes: "On the Whole, as I see no Reason to doubt of the Truth of the Fact, & no circumstances appeared to alleviate the guilt of it, I cannot take on my Self to represent him as an object of your Majesty's Mercy. But if your Majesty out of your great clemency shall be graciously pleased to extend your Royal Mercy to him, I humbly Submit it to your Majesty's wisdom whether it may not be on the Terms of Transportation for Life [as opposed to the seven or fourteen year terms otherwise current]": P.R.O., S.P. 36/128/77-8 (7 Sept. 1754).

hang. At Horsham assizes a few days earlier Ryder sentenced to death a man named Millet for horse-stealing. His diary records: "The clerk of assizes pressed me much to transport Millet, the hosteller, but I refused it because it seems to have been his practice [that is, he was a multiple offender], and nobody spoke to his character".[55] Ryder's handling of reprieve and pardon matters was principled. He was trying to take into account factors that ethical sentencing officers still consult.

King faults Hay for using "a small number of quotations from [the judges' reports to the monarch] to illustrate the importance of one particular factor — the role of respectability or respectable connections . . .".[56] To correct for that, King undertook to categorize all the factors mentioned in all the cases in the state papers for the period from 1784 to 1787. He identifies "five broad groups of factors", of which the respectability of the convict turned out to be the *least* important. The most frequent was good character, including previous good conduct. Although men of relatively high social standing supplied some of these references, King found that "the great majority of character witnesses were drawn from the middling sort or from the poorer but respectable sections of the local community".

Next in order of frequency, he found, was the youth of the offender, which reflected both sympathy and a belief in reformability. Third, King says, came the circumstances of the crime, especially whether violent. The fourth most commonly mentioned factor was the poverty of the culprit and his family. A little of this may have had to do with the desire to spare the ratepayers from having to support an executed convict's family, but the more usual concern was to recognize the lesser culpability of someone who acted in distress (and we remember Dudley Ryder's sympathy for the destitute highway robber Thomas Rolf). Furthermore, King says, wealth hurt. Judges were "very hard on prisoners who were relatively well off and could not therefore plead poverty at the time of the crime". He quotes a judge's report from a case in 1764, which says that it is better "that one man in good circumstances should suffer than 20 miserable wretches". Fifth and last in King's sample comes the factor Hay stresses, the respectability of the convict or his parents. King's totals for the five categories: (a) character and previous conduct, 126; (b) youth, old age and infirmity, 61; (c) circumstances of the crime, 56; (d) destitution or family poverty, 33; (e) respectability, 13. Radzinowicz directed attention several decades ago to the prevalence of a broad range of sentencing-type factors in the pardon process,[57] and

[55] Ryder Assize Diary, p. 13.
[56] King, "Decision-Makers and Decision-Making in the 18th Century Criminal Law", p. 22. The data quoted in text is from *ibid.*, pp. 22-8.
[57] Radzinowicz, *History of English Criminal Law*, i, pp. 115-16.

King has now done a great service in bringing new precision to the subject.

VI

LEGITIMATION

A staple of Marxist argumentation for dealing with contrary evidence is what I call the legitimation trick. Evidence that cuts against the thesis is dismissed as part of a sub-plot to make the conspiracy more palatable to its victims, to legitimate it. The Hay essay contains some splendid examples. Hay notices the pervasive legalism of English criminal procedure, including "the extreme solicitude of judges for the rights of the accused, [in which contemporary visitors from Europe saw such] a sharp distinction from the usual practice of continental benches".[58] Hay also mentions the tradition of strict construction against penal statutes and the recurrent quashing of strong prosecution cases for technical flaws. But Hay undertakes to reconcile this attention to safeguard with his thesis by arguing: "When the ruling class acquitted men on technicalities they helped instil a belief in the disembodied justice of the law in the minds of all who watched. In short, its very inefficiency, its absurd formalism, was part of its strength as ideology".[59]

Now the question that comes to mind is, simply, how does one test that proposition? A revealing manner, I think, is to hypothesize the exact opposite facts. Suppose that the rulers of eighteenth-century England had been operating banana-republic courts, coercing confessions or lynching paupers without trial. Obviously, the ruling-class conspiracy would be equally well evidenced. I have to ask, therefore, what kind of thesis it is that can be satisfied by any state of the evidence, and my answer is that it is not a thesis about the evidence, which means that it is not a thesis about history as I understand the discipline.

Consider another example, the celebrated case of Lord Ferrers, who as Hay tells us "killed his steward, was captured by his tenantry, tried in the House of Lords, sentenced to death, executed at Tyburn, and dissected 'like a common criminal' as the publicists never tired of repeating".[60] Hay dismisses such events as "part of the lore of politics that in England social class did not preserve a man even from the extreme sanction of death".[61] But suppose instead that Lord Ferrers had been privileged to slay as many social inferiors as he pleased, suppose, that is, that the English had immunized the élite from capital punishment. Well, of course, that would fit the thesis

[58] Hay, "Property, Authority and the Criminal Law", p. 32.
[59] *Ibid.*, p. 33.
[60] *Ibid.*, p. 34.
[61] *Ibid.*, p. 33.

just as conveniently. Consequently, the thesis is simply not testable. It floats above the evidence, it is self-proving. I am reminded of the way that some adherents of another economic-determinist school, the modern law-and-economics movement, are able to dismiss contrary evidence: the market makes everything efficient, and anything that is not is a consumption choice.

VII

THE STATUTES

Laying aside Hay's ruling-class conspiracy, what does explain the eighteenth-century paradox — the profusion of capital statutes in an era of declining capital punishment? I do not have a full answer, much less a thesis with the elegance of Hay's. I can, however, point to some factors that I believe bear on this great question.

My starting point is volume one of Radzinowicz's *History of English Criminal Law* published in 1948.[62] This work is not in fashion today, for reasons that I do not understand. In my opinion the burst of recent scholarship on eighteenth-century criminal procedure has done little to detract from Radzinowicz's awesome book. Radzinowicz derived his account from the contemporary tracts and legal literature, as well as from the parliamentary materials produced during the course of the reform movement that became prominent in the 1770s and ran into the middle of the nineteenth century. Rádzinowicz observes that Eden and Romilly, the legendary proponents of reform, followed the teaching of Beccaria and argued that punishment should be proportioned to the gravity of the crime.[63] (Blackstone advanced similar ideas in the 1760s.[64]) English law was wrong, they said, to invoke the death penalty for offences of vastly different seriousness. Excessive severity was counter-productive, it weakened deterrence by discouraging victims from prosecuting and by encouraging juries to down-charge or acquit. Nevertheless, adherents of what Radzinowicz calls the theory of maximum severity resisted the reformers' manifestly sensible position well into the nineteenth century. These people who supported the heavy English reliance on the threat of capital punishment were preoccupied with the deterrent policy of the criminal law, virtually to the exclusion of competing considerations such as proportionality. Why? They argued — and I think they believed — that England was uniquely dependent upon the deterrent effect of the capital threat because, alone of the great states of the day, England had neither a professional police force nor the system of non-capital sanctions known as penal servitude that had so widely displaced the death penalty on the Continent.

[62] Radzinowicz, *History of English Criminal Law*, i.
[63] *Ibid.*, pp. 231 ff.
[64] Blackstone, *Commentaries on the Laws of England*, iv, pp. 16-19.

A large chapter of English constitutional and administrative history underlies the eighteenth-century aversion to professional police forces and correction systems. Just as the prospect of a standing army evoked shivers in those who thought back to the days of James II, the suggestion that the police power in the localities be turned over to a corps of hirelings raised alarm. A tyrant might use this force to undercut or repress the liberties of the political community. The administrative challenge of organizing police and correction systems was also daunting to contemporaries. The English had scant experience in dealing with the problems of recruiting, training, financing, leading and controlling such forces. Ultimately, of course, as the urban-industrial age unfolded, the English had to abandon their attachment to amateur law enforcement, but that was the work of the next century; scarcely anyone foresaw it in the eighteenth century when the capital legislation was expanding so greatly.

Radzinowicz emphasizes the sense of insecurity that resulted from the want of effective policing.[65] Contemporaries felt that they needed every ounce of deterrence that they could get. They had to put so much weight on deterrence because they had so little chance of catching and convicting the undeterred. If the fear of hanging deterred some potential criminals, as most people thought it did, then the capital threat was worth making. Likewise, the want of any alternative to the capital sanction better than transportation had a great bearing on the extension of capital punishment to offences created in the eighteenth century.

I think that Radzinowicz's account of the explosion of capital statutes in an age of declining capital punishment has two major virtues when contrasted with Hay's.[66] First, Radzinowicz takes seriously the evidence of the people who were near, and in some cases quite influential in, the legislative events. Contemporaries struggled for decades over the relative merits of maximum severity versus proportionality, and I am persuaded that we should listen to them. Second, Radzinowicz has related his explanation to other, fundamental features of the legal system — that is, to the weaknesses in detection and corrections. In that respect the comparative dimension reinforces Radzinowicz. A notable weakness of Hay's account is that he points to ruling-class self-interest to explain a phenomenon that was distinctively English. Other states of the day had comparable ruling classes, yet the burgeoning of capital legislation in the later eighteenth century was an English peculiarity.

[65] Radzinowicz, *History of English Criminal Law*, i, pp. 23-35, 248 ff., 410.

[66] I should say, however, that I prefer Hay to Radzinowicz on the question of whether, as Radzinowicz contends, the declining penal death rate of the later eighteenth century was frustrating a legislative preference for higher levels of enforcement. Cf. Hay, "Property, Authority and the Criminal Law", p. 23, with Radzinowicz, *History of English Criminal Law*, i, pp. 158-64, esp. p. 164. Belief in the deterrent efficacy of capital punishment need not presuppose high levels of actual execution.

I wish to point to two other peculiarities of the English criminal justice system that help explain the burst of eighteenth-century capital legislation — benefit of clergy and the conceptual impoverishment of the substantive law.

From the middle ages into the eighteenth century, the remarkable institution of benefit of clergy underwent an incessant and contorted transmutation.[67] Originally a device for preserving ecclesiastical criminal jurisdiction over clerics, it became by 1706 a-privilege that anyone convicted of a common law felony could claim in order to obtain exemption from the imposition of the death penalty. Pursuant to legislation of 1717, almost all convicts who pleaded clergy after that date were transported to the British colonies in America for a seven-year term of indentured servitude. By the eighteenth century, therefore, benefit of clergy had drained most of the blood from the common law of crime. In order to preserve the capital threat for a crime that had been or would have been capital under the common law, special legislation had to be enacted making the offence non-clergyable. Some such statutes date from the sixteenth century, and a group of important ones appeared in the reigns of William and Anne, but most were Georgian.[68] Accordingly, the so-called expansion of the capital sanction in the eighteenth century was to some considerable extent only a restoration. This process of piecemeal restoration was a major force in the transformation of the law of crime from a common law field to a predominantly statutory one.[69]

This movement from common law into statute law occurred in a legal system that was ill-equipped to handle it. Milsom, speaking of the late medieval period, overstates this point, but let me quote him for the flavour of a notion that I think would repay careful study. "The miserable history of [the law of] crime in England can be shortly told. Nothing worthwhile was created".[70] Many aspects of the English medieval heritage had the effect of reducing the legal-scientific dimension of the criminal law by comparison with Continental law — we might mention the heavy use of laymen to decide and to prosecute criminal cases, the virtual absence of lawyers for prosecution and defence, the tiny number of royal judges, the decentralization of the assize system, and the opacity of the general verdict. English criminal law was primitive in matters of offence definition, especially

---

[67] See generally *The Reports of Sir John Spelman*, ed. J. H. Baker, 2 vols. (Selden Soc., xciii-xciv, London, 1977-8), ii, Introduction, pp. 327-34; James F. Stephen, *A History of the Criminal Law of England*, 3 vols. (London, 1883), i, pp. 458 ff. Hay dismisses benefit of clergy in a footnote: Hay, "Property, Authority and the Criminal Law", p. 22 n. 2.

[68] See the convenient list of these statutes in Jerome Hall, *Theft, Law and Society*, 2nd edn. (Indianapolis, 1952), pp. 356-63.

[69] See John Styles, "Criminal Records", *Hist. Jl.*, xx (1977), pp. 977, 980.

[70] S. F. C. Milsom, *Historical Foundations of the Common Law*, 2nd edn. (London, 1981), p. 403.

the general part, that set of notions about criminal responsibility that cuts across all criminal offences (for example, degrees of culpability, the law of attempts, aiding and abetting, capacity, and most of the affirmative defences). This underdevelopment of the scientific side of English law greatly affected the multiplication of capital statutes. The English did not have 200 separate crimes in the modern sense that could be punished with death. Rather, they lacked general definitions, especially for larceny and embezzlement, with the result that they were constantly having to add particulars in order to compensate for the want of generality.[71] The consolidation movement of the nineteenth century illustrates this point well; few offences were repealed, rather definitions were improved so that the number of separate offences could be reduced. Stephen, writing nearly a century ago, made the point that the 160 capital offences that Blackstone complained were in force in the 1760s "might probably be reduced by careful classification to a comparatively small number".[72]

Not only did English criminal law lack scientific sophistication, on the legislative side it had no central direction. No minister of justice oversaw the administration and amendment of the criminal justice system. Most of the capital statutes, like most of the rest of eighteenth-century legislation,[73] originated as members' bills. In such circumstances the extension of capital sanctions to new forms of property was natural enough, by sheer force of analogy. If the capital sanction suited offences against sheep under Elizabeth, then why not factories under George III? "For once the death penalty is established as the most effective instrument of crime-prevention", Radzinowicz remarks, "there can be no valid reason for invoking it to suppress one offence and not another".[74] Some larger reform of principle is needed to interrrupt that process. Legislatures incline to err on the side of severity when considering particular offences. Particulars are inflationary, because there is no counter-constituency to resist the analogy that extends penal sanctions from one thing to the next. Leniency and proportionality are considerations that come to the fore when a legislature has occasion to compare offences and sanctions — when, for example, it produces a penal code, or (as in nineteenth-century England) revises major segments of the law.

[71] See, for example, Radzinowicz's succinct account of the succession of larceny statutes: Radzinowicz, *History of English Criminal Law*, i, pp. 41-9.

[72] Stephen, *History of the Criminal Law of England*, i, p. 470.

[73] "In the eighteenth century, legislation was not . . . especially a matter for the ministers of the Crown. There was little government legislation apart from routine financial measures . . .": P. D. G. Thomas, *The House of Commons in the Eighteenth Century* (Oxford, 1971), p. 45. On the Treasury's oversight of revenue bills, see Sheila Lambert, *Bills and Acts: Legislative Procedure in Eighteenth-Century England* (Cambridge, 1971), pp. 71-4. See also Hugh Amory, "Henry Fielding and the Criminal Legislation of 1751-2", *Philol. Quart.*, l (1971), pp. 175, 191-2.

[74] Radzinowicz, *History of English Criminal Law*, i, p. 49.

We can, of course, trace the hand of commercial interests (who were often more petty bourgeois than élite, as I have said before) in a considerable fraction of the eighteenth-century criminal legislation, both capital and non-capital. I doubt whether anyone would argue with Jerome Hall's assessment that "it is in this century that one comes upon the law of receiving stolen property, larceny by trick, obtaining goods by false pretences, and embezzlement. Here, for the first time, the modern lawyer finds himself in contact with a body of substantive criminal law which he feels is essentially his own".[75] New forms of economic activity and commercial organization gave rise to new issues of definition. Yet the very fact that the solutions that were reached in the eighteenth century strike us as essentially modern (on issues of culpability, that is, rather than sanction) suggests that these measures were enacted because they were reasonable rather than because a ruling class wrested advantage from others. There is no social interest in failing to criminalize receiving stolen property, larceny by trick, obtaining goods by false pretences, and embezzlement. These offences persist with only technical refinement in modern English law, and comparable provisions grace the codes of modern socialist states.[76]

VIII
THE RULERS

In a recent essay Richard Sparks makes a point that helps us understand why the Hay thesis is so improbable.[77] The criminal law, says Sparks, is only important "at the *margins* of social life; . . . in day-to-day affairs it is not all that important to the maintenance of late industrial capitalism's social order . . . give me the law of contracts (including contracts of employment), and you can have all the rest of the statute book . . . the most generally useful laws are likely to be the ones that define . . . ownership and control [of the means of production], and not some ancillary laws that promise to thump individuals for rather trivial kinds of tampering with those means".[78] The criminal law is simply the wrong place to look for the active hand of the ruling classes. From the standpoint of the rulers, I would suggest, the criminal justice system occupies a place not much more central than the garbage collection system. True, if the garbage is not collected the society cannot operate and ruling-class goals will be frustrated, but that does not turn garbage collection into a ruling-

---

[75] Hall, *Theft, Law and Society*, pp. 34-5.
[76] For example, *Criminal Code of the Hungarian People's Republic*, trans. P. Lamberg (Budapest, 1962), pp. 108, 110, ss. 292 (embezzlement), 293 (criminal fraud), 301 (receiving goods unlawfully obtained).
[77] Richard F. Sparks, "A Critique of Marxist Criminology", *Crime and Justice: An Annual Review of Research*, ii (1980), p. 159.
[78] *Ibid.*, pp. 193-4.

class conspiracy. The Hay thesis, in a similar fashion, confuses necessary and sufficient conditions.

In this paper I have been maintaining two themes about the administration of the criminal law in the eighteenth century. First, most of the discretion was exercised by people not fairly to be described as the ruling class, especially the prosecutors and the jurors. Secondly, the discretion that characterized this system was not arbitrary and self-interested, but rather turned on the good-faith consideration of factors with which ethical decision-makers ought to have been concerned. The historian does not need a conspiracy theory to explain the discretion, and the discretion does not fit the theory. I concede fully that when men of the social élite came into contact with the criminal justice system in any capacity, they were treated with special courtesy and regard, just as they were elsewhere in this stratified society. To seize upon that as the *raison d'être* of the criminal justice system is, however, to mistake the barnacles for the boat.

University of Chicago　　　　　　　　　　　　　　*John H. Langbein*

[5]

(MARXIST) SOCIAL HISTORY AND (CONSERVATIVE) LEGAL HISTORY: A REPLY TO PROFESSOR LANGBEIN

PETER LINEBAUGH*

In an anthology entitled Albion's Fatal Tree *several social historians examined eighteenth-century English society through its laws and their application. In this article, Professor Linebaugh, one of the book's editors, responds to Professor Langbein's ferocious challenge to the Marxist interpretation of the century's criminal law provided by one of the essayists, Douglas Hay. Labeling Langbein's legal scholarship "ahistorical" elitism, Professor Linebaugh contrasts it with his colleagues' emphasis on customs and attitudes of ordinary people from the "bottom up." He proceeds to illustrate how Langbein's functionalist approach causes him to misconstrue Hay's point and misinterpret the evidence. Professor Linebaugh paints a world in which underpaid workers customarily took goods from their employers and corrupt trial jurors were drawn from propertied elite classes. He argues that Langbein's narrow vision prevents him from appreciating that because law was rooted in community custom, a more democratic jury may have sanctioned such appropriation. Finally, Professor Linebaugh rebuts Langbein's assertion that criminal law was no more central to society than was garbage collection by graphically illustrating eighteenth-century London's preoccupation with waste disposal. He ends by analogizing the century's criminal justice system to the flush toilet.*

INTRODUCTION

In this Article I contrast a legal view of social relations with a social view of legal relations by examining several issues that have emerged recently in a debate about eighteenth-century English law and society. The issues include the narrow and broad use of judicial records, the ambivalent role of the jury, the contrast between custom or common law and statute or Roman law, and the tendency of a superior social class to see the powerless in terms of garbage.

In particular I respond to Professor John Langbein of the University of Chicago, whose recent article, "Albion's Fatal Flaws,"[1] attacks *Albion's Fatal Tree: Crime and Society in Eighteenth-Century England*,[2] an anthology that E.P. Thompson, Douglas Hay, and I edited.

---

* Visiting Associate Professor of History, Tufts University. B.S., 1964, Swarthmore College; M.A., 1969, Columbia University; Ph.D., 1975, Centre for the Study of Social History at the University of Warwick.

[1] Langbein, Albion's Fatal Flaws, 98 Past & Present 96 (1983).

[2] D. Hay, P. Linebaugh, J. Rule, E.P. Thompson & C. Winslow, Albion's Fatal Tree: Crime and Society in Eighteenth-Century England (1975) [hereinafter Albion's Fatal Tree].

I

SOCIAL HISTORY AND THE LAW

"Albion" was the Greek name for England. By the eighteenth century this name became associated with a mythic, generous idea of a peaceful and harmonious society in very much the same way that the place known as "Jerusalem" has in the Christian tradition been associated with peace and salvation. In this respect the word hearkens to an earlier vision of England, which it counterposes to eighteenth-century England's chauvinism, war, and imperialism.[3] "Fatal Tree" refers to the gallows, especially the London gallows called "Tyburn," at the edge of town in Paddington. Many thousands lost their lives upon this "cheat," as it was familiarly known.[4] Our book began with a quotation from William Blake that expressed the contrast, as it was understood at the end of the eighteenth century, between the hopeful potentiality of human freedom and creativity and the actuality of death and destruction:

> What are those golden Builders doing
> Near mournful ever-weeping Paddington
> Standing above that mighty Ruin
> Where Satan the first victory won.

> Where Albion slept beneath the Fatal Tree
> And the Druids golden Knife,
> Rioted in human gore,
> In Offerings of Human Life.

> They groan'd aloud on London Stone
> They groan'd aloud on Tyburn's Brook
> Albion gave his deadly groan,
> And all the Atlantic Mountains shook.[5]

These lines from the 1790's express in a mixture of history, myth, and revolutionary aspiration real and vast historical forces that initiated the traffic in human beings on an enormous, epic scale: millions of people were thrown thousands of miles across oceans and continents to forced labor in America and Australia;[6] thousands were dispossessed from common land, Gaelic sept, or Scottish Highlands and torn from their roots

---

[3] See generally D. Erdman, Blake, Prophet Against Empire: A Poet's Interpretation of the History of his Own Times 14-16, 312-13, 479-87 (2d ed. 1969); T. Frosch, The Awakening of Albion: The Renovation of the Body in the Poetry of William Blake 60, 85 (1974).

[4] A New Canting Dictionary (London 1725), quoted in Albion's Fatal Tree, supra note 2, at 66.

[5] W. Blake, Jerusalem, in The Poetry and Prose of William Blake 170 (Erdman ed. 1965).

[6] The English people transported to the colonies for the violation of laws were, of course, not the only people forcibly removed from their homelands. One good source on transportation to the American colonies is A.E. Smith, Colonists in Bondage (1947). On the slave trade in African peoples, see, e.g., D. Mannix & M. Cowley, Black Cargoes (1962).

214   *NEW YORK UNIVERSITY LAW REVIEW*   [Vol. 60:212

and communities; whole towns and regions were expropriated in a revolutionizing of human labor in the process habitually, if lamely, called "industrialization." *Albion's Fatal Tree* did not analyze these forces directly or upon a world scale. Rather, we used a series of particular case studies of regional episodes to narrate strictly English conflicts between the murderousness of the eighteenth-century law and the people who not only suffered, but sometimes in their own ways struggled to survive and to maintain their own conception of "Albion." This was called "history from below" when the volume was published nine years ago, and it is this history that Professor Langbein attacks "from above."[7]

One American wrote about the Tyburn hangings and their relation to the development of anatomy.[8] Another wrote about the smugglers of southeastern England and their endemic wars against the excisemen.[9] A Cornishman wrote an essay about the practice of wrecking merchant ships upon the rocky coasts of western England.[10] A Canadian investigated the Game Laws and the poaching of rabbits in a midlands county.[11] E.P. Thompson, who from the Centre for the Study of Social History at the University of Warwick had assembled and guided this international group of scholars, contributed an essay on the "crime of anonymity" that summed up the historiographic problems of "history from below." (As a Newcastle collier wrote, "I Wauld Tel you My Name but My Simplicity Will Not Let Mee.")[12] We might have written about other subjects: piracy, clipping, highway robbery, embezzlement, and counterfeiting. However, because the essays included were so extensively researched, the questions they raised stirred activity in several academic disciplines; a more theoretical or abstract work might not have had the same academic versatility. The essays raised questions about property and the differences and relationships between those who created it and those who consumed it, about the diversity of regional and local attitudes towards the new law, about the class backgrounds of those who enforced it and those against whom it was enforced. Such questions were raised, but not completely answered, because we felt our conclusions had to be

---

[7] A. Calder, Revolutionary Empire: The Rise of the English Speaking Empires from the Fifteenth Century to the 1780s (1981), is a massive survey of these forces of "industrialization" and is by no means written "from below." On "history from below" see, e.g., Lemish, The American Revolution Seen from the Bottom Up, in Towards a New Past: Dissenting Essays in American History 3 (1968).

[8] Linebaugh, The Tyburn Riot Against the Surgeons, in Albion's Fatal Tree, supra note 2, at 65.

[9] Winslow, Sussex Smugglers, in Albion's Fatal Tree, supra note 2, at 119.

[10] Rule, Wrecking and Coastal Plunder, in Albion's Fatal Tree, supra note 2, at 167.

[11] Hay, Poaching and the Game Laws on Cannock Chase, in Albion's Fatal Tree, supra note 2, at 189.

[12] Thompson, The Crime of Anonymity, in Albion's Fatal Tree, supra note 2, at 255, 255.

limited by what was shown in the essays. We were aware that issues of great concern to legal, economic, and social historians were at stake, but we felt that practitioners of other disciplines might do this in a way more understandable to their particular discourses.

In the preface, however, E.P. Thompson did attempt to relate the narratives to a distinction commonly proposed in historiographical discussions of illegal behavior:

> It is rather easy, when taking a superficial view of eighteenth-century evidence, to propose two distinct kinds of offence and offenders. There are 'good' criminals, who are premature revolutionaries or reformers, forerunners of popular movements—all kinds of rioters, smugglers, poachers, primitive rebels in industry. This appears as 'social crime'. And there then are those who commit crime without qualification: thieves, robbers, highwaymen, forgers, arsonists, and murderers.[13]

We found no evidence of a sharp line between a "morally endorsed popular culture" and a "deviant subculture"; different communities appear to have opposed, tolerated, or sheltered varying kinds of offenders.[14] Despite our cautious conclusions, the essays became controversial among legal historians, among criminologists, among eighteenth-century specialists, and more generally among those working on both sides of the Atlantic in "popular history" or "social history." The volume also contributed to the revival of political economy, and Marxists of various persuasions found in it a source of disagreement or encouragement.[15]

The historian is affected by the kind of evidence used, and must therefore learn to be critical of its origins, the reasons for its survival, and the precise nature of its limitations. We turned to legal records because they are a prime source of documentation about the lives of people who left few written records of their own and attracted no attention from biographers. Just as Mary and John Leakey must be expert in paleontology and anatomy because their evidence for the early history of human beings is stones and bones, so we had to become interested in law and the judiciary.

Of the contributors to *Albion's Fatal Tree*, Douglas Hay became

---

[13] Thompson, Preface, in Albion's Fatal Tree, supra note 2, at 13-14.

[14] See id. at 14.

[15] See, e.g., Crime in England, 1550-1800 (J. Cockburn ed. 1977); Crime & Capitalism: Readings in Marxist Criminology (D. Greenberg ed. 1981); M. Ignatieff, A Just Measure of Pain: The Penitentiary in the Industrial Revolution, 1750-1850 (1978); An Ungovernable People: The English and Their Law in the Seventeenth and Eighteenth Centuries (J. Brewer & J. Styles ed. 1980); Horowitz, The Rule of Law: An Unqualified Human Good? (Book Review), 86 Yale L.J. 561 (1977); Pearson, Eighteenth Century English Criminal Law (Book Review), 3 Brit. J.L. & Soc'y 115 (1976); Rudé, Poachers and Protesters (Book Review), Times Literary Supp., Jan. 30, 1976, at 104 (*Albion's Fatal Tree* "open[s] up a rich field for further exploration and it is to be hoped that historians . . . who have in the past been somewhat slow to become engaged in this type of history 'from below', will be ready to take up the challenge.").

most interested in the law and the lawmakers. In the only essay that is entirely interpretive and analytical, he argued that in the eighteenth century the law replaced religion as the dominant form of ruling class ideological hegemony. The law with its costumes, its courtroom theatrics, its specialized jargon, and its internal, closed intellectualism came to dominate the discussion of property and social relationships.[16] The limits of that domination are implied in the other essays, which deal with proscribed behavior and with self-conscious "resistance" to legal norms. In a sense, therefore, Hay became more interested in the stones and bones than in what they might reveal about crime and criminals. Perhaps it is for this reason that Professor Langbein, a distinguished stone-and-bone man himself, has restricted his attack entirely to Hay's essay, an essay that powerfully conjoined the methods of legal and social history. Langbein is not interested in the other questions the volume raised; the stones and bones are ends in themselves: popular culture, social protest, material life, ruling class attitudes, the ownership and distribution of the "earthly treasury" are of no interest to him. Yet, by attacking Hay, Langbein seeks to discredit the volume as a whole, the deeper questions that it raises, and the view of the eighteenth century that our evidence led us to accept.

II

LANGBEIN'S ATTACK

Let us now turn to Langbein's eight-part attack. First, he attempts to controvert Hay's explanation of the essential paradox of eighteenth-century law—that while the statutory sanction of death expanded at an astonishing rate, from fifty to two hundred offenses, the actual numbers of hangings stabilized or declined. Langbein feigns evenhandedness at the Marxist overtones of Hay's essay,[17] but his rejection of Hay's "ruling class conspiracy" view not only takes a phrase out of context, but wholly misinterprets Hay's analysis. Hay argues that the increasing arsenal of death laws provided the Whig rulers of England with a functional combination of threat, terror, and mercy that established their hegemony over the "loose and disorderly" mass of the population.[18] He writes of "the private manipulation of the law by the wealthy and powerful," as a "ruling class conspiracy."[19] But he never confuses such behind-the-scene manipulations with the public operation of law, which he sees not in

---

[16] Hay, Property, Authority and the Criminal Law, in Albion's Fatal Tree, supra note 2, at 17.

[17] Langbein, supra note 1, at 97.

[18] Hay, supra note 16, at 17-18, 52.

[19] Id. at 52.

conspiratorial terms, but hegemonically: "The law was important as gross coercion; it was equally important as ideology. Its majesty, justice and mercy helped to create the spirit of consent and submission, the 'mind-forged manacles', which Blake saw binding the English poor."[20]

After badly mischaracterizing the thrust of Hay's historical analysis, Langbein suggests that the corpus of eighteenth-century death laws is one of those subjects, like the flush toilet, upon which Marxist historical method throws little light.[21] We shall return to Langbein's interest in sanitation.[22] Here we note only Langbein's refusal to consider the death laws in any terms—Marxist, Gramscian or otherwise—that would require him to move beyond the self-enclosed analysis commonly applied to legal and administrative subjects.

In the second section, attacking Hay's analysis of offenses and offenders, Langbein describes evidence from the *Old Bailey Proceedings*[23] of four of the sessions between 1754 and 1756 at which Londoners were tried for felonies. Although he acknowledges that this is not a statistically significant sample, and that the data are exclusively from London, rather than the countryside, where most English people lived and where Hay considered his case strongest, Langbein does not seem to consider his conclusions tentative. In defending his limited evidence, Langbein argues that the procedure of all courts was similar,[24] ignoring the numerous nonprocedural differences and demonstrating the narrowness of his analysis. His description of the offenders, or, as he would have it, the "little crooks,"[25] who were hanged or spared is similarly misleading, ideologically tendentious, and symptomatic of the limitations of narrowly legal inquiries into the history and meaning of law.

The third section analyzes the social class of private prosecutors and

---

[20] Id. at 49. Langbein apparently fails to notice that Hay is more influenced by Gramsci's notion of hegemony than by any "crude Marxist" notions of conscious ruling class manipulation of the working classes. See, e.g., Mouffe, Hegemony and Ideology in Gramsci, in Gramsci and Marxist Theory 168 (C. Mouffe ed. 1979). Langbein dramatically displays this misunderstanding when he alleges that "Hay takes it for granted that the criminal law lacked the adherence of the lower orders." Langbein, supra note 1, at 108. In fact, Hay's essay suggests how the criminal law secured the obedience of the working classes with terror and theater.

[21] Langbein, supra note 1, at 97.

[22] See text accompanying notes 121-40 infra.

[23] The Proceedings of the Peace, Oyer and Terminer, and Gaol Delivery in the City of London; and also the Gaol Delivery in the County of Middlesex, Held at Justice Hall in the Old Bailey [hereinafter Old Bailey Proceedings]. The Old Bailey Proceedings were pamphlets, with somewhat varying titles, containing accounts of recent trials. Professor Langbein has written about the Proceedings in several articles, including Langbein, Shaping the Eighteenth Century Criminal Trial: A View from the Ryder Sources, 50 U. Chi. L. Rev. 1 (1983). Though that article provides some useful information, it must be used carefully because it is flawed by some of the same unexamined and mistaken assumptions discussed in this article.

[24] Langbein, supra note 1, at 99 & n.14.

[25] Id. at 101.

attempts to show that these were rarely "gentlemen" or members of the elite, but were usually small propertied persons. Though Langbein notes that rewards were enacted to encourage prosecutorial activity by the lower orders,[26] he does not permit this system of "blood money" to interfere with his judgment that the system served the interests of crime victims in general rather than "self serving gentlemen" in particular.

The fourth section seeks to show that jurors were independent from influence by the gentry and urban oligarchs, and that their independence was exercised by the practices of undervaluing the goods that were stolen, acquitting defendants of major offenses and finding them guilty of lesser offenses.

The fifth section defends the Bench, arguing that it did not exercise its discretionary powers of sentencing for the purposes Hay suggested, but was entirely upright, compassionate, "firm," and socially responsible.[27]

The sixth section, called "Legitimation," casually dismisses as unverifiable Hay's explanation of the anomaly that occasionally a rich person was hanged—that such occasions lent an appearance of impartiality to the law. Langbein scoffs at what he calls a Marxist "legitimation trick," through which all practices inconsistent with naked class domination are chalked up to legitimation, making "the conspiracy more palatable to its victims."[28] He rejects Hay's argument that technical acquittals helped legitimate the law as ideology by giving the impression of justice, arguing that a system of "banana republic courts" would be equally good evidence of a ruling class conspiracy.[29] By relying on this repetitious and incorrect charge that Hay imagines a crude class conspiracy,[30] Langbein again misconstrues rather than refutes Hay's point. In fact, "banana republic courts" would do nothing to strengthen the ideology of law. Rather than attempt to understand the morality of the upper classes and the responses of the "lower orders" to their condition, Langbein simply writes off a basic part of Hay's analysis, choosing to meet him on exclusively institutional and legal grounds.

In section seven, Langbein considers the profusion of death statutes in an era of declining per capita hangings, the nub of Hay's concern. Langbein rejects Hay's thesis in part because "[o]ther states of the day had comparable ruling classes, yet the burgeoning of capital legislation was an English peculiarity."[31] But, as Langbein himself notes, England

---

[26] Id. at 102.
[27] Id. at 108-14.
[28] Id. at 114.
[29] Id.
[30] See text accompanying notes 17-20 supra.
[31] Langbein, supra note 1, at 116.

was unique among European nations because it had no police force and no system of noncapital criminal sanctions.[32] This peculiarity grounds Hay's hypothesis that the criminal law, with its growing store of capital statutes, "made it possible to govern eighteenth-century England without a police force and without a large army."[33]

Ignoring this, Langbein accepts the traditional explanation—that it was the want of policing, the weakness of detection, and the insufficiency of "corrections" that accounted for the expansion of the death laws[34]—and adds to it two of his own, involving the confused legal meaning of the doctrine of benefit of clergy[35] and the "conceptual impoverishment of the substantive law."[36] In this discussion his own theory of law is suggested: it shares more with canon law, Roman law, and Benthamite utilitarianism than with the common law and customs of England which, according to Langbein, lacked "scientific sophistication" and "central direction."[37]

Of the many issues raised in Professor Langbein's attack, I will not consider all here. Others may enjoy investigating the probity of eighteenth-century judges, or the interesting and obscure ways in which the big elite paid the little elite to prosecute in court. Here I wish to concentrate on the difference between how a legal historian and a social historian approach courtoom evidence, on Langbein's one-sided and partial interpretation of the jury, on the antidemocratic and ahistorical tendencies of his theory of law, and on his view of garbage.

III

OFFENSES

Because it is presented in statistical form and derived from a study of trial records, Langbein's analysis of offenses appears to be the most forceful and soundest part of his attack. In fact it is among the weakest. He analyzes the felonies tried at four Old Bailey sessions from 1754 to 1756, classifying the offenses in sixteen "lay" categories ranging from

---

[32] Id. at 115.

[33] Hay, supra note 16, at 56.

[34] See Langbein, supra note 1, at 115-19. Two of the traditional sources are 1 L. Radzinowicz, A History of English Criminal Law and Its Administration from 1750, at 3-40 (1948), and J.F. Stephen, A History of the Criminal Law of England 469-72 (1883).

[35] Benefit of clergy originally served to reserve for the ecclesiastical courts jurisdiction over certain defendants. During the eighteenth century, the doctrine permitted noncapital sentences for certain cases involving capital crimes. However, numerous statutes made certain crimes "unclergyable," making a guilty verdict a mandatory sentence of death. See Radzinowicz, supra note 34, at 3 n.2, 631-32.

[36] Langbein, supra note 1, at 117.

[37] Id. at 117-18.

homicide to perjury.[38] About these offenses Langbein makes two observations. First, they are "prosaic" and therefore surprising to readers who have accepted Hay's preoccupation with food riots and workplace insurrections.[39] Second, Langbein argues that "[v]irtually all of these offenses had been felonious even back into the middle ages."[40] This approach is most surprising, coming as it does from a legal historian, of whom we might expect some historical sensitivity. It is not enough to suggest that taking things that belong to another is and has long been a crime. The varieties of such crime and the way in which they are defined (for example, what does it mean for a thing "to belong to another"?) say much about the society that creates and enforces the criminal law. Consider, for example, Langbein's categories of "pocket-picking" and "shoplifting," which account for one-fifth of the crimes in his sample.[41] "Pocket-picking" requires pockets to be picked; "shop-lifting" requires shops to be lifted from. There is a history of shops and pockets, but neither was much a part of medieval life, when retailing was a matter not of shops, but of markets, peddling, and hawking, and when personal wealth was protected not by pockets, but by purses.[42] The legal historian will search in vain for laws against pocket-picking or shoplifting in the middle ages, because such offenses did not yet exist.[43] Historical sensitiv-

---

[38] The most numerous offenses are "theft under 40s.," "shop-lifting," "other theft 40s. or over," "theft from lodgings, inns, pubs," "theft from work-places or employers," "pocket-picking," and "receiving stolen goods." Id. at 99–101.

[39] In fact Hay writes little about workplaces. Moreover, had Langbein chosen to examine a session from, for example, 1768 or 1769, years of serious food shortages, he might have been less complacent about the "prosaic" nature of such offenses. See generally W. Shelton, English Hunger and Industrial Disorders: A Study of Social Conflict During the First Decade of George III's Reign (1973).

[40] Langbein, supra note 1, at 99 & n.16. Langbein contends that Hay concedes this point, but in fact Hay's "concession" is far more limited than Langbein suggests. Hay acknowledges that most capital prosecutions were brought under Tudor legislation, but it is a long way from the Tudors back to the middle ages. See Hay, War, Dearth, and Theft in the Eighteenth Century, 95 Past & Present 117, 146 (1982).

[41] Langbein, supra note 1, at 100.

[42] See generally D. Davis, A History of Shopping (1966); F. Kelly & R. Schwabe, Historic Costume: A Chronicle of Fashion in Western Europe, 1490-1790 (1925); 2 M. Davenport, The Book of Costume (1948).

[43] During the Renaissance, new statutes criminalized the acts of "cut purses" and "pick purses." An Act to take away the Benefit of Clergy from certain felonious Offenders, 8 Eliz., ch. 4 (1566), repealed by 7 & 8 Geo. 4, ch. 27, § 1 (1827). An Act that no Man robbing any House, Booth, or Tent, shall not [sic] be admitted to the Benefit of his Clergy, 5 & 6 Edw. 6, ch. 9, § 1 (1551), repealed by 7 & 8 Geo. 4, ch. 27, § 1 (1827), set penalties for "burglary in a tent or booth in a fair or market." Shoplifting was criminalized as such at the turn of the seventeenth century. An Act for the better apprehending, prosecuting, and punishing of Felons that commit Burglary, House-breaking, or Robbery in Shops, Warehouses, Coach Houses, or Stables, or that steal Horses, 10 Will. 3, ch. 12, § 1 (1698) (commonly known as the Shoplifting Act), repealed by 7 & 8 Geo. 4, ch. 27, § 1 (1827). An act to take away clergy from some offenders and to bring others to punishment, 3 W. & M., ch. 9, § 1 (1691), repealed by 7

ity should produce a sense of contingency, especially where property is concerned.

By the eighteenth century, the law of larceny had undergone certain changes.[44] Two were especially salient. First, the venue of the larceny assumed new importance: statutes provided different penalties for thefts depending on where they were committed. Such distinctions corresponded to new patterns of material and economic life. The shop, the warehouse, the stables, the workplace, and the home became, from the standpoint of the law of larceny, decisive to the fate of the offender, determining whether he or she would be hanged or transported.[45] The new importance of venue in the law of larceny reflects, in Marxist terms, new forms of commodity-capital whose value is created in production, realized in circulation, and consumed in final purchase.[46]

The second salient change in the law of larceny concerned not the economic environment of the commodity, but its monetary value. The most important consideration in determining whether an offender charged with larceny would live or die was the jury's evaluation of the monetary value of the misappropriated goods. When the larceny occurred from a shop, stable, or warehouse, the offender was spared his life

---

& 8 Geo. 4, ch. 27, § 1 (1827), addressed "robberies upon mens persons," but did not specifically refer to "pocket-picking."

(Where Statutes At Large (D. Pickering ed. 1762-1807) conflicts with later sources on the correct regnal year or chapter for statutes, citations follow 1 Chronological Table of the Statutes (1984).)

[44] 1 L. Radzinowicz, supra note 34, at 632-37, provides a summary of some major eighteenth-century larceny statutes. See also J.F. Stephen, supra note 34, at 121-76.

[45] Compare, e.g., An Act for the better apprehending, prosecuting, and punishing of Felons that commit Burglary, House-breaking, or Robbery in Shops, Warehouses, Coach Houses, or Stables, or that steal Horses, 10 Will. 3, ch. 12, § 1 (1698) (stealing from shop, warehouse, coach house or stable "not actually broke open by such offender" excluded from benefit of clergy where goods taken valued at more than five shillings), repealed by 7 & 8 Geo. 4, ch. 27, § 1 (1827), with An act for the more effectual preventing and punishing Robberies that shall be committed in Houses, 12 Anne, ch. 7 (1712) (stealing from "dwelling-house or outhouse thereunto belonging, although such house or out-house be not actually broken by such offender" excluded from benefit of clergy where goods taken valued at more than forty shillings), repealed by 7 & 8 Geo. 4, ch. 27, § 1 (1827). See also, e.g., An act for the further preventing robbery, burglary, and other felonies, and for the more effectual transportation of felons, 6 Geo., ch. 23, § 11 (1719) (seven years' transportation for offenders who "willfully and maliciously assault any person . . . in the publick streets and highways . . . and . . . tear, spoil, cut, burn or deface the garments or cloaths of such person"), repealed by 7 Geo. 4, ch. 64, § 32 (1826); An act for the more effectually preventing the stealing of linen, fustain [sic], and cotton goods and wares, in buildings, fields, grounds, and other places used for printing, whitening, bleaching, or drying the same, 18 Geo. 2, ch. 27 (1744) (theft of enumerated fabrics and yarns from specified places punishable by death or, at the judge's discretion, 14 years' transportation), repealed by 30 & 31 Vict., ch. 59 (1867).

[46] The greater care in the definition of venue that these statutes reflect parallels the growth of new centers of manufacture (production), new forms of transportation and the growth of banking (circulation), and the increased number of households containing small hoards of personal valuables (consumption).

222 *NEW YORK UNIVERSITY LAW REVIEW* [Vol. 60:212

if the jurors evaluated the goods at less than five shillings.[47] When the larceny occurred from a dwelling house, the suspect had not broken in or "put [the victim] in fear," and the misappropriated goods were valued at less than forty shillings, then again the offender's life was spared.[48] In the middle ages what had been legally important was not the monetary value of the property stolen, but the fact that theft indicated a violation of the feudal bonds.[49] Theft was a betrayal of the hierarchical personal relationship in a society where everyone was kept in his or her place, but there was a place for everyone. By the 1690's, in contrast, the personal relationship was concealed in and through the commodity-form.[50] Relationships that were formerly personal, such as those of lord and vassal, or master and apprentice, were converted into exchange relationships. These developments in the law of larceny may be understood, therefore, as allowing human sacrifice to the fetishism of commodities. In legally defined circumstances private property became so significant that its violation broke the most important taboo of capitalist society and required the sacrifice of life.

So, far from presenting the classification of felony in meaningful "lay" terms, Professor Langbein presents it ahistorically, suggesting that crime and specific crimes are eternal or inherent in human society. What he has eternalized, however, are only his legal categories which, under the guise of being "lay," are in fact quite ideological. He thus violates two main tenets of the historian's craft: the principle of historical specification, which examines everything, even legal ideas, in relation to the times when they arose, and the principle of historical periodization, which defines epochs, periods, and phases and accounts for changes

---

[47] An Act for the better apprehending, prosecuting, and punishing of Felons that commit Burglary, House-breaking, or Robbery in Shops, Warehouses, Coach Houses, or Stables, or that steal Horses, 10 Will. 3, ch. 12, § 1 (1698), repealed by 7 & 8 Geo. 4, ch. 27, § 1 (1827).

[48] An act for the more effecutal preventing and punishing Robberies that shall be committed in Houses, 12 Anne, ch. 7 (1712) (removing benefit of clergy from thefts of goods valued at forty shillings or more from a house), repealed by 7 & 8 Geo. 4, ch. 27, § 1 (1827). The distinction between grand and petty larceny dates from at least the thirteenth century, see Which Prisoners be Mainpernable, and which not, 3 Edw., ch. 15, § 4 (1275) (twelve pence), but by the early eighteenth century additional distinctions were made. See, e.g., An act to take away clergy from some offenders and to bring others to punishment, 3 W.& M., ch. 9, § 1 (1691) (removing benefit of clergy from daytime larceny from an occupied dwelling house, shop, or warehouse, when the goods stolen were valued at more than five shillings), repealed by 7 & 8 Geo. 4, ch. 27, § 1 (1827); P. Linebaugh, The London Hanged: Crime and Civil Society in Eighteenth Century London, ch. 2 (forthcoming in 1985). See also 13 W. Holdsworth, A History of English Law 397-98 (1952).

[49] See, e.g., 1 Dictionary of English History 465 (F. Hearnshaw, H. Crew & A. Beales ed. 1928).

[50] See generally G. Cohen, Karl Marx's Theory of History: A Defence 119-22 (1978).

among them.[51] The structures of historical periods and the social determinants of historical change are, of course, matters of interpretation, disagreement, and even controversy. But they cannot be analyzed if one's starting point is categories that conceal the problems of historical particularity and change. Had Professor Langbein simply classified offenses as they were classified in law at the time, readers might have been able to judge for themselves the degree to which seventeenth- and eighteenth-century offenses were historically specific.

IV

THE OFFENDERS

We now turn to Langbein's reflections upon the offenders. He finds it "hard to find figures worthy of romance, even social romance, among the shop-lifters, pickpockets, pilfering housemaids, and dishonest apprentices who populated the Old Bailey dock."[52] He does not call any of the offenders by name, nor attempt to follow any particular person's case. He does not attempt to recount any of their trials or travails, nor to reconstruct the social determinants of any of their offenses. Nothing could be further from the methods practiced by the authors of *Albion's Fatal Tree* who presented interpretation and analysis through the specific and concrete. For us the naming of names was essential not only for the narrative or the orderly presentation of evidence, but also as an antidote to the "crime of anonymity."

At his most vitriolic, Langbein writes, "to turn these little crooks into class warriors one must wear rose colored glasses of the deepest hue."[53] Neither Hay nor the other authors of *Albion's Fatal Tree* referred to offenders as "class warriors," partly because the authors did not all agree about the theoretical consequences of that phrase, and partly be-

---

[51] A good discussion of these principles may be found in M. Bloch, The Historian's Craft 27-35, 181-89 (1953).

[52] Langbein, supra note 1, at 100. We need not discuss in detail the differences Langbein chooses to ignore between "romance" and "social history." And if the population of the Old Bailey dock was not "romantic," perhaps there are other qualities that might stimulate our interest, as historians and other writers have recognized. See, e.g., B. Brecht, The Threepenny Opera (D. Vesey & E. Bentley trans. 1964); J. Gay, The Beggar's Opera: A Faithful Reproduction of the 1729 Edition (1961).

[53] Langbein, supra note 1, at 101. Langbein's choice of language is additional evidence of his careless, ahistorical approach. It is not until the nineteenth century that "crook" came to mean "criminal"; in the eighteenth century it meant "sixpence." E. Partridge, A Dictionary of the Underworld 163 (3d ed. 1968). See also 2 Oxford English Dictionary 1186-87 (J. Murray ed. 1893) (use of "crook" to refer to a dishonest person or swindler is United States colloquialism dating from 1880's). Langbein's use of language suggests not merely sloppiness, but a tendency to assume that crimes and criminals mean the same things to all people and in all times. This groundless assumption is fundamentally at odds with historical inquiry of a Marxist or any other nature.

cause they knew that to some others it was a red flag that might bait a bull.

But were they "class warriors"? Perhaps so, perhaps not. One cannot tell without actually examining some crimes and their circumstances, which Professor Langbein has chosen not to do. Here we suggest a few lines of inquiry, if only to raise questions about the offenders and to indicate lines of exploration, lines that Professor Langbein shuts off by his conclusory characterizations and by his ahistorical methods of analysis.

During the first part of the October 1754 Sessions at the Old Bailey,[54] forty-two people were indicted and tried. In thirteen of the cases the information is too scanty to suggest much about the social and occupational background of the offender or the circumstances leading him or her to commit the offense. The remaining cases fall easily into groups. Seven offenders were tried for work-related crimes: a journeyman loommaker who pawned his master's looking-glass, a cellarman who took thirty-two glass bottles and six gallons of white wine he had been entrusted to deliver, a stable boy who stole his master's cropt bay gelding and rode it towards Hounslow, a journeyman pewterer who took three plates from his master, two sailors who took sails and cordage from a vessel moored alongside their own, and a washerwoman's son who said he was returning to his mother's customers the four handkerchiefs he was alleged to have stolen.

Another five offenders at this Session were indicted for residence-related offenses: a waiter who stole his lodging-house neighbor's watch and coins, a husband and wife indicted for stealing linens and other goods from a lodging room let to them by contract, a sixteen- or seventeen-year-old "spinster" who stole some clothes from the keeper of a lodging house, and a lodger who stole a copper stew-pot and some linens from a "lodging room let by contract."

A third group consists of six offenses relating to the ambiguous transactions of sexuality:[55] a spinster who received a silver spoon from a baker's servant who had lain with her in the baker's cellar, a silk-winder who received a silver watch from a journeyman tailor who had lain with her, a scouring maid who took a silver watch from a drunken cabinet-

---

[54] Old Bailey Proceedings, supra note 23, for October 23-28, 1754. Linda Merrill's study of the Old Bailey Proceedings of December 1755 and December 1756 concluded: "The majority of cases in these sessions show that those who were convicted as well as those accused, were working people . . . and that judging by the small amounts stolen it appears that they were selling [the goods] for quick money in an effort to compensate for inadequate wages." (On file at New York University Law Review.)

[55] Were these thefts, appropriations, or exchanges? The cases were brought by male prosecutors, some of whom admit that they did or may have "lain with" the female defendants. The offenders assert that the goods were not stolen, but given or taken as compensation for sexual services.

maker who "had stripped [her] naked," a "spinster," alleged to be "one
of the most notorious whores in the whole ward," who took a silk handkerchief from a man to lie with him, an army officer's servant girl who
took the silver watch of a sergeant in the Chelsea guards in whose bed
she had lain, and a woman indicted for stealing silver and linen from a
watchman. He said he permitted the offender and her husband to "lie in
[his] bed when [he] was out watching." She said the watchman had told
her that if her "husband were dead he'd make [her] possess'd of all, and
gave her the key of the door," and that he prosecuted her because she
"would not leave [her] husband and come and live with him."

Then there is a fourth group of offenders whose crimes took place in
the public spaces of London. These include six who were indicted for
taking handkerchiefs from people in the streets, two who were said to
have stolen from public houses, and three who were alleged to have stolen during a fight in the streets.

Can these offenders be justly characterized as "little crooks" or
"class warriors"? A historian, perhaps, is less interested in the labels
than in exploring the nature of the offenders and their offenses within
their social and historical context. The grouping of the cases—work-related, residence-related, sex-related, and public appropriation—that is
suggested by even the most cursory historical investigation suggests a
dynamic of class relations that might explain the existence of the offenses
as a matter of contingent historical fact. Langbein's ahistorical and tendentious dismissals of the offenses and the offenders as minor, however,
obscures any possible historical explanations of the causes of the offenses.

V

TWO OFFENDERS IN PARTICULAR

Examining two cases from the *Old Bailey Proceedings*[56] shows how
further investigation might illuminate the circumstances behind the trial
records. First is Michael Harris,[57] a shoemaker's apprentice, who was
found guilty and sentenced to seven years' transportation for stealing
"three pair of callimanco shoes, value 9s., two pair of satten shoes, value
20s., one linen shirt, one lawn neckcloth, and one linen table-cloth."
Some of these he allegedly exchanged at a pawnbroker's, and the rest at
"Rag Fair." The case suggests several avenues of investigation. We may
examine monetary wage rates and discover that these could be below
subsistence.[58] English shoemakers fought at least fifteen wage disputes in

---

[56] Old Bailey Proceedings, supra note 23, for December 4-10, 1755.

[57] See id. at 2 for the record of Harris's trial; id. at 40 for the record of his sentence.

[58] See, e.g., M. George, English Social Life in the Eighteenth Century 19-25 (1923); J.
Rule, The Experience of Labour in Eighteenth Century English Industry 61, 124-43 (1981);

the eighteenth century.[59] Employers did not always pay in currency the wages due their employees in this period when little credit was available to small manufacturers and small denominations of coins were often scarce. In many industries workers customarily appropriated certain materials, which were perceived by both worker and master as payments in lieu of monetary wages well into the eighteenth century.[60]

Second, we need to examine the organization of production. In the putting-out system the fabricator could use materials or goods put out to him or her as collateral for raising money or credit for food and fuel until he or she was paid for other, completed work. As the structure of the shoemaking industry changed, this became a serious problem to eighteenth-century London capitalist cordwainers who in 1722 obtained an Act of Parliament to prevent "journeymen shoemakers selling, exchanging or pawning boots, shoes, slippers, cut leather or other materials . . . and for better regulating the said journeymen."[61] Legislation was unsuccessful in blocking this kind of customary appropriation; only the revolutionizing of the mode of production itself, from putting-out to factory production, could remove the physical conditions permitting such customary appropriations.[62]

Third, we might investigate some of the traditions and legends of these "Sons of Crispin." Saints Crispin and Crispinian were brother cobblers, legend ran, who came from Rome. In Paris whence they fled they labored by day as journeyman shoemakers, and by night to make shoes to be given freely to the unshod poor. After their martyrdom, their bones were enshrined in Kent.[63]

This is a single case. On the basis of the trial record we do not know whether Harris was poorly paid or paid at all. It would require other

Becker, Property in the Workplace: Labor, Capital, and Crime in the Eighteenth Century British Woolen and Worsted Industry, 69 Va. L. Rev. 1487 (1982). Langbein's readiness to find the defendants "yielding to temptation rather than necessity," Langbein, supra note 1, at 100, is curious but typically ahistorical. He seeks an easy contrast between employed people, who he presumes "yielded to temptation," and the unemployed. Evidence on the customary composition and timing of wages suggests that some working people sometimes earned far less than subsistence wages and that even those who earned living wages may have gone for long periods without income. See, e.g., J. Rule, supra; Becker, supra, at 1494-95.

[59] C. Dobson, Masters and Journeymen: A Prehistory of Industrial Relations 1717-1800, at 24, 154-70 (1980).

[60] Becker, supra note 58, at 1495, 1510. See also M. George, supra note 58; J. Rule, supra note 58.

[61] 9 Geo., ch. 27 (1722). Cf. Becker, supra note 58, at 1496-1500 (criminalization of woolen workers' takings).

[62] See, e.g., Becker, supra note 58, at 1515 (woolen workers); Oppenheim, The Royal Dockyards, in 2 The Victoria History of Counties of England 336, 347, 351, 374 (W. Page ed. 1926) (stockyard workers).

[63] Butler's Lives of the Saints 197-98 (H. Thurston & D. Attwater rev. ed. 1956) (1st ed. London 1756-1759).

types of historical evidence to find out. Edgar Furniss drew a conclusion about this period which suggests that the English laborer may have needed to take goods to survive: "for no considerable period did he receive much more than subsistence wages and for certain stretches of time his money wages were insufficient to supply him with the barest essentials of physical existence."[64] Was Harris's survival at stake? As the historian begins to ask such questions, evidence can accumulate until the "case" is no longer merely an example proving a point, or a datum composing statistics, or even a defendant requiring a judge to apply a statute or rule. With investigation a "case" can, if the historian is willing to listen, take on a life of its own that may, if the historian will explore, illuminate far more than this or that point, statistic, precept, or statute.

Our second case is that of Samuel Boroughs, who was sentenced to seven years' transportation for stealing ten pounds' weight of linen yarn, value twenty shillings, from his master, Josias Deponthien, a partner in a commercial firm which imported linen from Germany and owned three large warehouses.[65] Boroughs was one of the porters who made up bales and loaded them into carts. His case is interesting because it makes the ambiguities of the class relationships more explicit. Boroughs said that several years before the trial his master gave him "a whole fatt [vat] of damaged yarn; it was often troublesome, and the servants used to throw it up on heaps."[66] Boroughs found that by tediously picking through this damaged yarn, he could find yarn good enough to sell at a dye-house. The master said he had given Boroughs fourteen or fifteen hundred-weight of yarn that had been so damaged by bad weather that it "stunk like poison, and was rotten, which we tried skain by skain; some by shaking with a jerk, the ends would fly out, and discover them to be rotten; the others we pulled by twenty, thirty, or more threads at a time, and all that broke: we flung the skain down."[67]

As to the yarn Boroughs was accused of "stealing," he first said he had it from Deponthien's footman, and later that he had it from the firm's bookkeeper. Numerous witnesses, including two former employers, attested to Borough's honesty and industry. The trial records do not tell us how the employer paid the footman or the porter.

Boroughs said there were six good bundles of yarn, four of them sold at six shillings each, a figure that might be equivalent to between two or three weeks' wages.[68] Such "gifts" in an age of incomplete monetiza-

---

[64] E. Furniss, The Position of the Laborer in a System of Nationalism: A Study of the Labor Theorists of the Later English Mercantilists 24 (1920).

[65] Old Bailey Proceedings, supra note 23, for December 4-10, 1755, at 6-9, 40.

[66] Id. at 8.

[67] Id. at 7.

[68] See J. Rule, supra note 58, at 49-70.

tion of material transactions have a way of becoming customary over time. In other trades, we know, they were fundamental: "cabbage" to tailors, "vails" to servants, "birrs" to leather workers, "chips" to shipwrights, "sockings" to tobacco porters, "sweepings" to sugar lumpers, "wastages" to coopers, "thrums" to weavers—the lexicon of appropriation was as extensive as the names of the trades. Today such appropriations are "perquisites" or "shrinkage." Sometimes they are useful to employers, sometimes to employees. In the eighteenth century the evidence mounts suggesting that they were decisive to the class relationships.[69]

The growth of that evidence permits us to search for similar leads in the cases of Harris and Boroughs. What was regarded by the court as a felony may have been regarded by others as "usages of the trade." Even if it were positively discovered that neither Harris nor Boroughs was appropriating in a customary way, as a harvester might her gleanings or a forester his lops and tops, that would still not mean that, objectively or economically, Harris and Boroughs were not "class warriors." Nobody wishes to be a "class warrior" or to have to fight tooth and nail for subsistence. Eighteenth-century society forced millions of people to such positions where they had to fight by every means necessary. The aggregation of such struggles caused employers, legislators, capitalists—in short, the "elite"—to respond and to fight back.

In sum, Langbein's analysis of the offenders and their offenses is moralizing and unsympathetic.[70] His emphasis on "lay" categories causes him to overlook fundamental novelties in the material conditions of production and circulation (wage labor and the commodity-form), and to write about the law in such general terms that he forgets its historical determinants. His method of categorization and statistical presentation lends itself to such omissions, oversights, and errors. He writes, "[i]n my data we do not see offenses that exemplify the advance of pre-industrial capitalism."[71] But he could have seen much more in his "data" had he arranged it in less conclusory categories, or had he actually become interested in the people who were tried.

---

[69] See, e.g., R. Malcolmson, Life and Labour in England, 1700-1780, at 54-58 (1981); Linebaugh, Soc'y for the Study of Lab. Hist. Bull., No. 25, Autumn 1972, at 11, 13. See also authorities cited in note 58 supra.

[70] I suspect that this part of Langbein's argument is directed less against Hay than it is the other essays, because Hay actually considers law as a whole, and not in those parts directly affecting the *modus operandi* of such eighteenth-century workshops as Harris or Boroughs worked in.

[71] Langbein, supra note 1, at 99.

VI

THE JURY AND JURORS

Langbein charges Hay with underemphasizing the importance of jury discretion, finding that Hay's "theory of ruling class conspiracy is impossible to reconcile with the reality of jury discretion."[72] He describes methods by which London juries rendered "partial verdicts"[73] —by finding defendants guilty of lesser offenses than those charged, or by "downvaluing" the monetary expression of stolen goods.

The introduction of the sentence of transportation[74] and the emphasis on exchange value as the principal legal consideration in sentencing[75] made down-charging a frequent device in the eighteenth century.

The rendering of partial verdicts used to be called "pious perjury." Its ameliorative effects on the harshness of the law are well known.[76] Though there is much that might be learned from an examination of these partial verdicts,[77] Professor Langbein does not analyze them, but instead suggests that the simple use of "pious perjury" refutes Hay's thesis.

> If I were going to organize a ruling-class conspiracy to use the criminal law to terrorize the lower orders, I would not interpose autonomous bodies of non-conspirators like the petty juries. If, on the other hand, I were going to reckon the jurors among my conspirators, I would be troubled that they were so predictably humane by the standards of the day.[78]

This extraordinary passage requires several responses. First, Langbein's implication that jurors were not drawn from the elite classes is clearly inaccurate. Professor Schwarz has shown that less than five percent of eighteenth-century Londoners possessed taxable incomes exceeding two hundred pounds and that at least three-quarters of the popu-

---

[72] Id. at 106.

[73] On partial verdicts, see, e.g., Beattie, Crime and the Courts in Surrey, 1736-1753, in Crime in England, 1500-1800, supra note 15, at 155, 171-72.

[74] An act for the further preventing robbery, burglary, and other felonies, and for the more effectual transportation of felons, and unlawful exporters of wool; and for declaring the law upon some points related to pirates (Piracy Act), 4 Geo., ch. 11, § 1 (1717) (those formerly entitled to benefit of clergy to be transported for seven years; those excluded from benefit of clergy may be transported for fourteen years at the discretion of the monarch), repealed by 7 & 8 Geo. 4, ch. 27, § 1 (1827).

[75] See text accompanying notes 47-50 supra.

[76] See, e.g., 1 L. Radzinowicz, supra note 34, at 94-97.

[77] It would be interesting to know, for example, whether members of particular groups, such as young, female, or first offenders, were more likely to receive partial verdicts, whether their incidence correlated with the use-value of stolen goods, whether the characteristics of the juror, such as age, status, or past jury service, appear to have played any role.

[78] Langbein, supra note 1, at 107.

230   NEW YORK UNIVERSITY LAW REVIEW   [Vol. 60:212

lation had incomes of less than sixty pounds a year.[79] After 1730 only householders who owned estates of more than one hundred pounds were qualified to serve on London juries;[80] a leasehold of more than fifty pounds qualified a man for service on a Middlesex jury.[81] It is clear that at least the London jury pool was drawn from a small portion of the population—small and propertied.[82] On grounds strictly of income and wealth, without considering other evidence, it is misleading to suggest that such a jury was "autonomous."

Second, and more fundamentally, Langbein's strange framing of the issues precludes reasoned analysis. Langbein seems to envision a black-and-white choice: jurors were either "nonconspirators" or "coconspirators," either "autonomous" or possessing interests identical to those of the most elite. Langbein's simplistic dichotomy does not respond to Hay's more subtle analysis. Hay does not argue that the social status of jurors was identical to that of magistrates and judges, but rather that they were on a continuum defined by property whose social relations imposed dependency and clientage upon lesser property holders.[83]

It is symptomatic of Langbein's tendency to ignore or oversimplify the complex conflicts and interrelationships between classes that he finds in the verdicts of these allegedly class-neutral juries evidence that the "property crimes that were of major consequence in the workload of eighteenth century criminal courts . . . were those about whose blameworthiness there was a moral consensus that knew no class lines."[84] Langbein can make this statement only by ignoring the obvious: the jury was composed of a small, propertied portion of the population whose interests were more closely allied with those of the most elite class than

---

[79] Schwarz, Social Class and Social Geography: The Middle Classes in London at the End of the Eighteenth Century, 7 Soc. Hist. 167, 167-69 (1982).

[80] An Act for the better regulation of juries, 3 Geo. 2, ch. 25, §§ 19-20 (1731) (local statute, date of repeal unclear).

[81] An act to explain and amend an act made in the third year of his Majesty's reign, intituled [sic], An act for the better regulation of juries, so far as the same relates to the county of Middlesex, 4 Geo. 2, ch. 7, § 3 (1731), repealed by 6 Geo. 4, ch. 50, § 62 (1825).

[82] Property qualifications for jury service survived well into the twentieth century in England. As late as 1956, Sir Patrick Devlin remarked: "[I]t is an odd thing that if you stopped several men in the street or held up the Clapham omnibus while you interrogated the passengers, you would very likely find that only a few of them were qualified to serve as jurors." P. Devlin, Trial By Jury 17 (3d ed. 1966).

[83] This pattern of dependency of the lesser propertied classes upon the wealthier, established elite has been demonstrated in areas of credit, taxation, and politics, see, e.g., Schwarz, supra note 79, at 167-69, and it is likely that its effects spilled over into the courtroom as well. See also Rogers, Money, Land and Lineage: The Big Bourgeoise of Hanoverian London, 4 Soc. Hist. 437 (1979) (discussing how the system of clientage united the rich, plutocratic bourgeoisie, whose "fortunes ranged from tens of thousands to perhaps millions of pounds," with the gentry).

[84] Langbein, supra note 1, at 108.

with those of the working class that supplied the majority of offenders.[85] Langbein has no evidence on which to judge the participation of the working classes in this "moral consensus."

A third observation about Langbein's imaginary scenario relates to his perception that the jury was "predictably humane." He reports that one-third of the defendants were acquitted, another third or so transported, and only those engaged in truly serious crimes, such as livestock theft, or suspected of group criminality routinely sentenced to death. Was this "humaneness"? Surely we cannot expect any system to convict or execute all of the offenders, and Langbein suggests no other standard against which we might compare his statistics. In addition, we might pause before accepting the assertion that transportation, which subjected often petty offenders to at least seven years of indentured servitude in a disease-ridden colony thousands of miles from their homes and families, was "humane."[86] We might also consider whether the "humane" sentence of transportation served other needs of the elite. Perhaps the death penalty permitted them to do away with those criminals who they thought were most dangerous while transportation allowed them to rid themselves of the less dangerous characters and supply the labor needed to build their colonies across the sea. Without contemplating such possibilities, how can Professor Langbein suggest that the criminal law protected the poor as well as the rich from evils they all agreed upon?

A fourth comment arises from Langbein's style of expression—"if I were going to organize a ruling-class conspiracy"—which connotes a historical perspective that consigns itself to failure by the very narrowness with which it perceives the issue. No single person or group organized eighteenth-century class forces or created the jury, an institution whose development spanned many centuries.

We cannot understand the theory and practice of the eighteenth-century jury or the rhetoric of freedom to which it belonged if we limit ourselves to the terms that Professor Langbein offers us and the incomplete evidence he explores. An understanding of the eighteenth-century jury must be broad enough to handle contradiction, and Professor Langbein's rigid categories are incapable of doing this. On the one hand, the jury was neither democratic nor egalitarian in its social composition and it was manipulated by the ruling class; on the other hand, it was a bulwark of freedom in its potential and in the rhetoric used to defend it.

---

[85] See generally Beattie, supra note 73.

[86] For many convicts, transportation was a de facto death sentence. Ordinary felons were customarily chained below the deck during the entire voyage. An average of 15% perished on board, with the death rate reaching 30 or 40% on certain voyages. A.E. Smith, supra note 6, at 125-26. Many of those who survived the grueling voyage succumbed to "colonial fever" within days or weeks. Id. at 5-6.

As dependent small property holders—master craftsmen, inn-keepers, grocers, cattle dealers and the like—the jurors were corruptible by those more powerful on the continuum of property.[87] This was recognized in statutes, such as an act of 1730 which stated, "Whereas many evil Practices have been used in corrupting of Jurors . . . and many Neglects and Abuses have happened in making of the Lists of Freeholders."[88] "Special juries"[89] were impaneled for special cases, such as for the trials of the Windsor Blacks[90] and political dissenters,[91] in order to be especially compliant. An act of 1751 stated that "great and extravagant Fees [had been] paid to Jurymen" and prohibited judges from paying jurors more than one pound one shilling.[92] The venality of jurors was an object of spleen in the most popular of English books, *Pilgrim's Progress*. In a trial presided over by "Lord Hate-good," the accused was convicted of violating statutes of Pharaoh, Nebuchadnezzar, and Darius, and condemned to die by a jury consisting of "Mr. Blind-man, Mr. No-good, Mr. Malice, Mr. Love-lust, Mr. Live-loose, Mr. Heady, Mr. High Mind, Mr. Enmity, Mr. Lyar, Mr. Cruelty, Mr. Hate-light, and Mr. Implacable."[93]

The most persuasive advocates of the jury system criticized its corruptions. Sir John Hawles, a prominent seventeenth-century lawyer, wrote *The Englishman's Right: A Dialogue Between a Barrister at Law and a Juryman*,[94] whose plain and gentle style may partly explain its frequent republication. On the problem of jury corruption Hawles observed:

> There are some make a trade of being Jurymen; that seek for the office;
> use means to be constantly continued in it; will not give a disobliging

---

[87] Roberts, Jury Vetting in the Seventeenth Century, 32 Hist. Today 25, 26 (1982) (describing rampant corruption of the juries in the century preceding this study).

[88] An Act for the Better Regulation of Juries, 3 Geo. 2, ch. 25, § 1 (1730) (local statute, date of repeal unclear).

[89] The special jury was composed of citizens of a higher social station or of those deemed to have expertise in the subject matter of particular civil cases. W. Cornish, The Jury 31 (1968). Now used only in special kinds of civil cases, it was used during the eighteenth century in criminal trials as well. Id. at 32-33. Nineteenth-century reformers recognized the special jury as a vehicle for abuse and manipulation, see, e.g., J. Bentham, The Elements of the Art of Packing, as applied to special Juries, particularly in Cases of Libel Law (London 1821).

[90] See E.P. Thompson, Whigs and Hunters: The Origins of the Black Act 74, 78 (1975). The Windsor Blacks were a loose confederation of largely laborers and apprentices who defied a 1723 capital statute and continued their customary practice of hunting deer in Windsor Forest. Whenever packed juries failed to convict the Blacks, the trials were moved to London and conducted before "jurys of men of probity and well enclined towards their Kings and country's service and interest." Id. at 151 (quoting letter from D. DeFaye, Secretary to the Lords Justices, to Viscount Townshend, Oct. 1, 1783).

[91] See, e.g., W. Cornish, supra note 89, at 32, 131.

[92] An Act for the Better Regulation of Trials by Jury, 24 Geo. 2, ch. 18, § 2 (1751).

[93] J. Bunyan, Pilgrim's Progress 153 (J. Wharey ed. 1969) (1st ed. London 1678).

[94] J. Hawles, The Englishman's Right: A Dialogue, between a Barrister at Law and a Juryman (London 1793) (1st ed. London 1680).

verdict, lest they should be discharged, and serve no more: these
standing Jurors have certainly some ill game to play. There are others
that hope to signalize themselves, to get a better trade, or some prefer-
ment by serving a turn.[95]

Such "standing jurors" may have been those who dominated the other
jurors and "rashly deliver[ed] their opinions; and all the rest, in respect
to their supposed gravity, and experience, or because they ha[d] the biggest estates, or to avoid the trouble of disputing the point, or to prevent
the spoiling of dinner by delay, or some such weighty reason, forthwith
agree[d] blindfold . . . ."[96]

Other jurors succumbed to the judges' admonitions and instructions. According to Hawles, "slavish fear" induced them "to eccho back,
what the bench would have done."[97]

To the statutory evidence and the testimony of Hawles we may add
a statistic that should be understood in the context of the other evidence.
My study of thirty-eight different jury panels in London between 1714
and 1717 reveals that an average of two jurors on the City panels had
served at least once before. On the panel in Middlesex, the county jurisdiction of the London suburbs in which many poor and working-class
citizens lived, more than one-half of the "good men and true," an average
of 6.6 to be exact, had sat on the jury at least once before.[98] This evidence of the existence of professional jurors is only an indication of the
system of clientage and manipulation ("vetting") that operated at the
Old Bailey. London jurors were impaneled from a small but propertied
portion of the population, and within that propertied portion their selection was neither random nor disinterested, but mercenary, venal, and
corrupt.[99]

Yet the jury was a "bank," holding in "an ocean of oppression," as
Hawles said.[100] It was, to quote two authorities on the modern jury, "the
one institution . . . which stands between the people and abuse of authority by the state."[101] The jurors' honesty, independence, and impartiality were continuously encouraged in the libertarian rhetoric of the
eighteenth century. Occasionally the jury's power was exercised with

---

[95] Id. at 32. See also W. Cornish, supra note 89, at 131-32 ("regular special jurors . . .
lived off the guinea which each case brought, and . . . knew that continuance of this stipend
depended on bringing in a verdict for the crown").

[96] J. Hawles, supra note 94, at 31.

[97] Id.

[98] The names of the petty jurors were printed in the Old Bailey Proceedings, supra note 23.
My study involved comparing lists between the specified years. See also Beattie, supra note 73,
at 165 ("any one jury would be likely to contain a few men with some previous experience").

[99] See generally Roberts, supra note 87.

[100] J. Hawles, supra note 94, at 7.

[101] National Jury Project, Jurywork: Systematic Techniques x (E. Krauss & B. Bonora 2d
ed. 1984).

courage and fortitude. This rhetoric of freedom flourished especially in the "Wilkes and Liberty" years[102] and in the 1790's.[103] The jury's protection under Magna Carta and the Declaration of Rights, its associations with pre-Norman England, and its centrality to the complex notions of "the Englishman's birthright" distinguished England to the eighteenth-century contemporaries from arbitrary government and despotism.

There is no adequate historical and analytical study of the eighteenth-century English jury, so at this point it would be premature—for me or for Professor Langbein—to draw conclusions; a fuller exploration of the moving contradiction between the limited social basis of the jury and some of the rhetoric of liberty will have to wait.

VII

SOURCES OF LAW

Professor Langbein's treatment of law as institution and theory underscores the shortcomings of his brand of narrow legal scholarship. Langbein stresses elements of continuity, suggesting that law in the Middle Ages, in the eighteenth century, and in our own time played the stable role of protecting both rich and poor from a well-defined criminal element. His analysis of law, custom, and the jury's role not only distorts Hay's central arguments, but reveals the limits of his own static, narrowly functionalist approach.

Langbein finds weak and speculative Hay's assertion that eighteenth-century juries, had they been more democratically composed, might have refused to return convictions in certain prosecutions, especially for theft.[104] Ordinary citizens no less than the elite, Langbein asserts, wanted to punish thieves. To prove his point, he cites a study of twentieth-century American juries that demonstrates, in his view, that these juries, "long since democratized and freed of property qualifications," are not "hostile to the law of larceny."[105] In reading back into

---

[102] See G. Rude, Wilkes & Liberty 28, 30 (1962).

[103] London juries acquitted numerous political dissenters indicted during periods of oppression, both in the 1790's and the 1810's. See, e.g., E.P. Thompson, The Making of the English Working Class 19, 80, 468, 721-22 (1963). Thompson found the jury system, along with the political opposition led by Lord Fox, the "last defence of English liberties." Id. at 165. See also W. Cornish, supra note 89, at 129-31.

[104] See Langbein, supra note 1, at 107-08; Hay, supra note 16, at 38-39.

[105] Langbein, supra note 1, at 108 (citing H. Kalven & H. Zeisel, The American Jury 76-77 (1966)). Even apart from its ahistorical application, the Kalven and Zeisel study lends Langbein only tenuous support at best. Kalven and Zeisel remark that "[t]here is no crime category in which the jury is totally at war with the law . . . as it is said to have been in the eighteenth century with respect to prosecutions for seditious libel." H. Kalven & J. Zeisel, supra, at 76. First, this conclusion addresses wholesale nullification, whereas Hay claims only

eighteenth-century England contemporary American conceptions of the jury, Langbein both fails to rebut Hay's point and neglects crucial features of the early modern jury.[106] First, it was true then as it is now that juries had the power to deliver general verdicts, which could not be refused by the court.[107] Because this power requires that the jury draw a conclusion from a legal major premise in conjunction with a factual minor premise,[108] juries have long been said to have the power to decide the law as well as the facts.[109] Under the doctrine of jury nullification, juries are said to have not only the power but the *right* to judge the law as well as the facts. In the modern-day United States the controversy has been whether juries are entitled to an instruction from the judge as to their power to decide the law;[110] it was settled in England that they were not.[111]

No precise analogy to the contemporary debate about jury nullification is available in the context of the eighteenth-century criminal trial.

---

that a more democratic jury might not have convicted. Second, failure to nullify is not the same as wholehearted support. Third, Kalven and Zeisel's ultimate conclusion, that "[w]hat is required is the inspection of the individual case. . . . [T]he approach by way of analyzing crime categories, as such, was a mistake," id. at 76-77, is congenial to the approach of *Albion's Fatal Tree*.

Even without the reference to Kalven and Zeisel, Langbein's quarrel with Hay rests on simple mystification. Langbein gives away the game when he observes that it is not obvious that "the English poor of the eighteenth century generally condoned the theft of livestock and victuals, and Hay does not produce evidence that they did." Langbein, supra note 1, at 108. Hay is of course committed to no such claim. It suffices to show that the definition of *theft* was up for grabs in the eighteenth century because the very concepts of property and possession were in flux. Thus a jury selected democratically, in the absence of property qualifications, would likely take a different view of what constituted theft, see Hay, supra note 16, at 38 (quoting T. Gisbourne, An Enquiry into the Duties of Men in the Higher and Middle Classes of Society in Great Britain 284 n.b (1974)), from jurors selected under actual eighteenth-century property qualifications.

[106] Indeed, Langbein's charge that Hay underestimates the power of jury discretion, Langbein, supra note 1, at 105-06, sits ill with his own delvings into the Old Bailey sources in The Criminal Trial before the Lawyers, 45 U. Chi. L. Rev. 263 (1978), which suggest that Hay is, if anything, overenthusiastic about the power of juries during this period to acquit against the judge's will.

[107] See, e.g., 1 G. Duncombe, Trials per Pais: or, the Law of England Concerning Juries by Nisi Prius, &c. 283 (8th ed. London 1766) (1st ed. London 1665) (marginal squib); Howe, Juries as Judges of the Criminal Law, 52 Harv. L. Rev. 582, 583 (1939).

[108] See, e.g., J. Hawles, supra note 94, at 30-32 & n.*.

[109] Thus, for example, Duncombe speaks of juries "tak[ing] upon them the Knowledge of the Law." G. Duncombe, supra note 107, at 230. Cf. An Examination into the Rights and Duties of Jurors 2 (London 1785) (author's view that libel juries should be restricted to factual questions "opposes the general voice" and "carr[ies] an air of novelty").

[110] See, e.g., Scheflin, Jury Nullification: The Right to Say No, 45 S. Cal. L. Rev. 168 (1972).

[111] See, e.g., Howe, supra note 107, at 583 ("[I]t is probably the sound view, at common law, that this power of the jury in criminal cases does not and did not, in any distinct and modern sense, import a right on their part to determine the law.") (quoting J. Thayer, Preliminary Treatise on Evidence 169, 256 (1898)).

Langbein himself gives the simple reason: jury instructions of any kind were practically nonexistent at the typical Old Bailey trial, so that the question of the jury's right to an instruction about its power to acquit against the law scarcely arose.[112]

But for several reasons there was also no need for any such instruction. First, jury panels at the Old Bailey contained a surprisingly high proportion of repeaters.[113] Such semiprofessional jurors were familiar through repetition with the relevant criminal statutes. What was most needed from jurors was not bookish law, but "first, understanding to know your duty; and, in the next place, courage and resolution to practice it with impartiality and integrity, free from accursed bribery and malice or (what is full as bad in the end) base and servile fear."[114]

Far more importantly, in an age before the transition to a statutory criminal law was complete, the bulk of the law was known to every potential juror.[115] Recent historical scholarship has demonstrated the strong roots eighteenth-century English law had in the community's customs, that is, in recognized patterns of work, compensation, distribution, marriage, and culture.[116] Practices adhered to and honored by common

---

[112] Langbein, supra note 106, at 284. At least one defendant used his opportunity to address the jury to remind the jury of its power:

> [The jurors] I again declare by the law of England, are the conservators and sole judges of my life, having inherent in them alone the judicial power of the law, as well as fact: you judges that sit there being no more, if they please, but cyphers to pronounce the sentence, or their clerks to say Amen to them: being at the best in your original, but the Norman Conqueror's intruders. . . . And therefore I desire you to know your power, and consider your duty both to God, to me, to your ownselves, and to your country.

4 J. Howell, State Trials 1270, 1395 (London 1816) (quoting J. Lilburne, tried for treason in 1642).

[113] See note 98 and accompanying text supra.

[114] J. Hawles, supra note 94, at 2.

[115] Morris Arnold very acutely makes the point for the medieval jury:

> Positive legislation played a very small part in medieval law . . . custom, derived from shared societal assumptions, was the legal norm, not what some sovereign or his agent decreed. Law . . . was less law than life . . . . It would, of course, be a long time before the law of England became a learned law; it was not taught in the universities because as to much of it there was no need. Why teach life when all one had to do was simply to live it? For the same reason that law did not need to be taught it also did not, in the ordinary case, need to be told to jurors; likewise jurors would have no need to inquire of professionals. Custom, or a "logical" extension of custom, only dimly, if at all, perceived as different from a concrete, natural, and inevitable fact, bottomed on the bedrock of universal acceptance, will supply the answer.

Arnold, Law and Fact in the Medieval Jury Trial: Out of Sight, Out of Mind, 18 Am. J. Legal Hist. 267, 279 (1974). Although statutes certainly had gained a significant role by the eighteenth century, Arnold's explanation provides some insight into eighteenth- as well as fourteenth- and fifteenth-century juries.

[116] See, e.g., C. Fisher, Custom, Work and Market Capitalism: the Forest of Dean Colliers, 1788-1888, at vii (1981) ("To study customs, the social and economic relationships in which they have been embedded and the ways in which the body of custom has been altered over time, is to achieve an insight into the fundamental relations of property, production and law in

law courts over centuries gave rise to legal rights with which the sovereign could not interfere. This concept of customary rights had a profound constitutional dimension, lying at the core of the three great documents that embody the principle of parliamentary constraint on royal prerogative: Magna Carta, the Petition of Right and the Bill of Rights.

Against this backdrop the power of the eighteenth-century jury to decide questions of law takes on a significance unappreciated by Langbein. Jurors, more knowledgeable about and sensitive to custom than were judges, were in a superior position to judge the law. Here the existence of the property qualification becomes crucial. Jurors drawn from the limited pool available to the Old Bailey owned property. Unlike many criminal defendants, they had a relatively ample "margin of survival," and were not driven to crime by continual or occasional necessity. Many were employed laborers or servants, and thus had economic interests directly opposed to those of the propertyless. The groups that benefited from new definitions of property were, in short, those who were represented on juries while those who suffered were excluded by property requirements. As such they stood arrayed in their class interests: those on the juries against those in the dock. It would not have been in the interest of such as Deponthien to have vouchsafed legal recognition to the custom of fatting we examined in the case of Boroughs.[117] It is scarcely surprising that in the transition to an industrial economy such customs fell by the wayside. This example illustrates that the law, or rather the question of which customs would become codified, was unsettled. Can it seriously be doubted that jury panels composed of workers such as Boroughs would have found differently in the fatting case, giving legal sanction to the custom of fatting? It would, after all, have been in their own interest to do so. This is the meaning of Hay's point that a more democratic jury might not have convicted: a more democratic jury might not have been worse disposed toward the law of larceny, but would have allotted the law of larceny a different content. It might have interpreted that law, for example, as not containing sanctions against fatting. Or, had such a jury confronted a statute that on its face forbade

---

a society."). In the case of the coal miners of the Forest of Dean, a customary right to title over coal was taken away by statute in the nineteenth century. For other discussion of the importance of customary appropriations and their transformation into criminal offenses, see generally Becker, *supra* note 58, at 1514-15:

> While labor's takings were transformed from a customary right (or, at most, a private harm) into a public wrong, dismissal of workers in disregard of standard terms and reduction of their wages or rates below established minimums were transformed from public harms into accepted practices. A transformation of what were deemed protected rights reflected and hastened the development of a capitalist society and economy.

[117] See text accompanying notes 65-69 *supra*.

fatting, it might have recognized the customary status of ambiguous transactions such as the one we have described, in effect shifting the burden of proof to the propertied party that the transaction was indeed a statutory offense against property rather than, for example, a gift.

Langbein writes of "the conceptual impoverishment of the substantive [criminal] law."[118] He bemoans the "underdevelopment of the scientific side of English law," which helped make it "ill-equipped" to handle the transition from common law to statute law.[119] English law, he complains, lacked generality and "scientific sophistication."[120] These remarks clearly indicate a preference for laws that are clear commands serving the values of certainty and predictability. Langbein's is an elite, hermetic theory of law, masked as "professionalism." It makes few, if any, allowances for procedures, ideas, or judgments that do not spring from the "legal mind." It ignores the source of law most central to eighteenth-century English society.

Inasmuch as custom was fundamental at all levels of the debate about eighteenth-century society, whether about the law, production, or the family, it cannot be surprising that Langbein's narrow view of historical inquiry is incapable of leading him to other subjects of social life. As a consequence, Langbein ignores the most significant aspect of the jury: it was—at least potentially—a profound democratic check upon the arbitrary authority of the state, which could be exercised either capriciously or in the name of "scientific sophistication."

VIII

GARBAGE

The conclusion of Langbein's attack reverts to the question of sanitation with which, in his expressed doubts about the possibility of a Marxist interpretation of the flush toilet, it began. He may intend a kind of retentive wit by raising this question, but because it is among the most revealing and interesting parts of his essay, we may treat it seriously. He writes:

> The criminal law is simply the wrong place to look for the active hand of the ruling classes. From the standpoint of the rulers, I would suggest, the criminal justice system occupies a place not much more central than the garbage collection system. True, if the garbage is not collected the society cannot operate and ruling class goals will be frustrated, but that does not turn garbage collection into a ruling-class

---

[118] Langbein, supra note 1, at 117.
[119] Id.
[120] Id. at 118.

conspiracy.[121]

Just how central was the garbage collection system? Were we to bisect a map of eighteenth-century London[122] on both its axes, we would find ourselves in a location that was indeed central to both the criminal justice and the garbage collection systems. The main workhouse, the Bridewell, and the largest debtors' prison, the Fleet, were near the Fleet "River" (as it once had been) or "Ditch" (as it had become), which carried garbage and sewage through the center of the city to the River Thames.[123] The Old Bailey lay close by the slaughterhouses and meat markets, which were a huge and constant source of entrails and offal or "pudding."[124] These wastes were carted down Pudding Lane which, at the midpoint of London, fed Dung Wharf and Puddle Dock, two stinking, insalubrious places, with the human and animal wastes of London.[125] The intimate proximity of the prisons and courts to dung and "pudding" in the literal center of London supports Langbein's comparison.

The garbage collection system was also a central concern of municipal policy. An ordinance "For Preserving and Ordering the Streets of London Against Annoyances" described in elaborate detail the urban regulation of sewage and waste.[126]

---

[121] Id. at 119. Langbein argues that the criminal law is only important "at the *margins* of social life." Id. (quoting Sparks, A Critique of Marxist Criminology, in 2 Crime and Justice: An Annual Review of Research 159, 193 (1980)). In fact, Langbein takes this quotation out of context. Though Sparks does disagree with *Albion's Fatal Tree* on some points, he explicitly finds "Hay's and Thompson's arguments as to the ideological importance of the criminal law in England in the early eighteenth century . . . convincing." Sparks, supra, at 192.

[122] See, e.g., Jean Rocques's mid-eighteenth-century map, reprinted in J. Rocque, The A to Z of Georgian London (1982).

[123] M. George, supra note 58, at 86; P. Jones, The Butchers of London 78 (1976). Indeed, during the sixteenth-century reconstruction of the Old Bailey, the headquarters of the criminal justice system, it was decided to cover the Fleet Ditch, making it one of the first modern underground sewers. T. McLaughlin, Dirt: A Social History As Seen Through the Uses and Abuses of Dirt 60 (1971).

[124] P. Jones, supra note 123, at 83-99.

[125] In a seventeenth-century poem, Ben Jonson observed that these parts of the Thames were so thick that a boat's oars could not stir the slime that

    Belch'd forth an ayre, as hot,
        as at a muster
    Of all your night-tubs, when the
        carts doe cluster,
    Who shall discharge first his
        merd-urinous load.

B. Jonson, On the Famous Voyage (Epigramme 133), quoted in T. McLaughlin, supra note 123, at 61.

[126] For example:

    Goung-Fermour shall not carry any Ordure till after Nine of the clock in the Night.
    No Goung-Fermour shall spill any Ordure in the Street.
    The Pudding Cart of the Shambles shall not go afore the Hour of Nine in the Night.

Eighteenth-century Londoners lived close to animals, which were essential to their diet and transportation; sewage clogged their streets and rivers; the disposal of human and animal wastes was a central problem. Amid this picture of filth and stench, however, we should consider the observation of a historian of dirt: "Dirt is evidence of the imperfections of life, a constant reminder of change and decay. It is the dark side of all human activities—human, because it is only in our judgements that things are dirty: there is no such material as *absolute* dirt."[127] The eighteenth-century London elite sought to avoid some of these imperfections by using perfume, living indoors, riding in coaches and chairs, and wearing high patterns, all devices designed in part to elevate the elite from urban "wastes" or conceal wastes from them. For the mass of the people, however, these devices were unaffordable luxuries, so dirt was very much a part of their lives. For many working class people, wastes were essential. Nightsoil men and dung farmers earned their livings recycling London's animal and human wastes by removing them to Pimlico and Victoria to replenish the vegetable garden and orchard soils.[128] The mudlarks derived their livings from coal wastes.[129] Recall the case of Boroughs:[130] what was waste to Deponthien was life to Boroughs. As one author has written, "Nature admits no waste. Nothing is left over; everything is joined in the spiral of life."[131]

In the eighteenth century, that spiral became the source of satire directed against refined society. Swift's Yahoos shitting from the tree tops[132] are perhaps the central picture in his "excremental vision." Hogarth's "The Four Times of Day" depicts Sir Thomas DeVeil, a police magistrate, wincing as a urine bowl is emptied on his head from a window above.[133] It is tempting to examine Langbein's analogy in the same spirit: to compare the "Ordure Bole" to the watchman's lock-up, "jakes" (privies) to the magistrate's examining rooms, "laystalls" (dung and refuse piles) to the Old Bailey and the nitrogenuous properties of

---

No Man shall cast any Urine-Boles, or Ordure Boles into the Streets by Day or Night, afore . . . Nine in the Night: And also he shall not cast it out, but bring it down, and lay it in the Channel.

Quoted in W. Bohun, Privilegia Londini; Or the Rights, Liberties, Privileges, Laws and Customs of the City of London 108, 109, 111 (3d ed. London 1723). See also P. Jones, supra note 123, at 91-103 (regulation of slaughterhouse and markets).

[127] T. McLaughlin, supra note 123, at 1.

[128] Id. at 97.

[129] Henry Mayhew described this underside of the fuel economy in 2 H. Mayhew, London Labour and the London Poor 173 (1968).

[130] See text accompanying notes 65-69 supra.

[131] See S. Van der Ryn, The Toilet Papers: Designs to Recycle Human Waste and Water 5 (1978).

[132] J. Swift, 11 The Works of Jonathan Swift 272-73 (2d ed. 1883)(1st ed. London 1726).

[133] 1 R. Paulson, Hogarth: His Life, Art and Times 402 (1971).

excrementa. But satiric treatment of the analogy might belittle other relations implied by Langbein's insight.

The lectures that Adam Smith delivered in Glasgow in the early 1760's, which became a basis for portions of his *Wealth of Nations*, began with a description of the objects of law: justice, police, revenue, and arms. "Police" was not yet a common English word; it was French and associated with despotism, so Smith reminded his listeners of its Greek derivation, meaning "civil government," and divided it into its three "objects":

> cleanliness, security, and cheapness or plenty. The two former, to wit, the proper method of carrying dirt from the streets, and the execution of justice, so far as it regards regulations for preventing crimes or the method of keeping a city guard, though useful, are too mean to be considered in a general discourse of this kind.[134]

Garbage disposal and crime prevention are two of the basic components of civil government, but they are "too mean to be considered." Dirt and crime are both central and mean, inescapable yet not fit for discourse. Professor Langbein apparently seeks to resolve a similar ambivalence by irony. Yet why are dirt and crime "mean" or unfit for a "general discourse"?

Human waste played an important role in the relationship between the classes. Norbert Elias argues that civilization is only a history of increasing the mediations between the necessary productions of the body and interactions with others.[135] The handkerchief, the nightdress, and the fork exemplify the technology of these mediations.[136] Such buffers against bodily activities and other persons were both a form of class differentiation and a means of denying humanity to others, who could be seen in terms of "garbage," "dirt," or "scum." In challenging Marxists to a history of the flush toilet, Professor Langbein may have been joking, but in light of Elias's thesis, we may treat the suggestion more seriously than it perhaps was intended.

We may suggest four stages in the evolution of the water closet.[137] A rudimentary water closet designed in 1547 for Edward VI was covered with velvet and garnished with fringe, quilting, and 2,000 gilt nails. This was the monarchical phase of the water closet. An improved water closet that delivered water with enough force to completely wash the bowl signaled the beginning of the aristocratic or oligarchic phase, but

---

[134] See A. Smith, Lectures on Justice, Police, and Arms 3-4, 154-55 (1896).

[135] N. Elias, The Civilizing Process: The Development of Manners: Changes in the Code of Conduct and Feeling in Early Modern Times 134-43 (1978).

[136] Id. at 117-22, 148-52, 163-68.

[137] The source for the facts in this passage is T. McLaughlin, supra note 123, at 49-52, 110. The analysis of phases is my own.

the need for a ready supply of water prevented its becoming more than a curiosity in the homes of aristocrats. The third stage was bourgeois: numerous mechanical and hydraulic improvements were introduced, and one manufacturer made 6,000 water closets in the last decades of the eighteenth century. The fourth and final stage saw the spread of water closets to the mass of urban houses. It is of this period that a modern author writes: "The flush toilet made one person's waste equal to another's in the great stream of sewage."[138]

Besides relating its evolution to four stages of history and to four classes (monarchy, aristocracy, bourgeoisie, proletariat), can Marxism add anything further to our interpretation of the flush toilet? If we extend Marx's theory of alienation in the direction suggested by Norbert Elias, we may understand the history of the flush toilet as part of "civilization," or the alienation of humans from our bodies. To flush and forget is not to get rid of a problem, but only to remove it to another place. For the flushers and forgetters of eighteenth-century London, that place was the environment of other Londoners. The elite's new luxury was not accompanied by a new system for waste disposal. Instead,

> closets mostly discharged into sewers or even open gutters running through the streets, and ultimately into the rivers. A large amount of sewage that had previously been confined to earth closets or carted away by nightmen for use on the land was now added to the already foul waterways. In London, the Thames became so polluted . . . that the end of the century saw an increase in the number of deaths from typhoid that paralleled the installation of the closets.[139]

Reality in eighteenth-century London thus turned Swift's Yahoo story on its head: the rich defecated, almost literally, on the poor. "[T]he rich had water closets, the poor merely got more sewage in their drinking water."[140]

Professor Langbein may find garbage collection and criminal law of no great importance. To those who lived in fear of the hangman and of typhoid, however, such systems were important indeed. As the capital statutes and hangings kept the mass of English people in its place, so the elite's adoption of the water closet may have served, on a psychological level, to convince the masses that they were nothing more than human garbage. In both areas, the "active hand of the ruling class"—not in Langbein's sense of conscious conspiracy, but in Hay's sense of social control—was apparent and heavy.

---

[138] S. Van der Ryn, supra note 131, at 19-20.
[139] T. McLaughlin, supra note 123, at 110.
[140] Id. at 111.

CONCLUSION

Albion's Fatal Tree opened up new paths of historical investigation that others have followed in other studies,[141] studies that by no means accept all the interpretations of our early work. Our volume showed how legal materials could be used in new ways. We used trial records and statutes to construct narratives of aspects of eighteenth-century society such as smuggling, hanging, poaching, wrecking, and anonymous letter writing. As narratives, the essays attempted to introduce forgotten subjects in such a way that a reader might find evidence of causalities—as well as the casualties—of historical change. To us the law was neither a mere superstructure upon fact nor a closed system of intellectualism; it was a new kind of evidence. But it was, in the eighteenth century, not only that. We found, and this was Douglas Hay's particular contribution, that law had in itself ideological importance as well as functional purposes that largely served the class interests of the elite. Often the law—its practices, rules, precepts, theater, and punishments—was opposed to "custom," and *Albion's Fatal Tree* helped to reintroduce that ancient antagonism between law and custom into current scholarly discussion.

In this "Reply" to Professor Langbein, I have sought to show the limits of his historical approach. In his classification of criminal statutes, in his characterization of offenders, and in his presentation of evidence about the eighteenth-century jury, Langbein has been limited by his excessively intellectualized and self-enclosed view of the law. This view both isolates that discipline from other modes of historical inquiry, such as economic, social, and political history, and stifles any meaningful analysis of historical change. Langbein's is a conservative and self-enclosed theory of law that is both elitist (hence his stress upon "professionalism") and sanitized (hence his hands-off treatment of the flush toilet).

---

[141] See authorities cited in note 15 supra.

Part II
Social Histories of Crime

[6]

KARL MARX, THE THEFT OF WOOD, AND WORKING CLASS COMPOSITION: A CONTRIBUTION TO THE CURRENT DEBATE*

Peter Linebaugh**

* I wish to thank Norman Stein who provided me with some material assistance in the preparation of this article. My deepest thanks to Gene Mason, Bobby Scollard and Monty Neill, my comrades in the Northeast Prisoners' Association, for their criticism of an earlier draft of this paper.

** Peter Linebaugh received his doctorate from the Centre for the Study of Social History at the University of Warwick. With his colleagues there he edited and contributed to *Albion's Fatal Tree: Crime and Society in Eighteenth-Century England* (Pantheon: New York, 1975). He was once an editor of *NEPA News*, a newspaper of the Northeast Prisoners' Association. He is now a member of the editorial collective of *Zerowork* and currently teaches history at the University of Rochester.

I.

The international working class offensive of the 1960s threw the social sciences into crisis from which they have not yet recovered. The offensive was launched in precisely those parts of the working class that capital had formerly attempted to contain within silent, often wageless reserves of the relative surplus population, that is, in North American ghettoes, in Caribbean islands, or in 'backward' regions of the Mediterranean. When that struggle took the form of the mass, direct appropriation of wealth, it became increasingly difficult for militants to understand it as a "secondary movement" to the "real struggle" that, it was said, resided only in the unions and the plants. Nor could it be seen as the incidental reactions of "victims" to an "oppressive society," as it was so often by those organizations left flat-footed by the power of an autonomous Black movement and an autonomous women's movement.

This is not the place to elaborate on the forms that the struggles have taken in the direct appropriation of wealth, nor how these were able to circulate within more familiar terms of struggle.[1] We must note, however, that they thrust the problem of crime, capital's most ancient tool in the creation and control of the working class, once again to a prominent place in the capitalist relation. As the political recomposition of the international working class threw into crisis the capitalist organization of labor markets, so that part of traditional social science, criminology, devoted to studying one of the corners in the labor market, "criminal subcultures" and street gangs, had to face a crisis of its own.

George Jackson recommended burning the libraries of criminology. Young criminologists began to question the autonomous status of criminology as a field of study (Hirst, 1972:29; Phillipson, 1973:400; Melossi, 1976:31; Currie, 1974:113). Accompanying both the internal and external critique of criminology has been a recovery of interest in the treatment of crime within the Marxist tradition. Yet, that tradition is by no means accessible or complete and in fact contains contradictory strains within it, so that one cannot be completely unqualified in welcoming it.

In stating our own position let us try to be as clear as possible even at the risk of overstatement. We wish to oppose the view that fossilizes particular compositions of the working class into eternal, even formulaic, patterns. We must, in particular, combat the view that analyzes crime (or much else indeed) in the nineteenth century terms of a "lumpenproletariat" versus an "industrial proletariat." It is to be regretted that despite the crisis of criminology and the experience of struggle that gave rise to it, some militants can still speak of the "lumpenproletariat" *tout court* as though this were a fixed category of capitalist relations of power. When neither the principle of historical specification nor the concept of class struggle is admitted there can be no useful analysis of class strategy, howsoever exalted the methodology may be in other respects.[2]

In the rejection of various idealist interpretations of crime including their 'marxist' variants, there is, perforce, a revival of interest in the situation of the problem within specified historical periods, that is, within well constituted phases of capitalist accumulation. In this respect the recent work appearing in these pages that discusses the problem in terms of original accumulation must be welcomed (Melossi, 1976:26ff). At the same time we must express the hope that this analysis may be extended to the discussion of the appropriation of wealth and of crime at other periods of the class relation. The contribution of those whose starting point in the analysis of crime is the concept of "marginalization" (Crime and Social Justice Collective, 1976:1-4; Herman and Julia R. Schwendinger, 1976:7-26) leads us to an analysis of the capitalist organization and planning of labor markets, certainly an advance in comparison to those for whom capital remains de-historicized and fixed in the forms of its command. On the other hand one cannot help but note the unilateral

nature of the concept, the fact that it entails an approach
to the question that must accept capital's point of view
without adequately reconstituting the concept with
working class determinants. One remembers that the life
and works of Malcolm X and George Jackson, far from
being contained within incidental, "marginal sectors,"
became leading international reference points for a whole
cycle of struggle.

The recent publication of the English translation of
Marx's early writings on the criminal law and the theft of
wood provides us with a propitious moment for another
look at the development of Marx's thinking on the question
of crime.[3] We hope that some suggestions for placing those
articles within the context of the real dynamics of capitalist
accumulation may not only allow us to specify the
historical determinants of class struggle in the 1840s,
but—what is of far greater importance—may make a
contribution to the present debate, a debate which in its
abandonment of "criminology" as traditionally constituted
in favor of an analysis of the political composition of the
working class has more than a few similarities with Marx's
own development after 1842.

Lunch Hour: Käthe Kollwitz

II.

It would not be much of an exaggeration to say that it
was a problem of theft that first forced Marx to realize his
ignorance of political economy, or to say that class struggle
first presented itself to Marx's serious attention as a form of
crime. Engels had always understood Marx to say that it
was the study of the law on the theft of wood and the
situation of the Moselle peasantry that led him to pass from
a purely political viewpoint to the study of economics and
from that to socialism (Cornu, 1958:ii, 68). Marx's own
testimony is no less clear. In the 1859 preface to his
Contribution to the Critique of Political Economy he
wrote,

> In 1842-43, as editor of the *Rheinische Zeitung*, I
> found myself embarrassed at first when I had to take

part in discussions concerning so-called material
interests. The proceedings of the Rhine Diet in
connection with forest thefts and the extreme
sub-division of landed property; the official controversy about the condition of the Mosel peasants into
which Herr von Schaper, at that time president of
the Rhine Province, entered with the *Rheinische
Zeitung;* finally, the debates on free trade and
protection, gave me the first impulse to take up the
study of economic questions (Marx, 1904:10).

Faced with his own and Engel's evidence, we must
therefore beware of those accounts of the development of
Marx's ideas that see it in the exclusive terms of either the
self-liberation from the problematics of Left Hegelianism or
the outcome of a political collision that his ideas had with
the French Utopian and revolutionary tradition that he met
during his exile in Paris. The famous trinity (French
politics, German philosophy, and English political economy) of the intellectual lineages of Marx's critical analysis
of the capitalist mode of production appears to include
everything but the actual, material form in which class
struggle first forced itself to the attention of the young
radical in 1842.

Our interest, however, is not to add the footnote to the
intellectual biography of Marx that his ideas, too, must be
considered in relation to their material setting. Our purpose
is different. We wish to find out why, as it was his
inadequate understanding of crime that led him to the
study of political economy, Marx never again returned to
the systematic analysis of crime as such. As we do this we
shall also find that the mass illegal appropriation of forest
products represented an important moment in the
development of German capitalism, and that it was to the
partial analysis of that moment that a good part of the
work of some founders of German criminology was
devoted. The same moment of struggle in German agrarian
relations produced contradictory results among those
attempting to understand it: on the one hand, the
formation of criminology, and on the other, the
development of the revolutionary critique of capitalism.

III.

Between 25 October and 3 November, 1842, Marx
published five articles in the *Rheinische Zeitung* on the
debates about a law on the theft of wood that had taken
place a year and a half earlier in the Provincial Assembly of
the Rhine.[4] The political background to those debates has
been described several times (Cornu, 1958: ii, 72-95;
Mehring, 1962:37ff). Here we need only point out that the
"liberal" emperor, Frederick William IV, following his
accession, attempted to make good on a forgotten promise
to call a constitutional convention, by instead re-convening
the provincial assemblies of the empire. Though they had
little power, their opening, together with the temporarily
relaxed censorship regulations, was the occasion for the
spokesmen of the Rhenish commercial and industrial
bourgeoisie to stretch their wings in the more liberal
political atmosphere. The *Rheinische Zeitung*, staffed by a
group of young and gifted men, was their vehicle for the

first, hesitant flights against the Prussian government and the landed nobility. Characterized at first by "a vague liberal aspiration and a veneration for the Hegelian philosophy" (Treitschke, 1919:vi, 538), the journal took a sharper turn under Marx's editing and it was his articles on the theft of wood that caused von Schaper to write the Prussian censorship minister that the journal was now characterized by the "impudent and disrespectful criticism of the existing government institutions" (Marx, 1842:747).

Though containing passages of "exhilirating eloquence" (Wilson, 1940:124), the articles as a whole suffer from an uncertainty as to their central subject. Is it the appropriation of wood, legal or illegal? Is it the equity of the laws of property governing that appropriation? Or, is it the debates with their inconsistencies and thoughtlessness that took place in the assembly before the law was passed? Marx is least confident about the first subject; indeed, we learn little about the amounts and types of direct appropriation. He really warms to the second as it allows him to expound on the nature of the state and the law. On the third his characteristic wit and sarcasm come into full play. Despite these ambiguities, the articles as a whole are united by the theme of the contradiction between private self-interest and the public good. He objects, in particular, to nine provisions in the new law:

1. It fails to distinguish between the theft of fallen wood and that of standing timber or hewn lumber.
2. It allows the forest warden to both apprehend wrongdoers and evaluate the stolen wood.
3. It puts the tenure of the appointment of the forest warden entirely at the will of the forest owner.
4. Violators of the law are obliged to perform forced labor on the roads of the forest owner.
5. The fines imposed on the thief are remitted to the forest owner (in addition to compensation for damaged property).
6. Costs of defense incurred at trial are payable in advance.
7. In prison, the thief is restricted to a diet of bread and water.
8. The receiver of stolen wood is punished to the same extent as the thief.
9. Anyone possessing wood that is suspected must prove honest title to it.

Young Marx was outraged by the crude, undisguised, self-interested provisions of punishment established by this law. He was no less indignant with its substantive expansion of the criminal sanction. His criticism of the law rested upon an *a priori*, idealist conception of both the law and the state. "The law," he wrote, "is the universal and authentic exponent of the rightful order of things." Its form represents "universality and necessity." When applied to the exclusive advantage of particular interests—the forest owners—then "the immortality of the law" is sacrificed and the state goes "against the nature of things." The "conflict between the interest of forest protection and the principles of law" can result only in the degradation of "the idea of the state." We stress that this criticism applied to both the substantive and the procedural sections of the law. In the latter case, "public punishment" is transformed "into private compensation." "Reform of the criminal" is attained by the "improvement of the percentage of profit" devolving on the forest owner. The attack on the substantive part of the law rests on similar arguments. "By

applying the category of theft where it ought not to be applied you exonerate it." "All the organs of the state become ears, eyes, arms, legs, and means by which the interest of the forest owner hears, sees, appraises, protects, grasps and runs." "The right of human beings gives way to the right of trees." As he stated this, Marx also had to ask, which human beings? For the first time he comes to the defense of the "poor, politically and socially propertyless" when he demands for the poor "a customary right."

On what basis is the demand made? Some confusion results as Marx, only a few years away from his Berlin studies of the pandects and jurisprudence, attempts to solve the problem. First, he justifies it on the basis that the law must represent the interests of all "citizens," that is, he refers to the classical arguments of natural justice. Second, and not altogether playfully, he says that "human poverty ... deduces its right to fallen wood" from the natural fact that the forests themselves present in the contrast between strong, upright timber to the snapped twigs and wind-felled branches underneath an "antithesis between poverty and wealth." Third, in noting that the inclusion of the appropriation of fallen wood with that of live and hewn timber under the rubric of the criminal sanction is inconsistent with both the sixteenth century penal code and the ancient "Germanic rights" (*leges barbarorum*), he suggests the greater force of these feudal codes.

It is true that Marx understands that these changes of law correspond, over the centuries, to changes in property relations: "all customary rights of the poor were based on the fact that certain forms of property were indeterminate in character, for they were not definitely private property, but neither were they definitely common property, being a mixture of private and public right, such as we find in all the institutions of the Middle Ages." Accumulation has in these articles no separate existence apart from the law which indeed determines it as Marx implies when he says that it was the introduction of the Roman law that abolished "indeterminate property." Powerless to resist, as it were, the tide of a millenium of legal development, Marx seeks to defend the "customary right" by fleeing the seas of history altogether and placing his defense upon the *terra firma* of nature itself. There are objects "which by their elemental nature and their accidental mode of existence" must defy the unitary force of law which makes private property from "indeterminate property," and the forests are one of these objects.

Appeal as he might to the "universal necessity of the rightful order of things" or to the bio-ecology of the forest, neither of these lofty tribunals could so much as delay, much less halt, the swift and sharp swath that the nobility and burgomasters in Dusseldorf were cutting through the forests of the Rhineland. Fruitless as such appeals had to be, Marx could not even understand, by the idealist terms of his argument, *why* it was that the rich Rhenish agriculturalists found it necessary to pass such a law at that time thus expanding the criminal sanction. Nor—and this was far dearer to his interests—could he analyze the historical forces that propelled the Rhenish cotters to the direct appropriation of the wood of the forests. To be sure, we know from passing remarks made in other articles of the 1842-43 period that Marx understood that the parcelling of landed property, the incidence of taxation upon the vineyards, the shortages of firewood, and the collapsing market for Moselle wines were all elements of a single situation that he could, however, only see from the partial, incomplete standpoint of natural justice.

IV.

When looking at these articles from the standpoint of Marx's later works, we can see that he analyzes only the contradictory appearance of the struggle. Having no concept of class struggle or capitalist accumulation he treats the Rhenish peasantry with a democratic, egalitarian passion, but still as an object external to the actual forces of its development. Unable to apprehend the struggle as one against capitalist development, he assumes that a reasoned appeal to the agrarian lords of the forest, or to their sympathetic brethren in Cologne, will find sympathetic ears. Thus real development occurs, he thought, at the level of the state which only needed to be reminded of its own inherent benevolence to reverse the course of the law and of history.

Precisely this viewpoint, though in an inverted form, dominated the work of the early German criminologists.[5] Like the young Marx, they separated the problem of the state and crime from the class relations of accumulation. They saw crime from a unilateral, idealist viewpoint. However, for them it was less a question of state benevolence than it was of the malevolence of the working class. They sought to determine the "moral condition of the people" by the classification, tabulation, and correlation of "social phenomena." The work produced in this statistical school sought to find "laws" that determined the relative importance of different "factors" (prices, wages, extension of the franchise, etc.) that accounted for changes in the amounts and types of crime. Like the young Marx, they were unable to ask either why some forms of appropriation became crimes at specified periods and others not, or why crimes could at some times become a serious political force imposing precise obstacles to capitalist reproduction.

The problem of the historical specification of class relations and in particular those as they were reflected in Marx's articles, can be solved only from the standpoint of his later work, especially the first volume of *Capital.* There we learn that in discussing the historical phases of the class relation it is necessary to emphasize the forms of divisions within the working class that are created by combining different modes of production within the social division of labor. This is one of the lessons of Chapter XV. The effect of the capitalist attack managed by means of the progressive subordination of living labor to machines is to extend and intensify "backward" modes of production in all of their forms. This is one of the weapons capital enjoys in establishing a working class articulated in a form favorable to it. Another is described in Chapter XXV of *Capital,* a chapter that is often read as a statement of a dual labor market theory, i.e., that capital in maintaining both an active and a reserve front in its social organization of labor power creates the mechanism for reducing the value of necessary labor. In fact, the "relative surplus population" is maintained in several different forms, forms determined precisely by the combination of different

modes of production. With the reproduction of capital and the struggles against it, that combination constantly changes. The chapter begins with a difficult, apparently technical, section on the value composition of capital that reminds us that the configuration of the working class cannot be analyzed exclusively in terms of its attachments to different "sectors" or "branches" of the social division of labor. Even while accounting for divisions in the class that rest upon its relation to capitals with variant compositions, the political composition of the working class must always be studied from the additional viewpoint of its ability to use these divisions in its attack upon capital. These are divisions whose determinations are not merely the relation to the labor process (employed or unemployed), but divisions based upon the quantitative and qualitative form of the value of labor power.

Lenin, in his analysis of the development of capitalism in Russia and, generally, in his polemics with the "legal Marxists" of the 1890s, was forced to cover much of this ground. "As for the forms of wage-labor, they are extremely diverse in a capitalist society, still everywhere enmeshed in survivals and institutions of the pre-capitalist regime" (Lenin, 1899:590). In contrast to the Narodnik economists who considered the size of the proletariat exclusively as current factory employment, Lenin was forced to remind militants that the working class must be considered only in its relation to capital and in its ability to struggle against capital, regardless of the forms in which capital organizes it within particular productive settings. From a quantitative point of view the timber and lumber workers of post-Reform Russia were next in importance only to agricultural workers. The fact that these belonged to the relative redundant population, or that they were primarily local (not migratory) workers, or that a proportion of their income did not take the form of the wage made them no less important from either the standpoint of capitalist accumulation or from that of the working class struggle against it. Although "the lumber industry leaves all the old, patriarchal way of life practically intact, enmeshing in the worst forms of bondage the workers left to toil in the remote forest depths," Lenin was forced to include his discussion of the timber industry in his section on "large-scale machine industry." He did so not on the grounds of the quantitative scale of lumber workers within the proletariat as a whole, but because the qualitative extension of such work remained a condition of large-scale industry in fuel, building, and machine supplies. Under these circumstances it was not possible to consider the two million timber workers as the tattered edges of a dying "feudalism." Forms of truck payment and extra-economic forms of bondage prevailed not as mere remnants from a pre-capitalist social formation, but as terms of exploitation guaranteeing stability to capitalist accumulation. This was made clear in the massive agrarian unrest of the years 1905-1907 when the illicit cutting of wood was one of the most important mass actions against the landowners (Perrie, 1972:128-129).

Let us return, at this point, to the development of capitalism in the Rhineland and, in sketching some elements of the class relation, see if we can throw some light upon the historical movement of which Marx's articles were a partial reflection.

The Meeting on the Haymarket: Mitchell Siporin

V.

Capitalist development in Germany, at least before 1848, is usually studied at the level of circulation as the formation of a national market. In 1818, 1824, and 1833, at the initiative of Prussia, a series of commercial treaties were signed creating a customs union, the Zollverein, that sought to restore the larger market that Napoleon's "continental system" had imposed. The treaties removed restrictions on communications and transport. They abolished internal customs, established a unified external tariff, and introduced a common system of weights and measures. "In fact," as a British specialist stated in 1840, "the Zollverein has brought the sentiment of German nationality out of the regions of hope and fancy into those of positive material interests" (Bowring, 1840:1). In 1837 and 1839 treaties with the Netherlands abolishing the octroi and other Dutch harbor and navigation duties established the Rhine as the main commercial artery of western Prussia (Henderson, 1939:129-130). Indeed, the Zollverein was only the most visible aspect of the offensive launched by German capital, providing as it did the basis for a national banking and credit market, a precondition of the revolutions in transportation of the 1830s and 1840s, and the basis of the expansion in trade that found some of its political consequences in the establishment of Chambers of Commerce, the consolidation of the German bourgeoisie, and the liberal initiatives of the young Frederick William IV.

The reforms in internal and foreign commercial arrangements, together with the reforms of the Napoleonic period that created a free market in land and "emancipated" the serfs, provided the foundations not only of a national market but laid the basis within a single generation for rapid capitalist development. Older historians, if not more recent ones, clearly understood that those changes "far from bringing into being the anticipated just social order, led to new and deplorable class struggles" (Treitschke, 1919:vii, 201). The expropriation of the serfs and their redeployment as wage laborers are of course logically and historically distinct moments in the history of capital. During the intermediating period the articulation of the working class within and without capitalist enterprises must present confusions to those attempting to analyze it from the framework established during other periods of working class organization. A consideration of the working class that regards it only when it is waged or only when that wage takes an exclusively monetary form is doomed to misunderstand both capitalist accumulation and the working class struggle against it. To consider our period alone, those who find class struggle "awakened" only after the 1839 strike of gold workers at Pfortsheim and the Berlin cotton weavers' and Brandenburg railway workers' strikes will not be able to understand why, for all their faults, Marx's articles on the theft of wood expressed an important moment in the dynamics of accumulation and class relations. In the following pages we can only suggest some elements of those dynamics.

The recomposition of class relations in the Rhineland during the 1830s and '40s was not led, as in England at the time, by the introduction of large-scale machinery. German manufacture was nevertheless deeply affected. From the point of view of class relations, manufacturing capital was organized in two apparently opposite ways. On the one hand the changes in transportation required massive, mobile injections of labor willing to accept short-term employments. Under state direction the great railway boom of the 1830s more than quadrupled the size of the railway system. River transport also changed—steam-powered tugs replaced the long lines of horses pulling laden barges on the Rhine. These changes provided, as it were, the material infrastructure to the possibilities made available by the Zollverein. On the other hand, the capitalist offensive against traditional handicraft and small workshop production met setbacks that were partially the results of workers' power in the detail of the labor process or of the obstacles remaining in the traditional, often agrarian, relations that engulfed such productive sites.

What Banfield, the English free-trader, wrote of the foremen of the Prussian-owned coal mines of the Ruhr applied equally well to most forms of Rhenish manufacture in the 1840s: "Their business they generally understand, but the discipline, which is the element by which time is played off against money, and which allows high wages to co-exist with large profits, does not show itself" (Banfield, 1848:55-56). Only a visitor from England with two or three generations of experience in the organization of relative surplus value, could have so clearly enunciated this fundamental principle of capitalist strategy. In Prussia the height of political economy stopped with the observation that the state organization of the home market could guarantee accumulation. In the silk and cotton weaving districts of Elberfeld where outwork and task payments prevailed, workers' power appeared to capital as short-weighting of finished cloth, "defective workmanship," and the purloining of materials. The handworkers of the Sieg and Ruhr (wire-drawers, nail makers, coppersmiths, etc.) prevented the transition to large-scale machinery in the forge industries. Linen workers and flax farmers prevented the introduction of heckling and scutching machines. Alcoholism and coffee addiction were regarded as serious impediments to the imposition of higher levels of intensity in work. Of course, another aspect of this power to reject intensification in the labor process was a stagnation that brought with it low wages and weaknesses in resisting the prolongation of the working day which, in cotton textiles, had become sixteen hours by the 1840s. Such were the obstacles to accumulation throughout Rhenish manufacture—the Lahn valley zinc works, the sugar refineries of Cologne, the rolling mills and earthenware factories of Trier and the Saarbrucken, the fine steel trades of Solingen, as well as in coal, weaving, and forge work.

These apparently opposite poles of the labor market in Rhenish manufacturing—the "light infantry," mobile, massive, and sudden, of railway construction and the stagnant, immobile conditions of small-scale manufacturing—were in fact regulated by the rhythms of agrarian relations. The point needs to be stressed insofar as many tend to make an equivalence between agriculture and feudalism on one hand and manufactures and capitalism on the other, thus confusing a primary characteristic of the social (and political) division of labor under capitalism with the transition to capitalist dominance in the mode of production as a whole. Both the form of the wage and the labor markets of manufacture were closely articulated to agrarian relations. Remuneration for work in manufacturing was in part made either by the allotment of small garden plots or by a working year that permitted "time off" for tending such plots. Other non-monetary forms of compensation, whether traditional perquisites in manufacture or common rights in forests, provided at once an obstacle to capitalist freedom in the wage and, at the pivot of the capitalist relation, a nodal point capable of uniting the struggles of workers in both agrarian and manufacturing settings. This mutual accomodation between manufacturing and agriculture could sometimes present bottlenecks to accumulation, as in the Sieg valley, where village control over the woodlands guaranteed that timber exploitation would remain more an aspect of working class consumption than in industrial fuel in the metal trades. Macadamization of the roads to the foundries allowed owners to buy and transport fuels, at once releasing them from the "parsimony" of village controlled wood supplies and providing the basis for the re-organization of the detail of the labor process (Banfield, 1846:142). Thus we can begin to see that technical changes in transportation are as much a weapon against the working class as they are adjuncts to the development of circulation in the market.

The progressive parcelling of arable and forest lands in the Rhine, the low rates of agricultural growth, as well as the mixed and sometimes sub-subsistence forms of compensation provided a dispersed and extensive pool for the intensive and concentrated labor requirements of the railway and metallurgical industries, and concurrently established (what was well known at the time) a form of agrarian relations wherein political stability could be managed (Palgrave, 1912:ii, 814-816; and Lengerke, 1849). The "latent" and "stagnant" reserves of proletarians were regulated, in part, by the institutions designed to control mendicity and emigration.

The emigration of German peasants and handicraft workers doubled between 1820 and 1840. Between 1830 and 1840 it actually tripled as on average forty thousand German speaking emigrants a year jammed the main ports of embarkation (Bremen and Le Havre) awaiting passage (Droz, 1957:78). The areas with the most intense emigration were the forest regions of the upper Rhine (Milward & Saul, 1973:147). A lucrative business existed in Mainz for the factors who organized the shipping of the peasants of the Odenwald and the Moselle across the Atlantic to Texas and Tennessee. Pauperization records are no less indicative of active state control of the relative surplus population than they are of the magnitude of the problem. Arrests for mendicity increased between 1841 and 1842 in Franconia, the Palatinate, and Lower Bavaria by 30 percent to 50 percent (Mayr, 1867:136-37). In the 1830s one in four people in Cologne were on some form of charitable or public relief (Milward and Saul, 1973:147).

Emigration policies and the repression of paupers alike were organized by the state. The police of western Prussia were directed to prevent the accumulation of strangers. The infamous Frankfurt Assembly of 1848 devoted much of its work to the encouragement and regulation of emigration. What early German criminologists were to find in the inverse relation between the incidence of emigration and that of crime had already become an assumption of policy in the early 1840s. The agrarian proletariat of the Rhine was thus given four possible settings of struggle during this period: emigration, pauperization, the immiseration of the "dwarf economy," or the factory. Its history during that period is the forms of its refusal of the last, the least favorable terrain of struggle. Of course to many contemporaries these problems appeared to be the result of "overpopulation" whose solution might have been sought in Malthusian remedies were it not for the fact that the struggles of the Rhenish proletariat for the re-appropriation of wealth had already forced the authorities to consider them as a major problem of "crime and order."

The organization of agriculture in the Rhineland during the 1830s and 1840s was characterized by the open-field system regulated by the *Gemeinde* or village association on the one hand, and by the progressive parcelling (or even pulverization) of individual ownership on the other (Ibid.:82). Friedrich List called it the "dwarf economy" (Ibid.). Since the time of the French occupation of the Rhine when cash payments replaced labor dues, the first historic steps were taken in the "emancipation of the peasantry." The two forms of agrarian relations were complementary: the *Gemeinde* tended to encourage parcelling, and thus one would be mistaken to consider the property relation of the *Gemeinde* opposed to the development of private property. Parcelling and the concurrent development of a free land-market in Rhenish Prussia wrought "devastation among the poorer peasantry" (Treitschke, 1919:vii,301).

The village system of farming, still widespread in the 1840s, was the "most expensive system of agriculture" according to one of its nineteenth century students. It was argued that the distance separating the individual's field from his dwelling caused a waste of time, and that the tissue of forest and grazing rights and customs caused a duplication of effort, constituting an impediment to "scientific" farming. Similarly, common rights in the mill were an inefficient deployment of resources and an obstacle to innovations. Side by side with the *Gemeinde* existed the enormous number of small allotment holders who, living at the margin of subsistence, were intensely sensitive to the slightest changes in prices for their products and to changes in interest rates at seeding or planting time. On ten million arable acres in the Rhineland, there were eleven million different parcels of land (Cornu, 1958:ii, 78-79). As a result of the opening of the Rhineland to competition from east Prussian grain and the extension of the timber market, small allotment holders could neither live on the lower prices received for their products nor afford the higher prices required for fuel. Under this progressive erosion of their material power, a life and death struggle took place for the re-appropriation of wealth, a struggle that was endemic, highly price sensitive, and by no means restricted to timber and fuel rights.

"In summer many a cow is kept sleek on purloined goods" (Banfield, 1846:157). In the spring women and children ranged through the fields along the Rhine and its tributaries, the Mosel, the Ahr, and the Lahn, cutting young thistles and nettles, digging up the roots of couch-grass, and collecting weeds and leaves of all kinds to turn them to account as winter fodder. Richer farmers planted a variety of lucerns (turnips, Swedes, wurzel), but they had to be ever watchful against the industrious skills of their neighbors, skills that often "degenerated into actual robbery." It must be remembered that a good meal in the 1840s consisted of potato porridge and sour milk, a meal that depended upon the keeping of a cow and on access to fodder or grazing rights that had become increasingly hard to come by.

The terms of cultivation among the orchards were similar to conditions of grazing and foraging—operose work and a suspicious eye. The size of orchards was determined not by the topography of the land but by the walking powers of the *gardes champetres* who provided "inefficient protection against the youth or loose population of the surrounding country." At harvest time cherries, apples, pears, walnuts, and chestnuts were guarded by their owners who rested on beds of straw during evening vigils. The expansion of the field police in the 1830s did nothing to reduce the complaints of depredations. A "man of weight" in the Moselle valley provides us with this description:

The disorderly habits that have such an influence in after life, it may safely be asserted have their root in the practice of sending children to watch the cattle on the (uninclosed) stubbles. Big and little meet here together. The cattle are allowed to graze for the most part on other people's lands; little bands are formed, where the older children teach the younger their bad habits. Thefts are discussed and planned, fighting follows, then come other vices. First, fruit and potatoes are stolen, and every evening at parting the wish is entertained that they may be able to meet again the next. Neither fields, gardens, nor houses are eventually spared, and with the excuse of this employment it is scarcely possible to bring the children together to frequent a summer day-school, or to attend on Sundays to the weekly explanation of the Christian doctrines (quoted in Banfield, 1846:159).

We note that in these observations no fine distinction can be drawn between the struggle to retain traditional common rights against their recent expropriation and the endemic depredations that were executed without cover of that appeal to legitimacy. Nor should we expect it. In viticulture, garden, and orchard farming the transformation of the market, the fall of prices, the stringencies of credit, especially during the period of 1839-1842, intensified the immiserations of the Rhenish agrarian population which still accounted for about 73 percent of employments.

Traditionally, one of the most important cushions to natural and cyclical disaster was the widespread existence of common rights in private and corporate forests. Despite the relatively high levels of population density and manufacturing development in western Prussia, the proportion of forest to arable lands was three to four, in contrast to Prussia as a whole where it was about one to two. The riches of the forests could provide not only fuel, but also forage, materials for houses, farm equipment, and food. The crisis hitting the Rhenish farming population made these riches all the more necessary to survival. At the same time, access to them was becoming progressively restricted with the inexorable expropriation of forest rights.

The forest, one knows, had supported a complex society both within its purviews and in the neighboring terrain: woodcutters, charcoal burners, coopers, sabot makers, basket makers, joiners, tanners, potters, tile makers, blacksmiths, glass makers, lime burners—the list is limited only by the limits of the uses of wood. Particular use-rights in the traditional forest economy had a social life of their own prescribed in a "tissue of customary rights" that defy the norms and clarities of private property. All rights were governed by two principles. First, that "no Man can have any Profit or Pleasure in a Forest which tends to the Destruction thereof," in the words of a sixteenth century treatise (Manwood, 1717:2). Second, the forms of human appropriation were designed to guarantee and preserve the stability and hierarchy of class relations which guaranteed to the lord his liberty in the hunt and mastery of the chase and to the poor particular inalienable usages. Assart of the forest, rights of agistment, rights of pannage, estovers of fire, house, cart or hedge, rush, fern, gorze and sedge rights, rights to searwood, to windfalls, to dotards, rights of lops and tops—in all, the overlapping vocabulary of natural and social relations recall a forgotten world, easily romanticized by those first criticizing the simplicities of *meum et tuum.* Indeed such romanticism is provoked by the harshness of the opposite view that said the existence of such rights "hindered intensive sylviculture, disturbed the progress of orderly cutting, prevented natural regeneration of the forest and depleted the fertility of the forest soil" (Heske, 1938: 241).

Forest relations in the Rhineland had already changed considerably by the time that Karl Marx took up his angry pen in 1841. The parcelling off of large forest estates, the buying and selling of woodlands, the expropriation of forest usufructs had all well progressed by the 1840s. The movement to abolish forest rights really began with the French Revolution. The Prussian agrarian edict of 1811 removed all restrictions that encumbered the free, private exploitation of forest properties.

The first forty years of the century were characterized by a secular appreciation in the value of timber relative to the value of other agrarian products. This may be attributed to the markets encouraged by the Zollverein, to the demands of railway construction, to the increasing demand for machinery (oak was still widely used), and to the burgeoning market for both individual and productive fuel consumption, itself the result in part of the expropriation of forest usufructs. Dutch shipbuilding, traditionally dependent on the wide rafts of oak brought down the Rhine, remained active. British shipbuilding relied in part on Rhenish hardwoods—oak, elm, cherry and ash—for its supply of spars, masts, yards, staves, and knees (Bowring, 1840:137). Industrial and commercial building in Cologne and the Ruhr was dependent on Rhenish timber. The discovery of the deep seams in 1838 that launched the great expansion of the Ruhr coalfields brought with it an equally sudden rise in the demand for mining timbers (Henderson, 1975:54). Timber prices rose no less in the fuel market where beech was extensively used as an industrial firing fuel, and where timber remained the main source of working-class fuel consumption despite the growing importance of coal. The price of beech tripled between the beginning of the century and 1841. Between 1830 and 1841 it doubled, rising in part due to the demand for railway ties (Banfield, 1846:109). Constructional timber prices rose by 20 percent during the same period.

The Strike: Frans Masereel

This secular trend in forest prices and the struggle of the "peasant proletariat" against it (Noyes, 1966:23) brought about a real crisis in legitimate appropriation that required the active intervention of the state. That which exports to Belgium and Holland started, the wind and the sun completed, and hundreds of years of soil and mulch in the Rhenish broadleaf forests were destroyed in the first part of the century (U.S. Government, 1887:74). The free alienation of forest lands, their subdivision and parcelling, and the violent, unplanned clearing of the woods threatened both part of the livelihood of an entire class in the Rhineland and sound principles of sustained yield management. Without succumbing to the romanticism of the forest which seems everywhere to accompany its destruction (e.g., Chateaubriand—"forests preceded people, deserts followed them"), we must note that on the vanguard of the movement to "preserve" the German woods was the Prussian state anxious to socialize the capital locked up in private forest acres.

For a start, the state reduced the clearing of its own forests and expanded the proportion of forests it owned relative to private, corporate and village forests. By the summer of 1841 more than one half of the Rhenish forests were Prussian owned or controlled. Under state encouragement an apparatus, independent of particular capitalists, was developed for the scientific study and management of timber. G. L. Hartig (1764-1837), organizer of the Prussian Forest Service, and Heinrich Cotta (1763-1844), founder of the Forest Academy at Tharandt (the oldest such school in the world), pioneered the development of scientific sylviculture. Partially under their influence, the free assart and clearing of the forest was subjected to state supervision in order to prevent the further depredation of the woods. The schools established in this movement produced a forest police expert in soil rent theory, actuarial calculations, afforestation scheduling, and cutting according to age-class composition. Not until the end of the century had the Germans lost their pre-eminence in sustained yield management.[6]

Enforcing the plans developed by these specialists in sustained yield and capital turnover against a working population increasingly ready to thwart them, stood the cadres of the police and the instruments of law. "No state organization was more hated," a Prussian sylviculturist wrote, "than the forest police" (quoted in Heske, 1938: 254). At the end of the 19th century the mere listing of the manuals and books of the Prussian forest police filled 61 pages in a standard bibliography (Schwappach, 1894). The law that these cadres enforced, in state *and* corporate and village forests, was the result of some centuries of development. Nothing could be more misleading than to regard the legislation criticized by Marx as law that with a single stroke cut through the thicket of feudal rights in order to establish the property law of the bourgeoisie. That process had been going on for a long time, at least since the forest ordinances of 1515 which, more than anything else, had abolished the unwritten, communal norms of the Carolingian period. The revisions of the law which Marx criticized were modifications of the main legal instrument concerning Prussian forests, the Forestal Theft Act of 1837 (U.S. Government, 1887:53). Several other German states had recently reorganized their forest police and revised their written codes. That of Baden, for example, enacted in 1833, contained 220 sections establishing rules and punishments for nearly every detail of forest appropriation. In Thuringia and Saxe-Meiningen similar codes were established. Written permits were required for berry and mushroom gathering. Dead leaves and forest litter could be gathered for fodder only "in extreme cases of need." The topping of trees for May poles, Christmas trees, rake handles, wagon tongues, etc., was punishable by fine and prison. By the 1840s most forests of Prussia had become subject to the police and deputies of the *Forstmeister* of the Ministry of Interior in Berlin (Banfield, 1846:115). The moment of class relations reflected in Marx's articles was not that of the transition from feudalism to capitalism or even one whose reflection in the law marked a transition from Teutonic to Roman conceptions of property. Each of these had occurred earlier. Nevertheless, it was an important moment in class relations which is to be measured not only by its intensity for which there is ample evidence, but also by its victories, an aspect of which must be studied in the obstacles placed upon the creation of a factory proletariat in the 1840s.

Workmen in the Snow: Edvard Munch

The countryman had a tenacious memory. "The long vanished days when the in the teeming forests anyone who wished might load his cart with wood, remained unforgotten throughout Germany" (Treitschke, 1919: vii, 302). Of course, *anyone* could never have loaded his cart with wood. That some could think so is testimony to the power of the movement in the 1830s and 1840s that was able to confuse the issue of lost rights with the direct appropriation regardless of its ancient legitimacy. Lenin in a similar context warned against accepting those "honeyed grandmothers' tales" of traditional "paternal" relations, a point that must be stressed even while we note that such tales have a way of becoming a force in themselves.

One need not be a specialist in 19th century German folklore to recognize that much of the imagination of the forester expressed hostility to the forces transforming the forests and their societies. In these imaginary worlds the trees themselves took sides with the cotters against their oppressors. Michael the Woodman roamed the forests of the Odenwald selecting trees destined for export on which to place his mark. Such trees were fated to bring misfortune upon their ultimate users: the house built of them would burn, the ship would sink (Hughes, 1910: 36). Knorr in the Black Forest played pranks on travellers. The wild Huntress in the same place gave strangers wrong directions. Particular trees were endowed with marvelous powers. A cherry whose loose boughs provided the cradle of a lost infant, a walnut that withstood the sieges of tumultuous gales, these could confer unexpected generosities upon neighboring peasants. Others exercised capricious malevolence against wayfarers, travellers or others strange to the woods. The legends and stories of the forests testified to the fact that poor woods-people and the peasants of the purlieus could find friends in the densest regions of the forest against the oppressions not only of princes and seigneurs but also of their more recent enemies—the tax collector, the forest police, and the apostles of scientific forest management.

By the end of the 1830s the forests of the Rhineland were haunted by more effectual dangers than the evil spirits of popular imagination. Thus in 1842 a Prussian guidebook warned travelers:

> Keep as much as possible to the highways. Every side path, every woodway, is dangerous. Seek herbage in towns when possible, rather than in villages, and never, or only under the most urgent necessity, in lonely ale-houses, mills, wood-houses, and the like. ... Shouldst thou be attacked, defend thyself manfully, where the contest is not too unequal; where that is the case, surrender thy property to save thy life (quoted in Howitt, 1842:89-90).

The real dangers in the forests before the revolution of 1848 were not those that Michael the Woodman might effect upon wayfarers but those that a mass movement for the appropriation of forest wealth placed upon capitalist accumulation. In 1836, of a total of 207,478 prosecutions brought forward in Prussia, a full 150,000 were against wood pilfering and other forest offenses (Cornu, 1958:ii, 74; Wilson, 1940:41). In Baden in 1836 there was one conviction for woodstealing for every 6.1 inhabitants. In 1841 there was a conviction for every 4.6 inhabitants, and in 1842 one for every four (Banfield, 1846:111).

So widespread was this movement that it would not be much of an exaggeration to say that German criminology cut its teeth in the tabulation of this movement. From the standpoint of later bourgeois criminology their works appear crude methodologically and in their substance, so many trivialities. Dr. G. Mayr, for instance, one of the first academic statisticians of criminology and the Zollverein, discovered that the more difficult it is to gain a livelihood in a lawful manner, the more crimes against property will be committed. Hence property crimes will vary directly with the price of provisions and inversely with the level of wages. He discovered that wood pilfering was likely to be greater in regions where privately owned forests prevailed over corporate and communal forests (Mayr, 1867: chapter 4). W. Starke studied the theft of wood in Prussia between 1854 and 1878. He concluded that the theft of wood was greater during the winter than the summer, and greater in cold years than in warm ones (Starke, 1884:88). L. Fuld made painstaking calculations to show that in Prussia between 1862 and 1874 there was a significant positive correlation between the price of rye and the number of convictions for the theft of wood. Valentini, the director of prisons in Prussia, discovered that within the eight districts of Prussia that he studied, the amount of crimes recorded varied according to the forms of land tenure prevalent in each. He found that in the "dwarf economy" of the Rhineland, where the parcelling of land had been carried to its extremes, pauperism was highest and the pilfering of wood the greatest, though these high rates did not hold for other types of crimes "against property" (Valentini, 1869:58). However, objectionable as such work may appear to the more sophisticated calculators of crime, one must stress that it reflects in part a real social analysis of the wage, or a decisive form of income, for a large part of the western Prussian proletariat. It is just as much an indication of that struggle as the "honeyed grandmothers' tales." In fact, we could say that the development of scientific sylviculture and of positivist criminology were two sides of the same coin: one studying sustained yield and the other the endemic ("moral," as they would say) obstacles to that yield.

If we take a glance forward to the revolution of 1848 a number of our problems become clarified. First, the great rural jacqueries of March that swept southwestern Germany were in part united by their common attempts to reappropriate the wealth of the forests, sometimes under the slogan calling for the recovery of lost rights and other times not. The attempts were geographically widespread and common to several juridically distinct sectors of the agrarian population—feudal tenants, day laborers, crofters and cotters alike (Droz, 1957:151-155). Second, this movement defies a rigid separation between a class of "rural peasants" and "urban workers," as the coordination and leadership of them was the responsibility of itinerant handworkers, loggers, rivermen, bargemen, teamsters, and wagoners, precisely those categories of workers with a foot both in the "country" and the "city." Furthermore, the working class that was locked within "backward" settings of manufacture and domestic industry burst out in flashes of destruction against factories and machines, a movement that paralleled the struggle against the forest police, enclosures, functionaries, tax collectors, and forest owners, a movement that in the Rhineland certainly was often united by the same personnel (Adelmann, 1969: *passim*). This is not the place to consider the strengths and weaknesses of the revolutionary working class of 1848 as a whole, nor do we mean to replace as its revolutionary subject the eastern textile workers or the Berlin craftsmen with the south German agrarian masses. We only wish to indicate that the relation between the "latent" and "stagnant" labor reserves to capitalist development in the Rhineland, some of whose unities we've tried to suggest, had their political analogues in 1848. The Frankfurt Assembly of 1848 found that the work of its Agriculture and Forestry Commission overlapped with that on Workers'

Conditions and that the problems of repression of autonomous rural and urban movements were similar (Noyes, 1966: chapters 9 and 13).

The defeat of these movements, more than anything else, paved the way for the advanced assault of German industrialization. Only after 1848 do those familiar indices of capitalist power against the working class (spindles per factory, number of steam engines employed, output of pig iron, etc.) begin to "take off." In light of that it is especially poignant to find that it was not until late into the Nazi period that the full expropriation of forest rights was completed, a time, in other words, when they had long ceased to be a principal terrain of struggle (Heske, 1938: 240ff.). It is a fact worth considering nevertheless by those who consider the final expropriation of such rights as the decisive moment in the birth of capitalism!

VI.

In sketching the dynamics of the class struggle in western Prussia during the 1840s, we've tried to show that the problem of the theft of wood should be seen neither as a problem of Primary Accumulation in the expropriation of a feudal peasantry nor as a problem of an anarchic, individualized "lumpenproletariat." Instead, we've attempted to present the elements of an analysis that cast the problem in a different light. In particular, we've seen in it a struggle to maintain and increase one of the forms of value of the working class, a form that enabled it for a time to reject those terms of work and exploitation that German capital was seeking to make available in the factory. We recall that the detonators of the working-class explosion in the spring of 1848 were precisely various categories of workers, agrarian and urban, within different forms of the relative redundant population. Marginal, to be sure, from the point of view of Siemens or Krupps, but an historic mass vanguard nevertheless. Other recent examples come easily to mind. We may end by noting that the author of *Capital*, the work that is the starting point of the working-class critique of the capitalist mode of production and that provides us with the concepts for at once analyzing the forms of the divisions within the working class and the conditions for using these within the revolutionary struggle against capital, dedicated his work to a Silesian peasant, Wilhelm Wolff, "the brave, noble fighter in the vanguard of the proletariat."

Farmers Revolt: William Gropper

FOOTNOTES

1. I have found the article by Paolo Carpignano, "U.S. Class Composition in the Sixties," *Zerowork 1*, December 1975, invaluable in the development of this theme.

2. One thinks here of those "deviancy specialists" influenced by Althusser (see, for example, Hirst, 1972:28-56). It may be that Marx "never developed an adequate philosophical reflection of his scientific discoveries." However, some account of those discoveries is in order, especially when by Marx's own account one of his most important contributions over the advances made by Adam Smith and David Ricardo was that of the principle of historical specification of the categories of political economy (Marx, 1867: 52-54).

3. I would like to thank E. J. Hobsbawm and Margaret Mynatt at Lawrence and Wishart who kindly assisted me in making available the English translation of these articles before their publication.

4. There does exist a small literature on Marx's articles (see, for example, Cornu, 1958:ii, 72ff., and Vigouroux, 1965:222-233) but its chief interest is in the intellectual passage of Marx's thought from Kant, Rousseau and Savigny to Feuerbach and Hegel.

5. These works will be discussed in more detail below; see section V. See Fuld, 1881; Mayr, 1867; Starke, 1884; and Valentini, 1869.

6. Even at the end of the nineteenth century the Italian, French and English literature on forestry subjects presented a dearth in comparison to the German. This is the conclusion of the American sylviculturist Bernard Fernow (1902:492).

REFERENCES

Adelman, Gerhard
1969   "Structural Change in the Rhenish Linen and Cotton Trades at the Outset of Industrialization," in F. Crouzet, W. H. Chaloner and W. M. Stern, Essays in European Economic History, 1789-1914. London: Arnold.

Ainlay, John
1975-   Review of Ian Taylor, Paul Walton and Jock Young, The
76   New Criminology (1973) in Telos 26.

Banfield, T. C.
1846   Industry on the Rhine: Agriculture. London: C. Knight & Co.
1848   Industry on the Rhine: Manufactures. London: C. Cox.

Bonger, William Adrian
1905   Criminalité et Conditions Economique. Amsterdam: G. P. Tierie.

Bowring, John
1840   "Report on the Prussian Commercial Union," Parliamentary Papers, XXI.

Cornu, Auguste
1958   Karl Marx et Friedrich Engels: Leur Vie et leur oeuvre. 3 vols. Paris: Presses Universitaires de France.

Crime and Social Justice Collective
1976   "The Politics of Street Crime," Crime and Social Justice, 5 (Spring-Summer), pp. 1-4.

Currie, Elliott
1974   "Review: The New Criminology," Crime and Social Justice 2 (Fall-Winter), pp. 109-113.

Deveze, Michel
1961   La Vie de la Forêt Française au XVIᵉ siècle. 2 vols. Paris: S.E.V.P.E.N.

Droz, Jacques
1957   Les Révolutions Allemandes de 1848. Paris: Presses Universitaires de France.

Endres, Max
1905   Handbuch der Forstpolitik. Berlin: J. Springer.

Fernow, Bernhard E.
1902   Economics of Forestry: A Reference Book for Students of Political Economy. New York: T. W. Crowell & Co.

Fuld, L.
1881   Der Einfluss der Lebensmittelpreise auf dem Bewegung der Strafbaren Handlunger. Mainz: J. Diemer.

Hamerow, Theodore S.
1958   Restoration, Revolution, Reaction: Economics and Politics in Germany, 1815-1971. Princeton: Princeton University Press.

Henderson, W. O.
1939   The Zollverein. Cambridge: Cambridge University Press.
1975   The Rise of German Industrial Power 1834-1914. Los Angeles: University of California Press.

Heske, Franz
1938   German Forestry. New Haven: Yale University Press.

Hirst, Paul Q
1972   "Marx and Engels on law, crime and morality," Economy and Society, I, 1 (February).
1973   "The Marxism of the 'New Criminology,' " The British Journal of Criminology, XIII, 4 (October), pp. 396-98.

Howitt, William
1842   Rural and Domestic Life in Germany. London: Longman, Brown, Green and Longmans.

Hughes, C. E.
1910   A Book of the Black Forest. London: Methuen & Co.

König, H.
1927   Die Rheinische Zeitung von 1842-43 in ihrer Einstellung zur Kulturpolitik des Preussischen Staates. Munster: F. Coppenrath.

Lenin, V. I.
1899   The Development of Capitalism in Russia. Moscow: Foreign Languages Publishing House.

Lengerke, A. V.
1849   Die Landliche Arbeiterfrage. Berlin: Büreau des Königl. ministeriums für landwirthschaftliche angelegenheiter.

Manwood, John
1717   Manwood's Treatise of the Forest Laws. Fourth edition, edited by William Nelson. London: B. Lintott.

Marx, Karl
1842   Proceedings of the Sixth Rhine Province Assembly. Third Article. Debates on the Law of the Theft of Wood. Karl Marx and Frederick Engels: Collected Works, Volume 1. New York: International Publishers, 1975.
1859   A Contribution to the Critique of Political Economy, translated by N. I. Stone. Chicago: Charles Kerr, 1904.
1867   Capital: A Critical Analysis of Capitalist Production, Volume 1. Translated by Samuel Moore and Edward Aveling. London: George Allen & Unwin.

Mayr, G.
1867   Statistik der Gerichtlichen Polizei im Königreiche Bayern. Munich: J. Gotteswinter & Mösel.

Mehring, Franz
    1962   Karl Marx: The Story of his Life. Translated by Edward Fitzgerald. Ann Arbor: University of Michigan Press.

Melossi, Dario
    1976   "The Penal Question in *Capital*," Crime and Social Justice, 5 (Spring-Summer), pp. 26-33.

Milward, Alan S. and S. B. Saul
    1973   The Economic Development of Continental Europe 1780-1870. New Jersey: Rowman and Littlefield.

Noyes, P. H.
    1966   Organization and Revolution: Working Class Associations in the German Revolutions of 1848-1849. Princeton: Princeton University Press.

Palgrave, R. H.
    1912   Dictionary of Political Economy. 3 volumes. London: Macmillan and Co.

Perrie, Maureen
    1972   "The Russian Peasant Movement of 1905-1907: Its Social Composition and Revolutionary Significance," Past & Present, 57 (November).

Phillipson, Michael
    1973   "Critical Theorising and the 'New Criminology,'" The British Journal of Criminology, XIII, 4 (October), pp. 398-400.

Schwappach, Adam
    1894   Forstpolitik. Leipzig: C. L. Hirschfeld.

Starke, W.
    1884   Verbrechen and Verbecher in Preussen 1854-1878. Berlin: T. C. F. Enslin.

Stein, H.
    1972   "Karl Marx et le pauperisme rhénan avant 1848," Jahrbuch des Kölnischen Geschichtsvereins, XIV.

Taylor, Ian, et al.
    1973   "Rejoinder to the Reviewers," The British Journal of Criminology, XIII, 4 (October), pp. 400-403.

Treitschke, H. v.
    1919   A History of Germany in the Nineteenth Century. Translated by Eden and Cedar Paul. 7 volumes. New York: McBride, Nast & Co.

U.S. Government
    1887   Forestry in Europe: Reports from the Consuls of the United States. Washington, D.C.: Government Printing Office.

Valentini, H. v.
    1869   Das Verbrecherthum in Preussische Staat. Leipzig.

Vigouroux, Camille
    1965   "Karl Marx et la législation forestière Rhénane de 1842," Revue d'histoire économique sociale, XLIII, pp. 222-233.

Wilson, Edmund
    1940   To the Finland Station. New York: Harcourt, Brace and Co.

[7]

PERKS, PILFERAGE, AND THE FIDDLE:

The Historical Structure of Invisible Wages[1]

JASON DITTON

Everybody gets part of their wages in "kind." Money alone is never the sole satisfaction attached to or derived from work. Although this is obviously and institutionally so for some jobs (clergymen are not commonly held to be motivated by financial reward), and difficult to perceive for others (few dustmen feel the "call" to dispose of other people's rubbish), it is theoretically impossible to denude even the most inhospitable of work environments of some degree of satisfaction. For example, Lisl Klein mentions a researcher who once interviewed a female worker who spent all her working life in a factory picking up tiny circular pieces of cork and inserting them in toothpaste tube caps. The researcher asked her whether the work felt boring, and the girl replied: "Oh, no!.They come up different every time!"[2]

While indirect and "spiritual" satisfactions of this sort are available to all who work (indeed, their existence makes work possible), temporarily ignoring the value of these delicate existential "wages," a glance at the structure of material wages forges a crucial distinction. While we all may garner a material (as well as a spiritual) rake-off on top of the official pay-packet—every job has its "perks"—the meaning of material kind wages varies essentially with the class of the recipient. When blue-collar workers get side-benefits of various kinds, these benefits act as added occupational commitment, and are proffered *instead of* exclusively direct financial reward. When white-collar workers similarly benefit, the meaningful effect of that benefit is wholly different. White-collar workers never get part of their wages in kind: instead, they may receive kind *extras*, which do not displace an appropriate amount in their salaries, and which act as unofficial rewards rather than as added commitment.

Department of Sociology, University of Durham, Great Britain

40

1. The Historical Context of Employee Theft

The appropriate interpretive context of this discrepancy in the meaning of material kind-pay is historical. Some rights to kind-pay are both universal and antiquarian, as enshrined, for example, in Leviticus:

> And when ye reap the harvest of your land, thou shalt not wholly reap the corners of thy field, neither shalt thou gather the gleaning of thy harvest. And thou shalt not glean thy vineyard, neither shalt you gather the fallen fruit of thy vineyard; thou shalt leave them for the poor and the stranger.

In early 17th century England customary rights to kind benefits were extensive, and encased within a protective body of common legislation. Whilst "common" rights are specifically those by which one or more persons have the right to take or use some portion of the profit that another's soil produces,[3] they are more generally held to refer to the batch of common, reciprocal and joint rights in which pre-industrial communities were enmeshed. This intricate web of mutual privileges and obligations provided the basis for exchange in agrarian contexts. Of the various common rights, Common of Pasture protected the grazing and manuring rights of agricultural animals upon specified land, and Common of Shack guaranteed the right of cattle to glean hay after the harvest. In rural England, the rules of Leviticus emerged as the right to herbage and gleaning for certain specified persons and strangers on half-year lands. Reciprocally, the lord of the manor had right of sheep-walk (right to feed sheep on common land), and foldage (the right to demand that tenant's flocks manure the lord's fields). Gonner adds that various universal rights also made important contributions to the rural economy.[4] Rights of pannage and mast, for example, specified the range of protected users of nuts, acorns, and even various flowers.

Common of Estover was the right of common to take wood from common or the lord's lands and forests, and specified either Plough Bote (the right to wood to repair ploughs, carts and other instruments of husbandry), Hedge Bote (wood for the repair of gates and hedges) and House Bote, which not only specified the right to wood for domestic repairs but which added, at least for freehold manor tenants, the antiquarian right to "sticks, tops and clippings for fuel."[5] Common of Tubary was the right to cut peat and turf for fuel, and the batch of common rights also included those of following and warren (fowl and rabbits), and even to dig sand, gravel and clay. Gonner comments:

> Taken together they supply the means whereby the system of cultivation was maintained, the wants of the tenants other than those met by the

product of the arable and the meadow were supplied, and full use made both of the waste and of the land in cultivation at such time as the crops were not in the ground.[6]

Thus, the extended package of common rights not only cemented feudalist and community ties (the lord of the manor had a special set of rights which included that of arriage from the tenant's beasts, and fencing and ditching skills from the tenants themselves), it also made a significant material contribution to the domestic and household budgets of the tenants. Domestic consumption was guaranteed either directly from cultivation, or indirectly from the exercise of right.

The Acts of Enclosure of these common rights had obvious and far-reaching effects on the material benefits which tenants had customarily come to expect.[7] The annexation of common rights (and their subsequent replacement with legal rights)[8] naturally culminated in the simultaneous creation of "property," and the propertied classes, and the ultimate criminalization of customary practices. The criminalization of custom involved both moral attempts to define "common." as bad,[9] and savage repressive measures enacted to persecute those who attempted to continue to exercise erstwhile rights.[10] Acts of Enclosure were, in the main, forced upon an unwilling populace,[11] which in some cases was physically removed from the land, as well as spiritually from the protection of ancient right.[12] In this welter of legislation, kind-benefits emerged coated in a new meaning structure—one which crucially distinguished between the propertied and the non-propertied classes. From here on, extraction of kind-benefits was to become particularly problematic for the newly created working class. The gradual translation of "rights" (held in common) into "property," or "capital" (held in particular) which the elongated processes of rural enclosure and urban industrialization effected emerged in different structural contexts (rural and urban), with noticably similar effects.

Basically, in land, we can see the gradual emergence of property *per se* from the systematic limited specification and curtailing of common rights to use land. "Rights," in a very real sense, become translated into "property" as a result of the legal process of translating universality of applicability of such rights into specificity of applicability. Enclosure of land took two forms. The gradual areal abolition of common (uncultivated) land, and the reparcelling and literal enclosure of stripcultivated land which had been previously farmed on the basis of common right.

42

Thus, the feudal picture of a village and its surrounding lands—over which the manorial lord had exclusive "rights" to a large proportion, and the villagers common "rights" to farm a small part (together with reciprocal obligations to labor for the lord on "his" land), with the rest remaining as unfarmed commonland—is replaced (through enclosure) by a scene wherein the lord's "rights" to farm exclusively have become property, the villager's common strip rights have become rented allotments, and the remaining common land has diminished considerably in size. At the same time, some villagers were wholly disenfranchised—their release from any commitments on the land collectively creating a pool of potential labor for the growing urban industrial machine.

A crucial intermediary stage in the confiscation and criminalization of rights, was their initial "engrossing": a process through which the larger units inexorably swallowed smaller ones.[13] A crucial stage in this process was the subsidiary transmutation of "rights" into graspable monetary sums. For example, vague and archaic specifications of duties and obligations of tenants to labor for the lord, became literally exchanged for direct money-rent obligations.[14] This was essentially a direct change in the legal construction of common rights, whose rather idiosyncratic and archaic nature had some severe effects on many otherwise indistinguishable beneficiaries. Gonner claims that common rights were essentially one of four possible legal varieties: *Common Appendant* (rights limited by tenancy or possession, specifically ancient and generally universal), *Common Appurtenant* (rights granted by prescription to copyholders or freeholders), *Common in Gross* (the definition of common by number or amount instead of by immediate reference to the needs or capacity of the land or its tenants) and *Common by Vicinage* (an imitation of common, generally arising out of mutual agreements to disregard trespass).[15]

The Acts of Enclosure made the hitherto relatively unknown distinction between *common appendant* and *common appurtenant* into a dividing line of crucial significance. The ability of the comparison to draw a *de facto/de jure* distinction between the actual (appendant) and legal (appurtenant) villagers refused common rights to those who sought its protection by custom, and restricted it to the smaller category of those who had legal entitlement.[16] Thus, those whose prior use of common was by proximity and sufferance failed to receive the rented allotments which villagers with appurtenant rights had exchanged for their rights.[17] Although *de facto* users had previously been able to enjoy the small rights attached to their dwellings, when an allotment was made, the landlord took the allotment, and left the cottager with nothing. The summation of all such minor losses was huge. Gonner comments:

43

Thus with inclosure, the number of geese owned by the poor are said to have decreased: cows were given up; the poor lost fuel, being deprived of the privilege of turf-cutting; the commonage in the stubbles which enabled them to keep pigs and geese is theirs no more; and with these went other small advantages such as gleaning, which came to be more carefully restricted.[18]

Added to this deliberate creation of a class of "poor" was some voluntary recruitment from the ranks of *bona fide* allotment holders who became disenchanted with allotment life either because of various deleterious effects of the reparcelling process,[19] or simply because of the sheer expense of fencing in the allotted land.[20] Essentially this forced a categorization of the villagers into the righteous working class, and the feckless scrounging poor.[21] So, the natural result of the intermediary process of engrossing was the translation of rights into a legally purchasable commodity, swiftly followed by the actual purchase of the allotments[22] (where they were not simply confiscated), was augmented by the percolation of industrial techniques to the fields and the subsequent reduction of the agrarian labor force. In a very real way, then, the Acts of Enclosure released a large part of the agrarian working population just at the time when labor was needed in the industrializing towns.[23] Of crucial interest here, is that this process released into urban life a working population not only used to receiving part of their "wages" in kind (an antiquarian element specifically and pointedly absent from the capitalist conception of rational production) but also one still stinging from the effects of the abrupt and cruel negation of those practices in the countryside. As one might expect, and empirical evidence supports this,[24] a major source of irritation to factory owners who took on such "idle" rural laborers was their penchant for making off with parts of the workplace or the fruits of their labor there, in addition to their wages.

To present a picture of the total negation of kind-payment would be to over-simplify. "Rights" were transmuted by two different processes into three separable categories of kind-payment. First, there was a literal specification of the *amount* which previous rights would now represent; and secondly, there was a restriction, of the previous universal *applicability* of rights. While general rights became specific financial amounts, the beneficiaries were restricted to those actively engaged in production. In fact, these two processes eventually produced three classes of recipient, which ultimately became synonymous with three categories of kind-payment: "perks" (for employers and the white-collar employed), "pilferage" (for blue-collar employees) and unequivocal "theft" (for the unemployed poor).

44

The gradual process of translating "rights" into "crimes" was, then, one of restructuring the range of applicability (and thus definition) of customary practices. The immediate effect of the Acts of Enclosure (the first stage in the process of criminalization) through the annexation of *de facto* cottagers, was the automatic relabeling of "rights" as the "privilege" of *de jure* tenants.[25] Almost simultaneously, such "privileges" were withheld from even those tenants, but immediately redistributed on the basis of "license" issued by the owners of property. When kind-benefits are distributed on the basis of license rather than of right, then they may more easily be controlled.[26] However, not all customary rights were relicensed. Those which just didn't fit into the new role into which the landlords had recast the countryside were occasionally savagely criminalized,[27] although more regularly just treated as civil of-fenses,[28] and even, on occasion, accusations to which the claim of customary practices was an acceptable defeat.[29] Importantly, the "pilferage" of wood emerged as a description of over-exuberant collection of kind-benefits by employees, a crime much more morally acceptable than the out-and-out "theft" by the non-employed.[30]

Thus, in the process of transforming reciprocal feudal labor obligations into contractual ones (and, coincidentally, the annexing of common duties such as hedging and ditching) ancient "rights" became restricted to modern employ-ees. The translation of most of the free citizenry into employees, and the erosion of rights to (withdrawable) "privilege" and "license" status, effec-tively translated customary practices from being the legitimate exercise of right, to becoming employment in kind. The very power of kind-payments lies in the fact that kind-pay generates a greater commitment to a particular employer, and in the fact that whimsical redefinition- of its receipt by the "giver" may oppress the recipient.[31] Having restricted the range of appli-cability of rights/kind-payments to those involved in work, any vestige of demands of right by the non-employed poor were unequivocally defined as "theft."[32] For the employer and landlord (and special classes of their directly employed white-collar minions) kind-benefits become perquisites, or "perks," with abstraction of kind-benefits by employees resting ambiguously between these two extremes, being simultaneously defined as a cheap way of paying part of the wages, and also vaguely immorally as "pilferage."

Accordingly, in the countryside, exercise of Common of Estover (wood-gathering) became wood-theft,[33] game-rights degenerated into poaching,[34] grazing-rights into trespass,[35] and even archaic common gleaning (if and when the gleanings could be seen by a sharp eye to be a commercially viable proposition) could become theft by finding.[36] At this stage in English history, there existed what Mantoux refers to as an "intimate connection" between the rural and urban economies.[37] In the towns, the importation of a mass of dispossessed agrarian workers "set free" by enclosures, but both personally and culturally accustomed to having kind-rights, posed problems for their new employers. Additionally, those trades and types of industrial work which pre-dated capitalization had direct customary practices of their own. Welsh coal miners were accustomed to use company coal for domestic purposes,[38] coopers considered that their "samples"[39] of wines and spirits were an unalienable right, in the same way that their fellow dockers demanded their "spots" of drink from the cooper[40] and their traditional "sweepings" from the employer's cargoes.[41]

The historical context of the varieties of modern employee kind-pay emerges from this analysis. Within the structures of rural enclosure and urban capitalization, "perks," "pilferage," and "theft" may be viewed profitably as the lingering vestiges of the annexation of customary rights by the ruling class, rather than (as is usually assumed) an index of the growing amorality of the urban working class. But this context does not supply a sufficient analysis of the current situation. To specify the historical generation of conceptual difference between, for example, "pilferage" and "theft," does not adequately account for the current paradoxical interactional context of such kind-pay. Employees who are currently expected to take part of their wages in kind may simultaneously be prosecuted on some of those occasions when they do so. Workers who are involved in this contradictory form of wage-payment "can't win." The historical structure which I have described has itself been translated into a paradoxical interactional mesh through the exercise of capitalist power. The blue-collar employee is caught up in this mesh without access to legitimate interactional escape mechanisms.

The historical process of criminalization of rights is unfinished. Current employee-theft is not yet wholly drained of its original meaning as "right." The histories of individual occupations show that the subsequent development of the ambiguity of translated rights has been unequally paced. In analyzing current examples selected from the English industrial culture, three discernable stages of the development of this process emerge.[42] Taken chronologically, kind-wage-payment can either arrange itself in a young, harsh form of "wage-theft," an ambiguous middle form of "wage-pilferage," and a relatively mature, benign form of "wage-perk."

2. Invisible-Wage System

2.1 Wage-Perk Payment[43]

When "on the side" satisfaction is rigorously and extensively codified into officially institutionalized practices, we may talk of wage-perk payment.

46

Under a wage-perk system, an employee is openly and legally paid part of his
wages in kind. There are no circumstances in which an employee can be
prosecuted for taking advantage of this system, which is often institutionalized as such into public job advertisements. Quite often, wage-perk structures are the mature outcome of a long history of legitimizing a wage-pilferage
system, especially when pilferage (as with the bus conductor's leisure time
bus-pass, and the miner's coal) is particularly difficult otherwise to control.
When members of management benefit (as those who have company cars and
expense account lunches do), the perk is generally thought of as added
incentive, if, indeed, it is not merely defined as being a necessary part of the
job.[44] When the workforce are entitled to perks (such as those living in "tied"
cottages) the perks themselves subtly undergo a transformation from being
"extra" pay, to becoming just added commitment to the employer.[45] Those
who do not nicely fit into either of these two bland categories suffer an
ambiguous fate.[46]

Ultimately, wage-perk payment generally acts to the disadvantage of the
workforce, especially if the latter is unorganized. As soon as it is institutionalized, the perk instantly begins to unfurl as a wage-depressant. On top of
this, it systematically reduces the isolated worker's choice in the way that his
wages are spent. This affects those who "live in," or "over the shop" (their
wages are subsequently reduced to pay for this facility). Even more seriously,
it frequently depresses the wages of those who are alleged to be motivated by
higher things to absurdly cruel levels. For example, nurses and *au pairs,*[47]
both have good spiritual reasons for receiving most of their material wages in
kind.[48] Of course, this does not apply to consultants and archbishops who
apparently need large financial compensation for taking their part in equivalently high moral worlds.

Sometimes, blue-collar employees who deal regularly and commercially with
members of the public are craftily encouraged to extrude part of their wages,
in gratuity form, from the customer.[49] "Wage-tip" is thus an indirect form of
wage-perk. This practice costs the employer nothing (barring a disgruntled
workforce, and an irritated customer constituency), but it produces a tricky
conflict between server and customer. This conflict arises in the ambiguity of
the word "tip," which means "wages" (and thus something routinely and
regularly collected) to the employee, and "gratuity" to the customer, who
clings to its original London coffee house context wherein it stood for "To
Insure Promptness."[50] Of course, the only member of the public to refuse to
view tips in the traditional way is Her Majesty's Inspector of Taxes. Crespi,
talking of the American situation, adds: "No longer does this agency (the
I.R.S.) overlook tips as casual unpredictable cash. Now every effort is being
made to see tips as substantial and predictable sources of income."[51]

Attempts to aggressively "organize" tips by service workers,[52] and to "work" customers for them,[53] has spawned, as a reaction, such organizations as NOTIP (Nationwide Operation To Instill Pride) in America, the members of which, to the delight of service workers everywhere, leave little cards denouncing the practice in lieu of little coins supporting it.

Under a wage-perk regime, management/workforce distinctions are reasserted. As I have indicated, "perks" are either "extras" for management, or they are coolly defined as part of the company-supplied equipment for the job. Members of the workforce in receipt of perks face an altogether different ambiguity of definition. Perks may either be "fringe benefits" (ancient rights restricted to those members of the working class "licensed" by the fact and nature of their employment), which are generally, for example the N.C.B. coal allowance,[54] even obtainable during strikes—whereas wage-packets quite clearly are not. Or they may be *part* of wages, and thus distinctly unobtainable when employment exists but actual work is stopped. Quite frequently, in addition to this type of definitional ambiguity, some perks (for example, the bank clerk's cheap mortgage) are generally defined as part of wages (for recruitment and inducement purposes), but occasionally called fringe-benefits when they are arbitrarily reduced in a way that wages could not be.

Irrespective of this ambiguity, there are significant variations in the credibility of the costing of wage-perk kind-pay. The N.C.B., for instance, cost the coal-allowance in terms of its retail value rather than the production value (thus allowing them to make a little profit out of the fringe-benefit), but the concessionary travel allowances to which British Rail employees are entitled *are* restricted in various ways (for example, are not transferable)[55] and although "priceable" are virtually "uncostable." The principles of costing the usage of a vacant seat are arguable (should it be in terms of the full fare that might be obtained, or in terms of the actual marginal cost of adding an extra person to an otherwise unoccupied seat?) and it is also unlikely that the employee would make the journey if it were not free.

But at least such "perks" have a clear legal standing. When the "kind" payments of a wage-perk system are *un*official, then we may talk instead of a wage-pilferage system.

2.2 Wage-Pilferage Systems

A crucial distinction between "pilferage" and "perks" is that anybody caught pilfering is stopped, but not necessarily prosecuted. Pilferage is thus itself a

48

paradoxical state. Its immediate consequences are unpredictable, and, in historical terms, it is a transitional stage between wage-perk (which is officially institutionalized), and wage-theft (which is officially condemned). Consequently, pilferage is the name which we should logically attach to those occasions where blue-collar employees abstract value in kind from their employer under a regime where the treatment of this appropriation is unpredictable, and its *a priori* meaning thus ambiguous.

This ambiguity is not benign. It produces for the worker a theoretically and empirically strong "can't win" situation. This is not a simple mutual contradiction in demands made of the worker of the sort colloquially referred to, with increasing frequency, as a "Catch-22 situation."[56] Most importantly, the worker (enmeshed in a wage-pilferage system) is faced with incompatible demands (i.e., that he should, *and* that he should not pilfer), and on top of this, these incompatible demands are communicated in such a way as to make the contradiction "uncommentable." This is achieved by communicating incompatible demands simultaneously at different communicative levels. What happens in a wage-pilferage context is that within a single communication act, a primary negative injunction ("Don't steal"—don't take goods in kind) is expressed at the literal level, while at the more abstract, metaphoric (meta-communicative) level, a secondary and contradictory injunction ("Make up your wages"—take goods in kind) is simultaneously conveyed.

Thus, wage-pilferage systems are "Double-binds."[57] There is no theoretical or empirical escape for workers trapped in this way as there is a tertiary negative injunction prohibiting the worker-victim's pragmatic analysis of his contradictory situation, and thus obviating his escape. There are various ways that this double-bind can be thrown around the new worker. For example, an employee is told that the rate of wages is low, but this statement is accompanied by some sort of figurative or real wink.[58] Perhaps he is told that he can purchase products at "give away" (wink) prices. Or, that there are always "cheap" (wink), "spare" (wink) or "extra" (wink) goods to be had. Perhaps he is told, as I was at the Wellbread Bakery, that "they" would see that I didn't "go short" (wink), or "lose out" (wink) when I complained that the wages were low. Everybody else, I was told,[59] was able to "make a bit on the side" (wink), or, "have their little perks" (wink), or, "take the odd loaf" (wink). With the meta-communicative wink, the employer is able to craftily say something quite specific *about* the actual statements he has made. The wink eliminates the ambiguity in such "alerting phrases" as "spare," "cheap," and "extra," and settles their meaning quite definitely for those sufficiently competent or "wise" to so read the communication. Any reaction from the worker in the form of a "comment" immediately vanquishes and replaces the meta-communicative negative statement offered by the employer—*itself* a comment *on* communication. To query the meaning of the wink (in other words, any attempt to "open" up a "closed" meaning) is to effectively deny it. It is in *this* sense that the double-bind is uncommentable. A worker frankly complaining that he is being asked to pilfer part of his wages, will be told, equally frankly, that he is "imagining things," and that (here, the primary injunction is reasserted) he is *not* to take anything above his wages. Refusal of the secondary negative injunction (the wink) is simultaneously refusal of the material advantages which would accrue were the injunction not questioned.

The potential pilferer must himself qualify the possible advantages of his occupational theft with the *a priori* knowledge that what will happen to him should he be caught is, *apropos* of the employer's reaction to the theft, wholly uncertain. Of course, he may be able to solve this problem at the psychological level, and successfully define the theft *as* pilferage to himself, but this in no way guarantees a similar definition by those who stand to suffer the loss. Additionally, an equivalently ambiguous (in the sense that "pilferage" is ambiguous) legal reaction is impossible. There is no such legal offense as "Pilferage." Occupational theft is either proceeded against as "theft," or is not proceeded against because it is defined as a "perk."[60] *This* is the paradox of wage-pilferage systems. Whether or not the theft in question is defined as "theft" or as "just a perk" will depend upon quite arbitrary, extraneous and non-specifiable dictates of those in control. In other words, the "pilferer" cannot be held responsible for the meaning of his action: that meaning is decided by others, after the action has objectively occurred. For example, at Wellbreads, those employees exclusively concerned with production were accustomed to take a loaf home every day. In fact, the management catered for this contingency by making sure to bake enough bread to allow for what became collectively known as "the men's bread." However, this bread was not rationally distributed as a "perk," each man had to surreptitiously "pilfer" his loaf while the Despatch Manager (who had responsibility for baked bread) was at lunch. Despatch operatives maintained a cursory and nominal watch over the racks of stock bread from which the men took "their" bread (so as to give life to the lie that they were trying to prevent domestic pilferage) but simultaneously made sure that enough bread was freely available on the stock racks to contain unlicensed pilferage from the racks of issued bread. Presumably the general managerial policy informing this practice was that defining as "pilfering" (and, of course, processing the occasional culprit as a "thief") helped to prevent the escalation of the practice from domestic consumption. The actual zealousness of the Despatch Manager was informed by what he considered to be his "perk" of office: if he could persuade at least some of the men to buy their bread from him (the

50

official process), then he could divert some of this cash to his own pocket, and cover the loss by stealing bread from the salesmen.

There is an historical, as well as a structural sense in which pilferage is "paradoxical." At one time, pilferage was a label strictly employed only in connection with the theft of indeterminate or "ambiguous" items. Indeed, in many cases, there are still grounds for claiming that this is so.[61] Generally, however, the paradoxical nature of pilferage is currently metaphorical, whereas once it was a real issue. For example, Marx is quite right to see that the difference between "theft" and "pilferage" is a question of fact, and not one of euphemism.[62] Referring to the thefts of wood, Marx isolates three categories of theft-object: the theft of live timber (an offense against forest regulations); the theft of hewn and felled wood (*prima facie* theft of material which has been converted into property); and an intermediate, ambiguous category: the picking up and consequent "pilferage" of fallen, "dead" wood. This latter, indeterminate category lies ambiguously between live and felled wood, and is, thus, a symbolically dangerous and marginal object.[63] It was precisely at this indeterminate level that the rights of the poor were located. Marx points out:

> All customary rights of the poor were based on the fact that certain forms of property were indeterminate in character, for they were not definitely private property, but neither were they definitely common property, being a mixture of private and public right . . . It will be found that the customs which are customs of the entire poor class are based with a sure instinct on the *indeterminate* aspect of property.[64]

Some vestige of this archaic indeterminancy remains in modern formulations. Whether or not employee theft is defined as "pilferage" or "theft" varies for different industries, on different days,[65] and even, crucially, between different individuals.[66] Now, while for some practical intents and purposes, the broad empirical outlines of the criteria of everyday current distinction are clear, the situation is specifically and indefinitely ambiguous. Martin, in an extensive study of the criteria used to distinguish between pilferage and stealing by various firms, emerges with the following summary:

> *"Pilfering"* (when "legitimate") involves one or more of the following features — the items taken are of "small" value, they are taken for the worker's own use, the quantities involved are small, and the act is unpremeditated. *"Stealing"* is any taking of cash (the only definition with which no one disagreed), or one or more of the following — taking of stamps, items from "stock" goods in large quantities (by the box, sack of crate),

items over a given value, small items taken repeatedly, taking for resale, taking with premeditation and unauthorised taking when it is known that the items would be given away on request.[67]

This is a summary of all possible criteria. It does not represent a set of criteria used by any one firm in Martin's sample. It is a summary of the possible "reasons" for labeling a theft as either "pilferage" or "stealing." Interestingly, the necessity for tabulating the possibilities testifies to the very absence of a universal distinction between the two labels. Taken together, the separate criteria provide an ostensive and weak definition: it settles upon no particular criteria as crucial (except the theft of cash) and while dressed to look specific, actually contains several elastic "weasel" words like "small."[68]

Employee thefts remain ambiguous at the time of the theft. We cannot specify *a priori* whether or not they will be defined as "pilferage" or as "theft."[69] Nevertheless, this ambiguity has a systematic rather than a random effect: it disadvantages the workforce and advantages the management. This systematic distinction is traceable to the workings of a crucial hidden dimension of double-binds: power. In any double-bind, it is axiomatic that the bound has *less* interactional power than the binder. But this specific situation may or may not be compatible with the power discrepancy existing generally between the two actors. This incompatibility may be of three types. The specific situation may mirror the general, and thus be symmetrically "orthodox." This is the case when members of management pilfer. There is a power symmetry between management (the enforcers) and management (the thieves), and thus the meaning of the pilferage becomes distinctly that, as Dalton suggests,[70] of relatively unstable and individualistic "supplementary (salary) rewards." Power incompatibility between the binder and the bound may either be asymmetrically contradictory ("paradoxical"), such as when archaic custom lingers to constrain management to allow worker pilferage, or it may be exaggeratedly asymmetrical ("heterodoxical"), such as when the specific pilferage situation merely parodies the general power discrepancy between management and worker. These two latter types of incompatibility produce the second main meaning of pilferage. For members of the workforce, pilferage means collective and relatively stable "customary (wage) pilferage."

"Customary pilferage" traps the worker in a double-bind. His wages are geared down to an invisible pilferage value of his job, but his attempt to secure this invisible value could well lose him his job, and land him in court. This double-bind is heterodoxical (since there is an obvious power difference between management and worker), but is in practice weakened by the

52

simultaneous presence of various workplace "customs" which, paradoxically, bind management to allow some pilferage.[71]

It seems that pilferage for workers may become "customary" (although not yet officially a "perk") under various structurally recognizable conditions. Management often turn a blind eye to pilferage when the pilfered goods do not really constitute a loss to the firm (as Martin rather nicely asks, what is the waiter *supposed* to do with the half-empty bottles of wine?). As Mars and Hutter note, the management is especially lenient if worthless items are consumed on the premises.[72] The management may be similarly genial even if goods with some real value are pilfered as long as the loss may be euphemistically and alternatively categorized at inventory time (i.e., the pilferage must be of "kind," as inventories do not contain categories for "broken," "damaged" or "reject" money). Pilferage may also be allowed to degenerate into custom when the loss may be systematically organized into production (such as the extra 40 loaves which are baked at Wellbreads everyday to provide the "men's bread"), or when the loss is of repeatable or disposable goods.

Management may be actually keen to institute and encourage customary pilferage if they feel the act of theft will generate a hedonistic surplus (in addition to the actual value of the goods taken) and as long as they are able to simultaneously retain the right to define it as "stealing" should the need arise. In this spirit, Zeitlin considers that a "system of controlled larceny" may well be actually cheaper than paying higher wages,[73] and Aufhauser notes how slave-owners shrewdly allowed the expression of their rebelliousness through minor thefts.[74] Aside from such imaginary emotional extra "wages" accruing from the pilferage of items rather than the purchase of them on the market, there is a real sense in which (because pilfered wages are untaxed wages), illicit kind-payment is actually cheaper for both management and worker.

However, when pilferage is institutionalized and common among members of management, it is a gross mistake to similarly label it "institutionalized theft," as Dalton so accurately and eloquently argues.[75] Managerial "organised pilfering rights" are explicitly, albeit unspokenly, "unofficial rewards" for the minutiae of individual managerial achievement.[76] As Dalton shows, formal ranking is too rigid and too slow to accurately recompense managerial effort, and informal rewards supplement wages and simultaneously support the *status quo*. The unofficial reward system functions as what Dalton calls an "elastic incentive." Effort can be recognized without disrupting the more cumbersome and symbolic procedures of promotion. In addition to this, "dirty work," which it would be unwise to reward directly, can be obtained. Dalton's managers obtained these rewards in kind rather than in cash, often either in the form of "foreigners" (using the company's time and resources to produce items for domestic use), or as "extras" like free petrol.

These managerial "supplementary reward systems" *are* double-binds, but their orthodox power structure makes them weak. While there is little chance of managers being prosecuted for accepting these informal rewards (at least under normal circumstances), the system *is* subterranean.[77] If formalized, it would conflict with the official reward system, and so it is generally shrouded in what Dalton refers to as "double-talk."[78] Each manager who takes advantage of the system cannot simultaneously benefit from it *and* refuse to accept personal responsibility for managing the ambiguity which is inevitably involved. Dalton cites two cases of female managers unable to thus benefit:

> Some female heads regularly., but discretely, gave certain items a "damaged" appearance. Division heads unofficially knew of this, and set no limit to the markdown that could be made, other things being equal. However, those department heads who shrank from the ambiguities of exercising their authority and asked a division manager the limit for a markdown were usually told, "30 percent" ... (another female department head) "worried the life out of" her division heads because only rarely could she "make decisions on her own." She, too, desired "shopworn" items, including jewelry with chipped stones, but she called upon the merchandising chief for judgements on the markdown she should make, and was repeatedly given the official "30 percent." Knowing that others more than doubled this figure, she caused trouble by her gossip and insinuations.[79]

Thus, in Dalton's cases, the reward for personally accepting the management of unofficial-reward-ambiguity was an extra thirty percent on top of the standard markdown. As Martin points out, the nearest real equivalent to these unofficial managerial rewards for the workforce are the cut-price concessions for purchasing company-produced goods, and *not* items customarily pilfered.[80]

Although wage-pilferage has its advantages for management, the pilfered items may well constitute a real loss to the company. In addition, it may be, in some employment situations, difficult to meta-specify the ceiling (or, the grounds of applicability) of the secondary injunction to pilfer. A classic solution to these problems is for the management to recommend that their workers indulge in a little indirect wage-pilferage from customers.[81] Here, the firm's financial worries about amounts pilfered may be ignored safely, and

54

yet high wages do not become necessary to maintain a stable workforce. An example of such a wage-fiddle context is reported at length in my "The Fiddler."[82] At the Wellbread Bakery, the salesmen were unequivocally incarcerated in an occupational trap which specified that they be paid low wages, which could be made up either by wage-theft from the firm (which would be treated as actionable), or by indirect wage-pilferage from customers (fiddling), which only *might* lead to trouble.[83]

This occupational trap arises as a managerial decision to shift an awkward organizational dilemma onto the shoulders of the workforce. The irreconcilable demands of profit and error,[84] when coupled with the prospective difficulties of an unstable workforce,[85] have convinced the Wellbreads management to operate a recruitment policy based upon the induction of men of sufficiently worldly character to be appropriately impressed by the eventually displayed organizational rationale for fiddling customers. Once the newcomer has been committed to the firm through subtle deployment of organizational side-bets such as the (honesty) insurance-bond (which the management threaten to revoke for quitters), and the non-legal but otherwise impressive employment "contract," to which the men sign their agreement to pay shortages; and also, once he has discovered that profits are essential and mistakes inevitable, *then* he is ripe for interpreting the sly wink that accompanies supervisors' suggestions that he overcharge customers. The normal justification that it is quite safe is only too just.[86] For most of the salesmen, the relief at finding a solution dilutes any remaining moral qualms, and many salesmen go on from overcharging a bit and paying it in to the firm to cover mistakes, to making an additional bit for themselves. But fiddling, once begun, produces an income which is swiftly transformed from being "extra," to being "instead of" (wages). Although making a bit extra for themselves was "unofficial," the salesmens' salaries would have been ridiculously puny without their invisible fiddled component.[87]

We may characterize this situation as being an example of the way that strategically managed "disengaged involvement" by the powerful (power overrides the apparent contradiction in that phrase by *fiat*) produces the effect of an "illusory partnership"[88] in crime, which, when the chips are down, becomes wholly one-sided collusion. The Wellbread's managers implicitly encourage the fiddling activities of their men, but they do so with the crucial meta-communicative wink: a secondary injunction ("fiddle") actually contradicting the primary injunction ("don't fiddle"), making it simultaneously clear that the second part of the communication will be denied in any dangerous situations. Those among the men perceptive enough to read accurately the accompanying meta-message, find no solace in

the hidden rider which prevents them from successfully exposing the contradictory nature of their employment: ultimately, in any enforcement situation, the management is more likely to be believed than the men.

Generally speaking then, wage-pilferage and wage-fiddle systems (inasmuch as
they function as what Zeitlin refers to as a "system of controlled larceny")[89]
can actually benefit those who *lose* the goods in question more than they
benefit those who stand to gain them. The advantage of these systems is the
power which accrues to those who control them. It does *not* lie in the
possession of the material goods and services in question. This is especially so
when workers (rather than members of management) pilfer or fiddle as they
often have to deduct the cost of "sweeteners" from their invisible earnings in
order to secure services from fellow workers who have no access to pilferage,
or to customers.[90] In the "spiritual" rather than "material" sense of kind-
benefits, the invisibility of invisible wages means that, for prestige and status
purposes, workers may only claim that they are worth the visible portion.[91]

Crucially, in all unofficial wage-pilferage agreements, there is the "of course"
clause. This rider specifies that: "Of course, this may turn out to be theft." In
other words, the primary injunction *not* to pilfer may be emphasized, and the
secondary negative injunction to pilfer may be denied. It is this ambiguity of
outcome which is the ultimate message of wage-pilferage. The will of the
pilferer is mortgaged to the manager to whom he is "technically" (as they
say) a "thief." Unfortunate disobedience of concealed, ambiguous, non-
specific and relatively *ad hoc* meta-rules (such as "too much" theft, of
"large" items, or the "wrong" sort, "open," and so on) can transform
pilferage or fiddling into outright "theft." When this happens, the wage-
pilferage system becomes a wage-theft structure.

2.3 Wage-Theft Structure

In a wage-theft structure, harsh consequentiality replaces uncertainty.[92] The
structure is wholly unambiguous, but on the other hand, there is no chance of
this ambiguity being resolved positively for the thief as there is for the
pilferer whose misapplications may later be redefined as a "perk."[93] On *all*
occasions of unauthorized taking of kind-benefit in a wage-theft structure,
the offender will be defined as a thief. *This* is the category of "pure theft"
which Dalton tries to distinguish from "supplementary rewards."[94]

How does wage-theft compare with wage-pilferage? Two crucial differences
are that first, contradictory imperatives are given on the same communicative level, and second, the contradiction is not uncommentable. Wage-

56

theft constitutes an empirical example of what we may refer to as Merton's Contradiction. Rather than a "can't win" situation for the actor, Merton's Contradiction proposes a "probably lose" situation for him.[95] For the working class employee, the general cultural availability of goals is in disjunctive coupling with a class-based relative unavailability of means for legitimately securing them. In action terms, the specification that the means should be legitimate ones is weaker than the specification that the goals should be attained. In some occupational situations,[96] for example, low wages are in harness with either direct (occupational) or indirect (societal) imperatives to maintain a certain standard of living which the visible component of the wage cannot support. In other occupational situations, managerial situations, managerial policy can arbitrarily create a harsh wage-theft structure. Martin offers a nice example:

> There would be trouble here if an employee took anything. He would be dismissed. I don't think there is any distinction. If he had only pinched something worth a shilling, we would dismiss him.[97]

So, compared with wage-pilferage, where the employer is in wage-supplement collusion with the employee, in a wage-theft structure, the worker has to steal part of his own wages. Leibow provides an excellent example of this. "Tonk," one of Leibow's subjects, was paid $35 per week and expected by the store owner to steal an additional $35 to make up his wages. Leibow continues:

> The employer is not in wage-theft collusion with the employee . . . Were he to have caught Tonk in the act of stealing, he would, of course, have fired him from the job and perhaps called the police as well . . . The employer knowingly provides the conditions which entice (force) the employee to steal the unpaid value of his labor, but at the same time, he punishes him for theft if he catches him doing it.[98]

There is not really a palpably separate form of indirect wage-theft. This, of course, does not mean that employees in the service industries do not "steal" from the customer, but rather that "thefts" from customers are chiefly fiddle-occasions which have misfired, and to which a rather severe control reaction has occurred.

Conclusion

History lives on. The perpetual and perpetuating myth of the present is to believe that we are liberated from the anguish of the past. On the contrary, the greatest source of history is impregnated in the mundane and everyday

57

world of the present. The meaning of the world of work, for example, is revealed in its relationship to its past. Workers are not only, on the whole, paid as a *class*,[99] those situated at structurally disadvantaged parts receive large segments of their wages "invisibly" — as tips or fiddles from customers, or pilferage and perks from employers. The crucial common factor in these forms of "invisible wages" is the added *power* which accrues to employers through their establishment. They are meaningfully located, however, not simply as archaic relics in the gradual rational liberation of the present from the feudal bond, but as forms of domination crucial to the persistence and growth of modern capitalism because of their solution to those disciplinary problems not soluble in money alone.

NOTES

1. The research for this article was financed by S. R. C. Grant No. HR 3603. The analysis suggested here will theoretically inform the continuing research. Richard Brown and Philip Corrigan (both of the University of Durham) have been particularly helpful in clarifying some of the ideas presented here.
2. Lisl Klein, "The Meaning of Work," *Fabian Tract 349* (1964), p.l.
3. E. C. K. Gonner, *Common Land and Inclosure* (London, 1912), p. 7.
4. *Ibid.*, p. 14.
5. *Ibid.*, p. 15.
6. *Ibid.*, p. 16.
7. Examination of particular cases has led Thompson to suggest that law: "is clearly an instrument of the *de facto* ruling class: it both defines and defends these rulers' claims upon resources and labour-power — it says what shall be property and what shall be crime — and it mediates class relations with a set of appropriate rules and sanctions, all of which, ultimately, confirm and consolidate existing class power. Hence the rule of law is only another mask for the rule of a class ... But this is not the same thing as to say that the rulers had need of law, in order to oppress the ruled, while those who were ruled had need of none. What was often at issue was not property, supported by law, against no-property; it was alternative definitions of propertyrights: for the landowner, enclosure — for the cottager, common rights; for the forest officialdom, 'preserved grounds' for the deer; for the foresters the right to take turfs." *Cf.* E. P. Thompson, *Whigs and Hunters* (London, 1975) pp. 259–261.
8. Marx (MEW, Vol. 1, pp. 231–232) himself suggests: "The customary rights of the aristocracy conflict by their *content* with the form of universal law ... The fact that their content is contrary to the form of law—universality and necessity— proves that they are *customary wrongs* ... At a time when universal laws prevail, rational customary right is nothing but the *custom of legal right*, for right has not ceased to be custom because it has been embodied in law, although it has ceased to be *merely* custom ... Customary right as a *separate domain* alongside legal right is therefore rational only where it exists *alongside* and *in addition to law*, where custom is the *anticipation* of a legal right ... But whereas these customary rights of the aristocracy are customs which are contrary to the conception of rational right, the customary rights of the poor are rights which are contrary to the customs of positive law."
9. George (*England in Transition*, p. 90) notes how enclosures were retrospectively seen as a way of dealing with crime and idleness, and Gonner (*op.cit.*, p. 360) recalls the common feeling that there was: "a disproportionate amount of crime

58

originated among those living near commons or in uninclosed parishes. Of still more gravity was the contention that, so far as these latter were concerned, commons, and to a lesser degree common right, increased idleness, proved an obstacle to industry, and led to greater poverty and wretchedness."

10. Those who *did* attempt to continue to secure ex-rights were successfully (even as far as many commentators were concerned) branded as criminal. Thompson, however, successfully shows that "blacking" was not of ordinary criminals, but of the general agrarian populace: "These Blacks are not quite (in E. J. Hobsbawm's sense) social bandits, and they are not quite agrarian rebels, but they share something of both characters. They are armed foresters, enforcing the definition of rights to which the "country people" had become habituated, and also (as we shall see) resisting the private emparkments which encroached upon their tillage, their firing and their grazing . . . The lamentable thing about this account (an account of the hanging of some Blacks which cited them as part of a criminal subculture) . . . is that they are nothing of the sort; they are simply accounts of the commonplace, mundane culture of plebian England—notes on the lives of unremarkable people, distinguished from their fellows by little else except the fact that by bad luck or worse judgement they got caught up in the toils of the law." In Thompson's analysis of the occupations of the Windson Blacks, he found that far from being a notorious gang, the offenders were made up of approximately 50 percent laborers; 21.5 percent urban and rural craftsmen; 15.5 percent farmers; 8 percent tradesmen; and 4.5 percent gentry.

11. Mantoux claims: "Once enrolled in Chancery, the agreements could be enforced without any further formality . . . If the consent of some small landowner was indispensable, he was asked for it in such a manner that he could scarcely refuse . . . The unlimited authority of the commissioners was no other than their own. It is not very surprising that they should have used it to their own advantage." *Cf.* Paul Mantoux, *The Industrial Revolution in the Eighteenth Century* (London, 1928) pp. 165–168. Gonner (*op.cit.*, 182) adds: "Unwilling commoners are threatened with the risks of long and expensive lawsuits; in other cases they are subject to persecution by the great proprietors, who ditch in their own demense and force them to go a long way round to their own land, or maliciously breed rabbits or keep geese on adjoining ground, to the detriment of their crops."

12. Marx (*Capital* Vol. I) noted: "The last process of wholesale expropriation of the agricultural population from the soil is, finally, the so-called clearing of estates, i.e., the sweeping men off them. All the English methods hitherto considered culminated in 'clearing' . . . (the Duchess of Sutherland resolved) to effect a radical cure, and to turn the whole country, whose population had already been, by earlier processes of the like kind, reduced to 15,000, into a sheepwalk. From 1814 to 1820 these 15,000 inhabitants, about 3,000 families, were systematically hunted and rooted out . . . Thus this fine lady appropriated 794,000 acres of land that had from time immemorial belonged to the clan. She assigned to the expelled inhabitants about 6,000 acres on the sea-shore."

13. Mantoux (*op.cit.* p. 172) offers the following examples: "Almost everywhere the enclosing of open fields and the division of common land were followed by the sale of a great many properties . . . the total number of farms had become much smaller in the latter half of the (18th) century. One village in Dorsetshire where, in 1780, as many as thirty farms could be found, fifteen years later had the whole of its land divided between two holdings; in one parish in Hertfordshire three landowners had together engrossed no less than twenty-four farms, with acreages averaging between 50 and 150 acres." Mantoux estimates that the number of small farms absorbed into smaller ones between 1740 and 1688 to be about four or five in each parish. This suggests a total of between 40,000 and 50,000 for the

whole of the United Kingdon, Crucially, these sales were carried out by private deed, and suffered no intervention by Parliament or from local authorities.

14. Thompson views these unintended consequences of engrossing as a phase in yet another transition: that simultaneous translation of existing "servants" into "employees." He says: "First was the loss of non-monetary usages or perquisites, or their translation into money payments. Such usages were still extraordinarily pervasive in the early eighteenth century. They favored paternal social control because they appeared simultaneously as economic and as social relations . . . In such ways economic rationalisation nibbled (and had long been nibbling) through the bonds of paternalism." *Cf.* E. P. Thompson, "Patrician Society, Plebeian Culture," *Journal of Social History*, 4 (1974), pp. 384–385. E. P. Thompson is by far the most sophisticated and subtle commentator in this area. I have profited a great deal from his writings. However, I think he does tend to assume that the gradual exchange of perks for money is an historical process, the rational conclusion to which is faithfully reflected in the modern structure of wage-payment. This paper challenges that implied assumption, and as such, attempts to go beyond Thompson, and view the historical setting as the interpretative context for modern life.

15. Gonner, *op.cit.*, pp. 96–100.

16. Custom was a broader category than right. Simon suggests that for a customary practice to be accepted an such, it has to be: "uniform, certain, of reasonable antiquity and so notorious that persons would contract on the basis of its existence."

17. Gonner (*op.cit.*, pp. 367–8) states: "Allotments, when made, vested in the owners, to whom they were a more tangible property than the small common right, the use of which in many cases was allowed by grace to the tenants. As the owner usually possessed several of these tenements, the compensation in land added materially to his property; and he was under the disadvantage besetting the poor owner who dwelt in his own cottage."
Mantoux (*op.cit.*, p. 170) adds: "As for the cottager who was traditionally allowed to live on the common, to gather his firewood there and perhaps keep a milch-cow, all that he considered as his possession was taken away from him at a blow. Nor had he any right to complain, for after all the common was the right of other men. The possessing classes were unanimous in thinking that the 'argument of robbing the poor was fallacious. *They had no legal title to the common land.*' This was so, no doubt, but they had until then enjoyed the advantages of a *de facto* situation, sanctioned by long tradition."

18. Gonner, *op.cit.*, p. 364.

19. Gonner (*op.cit.*, pp. 362–366) lists the various drawbacks of the allotments: "In some cases the allotments were too small to be of any value, even when they came to the inhabitant of the cottage. In others the expense of fencing proved too great, while in other instances the very inclosure might occasion a change in the actual as distinct from the legal ownership . . . and when common allotments were made to mitigate the hardships of a class, they were unfortunately made in a form which partook in some measure of the old wils attaching to uncertain charity, and did little to foster the habits of industry or to provide a means of a self-reliant life."

20. Mantoux (*op.cit.*, p. 170): "Once in possession of his new land the yeoman had to fence it round, and this cost him both labor and money. He had to pay his share of the expenses incurred in carrying out the Act—and those expenses were often very heavy. He could not fail to be left poorer than before, if not actually burdened with debt."

21. George feels that Enclosure produced the "squatters, the victim of the resentment of those with common rights."

60

22. Mantoux (*op.cit.*, p. 175) puts it even more strongly:
"The enclosures resulted in the buying up of the land by the wealthier class; they lay at the root of all evils of the period – the high cost of necessaries, the demoralisation of the lower classes and the aggravation of poverty. 'It is no uncommon thing for four of five wealthy graziers to engross a large enclosed lordship, which was before in the hands of twenty or thirty farmers, and as many smaller tenants and proprietors. All these are thereby thrown out of their livings, and many other families, who were chiefly employed and supported by them, such as blacksmiths, carpenters, wheelwrights and artificiers and tradesmen, besides their own labourers and servants.' "

23. Marx (*Capital* Vol. I) claims:
"the law itself becomes now the instrument of the theft of the people's land, although the large farmers make use of their little independent methods as well. The parliamentary form of the robbery is that of Acts for enclosures of Commons, in other words, decrees by which the landlords grant themselves the people's land as private property, decrees of expropriation of the people . . . the systematic robbery of the Communal lands helped especially . . . to swell those large farms, that were called in the 18th century capital farms or merchant farms, and to 'set free' the agricultural population as proletarians for manufacturing industry. . . . 'Working men are driven from their cottages and forced into the towns to seek for employment, but then a larger surplus is obtained, and thus capital is augmented.' "

24. Tobias noted that in Birmingham in the early part of the 19th century, "the most prevalent crime was larceny from their masters or from shops and so forth committed by youngsters who had an honest job . . . The large number of small workshops meant that many opportunities for theft existed." In addition, in the first decades of the century, "domestic servants were often involved in criminal enterprises against their masters" *Cf.* J. J. Tobias, *Crime and Industrial Society in the Nineteenth Century* (Harmondsworth, 1967).

25. Mantoux (*op.cit.*, p. 171) notes how this was achieved by retrospective reinterpretation:
"The poor inhabitants of open-field parishes frequently enjoy the privileges of cutting furze, turves, and the like, on the common land for which they have rarely any compensation made to them upon enclosure. The selfish proprietor insists that they had no right to such privileges, but were only permitted to enjoy them by indulgence or connivance."

26. Thompson (*op.cit.*, 1975 pp. 130–1, 134–5) offers a nice example in the "moral career" of aged timber rights in Hampshire:
The other critical issue was that of timber rights. . . . A case was tried at Surrey Assizes, and decided against the tenants: they could not cut timber (unless for necessary repairs on their own lands) without license. But ambiguities remained (as well as illfeelings); what was 'timber'? What constituted 'repairs'? There was also the question of the license, which was to be granted not by the lord's Steward but by Kerby, the Woodward. Upon each license, the Woodward too a fee in bark and 'lops and tops' . . . but Heron claimed . . . the loss sustained by the Bishop through the waste of his tenants was nothing to the loss sustained through the perquisites of the Woodward . . ."
A new Steward introduced several "improvements," which, Thompson continues, successfully extinguished what remained of common rights:
"The common rights in dispute here probably included grazing, and access to clay, marl, chalk, earth, stones, peat, turf and heath . . . (but) If the tenants' right to cut timber on their own farms remained ambiguous (limited to wood for repairs) and bought them under menace of forfeit, and if in any case this timber was scarce, it was inevitable that they should assert more stubbornly customary rights (or claims) over the common land and chases."

27. For example, the notorious 1723 Black Act instantaneously transformed game-rights (which had become felonies) into capital offenses.

28. Marx (MEW, pp. 225, 235) notes how wood-theft (the instant transformation of Common of Estover) was processed as a civil, rather than as a criminal offence. He continues:
   "In short, if popular customary rights are suppressed, the attempt to exercise them can only be treated as the simple *contravention of a police regulation*, but never punished as a crime."

29. Jones shows that as late as 1849 in Wales, miners accused of coal-stealing could successfully use the defense that the mineowner was attempting to deprive them of traditional rights to free coal.

30. Marx noticed this crucial distinction between "pilferage" and "theft," (although at that stage, the distinction was based still upon the different types of regulation upon which each depended—forest regulations, and the criminal code respectively), and argued against the common suggestion that "pilferage" was *really* "theft," and that resistance to that uniformity is merely grammatical purism. While it was still common in England in the 19th century to use "pilferage" as distinct from "theft," any legal distinction is certainly missing from the 1968 Theft Act.

31. This is not to say that "employee" was a freely given status. The "masters" preferred the term "servant." Thompson (*op.cit.*, 1974, pp. 383–4) continues: "They clung to the image of the laborer as an *un*free man, a "servant": a servant in husbandry, in the workshop, in the house. (They clung simultaneously to the image of the free or masterless man as a vagabond, to be disciplined, whipped and compelled to work.) But crops could not be harvested, cloth could not be manufactured, goods could not be transported, houses could not be built and parks enlarged, without labor readily available and mobile, for whom it would be inconvenient or impossible to accept the reciprocities of the master-servant relationship. The masters disclaimed their paternal responsibilities."

32. Thompson (*op.cit.*, 1975, pp. 240–1) gives the example of the Windson foresters: "The unrestricted grazing rights they enjoyed were exceptional . . . in these great forests, concepts of property remained archaic . . . The foresters clung still to the lowest rungs of a hierarchy of use-rights . . . Little money passed among foresters; they did not go to a butcher for their meat. It was because they pursued not a luxury but a livelihood that encounters between them and the keepers were so grim . . . the law abhorred the messy complexities of coincident use-right. And capitalist modes transmuted offices, rights and perquisites into round monetary sums, which could be bought and sold like any other property. Or, rather, the offices and rights of the great were transmuted in this way—those of the Rangers, bishops, manorial lords. The rights and claims of the poor, if inquired into at all, received more perfunctory compensation, smeared over with condescension and poisoned with charity. Very often they were simply redefined as crimes: poaching, wood-theft, trespass."

33. Marx (MEW, p. 227) tries, on behalf of the wood-gatherer, to force a distinction between "live" and "dead" wood, and attempts to show the irony behind the forest-owner's treatment of gathering dead wood in the same way as he would treat somebody apprehended tearing a tree down: "In order to appropriate growing timber, it has to be forcibly separated from its organic association. Since this is an obvious outrage against the tree, it is therefore an obvious outrage against the owner of the tree. Further, if felled wood is stolen from a third person, this felled wood is material that has been produced by the owner. Felled wood is wood that has been worked on. The natural connection with property has been replaced by an artificial one. Therefore, anyone who takes away felled wood takes away property. In the case of fallen wood, on the contrary, nothing has

62

been separated from property. It is only what has already been separated from property that is being separated from it . . . The gathering of fallen wood and the theft of wood are therefore essentially different things."

In England, Thompson notes that in 1717, New Forest wood thieves faced a standard £5 fine (no mean sum for a poor man), but that by the latter half of the 18th century, the new perquisites of the ruling classes began to garner more significant legal protection. Thompson (*op. cit.*, 1975, pp. 244–5) continues:

"In 1741 the 'pretended right' of the poor was tried at Winchester Assizes, and they lost their case. But they asserted it again and again . . . Nevertheless, in 1788 at the next fall: 'The offal wood, after having been made into faggots, and a day appointed for the sale of it, was openly carried off by the people of Frensham, to the number of 6,365 faggots in one day and night.' The value of these perquisites, pretended or allowed, was unequal. In 1777 the stack wood taken by all the poor villagers was valued at £80, whereas the Ranger claimed for himself £250 (or one fifth of the fall). But the decisive inequality lay in a class society, wherein non-monetary use-rights were being reified into capitalist property rights, by the mediation of the courts of law. When the people of Frensham claimed their 'rights,' openly, and with a solidarity so complete that in 1788 no tithingman could be found to execute a warrant, they were subject to prosecution . . . It is astonishing the wealth that can be extracted from territories of the poor, during the phase of capital accumulation, provided that the predatory elite are limited in number, and provided that the state and the law smooth the way of exploitation."

34. Jones notes how, in rural Wales, the withdrawal of fishing rights produced many "crimes" of poaching, and from an examination of 60 cases of poaching, suggests that firstly, most of the incidents had occurred on land that had been recently enclosed; secondly, most cases were prosecuted by absentee landlords (chiefly members of the "English Shooting Gentry"); and thirdly, almost half of the defendants didn't turn up for the trial. Jones suggests that it seems that:

"For certain landowners poaching was a crime worthy of social excommunication. On several occasions farm labourers were sacked as soon as their children were arrested for catching rabbits, even though the subsequent court case was sometimes dismissed." *Cf.* David J. V. Jones, "Crime, Protest, and Community in 19th Century Wales, *Llafur*, 1,3 (1974), pp. 5–15.

35. Jones adds:

"It has been customary for local inhabitants to graze sheep and ponies on the mountain slopes during the summer, and they were clearly determined to protect their 'rights.' When the landowners tried to carry out the award (an Enclosure Act of 1858) by building walls around their allotments, they were repeatedly torn down by gangs of men."

36. Marx (MEW, p. 234, 235) refers to the fruits of gleaning as the "alms of nature," and adds: "By its act of *gathering*, the elemental class of human society appoints itself to introduce order among the products of the elemental power of nature. The position is similar in regard to those products which, because of their wild growth, are a wholly accidental appendage of property and, if only because of their unimportance, are not an object for the activity of the actual owner. The same thing holds good also in regard to gleaning after the harvest and similar customary rights . . . the gathering of bilberries and cranberries is also (now) treated as theft."

Marx goes on to say that the bilberry and cranberry pickers have now become thieves chiefly because it is now possible to extract some commercial value from them. He continues:

"In *one locality*, therefore, things have actually gone so far that a customary right of the poor has been turned into a *monopoly* of the rich."

63

In other words, the acts of theft create capital for the owner of the property concerned. Taking wood-thefts as an example, the value of the wood is only turned into substance by its theft. Marx adds: "For the wood thief has become a capital for the forest owner . . . By reform of the criminal is understood *improvement of the percentage of profit* which it is the criminal's noble function to provide for the forest owner."

Outworkers were in a similar situation. Simon reports that under the Acts of 1843, outworkers were liable to prosecution if they failed to finish all their work on time, or failed to return all the materials given out. This amazing liability managed to blur the normal line between "idleness" and "pilferage," but criminalize both.

37. Mantoux, *op.cit.*, pp. 184–185. He reports:
"The village artisan, when deprived of his field and of his rights of common, could not continue to work at home. He was forced to give up whatever independence he still seemed to have retained, and had to accept the wages offered to him in the employer's workshop . . . There is, then, an intimate connection between the movement by which English agriculture was transformed and the rise of the factory system."

38. See Jones, *op.cit.*, p. 6, 10.

39. Gilding claims that coopers have plenty of opportunity to "sample" the contents of the casks and barrells which they repair and maintain. For example, a "waxer" is a cooper's term for "his unofficial drink, gleaned or siphoned from a wine tub," and "bull" was the name of a drink unofficially created by pouring boiling water into a cask which had held liquor, and leaving it to stand for a couple of days, until the alcohol was satisfactorily gleaned from the woodwork of the tub. It was then drained into a drip-tub and kept for occasional use.

40. Most coopers share their "waxer" with gangs of dockers. *Cf.* Bob Gilding, "The Journeymen Coopers of East London," *History Workshop Pamphlet* No. 4 (1971).

41. Gilding refers to the coopers' traditional allowance system as "sweepings," and cites the attempts by the dock authorities to redefine these practices as "wholesale plunder," and thus eradicate them. Gilding then quotes George Pattison ("The Coopers' Strike at the West India Dock 1821," *Mariner's Mirror*, 12.9.1850):
"When rum was plundered it was drunk on the quay, but sugar was an easier object to conceal and to convey through the dock gates, while the fact that sugar casks were frequently found on arrival to be broken to pieces gave sugar coopers special opportunities for plunder."

42. This typification of development is somewhat optimistic. It would be a little more realistic, perhaps, to set these types of everyday, current contradiction in the grander historical context of interminable criminalization, and subsequently new "wage-theft" as a considerably more mature form than "wage theft." To do so would be to meekly deny the bitter counter struggles of working men in attempts to halt, and turn back the processes of history, inasmuch as the latter are seen purely as oppressive. Current occasions of (weak) "wage-perk" material kind-payment are derived from workforce *re*-definition of more severe forms of contradiction, and not merely unattended contextual throwbacks waiting in the wings of history.

43. Webster defines a "perk" as "a gain or profit incidentally made from employment in addition to regular salary or wages . . . especially one made by custom expected or claimed." A "perk" may here be defined as "Preferential or concessionary access to goods or services conventionally supplied non-preferentially to the public."

64

44. Of course, sometimes, if the "perks" come from the wrong people, or if the Law's claim to universality needs a little direct bolstering, then "perks" become "bribes." Blue-collar workers rarely achieve occupational or professional positions where bribes are possible, and so bribes become almost exclusively the scourge of the working middle classes. Nevertheless, is has recently been estimated (CUTTING 211, 30.1.76) that a $4\frac{1}{2}$ litre company car is worth a 2–4% salary increase to a managing director on £16,000 a year. (I shall bolster the arguments presented here with examples clipped from the British national daily press. These are either quoted as CASES—court reports where the offender matches a definition of an individual occupational thief—or as CUTTINGS, reports of varying status not quite or not even remotely satisfying that definition, but of vague general interest.)

45. A nice recent example being the $2\frac{1}{2}$% mortgage interest rates traditionally the perk of bank employees. When Lloyds Bank recently announced that these were to be increased to 5% and NUBE complained (CUTTING 164: 24.12.75), the bank retorted that the rate was not a "negotiable" item (i.e., not part of wages).

46. For example, a council official (CASE 12: 16.5.73) who was found with 80 tins of food (destined for a council pulverisation plant) in the boot of his car, was unsuccessfully prosecuted. He had claimed that "this practice of taking things home is accepted by many local authorities as a perk of the job." Although he was cleared, the council suspended him. In another case (CASE 155: 11.11.75) a British Rail chef was accused of 12 charges of theft of items of British Rail cutlery (including cutlery from the Royal train) worth £2,472. He claimed in his defence to have had written permission to use the cutlery for private functions, but had lost the note. He was cleared, and the judge commented (that, presumably only for British Rail employees) "it is not an offense to borrow your employer's property—even the Royal crockery—to use for a private function." In both cases, the defendant occupied an ambiguous occupational position, half-way between manager and worker.

47. In CASE 10 (12.5.73) a French *Au pair* was conditionally discharged for stealing 3 dresses from her employers who paid her £7.50 per week—and took £5 of that back in rent. In CASE 20 (28.8.73), a cleaning lady was put on probation for stealing £16 from offices which she cleaned professionally. She was given a small room, free electricity, and £1.50 as a week's wages.

48. Unscrupulous employers use this opportunity to make profit not only out of the goods that their employees are allowed as perks, but also by overcharging them. In "The Political Economy of Nursing Homes," (*Annals A.A.S.P.S.* Vol. 415, Sept. 1974) Mary Mendelson and David Hapgood note how nursing home proprietors have been known to charge the government $14 per day to feed their inmates whom they subsequently manage just to keep alive on $0.78 per day. Hutter similarly adds: "Free meals and lodgings are, of course, included in calculating an employee's salary. The ... owner prefers to deduct the cost of the employee's meal and lodgings—the cost according to his own calculations—rather than pay the employee's actual value. If the employee requests cash instead of meals or the lodgings, his request is denied." *Cf.* Mark Hutter, "Summertime Servants: The 'Schlockhaus' Waiter," in Glenn Jacobs, ed., *The Participant Observer: Encounters with Social Reality* (New York, 1970).

49. As I have already suggested, white-collar employees cannot receive tips, they can only get "bribes." Davis suggests that some "tip-sensitive" blue-collar employees get as much as 40% of their real wages from tips. *Cf.* Fred Davis, "The Cabdriver and his Fare: Facets of a Fleeting Relationship," *American Journal of Sociology*, 65 (1959), pp. 158–165.

50. Leo P. Crespi, "The Implications of Tipping in America," *Public Opinion Quarterly*, 11 (1947), pp. 424–435. In Crespi's study, only 13% of a tipper-public

sample of 300 tip because they feel that the recipient gets a "poor salary," although over 69% agree that tipping could be eliminated if service workers got a "fair wage."

51. Crespi, *op.cit.*
52. To "organize" means to remove picturesque ambiguity and uncertainty from the practice. Davis (op.cit., p. 267) comments: "No regular scheme of work can easily tolerate so high a degree of ambiguity and uncertainty in a key contingency. Invariably, attempts are made to fashion ways and means of greater predictability and control; or failing that, of devising formulas and imagery to bring order and reason into otherwise inscrutable and capricious events."
53. To "work" a customer means to manipulate her in order to increase the probability of a tip. This may be done, for example, by "making change," i.e., to give change in small denominations so as to encourage and facilitate tips.
54. The N.C.B. (N.C.B. Statistical Tables, 1973–74) give £2.56 per week (6.4% of average weekly earnings of all workers at £40.09 per week) as the actual retail value of all allowances in kind. Interestingly, there have been no moves either from the N.C.B., or from the N.U.M. to exchange these legitimate perks for a fixed weekly sum in cash. This is not altogether surprising when it is realized that the office staff and management are *also* entitled to the same coal-allowance (albeit on a slightly reduced basis). The coal-allowance constitutes most of the N.C.B. employee's allowances in kind, although, for some, there is also a small rent allowance in lieu of a colliery tenancy. Those in non-coal-fired houses may instead have a financial allowance (for example, in North Durham, of £175 p.a.). It should be noted that in an inflationary situation, when prices rise faster than wages (as the outcome of a wages policy), wages-in-kind are better value than "real" money. It is possible that the N.C.B. employee's entitlement to his coal allowance, and the B.R. employee's entitlement to free and concessionary travel during strikes reflects the nationalized status of those industries, rather than the "fringe benefit" status of the perk.
55. Permanent British Rail salary, and wage-earning employees have preferential access to travel. Staff (who have an identity card) may purchase tickets at privileged rates—usually one quarter of the public fare—except for travel to and from work, where the first 12 miles of daily travel is free, but the remainder payable at the standard rate. On top of this, full-time staff are entitled to a variety of free tickets: none of those with less than 6 months service, 4 for those with up to 10 years, and 7 for those with over. One free ticket may even take an employee across Europe. These concessions are considered to be part of the wages of the employee inasmuch as they are his *right*, but they are fringe benefits to the extent that they are supposed to act as an inducement (or commitment).
56. A "Catch-22" situation is a theoretically strong "can't win" one. It crucially differs from the double-bind in that the contradiction involved occurs *at* one communicative level, rather than between two levels. It is theoretically strong and generates a structural impossibility for the trapped actor, whereas weaker "catches" (for example, Merton's Contradiction) merely offer structural difficulties. Catch-22 is derived from Heller's novel of the same name, wherein it functioned as a clause preventing hasty escape from the armed forces. Heller: "There was only one catch and that was Catch-22, which specified that a concern for one's own safety in the face of dangers that were real and immediate was the process of a rational mind. Orr was crazy and could be grounded. All he had to do was ask; and as soon as he did, he would no longer be crazy to fly more missions and sane if he didn't, but if he was sane he had to fly them. If he flew them he was crazy and didn't have to; but if he didn't want to he was sane and had to."
    To summarize, Catch-22 was a set of three, mutually contradictory rules: (1) Crazy people may be grounded, (2) One can only apply for grounding oneself,

66

and (3) To apply for grounding indicates sanity. In terms of a means-end schema: inevitably built into the legitimate means of goal-achievement is a logically inevitable disqualification. A particularly nice everyday mundane example of the Catch-22 in operation is given by Birdwhistell where a typical domestic scene is described and minutely analysed to show that a mother putting on a baby's nappy can accustom the child to raise or lower its arm by applying two different sorts of bodily pressure. At one instant, pressure is simultaneously applied at both points thus sending two contradictory messages in one frame. *Cf.* Ray L. Birdwhistell, *Kinesics and Context: Essays on Body-Motion Communication* (Harmondsworth, 1970), pp. 11–23.

57. In terms of the means-end imagery, the "double-bind" is a situation wherein attempts to reach the goal by deliberately specified means are stymied by a meta-qualification which prevents the use of those means. The resulting contradiction (which amounts to a theoretically strong structural impossibility) may be held to occur *between* two communicative levels. For example, Brooks (1969; 213 *et seq*) reports that the conspirators in the General Electric/Westinghouse price-rigging conspiracy had all previously received a memo warning them not to form cartels with the competition. Amazingly, some of the subordinates felt that it was not "serious," or that it was "window dressing," they assumed: "that often when a ranking executive ordered a subordinate executive to comply with 20.5 (the memo on cartels), he was actually ordering him to violate it. Illogical as it might seem, this last assumption becomes comprehensible in the light of the fact that, for a time, when some executives orally conveyed, or reconveyed the order, they were apparently in the habit of accompanying it with an unmistakable wink." *Cf.* John Brooks, *Business Adventures* (Harmondsworth, 1969), p. 213 ff. Although the double-bind has become over-associated with analyses of schizophrenia through Laing's work, both the original formulation and the epistemological basis of its applicability demand that it possibly be a feature of normal situations. A particularly clear statement of the logical structure of the double-bind is given in Batenson (*Steps to an Ecology of Mind*, 1972, pp. 177–188). The irony of the situation has been adopted both by Merton (*Social Theory and Social Structure*, p. 486) with his "circle of paradox," and by Goffman (*Frame Analysis*, pp. 480–486) in his discussion of the "frame trap." A particularly clear statement of a relatively ordinary example is given in Sprand, Ney and Mann (*The Cocktail Waitress: Woman's Work in a Man's World*, 1975, pp. 139–141). Here, it was noted that in some American bars customers occasionally ask for the "wrong" drink. In other words, they ask for one drink, receive another, but do not complain. This is considered funny in America. The customer jovially asks publicly for a rudely named drink, but manages to convince the waitress using various meta-channels of communication, that this drink *isn't* required, and that he wants the "usual." But how comical is this for the waitress?? She can either underread the situation and supply the drink that is verbally and literally asked for, or she can overread the situation, avoid supplying the rudely-named drink and pour that metaphorically requested. But either of these courses of action *can* be wrong. There is no theoretical exit from the double-bind, although experience (as in the waitresses' case) can convert actual loss into a low probability.

58. Goffman (*op. cit.*, p. 84) notes that the wink is a collusive one with a long social history, and that the many meanings which it once could convey are now telescoped into the usual negative meta-statement.

59. Jason Ditton, "The Fiddler: A Sociological Analysis of Forms of Blue-Collar Employee Theft amongst Bread Salesmen," Unpublished Ph. D. Thesis (Durham, 1976), p. 12.

60. At least, this must be the outcome of the official disposition. Unofficially, many shades of treatment are possible. Some cases are treated as neither "theft" nor

"perks," and are called (petty) "pilferage." In other words, the ambiguity need not be resolved at the reaction stage. It is even possible for the ambiguity to be officially sanctioned, and for the action to be defined (in actuality) as "theft," but not proceeded against because this verdict is qualified by its "pettiness." For example (CUTTING 0.1: 29.1.73) Cadbury-Schweppes and Rowntree-Mackintosh (quite legally) set up their own courts to try employee offenders, and have been doing so, with the blessing of the local Birmingham constabulary, since 1920.

61. This is at least the case in terms of the meanings attached to the world by the "pilferers." Horning found that a crucial definition which rendered objects available for pilferage by the workers in his study was their definition of those objects as being "property of uncertain ownership." Some of these objects *are* of questionable ownership (for example, broken parts in the scrap barrel) but most are clearly legitimately owned, although for various reasons, have slipped into the limbo of uncertainty in the worker's eyes. In a very similar way I found that bread salesmen found it psychologically "easier" to steal bread while it was labeled "stock": a category of intermediate factory responsibility for bread. As "stock," bread was neither clearly the responsibility of despatch workers, nor yet obviously issued to the salesmen.

62. Marx (MEW, p. 225) further claims that to claim that pilfering *"is"* theft: "mistakes the conversion of a citizen into a thief for a mere negligence in formulation and rejects all opposition to it as grammatical purism."

63. Douglas claims that marginality is untidy experience, and that it is precisely this untidiness which is dangerous. She suggests: "Danger lies in transitional states; simply because transition is neither one state nor the next, it is undefinable." *Cf.* Mary Douglas, *Purity and Danger* (Harmondworth, 1966) p. 116.

64. Marx, MEW, p. 232–233.

65. I once asked one of the Wellbreads managers what sort of overall daily shortage figure would be acceptable for the production department. He replied: "Anything up to £100, but it's very hard to say, because on some occasions, we've been £30 or £40 short, and they've not said a word, and sometimes, we're £35 or £45 short, and they'll say: 'You're short' . . .-you see, you can't really pin this down to a specific amount."

66. One employer told Martin that deciding whether to label an action "pilferage" or "theft": "depends on the person, if you know a chap is a bit of a rogue, it is different from an honest man." It is also possible that "ambiguous" employees, for example gamekeepers who combine manorality with servility, have a sort of portfolio of kind-benefits comprising half of perks (representing their white-collar status) and half of pilferage (showing their blue-collar status). For example, Thompson (*op.cit.*, 1975, p. 34) notices: "These posts (gamekeepers) carried small salaries–for underkeepers £20 per annum–and if not supplemented from other sources would scarcely have constituted a livelihood. But the best posts were in fact lavishly supplemented by perquisites. Some of these were expressed, such as the use of their own sub-lodges, a hay allowance for the deer, a scale of payment for each stag, buck or hind officially killed, the use of old fence posts for firing, etc; others were unexpressed but perfectly well understood and sanctioned by usage, such as the culling for their own use of the occasional ('wounded') deer, a fairly free hand with timber, small game and herbage; still others were the wages of customary corruption (the covert sale of venison on their own account, or the acceptance of bribes from poachers as a payment for silence."

[*Footnote here:* "It is impossible to set an exact value of the perquisites of keepers; the best attempt was made later in the century in the New Forest (*Commons Journals*, XLIV, 1789: 558). A keeper who started off with a salary of

68

£20 p.a. would be unlucky, when he added to this fees for driving the walks, fuel wood (or allowance in lieu), allowance for repair of lodges, use of lodge, fees for killing deer, profit from the sale of browse wood, sale of rabbits, use of his own grazing in the forest, etc., to emerge with less than £100 p.a., and this on his own confession, before undeclared advantages are considered. Many gained very much more."]

67. Martin, *op.cit.*, pp. 125–126.

68. A "weasel" word is one cunningly inserted into advertising copy in order to evade the spirit, but not the letter of the law. It is difficult to sustain common-sense definitions of what "small" means when we examine the offenses for which several meat-inspectors from Boston were indicted in 1971. Among other things, the inspectors were indicted for the theft of a "handful of screws," a "spiritual bouquet" (?), a "light bulb," "half a can of shoe polish," and a "photograph." Contrarily, what does "large" mean? In CASE 37 (7.7.74) an absolute discharge was given to a man who had taken a worthless box from his employers. The judge accepted that the defendant did not know that there was a sextant inside the box.

69. On one occasion, even Thompson's under-keepers were produced against (*op.cit.*, 1975 p. 97):
"In the case of the under-keepers, known perquisites included the use of lodges, often with orchards, gardens, grazings, fees for the unwarranted killing of deer; important timber perquisites." [*Footnote Here:* "the keepers of Cranbourne Chase (in Windsor forest) had 'all profits arising by the herbage and browse-wood windfall tree and dead branchles mastage and chimage, as well as fuel and wood for repairs.' "] "the sale of browse-wood; and the exploitation of the influence that went with office. In the aftermath of the tragedy of the Blacks, the normally compliant regarders of the forest court showed, at the last two swanimotes to be held for Windsor Forest, a flurry of guarded independence. They presented the under-keepers as a group for taking down dead trees without view (i.e., without licence or notice to a Regarder) and lopping too many branches from the trees under the pretence of browse-wood. In addition the taking for their own use of deer found wounded or accidentally killed 'is grown to be a pernitious custome.' "

70. M. Dalton, *Men Who Manage* (New York, 1964), p. 212.

71. For example, in the building industry, "custom" weakens the law to such an extent that (Martin, *op.cit.*, p. 117):
"The building industry always accepts that no man ever pays for nails, screws, or firewood, but if he took something bigger, it would be theft."
It is similarly traditional that meat-inspectors (who have to temper bureaucratic regulations with commercial "good sense") are entitled to extra rewards called "cumshaw" (meat for their domestic use) for thus oiling the wheels of commerce. Zurcher notes that "cumshaw" was originally a Chinese word for tip. The meat inspectors are employed by the government, but "tipped" by the companies they are allegedly checking.

72. *Cf.* Gerald Mars, "Chance Punters and the Fiddle: Institutional Pilferage in a Hotal Dining Room," in M. Warner, ed., *The Sociology of the Workplace* (London, 1973), p. 202.; Mark Hutter, *op.cit.*, p. 206.

73. Lawrence R. Zeitlin, "A Little Larcency Can Do a Lot for Employee Morale," *Psychology Today*, V, (June 1971), p. 26.

74. R. Keith Aufhauser, "Slavery and Scientific Management," *Journal of Economic History*, 33 (1973), p. 819.

75. Dalton, *op.cit.*, p. 212, 215.

76. *Ibid.*, pp. 198–199.

77. There is a nice historical basis for this processing distinction between management and worker. Simon reports that: "Whereas the master who broke his contract was

only liable in a civil action for damages or wages owing, the servant who broke his contract was punished as a criminal with imprisonment and hard labor up to three months." (in 1875). *Cf.* Daphne Simon, "Master and Servant," in J. Saville, ed., *Democracy and the Labour Movement* (London, 1954), p. 160.

78. Dalton, *op.cit.*, p. 195.

79. *Ibid.*, p. 208, 211.

80. Martin, *op.cit.*, p. 23, 126.

81. I am not here concerned with the other side of the fiddler's coin—either "dodgers" (customers who do not pay their dues, T.V. license dodgers and so on) or, "flankers"—members of the public who defraud corporations or state institutions. An interesting possibility arises, however, when members of the public depend for their means of subsistence upon financial negotiations with state institutions. This gives us, on occasion, two sorts of flankers—"scroungers" (those who defraud the D.H.S.S.), and "evaders" (those who defraud H.M. Tax Inspectors). Sometimes, those of the Right can see no distinction between "scroungers" and claimants; and those of the Left no difference between "evaders" and avoiders. A nice financial note is possible however. The D.H.S.S. estimate fraudulent benefit claims at £3.7 millions in 1974 (0.4% of the benefit total of £843 millions), and Anthony Christopher of the Inland Revenue Staff Association claims that tax-owed but written-off in 1970 amounted to between £235 and £535 millions (CUTTING, 206: 26.1.76). Taylor, Walton and Young estimate that in 1972 there were only 17 prosecutions for false income tax returns (as against 80,000 cases settled without prosecution), although there were 12,000 prosecutions for fraudulent claims from the D.H.S.S. The amounts reclaimed in these 12,000 cases was only 15% of that recovered in the 17 tax cases. Titmuss adds that of 7,937 cases of tax-evasion investigated between 1948 and 1951, £4 millions was recovered in imposed penalties, but there was not a single prosecution. While we may suggest that Social Security fraud is the prerogative of the "working" classes, the community and the country stands to lose far more through the rascally peculations of the white-collar, diligent but evasive employer.

82. Ditton, *op.cit.*

83. "Fiddling" is an ambiguous category like "pilferage." The bakery management tolerate the practice as long as irate customers do not complain. Interestingly, the salesmen at the bakery do *not* have the same pilfering rights as the production workers. It is assumed that the production staff have no outlet other than domestic consumption, and that this empirical feature of the practice will *de facto* limit the amount of bread that they will take. Salesmen, on the other hand, are assumed to have guaranteed occupational access to facilities (a round of customers) with which they could easily violate the meta-injunction of domestic usage.

84. On the one hand (profit) the sales department is strictly accountable for all the goods which its salesmen are debited with, but on the other (mistake), the process of transforming bread into money is fraught with inevitable and unintentional mistakes which will, on balance, disadvantage the firm.

85. Recruitment is expensive, so recruits must be both brought to peak efficiency quickly, and encouraged to stay there. "Fiddling" will simultaneously remove worries about being short in accounting losses, and increase wage-packets, thus decreasing labor turnover.

86. Court prosecutions (which transform the fiddle into theft) are rare, as customers only infrequently officially complain. In my current collection of over 200 CASES of employee theft taken from U.K. national newspapers over the last 4 years, only two (CASE 165: 25.11.75, taxidriver overcharging; and CASE 174: 2.12.75, London dustmen demanding tips with menaces for emptying extra dustbins) involved prosecutions for workers stealing from customers.

70

87. In the research summer of 1973, salesmen were paid an average wage of £32.50 p.w. I asked one of the salesmen if he felt guilty about fiddling, and he replied: "I don't bother about it at all . . . I just think of it as subsidising my wages, that's all." A hotel waiter in a similar position (Mars, *op.cit.*, p. 202) said: "Who'd work for £12. 10s a week for the hours I put in? No one but a bloody fool, I can tell you. Fiddles are part of wages. The whole issue runs on fiddles, it couldn't work otherwise."

88. The Wellbreads situation is an *active* "illusory partnership." In other words, the managers are personally involved in, and then disengaged from each recruit, and do not *passively* rely upon historical precedent and workforce custom to produce the rewards that they gain from workforce fiddling.

89. Zeitlin, *op.cit.*, p. 64.

90. *Cf.* Hutter, *op.cit.*, p. 213; Davis, *op.cit.*, p. 27.

91. *Cf.* Elliot Leibow, *Tally's Corner* (Boston, 1967), p. 40.

92. For example, CASE 3 (31.1.73) a railway porter convicted of stealing newspapers worth 57p from a train was fined £20 and asked to pay £20 costs; CASE 6 (17.2.73) a barman convicted of stealing from the till was given a £500 fine and an 18-month suspended prison sentence; in CASE 194 (23.12.75) a sheet metal worker was successfully prosecuted and fined £25 for the theft of 10p's worth of scrap metal which he had taken 15 years before.

93. For example, CASE 29 (25.1.74). A store employee who stole store goods was fined. He claimed that he took the goods because he was underpaid. In CASE 34 (19.6.74), a coal-board official who took some envelopes worth £1.25 was discharged—but he lost his job.

94. Dalton, *op.cit.*, p. 201.

95. Merton's Contradiction is derived from Merton. Briefly, the same body of success-goals is held to apply to all, but social organization is such that there exist class differentials of goal accessibility. The "open-class ideology" is never sufficient to wholly mask this disjunction.

96. Salesmen and bank clerks, for example, are particularly prone to being paid as blue-collar employees, but asked to appear at work as whitecollar ones. Abramson notes that this is often referred to as being asked to "put on the dog." Inevitably, there are those who will read the secondary injunction (to appear well) as more important than the primary injunction not to steal. Many complain of the difficulty of balancing reality with the impressions of it that are occupationally essential. An ex-bank president complained:
"A person who works in a bank is generally regarded as wealthy, no matter how small his salary. He is expected to subscribe to everything . . . live on a fairly high standard. He is compelled to look prosperous for the sake of the bank. He has to 'live up to his position.' " *Cf.* Donald Cressey, *Other People's Money* (London, 1953), pp. 56–57.
However, in banks it is not so much that there is not theft (as is commonly supposed) it is rather than all theft is unambiguously defined as stealing. This has always been so, and accordingly, there is no culture of pilferage as an employee-transmitted workplace tradition. A bank contacted by Martin commented: "In a bank there is no line (between pilferage and stealing) you just don't do it. One thing leads to another and we do ask for a high standard and maintain it." Since banks only handle money, and since there would be no way to, for example, define what "domestic consumption," or a "small" amount of money might be, allowing clerks to dip into the till on their own account would inevitably lead to a situation where, as was suggested, "one thing leads to another." On top of this, there is no inventory euphemism (such as "damaged") where "lost" money might be alternatively located. No "pilferage," then, by definition, but a considerable amount of "theft." Robin notes how banks as a whole tend to prosecute up to

71

87% of their embezzling employees, whereas department stores only bother to take about 17% to court. *Cf.* Gerald D. Robin, "The Corporate and Judicial Disposition of Employee Thieves, " *Wisconsin Law Review,* 642 (1967), pp. 685–702.

97. Martin, *op.cit.* p. 117.

98. Leibow, *op.cit.,* pp. 38–39. Judicial disposition of employee thieves is likely to be light although employee theft presents good opportunities for activating victim compensation. Recently (CUTTING 204: 24.1.76) a petrol pump attendant, convicted of false accounting and theft in 1972 was released from an order to repay £2,852 because she was living, with one daughter, on £8 p.w. from Social Security benefits.

99. *Cf.* Jason Ditton, "Moral Horror vs. Folk Terror: Class, Output Restriction and the Social Organization of Exploitation," *Sociological Review* 24 (August, 1976).

Theory and Society, 4 (1977) 39–71
© Elsevier   Scientific Publishing Company, Amsterdam – Printed in the Netherlands

[8]

Hunting, Fishing, and Foraging: Common Rights and Class Relations in the Postbellum South

Steven Hahn

I

When the Beech Island Farmers' Club, a planter organization in Aiken, South Carolina, met in January, 1875, it passed resolutions instructing members to "prosecute all trespassers and violators of the game laws" and prohibit "tenants and laborers" from keeping "stock of any kind on any enclosed or unenclosed land" not "specifically allotted to" them. The club further implored that livestock "trespassing beyond [the] allotted land be impounded" at the laborer's expense "for the first offense and...forfeited or destroyed" for the second and urged "the adoption and enforcement" of these "conditions by all persons in our community." Three years later the club overwhelmingly supported the enactment of a general stock law that would require the enclosure of animals rather than crops.[1]

Trespassers, enclosures, stock and game laws—the stuff of local skirmishes often obscured by the broader and imposing events of the postbellum era. But in an agricultural society the grid of use rights in the land underlies basic social relationships, and in the turbulent aftermath of the Civil War skirmishes over such rights helped define the larger meaning of the sectional reconciliation. The Aiken planters and their counterparts throughout the South knew this well enough. Reeling from the twin jolts of military defeat and abolition, though having avoided general land confiscation, they moved to reclaim the labor of ex-slaves who hoped to farm for themselves or, at least, to escape the rigors of plantation life.[2] In the South, as in other post-emancipation societies, the fists of coercion and repression came down in efforts to restrict the freedmen's mobility, alternative employment opportunities, and access to the means of production and subsistence, tying them to the land as a propertyless work force.[3] Thus, the all-too-familiar black codes, vagrancy laws, enticement statutes, apprenticeship arrangements, and vigilante violence. Yet the appeal for a toughened stance against tresspassers, and particularly the agitation for game and stock laws, suggests that the strong arm of compulsion did not easily hold sway, that confrontations and competing claims went into the making of new class relations in the South. And it was a process that soon extended beyond the Plantation Belt, setting the stage for wide-ranging social and political conflict.

It is the very breadth of these struggles that compels our attention. For if the high drama—not to mention the historiography—of the Southern transition from slavery focused upon the reorganization of the plantation sector, the repercussions touched all corners of the region.[4] Any overall assessment of the nature of this transition must, therefore, link the experiences of planters and Afro-Americans with those of other social groups, most notably white family farmers. Although the majority of these farmers had owned no slaves and resided in non-plantation areas, the postwar period saw growing numbers drawn into the cotton economy, eventually leaving the South with an unprecedented level of economic integration.[5] The connections between Emancipation and the absorption of white yeomen into the market have not been examined fully, but of central importance was the transformation of productive relations. Here, the issue of use rights, of common access to unenclosed land —embodied in the movement for game and stock laws—resonated with a special intensity.

What follows, then, is a preliminary exploration of mounting contentions over common rights and their role in the reshaping of Southern class relations. It will raise many more questions than it will answer, partly because the subject has received scant attention and partly because the subject demands highly localized research.[7] While state assemblies ratified enabling legislation, counties, militia districts, and, at times, individual plantations became the theaters of activity and strife. Enough information is readily available, however, to make for a promising venture, and the obvious comparative implications make the venture all the more intriguing.[8]

II

Fee-simple landownership prevailed in the antebellum South. Real property, unencumbered by primogeniture, entail, or other formal obligations, could be bought and sold at will, its purchaser entitled to full possession.[9] But from earliest settlement, custom and law circumscribed exclusivity and widened use rights. Unimproved, and thus unenclosed, land, which constituted most of the acreage on Southern farms, won sanction as common property for hunting, fishing, and grazing. 'Though it is the broad common law maxim, 'that everything upon a man's land is his own'. . .and he can shut it out from his neighbor without any wrong to him," wealthy South Carolina planter William Elliott grumbled in 1859, "yet custom, with us, forfeited by certain decisions of the court, has gone far to qualify and set limits to the maxim."[10]

While Elliott, an avid sportsman, disapproved of customary practices, he left little doubt that his sentiments ran against the grain of public opinion. 'The right to hunt wild animals is held by the great body of the people, whether landholders or otherwise, as one of their franchises," he observed, bemoaning that the land one acquired must be enclosed or it was one's "neighbors' or anybody's." A court case, which Elliott disdainfully recounted, attested further to the nature and tenacity of popular attitudes on hunting rights. An action for trespass, growing out of the conflicting claims of hunter and landholder, came to trial in South Carolina. One of the hunters, himself a landowner, took the stand and was asked by the prosecuting attorney, "Would you pursue a deer if he entered your neighbor's enclosure?"

> *Hunter:* Certainly.
> *Counsel:* What if his fields were planted, and his cotton growing or his grain ripe?
> *Hunter:* It would make no difference; I should follow my dogs where they might.
> *Judge:* And pull down your neighbor's fence, and trample on his fields?
> *Hunter:* I should do it—though I might regret to injure him!
> *Judge:* You would commit a trespass; you would be mulcted in damages. There is no law for such an act!
> *Hunter:* It is hunter's law, however!

"And hunter's law is likely somewhat longer to be the governing law of the case in this section of the country," Elliott groaned, "for the prejudices of the people are strong against any exclusive property in game...".[11]

Elliott and like-minded planters feared that unregulated common rights would lead to a depletion in the supply of game and, thereby, threaten one of their favorite sports. Hunting, with its occasional pageantry and ostentatious display, reinforced the cultural prestige of the master class.[12] During the 1850s pressure for game laws began to surface. Legislation was local and the greatest inroads came in Maryland and Virginia, although several counties in Mississippi, Alabama, and Georgia also established hunting seasons for deer, turkeys, partridge, and quail.[13] Overall, however, the impact of such laws remained quite limited, for they met with deep popular resistance. As Elliott could again note, the "laboring emigrants" from Britain brought a profound "disgust at the tyranny of the English game laws.... The preservation of game is thus associated...with ideas of aristocracy—peculiar privileges to the rich, and oppression toward the poor."[14]

Common right to unenclosed land had even greater significance for livestock raising. Rather than provide pasture, Southerners customarily turned their hogs, cattle, and sheep out in the woods to forage. "The cows graze in the forest...[and the hogs] go daily to feed in the woods," traveler John Pinkerton found in mid-eighteenth century North Carolina, and reports of what was known as the "open range" came from all over the nineteenth-century South.[15] "Many people [in the piney woods of Mississippi] are herdsmen," J.F.H. Claiborne recorded, "owning large droves of cattle...[which] are permitted to run in the range or forest." Northern Alabama, a United States Patent Office correspondent wrote in 1851, had "no system of raising stock...of any sort. The cattle live half the time on Uncle Sam's pasture." So, too, in the South Carolina Piedmont. "We really raise [cattle] with so little care, that it would be a shame to charge anything for their keep up to three years," one resident claimed. "We raise our hogs by allowing them to range in our woods, where they get fat in the autumn on acorns."[16]

Widespread in Britain, continental Europe, and Africa before capitalist agriculture fully penetrated the countryside, these grazing practices entered Southern statute books during the colonial period in the form of fence laws.[17] An act passed as early as 1759 in Georgia, for example, established guidelines that would persist throughout the antebellum era. It required farmers to enclose their crops, thereby permitting livestock to roam freely upon uncultivated land. The specifications were detailed and precise:

> ...all fences or enclosures...that shall be made around or about any garden, orchard, rice ground, indigo field, plantation or settlement in this province, shall be six feet high from the ground when staked or ridered and from the ground to the height of three feet of every such fence or enclosure, the rails thereof shall not be more than four inches distant from each other; and that all fences or enclosures that shall consist of paling shall likewise be six feet high from the ground and the pales thereof not more than two inches asunder: *Provided always*, that where any fence or enclosure shall be made with a ditch or trench, the same shall be four feet wide, and in that

case the fence shall be six feet high from the bottom of the ditch.

Although Georgia's Assembly reduced the legal height of fences by a foot during the nineteenth century, the other provisions stood. Should animals break into a farmer's field, his fencing had to measure up to these standards if he hoped to collect damages. "If any trespass or damage shall be committed in any enclosure, not being protected as aforesaid," the *Georgia Code* flatly decreed, "the owner of such animal shall not be liable to answer for the trespass, and if the owner of the enclosure shall kill or injure such in any manner, he is liable in three times the damages." Other Southern states enacted similar laws.[18]

Decisions rendered by antebellum state courts upheld the dictates of statute law. In a series of damage suits brought against railroad companies by farmers and planters whose animals had been struck by trains, judges invariably found for the plaintiffs on the grounds of legal and customary public access to private, albeit unenclosed, land. Thus, when the Nashville and Chattanooga Railroad Company appealed such a lower court verdict in 1854 by contending that common law precedent absolved it from responsibility, the Alabama Supreme Court demurred. The common law was not operative in Alabama, Judge J. Ligon declared, noting that the state code prescribed that "unenclosed lands . . . are to be treated as common pasture for the cattle and stock of every citizen." The Mississippi High Court of Errors and Appeals issued much the same ruling in an almost identical case two years later, reasoning that "by common consent [the woods and prairies] have been understood . . . to be a common pasture." Any shift in the burden of obligations "would require a revolution in our people's habits of thought and action," Judge Stephens of the Georgia Supreme Court proclaimed in 1860. "Our people . . . would be converted into a set of trespassers."[19]

Dissident voices could be heard. As the antebellum era wore on, agricultural reformers and "progressive" planters blamed the custom of open-range foraging for the poor quality of Southern livestock. They also argued that the fence laws worked a special hardship on farmers as expanded cultivation led to timber shortages and made fencing unduly expensive, not to mention laborious and time-consuming. "In some parts," one critic insisted, "timber is becoming so scarce that it will be a serious question how we are to provide fences for our fields." Another complained that "custom and the example of our fathers have riveted upon us practices, which although they are injurious to our interests, are nevertheless unnoticed, because they are familiar." And, in the words of a Virginia planter, the prevailing fence laws represented the "heaviest of all taxes on farmers." The *Southern Cultivator*, an agricultural journal, suggested the use of wire fences or thorn hedges, but agitation eventually turned to a call for new statutes requiring the enclosure of livestock rather than crops.[20]

Reformers not only pressed for conservation and agricultural improvement; they challenged the validity of common rights. "Justice and policy have concurred in fixing as a general principle in the laws of civilized nations, that every individual should be compelled to refrain from trespassing on the property [of]. . .other persons," one of them told the Virginia General Assembly, but in the case of fencing "the rule is just reversed. . .[and] every individual shall guard and protect his property from depredators and everyone is permitted to consume or destroy all that may not be well guarded." More succinctly, another proponent asked, "Why. . .should my land which I choose to turn out to improve by rest, be taken possession of and impoverished by other people's stock."[21] These arguments, however, won little support, partly because of the issue's sensitivity. Poorer farmers, the reformers admitted, derived special benefits from common rights and would not surrender easily. "It is notorious," one vocal reformer sneered, "that those frequently have the largest stock who have the least land to graze." The Committee on Agriculture and Manufactures in the Virginia Assembly made the same point in a different way when rejecting petitions for a "Change of the General Law of Enclosures": "Many poor persons have derived advantage from grazing their stock on the commons and unenclosed lands, and to whom the obligation to confine them, or a liability to damages if not confined, would operate as a great hardship." Several Virginia counties made adjustments in the fence law, but limited advance could be seen there or elsewhere in the South before the Civil War.[22]

The commitment of yeomen and poorer whites to common rights reflected more than strictly economic considerations. The majority of them resided on small farms outside the Plantation Belt where a household economy predominated. Farm families primarily grew food crops, made much of their own clothing and furnishings, and raised substantial numbers of livestock, supplementing their efforts with local exchanges of goods and labor. Like petty producers in many parts of the United States, these yeomen viewed property ownership as the foundation of independence. Yet, also like other petty producers, they understood that independence could not be achieved through individual enterprise alone. In this regard, common hunting and grazing rights took their place beside other "habits of mutuality"—various forms of "swap work," for instance—as important features of productive organization. Common rights, in short, not only enabled small landowners and the landless to own livestock, but they fit comfortably into a setting where social relations were mediated largely by ties of kinship and reciprocity rather than the marketplace.[23]

Unquestionably, the planters' desire to mitigate class conflict within the South as the sectional crisis deepened afforded protection to these popular customs. William Elliott and members of the Virginia Assembly were not alone in forecasting explosive consequences should hunting and grazing rights be curtailed. More than political pragmatism was at work, however, for the dominant relations of the Plantation Belt provided essential room. With an enslaved labor force, planters did not have to confront the problems that common property rights posed for labor supply and discipline—problems that, historically, set the economic and intellectual underpinnings for exclusivity.[24] Indeed, save for the handful of agricultural reformers and their sympathizers, planters themselves found advantage in the "commons." Thus, Mississippi slaveowner William L. Patton was "in the habit of pasturing [his animals] upon unenclosed lands. . . owned by other persons and. . . used by the neighborhood generally." It was then with some force that pro-slavery spokesmen could argue that black bondage secured the independence of all whites by obstructing the development of market relations.[25]

III

Emancipation effected a fundamental alteration in Southern race relations. In a manner more sweeping and imposing than anywhere else in the Western Hemisphere, forms of racial subordination, nearly two centuries old, were dissolved. Yet, slavery was not simply a system of race relations; it was also a system of labor exploitation and, thus, of class relations. And however much discussions of its aftermath were cast in racial terms, abolition brought planters squarely up against what they, themselves, called "the labor question." Their fortunes as a class resting on the surpluses that flowed from staple agriculture, the planters understood that the civil, political, and economic status of the ex-slaves were intimately related. Fears of "Negro rule" and "racial amalgamation" notwithstanding, the "question of labor control," as South Carolinian William H. Trescott put it in 1865, "underlies every other question of state interest."[26]

The old masters confronted the issue with little optimism. Experience had demonstrated, they believed, that blacks were inherently lazy, indolent, and unreliable and would never submit voluntarily to the demands of a plantation regime. "As a general rule the world over, in freedom or in bondage," the *Southern Cultivator* declared, "labor can be extracted from the Negro only by compulsion."[27] The freedmen had their own version, but it spoke to the planters' dilemma nonetheless. Emancipation saw a large-scale black exodus from the plantations as the ex-slaves tested the new waters of freedom. They roamed the countryside, made their way to cities and towns, squatted on unenclosed land. Reluctant to sign contracts and return to regimented field work, they looked to—and felt they had a right to—set up for themselves. "The greater number," a Mississippi Freedmen's Bureau agent reported, "are determined to try farming on their own responsibility." And when the opportunity presented itself, according to another Federal official, the blacks acquitted themselves "with good success." "All I wants," one freedman explained, "is to gits fo' or five acres ob land, dat I can build me a little house on and call my home."[28]

The "labor question," therefore, became linked inextricably with the "land question." Many planters worried, and many freedmen expected, that the Federal government would confiscate and redistribute the land of wealthy ex-Confederates. Although prospects for such a radical measure faltered in Congress, the enfranchisement of the freedmen and the struggle to build a Southern wing of the Republican party kept the issue alive and contributed to the surge of white vigilante violence.[29] More immediately, planters recognized that customary use rights, along with the availability of public domain in some states, jeopardized labor supply and discipline and, by extension, the revitalization of the cotton economy. The travail of the plantation system in much of the post-emancipation Caribbean, they were well aware, stemmed largely from the success of ex-slaves in taking up former provision grounds and other uninhabited land that proved unsuited to staple crops.[30] Freedmen in the South evinced similar proclivities: They seemed ready to spurn wage and sharecropping incentives in favor of a rude subsistence on game and raised foodstuffs rather than cotton when able to farm on their own account. Tidewater planters, the Richmond *Times* charged in 1866, "suffer great annoyance and serious pecuniary loss from the trespasses of predacious negroes and low pot hunters, who with dogs and guns, live in the fields . . . as if the whole country belonged to them." A more sedentary independence apparently promised little better. Should "the negroes . . . become possessed of a small freehold," Alabama's Clark County *Journal* warned, they "will raise their corn, squashes, pigs, and chickens, and will work no more in the cotton, rice, and sugar fields." The freedmen's "disposition is to be content with the most precarious subsistence," a Louisiana planter complained, "where left to themselves they reside in huts, and live upon small game and corn meal."[31]

Proscriptions against "vagrancy" and the renting of land to freedmen, which some Southern legislatures enacted as part of their "Black Codes" during Presidential Reconstruction, represented the planters' initial, if temporary, steps to use state authority to control the black labor force.[32] At the same time, planter spokesmen, citing the "depredations" of "wandering" freedmen, began to press for stricter definitions of and

Edward King, The Great South *(Hartford, 1875)*

stronger safeguards for private property. "Negroes have a notorious propensity to appropriate what belongs to another," the *Countryman* lectured, arguing that while under "slavery they could be checked by their masters in the indulgence of this propensity [n]ow . . . the strong arm of the law must protect all property-holders." By 1866 the Louisiana and Georgia Assemblies had passed "trespass laws" and a bill to the same effect was under consideration in Virginia. The laws imposed stiff fines or prison terms on anyone convicted of entering "enclosed or unenclosed land" to cut timber or collect anything growing with the owner's permission. The Georgia law also prohibited "squatting or setting upon enclosed or unenclosed land of another whether public or private without bonafide claim, title, or consent."[33]

The perception that a redefinition of traditional use rights was essential for a successful adjustment to free labor gave agricultural reformers and conservationists an increasingly receptive audience. Pointing to the "wholesale and ill-seasoned destruction" of fish and wildlife, the diminishing supply of timber, the costs and inefficiencies of fencing practices, and the benefits of improved animal husbandry, they renewed agitation for game and stock laws. And they spirited a substantial following, as newspapers and agricultural journals filled with similar refrains. In the face of "straitened circumstances" and "the altered system of labor," planters from Mississippi, South Carolina, Louisiana, and

Georgia cried that the "old habits" were too "expensive" and "burden-some," and demanded that "every person who owns any kind of stock" be required "to keep such stock within their own enclosures." "Why in the name of common sense," one asked, "am I compelled to maintain 12 or 13 miles of hideous fence around my plantation at an annual cost of up-wards of a thousand dollars, in order to prevent the cattle and hogs which my neighbors turn loose...from destroying my crops and robbing my property?"[34]

The concerns for conservation and agricultural rehabilitation were quite genuine, as before the war. But it was the connection between these concerns and new labor relations that won growing numbers of large landowners to the cause. South Carolina planter Henry Hammond thus voiced his support for game laws by asserting that while he "was not op-posed to amusements," hunting and fishing only "demoralized man, and in many cases led to crime." A contributor to *The Countryman* heartily agreed, insisting that "stringent trespass laws" be supplemented with "stringent game laws." "We are just as much entitled to the possums, rab-bits, squirrels, and partridges on our land, as we are to our chickens and turkeys," he proclaimed. Strict observance of such laws "would remove many temptations," another South Carolinian believed. "It would keep the negroes more confined."[35]

Much the same was said in regard to fencing. According to the Beech Island Farmers' Club, "the present laws of enclosure," which permitted common grazing, weighed heavily upon "the landed interest," protecting only "whites and blacks, poor, lazy, worthless people...living mainly off to themselves, who eke out a living on a few hogs and other stock run-ning at large." John H. Dent, the Georgia planter and agricultural re-former stated it bluntly: "Our greatest trouble is Labor and Fencing." In-deed, the Memphis *Southern Home and Farm* included the regulation of hunting, fishing, and foraging on a list of "needed laws" that could serve as an agenda for restoring the plantation system. Along with preventing any person from "ranging livestock...hunting, fishing, trapping, net-ting, or seining on another's land without permission," the journal called for measures enforcing all labor contracts, outlawing the enticement or harboring of any laborer who had broken an agreement, giving landlords first lien on the crops of laborers and tenants, restricting merchants' transactions with laborers, taxing dogs, and prohibiting "any person from tampering with fences."[36]

The laws were easier to discuss than implement, however. Black Belt advocates initially met a cool reception from the Hill Country, where commercial agriculture had made limited inroads, and from the Wire-grass and Pine Barrens, where open-range stock raising assumed consid-erable importance, making statewide statutes unfeasible. As one Low

Country planter admitted, 'No uniform fence law throughout the state can operate justly. The present law is very well adapted to the pine and sand country and also to the mountain country, but ruinous to the middle country."[37] Consequently, legislation was localized, authorizing counties, or militia districts within counties, to carry out the law or provide for some means of public deliberation, whether by petition or ballot. And the early postwar years saw a scattered and tentative beginning. In 1865 the Mississippi General Assembly passed two bills: one enabling the "Citizens of Hinds County," where seventy percent of the population was black, to require the fencing of livestock, and one making it a misdemeanor to hunt on privately owned land without consent in all counties outside the south-eastern piney woods and the northeastern hills. The next year the Virginia Assembly followed suit, establishing procedures for "any county" to deem "land boundaries legal fences" for crops, thereby prohibiting stock from "running at large," and defining as a trespass the act of hunting on unenclosed land without permission. Coincidentally, game restrictions took hold in parts of South Carolina and between 1866 and 1868 several counties in the Alabama Black Belt obtained the right to adopt a new fencing, or stock, law.[38]

Yet, planters bent upon limiting public access to landed property met another challenge—this time from within their own locales. Although the social structure and relations of the Plantation Belt had linked the fortunes of many whites through slave ownership, economic interchange, aspiration, and kinship, the campaign on behalf of conservation, progressive agriculture, and the sanctity of private property did little to win the support of numerous small landholding and landless farmers who depended on common hunting, fishing, and grazing for sustenance.[39] To be sure, these poorer whites feared that abolition would unleash "thieving negroes" and often rode with vigilante bands to keep the freedmen in check. But the game and stock laws struck at their own welfare and sense of justice. A planter from Greene County, Georgia found that the "stock law would meet with much opposition, if it could pass at all. The opposition is bitter, made up more of prejudice than reason." A similar report came from Sumter County, Alabama: "We have a class of farmers and stock owners among us [who] . . . are opposed to any innovation on the practice of their fathers, from the use of the subsoil plow to the enactment of a no-fence [stock] law." Not simply economic interest, but, from the planters' point of view, "strange ideas of individual rights" appeared to inspire opponents.[40]

Poorer whites were joined in this battle by their long acknowledged adversaries, the ex-slaves. Antebellum law prohibited slaves from freely using the forests to hunt, from carrying firearms and other weapons, from owning property, and from marketing produce. Formal law did not necessarily reflect day-to-day reality, however, and what masters might have seen as paternal indulgences the slaves transformed into expectations and rights. Slaves commonly hunted and fished, both to supply the plantations and augment their provisions, acquiring a reputation for their skill. If unable to use guns, the blacks relied on dogs to trap prey and, in the words of one historian, enjoyed "indiscriminate permission to fish at large." Indeed, so proficient were the slaves that in certain areas they "monopolized all the good fishing holes" and sold their catches, despite the grumblings of some locals.[41] What is more, scattered evidence suggests that the slaves were not only familiar with open-range grazing; they had livestock and other possessions recognized by their owners as personal property. Most impressive was the situation in the rice districts of coastal South Carolina and Georgia where the task system provided special room for slave accumulation. But as far away as Louisiana a group of recently liberated slaves could ask a prospective employer if they might "keep their pigs." Seeking to curtail their dependence on whites, the freedmen thus rankled at the prospect of game and stock laws. Traveler Edward King observed that the blacks "are fond of the same pleasures which their late masters gave them so freely—hunting, fishing, and lounging." And one ex-slave remarked: "I tell you one thing. This here no fence law was one of the lowest things they ever did."[42]

The opposition of the white and black lower classes came to notable effect with the advent of Radical Reconstruction. Holding newly-conferred political rights, the freedmen—along with Unionist whites— flocked to the Republican party standard and made their presence felt. They voted in large numbers, soon sat in state legislatures, and, in many parts of the Black Belt, took command of county government. The momentum of restrictive legislation wound down during their tenure and, in some cases, laws already on the books were repealed.[43] The proliferation of Republican local officials, of both races, had especially telling repercussions. Now in a position to adjudicate labor contracts and oversee the implementation of coercive statutes, these office-holders and judges often clipped the planters' wings. One South Carolinian fretted that the game laws "would be of great benefit . . . but with such trial justices as we now have, they are not enforced." The adoption of stock laws stood in doubt, another believed, for "the negroes will defeat any [such] measures." Small wonder that a planter spokesman could declare that penalties for various forms of trespass "should be definite and certain, and not be left to a court to decide what the damages are." Small wonder, too, that a Georgia proponent of fencing reform could insist that the issue be decided by "the freeholders of each county" who "alone have a direct interest."[44]

The Black Belt counter-offensive proved short-lived. By the early

1870s white conservatives had "redeemed" most Southern states and even in Louisiana, South Carolina, and Mississippi the Republicans tread a thin balance.[45] Taking their cue from national developments which signalled a declining commitment to the protection of black civil and political rights, planter-dominated legislatures moved forcefully to recapture the initiative in regulating labor relations. In the process, the attack on common hunting, fishing, and grazing privileges intensified. Game laws multiplied in Black Belt counties of Georgia, Alabama, South Carolina, Tennessee, and Virginia; by the end of the decade they operated on a state-wide basis in Mississippi, Louisiana, and Arkansas.[46] The laws prescribed hunting seasons for deer and fowl, prohibited certain methods of trapping game and fish (some of which had West African roots), and curtailed access to woods and waterways. In Georgia, for example, where Republican rule ended in 1871, three plantation counties enacted game laws in 1872, six in 1875, eighteen in 1876, six in 1877, and six in 1878. An act passed for Burke, Taylor, and Jefferson counties was typical, deeming it a misdemeanor to "kill or destroy" deer or partridges between April and October, to "trap, snare, or net" partridges, to catch fish by means of drugs or poison, and to "hunt, trap, or fish" on an individual's land without permission.[47] Alabama witnessed a similar trend. The Reconstruction legislatures repealed game laws adopted by several counties before 1874. That year brought "redemption" and by 1877 most of the Black Belt had such laws in effect.[48]

The progress of new fencing laws also received a boost in the latter years and aftermath of Reconstruction, as local and state agricultural societies, the Grange, and railroad companies joined to press the issue.[49] In response, the Georgia, North Carolina, and South Carolina Assemblies ratified local-option stock laws in 1872, 1873, and 1877 respectively.[50] Elsewhere, individual counties petitioned for enabling legislation. Procedures for implementation were not uniform. In some areas the matter was left to the discretion of local officials; in some to the decision of landowners; and in some to the deliberation of all eligible voters. Although it is impossible at this point to determine the results with precision, it can be said that by 1880 the stock law was under active consideration, if not in operation, in at least 30 Georgia, 17 Alabama, 26 North Carolina, 12 Mississippi, and 18 South Carolina counties, most of which had black majorities.[51]

Further signs of the mounting attack on common rights could be seen in the rulings of Southern judges. Thus, when the Georgia Supreme Court heard a relevant case for damages in 1876, it found the plaintiff's claim "that he had in the woods...the right of common pasture for his cattle which are numerous and which have been accustomed to range heretofore...wholly insufficient," as "he does not set forth any contract, prescription, or other lawful basis for the right." In a dramatic departure from previous policy, the justices expressed incredulity "as to common of pasture upon lands which are all private property" and ruled that "citizens generally have no strict right of common pasture in the 'woods' or upon the unenclosed lands of others...". Courts in other states moved with greater caution, hedging on the question of general principle while upholding the constitutionality of legislative statutes. "The common-law doctrine, which requires the owner of stock to keep them off the land of others...does not prevail in this state," the Supreme Court of Mississippi could announce in 1887. "But the subject is within the power and control of the legislature; and no legal right is violated...when one is required by law to keep his stock off the land of others." Judges in Alabama, North Carolina, and South Carolina rendered similar decisions.[52]

The resistance to game and, especially, to stock laws that surfaced in the Black Belt during Reconstruction by no means entirely collapsed. North Carolina's Charlotte *Democrat* observed that the prospect of a "no-fence law" in one county prompted threats by local freedmen "to leave." The Atlanta *Constitution* found numerous counties "unfriendly to the stock law" due primarily to the fact that "blacks opposed." And in South Carolina a major political controversy was stirred. As an Aiken County planter exclaimed: "The passage of the 'stock law' by our legislature is creating much excitement and angry comment. Threats of a new party are made and fears entertained by some that it will unharmonize the Democratic party...". The planter's fears were justified, for Independent candidates seized the issue and rallied noteworthy support among poor whites and blacks.[53] Nonetheless, much of the Black Belt, in South Carolina and other states, came to heel by the early 1880s. Indeed, South Carolina, where planter power loomed particularly large, stood alone among Southern states during the nineteenth century in passing a "general" stock law—which eliminated local prerogatives—in 1881.[54]

On an elementary level, the spread of game and stock laws attests to the planters' efforts, and success, at re-asserting their authority over black labor—attests, in short, to the re-establishment of economic power relations in the Black Belt despite Emancipation and Reconstruction. Even Henry Grady, the leading spokesman for a new, industrial South, conceded in 1881 that a "landholding oligopoly" lorded over vast acres "through all the cotton states."[55] But from a wider vantage point, the movement to eradicate common rights pointed, as well, to an important metamorphosis in the character of the planter class and of basic social relationships. And the metamorphosis came as the result of intense social conflict.

If the planters had had their way, a formal system of dependent labor would have been erected in the postwar South, giving "the land-

owner an absolute control over the freedman as though he was his slave."
Planters believed it beneath their dignity to bid for the labor of ex-slaves.
The Federal government made such a repressive system difficult to install; the freedmen made it impossible. Resisting gang labor, withdraw-
ing women from the fields, seeking their own land and subsistence, and
moving from plantation to plantation to strike better contracts, blacks
forced their old masters to come to terms with free labor. For some members of the elite, this was too much to bear: They sold out and, perhaps,
left for Brazil or Cuba. Others met the challenge.[56]

It was an unequal confrontation, to be sure, yet one that gradually
brought forth a structure of market relations in agriculture. The redefinition of property rights, which strengthened the planters' control over
productive resources and eroded the claims of their laborers, paved the
way. Lien laws limited tenants' property in their growing crops; court
decisions fully eliminated such property for sharecroppers and categorized them as wage laborers; constitutional and legislative reforms
ended protections that certain property had from levy for debt.[57] And, of
course, the game and stock laws greatly narrowed use rights in landed
property, further circumscribing access to the means of subsistence and
threatening ownership of livestock and draft animals among the poor.
The planters were increasingly transformed into agricultural employers
and the freedmen into agricultural employees. The compulsions of
necessity replaced the compulsions of the lash.

The metamorphosis of Black Belt social relations, which the game
and stock laws highlighted, also had significant cultural and ideological
ramifications. The Southern defense of slavery always rested, in large
part, on doctrines of racial inferiority. Over time, however, Southern intellectuals and politicians alike linked the racial defense of slavery with
the defense of slavery in the abstract: with notions that inequality was the
natural condition of humankind, that natural inequalities were reflected
in social stratification, that free society left the poor and inherently disadvantaged to the mercy of the labor market, and that organic relations of
dependency and mutuality offered the best means for security and social
peace. The most conservative theorists argued that slavery was the proper status for the poor of both races.[58] But even those who spoke the
language of "*Herrenvolk* democracy" mixed conservative theory with
racism and insisted that only the enslavement of blacks stood between
poorer whites and the ravages of the marketplace. It seemed to strike a
responsive chord among the majority of white Southerners who were
outside the mainstream of the staple economy and who cast their votes
for a political party that depicted the expansion of commerce and the
market as a threat to independence.[59]

With Emancipation the planters' outlook and world-view, much as the relations they entered into, were gradually transformed. The racism remained and grew more vociferous. Yet, drawing upon ideas previously advanced by the small brigade of antebellum agricultural reformers, the planter class slowly embraced the market, not dependency or reciprocity, as the proper arbiter of social relationships. The new ideology began to surface with special force in the agitation for game and stock laws, as advocates dismissed the "strange ideas" associated with common rights in favor of the logic of absolute property. "The land outside a farm is as much the property of the farmer as that he may cultivate," a Georgia newspaper proclaimed, "and truly in essential justice [no person]...has any right thereon without express permission." Similarly, a Virginian maintained that "we are just as entitled to [the wildlife] on our land as to the domestic animals." Or, as an Alabama planter asked rhetorically, "Is there any reason or right that A should furnish land for B's cattle to graze upon?"[60] The logic melded easily with the dominant bourgeois currents of postwar America, suggesting the dimensions of the emerging postwar settlement. But the "strange ideas" held on and helped thrust the South into deeper social and political turmoil.

IV

The locus of contention over common rights, and particularly over common grazing rights, shifted from the Black Belt to the Hill Country during the late 1870s and 1880s, reflecting the advance of commercial agriculture into areas previously dominated by semi-subsistence farming. Indeed, the absorption of the Southern Hill, or Upcountry, into the cotton economy was one of the significant developments of the postwar period. Inhabitants of this region had been hard hit by wartime privation, drought, and pillaging; destitution was widespread in 1865 and for a while thereafter. Local officials of the Freedmen's Bureau spent much of their time distributing needed rations to whites, not blacks. By the first years of the next decade, however, a new orientation seemed evident. "Cotton," a county newspaper reported in 1872, "formerly cultivated on a very limited extent, has increased rapidly in the last few years in production...". And the trend would continue so that by century's end white labor raised most of the cotton in the South.[61]

The initial thrust toward market production likely came from yeomen farmers hoping to avail themselves of relatively high cotton prices and recoup war-related losses. Railroads, which began to penetrate the Upcountry during the 1870s, offered added inducement by easing access to supra-local markets. But most importantly, the transition came as a product of new social relations and credit arrangements. Like many peasantries, Upcountry yeomen normally cultivated a limited cash crop along with foodstuffs; the dynamic of the household economy, itself, encouraged the pattern. Even in 1873, a Black Belt paper could note that these farmers attended to "their grain, provender, and provisions and then bestowed their surplus labor on cotton."[62] What turned cotton from one item in a crop mix into a defining feature of the region's economy was a process that tied yeomen firmly to the export market, made vulnerable their productive property, and eventually reduced many of them to tenants and laborers. Expanded lines of transportation and communication and legislation bearing on production and exchange laid the foundation for the transformation; supply merchants carried it through.

The 1870s witnessed a considerable influx of merchandisers into Upcountry towns and hamlets. Prospects of a large clientele along with the developing lien system provided the lure and enabled them to establish a foothold. The Southern lien laws, passed after Emancipation, permitted suppliers to obtain mortgages on the crops of their customers to secure advances of money and provisions. After a series of twists and turns, most legislatures gave landlords superior lien rights for both rent and advances; merchants could get first lien only on the crops of proprietors. Since the majority of Black Belt customers were tenants and croppers and since landlords began to move into the supply business to bolster surpluses, the opportunities of landless merchants diminished. In the Upcountry, on the other hand, the majority of customers were freeholders and the planter element was small. Growing numbers of merchants, thereby, hoped to capitalize on the legacy of wartime hardship and short food crops. As one Upcountry resident recalled: "When the lien law was passed the town merchant became an important factor in farming."[63]

Merchandisers decisively shifted the energies of Upcountry producers to commercial agriculture. Farmers wishing to purchase goods on credit—the norm—now had to mortgage their crops as security, and storekeepers made plain their preference for cotton, it being the most likely to bring a return. High interest rates charged for credit further impelled yeomen to raise the staple, if only to keep their heads above water.[64] Soon, by virtue of legislative initiative, real and personal property could also serve as collateral, thus placing land, tools, and livestock in jeopardy of attachment and offering merchants greater control over the productive process. As cotton prices slid in the 1870s and 1880s, the auction block became the resort for the hopelessly indebted, and a new class of merchant-landlords, based in the Upcountry towns, began to emerge.[65]

It is not surprising, then, that merchants, landlords, and other interests associated with these towns seized upon the stock law as they pushed to consolidate their command of the developing cotton economy. By 1880 the law was being discussed "fiercely" and during the next decade a bitter struggle erupted over its adoption. Hill counties in South Carolina, Georgia, Alabama, and Mississippi entered the fray.[66] While little more is known about the episode on a south-wide scale, the story in Georgia is rich and revealing, and, in its main lines, probably representative.

Following their counterparts in the plantation districts, advocates in the Georgia Upcountry linked the stock law to the cause of agricultural improvement and the ideals of exclusivity in property, which they saw as fitting hand-in-glove. Open-range foraging, they submitted, was "sad

evidence of old fogyism, general ignorance, and backwardness of agri-culture," contributing to timber scarcity, inefficiency, and the prolifera-tion of "useless, scrubby stock."[67] It was a custom dignified by no more than peculiar circumstances and hard-headedness, a sap on economic progress and prosperity, and a violation of "natural rights." Indeed, many supporters of fencing reform viewed common grazing as a "priv-ilege or favor" bordering upon theft. "My neighbor has as much right to pasture my enclosed land as my unenclosed," one of them put it, "as his stock robs it of its vegetable matter...making it poorer everyday."[68]

Compelling as these arguments appeared to be, they failed to win much popular acceptance. The Georgia local-option statute of 1872 provided for county elections, and when the vote came the stock law met resounding defeats. Only the towns and militia districts boasting the highest per capita wealth and the largest farm units lent the law substantial backing; elsewhere it was routed.[69] Opponents had no objection to the cause of agricultural progress *per se*. Rather, they perceived it as window-dressing for class exploitation. "The law would benefit the extensive landowners," one insisted, and, in turn, "would be the greatest curse to the poor laboring men that ever befell them." Not prosperity but expropriation and dependency would be in store for yeomen and tenants alike, who "will be relieved of the privileges our fathers established, of the care and use of the hog, the cow, and all the necessities, only as they are furnished by the" large landowners and merchants. Thus, one Upcountry smallholder predicted that "the stock law will divide the people into classes similar to the patricians and plebians of ancient Rome." Another concluded that it "would be proof of insanity for a poor man that don't own as much as 100 acres of land to vote" for the measure.[70]

The stuff of popular resistance ran deeper. Opponents not only challenged the stock law on economic grounds; they "controverted" the principles of ownership upon which it rested, "the proposition that 'What is mine I have a right to do as I please with.' " "The woods were put here by our Creator for a benefit to his people," they declared, endowing "custom to the range" with "legal, moral, and bible" sanction—sanction that could not be abrogated by private title.[71] Arguing that stock law supporters were "men who never split but few, if any rails" and that no man was properly a "farmer until he does keep his fields fenced," they expressed the abiding logic of the open-range: "While my cow is on my neighbor's land eating grass, his is on mine, that makes it alright." Reciprocity, not exclusivity, promoted "equal rights, equal liberty, and equal privileges," and sustained the community of producers.[72] In sum, stock law opponents began to articulate the values of cooperative commonwealth and counterpose them to the hegemony of the marketplace.

Finding in such attitudes "the spirit of communism fully displayed," disappointed reformers attributed their defeats to the workings of "pauper" democracy. "Agrarianism rules," one of them cried, and "nothing but a restriction on the voters' qualifications will ever protect capital from such injustice and wrong."[73] Disfranchisement did not come to pass in this instance, but since legislation made additional contests possible, stock law proponents prepared themselves to carry the issue. Utilizing the machinery of the Democratic party, which they had come to dominate, and particularly the vehicles of local agricultural clubs, they waged a campaign throughout the counties. Electoral fraud and coercion, so familiar to postbellum politics, also came into play. While neither side could claim innocence, most of the complaints emanated from opponents who cited cases of bribery, threats, ticket-fixing, ballotbox stuffing, and the tossing out of votes.[74]

Yet, even these efforts failed to bring victory. Despite increasing its share of the vote somewhat, the stock law was beaten again and again in countywide elections during the 1880s as white yeomen and tenants, along with blacks, scotched the drive of commercial interests. In the words of one landlord, "the Niggers and white trash" voted against the law.[75] Agitation then shifted to individual militia districts within counties, where reformers made some headway. Not surprisingly, town and village districts, which included many of the largest farms and most highly-assessed acres, often led the way, followed by wealthier rural districts. Other rural areas proved far more troublesome, and adversaries locked horns in a battle that saw voting results overturned, district boundary lines changed, law suits filed, and outbreaks of violence before formal resolution.[76] And although by 1890 a majority of districts in most Upcountry counties had come under the law's jurisdiction, enforcement was another matter. County newspapers charged that "outlaws" occasionally tore newly constructed enclosures "to smash," and that in a few places opponents were "doing their best to evade the law and warning that if any man takes up their stock, they will use their little guns on him." It would be another sixty-five years before a blanket, state-wide stock law entered the books.[77]

V

If Upcountry farmers resisted the attack on common rights more successfully than did poorer whites and blacks in the Plantation Belt, the conflict in both regions illuminated the new relations and fissures spreading throughout the postbellum South. Quite significantly, it suggests that the struggle for control of production may be the key link between the post-emancipation experiences of diverse Southern locales: from the Upper to the Lower South, from the plantation to the small farming districts.[78] In an important sense, too, the conflict suggests how much a part of Gilded Age America the South had become. Landlords, merchants, and other commercial types remained junior and, at times, disgruntled partners, but they came to share with Northern elites a language, outlook, and set of concerns that increasingly put them on one side of a great historical divide. The Southerners, of course, handled these concerns—most conpicuously the "labor question"—in what seemed to be their own peculiar way, to a certain extent because race intervened at so many levels. Yet, it should also be remembered that this very period saw Northern industrialists rely on force, or the threat of force, to settle labor disputes, saw the "best men" call for voting restrictions and other political reforms designed to "cleanse" government, and saw segregation become institutionalized nationally.[79]

At the same time, petty producers in the South came to share with their Northern counterparts another language, outlook, and set of concerns. However different their backgrounds and specific circumstances, they faced similar problems and joined, at least in spirit, in defending a version of the Revolutionary heritage that associated freedom with economic independence and tyranny with massive concentrations of wealth and power. One cannot read arguments opposing the stock law and not be reminded of the Greenbackers and the Knights of Labor. Thus, a dirt farmer in the Georgia Upcountry could declare that "we as poor men and negroes do not need the law but we need a democratic government and independence that will do the common people good." And the inhabitants of northwestern Alabama and northeastern Mississippi could celebrate the maintenance of open-range grazing by dubbing their locales "freedom hills."[81] Such sentiments and sensibilities formed the heart of an emergent popular radicalism that would be harnessed by Populism. □

Notes

An earlier version of this essay was presented to the Shelby Cullom Davis Center Seminar at Princeton University (February, 1981) where it was subjected to searching criticism. I am grateful to those in attendance and, especially, to Stanley Katz. For their comments and suggestions I should also like to thank Tom Dublin, Drew Faust, Tony Freyer, and Walter Licht.

1. Beech Island Farmers' Club, Aiken, South Carolina, Minutes, January 1875, 210, 279, South Caroliniana Library.

2. As a consequence of the Second Confiscation Act of 1862, Federal taxation, and General William T. Sherman's Field Order No. 15 of 1865, the Federal government had control of nearly 900,000 acres of Southern land at war's end. President Johnson subsequently restored most of this land to its former owners. While a handful of Radical Republicans hoped to carry out a general program of land confiscation and redistribution, they met defeat in Congress. Only on the sea-islands and coast of South Carolina and Georgia, where freedmen had established claims and defended them even against Federal troops, did a significant shift in the structure of landownership take place. See Claude F. Oubre, *Forty Acres and a Mule: The Freedmen's Bureau and Black Landownership* (Baton Rouge, 1978), 1-45; James M. McPherson, *The Struggle for Equality: Abolitionists and the Negro in the Civil War and Reconstruction* (Princeton, 1964), 246-259; Willie Lee Rose, *Rehearsal for Reconstruction: The Port Royal Experiment* (New York, 1964), 320-331; Eric Foner, "Thaddeus Stevens, Confiscation, and Reconstruction," in Stanley Elkins and Eric McKitrick, eds., *The Hofstadter Aegis: A Memorial* (New York, 1974), 154-183; Manuel Gottlieb, "The Land Question in Georgia During Reconstruction," *Science and Society,* 3 (Summer, 1939), 356-388.

3. For comparisons from Latin America and continental Europe see C. Vann Woodward, "The Price of Freedom," in David Sansing, ed., *What Was Freedom's Price?* (Jackson, Miss., 1978), 93-113; Wilhemina Kloosterboer, *Involuntary Servitude Since the Abolition of Slavery: A Survey of Compulsory Labour Throughout the World* (Leiden, 1960); William A.

Green, *British Slave Emancipation: The Sugar Colonies and the Great Experiment, 1830-1865* (Oxford, 1976), 99-161; Jerome Blum, *The End of the Old Order in Rural Europe* (Princeton, 1978), 357-441.

4. For an excellent survey and critique of the very recent historiography see Harold D. Woodman, "Sequel to Slavery: The New History Views the Postbellum South," *Journal of Southern History,* 43 (November, 1977), 523-554.

5. C. Vann Woodward, *Origins of the New South, 1877-1913* (Baton Rouge, 1951), 175-188, 291-321; Gavin Wright, *The Political Economy of the Cotton South: Households, Markets, and Wealth in the Nineteenth Century* (New York, 1978), 158-184; Stanley L. Engerman, "The Legacy of Slavery," (Paper presented at the Duke University Symposium on "One Kind of Freedom," February 1978).

6. Harold D. Woodman, "Post-Civil War Southern Agriculture and the Law," *Agricultural History,* 53 (January, 1979), 319-337.

7. Forrest McDonald and Grady McWhiney have discussed briefly the importance and eventual demise of "open-range" grazing in two major articles, "The Antebellum Herdsman: A Reinterpretation," *Journal of Southern History,* 44 (May, 1975), 147-166 and "The South From Self-Sufficiency to Peonage: An Interpretation," *American Historical Review,* 85 (December, 1980), 1095-1118. Also see Jack P. Maddex, *The Virginia Conservatives, 1867-1879: A Study in Reconstruction Politics* (Chapel Hill, 1970), 176-177; J. Crawford King, "The Closing of the Southern Range: An Exploratory Study," *Journal of Southern History,* 48 (February, 1982), 53-70.

8. On the struggle over common rights to forage, woodland, waste, and game in Europe see Blum, *End of the Old Order,* 262-271; Marc Bloch, *French Rural History: An Essay on its Basic Characteristics* (Berkeley, 1966), 197-213; E.P. Thompson, *Whigs and Hunters: The Origin of the Black Act* (New York, 1975); Douglas Hay, "Poaching and the Game Laws on Cannock Chase," in Douglas Hay, Peter Linebaugh, John G. Rule, E.P. Thompson, and Cal Winslow, eds., *Albion's Fatal Tree: Crime and Society in Eighteenth Century England* (New York, 1975), 189-253.

9. C. Ray Keim, "Primogeniture and Entail in Colonial Virginia," *William and Mary Quarterly,* 3rd series, 25 (October, 1968), 554-586; Lawrence M. Friedman, *A History of American Law* (New York, 1973), 205-215; Roy M. Robbins, *Our Landed Heritage: The Public Domain, 1776-1970* (Lincoln, Neb., 1976), 3-58.

10. William Elliott, *Carolina Sports By Land and Water Including Incidents of Devil-Fishing, Wild-Cat, Deer, and Bear Hunting, Etc.* (New York, 1859), 254-255. For statistics on improved and unimproved acreage see Donald B. Dodd and Wynelle S. Dodd, *Historical Statistics of the South, 1790-1970* (Tuscaloosa, Ala., 1973), 2, 18, 26, 34, 38, 50, 54, 58.

11. Elliott, *Carolina Sports,* 254-255, 257-258. Also see Sam B. Hilliard, *Hogmeat and Hoecake: Food Supply in the Old South, 1840-1860* (Carbondale, Ill., 1972), 71-83; "Fox Hunting Fever," in B.A. Botkin, ed., *A Treasury of Southern Folklore: Stories, Ballads, Traditions, and Folkways of the People of the South* (New York, 1949), 610-611.

12. Dickson D. Bruce, *Violence and Culture in the Antebellum South* (Austin, 1979), 197.

13. *Fur, Fin, and Feather: A Compilation of the Game Laws of the Principal States and Provinces of the United States and Canada* (New York, 1871), 112, 141-147; Augusta (Georgia) *Chronicle and Sentinel* quoted in Athens (Georgia) *Southern Watchman,* April 29, 1858.

14. Elliott, *Carolina Sports,* 250-253, 260.

15. Pinkerton quoted in Rupert P. Vance, *Human Geography of the South: A Study in Regional Resources and Human Adequacy* (Chapel Hill, 1932), 146-147; Lewis C. Gray, *History of Agriculture in the Southern United States to 1860* (2 vols; Gloucester, Mass., 1958), I, 146; Terry G. Jordan, *Trails to Texas: Southern Roots of Western Cattle Ranching* (Lincoln, Neb., 1981).

16. J.F.H. Claiborne, "A Trip Through the Piney Woods," *Publications of the Mississippi Historical Society,* 9 (Oxford, Miss., 1906), 521; U.S. Patent Office, *Report to the Commissioner of Patents for the Year 1851* (Washington, D.C., 1851), 331; *Report to the Commissioner of Patents for the Year 1850* (Washington, D.C., 1851), 233-234. Also see Gray, *History of Agriculture,* 2, 836 843; Hilliard, *Hogmeat and Hoecake,* 98-100; Cornelius O. Cathay *Agricultural Developments in North Carolina, 1783-1860* (Chapel Hill, 1956), 28,

159; Alfred G. Smith, *Economic Readjustment of an Old Cotton State: South Carolina, 1820-1860* (Columbia, S.C., 1958), 76; McDonald and McWhiney, "Antebellum Herdsman," 156-158.

17. McDonald and McWhiney, "Antebellum Herdsman," 156; Herbert Heaton, *Economic History of Europe* (New York, 1936), 406, 415, 428-429; Eugen Weber, *Peasants into Frenchmen: The Modernization of Rural France, 1870-1914* (Stanford, 1976), 128; Blum, *End of the Old Order*, 123-125; J.L. Hammond and Barbara Hammond, *The Village Labourer, 1760-1832* (London, 1911), 2-18; Peter H. Wood, *Black Majority: Negroes in Colonial South Carolina From 1670 Through the Stono Rebellion* (New York, 1974), 30; Jordan, *Trails to Texas*, 1-15.

18. Thomas R.R. Cobb, *A Digest of the Statute Laws of the State of Georgia* (Athens, 1851), 18-19; R.H. Clark, T.R.R. Cobb, and David Irwin, *The Code of the State of Georgia* (Atlanta, 1861), 271-272; David J. McCord, *The Statutes At Large of South Carolina* (Columbia, S.C., 1839), 331-332; A. Hutchinson, *Code of Mississippi, 1798-1848* (Jackson, Miss., 1848), 278-280; John J. Ormond, Arthur Bagby, and George Goldwaite, *Code of Alabama* (Montgomery, 1852), 250-251; Williamson S. Oldham and George W. White, *A Digest of the General Statute Laws of the State of Texas* (Austin, 1859), 217-218.

19. Nashville and Chattanooga Railroad Company v. Peacock, 25 *Alabama Reports*, 229; Vicksburg and Jackson Railroad Company v. Patton, 31 *Mississippi Reports*, 156; Macon and Western Railroad Company v. Lester, 30 *Georgia Reports*, 911.

20. *Southern Agriculturist* quoted in *Southern Cultivator*, 2 (October 30, 1844), 173; *Farmer's Register*, 1 (January, 1834), 450-452; *Farmer's Register*, 1 (May, 1834), 753-754; *Southern Cultivator*, 3 (January, 1845), 10; *Southern Cultivator*, 8 (April, 1850), 55-56. In Demopolis, Alabama, the president of the State Agricultural Society won a prize for "An Essay on the Propriety and Policy of Abolishing Fences" in 1859. He pointed to the "large and unnecessary expense of fencing," and argued that improved stock required enclosures rather than the practice of turning them out "to make their subsistence on the public commons or pasture." He, thereby, urged the legislature to pass special or private laws establishing fence law districts. See Thomas McAdory Owens, *History of Alabama and Dictionary of Alabama Biography* (4 vols; Chicago, 1921), 2, 895.

21. *Farmer's Register*, 1 (December, 1833), 388-396; *Farmer's Register*, 1 (January, 1834), 450-452.

22. *Farmer's Register*, 1 (January, 1834), 450-452; *Farmer's Register*, 2 (April, 1835), 712; Smith, *Economic Readjustment*, 73, 106. It is not incidental that pressure for new fence laws was more pronounced in the Upper South. Virginia, in particular, saw a declining slave population and an extended transition, dating back to the eighteenth century, from tobacco to grain crops.

23. For a more detailed discussion see Steven Hahn, 'The Yeomanry of the Non-Plantation South: Upper Piedmont Georgia, 1850-1860," in Robert C. McMath Jr. and Vernon Burton, eds., *Class, Conflict, and Consensus: Antebellum Southern Community Studies* (Westport, Conn., 1982) and *The Roots of Southern Populism: Yeomen Farmers and the Transformation of the Georgia Upcountry, 1850-1890* (forthcoming, Oxford University Press).

24. C.B. Macpherson, "Capitalism and the Changing Concept of Property," in Eugene Kamenka and R.S. Neale, eds., *Feudalism, Capitalism, and Beyond* (New York, 1975), 112-113; Richard Schlatter, *Private Property: The History of an Idea* (New Brunswick, N.J., 1951), 205-249.

25. Vicksburg and Jackson Railroad Company v. Patton, 31 *Mississippi Reports*, 156.

26. Trescott quoted in Eric Foner, "Reconstruction and the Crisis of Free Labor," in *Politics and Ideology in the Age of the Civil War* (New York, 1980), 98. Also see Darlington County Agricultural Society, Darlington, South Carolina, Minutes, August 29, 1865, South Caroliniana Library.

27. *Southern Cultivator* quoted in Paul S. Taylor, "Slave to Freedman," *Southern Economic History Project*, 7 (Berkeley, 1970), 27. Also see James L. Roark, *Masters Without Slaves: Southern Planters in the Civil War and Reconstruction* (New York, 1977), 157-169.

28. Whitelaw Reid, *After the War: A Southern Tour* (New York, 1866), 564-565; John Eaton, *Grant, Lincoln, and the Freedmen: Reminiscences of the Civil War* (New York, 1907), 163-164; John Moore to Lt. Merritt Barber, Lauderdale, Mississippi, February 29, 1868,

Bureau of Refugees, Freedmen, and Abandoned Lands, Records of the Assistant Commissioner, Mississippi, Record Group 105, National Archives. Also see Leon F. Litwack, *Been in the Storm So Long: The Aftermath of Slavery* (New York, 1979), 292-335.

29. W.R. Brock, *An American Crisis: Congress and Reconstruction, 1865-1867* (New York, 1966), 284-304; Foner, "Thaddeus Stevens," 154-183; Gottlieb, "The Land Question," 356-388.

30. Vernon Burton, "Race and Reconstruction: Edgefield County, South Carolina," in Edward Magdol and Jon L. Wakelyn, eds., *The Southern Common People; Studies in Nineteenth Century Social History* (Westport, Conn., 1980), 216-217; Robert A. Gilmour, "The Other Emancipation: Studies in the Society and Economy of Alabama Whites During Reconstruction" (Ph.D. diss., Johns Hopkins University, 1972), 119-120. On the post-emancipation Caribbean see Green, *British Slave Emancipation*, 99-228; Phillip D. Curtin, *Two Jamaicas: The Role of Ideas in a Tropical Colony, 1830-1865* (New York, 1970), 106-112; Woodward, "The Price of Freedom," 105-106; Stanley L. Engerman, "Economic Aspects of the Adjustments to Emancipation in the United States and the British West Indies (Unpublished paper courtesy of the author).

31. Richmond *Times* quoted in *Southern Cultivator*, 24 (February, 1866), 29; Clark County *Journal* quoted in Gilmour, "The Other Emancipation," 119-120; U.S. Department of Agriculture, *Report of the Commissioner of Agriculture for the Year 1867* (Washington, D.C., 1867), 421. Also see Rose, *Rehearsal for Reconstruction*, 79-84; Lawrence Powell, *New Masters: Northern Planters During the Civil War and Reconstruction* (New Haven, 1980), 73-122; Foner, "Reconstruction and the Crisis of Free Labor," 106-112.

32. Theodore B. Wilson, *The Black Codes of the South* (University, Ala., 1965).

33. *The Countryman* quoted in *Southern Cultivator*, 24 (April, 1866), 86; Albert Voorhies, *Revised Laws of Louisiana* (New Orleans, 1884), 136-137; Athens *Southern Watchman*, April 18, 1866. Violations of the trespass laws brought fines ranging between $100 and $200 or jail terms of between one and two months.

34. Hinds County (Miss.) *Gazette*, May 10, 1867; *Rural Carolinian*, 2 (April, 1871), 381-382; *Rural Carolinian*, 2, (May, 1871) 516-519; *Southern Cultivator* 25 (June, 1867) 172; *Southern Cultivator* 25 (September, 1867), n.p.; Memphis *Southern Home and Farm*, 3 (December, 1871), 52-53; *Acts and Resolutions of the General Assembly of the State of Georgia, 1873* (Atlanta, 1873), 235.

35. Beech Island Farmers' Club, Minutes, June 1875, June 6, 1876, 221-239; *The Countryman* quoted in *Southern Cultivator*, 24 (April, 1866), 86.

36. *Rural Carolinian*, 2 (May, 1871), 516-519; Beech Island Farmers' Club, Minutes, April 2, 1881, 318-320; *The Plantation*, 2 (December 27, 1871), 755; Memphis *Southern Home and Farm*, 3 (January, 1872), 90-91.

37. *Rural Carolinian*, 2 (June, 1871), 593-594. Also see *Southern Cultivator*, 31 (May, 1873), 164.

38. *Laws of. . . the State of Mississippi, 1865-1866* (Jackson, Miss., 1866), 199-200, 289-290; *Acts of. . . the State of Virginia, 1865-1866* (Richmond, 1866), 202-204; *Acts of. . . the State of Alabama, 1866-1867* (Montgomery, Ala., 1867), 586-587; *1868*, 473-474, 557-560. In 1866 Mississippi extended provisions for adopting the stock law to seven additional Plantation Belt counties, and in early 1867 increased the fine for violating restrictions on hunting. See *Mississippi Laws, 1866*, 141-142; *1867*, 271.

39. Studies have shown that a majority of whites in many counties of the antebellum Plantation Belt owned slaves. Participation in the cotton economy and, perhaps, the hope of one day becoming a slaveholder brought others within the plantation orbit. But relations between rich and poor could have explosive qualities and even within such counties there existed relatively isolated enclaves of slaveless whites who seem to have forged a culture of their own. See Eugene D. Genovese, "Yeomen Farmers in a Slaveholders' Democracy," *Agricultural History*, 49 (April, 1975), 331-342; Hilliard, *Hogmeat and Hoecake*, 151; James D. Foust, *The Yeomen Farmer and the Westward Expansion of United States Cotton Production* (New York, 1975); Wright, *Political Economy of Cotton South*, 55-56.

40. *Southern Cultivator*, 30 (May, 1872), 176; *Southern Cultivator*, 28 (July, 1870), 203; *Southern Cultivator*, 27 (September, 1869), 274.

41. Eugene D. Genovese, *Roll, Jordan, Roll: The World the Slaves Made* (New York, 1974),

486–490; Wood, *Black Majority*, 28–83, 122–123, 127; Guion Griffis Johnson, *Antebellum North Carolina: A Social History* (Chapel Hill, 1937), 555–556.

42. Edward King, *The Great South: A Record of Journeys* (Hartford, Conn., 1875), 274, 371; George P. Rawick, ed., *The American Slave: A Composite Autobiography* (19 vols; Westport, Conn., 1972), *Arkansas Narratives*, X, Part 5, 105; Litwack, *Been in the Storm So Long*, 393. Also see Thomas Holt, *Black Over White: Negro Political Leadership in South Carolina During Reconstruction* (Urbana, Ill., 1977), 190–191. I am greatly indebted to Professor Leslie Rowland, presently at the University of Virginia, for sharing her pioneering research on Emancipation in the coastal rice areas with me, for it promises to recast the way we think about the Afro-American experience before and after slavery. Rowland has found that, despite legal restrictions, many of the slaves accumulated personal property (livestock, furnishings, tools, and even carriages) and established a system of inheritance which the planters formally sanctioned. Furthermore, the slaves seem to have dominated local marketing networks by selling some of the produce from their garden plots, thereby obtaining cash much in the way their Jamaican counterparts did. Rowland makes no claim that this marketing system had much importance beyond the coast and, indeed, attributes its vitality to the task system associated with rice production. But my own work with postbellum tax records in Georgia suggests that slave property ownership, including livestock, may have been more widespread. Rowland's preliminary findings are presented in "Rice and Freedom: Emancipation in the Georgia and South Carolina Lowcountry" (Paper presented at the Annual Meeting of the American Historical Association, Washington, D.C., December 1980). I should also like to thank Professor Vernon Burton, of the University of Illinois, for drawing my attention to relevant material in the W.P.A. exslave narratives.

43. See, for example, *Alabama Acts, 1870*, 93–94, 96–97; *Mississippi Laws, 1873*, 200. Also see Holt, *Black Over White*, 9–40, 95–151.

44. Foner, "Reconstruction and the Crisis of Free Labor," 115–117; *Southern Cultivator*, 24 (April, 1866), 86; Georgia Department of Agriculture, *Annual Report of Thomas P. Janes, Commissioner of Agriculture of the State of Georgia for the Year 1875* (Atlanta, 1876), 66. Also see Burton, "Race and Reconstruction," 219–222.

45. Joe Gray Taylor, *Louisiana Reconstructed, 1863–1877* (Baton Rouge, 1974), 253–313, 480–505; Holt, *Black Over White*, 173–207; William C. Harris, *The Day of the Carpetbagger: Republican Reconstruction in Mississippi* (Baton Rouge, 1979), 623–690.

46. *Georgia Acts and Resolutions, 1872*, 469; *1875*, 296–303; *1876*, part II, title IV; *1877*, part II, title II; *1878–1879*, part III, title V; *Alabama Acts, 1870*, 96–97; *1871*; 171; *1876–1877*, 136, 226; *Acts and Resolutions of . . . the State of South Carolina, 1871* (Columbia, S.C., 1871), 660; *1879*, 84; *General Statutes of South Carolina* (Columbia, S.C., 1882), 491–498; *Acts of the State of Tennessee . . . 1869–1870* (2 vols; Nashville, 1870), 2, 68–69, 152, 159; *1871*, 3; *1873*, 121; *1875*, 19, 214–215; *1877*, 39; *1879*, 241–242; W.A. Milliken and John V. Vertress, *The Code of Tennessee* (Nashville, 1884), 385–388; George W. Munford, *The Code of Virginia* (Richmond, 1873), 805; *Mississippi Laws, 1876*, 49–51; *Acts of the . . . State of Louisiana, Extra Session, 1877* (New Orleans, 1877), 100–101; *1880*, 64–65; *Acts, Resolutions, and Memorials . . . of the State of Arkansas, 1875* (Little Rock, 1875), 158–159; *1879*, 60–61.

47. *Georgia Acts and Resolutions, 1875*, 296–303.

48. *Alabama Acts, 1876–1877*, 136, 226.

49. *The Plantation*, 2 (June 17, 1871), 323–324; *Southern Cultivator*, 28 (May, 1870), 137; *Southern Planter and Farmer* quoted in *Southern Cultivator*, 30 (May, 1872), 172; Edgefield (S.C.) *Advertiser* quoted in *Southern Cultivator*, 35 (August, 1877), 300; Darlington County Agricultural Society, Minutes, August 14, 1877, 41; Patrons of Husbandry, State Grange of South Carolina, Minutes, January 15, 1873, South Caroliniana; *Proceedings of the State Grange of the Patrons of Husbandry of Alabama, 1874* (Montgomery, 1875), 25; Memorial of the State Grange, Atlanta, February 4, 1874, Legislative Department, Petitions, Record Group 37/Series 12, Georgia Department of Archives and History; Carroll County (Ga.) *Times*, January 10, 1873.

50. *Georgia Acts and Resolutions, 1872*, 34–35; *Laws and Resolutions of the State of North Carolina, 1872–1873* (Raleigh, 1873), 314–316; *South Carolina Acts and Resolutions, 1877*, 251–254.

51. Atlanta *Constitution*, November 11, 1883; *Alabama Acts, 1880-1881,* 163-165, 175-177, 223, 260-263; *North Carolina Laws and Resolutions, 1874-1875,* 70-77, 267-269; *1879,* 252; *Mississippi Laws, 1871,* 693-696; *1876,* 294-298; *1878,* 305-310; *1880,* 376-380; *South Carolina Acts and Resolutions, 1878,* 361-362, 484-485, 689-691, 733; *1879,* 41-42, 100-101, 243-244, 247-248; *1880,* 323-236, 401-404, 473-474; Spartanburg (S.C.) *Carolina Spartan,* February 17, 1875; Anderson (S.C.) *Intelligencer,* August 23, 1877; Yorkville (S.C.) *Enquirer,* December 18, 1879. I am grateful to Lacy Ford of the University of South Carolina for sharing some of his research on the South Carolina Upcountry with me.

52. Harrell v. Hannum and Coleman, 56 *Georgia Reports,* 508; Anderson v. Locke (Miss.), 1 *Southern Reporter,* 251; Spigener v. Rives (Ala.), 16 *Southern Reporter,* 74; Rose v. Hardie (N.C.), 4 *Southeastern Reporter,* 41; Utsey v. Hiott (S.C.), 9 *Southeastern Reporter,* 338.

53. Charlotte *Democrat* quoted in *Southern Cultivator,* 34, (May, 1876), 178-179; Atlanta *Constitution,* November 11, 1883; Beech Island Farmers' Club, Minutes, January 7, 1882; New York *Times,* January 2, 1882; William Watts Ball, *The State That Forgot: South Carolina's Surrender to Democracy* (Indianapolis, 1932), 175; David D. Wallace, *History of South Carolina* (3 vols; New York, 1935), 3, 328.

54. *Southern Cultivator,* 34 (May, 1876), 178-179; Atlanta *Constitution,* November 11, 1883; *South Carolina Acts and Resolutions, 1881,* 591-594.

55. Grady quoted in Jonathan M. Wiener, "Class Structure and Economic Development in the American South, 1865-1955," *American Historical Review,* 84 (October, 1979), 986.

56. Foner, "Reconstruction and the Crisis of Free Labor," 103; Roger Ransom and Richard Sutch, *One Kind of Freedom: The Economic Consequences of Emancipation* (Cambridge, 1977), 56-78, 81-87; Michael Wayne, *Antebellum Planters in the Postwar South: The Natchez District, 1860-1880* (Baton Rouge, forthcoming); Roark, *Masters Without Slaves,* 120-131.

57. Woodman, "Post-Civil War Southern Agriculture and the Law," 319-337. The so-called "homestead exemption," which prevailed until the 1870s, secured varying amounts of real and personal property from attachment. Post-Reconstruction reforms whittled the homestead's coverage and gave debtors the option to waive its protection entirely.

58. Eugene D. Genovese, *The World the Slaveholders Made: Two Essays in Interpretation* (New York, 1969), 156-234; William S. Jenkins, *Pro-Slavery Thought in the Old South* (Gloucester, Mass., 1960), 285-295; C. Vann Woodward, "A Southern War Against Capitalism," in *American Counterpoint: Slavery and Race in the North-South Dialogue* (Boston, 1971), 107-139.

59. J.D.B. DeBow, *The Interest in Slavery of the Southern Non-Slaveholder* (Charleston, 1860); Milledgeville (Ga.) *Federal Union,* December 11, 1860; J. Mills Thornton III, *Politics and Power in a Slave Society: Alabama, 1800-1860* (Baton Rouge, 1978), 58-59, 273-274. On "Herrenvolk democracy" see George M. Fredrickson, *The Black Image in the White Mind: The Debate on Afro-American Character and Destiny, 1817-1914* (New York, 1971), 30-60.

60. Jefferson (Ga.) *Forest News,* April 23, 1880; *Southern Cultivator,* 24 (April, 1866), 86; *Proceedings of the Second Annual Session of the Alabama Agricultural Society, 1885* (Montgomery, Ala., 1885), 18-22.

61. *Carroll County Times,* February 2, 1872; Roger W. Shugg, *Origins of Class Struggle in Louisiana: A Social History of White Farmers and Laborers During Slavery and After, 1840-1875* (Baton Rouge, 1939), 269-272; Robert P. Brooks, *The Agrarian Revolution in Georgia, 1865-1914* (Madison, Wis., 1914); Ransom and Sutch, *One Kind of Freedom,* 104-105; Wright, *Political Economy of Cotton South,* 164-184; Engerman, "Economic Aspects of the Adjustment to Emancipation," 19.

62. Columbus (Ga.) *Sun* quoted in *Carroll County Times,* October 10, 1873.

63. Testimony of H.J. McCormick in Robert P. Brooks, *Inquiries Concerning Georgia Farms,* I, University of Georgia Archives.; Jonathan M. Wiener, *Social Origins of the New South: Alabama, 1860-1885* (Baton Rouge, 1978), 77-102; Michael Schwartz, *Radical Protest and Social Structure: The Southern Farmers' Alliance and Cotton Tenancy, 1880-1890* (New York, 1976), 62; Woodward, *Origins of the New South,* 180-184; Woodman, "Post-Civil War Southern Agriculture and the Law," 327-332.

64. Harold D. Woodman, *King Cotton and His Retainers: Financing and Marketing the*

Cotton Crop of the South, 1800-1925 (Lexington, Ky., 1968), 295-314; Ransom and Sutch, *One Kind of Freedom*, 106-148; Woodward, *Origins of the New South*, 180-181.
65. For a more detailed discussion see Hahn, *Roots of Southern Populism*.
66. King, "Closing of the Southern Range," 63-70; *Alabama Acts, 1882-1883*, 538-609; *Mississippi Laws 1884*, 366-372; *1888*, 199; Yorkville *Enquirer*, December 18, 1879; Spartanburg *Carolina Spartan*, November 26, 1879. Forthcoming dissertations on the South Carolina and Alabama Upcountries by Lacy Ford and Michael Hyman will be important contributions in this regard.
67. Cherokee (County) *Advance*, April 21, 1880; Carroll County *Times*, September 1, 1882; Jefferson *Forest News*, April 23, 1880; Jackson (County) *Herald*, March 20, 1885; Cottage Home Farm Journal, Floyd County, January 14, 1878, John H. Dent Papers, Georgia Department of Archives and History.
68. Jackson *Herald*, May 27, 1881, April 3, 1885; Carroll (County) *Free Press*, May 8, 1885; Carroll County *Times*, January 6, 1882; Gwinnett (County) *Herald*, August 30, 1882.
69. Carroll County *Times*, January 11, 1882; Jackson *Herald*, July 8, 1881; Cartersville (Bartow County) *Express*, July 15, 1880; Gwinnett *Herald*, July 14, 1885; Carroll County Tax Digests, 1880, 1890; Jackson County Tax Digests, 1880, 1890, Georgia Department of Archives and History. Thus, when Carroll county voters went to the polls in 1882, they defeated the stock law by 1616 to 620. Yet two districts turned majorities in its favor: the Tenth district where the largest town of Carrollton was located and the Second district which contained the town of Villa Rica. Over half the county-wide votes came from these two districts alone. All the town and village districts together provided the stock law with 80 percent of its votes. The eight remaining rural districts collectively defeated the statute by a margin of over 6:1, with some delivering over 90 percent of their votes to the retention of common grazing rights. Although race and land tenure bore less direct relationship to voting alignments, strong anti-stock law districts had fewer large landowners (500 or more acres) and these large landowners controlled a smaller share of the total acreage than was true in districts more favorably inclined to the stock law.
70. Gwinnett *Herald*, September 20, 1882, June 29, 1885, October 18, 1882; Carroll *Free Press*, June 19, 1885, June 26, 1885, May 15, 1885; Jackson *Herald*, June 17, 1881, August 3, 1883; Cartersville *Express*, June 21, 1880; Carroll County *Times*, May 17, 1878, September 8, 1882, August 25, 1882; Cherokee *Advance*, July 1, 1882.
71. Carroll *Free Press*, May 8, 1885, June 5, 1885, June 25, 1885.
72. Jefferson *Forest News*, January 14, 1881; Carroll *Free Press*, n.d.
73. *Cottage Home Farm Journal*, Floyd County, January 14, 1878, December 15, 1881, October 24, 1883, November 17, 1886, Dent Papers; Georgia Department of Agriculture, *Report of Thomas P. Janes*, 66; Jackson *Herald*, April 3, 1885, June 24, 1885; Carroll County *Times*, May 3, 1878, June 7, 1878.
74. Carroll County *Times*, September 23, 1881, October 7, 1881; Carroll *Free Press*, June 19, 1885, April 8, 1887, April 15, 1887; Gwinnett *Herald*, January 3, 1891; Jefferson *Forest News*, November 19, 1880; Jackson *Herald*, September 2, 1887.
75. Gwinnett *Herald*, July 14, 1885, July 7, 1891; Jackson *Herald*, July 8, 1881, September 14, 1883; Carroll *Free Press*, July 3, 1885, July 8, 1887, June 4, 1890; Carroll County *Times*, September 9, 1882; Cottage Home Farm Journal, Floyd County, December 15, 1881, October 24, 1883, Dent Papers.
76. Carroll *Free Press*, July 4, 1884, March 26, 1886, September 23, 1887, March 1, 1889, July 4, 1890; Jackson *Herald*, March 27, 1885, July 1, 1887, November 11, 1887; Gwinnett *Herald*, October 17, 1883, October 14, 1884, September 27, 1887, August 29, 1890, July 7, 1891; Cherokee *Advance*, April 16, 1886, November 4, 1887, August 9, 1890, August 26, 1887.
77. *Publications of the Georgia Department of Agriculture*, XV (1889), 117-123; Carroll *Free Press*, July 12, 1889, March 26, 1886, February 3, 1888, March 14, 1890; King, "Closing of the Southern Range," 60-61
78. Very important forthcoming studies on Maryland by Barbara Fields; Kentucky by Leslie Rowland; Georgia by Joseph Reidy; and South Carolina by Lacy Ford and Scott Strickland will, I think, bear this out. Also see Armstead L. Robinson, "Beyond the Realm of Consensus: New Meanings of Reconstruction for American History," *Journal of American*

History, 68 (September, 1981), 276-297.

79. Woodward, *Origins of the New South*, 321-395 and passim; John G. Sproat, *"The Best Men"–Liberal Reformers in the Gilded Age* (New York, 1968).

80. Leon Fink, *Workingmen's Democracy: The Knights of Labor in American Politics* (Urbana, Ill., forthcoming); David Montgomery, *Beyond Equality: Labor and the Radical Republicans, 1862-1872* (New York, 1967), 340-447; Lawrence Goodwyn, *Democratic Promise: The Populist Moment in America* (New York, 1976).

81. Carroll *Free Press*, May 15, 1885; Robert R. Madden, "Freedom Hills," *Alabama Historical Review* (1965), 196; Marie B. Owen, *Alabama: A Social and Economic History* (Montgomery, Ala., 1938), 102; King, "Closing of the Southern Range,"; Hahn, *Roots of Southern Populism*, chap. VII.

[9]

"Southern Violence" Reconsidered: Arson as Protest in Black-Belt Georgia, 1865–1910

By Albert C. Smith

MOST SCHOLARS AGREE THAT EXCESSIVE VIOLENCE HAS CHARAC-terized crime in the American South, a region once described as "that part of the United States lying below the Smith and Wesson line."[1] Indeed, a number of studies confirm the theory that, compared to the non-South, the South has high rates of homicide and assault and moderate, or even low, rates of crime against property.[2] To date, the most influential authors, practically all of whom have examined only traditional crimes of violence such as homicide and assault, have agreed that cultural influences best explain the distinctly regional propen-

---

[1] H. C. Brearley, "The Pattern of Violence," in *Culture in the South*, edited by W. T. Couch (Chapel Hill, 1935), 678. The following represent a sample of works that reflect the theme of violence in southern history: Horace V. Redfield, *Homicide, North and South: Being a Comparative View of Crime Against the Person in Several Parts of the United States* (Philadelphia, 1880); Clement Eaton, "Mob Violence in the Old South," *Mississippi Valley Historical Review*, XXIX (December 1942), 351–70; John Hope Franklin, *The Militant South, 1800–1861* (Cambridge, Mass., 1956); John Richard Alden, *The South in the Revolution, 1763–1789* (Baton Rouge, 1957); Wilbur J. Cash, *The Mind of the South* (New York, 1960); Clement Eaton, *The Growth of Southern Civilization, 1790–1860* (New York, 1963); Frank E. Vandiver, "The Southerner as Extremist," in *The Idea of the South: Pursuit of a Central Theme*, edited by Frank E. Vandiver (Chicago, 1964), 43–55; David Bertelson, *The Lazy South* (New York, 1967); John Shelton Reed, *The Enduring South: Subcultural Persistence in Mass Society* (Lexington, Mass., 1972), especially Chapter 5; Bertram Wyatt-Brown, *Southern Honor: Ethics and Behavior in the Old South* (New York, 1982).

[2] "Explaining our Homicide Record," *Literary Digest*, XLV (October 19, 1912), 665; H. C. Brearley, *Homicide in the United States* (Chapel Hill, 1932), 19–22; Stuart Lottier, "Distribution of Criminal Offenses in Sectional Regions," *Journal of Criminal Law and Criminology*, XXIX (September-October 1938), 329–44; Austin L. Porterfield, "A Decade of Serious Crimes in the United States: Some Trends and Hypotheses," *American Sociological Review*, XIII (February 1948), 44–54; Porterfield, "Indices of Suicide and Homicide by States and Cities: Some Southern–non-southern Contrasts with Implications for Research," *ibid.*, XIV (August 1949), 481–90; Lyle W. Shannon, "The Spatial Distribution of Criminal Offenses by States," *Journal of Criminal Law and Criminology*, XLV (September-October 1954), 264–73; Marvin E. Wolfgang, *Patterns in Criminal Homicide* (Philadelphia, 1958), 31–56; William D. Miller, "Myth and New South City Murder Rates," *Mississippi Quarterly*, XXXVI (Spring 1973), 143–53.

The late MR. SMITH received his Ph.D. from the University of Georgia in 1982.

THE JOURNAL OF SOUTHERN HISTORY
Vol. LI, No. 4, November 1985

sity for aggression. Enduring frontier conditions, a persistent tradition of honor, and, especially for white southerners, an acute sense of grievance prompted by intense psychological reactions to the region's unparalleled history of defeat, occupation, and national ostracism are the most frequently mentioned causes of violent crime.[3]

This study, in examining arson in Black-Belt Georgia, argues for a reconsideration of assumptions concerning southern violence and its relationship to culture.[4] The evidence presented here indicates that arson, although a nontraditional form of violence, fitted into overall patterns of violent crime on the community level during the Reconstruction and New South eras. Moreover, the research suggests that property crime resulted in large part from cultural influences typical of the American South during much of its history. In fact, arson was violent, interracial protest, a form of revenge for the racism and poverty that defined the region's race relations.

Since one of the unique characteristics of most southern states has been the presence of a large, geographically compact black population, the specific focus here is the Black-Belt region of Georgia. In that part of Georgia, as in other areas of the Black-Belt South, the majority of the state's nonwhite population lived in rural, agricultural communities that were at least 50 percent black. Two counties were chosen from the area illustrated in Figure 1: Baldwin, in the lower Piedmont section of central Georgia; and Terrell, located in the southwest plains region of the state.[5] The years selected for analysis are 1865 to 1910. Throughout these decades of Reconstruction and

[3] For the most important works that utilize the cultural thesis, see Brearley, *Homicide*, 51–56, and "The Pattern of Violence," 678–92; Cash, *The Mind of the South*, 32–34, 42–44, 115–25; Raymond D. Gastil, "Homicide and a Regional Culture of Violence," *American Sociological Review*, XXXVI (June 1971), 412–27; Reed, *The Enduring South*, Chapter 5; Wyatt-Brown, *Southern Honor*; and, most significantly, Sheldon Hackney, "Southern Violence," in *The History of Violence in America: Historical and Comparative Perspectives*, edited by Hugh Davis Graham and Ted Robert Gurr (New York, 1969), 505–27.

[4] Arson is broadly defined here as the burning of the property of another in the night or day. "Property" includes, among other things, a house, crib, smokehouse, outhouse (*i.e.*, a kitchen built separately from a home), building, business, or privately owned woods. See *The Code of the State of Georgia*, Sec. 4272-4281 (1861); Sec. 4375-4385 (1873); Sec. 135-146 (1896).

[5] From 1880 to 1910 the percentage of blacks decreased each decade from 67 percent to 60 percent of Baldwin County's total population, while in Terrell, the black percentage of total population over the same period increased each decade from 59 percent to just over 75 percent. Statewide, during these decades, blacks consistently averaged 46 percent of Georgia's population, and as late as 1910 the overwhelming majority (81 percent) lived in rural areas. In the southern region proper, South Carolina and Mississippi were the only states where blacks were a majority of the total population during the half-century following the Civil War. By 1910, 79 percent of all southern blacks still lived in rural areas. In Georgia, the Black Belt contained 75 percent of that state's black population in 1880 and 63 percent by 1910. Geographically, the region constituted 47 percent of the entire area of the state. Source: *Negro Population in the United States, 1790-1915* (Washington, 1918), 36, 48–51, 90–96, and 125–27, 134, 778, 780.

FIGURE 1
BLACK-BELT GEORGIA, 1910

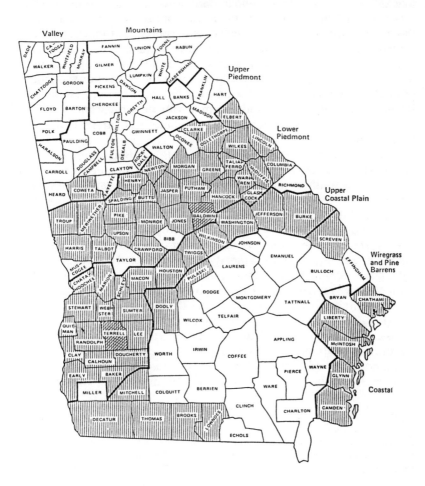

the New South, the entire region was greatly concerned with defining the political, social, and economic relationships between whites and blacks,[6] an essential and obvious part of which was the impact of race, or skin-color.[7] Another crucial part of postwar race relations, though, was economic, specifically the property relations and widespread poverty that evolved from institutional changes in the antebellum labor system, such as the development of sharecropping and farm tenancy.[8] These property relations and the status derived from property ownership ultimately defined political power and social influence. Therefore, this study examines the importance of race and class, defined here as economic status, in patterns of arson in Black-Belt Georgia.[9]

An examination of counties in Georgia's Black-Belt region reveals the relationships among race, class, and violent property crime in one area of a southern state that exhibits many of the salient cultural features of the larger Black-Belt South. Historically the most "southern" part of the American South, the Black Belt served as the center of the region's cotton culture and its sharecropping and farm tenancy labor system. As the area with the largest concentration of blacks, the Black Belt and its white minority consistently led the South in the fight over secession, redemption, disfranchisement, and Jim Crow laws. A brief review of postwar Baldwin and Terrell counties indicates the importance of developments in the Black Belt to the historiography of the larger southern region.

Like much of the Black-Belt South in the Reconstruction and New South eras, Baldwin and Terrell counties were essentially rural, plantation societies of extensive farm lands and small crossroads villages.[10] Economic activity in these communities centered on

---

[6] The following represent a few of the works which deal with this theme: George Brown Tindall, *South Carolina Negroes, 1877–1900* (Columbia, S. C., 1952); Vernon Lane Wharton, *The Negro in Mississippi, 1865–1890* (New York, 1965); Joel Williamson, *After Slavery: The Negro in South Carolina During Reconstruction, 1861–1877* (Chapel Hill, 1965); C. Vann Woodward, *Origins of the New South, 1877–1913* (Baton Rouge, 1951); Woodward, *The Strange Career of Jim Crow*, 2d rev. ed. (New York, 1966); Howard N. Rabinowitz, *Race Relations in the Urban South, 1865–1890* (New York, 1978).

[7] For a discussion of the idea of race as a social reality, see Raymond W. Mack, *Race, Class, and Power* (New York, 1963), 91–94.

[8] For discussion of this theme, see Jay R. Mandle, "The Plantation Economy: An Essay in Definition," *Science and Society*, XXXVI (Spring 1972), 49–62, and *The Roots of Black Poverty: The Southern Plantation Economy After the Civil War* (Durham, N. C., 1978); Robert Higgs, *Competition and Coercion: Blacks in the American Economy, 1865–1914* (Cambridge, Eng., and other cities, 1977); Roger L. Ransom and Richard Sutch, *One Kind of Freedom: The Economic Consequences of Emancipation* (Cambridge, Eng., and New York, 1977); Harold D. Woodman, "Sequel to Slavery: The New History Views the Postbellum South," *Journal of Southern History*, XLIII (November 1977), 523–54; and Woodward, *Origins of the New South, passim*.

[9] See Mack, *Race, Class, and Power*; H. Edward Ransford, *Race and Class in American Society: Black, Chicano, Anglo* (Cambridge, Mass., 1977), Chapters 1–2.

[10] Terrell grew from 6,232 inhabitants in 1860 to 22,003 by 1910. Baldwin claimed a popu-

staple-crop agriculture, and the underpinning of that agrarian economy was cotton. In 1881, 45 percent of Baldwin County's tilled acreage was planted in cotton, and for Terrell the percentage was 43. By 1910 more than half of the tilled acreage in Terrell was planted in cotton. While in Baldwin the percentage dropped to 38, the number of tilled acres planted in cotton increased 25 percent from 1890 until 1910.[11]

An economic system based on staple-crop agriculture and the primacy of land ownership caused poverty and dependency for most blacks. An analysis of property ownership and occupational structure in these two counties shows that opportunities for the black majority were very restricted. In 1870 blacks owned less than 1 percent of all privately owned lands in Baldwin and Terrell. By 1910 whites owned more than 90 percent of all real estate there, even though blacks constituted 60 percent of the population in Baldwin and 75 percent in Terrell.[12] Propertyless and without an economic base, blacks consequently had very limited options for employment, which helps to explain why the overwhelming majority (95 percent) worked as unskilled laborers, domestic servants, or landless farm workers.[13] Without real property, all that blacks had to "sell" in this

---

lation of 9,078 at the beginning of the period, and 18,354 by the second decade of the twentieth century. Although population density steadily increased in both counties, most inhabitants lived in farming precincts outside the town districts of Milledgeville and Dawson, the county seats and the only population centers of any size in Baldwin and Terrell, respectively. During the postwar decades, the population of Milledgeville consistently averaged no more than 24 percent of the entire county population. By 1910, the town of Dawson claimed 17 percent of Terrell's populace. *Negro Population*, 131; U. S. Census Office, *Population of the United States in 1860 . . .* (Washington, 1864), 72, 73, 74; *Thirteenth Census of the United States . . . 1910.* Vol. I: *Population* (Washington, 1913), 88, 105, 106. For a more detailed analysis of socioeconomic and political developments in Baldwin and Terrell during the Reconstruction and New South decades, see Albert Colbey Smith, "Down Freedom's Road: The Contours of Race, Class, and Property Crime in Black-Belt Georgia, 1866–1910," (unpublished Ph.D. dissertation, University of Georgia, 1982), Chapter 3; James C. Bonner, *Milledgeville: Georgia's Antebellum Capitol* (Athens, Ga., 1978), Chapters 10–11; Ella Christie Melton and Augusta Griggs Raines, *History of Terrell County, Georgia* (Roswell, Ga., 1980).

[11] U. S. Census Office, *Report on Cotton Production in the United States*, Part 2 (Washington, 1884), 270–72; *Report on the Statistics of Agriculture in the United States* (Washington, 1895), 393–94; *. . . Twelfth Census of the United States.* Vol. VI: *Crops and Irrigation* (Washington, 1902), 431; *Negro Population*, 678–81.

[12] From 1871 to 1909 whites owned an average of 94 percent of *all* valued property in Baldwin, both real and personal. Terrell whites owned slightly more: 95.3 percent. Annual Tax Digests, Baldwin and Terrell Counties, 1870–1910 (Georgia Department of Archives and History, Atlanta; hereinafter cited as GDAH); *Negro Population*, 131, 134. See also Robert P. Brooks, *The Agrarian Revolution in Georgia, 1865–1912* (Madison, Wisc., 1914), 44 and 87; Enoch M. Banks, *The Economics of Land Tenure in Georgia* (New York, 1905), 119–22 and 141. The low percentage of black landowners in consistent with the pattern for Georgia; generally, Georgia lagged behind all other southern states in the extent of black land ownership at the turn of the century. *Twelfth Census of the United States, Agriculture*, Part I (Washington, 1902), 40–53 and 69–71.

[13] Manuscript Census Returns, Twelfth Census of the United States, 1900, Baldwin and Terrell Counties (University of Georgia Microfilm Library, Athens, Ga.). In 1900 fewer than

agricultural economy was their labor.[14]

The concentration of wealth and property in the hands of the white minority caused the blacks to be economically dependent upon the whites; in turn, an ideology of white supremacy complemented and reinforced that dependency. In both counties *de facto* segregation of the races emerged before the end of the nineteenth century. Not surprisingly, Milledgeville's Opera House — the site of Baldwin County's court proceedings, popular entertainment, and political rallies — contained separate balcony seating for blacks. The impact of racial separation in Baldwin County extended far beyond public accommodations and included everyday social situations. For instance, when T. F. Newell's "black mammy" died in 1886, the "Captain" conducted funeral services in his parlor — "white friends in one room, colored in another." At J. M. D. Webb's annual barbecue outside of Milledgeville in 1879, "dinner for the whites being over, the colored people occupied their places and feasted."[15] Although Dawson, the county seat of Terrell, developed later than Milledgeville, Georgia's antebellum capital, segregated public facilities were commonplace in Dawson well before the end of the century. In addition to racially separate schools and cemeteries, blacks were required to sit in the gallery at political rallies in the courthouse. Social interaction between blacks and whites likewise reflected the nuances of racial segregation. On occasion, blacks used a popular Dawson "swimming hole," but only when whites were not present. In the spring of 1890 a Dawson merchant built "separate departments for . . . white and col-

---

4 percent of the blacks in either county's work force held skilled or professional jobs. Smith, "Down Freedom's Road," 93. See Lorenzo J. Greene and Carter G. Woodson, *The Negro Wage Earner* (New York, 1969), 41 and 338 for nationwide trends that parallel the concentration of blacks in agricultural and/or unskilled jobs locally. See also Mandle, *Roots of Black Poverty*, 59; Gavin Wright, *The Political Economy of the Cotton South: Households, Markets, and Wealth in the Nineteenth Century* (New York, 1978), 160–64.

[14] For a thorough discussion of the idea of a laborer's "value," see Ransom and Sutch, *One Kind of Freedom*, 2–4; Wright, *Political Economy of the Cotton South*, 176–79. When discussing the relative lack of black property ownership, it is important to note that, even when blacks acquired enough money to purchase land, some whites opposed the sale of property to them. See Claude F. Oubre, *Forty Acres and a Mule: The Freedmen's Bureau and Black Land Ownership* (Baton Rouge, 1978), 195–98.

[15] Milledgeville *Union and Recorder*, December 5, 1882; January 23, 1883; February 23, 1886; August 12, 1879 (second quotation); Milledgeville *Union Recorder*, October 12, 1886 (first quotation). Other examples of *de facto* segregation in postwar Baldwin include teachers' institutes that were housed in racially separate facilities: see Milledgeville *Union and Recorder*, August 15, 1882; Milledgeville *Union Recorder*, July 9, 1889; August 19, 1890; August 4, 1891; February 23, March 29, June 14, 1892; February 21, 1893. During an 1886 Prohibition election, women's auxiliaries sponsored "lunches" for voters in separate rooms, one for whites and the other for blacks — "the latter having good colored women to wait on those of their race." Milledgeville *Union and Recorder*, March 23, 1886. The first instance of *de jure* segregation occurred in 1902, when the Milledgeville City Council enacted ordinances providing for "separate counters" with "partitions" to eliminate the "close personal contact" between blacks and whites in saloons. See City of Milledgeville, City Council Ordinances, June 9, 1902 (GDAH, Microfilm Collections).

ored" in his ice-cream parlor. When one of Terrell's black churches held its annual camp meeting beside the Kinchafoonee River in 1882, the congregation "reserved" seats "for all whites who wish to attend."[16]

Blacks in neither county achieved political influence comparable with their numerical superiority, although Baldwin blacks enjoyed temporary success in Reconstruction when they elected a state representative.[17] In both counties Ku Klux Klan terrorism and economic coercion quickly undermined the postemancipation political efforts of blacks. Terrell blacks accounted for a majority of the registered voters in the first postwar election—the 1867 constitutional referendum—but conservative, anticonstitution forces carried the county with the support of an aggressive vigilante organization that included a prominent doctor, a judge, and the county sheriff.[18] Democrats won even more impressive victories in 1868, defeating the Republican candidates by better than two-to-one margins, despite a black voter registration majority of 864 to 601. Economic and physical intimidation no doubt contributed to that victory. Newspaper editors urged employers to discharge from employment "all those . . . who are striving by their votes . . . to destroy us . . . ." Following the November presidential balloting, a grand jury report lamented the

[16] Dawson *Weekly Journal*, June 8, 1876; July 24, 1873; August 7, 1879; September 28, 1882 (second quotation); Dawson *News*, December 11, February 20, 1895; September 23, 1896; May 14, 1890 (first quotation). In the large towns of the Black Belt segregated housing patterns reinforced the exclusionary nature of public accommodations. By 1900, 72 percent of all blacks in Dawson lived on black-majority streets; 92 percent of the city's whites lived on white-majority streets. In 1880, 86 percent of Milledgeville's blacks lived on predominately black streets; 71 percent of the town's white population lived on white-majority streets in 1900. Manuscript Census Returns, Tenth and Twelfth Censuses, 1880 and 1900, Baldwin County; Manuscript Census Returns, Twelfth Census, 1900, Terrell County.

[17] Georgia enacted *de jure* disfranchisement in 1908; the best studies of the state's politics during the Reconstruction and New South years are C. Mildred Thompson, *Reconstruction in Georgia: Economic, Social, Political, 1865-1872* (New York, 1915); Alan Conway, *The Reconstruction of Georgia* (Minneapolis, 1966); Elizabeth Studley Nathans, *Losing the Peace: Georgia Republicans and Reconstruction, 1865-1871* (Baton Rouge, 1968); John Dittmer, *Black Georgia in the Progressive Era, 1900-1920* (Urbana, 1977); Edmund L. Drago, *Black Politicians and Reconstruction in Georgia: A Splendid Failure* (Baton Rouge, 1982); Howard N. Rabinowitz, ed., *Southern Black Leaders of the Reconstruction Era* (Urbana, 1982).

[18] Dawson *Journal*, July 26, November 8, 1867. For references to newspaper advertisements by a local gunsmith who sought Klan patronage in Terrell, see Dawson *Weekly Journal*, October 22, December 17, 1868. A list of Klan members is contained in Chapter 14 of the D. A. R.-sponsored *History of Terrell County, Georgia* by Ella Christie Melton and Augusta Griggs Raines. The original, undated manuscript is located in the probate judge's office in the Terrell County Courthouse, Dawson, Georgia; the Kinchafoonee Regional Library, Dawson, Georgia, and the Georgia Department of Archives and History in Atlanta have copies of the manuscript. Generally, historians have discounted the Klan presence in the lower Black Belt. See Allen W. Trelease, *White Terror: The Ku Klux Klan Conspiracy and Southern Reconstruction* (New York, 1971), 74–75, 118, and 242; Thompson, *Reconstruction in Georgia*, 361–94; *Report of the Joint Select Committee to Inquire into the Condition of Affairs in the Late Insurrectionary States* (13 vols., Washington, 1872), House Reports, 42 Cong., 2 Sess., No. 22 (cited hereinafter as *Ku Klux Conspiracy*), Georgia, II, 1121.

"secret murders committed at night in the county . . . ."[19] In subsequent decades the supremacy of the Democratic party went virtually unchallenged by the country's G. O. P.: between 1870 and the enactment of *de jure* disfranchisement in 1908, Republicans fielded only one candidate in local elections.[20]

Several factors prompted a brief period of black political influence in Reconstruction Baldwin. The presence of federal troops and an active Loyal League organization encouraged cohesion within the black population. Blacks in Baldwin organized their own welfare societies; the community also had an active "Axe Company" to assist in fire fighting and a Farmer's Club to help tenants and freeholders.[21] In time, though, economic coercion and vigilante violence destroyed black political solidarity. White employers were urged to "make every freedman show his hand" by joining the Democratic party. "If he refuses," the press declared, "it will be prima facie evidence that he is against us . . . ."[22] In 1871 after months of Klan terrorism in the Black-Belt counties surrounding Baldwin, a mass meeting of the county's blacks voted to emigrate to Liberia. In September 1871 Democrats won a special election that broke "the power of the Union League . . . and scalawags." In 1872 the Republican vote fell to 12 percent of the total, compared to the 64 percent garnered by black representative Peter O'Neal in the 1870 state elections. Thereafter, except for a brief flirtation with Populism during the 1890s, Baldwin's politics, like Terrell's, remained Democratic and influenced primarily by whites, despite continued black voter participation.[23]

In addition to demographic similarities with other counties in the Black-Belt South, Baldwin and Terrell have numerous and well-preserved sources that are necessary for an extended study of crime. Original and chronologically complete Superior Court Records pro-

[19] Dawson *Journal*, April 30, 1868; Milledgeville *Federal Union*, May 5, 1868; Dawson *Journal*, April 16, 1868 (first quotation); Dawson *Weekly Journal*, December 10, 1868 (second quotation). Concerning editorial support for economic coercion against blacks, see *Journal*, November 8, 1867.

[20] Smith, "Down Freedom's Road," 64–66.

[21] Milledgeville *Federal Union*, May 7, 1867; January 7, 1868; August 18, 1868; December 6, 1870; May 17, 1870; June 7, 1870; August 9, 1870; August 9, 1871.

[22] Milledgeville *Federal Union*, May 5, 1868 (first quotation); August 11, 1868 (second quotation); Bonner, *Milledgeville*, 208.

[23] Trelease, *White Terror*, 321–23; *Ku Klux Conspiracy*, Georgia, II, 1036; Milledgeville *Federal Union*, July 26, 1871; September 13, 1871; September 20, 1871 (quotation); September 27, 1871; Milledgeville *Union Recorder*, October 9, 1872. See also Ethel Maude Christler, "Participation of Negroes in the Government of Georgia, 1867–1870," (unpublished M.A. thesis, Atlanta University, 1932). Following the destruction of Republican political organizations during Reconstruction, blacks continued to vote in a variety of elections in both counties until the late 1890s, when *de facto* disfranchisement in the form of all-white primaries eliminated black voter participation. See Smith, "Down Freedom's Road," 65–69 and 71–74.

TABLE 1

VIOLENT CRIME IN BALDWIN AND TERRELL COUNTIES, GEORGIA,
1865–1910

	Baldwin		Terrell	
	N	%	N	%
Arson	74	12.7	143	19.4
Rape	40	6.9	53	7.2
Homicide	137	23.6	147	19.9
Serious Assault	330	56.8	396	53.6
Total	581	100.0	739	100.1

SOURCE: Court Records and Newspaper Crime Reports

vide the standard source for determining indictment numbers; however, because of the unusual circumstances inherent in the crime of arson, court records alone do not provide an accurate index of violent property crime.[24] Since almost all alleged arson incidents occurred at night in isolated rural areas, there were rarely witnesses; as a result, the courts frequently could not indict anyone in suspected arson cases. For this reason, newspaper crime reports represent an alternative source for determining the occurrence of violent property crime.[25] Because local court records lack transcripts of trial proceedings, newspapers are sometimes the only source of data on the kind of

[24] The following court records constitute part of the primary source material for this study: Minutes of the Superior Court: Baldwin County, Georgia, 1865-1910 (GDAH); Minutes of the Superior Court: Terrell County, Georgia, 1865-1900 (GDAH); Minutes of the Superior Court: Terrell County, Georgia, 1900-1910 (Terrell County Courthouse, Dawson, Ga.); Minutes of the Inferior Court: Baldwin County, Georgia, 1866-1868 (GDAH); County Court Criminal Docket: Baldwin County, Georgia, 1900-1910 (Baldwin County Courthouse, Milledgeville, Ga.); Minutes of the County Court: Terrell County, Georgia, 1887-1895 (GDAH); Minutes of the County Court, Terrell County, Georgia, 1895-1898 (Terrell County Courthouse); Minutes of the City Court: Dawson, Georgia, 1898-1910 (Terrell County Courthouse). In Georgia the indictment process began with the grand jury, which met twice a year—at the beginning of biennial Superior Court sessions—to consider evidence in criminal offenses. If the jury determined that an offense indeed took place and that there was probable cause that a given individual committed the offense, a true bill of indictment was returned to the court naming the individual and the crime of which he or she was accused. The true bill represented the formal "labeling" process at the court level of the criminal justice system. The labeling process could occur at an earlier stage, however; police officials, such as sheriffs and constables, had the authority to arrest and bring the suspect before a magistrate. Upon hearing evidence, the magistrate, often a justice of the peace, could release the suspect on bond or remand the suspect to the custody of the sheriff—that is, place the suspect in jail without bond—until the grand jury met. In addition, the magistrate could release the suspect for lack of sufficient evidence to implicate the suspect in the alleged offense. See Georgia *Code*, Sec. 218, 246, 3241, 3900-3935 (1873).

[25] From 1866 to 1910, 17 arson cases were brought before the grand juries in Baldwin and 32 in Terrell. During the same period the press reported 57 other cases of suspected arson in Baldwin and 111 in Terrell. Although one must be careful in aggregating data from two different sources, newspaper crime reports are a reliable alternative souce for determining the incidence of arson. In a rural community, crime—particularly violent crime—was major news. For example, from 1866 to 1910 at least 80 percent of all homicides in Baldwin and Terrell dealt with by the grand juries were reported in newspapers either at the time the crime

property destroyed as well as the name and race of arson victims and, occasionally, suspects.[26] Annual tax digests permit further identification of suspects and victims; the digests also enable the researcher to construct profiles, based on economic status, of the subpopulation of arsonists.[27]

Earlier studies of southern violence focus exclusively on crimes against the person; thus there is a need for some measure of the extent to which arson contributed to the overall incidence of violent crime on a community level. Using crime statistics from grand jury indictments and newspaper crime reports, Table 1 indicates that during the years covered by this study arson constituted 13 percent of recorded acts of violent crime in Baldwin and 19 percent in Terrell. There were substantially more incidents of arson than reported cases of rape. Homicide — the most traditional index of southern violence — occurred less than twice as often as arson in Baldwin. In Terrell there were almost as many incidents of arson as homicide. It seems fair to conclude, therefore, that acts of arson figured prominently in overall levels of violent crime on a community level.[28]

---

was committed or when the grand jury was in session. Of the arson cases considered by those same grand juries, the press reported on 53 percent in Baldwin and 80 percent in Terrell. Smith, "Down Freedom's Road," 46–48 and 292. Police statistics are not available because the localities examined here had no police *per se* during the years 1865-1910. In rural Black-Belt counties the elected county sheriff and appointed deputies constituted the equivalent of an official police force. The towns that served as county seats had a marshal and deputies, who were appointed by the town council. In outlying districts these officers were supplemented by constables in crossroads villages. These various officers of the criminal justice system performed a variety of duties: executing warrants, arresting those accused of violating the law, and operating the jail and county chaingang, when it developed. See Georgia *Code*, Sec. 349, 5, 445, 473, and 478 (1873).

The following newspapers were used in this study: Milledgeville, Georgia (Baldwin County) *Federal Union*, January 2, 1866, to August 28, 1872; Milledgeville *Union Recorder* (listed as *Union and Recorder*), September 4, 1872, to December 27, 1910; Dawson, Georgia (Terrell County) *Weekly Journal* (also listed as *Journal*), February 2, 1866, to April 1887; Dawson *Southwestern News*, May 4, 1887, to March 6, 1889; Dawson *News*, 13, 1889, to December 28, 1910. Microfilm copies of these newspapers are located in University of Georgia Library. An extensive search for county-level court records in post-war Georgia reveals that, generally, trial reports lack recorded testimony until after It's uncertain whether this situation results from a failure to transcribe trial testimony, or the nineteenth-century equivalents of the later Evidence Books were not preserved house archives.

Excellent copies of tax digests for many Georgia counties, beginning with the early are kept in the State Department of Archives and History. The digests list the race of property owner, the kinds of property he or she owned, the dollar value of that real or al property, the exact number of acres an individual owned, and the names of many males who did not own real or personal property.

The crime categories listed in Table 1 reflect the categories and definitions established in published editions of the Georgia *Code* from 1865 through 1910. "Homicide" includes murder, voluntary and involuntary manslaughters, infanticides, and justifiable homicides. "Rape" incorporates rapes and attempts at rape. "Serious Assault" includes aggravated assaults, stabbings, and shooting at another. For examples of these definitions, see relevant sections of the Georgia *Code* for 1873 and 1896. The sources for the incidents of arson listed in Table 1 are as follows: Baldwin: newspaper cases, 57; court cases, 8; court cases linked

ARSON AS PROTEST

FIGURE 2

ARSON RATE IN BALDWIN AND TERRELL COUNTIES, 1867–1909

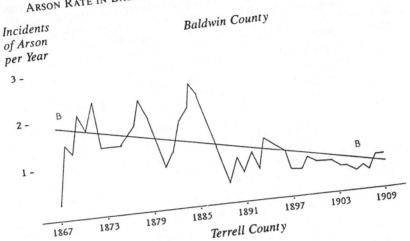

Baldwin County

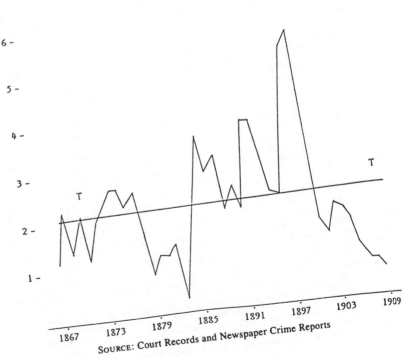

Terrell County

SOURCE: Court Records and Newspaper Crime Reports

Yet, an examination of long-term trends in arson qualifies, to an extent, the suggested statistical importance of the crime. From 1867 to 1909 in Baldwin the overall trend of arson incidents (indicated by Line B in Figure 2) declined. Based on available evidence, arson occurred most frequently during the first two decades of this study; after the 1890s, by comparison, the level of offenses decreased steadily. Although Terrell's arson rate increased sharply during the late nineteenth century, the number of recorded incidents abated precipitously in the early years of the twentieth century. Despite this pronounced decline, Terrell County's overall arson trend (indicated by Line T) remained essentially constant from 1867 to 1909.[29] In both counties the incidence of arson reflects a cyclical pattern that seems to correspond with periods of intense economic fluctuation, but the observed pattern is somewhat inconsistent. Baldwin and Terrell experienced arson more frequently in the depression of the 1870s than in the years immediately after the Civil War; in both counties, though, the incidence of arson was even greater during the recession the 1880s than in the 1870s. Baldwin had a slight increase in arson incidents in the 1890s depression, but the level of offenses remained er than that documented for the previous decade's recession. In ell the rate of arson accelerated dramatically in the 1890s, and depression decade's peak also surpassed all previous levels of it property crime.[30]

---

spaper reports, 9; total cases, 74. Terrell: newspaper cases, 111; court cases, 8; es linked with newspaper reports, 24; total cases, 143. For a discussion of the meth- sed in compiling statistics, see Smith, "Down Freedom's Road," Appendix B. One in each county, and subsequent proceedings of a magistrate's hearing, were the press but not in available court records. Thus, the author counted these two s newspaper cases, rather than as linked cases. See Milledgeville *Union and*)ctober 14, 21, 1879; Dawson *News*, February 2, 9, 16, 1898.

phs in Figure 2 were constructed by computing a three-year moving average of the er of reported arson cases. In utilizing a moving average, data for the years 1866 discarded. The figure excludes the year 1865, since newspaper records are iowever, it should be noted that court records for both counties indicate no arson r that year. The moving average eliminates erratic fluctuations from one year to it affecting possible cyclical trends in the data. Crime rates were computed for f 10,000 with this formula: $CR = N (10,000)/P$, where CR is the crime rate, N :d number of crimes for a given year, and P is the population for a given year. ation data cited in footnote 10, the population for each year was computed as $Pn - Po/N$, where r is the estimated annual rate of population increase, Pn is the ation at the end of the decennial period, Po is the population at the beginning of a period, and N is the number of years in between the beginning and terminal dates. is were computed with a variation of linear regression, which determines the line fits" the data points consisting of all the values of the Y-variables, or the yearly , and the X-variables, or the given year. ivenience, economic fluctuations are designed as periods of economic instability is in which expansion results in economic "upturn") and economic instability (*i.e.*, hich contraction results in economic "downturn," or recessions and depressions). on of this terminology, see Rendigs Fels, *American Business Cycles, 1865–1897* 1959); Milton Friedman and Anna Jacobson Schwartz, *A Monetary History of*

Despite indications that arson patterns coincided with periods of national economic fluctuation, one should not assume that economic fluctuations alone fostered violent property crime. In the half-century following the Civil War, cotton prices throughout the South declined steadily until just prior to World War I. If economic fluctuations affect the incidence of crime, one might expect that arson offenses would have exhibited an upward trend in agricultural Baldwin and Terrell. Accurately measuring the impact of national economic fluctuations on local economies presents conceptual problems for the historian. Exactly what national economic indicators does one use in measuring economic fluctuations on a community level? How does one measure the degree to which Baldwin and Terrell "suffered" depressions and recessions compared to the rest of the nation? These questions are difficult to answer because local indices of economic fluctuation are often difficult to obtain. Nevertheless, there is little reason to doubt that some communities escaped the impact of national and even international economic fluctuations, especially Black-Belt counties like Baldwin and Terrell where the economy depended in large part on the sale of cotton on a world market.[31]

The real significance of violent property crime in these counties lies in the complex of factors that appears to have precipitated the "willful and malicious" destruction of private property. In order to assess the importance of violent property crime in Baldwin and Terrell, the following analysis first determines the race, sex, and class of arson suspects and their victims. Next, several factors that suggest a

---

the United States, 1867–1960 (Princeton, 1963); and Charles Hoffmann, "The Depression of the Nineties," *Journal of Economic History*, XVI (June 1956), 137–64.

[31] Some evidence exists to suggest that local economic fluctuations coincided with patterns on a national level. Between 1892 and 1896 the Baldwin tax digests note a 17 percent decrease in the value of county property. After an increase in 1897 that followed the brief recovery in the middle of the 1890s depression, the dollar value of property declined again until 1900. Only in 1903 did the value of real and personal property exceed the 1892 total. Terrell County experienced a similar pattern of declining property values in both the 1870s and 1890s depressions. See Baldwin County Tax Digests, 1892–1903; Terrell County Tax Digests, 1870–1900. Interestingly, trends in nonviolent property crimes reveal a distinct cyclical pattern in both counties: acts of larceny and burglary increased dramatically during periods of recession and depression and decreased in periods of relative economic stability. Smith, "Down Freedom's Road," 168–73. Two other studies suggest a strong relationship between the incidence of crime and "national" economic fluctuations. J. S. Cockburn closely correlated property crimes (specifically, larcenies, burglary, and robbery) and wheat prices in late sixteenth- and early seventeenth-century England. Cockburn, "The Nature and Incidence of Crime in England, 1559–1625," J. S. Cockburn, ed., *Crime in England, 1550–1800* (Princeton, 1977), 49–71. Barbara A. Hanawalt's excellent survey of fourteenth-century English communities illustrates that changes in wheat prices correspond "very closely" with yearly indictments for crimes against property and person (specifically, larceny, burglary, robbery, homicide, receiving stolen goods, counterfeiting, arson, rape, and treason). Hanawalt, *Crime and Conflict in English Communities, 1300–1348* (Cambridge, Mass., 1979), especially 238–60.

JOURNAL OF SOUTHERN HISTORY

TABLE 2

A. RACE OF ARSON SUSPECTS:
N AND TERRELL COUNTIES, 1865–1910

Baldwin		Terrell	
N	%	*N*	%
36	92.3	45	84.9
3	7.7	8	15.1
39	100.0	53	100.0

B. RACE OF ARSON VICTIMS:
N AND TERRELL COUNTIES, 1865–1910

Baldwin		Terrell	
N	%	*N*	%
60	92.3	107	81.1
5	7.7	25	18.9
65	100.0	132	100.0

HIP OF RACE TO SUSPECT-VICTIM DICHOTOMY:
N AND TERRELL COUNTIES, 1865–1910

Baldwin		Terrell	
N	%	*N*	%
13	81.3	26	66.7
1	6.3	10	25.6
2	12.5	3	7.7
0	-	0	-
16	100.1	39	100.0

lewspaper Crime Reports, and Tax Digests.

ious differences between the suspect and the vic-
Among these factors are the kinds of property
alleged incendiarism and a seasonal pattern that
kably with the ebb and flow of the cotton econ-
factors in particular—the suspect-victim dichot-
arsoned property, and the distinctive seasonal
nitial evidence for the contention that arson origi-
violent protest in Black-Belt Georgia.

scholars have discounted the impact of race and
uth's penchant for personal violence, an analysis of
nd victims suggests that these factors played an
mplementary role in the patterns of violent property
terized Baldwin and Terrell.[32] Table 2-A shows that

ttern of Violence"; Hackney, "Southern Violence," 511–15; Lottier,

ARSON AS PROTEST   541

in both counties at least 85 percent of the suspected arsonists were black. It should be noted here that the 92 racially identified suspects collectively account for only 31.8 percent (or 69) of the arson cases recorded in both Baldwin and Terrell. In 144 other instances of arson, or 66.4 percent of all cases, arson suspects were not identified by name or by race.[33] Newspaper crime reports, which provide the only source of information for these cases, did not speculate about the race or name of arson suspects, although the authors of these reports consistently noted possible motivations for specific incidents of arson.[34] The generally uniform lack of reference to arson suspects in the press contrasts noticeably with newspaper coverage of other violent crimes. When discussing cases of homicide, assault, and rape, editors often identified suspects in some manner. For all intents and purposes, then, most arsonists seemingly remained "anonymous" in Baldwin and Terrell.

Examining victimization in acts of arson (Table 2-B) also illustrates the importance of race in patterns of violent property crime. The great majority of arson victims were white: 81.1 percent in Terrell and 92.3 percent in Baldwin.[35] Analyzing the racial relationship between arson suspects and victims in specific cases further clarifies the distinctive racial dichotomy in violent crimes against property (Table 2-C). The largest category of offenses involved black suspects and white victims: 66.7 percent of all cases in Terrell and 81.3 percent in Baldwin. No white-on-black offenses were reported in either county. White arsonists, it seems, always attacked the property of other whites. Apparently, arson was a primarily interracial, black-on-white crime in Baldwin and Terrell counties.[36]

"Distribution of Criminal Offenses"; Shannon, "The Spatial Distribution of Criminal Offenses"; Edwin H. Sutherland and Donald R. Cressey, *Criminology* (Philadelphia, 1970), 220–29; Van B. Shaw, "Relationship Between Crime Rates and Certain Population Characteristics in Minnesota Counties," *Journal of Criminal Law and Criminology*, XL (May-June 1949), 43–49; John Dollard, *Caste and Class in a Southern Town* (New Haven, 1937), Chapters 13–14. In contrast, Colin Loftin and Robert H. Hill argue that poverty is indeed highly correlated with the southern region's tendency to violence. "Regional Subculture and Homicide: An Examination of the Gastil-Hackney Thesis," *American Sociological Review*, XXXIX (October 1974), 714–24.

[33] These 144 cases were distributed as follows: in Baldwin, 49 cases, or 66.2 percent of the recorded incidents of arson; and 95 incidents in Terrell, or 66.4 percent of recorded arson offenses.

[34] In four other arson cases (one in Baldwin and three in Terrell) where records indicate the name of the suspect, the individual's race could not be identified. These four cases represent fewer than 2 percent of all cases.

[35] The 197 identified arson victims account for 90.8 percent of all reported cases.

[36] Table 2-C only includes those cases in which records indicate the race of both suspect and victim. Because of the difficulty in identifying arson suspects, therefore, the number of cases, a total of fifty-five, represents only 25.3 percent of all offenses. To avoid overcounting, cases with multiple suspects were calculated as a single incident. For example, including multiple suspects for Baldwin increases the number of black-white cases in that county to twenty-three.

TABLE 3

PROPERTIED STATUS OF ARSON SUSPECTS:
BALDWIN AND TERRELL COUNTIES, 1865–1910

	Baldwin		Terrell		Total	
	N	%	N	%	N	%
No Property	30	83.3	27	67.5	57	75.0
Personal Property	4	11.1	13	32.5	17	22.4
Real Property	2	5.6	-	-	2	2.6
Total	36	100.0	40	100.0	76	100.0

SOURCE: Court Records, Newspaper Crime Reports, and Tax Digests.

An analysis of the sex of arson suspects shows that, in Baldwin and Terrell, women were represented more often in incidents of violent property crime than in other crime categories. Females constituted nearly 11 percent of all suspects in Terrell and one-third (32.5 percent) of the identified suspects in Baldwin.[37] All of the female suspects were black, but more significantly, most female arsonists acted on their own, like Ella Carswell and Dolly Robinson, both of whom were accused in separate incidents of barn burning.[38] These patterns contradict traditional assumptions about the noninvolvement of women in serious crimes and about the dependent role of female participants in such offenses.[39]

Table 3 suggests that most arson suspects were propertyless. Of seventy-six suspects, only two owned any real estate, and both of these suspects lived in Baldwin. Barely one-fifth (22.4 percent) of the suspects claimed any personal property. Charles James and Easter May were typical of this latter category. James, a black resident of Baldwin County, owned $75.00 in stock animals and $6.00 worth of household goods. Like many blacks who lived in Terrell's farming districts, Easter May had very little personal property: $2.00 in stock and household items valued at $10.00.[40] In Baldwin and Terrell the

[37] Thirteen of forty suspects identified by sex in Baldwin were women; in Terrell, six of fifty-six identified arson suspects were women. For Baldwin, female suspects accounted for 5.4 percent of all homicide cases, 6 percent of serious assaults, and 7.5 percent of all larcenies and burglaries in which the sex of the suspect could be identified. The corresponding percentages for Terrell were as follows: homicide, 9.9 percent; serious assault, 4.8 percent; larceny and burglary, 8.0 percent.

[38] Milledgeville *Union Recorder*, May 2, 1905; March 5, 1907; Minutes of the Superior Court: Baldwin County, 1905 and 1907. Nine of the female suspects acted independently in single acts of arson; four other women were involved in one Baldwin case. Six female suspects acted in conjunction with male companions; in four of these cases, the suspects were apparently related to one another.

[39] Sutherland and Cressey, *Criminology*, 126–31; Otto Pollak, *The Criminality of Women* (New York, 1950), 44–56.

[40] Minutes of the Superior Court: Baldwin County, 1892; Minutes of the Superior Court: Terrell County, 1895; Baldwin County Tax Digest, 1891; Terrell County Tax Digest, 1895.

great majority of arson suspects did not own property of any kind.[41]

One should be careful, though, not to overemphasize the racial or class parameters of the suspect-victim dichotomy in acts of arson. That most arson suspects in Baldwin and Terrell were black and propertyless is not very startling, especially if one considers that these counties were predominately black and that few blacks owned property. Furthermore, since arson is by definition a crime against property and since one must obviously have property in order to be an arson victim, it is not surprising that arson victims were almost always white and propertied. Nevertheless, overall consistency in the suspect-victim dichotomy of these counties provides the first clue as to the origins of arson in Black-Belt Georgia. An examination of the objects destroyed in violent attacks against property helps to explain why generally poor blacks allegedly burned the material possessions of the propertied white minority.

Despite some variations in the focus of specific attacks, arsonists displayed similar preferences when selecting their targets: almost always, they burned structures identified with the dominant economic activities of each county (Table 4-A). Cotton gins, barns, stables, and storehouses (or cribs) for food, cotton, and fodder accounted for 60.8 percent of all property identified for Baldwin arson reports. For Terrell, the corresponding figure was 51.4 percent. A substantial percentage of that county's arsonists also attacked private residences (25.3 percent), but in virtually every instance the houses were owned or rented by farmers. By consistently destroying such property, these arsonists were attacking the very symbols of power and status that differentiated the propertied from the propertyless and sustained and perpetuated that inequality.[42]

Arson in these counties occurred in seasonal patterns. Approximately two-thirds of the arson cases occurred during the fall and winter months, while the spring and summer months were apparently the periods of least arson activity (Table 4-B).[43] This seasonal pattern coincided with important stages in the cotton economy. The cotton economy's peak labor needs developed at the fall harvest, between

---

[41] In compiling Table 3 each suspect's name was cross-checked with the list of names contained in tax digests for the year in which the offense occurred and for the year preceding and following the incident.

[42] The 215 examples in Table 4-A account for 202 (or 93.9 percent) of recorded arson cases The object of the arson attack could not be determined in 7 Baldwin cases and 8 Terrell cases which appear in court records. In Table 4-A data for Terrell include 10 cases in which arsonists destroyed more than one object (a total of 21 buildings) and 2 Baldwin cases in which 4 buildings were burned. The "other" category included such items as privately owned woods, a public bridge burned in Baldwin just prior to the harvest season, and the Terrell County jail.

[43] Since the concern here is with the pattern of seasonality of the most frequently burned structures, Tables 4-B and 5 exclude items from the "other" category and cases, especially those based only on biannual court records, where seasonality could not be accurately determined.

TABLE 4

A. OBJECTS DESTROYED BY ARSON:
BALDWIN AND TERRELL COUNTIES, 1866–1910

	Baldwin		Terrell	
	N	%	N	%
Cotton Gin	17	24.6	21	14.4
Storehouse	7	10.1	35	24.0
Barn/Stable	18	26.1	19	13.0
Business	11	15.9	17	11.6
House	10	14.5	37	25.3
Other	6	8.7	17	11.6
Total	69	100.0	146	99.9

B. SEASONAL DISTRIBUTION OF ARSON OFFENSES:
BALDWIN AND TERRELL COUNTIES, 1866–1910

	Baldwin		Terrell	
	N	%	N	%
Fall	30	48.4	41	31.8
Winter	14	22.6	41	31.8
Spring	8	12.9	24	18.6
Summer	10	16.1	23	17.8
Total	62	100.0	129	100.0

SOURCE: Newspaper Crime Reports

mid-September and mid-December, when field laborers, share-croppers, and tenant farmers alike performed the tedious, physically demanding task of picking the lint from the boll, after which the cotton was transported to local gin mills and warehouses for processing and storage.[44] These were also the months when planters, other agricultural employers, and merchants generally concluded contractual relationships with their tenants and sharecroppers; during this time, day laborers received their wages for harvesting cotton and other crops.[45] As Table 5 demonstrates, it was precisely during these

[44] Alfred B. Shepperson, *Cotton Facts* (New York, 1906), 1; Wright, *The Political Economy of the Cotton South*, 60–61; Joseph B. Lyman, *Cotton Culture* (New York, 1868), 59–68; Gilbeart H. Collings, *The Production of Cotton* (New York, 1926), 144–48, 155; *Report on Cotton Production*, Part 2, pp. 324–25, 434. See also William B. Dana, *Cotton from Seed to Loom: A Handbook of Facts for the Daily Use of Producer, Merchant, and Consumer* (New York, 1878); Lewis Cecil Gray, *History of Agriculture in the Southern United States to 1860* (2 vols., New York, 1958), II.

[45] Collings, *Production of Cotton*, 155, 160; *Report on Cotton Production*, Part 2, p. 324; Rupert B. Vance, *Human Factors in Cotton Culture: A Study in the Social Geography of the American South* (Chapel Hill, 1929), 169–70. See in particular, Steven W. Engerrand, "'Now Scratch or Die': The Genesis of Capitalistic Agricultural Labor in Georgia, 1865–1880" (unpublished Ph.D. dissertation, University of Georgia, 1981), 64–95 and the contracts cited therein.

TABLE 5

SEASONAL DISTRIBUTION OF OBJECTS DESTROYED BY ARSON:
BALDWIN AND TERRELL COUNTIES COMBINED, 1866–1910

| | Cotton Gin | | Storehouse | | Barn/Stable | | Business | | House | | Total | |
	N	%	N	%	N	%	N	%	N	%	N	%
Fall	27	71.1	17	41.5	10	27.0	9	32.1	8	17.0	71	37.2
Winter	6	15.8	9	22.0	15	40.5	9	32.1	16	34.0	55	28.8
Spring	1	2.6	7	17.1	6	16.2	3	10.7	15	31.9	32	16.8
Summer	4	10.5	8	19.5	6	16.2	7	25.0	8	17.0	33	17.3
Total	38	100.0	41	100.1	37	99.9	28	99.9	47	99.9	191	100.1

SOURCE: Newspaper Crime Reports

fall months that 71 percent of the ginhouse fires occurred. It was also in the fall and winter months that the majority of all storehouses (63.5 percent), barns and stables (67.5 percent), and businesses (64.2 percent) were burned.

Together, the decidedly seasonal pattern of arson offenses, the kinds of property destroyed, and the distinctive dichotomy between suspects and victims suggest that arson represented a dramatic form of protest in Black-Belt Georgia. An examination of specific cases lends additional credence to this theory. In Baldwin and Terrell arson essentially served as an outlet for vengeance and a sense of grievance fostered by the impact of the racism and poverty which permeated Black-Belt society. One incident in Baldwin illustrates how the inability of blacks to receive justice through established institutions fostered vengeance and, ultimately, violent retaliation.

In October 1891 C. W. Ennis of Baldwin shot and killed Crawford Vasser, another county resident, in Macon, Georgia, nearly 30 miles south of Milledgeville. Vasser, a black man, had escaped from the Baldwin jail in April following his conviction for burglary in the local courts. Ennis went to Macon, perhaps on official business as the county sheriff, and while there encountered Vasser and attempted to arrest him. According to the press, Vasser resisted, the sheriff shot him, and a coroner's jury declared the death a justifiable homicide. Yet, based on available evidence, the coroner's jury erred in its decision, exonerating what was in effect an act of extra-legal violence against a man who was apparently unarmed. If one considers these circumstances, it is not too surprising that some Baldwin County residents subsequently sought "justice" in their own way. Following the jury's verdict, a number of Vasser's friends requested that his body be returned to Baldwin for burial. Several days after the incident, Ennis's cotton mill and ginnery complex in Milledgeville burned to the ground. For several months there were no further press reports concerning the Ennis case, but in the spring of 1892 authorities finally arrested two black Baldwin residents, one of whom implicated other county blacks. In all, the grand jury considered evidence against five suspects, including four men and one woman; the courts later convicted the two black men who had been arrested first.[46]

The most frequent and direct form of protest in attacks against private property developed out of class tensions between the propertied and the propertyless, more specifically, in conflicts involving white employers and their black employees. Generally, these disputes also illustrate the importance of the seasonal pattern in arson offenses. In December 1896, at the conclusion of cotton-picking in

[46] Milledgeville *Union Recorder*, April 28, November 3, 1891; February 2, 23, April 26, May 3, September 13, 1892; Minutes of the Superior Court: Baldwin County, 1892.

Terrell, a black family was "made to vacate" their tenant house on Mrs. R. G. Jones's plantation, located two miles south of Dawson. Before dawn, on the day after the eviction, fire destroyed the empty structure and an adjoining kitchen and smokehouse. Apparently authorities never found the evicted tenants, for the grand jury returned no indictments in the case. The following January a similar incident occurred on a farm near the Bronwood area of Terrell County. A tenant moved out of a two-room dwelling during the day; that night an unknown party, or parties, burned the vacant building.[47]

Even more damaging were the frequent and distinctly seasonal attacks on cotton gins, on storehouses and "cribs" containing food, cotton, and fodder, and on barns and stables. Granted that these incidents resulted in the destruction of valuable buildings, machinery, and equipment, but such acts were costly as well because the structures invariably housed the products of the agricultural harvest. A careful scrutiny of these cases indicates the possibility of sabotage by disgruntled farm laborers and other individuals who ostensibly found in arson an outlet for the frustrations engendered by an exclusionary and exploitative society.

From the end of September until mid-December, the Dawson *Weekly Journal* observed in 1873, fifty-six ginhouses had burned throughout the state of Georgia.[48] More than a decade later, in the midst of the 1886 cotton harvest, the county's newspaper again cited press reports "from all directions" concerning the "usual returns of torn hands by cotton gins" and the "usual number of gin house fires."[49] When discussing the origins of local ginhouse fires and other cases involving the allegedly deliberate burning of private property, editors generally used such terms as "arsonists" or "incendiaries." Often the press in Baldwin and Terrell also blamed "matches in the cotton" or just plain "matches." Commenting on an 1881 gin fire in Milledgeville, the Baldwin reporter attributed the October incident to a "match in the seed cotton" that ignited when "passing through the gin."[50] Another fall ginhouse fire in Terrell produced an equivalent response from the *Journal* editor, who "thought" that the fire "originated from a match" in a bale of cotton.[51] Following the burning of a Terrell farmer's corn crib and wagon house in September 1899, the press asserted that the fire had been caused by "a match being dropped in the hay."[52] Press reports about other fires were more specific. Four hundred bushels of harvested corn were ruined when

[47] Dawson *News*, December 16, 1896; January 13, 1897.
[48] Dawson *Weekly Journal*, December 18, 1873.
[49] Dawson *Journal*, October 28, 1886.
[50] Milledgeville *Union Recorder*, October 11, 1881.
[51] Dawson *Journal*, October 21, 1886; see also Dawson *News*, September 13, 1899.
[52] Dawson *News*, September 27, 1899.

W. A. McRea's crib burned near Dawson. According to the Dawson *News*, the November fire started "in the middle of the crib," supposedly due to "matches dropped in the corn by some of the hands."[53] In September 1896 fire also consumed a crib in which a Terrell farmer had stored 150 pounds of cotton. According to the press account, a young black woman had entered the crib "with a match in her hair, and by some means the match became ignited and set the cotton on fire."[54]

These cases, like all incidents of alleged arson, raise important questions regarding the veracity of newspaper crime reports and causation. Were editors correct in labeling ginhouse and other fires as acts of arson, or did the press merely assume that frequent fires were the result of "incendiarism"? As noted earlier, newspaper crime reports were quite specific in discussing the origins of various fires. Despite a Terrell editor's declaration in 1889 that in "*nearly every instance* they are undoubtedly of incendiary origin," the press in both counties rather consistently distinguished between "suspected" or even "certain" cases of arson and clearly "accidental" or "unknown" fires.[55] In a December 1888 issue of the *Southwestern News*, for instance, the Terrell editor commented on three "fires" from the previous week. He labeled two of the incidents simply as "fires" but blamed the third on an "incendiary."[56] A Terrell editor directly attributed another fire in 1869 to an "incendiary" since the ginhouse owner had observed the building and ostensibly found it unharmed "but a few minutes before he discovered it on fire."[57] After a Milledgeville ginhouse burned in November 1867, the *Federal Union* explained that the cause was "unknown"; the editor termed "accidental" another ginhouse fire that took place the following month.[58] On a different occasion the Baldwin press initially listed "arson" as the cause of a grist mill and cotton gin fire. Although the grand jury later indicted three black males, prosecutors withdrew the charges when trial testimony showed that the fire was "accidental." The men had gone to the mill to steal, the press duly noted, and while in the building they lit a match to see, not to destroy. Thus, no arson occurred.[59]

[53] *Ibid.*, November 9, 1898.
[54] *Ibid.*, September 16, 1896.
[55] Dawson *Southwestern News*, January 16, 1889 (italics my own).
[56] *Ibid.*, December 19, 1888.
[57] Dawson *Weekly Journal*, October 21, 1869.
[58] Milledgeville *Federal Union*, November 26, December 3, 1867.
[59] Milledgeville *Union Recorder*, November 7, December 5, 1893. For additional examples illustrating newspaper classification of accidental or unknown fires, see Milledgeville *Federal Union*, October 2, 1866; Milledgeville *Union Recorder*, November 5, 1873; October 2, 1888; Dawson *Weekly Journal*, April 9, 1874; Dawson *News*, November 1, 1893; December 29, 1897. In one instance, information from the diary of a Baldwin planter confirmed a newspaper report designating a hotel fire as an act of arson. See Milledgeville *Federal Union*, December 28, 1869; Archibald C. McKinley Diary, December 7, 1869 (University of Geor-

More importantly, even if editors were correct in distinguishing between accidental "fires" and incidents of "arson," how could they determine causation in alleged acts of violent property crime? How, for example, did newspaper editors "learn," after the fact, that arson resulted from "matches in the cotton"? Obviously, in these cases especially, there could not possibly have been any firm evidence to support such a contention. Even if the reporter's information came directly from police authorities rather than from "unofficial" sources, the primitive investigative techniques of the time no doubt hindered accurate assessment in arson detection.[60] Rare, indeed, were the news reports that gave information as detailed as that provided in the Dawson *News*, wherein the editor attributed the burning of a grist mill in 1896 to arson because the floor had been "saturated with kerosene oil."[61]

For the historian the problems associated with identifying arson cases as opposed to mere "fires," and the difficulty of determining causation as well as motivation, present admittedly perplexing tasks — each further compounded by the absence of court records containing trial testimony. Yet, even in the absence of official transcripts, there is additional evidence to suggest that property fires in Baldwin and Terrell may very well have represented acts of violent protest against the status quo and those who maintained it. This evidence stems primarily from an analysis of the dynamics of fire combustion and from the criminal justice system's response to arson cases as well as from the procedural requirements of the law.

Several factors minimize the possibility that gin and cotton house fires, in particular, resulted from the accidental "combustion" of dry cotton in the often closed confines of these structures. First, by definition, combustion is the "chemical union of a fuel with oxygen at a rapid rate," and combustion cannot take place without the completion of the "fire triangle's" third ingredient: heat. Together, oxygen, fuel,

---

gia Manuscript Collections, Athens, Ga.). Some fires could easily have been started by lightning; however, the press never attributed a local fire to the effects of lightning, nor did the press speculate that lightning *might* have caused destructive fires. See also Richard D. Fitch and Edward A. Porter, *Accidental or Incendiary?* (Springfield, Ill., 1968). In a study of post–World War I Austria, Roland Grassberger found that the number of arson cases in which lightning was "merely suspected as a cause" was so rare that he could not use them for statistical purposes. Grassberger, *The Crime of Arson*, translated from the German by Alfred Bruege (Berkeley, Calif., 1938), 34.

[60] Even today, and especially in rural areas that lack organized fire departments, arson detection remains exceedingly difficult. Robert E. Carter, *Arson Investigation* (Encino, Calif., 1978), 35, 62, and 124–40; Brendan P. Battle and Paul B. Weston, *Arson: Detection and Investigation* (New York, 1978), 9–20 and 177–93; Raymond L. Straeter and C. C. Crawford, *Techniques of Arson Investigation* (Los Angeles, 1955); Grassberger, *Crime of Arson*, 79; John F. Boudreau *et al.*, *Arson and Arson Investigation: Survey and Assessment* (Washington, 1977), 34.

[61] Dawson *News*, November 4, 1896; see also Milledgeville *Union Recorder*, January 23, 1894.

and heat make "combustion" possible, but not until the fuel (in this instance, cotton) reaches its ignition temperature. That most gin and cotton house fires occurred in the fall months, when temperatures progressively cooled, increased the likelihood of "external intervention," as it were, in the combustion process: that is, the use of a match or a candle to "ignite" a fire.[62] Second, cotton frequently remained in a damp condition at the time of picking due to early morning moisture or even rain. In this situation, it was common practice to place loose cotton on the floor of cotton houses, mills, or other storage facilities in order for it to dry, a necessary process prior to ginning. Thus, "accidental" combustion would have been difficult in any facility as long as cotton remained damp.[63] Third, numerous writers, including contemporary authors, who examined cotton production make no mention of "combustion" as a potential fire hazard in gin mills, warehouses, or other storage facilities.[64] One contemporary writer, though, William B. Dana in *Cotton from Seed to Loom*, suggested that planters marketed their cotton crop soon after it had been picked because "while the cotton is on the plantations it is . . . exposed to an absolute loss through fire from accident or malice."[65]

The response of the criminal justice system to property crime further supports the contention that arson represented an act of protest. In Baldwin and Terrell the courts dealt firmly with nonviolent property crimes, *e.g.*, larcenies and burglaries. In such cases, the courts convicted 75.9 percent and 66.4 percent of identified suspects in Baldwin and Terrell respectively from 1866 to 1910.[66] These conviction percentages include two categories: suspects convicted of the offense as originally charged by the grand jury and suspects convicted of a lesser offense.[67] Since the potential financial losses in acts

---

[62] See Carter, *Arson Investigation*, 46–49.

[63] See D. A. Tompkins, *Cotton Mill Processes and Calculations: An Elementary Textbook for the Use of Textile Schools and for Home Study* (Charlotte, N. C., 1902), 9; Lyman, *Cotton Culture*, 67–68; Collings, *Production of Cotton*, 149.

[64] See for example, Vance, *Human Factors in Cotton Culture*; F. L. Lewton, *Historical Notes on the Cotton Gin* (Washington, 1938); Charles William Burkett and Clarence Hamilton Poe, *Cotton: Its Cultivation, Marketing, Manufacture, and the Problems of the Cotton World* (New York, 1906); Edna Turpin, *Cotton* (New York, 1924); Lyman, *Cotton Culture*.

[65] Dana, *Cotton from Seed to Loom*, 158. See also Tompkins, *Cotton Mill Processes*, 10, regarding "danger from fire speading in the loose cotton" on a cotton mill floor. Also, the U. S. Census Bureau's 1884 *Report on Cotton Production*, Part 2, p. 440 notes that in the region of "middle" Georgia—where Baldwin County is located—some farmers "insured" ginhouses "in which cotton is stored." No references could be found concerning fire hazards resulting from use of steam gins, as opposed to hand-turn, oxen, horse, or water-powered gins. See Lewton, *Historical Notes on the Cotton Gin*.

[66] See Smith, "Down Freedom's Road," 166 and 190–91 for a discussion of limitations in these data.

[67] Final adjudication of theft indictments could not be determined in 253 Baldwin cases (41.1 percent of those indicted) and 198 Terrell cases (23.7 percent of those indicted). Almost all of these cases were petty larcenies that the judge, after grand jury indictment, transferred to lower courts.

TABLE 6

A. Response of the Courts to Arson Cases: Baldwin and Terrell Counties, 1865–1910

	Suspects Indicted			Suspects Convicted	
	% of Identified	% of All		% of Indicted	% of All
N	Suspects	Arson Cases	N	Suspects	Arson Cases
Baldwin	21	61.8	16.2	9	42.9	6.8
Terrell	29	70.7	15.4	2	6.9	1.4

B. Attrition of Justice in Arson Cases by Decades: Baldwin and Terrell Counties, 1865–1910

	Number of Cases	Number of Indictments	Number of Convictions
Baldwin			
1860s	5	0	0
1870s	22	1	0
1880s	21	4	3
1890s	14	7	5
1900-1910	12	9	1
Total	74	21	9
Terrell			
1860s	6	3	0
1870s	20	2	1
1880s	28	5	0
1890s	59	10	1
1900-1910	30	9	0
Total	143	29	2

SOURCE: Court Records and Newspaper Crime Reports

of violent property crime were far more devastating than incidents of larceny or burglary, one would expect the courts to have been at least as vigilant in prosecuting suspected arsonists; however, the criminal justice system proved surprisingly inefficient in adjudicating these offenses.

Table 6-A examines the response of the criminal justice system to incidents of violent property crime. Most of the suspects brought before the courts were indicted: in Baldwin, 61.8 percent (or twenty-one of thirty-four suspects) and in Terrell, 70.7 percent (or twenty-nine of forty-one suspects). More significantly, the arson suspects indicted by grand juries collectively account for very few of the total number of recorded arson cases. The twenty-one Baldwin suspects represent only 16.2 percent (twelve) of the documented cases in that county. Grand juries in Terrell—with nearly twice as many arson incidents as Baldwin—fared no better, indicting suspects in only twenty-two cases, or 15.4 percent of all recorded incidents of violent property crime. Thus, in the great majority of arson cases, grand juries did not identify a suspect much less indict one. Even when grand juries did identify and indict suspected offenders, conviction rates were low. In neither county did the courts convict a majority of the indicted arson suspects. Baldwin juries returned guilty verdicts against 42.9 percent of those indicted for arson. Terrell County had a remarkably lower percentage of convictions, at 6.9 percent.[68]

The criminal justice system's failure to respond effectively to violent property crime does not reflect a nonchalant or lax attitude on the part of elites towards the crime of arson during the half century following the Civil War. If anything, an analysis of developments in the criminal law suggests an increased concern for and awareness of the problem of incendiarism. In antebellum Georgia arson constituted a felony punishable by death, but only if the incendiary act occurred within a city, town, or village. The Georgia *Code* provided for prison terms of five to twenty years for the burning of a house on a farm or plantation and two to seven years for the firing of a barn or stable on a farm or plantation.[69] Most likely, the lighter penalties for arson on a farm or plantation reflect the impact of "plantation justice" and the prerogatives of slaveowning elites to "adjudicate" offenses within their own "domain."[70] After 1865, however, the criminal code in Georgia changed dramatically, largely in response to white concerns about the effects of emancipation. Between 1865 and 1866 the Georgia legislature strengthened the penalties for burning a house on a farm or plantation: instead of a five-to-twenty-year sentence for this offense, the legislature imposed the death penalty.[71] In 1874 the legislature expanded the scope of the criminal law in arson cases to include the burning of an unoccupied house on a farm or plantation; the imposition of a five-to-twenty-year prison sentence for this offense paralleled the antebellum code's provision for burning an

---

[68] Occasionally, careful scrutiny of court records did not yield the final outcome of court proceedings. Final adjudication could not be determined in the cases of two suspects indicted in Baldwin (10.0 percent of all indictments) and four indicted suspects in Terrell (14.3 percent of all indictments).

[69] Georgia, *Code*, Sec. 4273-4281 (1860).

[70] Michael Stephen Hindus, *Prison and Plantation: Crime, Justice, and Authority in Massachusetts and South Carolina, 1767–1878* (Chapel Hill, 1980), Chapter 6; Charles S. Sydnor, "The Southerner and the Laws," *Journal of Southern History*, VI (February 1940), 10; Eugene D. Genovese, *Roll, Jordan, Roll: The World the Slaves Made* (New York, 1974), 635-37; Ulrich Bonnell Phillips, *American Negro Slavery: A Survey of the Supply, Employment and Control of Negro Labor as Determined by the Plantation Regime* (New York, 1918), Chapter 23.

[71] Georgia, *Code*, Sec. 4377 (1873); see *Acts of the Georgia Legislature, 1865–1866*, p. 232 (cited in the 1873 edition of the *Code*); hereinafter cited as Georgia, *Acts* with appropriate date and page. The legislature also sanctioned the death penalty for burning a railroad bridge. See Georgia, *Acts, 1866*, p. 150 (cited in the Georgia *Code* for 1873).

occupied dwelling. Lawmakers added still another refinement to the criminal code during the 1878–1879 legislative sessions, providing a prison term of two to seven years for the burning of a ginhouse on a farm or plantation.[72]

Since almost all alleged arson incidents occurred at night in isolated, rural places, there were rarely any witnesses, a situation that severely hampered the identification of suspects. After a disastrous fire in the Dawson business district in September 1871, an exasperated Dawson *Weekly Journal* editor acknowledged this dilemma. No one doubted that the conflagration was "the work of an incendiary"; nevertheless, he complained, "It is a difficult matter to bring to justice the demon who puts the torch to a building *under cover of night* . . . ."[73]

Even when suspects were successfully identified and indicted, prosecutors generally could not obtain a conviction, partly because under rules of evidence practiced in Georgia during the late nineteenth and early twentieth centuries, neither "mere suspicion" nor entirely "circumstantial" evidence was sufficient to convict an arson suspect.[74] No wonder, then, that a frustrated Dawson businessman posted a $500.00 reward not merely for information but for "*evidence sufficient to convict*" the "man or men" who set fire to his store.[75] Because the criminal justice system seemed unable to contend with arson, newspaper editors occasionally advocated extralegal methods. "A few gin house burners swung to a hickory limb," argued a Dawson journalist, "would have an amazing effect on the business."[76] When unknown parties apparently burned stables belonging to a prominent Terrell farmer, the press concluded that "If this thing continues we will be forced to have either a paid department or a vigilante committee."[77]

At least once citizens did resort to extralegal violence against individuals suspected of arson. In February 1898 sheriff's deputies in Terrell County arrested Charlie Chambliss, a landless black man who lived in one of the county's farming districts. Chambliss was accused

[72] Georgia, *Code*, Sec. 141 (1896); see Georgia, *Acts, 1874*, p. 21 and Georgia, *Acts, 1878-1879*, pp. 61-62 (cited in the Georgia *Code* for 1896).

[73] Dawson *Weekly Journal*, September 7, 1871 (italics my own); see also Carter, *Arson Investigation*, 13 and 33; Battle and Weston, *Arson*, 36.

[74] If the "evidence be circumstantial, it must connect the accused with the offense so as to exclude every other reasonable hypothesis than that of guilt." See George F. Gober, *Gober's Georgia Evidence* (Atlanta, 1928), Sec. 50, pp. 77-78. To constitute a felony, notes John C. Reed in *A Handbook of Georgia Criminal Law and Procedure* (Macon, 1873), 30, the arson must be a " 'malicious and voluntary burning . . . .' " Without an actual witness, it was difficult for the courts to prove "willful and malicious" intent. See also Carter, *Arson Investigation*, 12; John L. Hopkins, comp., *Annotated Penal Laws of Georgia* (Macon, 1875), 264–68 (bottom script); Boudreau *et al.*, *Arson and Arson Investigation*, 35.

[75] Dawson *Weekly Journal*, September 14, 1871 (italics my own).

[76] *Ibid.*, December 3, 1874.

[77] Dawson *Southwestern News*, January 16, 1889.

of burning a white farmer's corncrib containing 400 bushels of harvested corn. En route to the Dawson jail, a party of masked men, some of whom wore women's clothing, intercepted Chambliss and the deputy and took the black man into nearby cypress swamps. The deputy claimed that he could not determine the race of Chambliss's abductors in part because of the masks and because the incident occurred at night. Although the press initially contended that the black man most likely had been "rescued by a party of friends," the *News* editor later confirmed that Chambliss had been severely whipped by his captors. After tying and blindfolding Chambliss, the masked men "removed his lower garments, bent him across a log and severely whipped him" with a "buggy trace," leaving gashes "four or five inches long and an inch wide . . . ." More than two weeks after the incident, some of the wounds had not healed. At Chambliss's commitment trial the magistrate released him "for want of evidence."[78]

In part because of the procedural limitations of the law and because of the unique context within which arson occurred, most arsonists went unpunished, remaining anonymous and almost invisible to the criminal justice system. It is this anonymity that provides the most plausible rationale for understanding the origins of arson as protest in Black-Belt Georgia. Historian E. P. Thompson has observed that in a "prescriptive society which, in myth if not in actuality, rested upon relations of . . . domination and subordination, there were many reasons why men might wish to remain anonymous." For the dominated, in particular, "anonymity was of the essence of any . . . form of . . . social protest." Although Thompson described conditions in rural England of the late eighteenth and early nineteenth centuries, his construct applies equally well to the American South during the half-century following the Civil War.[79] Especially in Baldwin and Terrell, the large black majority lived a subordinated existence sharply circumscribed by the dual impact of racism and economic exploitation. At times these conditions may have proved unbearable and, quite possibly, fostered bitterness and resentment toward the dominant white minority, particularly those who controlled the symbols and the means of power and production in an agrarian society.

Yet, for the poor, especially the black poor, there were few outlets for the frustrations of the Black-Belt culture. Scholars generally

---

[78] *News*, February 2, 9, 16, 1898.

[79] E. P. Thompson, "The Crime of Anonymity," in Douglas Hay, Peter Linebaugh, John G. Rule, E. P. Thompson, and Cal Winslow, *Albion's Fatal Tree: Crime and Society in Eighteenth-Century England* (London, 1975), 272. Thompson's essay and the brilliant study by Douglas Hay in the same book ("Property, Authority, and the Criminal Law," 17-63) represent some of the finest scholarship published to date in the area of crime as social history.

agree that, historically, black aggression against whites—in the form of assault or homicide—has been infrequent because such acts would result in extremely harsh penalties.[80] In arson, however, some blacks may have found an alternative to interracial, personal violence. Racism and poverty may very well have nurtured vindictiveness that often found expression in the burning of gins, barns, stables, and other properties of those who dominated an exclusionary society. As an act of protest, violent property crimes—the "minatory anonymous 'voice of the poor'"—were simply one manifestation of how society felt from below.[81] For some who lived in the Black Belt's debilitating environment, the drama of arson fulfilled a need, much like that of the sharecropper in William Faulkner's "Barn Burning," to whom "the element of fire spoke to some deep mainspring of his . . . being, as the element of steel or of powder spoke to other men, as the one weapon for the preservation of integrity, else breath were not worth the breathing . . . ."[82]

Not all violent property crimes fit this pattern, though. In a few instances arson may have represented a desire for profit on the part of the offender. When separate fires destroyed three homes in "Rosstown"—an all-black section of Dawson—the local press noted the owners' names and the amount of insurance each had acquired on the property. No charges were filed.[83] Other arson incidents may have resulted from attempts to disguise burglaries. The *Union-Recorder* declared in 1891 that L. L. Smith's store had been "arsoned" in order to "protect a burglary." Another issue of the Baldwin press reported that a plantation store had been "robbed and set on fire."[84] Rev. W. D. Stewart of Dawson lost most of his property in 1881 when two men burglarized "first [and] then burned" his home. After Terrell burglars robbed a safe inside R. Cannon's store in 1907, they "burned" the building, according to the press.[85]

[80] Hackney, "Southern Violence," 521; Wolfgang, *Patterns in Criminal Homicide*, 234–36; Dollard, *Caste and Class*, Chapter 14, especially p. 290.

[81] Thompson, "The Crime of Anonymity," 272.

[82] William Faulkner, "Barn Burning," in *Collected Stories of William Faulkner* (New York, 1950), 7–8. It should be noted that Faulkner, in his treatment of barn-burning, portrays this form of arson exclusively within the context of class, *i.e.*, as an intraracial, white-on-white crime.

[83] Dawson *News*, May 9, 1900; Minutes of the Superior Court: Terrell County, 1900. In another case, Dawson businessman D. W. Brown was initially accused of burning his "own store for insurance" in 1903, but the Terrell courts "dismissed" the charge. Dawson *News*, July 8, 1903; Minutes of the Superior Court: Terrell County, 1903. The four apparent "arson for profit" cases cited here represent less than 2 percent of all recorded offenses.

[84] Milledgeville *Union Recorder*, February 3, 1891; January 28, 1896.

[85] Dawson *Journal*, April 7, 1881; Dawson *News*, January 2, 1907. A cotton house "burned, too," according to the 1907 *News* report, as a "result of the arson of the store." Therefore, using available information from newspaper sources, this author did not count the cotton house as an object of arson. See also Milledgeville *Federal Union*, August 31, 1869; Milledgeville *Union and Recorder*, December 30, 1884; Dawson *Journal*, September 30,

In addition to these distinctions, the pattern of black victimization also differs from most instances of arson. For example, the types of black-owned property destroyed by fire contrast with those of white owners. Of twenty-nine arson cases in which blacks were identified as the victims, over one-half (fifteen or 51.7 percent) involved the destruction of homes, either rented or owned. Only 20.7 percent (six) of the cases involved the burning of property directly related to the agricultural economy, which is not very surprising since so few blacks owned corn cribs, cotton houses, or barns.[86] Moreover, in all instances where blacks were arson victims, the offenses were apparently intraracial, not interracial: of eleven cases where records indicate the race of both suspect and victim, all were black-on-black offenses. These incidents included the burning of a black church, supposedly prompted by a division within the congregation, and the destruction of two schools which, the press speculated, resulted from internal disputes in Dawson's black community.[87] In several instances domestic squabbles apparently led to arson. When Lou Thompson, a black female resident of Terrell, discovered that Mariah Lewis, another black, had "estranged" her [Lou's] husband, she burned three different dwellings that Lewis had rented. Although the press casually explained Thompson's motivation for these incidents, the grand jury never indicted her, primarily because prosecutors did not have "proof sufficient."[88]

These examples, however, represent exceptions to the overall patterns of violent property crime typical of Baldwin and Terrell. As an act of protest in the half-century following the Civil War, arson generally constituted a means by which the poor and the propertyless could strike out against those who dominated a racist and economically exploitive society. To be sure, attacks against private property were not limited to the Black Belt of Georgia. "White Caps" in the Appalachian mountain counties of northwest Georgia occasionally resorted to arson as a form of punishment against suspected revenue informers.[89] Even in the Black Belt, arson was not an offense attributable only to propertyless blacks. Occasionally in Baldwin poor

---

1867; Dawson *News*, January 11, October 18, 1893; November 23, 1898. These ten apparent incidents of burglary-arson account for only 4.6 percent of recorded cases.

[86] For both counties, the destruction of black-owned property included the following identified structures: houses (fifteen); churches (six); corn cribs (four); schools (two, both in Terrell); cotton house (one); and one barn. It should be noted that the destruction of a church or a school actually "victimized" numerous individuals. In this sense, then, Table 2-B undercounts blacks as victims in arson cases.

[87] Dawson *News*, May 31, June 28, August 9, 1899. See also Dawson *Journal*, May 19, 1881, regarding arson and a Terrell lawsuit concerning ownership of a building used as a black church.

[88] Dawson *News*, February 22, 1893; see also *News*, May 17, 1893.

[89] William F. Holmes, "Moonshining and Collective Violence: Georgia, 1889–1895," *Journal of American History*, LXVII (December 1980), 602.

whites also may have attacked the symbols of power that relegated the propertyless—regardless of race—to the lowest economic class. In October 1879 fire destroyed Luke Robinson's tannery, barn, and stables located in one of the county's outlying farm districts. Previously, Robinson's life had been threatened. Local officials brought a propertyless white man, named Bonner, before a justice of the peace to determine if enough evidence existed to bind him over to the grand jury. At least one person positively identified Bonner as the tannery arsonist, but the justice discharged the case. Although the main witness, a black youth, had been raised "from infancy" by Robinson, the court apparently could not accept his testimony against a white man.[90] In another, apparently unrelated Baldwin arson incident that occurred one week before the tannery fire blacks and whites allegedly joined together in attacking private property. During the height of the cotton-picking season, according to newspaper reports, a group of blacks and whites burned J. A. P. Robson's ginhouse, firing guns at him as they made their escape. Several nights later, arsonists visited Robson's farm again, destroying a cotton house and several stacks of fodder. No suspects were ever identified by name in either instance.[91]

Quite possibly, these cases represent isolated incidents. Perhaps class conflict between whites rarely prompted violent attacks against private property. On the other hand, these incidents may also be symptomatic of more widespread intraracial, white-on-white tensions. It is possible that whites were involved in some of the large number of arson cases that never received the attention of the courts. If at times blacks resorted to arson against whites as a safer means of protest than personal violence, poor whites, too, may have preferred arson as an outlet for frustrations against their socioeconomic betters.[92]

[90] Milledgeville *Union Recorder*, October 14, 21, 1879. The Bonner case, in particular, illustrates the racial bias that confronts any social historian who examines the operation of the criminal justice system, its accompanying records, and newspaper reports of "criminal" offenses during the Reconstruction and New South decades. Blacks were more likely to be labeled as suspects by the courts; for the same reasons, the press might more frequently report interracial rather than intraracial crimes, particularly those in which blacks victimized whites. See Marvin E. Wolfgang and Bernard Cohen, *Crime and Race: Conceptions and Misconceptions* (New York, 1964). In a Terrell County case, for example, the press initially identified two whites as suspects in the burlary-arson of a minister's home; the courts, however, indicted, and subsequently acquitted, three black males. See Dawson *Journal*, April 7, 1881; Minutes of the Superior Court: Terrell County, 1881. See also Dawson *News*, December 29, 1897.

[91] Milledgeville *Union Recorder*, October 7, 1879.

[92] One important qualitative study suggests that, in the antebellum South, arson did indeed reflect latent class conflict between propertied and nonpropertied whites. Bertram Wyatt-Brown argued persuasively that elites tolerated occasional acts of violent property crime because they viewed it as a "safety-valve" that mitigated intraracial class tensions. See Wyatt-Brown, "Community, Class, and Snopesian Crime: Local Justice in the Old South," in Orville

To find more class-oriented patterns of violent property crime one might consider a non–Black-Belt county such as Whitfield, located in northwest Georgia at the base of an Appalachian landscape of hills, valleys, and small mountains. In an economy dominated by commercial and subsistence farming, landowners greatly outnumbered sharecroppers and renters. Wheat, corn, oats, rye, sheep, milk, and butter accounted for most of this hill county's agricultural production. Dalton, the county seat and one of the largest towns in the north Georgia region, had 5,324 inhabitants by 1910, fully one-third of Whitfield's population. As an important trading center through which the Western and Atlantic Railroad connected with Rome, Georgia, and Chattanooga, Tennessee, Dalton gradually developed manufacturing and light industries; by 1890, there 101 manufacturing establishments in the county representing a capital investment of nearly $500,000 and product value of over $1,000,000.[93]

Although Whitfield's black population, most of whom lived in Dalton, decreased from 18.6 percent of the total population in 1880 to 10.8 percent in 1910, the black minority's presence was crucial to the history of the region, for blacks experienced racism that was as pervasive as that imposed in Baldwin and Terrell, and despite declining numbers, their presence created constant concern among the white majority. The press frequently used racist slang to describe the black community, and editors often advocated violence as a means of social control. Signed and anonymous letters attacking blacks by name periodically appeared in the press and on public buildings in Dalton. Moreover, nonwhites were disproportionate victims of the vigilante violence and nightriding terrorism that characterized Whitfield during Reconstruction and New South years.[94] Yet, the use of

Vernon Burton and Robert C. McMath, Jr., eds., *Class, Conflict, and Consensus: Antebellum Southern Community Studies* (Westport, Conn., 1982), 173–206.

[93] U. S. Census Office, *Statistics of the Population of the United States at the Tenth Census . . . 1880* (Washington, 1883), 383; *Thirteenth Census.* Vol. I: *Population, 1910,* 232–33; *Report on Manufacturing Industries in the United States at the Eleventh Census, 1890: Part 1, Totals for States and Industries* (Washington, 1895), 382–85; *Report on the Statistics of Agriculture . . .* (1895), 128–33 and 190–93; see also Whitfield County History Commission, *Official History of Whitfield County, Georgia* (Dalton, Ga., 1936), 39–62, cited in Holmes, "Moonshining and Collective Violence," 592n. Whitfield County's tax assessments in 1880 were on property valued at $1,225,746, which greatly exceeded estimates for Baldwin and Terrell. See Whitfield County Tax Digest for 1880 (GDAH).

[94] *Negro Population,* 96, 480, 780. For typical references describing Dalton's black community, see Dalton *Argus,* August 12, 1882; August 30, 1884; Dalton *North Georgia Citizen,* June 24, 1869. For examples of handbills and letters attacking blacks, see Dalton *Argus,* May 9, 1891; August 5, 1893; Dalton *North Georgia Citizen,* January 19, 1893; February 11, 1897; October 11, 1906; January 17, 1907. From 1868 to 1910 these newspapers recorded at least twenty-seven separate vigilante attacks in Whitfield County. Fifteen of these incidents involved blacks who were victims of lynching, whipping, or arson. See, for example, *Argus,* January 21, February 4, 11, April 15, 29, 1909. See also, Holmes, "Moonshining and Collective Violence," 602.

violence represented only one facet of the white majority's efforts to intimidate and control the black minority. As anxious to impose *de facto* segregation in social relations as their counterparts in the Black Belt, Whitfield whites established a separate teachers' institute, skating rink, cemetery, pool for baptisms, and segregated counters in stores well before the turn of the century.[95]

Against this backdrop of a highly race-conscious community, a brief examination of arson patterns produces some surprising conclusions.[96] Several contrasts with Baldwin and Terrell should be noted initially. Most arson incidents in Whitfield occurred during the winter and spring months, and the objects most frequently attacked by arsonists were businesses, barns and stables, and private homes. The impact of Dalton's commercial activity and the concomitant absence of the cotton culture's influence help explain not only the contrast with the Black Belt's distinct fall seasonal pattern, but also the lack of arson attacks on structures associated with a cotton economy.

Additionally, an analysis of available newspaper and court data demonstrates how difficult it is to make generalizations about suspects and causation. Almost all arson victims were white and, obviously, propertied, but neither the courts nor the newspapers successfully identified enough suspects to warrant concise observations. Newspaper reports listed only 15 suspects, 6 of whom were black, and these suspects accounted for only 10 arson cases (10 percent of a total of 101). Court records provide even fewer clues as to the motivation or background of suspected arsonists, since from 1866 to 1903 only 10 additional cases were brought before the grand jury, and in every instance the defendants were either dismissed or found not guilty. Still, there is some evidence that arson occasionally resembled the Faulknerian class-conflict model described in previous studies. Although few arson incidents involved cribs, storehouses, cotton gins, or other structures associated with an agrarian economy, arsonists regularly attacked barns and stables (26.5 percent of all cases). Evidence from these incidents suggests that class was the primary factor in incendiary activity. Many of the barns and stables destroyed by arsonists were of great value and owned by prominent commercial farmers. In 1893, for instance, someone burned a large storage barn in a rural Whitfield district, destroying nearly $2,500 in horses, mules, hay, and corn. W. H. Kenner's barn

[95] See Dalton *Argus*, July 14, 1883; April 11, 1885; July 18, 1891; July 16, 1893; August 18, 1894; Dalton *North Georgia Citizen*, February 18, 1875; September 22, 1881; March 29, April 12, 1883.

[96] The primary sources for the accompanying data are Dalton *Argus*, May 27, 1882, to December 15, 1910; Dalton *North Georgia Citizen*, June 18, 1868, to January 5, 1911; and Minutes of the Superior Court: Whitfield County, Georgia, 1866–1903 (GDAH).

was burned in 1904, with 25 tons of hay and 7,000 bushels of fodder.[97] Other incidents of arson seem to have been related to vendettas involving white residents of the county. Jim Shinholser's barn was torched in 1900, apparently by "some of his enemies," according to the press. "Enemies" also allegedly burned the house of a Dalton policeman assigned to "special duties" within the town district.[98]

Extant records identify both suspect and victim in only very few cases. Such identification is necessary in order to discover the relationship between victim and arsonist and to determine that class conflict played a role in a particular case.[99] Based on available evidence, therefore, the condition of class played a role in Whitfield's arson patterns, but it is uncertain to what extent considerations of class fostered violent property crime. What seems apparent, ironically, is that even in this non–Black-Belt hill county, race played a more obvious role in patterns of arson than one might have expected.

White vigilantes seven times resorted to arson as a means of coercing Dalton's black population, occasions in which threatening letters and handbills in the local press often preceded the incendiary attack. In one instance the press made references to the appearance of the "Klan" and commented that a black restaurant and social hall had been a neighborhood "nuisance" for some time prior to its destruction in 1909.[100]

Even more intriguing is the possibility that arson served as a form of protest by Whitfield's black minority. The evidence is scanty, but several factors indicate a plausible connection between a rising incidence of arson, especially from 1900 to 1910, and retaliation by blacks incensed at the harshness of that decade's racism.[101] Throughout the years covered by this survey there were few indictments and no convictions for arson in Whitfield County courts. Like arsonists in the Black Belt, most hill county incendiaries remained anonymous and seemingly beyond the reach of the criminal justice system. For Whitfield blacks, most of whom lived in Dalton, the town environment may have provided a "safe" outlet for vengeance, just as the rural environment encouraged incendiary acts in Baldwin and Terrell.[102] It is extremely important to note that nearly two-thirds of all recorded arson incidents took place at night within the town district. More importantly, the biggest outbreak of incendiarism occurred in

[97] Dalton *Argus*, April 8, 1893; November 5, 1904; Dalton *North Georgia Citizen*, April 13, 1893.

[98] Dalton *Argus*, January 6, 1900; January 27, 1910; Dalton *North Georgia Citizen*, January 4, 1900.

[99] Suspects and victims were clearly linked in only five cases.

[100] Dalton *Argus*, October 7, 1909.

[101] The following number of arson incidents were recorded by decade: 1870, five; 1880, nineteen; 1890, twenty-seven; 1900, fifty.

[102] See Richard C. Wade, *Slavery in the Cities: The South 1820–1860* (New York, 1964).

1908, at the height of a rising tide of white racism, illustrated by the statewide movement for disfranchisement, the establishment in Dalton of a white Law and Order League to supplement the town's police authorities, and the burning of black homes, a church, and school by nightriders.[103] One cannot be certain, but considering the harshness of the black experience in Whitfield, it is not unreasonable to suggest that, just as arson may have served as an outlet for class conflict, so also could arson have provided a vehicle for racial protest, even in the foothills of the Appalachians.

It should be noted again that arson over time declined gradually in Baldwin and probably remained at best constant in Terrell, where there was a sharp decrease in the number of recorded acts after 1899. These patterns are admittedly difficult to explain, especially because racism and poverty, which seem to have contributed substantially to violent crime, became progressively worse in those counties during the latter decades of this study.

Two factors—the criminal justice system's response to arson after 1890 and long-term demographic developments—provide a partial explanation for the observed trends in violent property crime. First, although the data presented above indicate that the courts proved inefficient in identifying, indicting, and convicting arsonists, the criminal justice system did adopt a more aggressive posture toward arson offenders after 1890. In Baldwin there were only five indictments and three convictions for arson from 1865 to 1889 (Table 6-B), years in which newspapers and court records cited forty-eight incidents of violent property crime. During the following two decades, only twenty-six cases of arson were reported; interestingly, most indictments and convictions also occurred in this time period. An analysis of Terrell County does not provide as clear a pattern. Grand juries returned as many indictments in the 1890s as in the preceding twenty-five years, but there were also more cases of arson during that depression decade than in previous years. From 1900 to 1910 juries continued to indict arson suspects more frequently than in the years prior to 1890; yet, it seems unlikely that indictments alone would have caused the dramatic decrease in that county's arson rate in the early years of the twentieth century. A declining rate of arson from 1900 to 1910 would make more sense if Terrell had also experienced a high conviction rate, but criminal court juries returned no guilty verdicts during these years.

Local socioeconomic developments offer a second possible explanation for changes in the incidence of arson. Based on available evidence, it would appear that violent property crime was closely

[103] Dalton *Argus*, April 9, 1908; January 21, February 4, 11, April 15, 29, 1909; Dalton *North Georgia Citizen*, December 31, 1908; February 25, April 29, 1909.

associated with the agrarian economy that characterized the Black-Belt counties of Baldwin and Terrell. In Terrell especially, an association between arson and a predominately agricultural or cotton economy—or an association between arson and economic deprivation—might explain the tremendous increase in the incidence of arson between 1865 and 1899, decades when that county's cotton economy expanded rapidly and when economic opportunities became more elusive for blacks. Yet, the cotton culture and economic deprivation became more pervasive after 1900, at the time when arson abated sharply. From 1900 to 1910, for example, the black percentage of real estate and personal property in Terrell increased slightly from 6.2 percent to 8.5 percent, but, overall, the poverty of the black majority worsened in these years when both the total number of blacks and the black percentage of the entire population increased.[104] Throughout the post-Reconstruction years Terrell's cotton economy also expanded dramatically in both the number of cotton acres (a 190 percent increase from 1880 to 1910) and in the total acres allotted to cotton production (from 43.7 percent in 1880 to 57.0 percent by 1910).[105] Although Baldwin also remained predominately agricultural during these years, its economy did change over time. Compared to Terrell, cotton production in Baldwin expanded at a much slower rate, and the percentage of tilled land committed to cotton-growing decreased. In addition, substantial increases in the number of domestics, porters, other service-related workers, and in the number of black homeowners in Milledgeville paralleled an apparent decrease in the number of agricultural laborers. One cannot be certain, but the gradual decline in Baldwin's arson rate might be related to these demographic changes.[106]

A more aggressive criminal justice system and evolving economic institutions provide some insight into changes in the rate of arson over time, but a definite relationship is difficult to establish since these factors do not form entirely consistent patterns. Nevertheless, despite the apparent decreasing incidence of violent property crime in Baldwin and Terrell during the latter years of this study, arson represents an important dimension to the patterns of violent crime

[104] The black percentage of total population rose from 70.2 percent in 1900 to nearly 76 percent a decade later. One illustration of the extent of black poverty is the number of black landowners contrasted with the total black population. In 1900, 101 blacks owned real estate in Terrell out of a black population of just over 13,000; in 1910, 131 blacks owned land in a county with nearly 17,000 blacks. Terrell County Tax Digests for 1900 and 1910; *Negro Population*, 134 and 780.

[105] *Report on Cotton Production*, Part 2, p. 270; *Report on the Statistics of Agriculture . . .* (1895), 393-94; *Twelfth Census . . .* Vol. VI: *Crops and Irrigation* (1902), 431; *Negro Population*, 680.

[106] See census reports cited in previous footnote and Smith, "Down Freedom's Road," 88, 93-94, and 115n81.

that characterized these Georgia counties during the late nineteenth and early twentieth centuries. First, by documenting its very occurrence, and in substantial numbers, this study of arson enables the historian to take a first step toward reconsidering our perception of what constitutes "violence." If one adheres solely to the criteria of previous studies, then arson cannot be included in definitions that limit violence to acts of direct, personal contact, such as homicide or assault. Yet, though admittedly nontraditional, arson, because it is deliberate and destructive, should be included in discussions of violent crime.

Second, and more important, examining arson enables the historian to broaden the understanding of violence and its relationship to culture. Indeed, this study suggests strongly that arson is significant because it reflects the influence of cultural stimuli and historical experiences. In Baldwin and Terrell the distinctive seasonal pattern of arson offenses as well as the kinds of property destroyed in acts of violent property crime underscore the impact of the agrarian economy that dominated these counties from 1865 to 1910.[107] In a broader sense, this analysis avoids the limitations of previous crime studies and illustrates the important effects of race relations in the social history of the Black Belt. Examining in particular the association between criminality and victimization highlights the affinity between race and class, between the contours of black and white and of the propertyless and the propertied. Indeed, violent property crime seems to have resulted from the restrictive impact of those relationships, or more specifically, from the racism and poverty that permeated race relations in the Reconstruction and New South eras. Since these influences were not limited to the confines of two Georgia counties, it would not be surprising if additional studies found that arson figured prominently in the crime patterns of the larger Black Belt and, moreover, that developments in race relations help to explain those patterns.[108]

[107] Examining arson during these years supports the contention that if crime results from cultural influences, then statistics should be analyzed within a time frame when such influences were developing. Most previous studies rely on statistics compiled primarily after 1918, a procedure that presents a problem of perspective for those who argue that twentieth-century crime rates result from nineteenth-century cultural developments. See, for example, Brearley, *Homicide*, 19–20, 99, and 153, and "Pattern of Violence," 682–83; Hackney, "Southern Violence," 508–14; and Gastil, "Homicide and a Regional Culture of Violence," 412–27. Gastil used data primarily from the year 1960 to support the idea that a regional culture of violence developed in the South prior to 1850; in his analysis Hackney relied on data for 1940.

[108] Since twentieth-century southern white homicide rates are greater than rates for blacks, these writers focus on instances of white homicide when examining causation in acts of personal violence. By using such a limited data base, these writers have presented a cultural explanation not so much for southern violence but for southern white violence. Even that perspective is limited because such examinations perpetuate the notion that interracial vio-

Finally, as one possible manifestation of race relations in the Black Belt, arson as protest would add another, unique dimension to the historiographical perspectives on southern violence, especially if one considers the assumptions of most previous studies. Historians may very well be correct in asserting that the South's proclivity for personal violence results in large part from psychological reactions to cultural and historical influences. The evidence presented here, however, suggests that the effects of cultural and historical forces and the response to those influences have varied within distinct groups of southerners. If a sense of grievance (or a paranoidal perception of the environment) explains the white southerner's tendency to locate threats to the person outside the self and to satisfy that frustration through personal violence, then perhaps historians should distinguish between the white sense of grievance and the frustrations of black southerners, between white grievances towards real or imaginary threats to their status and the manner in which some blacks perceive the status quo as the factor that relegates them to a lesser socioeconomic position. Certainly, the experience of Black-Belt counties in Georgia suggests that a reaction to cultural and historical influences fostered a sense of grievance with dynamics quite different from those described in previous studies of southern violence. [109]

---

lence, especially black-on-white offenses, is rare in the South and that race, and the interaction between races, plays no role in patterns of violent crime. Yet, there are no studies of the Reconstruction and New South decades that confirm this notion. Indeed, previous studies cannot assess either the incidence of or that lack of interracial violence because these investigations do not consider the connection between criminality and victimization—a conceptual weakness that also excludes race relations from consideration as a possible factor in regional patterns of violence. See Lottier, "Distribution of Criminal Offenses"; Porterfield, "A Decade of Serious Crimes"; Shannon, "The Spatial Distribution of Criminal Offenses"; Hackney, "Southern Violence."

[109] Hackney, "Southern Violence"; Hackney's article—the best and most important work on postbellum southern violence published thus far—may have been prompted by an earlier study that earnestly solicited theoretical research on the phenomenon of regionally distinctive homicide rates. See J. S. Wilks, "Ecological Correlates of Crime and Delinquency," in *The President's Commission on Law Enforcement and Administration of Justice Task Force Report: Crime and Its Impact—An Assessment* (Washington, 1967), 138–56.

[10]

PROPERTY OFFENSES, SOCIAL TENSION AND RACIAL ANTAGONISM IN POST-CIVIL WAR RURAL LOUISIANA

By Gilles Vandal   Université de Sherbroke

The parish of Lafayette was the scene in June 1873 of a particularly brutal double murder. Daniel Lanet, a Frenchman, and Alexander Snaer, a black justice of the peace, who were also business partners, were murdered in their store by four blacks. The two killings took place in the course of a robbery and in order to dissimulate their deed, the four confederates set fire to the store. Although the store burned to the ground, their brutal action was discovered. Three of them were caught and summary executed by a lynch mob of over a thousand people. The fourth only escaped the rope by confessing the deed.[1] This case could be seen as an isolated incident. And yet, it takes on greater significance when we consider that brutal murders in the course of robbery were a rather new phenomenon and were seen by contemporaries as a major characteristic of the post-Civil War era. Such crimes were seen as the direct consequence of emancipation. No longer under the tight control of the whites, many blacks refused to submit any longer to the plantation discipline. As blacks could rarely find alternative work for making a living, petty thefts, grand larceny and robbery often became part of their day-to-day life. Meanwhile, whites who struggled to adjust to the new social and economic conditions, felt increasingly insecure before what they perceived as the inability of the civil authorities to cope with the wave of property crimes. As a consequence, hundreds of whites periodically joined lynching parties as they saw mob violence as their only resort to correct an intolerable situation.[2]

Although theft, the most common property offense, represents a social phenomenon common to traditional society, it was particularly common in rural Louisiana during the second half of the nineteenth century. The Civil War brought not only the emancipation of slaves, but a new land of economic ruin and social disruption. An increasing number of rural inhabitants, unable to adjust to the post-War conditions, lived off robbery and marauding. While tensions between planters and freedmen were an individual matter in most cases, a minority of whites and blacks turned to crime and joined gangs of outlaws and robbers which plundered the countryside. Consequently, petty thefts, robbery, burglary and other property offenses reflect more than simply the activity of common criminals acting alone or in groups. These particular criminal activities revealed the deep social contradictions, conflicts and disequilibrum of the post-Civil War Southern society. And yet only a few historians have paid attention to the significance of property offenses in Louisiana, or in other Southern states during that troubled period.[3]

In focusing on rural Louisiana[4] during the crucial years of the post-Civil War period, the goal of this study is threefold: first, to analyze the various patterns of property offenses, to examine the social context in which those crimes were committed, and determine whether or not blacks were disproportionately responsible; secondly, to investigate the various networks of robbers and to determine the significance of the appearance and disappearance of outlaw and robber gangs; and finally, to determine whether the emergence of viligance committees was rooted largely in the failure of the judicial authorities to deal with property crimes, or if it represented a desperate attempt by whites to regain the rights they had once enjoyed over the land and the black population. In the process, we shall be able to demonstrate how the various patterns of property crimes were exacerbated by the larger issue of racial antagonism.

The Patterns of Property Crimes in Rural Louisiana

It is impossible to pick up a country paper from mid-nineteenth century Louisiana without noticing the epidemic nature of crimes of all types and grades, particularly burglaries and robberies, that were committed. Property crimes became so frequent after the War that many local papers stopped reporting petty thefts and mentioned other property offenses only of an aggravated nature. Still, a quick look at local newspapers under the headings of "District Court" or "Local Items" and the several congressional, district attorney and penitentiary reports, reveals numerous cases of indictments for arson, breaking into stores and houses, burglary, embezzlement, forgery, fraud, larceny, petty theft, robbery, etc., that regularly afflicted most country parishes. Although sketchy, the variety of the sources made it possible to develop such a study on post-Civil War Louisiana by using contemporary reports and collecting data on property offenses (Appendix). Despite inevitable gaps, this property criminal index represents a significant record of the amount of property crime in post-Civil War Louisiana (Table 1).

Table 1

Crimes Against Property in Rural Louisiana, 1866 to 1876

	(1)	(2)	(3)	(4)	(5)	(6)	(7)	(8)	total
1866	14	4	2	29	6	40	10	219	324
1867	12	15	2	28	10	25	12	165	269
1868	13	28	10	42	3	13	5	182	296
1869	9	2	2	33	1	24	2	135	208
1870	4	9	1	21	4	14	1	69	123
1871	10	14	4	21	6	27	7	154	243
1872	9	14	1	10	2	10	2	37	85
1873	8	20	2	10	7	20	6	95	168
1874	11	47	7	25	4	16	3	112	225
1875	14	31	3	9	0	14	12	62	145
1876	14	22	32	36	5	25	3	163	300
Total	118	206	66	264	48	228	63	1393	2386

(1)   Robbery and murder
(2)   Robbery and personal violence
(3)   Arson or destruction of property
(4)   Robbery, burglary or breaking and entering
(5)   Bribery, embezzlement, forgery or fraud
(6)   Horse stealing
(7)   Cattle, mule, hog stealing
(8)   Petty theft and larceny

Stealing in traditional and modern societies was closely related to the precarious condition and vulnerability of the lower classes who were most sensitive to economic depressions or to increases in the price of goods.[5] Property crimes, in particular petty thefts and larceny, had similar roots in post-Civil War Louisiana. Following the destruction and the economic disruption caused by the War, thousands of people, both whites and former slaves, were reduced to poverty in rural parishes. Malnutrition became particularly evident during the years immediately after the War and the economic depression of the mid 1870s. Trapped in a life of stealing or starving, thousands of people without regular employment were left with little to do besides loafing on town squares. The prevaling economic conditions were worsened by poor harvests that periodically struck Louisiana after the War. That most property crimes were closely related to misery is further shown by the nature of the stolen goods. Black and white indigents suffering from hunger regularly made raids on livestock, poultry yards, gardens, pantries, and kitchens; stealing important goods for their daily life.[6]

The theft of farm animals did occur occasionally during the antebellum period, but after the War such thefts took on almost epidemic proportions, as pigs and cattle were run off to concealed places and killed for food. Cattle stealing became so common in the late 1860s that it was considered the most serious obstacle to raising stock in many regions. In some parishes, the number of animals killed would have been sufficient to supply local towns with milk, butter and meat. In the prairies of Southwestern Louisiana three quarters of the livestock roaming at large had been illegally slaughtered by 1868.[7] In a period when the demand for stock was particularly high, cattle thefts represented a great loss for planters and farmers. In many instances, the parties losing their stock were deprived of their sole draft labor for cultivating their farms and of their sole means for supplying their family with meat.[8]

Hogs and cattle were not the only farm animals stolen for food. The stealing of mules and horses reached very high levels. The loss of mules, the common draft animal in rural Louisiana, was so great that many owners offered up to $50 in the hope of recovering their stolen animal. Although horses were worth less than mules, horse-stealing also represented a heavy loss for planters and farmers. The theft of horses was aggravated by the death of thousands from the "epizootic" and the "charbons" diseases, both of which spread through the South with a fearful rapidity.[9]

Stealing was not limited to goods of necessity: horses, mules, hogs, cows, steers, heifers and young calves attracted the attention of thieves. Louisiana planters regularly complained that thievery had become a profession for many rural residents; their criminal activity had gone beyond the need to survive. On many plantations, many articles made of wood, iron, lead and copper, along with harnesses, machinery and pipes attached to the gins and sugar houses were packed off by field hands and brought to towns and country stores or sold to foundry shops.[10]

Thieves and robbers did not limit their predatory activities to plantations or isolated houses and country stores. Small towns and cities which underwent a considerable growth in the second half of the nineteenth century were constantly plagued by burglars. After the War, thousands of rural people, particularly blacks, moved to towns which became invaded by tramps and beggers who could only survive through stealing. White and black thieves flocked the cities of Baton Rouge, Donaldsonville, Shreveport, and other smaller towns. Barely a night passed without some evidence of the thieves' daring escapades. Nearly every store and residence in these towns was struck, and the thieves often succeeded in escaping with considerable bounty.[11]

Thievery and robbery were not simply a regional phenomenon; every parish and town had its thieves. Rural parishes were full of scoundrels who made a good living travelling from town to town, using different aliases and deceiving people. Since the countryside was overrun by bands of thieves, local evil-doers took advantage of the opportunity to steal and cast the blame on travelling criminals.[12] Although sketchy, the regional distribution of property crimes reveals how offenses against property changed with regions (Table 2 and Figure I). While no rural districts[13] were protected from major crimes, most of them suffered primarily from simple theft. Moreover, the data show that the Red River Delta and the Eastern Bluff were the only two districts where the percentage of property offenses exceeded the levels of population in rural Louisiana. These two regions also had the unenviable record of being two of the most violent areas during Reconstruction.[14]

Black and white thieves were often very cunning and bold. They became acquainted with a building and the habits of its occupants and devised ways to open the door without a key. Some brazenly entered the owner's room, took the keys from his clothes while he slept and opened the front door to the store. Other thieves packed trunks of their victim's goods, put them on wagons and got away. Some stole spades and other tools from stables. The burning of stores or houses to destroy evidence of the robberies was not uncommon. Black field hands often took horses and mules from plantations, worked them for a time then reported them as strays to the local constable.[15]

While many blacks did not think it a crime to rob a white, most whites considered it even less of a crime to rob or kill a black.[16] Consequently, blacks were regularly defrauded of their wages, saw their crops and farm animals stolen, or were beaten, wounded and sometimes killed because had they asked for a fair settlement for their crops, refused to continue to work on a plantation or sued planters for money they owed them.[17] Blacks were also killed because they rented land and wanted to live on their own without any white control.[18]

Not surprisingly, not all blacks accepted or conformed with the whites' wishes. Many blacks reacted to white policies by refusing to work and began to live off the planters's stock, stealing mules, horses, cattles, hogs and corn.[19] Blacks were arrested in Bossier parish in late August 1868 when rumors of a black insurrection were circulated. The sheriff with a posse of 150 men went to put it down and arrested forty-eight blacks who were charged with riot and sedition. The whole affair began when the sheriff attempted to arrest several blacks charged with stealing cattle, although they had not committed any crime. A similar situation occurred in Caddo parish when whites attempted to arrest thirty families of black squatters.[20]

After economic crisis, political turmoil was the second most important factor that reduced blacks to stealing as a means of survive. During the electoral cam-

Table 2

Regional Distribution of Property Offences in Rural Louisiana, 1866–1876

(A)	(B)	(C)	(1)	(2)	(3)	(4)	(5)	(6)	(7)	(8)	Total	%
1.	13.5	72.9	31	138	10	39	2	57	11	241	529	27.1
2.	1.9	19.5	3	3	0	1	0	0	0	5	12	0.6
3.	2.4	22.3	1	0	0	3	0	2	0	14	20	1.0
4.	9.4	47.0	5	18	4	15	1	5	1	42	91	4.6
5.	5.6	41.1	4	6	1	4	1	3	5	21	45	2.3
6.	5.8	63.3	6	4	5	21	1	8	0	52	97	5.0
7.	10.1	83.0	1	6	4	5	3	14	6	49	88	4.5
8.	9.1	46.5	2	10	4	12	2	31	21	105	187	9.6
9.	23.2	59.3	17	18	11	43	9	70	11	238	417	21.4
10.	7.8	70.9	1	27	27	37	9	22	5	174	302	15.5
11.	4.9	37.9	3	0	1	5	2	1	0	14	26	1.3
12.	5.9	62.0	2	6	2	16	1	8	1	103	139	7.1
Total	99.6	62.0	76	236	69	201	31	221	61	1058	1953	100.0

A) Regions: 1 = Red River Delta Area; 2 = Western Frontier Area; 3 = Southwestern Frontier Area; 4 = Northern Frontier Area; 5 = North Central Hill Area; 6 = Northern Bluff Land Area; 7 = Mississippi Delta Area; 8 = South Central Prairies Area; 9 = Sugar Bowl Area; 10 = Eastern Bluff Land Area; 11 = Florida Parishes Area; 12 = Bayou Area

B) % of regional population has been compiled from the 1870 Federal census on the basis of a rural population of 533,451.

C) Regional % of blacks

(1) Robbery and murder	(5) Bribery, embezzlement, forgery or fraud
(2) Robbery and personal violence	(6) Horse stealing
(3) Arson or destruction of property	(7) Cattle, mule, hog stealing
(4) Robbery, burglary or breaking and entering	(8) Petty theft and larceny

131

Figure 1

Geographic and Cultural Regions of Louisiana in 1870

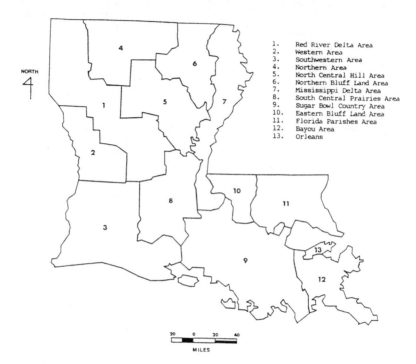

1.   Red River Delta Area
2.   Western Area
3.   Southwestern Area
4.   Northern Area
5.   North Central Hill Area
6.   Northern Bluff Land Area
7.   Mississippi Delta Area
8.   South Central Prairies Area
9.   Sugar Bowl Country Area
10. Eastern Bluff Land Area
11. Florida Parishes Area
12. Bayou Area
13. Orleans

paign of 1874, white conservatives across the state, determined to carry their districts, did not hesitate to apply economic pressure. Consequently, calls were made on planters in several parishes to discharge all blacks who had voted republican. As a result, some 500 black families, an aggregate of about two thousand people, were left roaming around Caddo parish during the winter of 1875 and contributing to much social chaos. Starving and prowling in the country for days without any means of subsistence, they gained a livehood only by stealing from the store houses, chicken coops and vegetable gardens of the planters in their neighborhood. These thefts created a high level of indignation among the planters, who threatened summary reprisals unless the petty larcenies abated.[21]

The post-Civil War period witnessed a significant change in criminal behavior as thieves and robbers became more willing to resort to violence. The years after the War also saw burgeoning incidences of armed robbery as guns become more widespread. Regularly carrying concealed weapons, thieves were less hesitant than their antebellum counterparts to use firearms in cases of emergency, even if this meant commiting murder.[22] Although newspapers charged blacks with using firearms upon the slightest provocation,[23] evidence shows that blacks rarely committed murder while perpetrating robberies. Whites tended to resort to murder during a robbery three times as often as blacks (Table 3). Still, the number of people killed during robberies represented only a small portion of all murders committed in Louisiana during this period.[24] Of 2943 homicides that occurred in rural Louisiana in the years 1866 to 1876, only 118 (4.0%) were committed by robbers. That so few homicides were related to robbery is in itself rather surprising. Still, this percentage is sustained by contemporary analysis.[25]

While stealing only occasionally degenerated into physical violence, other forms of violent crimes evolved out of rural criminality. Arson became one of the most serious crimes in post-Civil War Louisiana. It was usually commited at night and although it aroused the whole community the perpetrators were rarely caught. Rural society appeared defenseless in the face of arsonists. When a suspicious fire erupted in a particular town, village or parish, protective associations or vigilance committees were set up to discover the arsonist and to prevent the repetition of such acts. When an arsonist was caught by the law, he was usually sentenced to the state penitentiary for life, if he had not previously suffered at the hands of a vigilance committee.[26] Still, arson, like other property offenses represented an important manifestation of the aggressiveness and social tension that prevailed in rural Louisiana.

Although blacks were charged by whites with being responsible for most larcenies, robberies and arsons,[27] the present data show that whites had a greater propensity to commit property crimes than blacks. Whites composed only 38% of the rural population, but committed 60% of all property offenses in countryside parishes (Table 4). Moreover, black thievery differed from white in the nature of the offenses. Blacks were more often charged with petty thefts and stealing cattle, horses, hogs and mules for food consumption, while whites were more often charged with violent and aggravated property crimes. Finally, people who robbed did not come only from the lower classes of society. Some of them went around after having committed their villanous deeds sporting a cane as any ordinary gentlemen.[28]

Table 3
Number of People Killed By Robbers, 1866 to 1876

Race of Victims	Race of Assailants	Number	%
Unknown	Unknown	1	0.8
Whites	Unknown	3	2.5
Blacks	Unknown	3	2.5
Unknown	Whites	4	3.4
Whites	Whites	38	32.2
Blacks	Whites	42	35.6
Unknown	Blacks	2	1.7
Whites	Blacks	11	9.3
Blacks	Blacks	14	11.8
Total		118	99.8

Table 4

Racial Distribution of People Involved in Crimes Against Property,
1866 To 1876

Type of Offense	Number	% Whites	White Propensity
Robbery and murder	228	62.7	2.7
Robbery and personal violence	293	89.0	13.7
Arson or destruction of property	52	80.7	6.8
Robbery, burglary or breaking and entering	163	73.6	4.6
Bribery, embezzelment, forgery or fraud	26	57.7	2.2
Horse stealing	127	43.3	1.2
Cattle, mule, hog stealing	64	26.5	− 1.7
Petty theft and larceny	634	46.2	1.4
Total and average	1587	59.6	2.4

Confronted with white violence, blacks did resort occasionally to violence as a way to correct wrongs committed against them. In these cases, violence was used either to obtain a just settlement for sale of crops or to rescue blacks arrested and charged with stealing.[29] But destruction of property and arson became the preferred response of blacks. Not only did arson provide a complete revenge, but blacks felt less liable to retaliation as arsonists were rarely caught.[30] Still, arson represented a two-edged sword as white conservatives often used it as a means to intimidate black and white Republicans.[31]

Generally, newspapers, congressional reports, or district attorney reports did not mention whether or not the person charged with committing a property offense acted alone or with someone else. Still, despite its sketchy character, evidence shows that in more than 16% of the cases, individuals who committed a crime against property did not act alone. In the case of burglary, fraud or forgery, horse theft, cattle and other animal theft and the usual robbery, offenders rarely tended to act collectively. But people who resorted to violence while committing property offenses usually did not act alone. Robberies involving more than one thief accounted for more than half of all robberies that resulted in murder. This number dropped to a little below 50% for robberies in which the offenders resorted to violence, and rose above 50% for cases involving destruction of property (Table 5).

The Outlaw and Robber Gangs

In rural Louisiana, stealing, robberies and petty thefts were often committed by several people acting together in ephemeral associations which periodically yielded gangs of outlaws and robbers. The development of outlaw bands was favored by a series of independent factors: the prevailing frontier spirit of some regions, the ease of finding refuge, or the authorities' inability to maintain law and order. Louisiana also suffered from more particular conditions: the economic destruction caused by the War, social dislocation generated by emancipation and post-Civil War political turmoil. These factors created conditions favorable for the proliferation of criminal activities in Louisiana and in some other south-

PROPERTY OFFENSES   135

Table 5
The Collective Nature of Crimes against Property

	Number	% Collective
Robbery and murder	114	54.2
Robbery and personal violence	203	46.8
Arson or destruction of property	57	57.9
Robbery, burglary or breaking and entering	251	16.9
Bribery, embezzlement, forgery or fraud	48	8.4
Horse stealing	228	4.9
Cattle, mule, hog stealing	62	22.6
Petty theft and larceny	1367	7.9
Total and average	2330	16.4

ern states such as Texas. Consequently, although bands of outlaws[32] were fairly common before the Civil War, they posed an even greater problem afterward. The large number of outlaw bands reflected the prevailing economic conditions. Thirty-eight bands were reported during the 1866–1869 post-War depression, but with the return of relative economic prosperity during the years 1870–1872, this number dropped to only seven. However, it rose again to thirty-seven with the 1873–1877 depression (Table 6).

In post-Civil War rural Louisiana, the advantages of belonging to a band of thieves were enormous: alibis were more easily arranged, large numbers of men could be employed to protect each other, risky schemes could be more successfully executed, stolen goods could be more easily disposed of, security and solidarity among the confreres were greater, etc. Moreover, the larger the band became, the bolder were its operations. Once a band had selected a store, a plantation or a house, its leader often devised ways to become aquainted with the selected target and the habits of those who occupied it. In some cases, a member checked the veranda or the windows. In other cases, a member took the key to the store

Table 6
Annual Distribution of Gangs of Robbers In Rural Louisiana, 1850–1884

Antebellum year	number	Reconstruction year	number	Early Bourbon year	number
1850	1	1866	6	1877	11
1851	0	1867	10	1878	2
1852	0	1868	11	1879	2
1853	1	1869	11	1880	5
1854	0	1870	4	1881	1
1855	0	1871	2	1882	1
1856	1	1872	1	1883	2
1857	2	1873	4	1884	2
1858	3	1874	8		
1859	10	1875	7		
1860	1	1876	7		
Total	19		71		26

from the clerk's pocket and opened the front door without breaking in. Finally, gangs not only accumulated large quantities of goods during their forays, but often assured the cohesion and survival of their organizations by sharing the booty after each robbery.[33]

Bands of outlaws and robbers functioned outside of the regular political society. By their very nature, bands lived in a parallel or underground world. Consequently, little information leaked out about their activities and organization. Only the most prominent figures became publicly known and these were both abhorred and glorified. For most common bands, the name of the leader, the exact composition and the number of members remained a mystery for contemporary officials. Moreover, the study of criminal bands is further complicated because many lasted for only a short period of time, before they dissolved or regrouped to start again.[34] Still it is possible to draw some general conclusions about post-Civil War Louisiana.

The numerous criminal fraternities that plundered rural Louisiana during the post-Civil War period were loosely organized in small robber bands that rarely grew beyond ten people. They usually originated with a local robber or outlaw who had become notorious for his daring exploits. The more successful a robber was, the more men chose to join him—as the history of the Damon Fontenot, Cyriaque Guillory, or Lawson Kimball bands showed. Bands rarely lasted more than two or three years. Although some bands limited their membership to whites or blacks only, many bands were biracial in their composition. Seeing bands headed by blacks was not unusual as leaders were chosen not on the basis of their race but on their leadership qualities and their ability to plan further criminal operations.[35]

The Beaver, the Black Horse Cavalry, the Fontenot, the Guillory, and the Kimball and West gangs were the most notorious of the bands that plundered rural Louisiana for years with total impunity. They shared a common root; they originated from rebel deserters and their leaders had been jayhawkers during and after the War.[36] That many bands were composed of rebel deserters and were the byproduct of the semi-guerrilla bands and jayhawkers is not surpising. War and gang robbery often appear as one and the same thing. Moreover, the War and its aftermath did accelerate social disintegration. As a consequence, former soldiers and rebel deserters—men who had spent years in a violent profession—represented a specially trained post of recruits for outlaw gangs. These men not only found it difficult to adapt to civilian life, but they had learned to live on the surrounding country, pillaging and robbing while members of guerrilla bands during the War. By transforming themselves at the end of the War into gangs of marauders and robbers, they simply continued to practice what they knew best. As Federal authorities did not have enough troops in Louisiana to maintain law and order in rural areas, these gangs were largely responsible for the general atmosphere of lawlessness that prevailed in the Pelican state after the War; they rode around the countryside, whipping and robbing freedmen and defying the military and civil authorities before retreating to the swamps which offered a secure hiding place.[37]

Freedmen represented the second most important sources of recruitment for bands of thieves and robbers. Many parishes were overrun after the War with bands of black thieves whose operations were as bold and mysterious as those of white bands. Often headed by shrewd and cunning blacks, these bands were governed by precise rules in robbery procedures and in disposing the stolen goods afterwards. Usually one member of the gang visited the store they intended to rob, bought a few things, and got to know where the safe was and if it contained any money. During the break in, two or three of the gang members served as lookouts. Nothing could stop them as they did not hesitate to blow holes in brick walls to get into a store. They often burned the store after a robbery to destroy any trace of evidence. Members of black robber gangs were usually asked to share the booty of a robbery even if they had acted alone. They rode through the surrounding country and developed large networks for disposing of the stolen property. One gang of black thieves during the early 1870s extended its operations throughout the region from New Iberia to Brashear City.[38]

Gangs of robbers and outlaws were found in all regions of Louisiana (Table 7 & Figure 1), but their strength and importance depended on the condition of the territory. Southern Louisiana with its numerous lakes, bayous and swamps was, in large part, almost impenetrable and offered an ideal refuge where criminal bands could flourish.[39] With few roads, thinly populated parishes, and proximity to Texas, Northwestern Louisiana became the second most important sanctuary for outlaw gangs.[40]

Table 7
Regional Distribution of Gangs of Robbers

	Antebellum		Reconstruction		Bourbons		Total	
	N	%	N	%	N	%	N	%
Red River area	1	5.2	17	23.9	6	23.0	24	20.7
Western area			1	1.4	1	3.9	2	1.7
Southwestern area	1	5.2	3	4.2	3	11.5	7	6.0
Northern area			1	1.4	1	3.9	2	1.7
N. Central Hill	1	5.2	3	4.2	2	7.7	6	5.2
Northern bluff land			2	2.8	1	3.9	3	2.6
Mississippi delta	3	15.7	3	4.2	3	11.5	9	7.7
South Central prairies	6	31.5	5	7.0	2	7.7	13	11.2
Sugar Bowl area	6	31.5	23	32.4	6	23.0	35	30.2
Bluff Land area			7	9.8	1	3.9	8	6.9
Florida parishes	1	5.2	4	5.6			5	4.3
Bayou area			2	2.8			2	1.7
Total	19	99.5	71	99.7	26	100.0	116	99.9

Many bands reflected the peculiar characteristics of their region. These bands were unlikely to abandon their home base where they learned to live on the territory and benefited from the complicity, or at least the passive support, of the local population who found this the best protection against being robbed, molested or murdered by local outlaws. No bands of outlaws or robbers could pursue their nefarious trade and survive without some protection. Indeed, gangs of robbers, outlaws and murderers, independent of their numbers or the cunning of their leaders, could not operate alone for long. Ostensibly, outlaws and robbers were able to remain at large and to continue to prey upon the community only because they recruited many men who were of good standing in the community which furnished them with harboring facilities. The protection that local bands received from prominent members of society not only made it more difficult for the authorities to muster aid in apprehending local criminals, but it was also seen as one of the main causes of the general atmosphere of lawlessness that prevailed in rural Louisiana after the War.[41]

Other bands developed extensive networks that covered a large territory. These bands maintained ties with several parishes and exercised their nefarious trade for years. Still other bands went beyond their regional base and expanded their activity throughout the whole state. Moreover, some bands extended their operations into the border states of Arkansas, Mississippi and Texas.[42] Finally, a few bands from other states, particularly Texas, operated in Louisiana, robbing, destroying property and murdering blacks.[43]

The kind of products stolen differed greatly depending on whether robberies were committed by an individual or by a band. The difference was not only in the quantity but also in the nature of the goods stolen. Louisiana robbers, and more particularly gangs of robbers, formed a criminal fraternity whose members were determined not only to survive, but to get a better life. Individual robbers stole cattle, hogs, mules and consumption goods as a means to feed themselves, but many bands broke into stores and selected goods for their market values.[44] Moreover, bands of robbers were developed within the historical circumstances specific to each region.

Bands of cattle thieves were mainly concentrated in Southwestern Louisiana where cattle raising was most extensive. For more than a quarter of century, the Attakapas country and the Opelousas prairies were populated by a group of men who contended that the cattle which fed upon the prairie were the property of those who caught them. These men made Abbeville their center of operations.[45] The stealing and illegal traffic of cotton and corn predominated in the Florida parishes after the War and was mainly responsible for the turmoil that particularly troubled the parishes of East Baton Rouge, East Feliciana and West Feliciana during the mid 1870s.[46] Horse-stealing was clearly one of the most lucrative criminal businesses in Louisiana after the War. Although dens of daring horse thieves were found in every section and region of the state, they were mainly concentrated in the northern regions of the state from where stolen horses could be smuggled into Arkansas and Texas. The civil authorities were so inefficient in pursuing and breaking up horse thief gangs in Northern Louisiana that on several occasions they asked the military to send troops into the area.[47]

The appearance and disappearance of these bands, as was the case for the robbery and petty theft epidemic, coincided with times of economic crisis. During the course of their existence, these bands preyed on the local population, terrorizing the surrounding countryside and often plundering the houses of both poor whites and innocent blacks. It did not matter if these bands were composed of only whites, only blacks, or blacks and whites, they followed the same criminal behavior towards blacks and poor whites.[48]

The only bands who could claim some sort of political program were those such as the "Black Horse Cavalry" who originated from semi-guerrilla bands. Even if a close link could be established between former guerrilla bands such as the "Black Horse Cavalry" and the "Knights of the White Camelia" that terrorized Louisiana in the summer and fall of 1868, the latter never adopted any program of social reform because they were completely dedicated to the restoration of the Pelican state as a white man's country.[49]

Property Offenders and Vigilance Committees

Robberies, murders and other depredations committed by gangs and individual thieves created a general atmosphere of suspicion and fear in rural areas. When a band of robbers appeared in a region or moved to a new area and began to operate its villanous trade, the most improbable stories about them arose and became exaggerated. Rumors could swell the size of a five-member band to fifty, describing the thieves as armed to the teeth and eager to perpetrate any act of violence. The whole country would then became worked up to a pitch of excitement. People were warned to become more watchful, to "sleep with one eye on watch, have a good-barrell gun, well loaded with sixteen, whistlers in each barrels, always at your bed side and and don't bother the judiciary with an investigation." Many papers advised rural people to keep their guns fully loaded and to resort to summary punishments whenever a thief was caught stealing.[50]

When a high rate of theft occurred in a parish, calls were issued for a vigorous enforcement of the laws and to have every idle vagrant arrested and put to work on the chain gang if necessary.[51] Not surprisingly, arson, burglary, larceny, petty theft, robbery and other crimes against property dominated the judicial calendar as they represented more than 50 percent of all cases prosecuted and tried in local parish and district courts in rural Louisiana. Crimes against property were considered by district attornies and judges to be the most heinous offenses, and burglars, forgers, highway robbers and petty thieves were not only promptly tried and convicted but also more severely punished than those convicted of violent crimes against a person.[52] Still, in spite of the efforts of local law enforcement officers in apprehending robbers and the severity of the court, most people who committed property crimes escaped the heavy hand of the law (Table 8).

It was fashionable during the period to blame the state administration and its law enforcement officers for this unfortunate state of affairs. Newspapers all over the state complained about the inefficiency of the authorities in arresting and prosecuting thieves and burglars. The Democratic press asserted that filling civil offices with "unprincipled vagabonds and ignorant negroes" was the first cause for the general atmosphere of lawlessness.[53] But the problem was more complex. Louisiana lacked the coherent centralized police force to repress banditry and brigandage in the countryside that Texas and most other states had. The state militia rarely operated outside of New Orleans, and local law enforcement officers were at the mercy of whatever local support they could muster to repress outlaws.[54]

Table 8

Distribution of Sentencing for Crimes Against Property in Rural Lousiana, 1866 to 1876

	(1)	(2)	(3)	(4)	(5)	(6)	(7)	(8)	Total
no action	196	291	53	113	22	60	35	323	1093
acquitted	3	2	1	1	0	0	32	40	79
escapees	14	1	1	0	0	3	1	1	21
liberated on bonds	16	24	24	–	–	–	–	–	64
found guilty	11	1	57	5	13	6	36	88	217
to pay a fine	0	0	1	0	1	0	3	9	14
less than a month	0	0	0	0	0	1	2	2	5
1 to 6 months	0	1	1	6	6	3	4	4	25
6 months to 1 year	0	0	0	3	1	2	0	0	6
1 to 2 years	17	56	1	67	18	81	14	14	268
2 to 5 years	0	0	0	83	5	77	10	10	185
6 to 10 years	0	0	2	19	0	0	0	0	21
11 to 20 years	2	1	7	10	0	0	0	0	20
more than 20 years	0	0	0	1	0	0	0	0	1
hard labor for life	15	0	1	4	0	0	0	0	20
death sentence	16	0	0	0	0	0	0	0	16
lynched	4	0	0	0	0	2	3	3	12
Total	294	377	149	312	66	235	140	494	2067

(1)	Robbery and murder
(2)	Robbery and personal violence
(3)	Arson or destruction of property
(4)	Robbery, burglary or breaking and entering
(5)	Bribery, embezzlement, forgery or fraud
(6)	Horse stealing
(7)	Cattle, mule, hog stealing
(8)	Petty theft and larceny

The lax state of affairs hampering law enforcement was further complicated by the unwillingness of whites to sit with blacks on juries. The judicial system was also disrupted by legal technicalities which allowed many criminals to escape justice. Moreover, corruption overrode the selection of jurors in criminal trials. Social and pecuniary influences were brought to bear on jurors by influential offenders. Finally, the fear of reprisal by desperate criminals influenced many jurors. Few people were willing to lay charges against criminals who, as a consequence, were allowed to go free. The detention, trial and punishment of offenders became more and more farcical and uncertain. Although robberies and murders were regularly committed, most people doubted that the perpetrators of those deeds could be brought to justice.[55]

Moreover, various parish newspapers and grand juries noted that the notorious inadequacies of the local jails and prisons throughout the state were an important factor in the inability of officials to cope with crime. Men indicted for arson, burglary, larceny, horse stealing, and even murder, often escaped trial by breaking out of jails. However, the reluctance of country residents to pay higher taxes for larger and more secure jails made the task of keeping offenders who awaited trial almost impossible.[56]

Faced with the inability of state and local authorities to put an end to theft and

PROPERTY OFFENSES   141

other crimes committed by gangs of robbers in the countryside, vigilance committees were organized as last resort. The rumor that a band of robbers was operating
in a region was often enough to generate the formation of preventive vigilance
committees before any crimes had been committed.[57] Consequently, associations
of citizens periodically formed vigilance committees or protective associations
all over the state to hold in check robbers and other property offenders.[58]

State laws and parish regulations were enacted during the 1850's to check
the illegal trade of local storeowners and merchants with slaves, but to no avail.
As a consequence, vigilance committees had already been formed in several
parishes.[59] When illegal traffic and contraband activities increased after the War,
becoming particularly widespread in the parishes of East Baton Rouge, and East
and West Felicianas between 1874 and 1876, the planters organized committees
to find the freedmen who were stealing and the merchants who were buying the
stolen property. The planting classes considered that the storeowners involved
in this criminal trade were disgracing the name of all merchants and ought to
be hung. Groups of white regulators conducted a campaign of terror—roaming
around parishes, killing, burning stores and ginhouses, and compelling black
laborers and white local merchants to quit the seed-cotton traffic. The problem
persisted beyond the Reconstruction period and in some regions became so grave
that merchants in Madison and Ouachita signed a pledge not to buy cotton after
a certain hour at night.[60]

Vigilance committees continued to resort to banishment for a first offense,[61]
which had been their main means of punishment during the 1850s[62] but after the
War their activities often took a swift and brutal character. In many instances,
they did not hesitate, particularly if those people accused of robbery had murdered
a white, to resort to summary justice and lynch the alledged guilty party.[63]
Vigilance committees were particularly active in Southern Louisiana where they
represented the local response to the problem of cattle and horse stealing during
the second half of the century.[64] The most notable of these cases of vigilante
violence occurred in Vermillion parish in September 1873 when twelve alleged
outlaws who had resisted the vigilance committee were lynched.[65]

In Louisiana, as elsewhere, the emergence of a strong opposition to vigilantes
often took the form of anti-vigilance committees and reflected deep social and
economic conflicts.[66] The proceedings of these committees created a climate
of terror in the lower parishes and met with stiff opposition from the press.[67]
And yet, even as many people came to deplore lynching and vigilantism, many
others continued to consider them as necessary evils. Some law officers did
occasionally try to resist vigilance committees or lynching mobs, but the plain
truth is that lynching was usually endorsed by local notables and occurred with
the compliance of law officials.[68]

Meanwhile, following emancipation, lynching and other forms of summary
executions became a disturbing feature of race relations in Louisiana and in
the South, as blacks were no longer protected by their market value. Many
blacks were caught and brutally murdered by vigilance committees for allegedly
stealing chickens, hogs, horse or cattle, and others were killed for such trivial
reasons as stealing an onion or an apple from the planter's garden, stealing meat
from a smokehouse or simply for going into the smokehouse, or being accused
of stealing a box of sardines.[69] But the lynching of blacks for alledged stealing

or arson was not limited to offenses against white property. On one occasion, a black reputed to be a notorious thief was lynched after a summary trial for stealing a cow from another black.[70] In another instance, a black in Ascension parish was brutally murdered in 1875 by "white ruffians" for refusing to confess complicity in a robbery with which it was later learned that he had nothing to do.[71] But lynching to protect property was not only a brutal and summary way to administer justice, it was also an important tool in converting Louisiana into a white man's territory.

Many alleged charges of larceny, robbery and other property offenses against white Republicans were politically motivated. In many instances, the charge of stealing chickens was used to justify the lynching of white Republicans. Many eminent black politicians also met with the same fate on trumped up charges of stealing hogs, chickens and cattle.[72] By regularly accusing white radicals of inciting blacks to murder and robbery, Democratic newspapers all over the state justified attacks against white Republicans and Republican newspapers which, as a result, became targets of the whites' fury.[73]

Conclusion

It is unquestionable that the general atmosphere of violence and lawlessness that prevailed in the South after the Civil War represented a fundamental factor in determining the significance of that troubled period. Political riots, social and labor disturbances, murders and others personal affrays reached an unprecedent level. Property crimes, as the present study shows, constituted the second largest type of offense and equally reflected the social climate of the Reconstruction, playing a major role in the spiralling cycle of violence.

If petty thefts and other forms of property offenses were regularly committed by both whites and blacks, they are most revealing about the adjustment of blacks to freedom and the white response to the post-Civil War economic and social conditions. With emancipation, Louisiana along with the rest of the South saw the emergence of a new economic order that introduced blacks into the new national and world economy. Freed from their masters who had been obliged to feed their slaves, blacks were no longer protected from financial crisis and became as vulnerable as planters and merchants to changes or fluctuations in the market economy. Meanwhile, economic depressions reduced many blacks to crime and stealing through desperation or destitution. A life of robbery could furnish blacks not only with a means of subsistance and avoiding misery, but also a way to escape the exploitation on plantations. Being a thief was not therefore an abstract phenomenon for freedmen, but an alternative mode of industry to satisfy their hunger, even if it meant living outside the abstract rules of law.[74] Meanwhile, as most Southern whites were determined to preserve as much as possible the moral values of the old social order, they punished more severely blacks charged with property offenses than whites who committed similar offenses.[75]

The variation in the frequency of property crimes suggests a breakdown of social organization. The patterns of property crimes show how post-Civil War Louisiana was affected by a strong sensitivity to the social and political turmoil of the period. The present study shows the need not only to establish the link

PROPERTY OFFENSES   143

between property crimes and such factors as the lack of police force or the periodic economic depressions. It also suggests that the curve of property crimes was also strongly influenced by the prevailing political disorders and the general atmosphere of racial antagonism. Indeed, regions that suffered the largest number of property crimes were also the areas of the state most affected by political violence. Further study on property crimes from local and regional perspectives are urgently needed in order to gain a more comprehensive understanding of the turbulent history of Reconstruction.

Département d'histoire et de sciences politiques
Sherbrooke, Québec, Canada J1K2R1

Appendix

Methodology and Scope of the Investigation

Historians who attempt to investigate property crimes are faced with the problem of finding reliable sources. Official data are often biased and do not indicate the real extent of the crimes. Consequently, many historians conclude that the general problem of under-reporting makes it difficult to go beyond an impressionistic portrayal of most forms of criminality.[76] The problem of under-reporting is further complicated by the large number of people who committed property crimes but were never caught. Nonetheless, it is possible to avoid the pitfalls contained in official data by identifying individual cases and collecting one's own data. This is the approach that I have followed here.

Collecting information on every case of property offense that occurred in Louisiana between 1866 and 1876 represents a difficult and hazardous task. The whole operation depends on the quality of sources available. Fortunately, a rich and diversified body of historical documentation makes such a study of post-Civil War Louisiana possible. Although I did consult some fifty congressional reports and miscellaneous documents and the general correspondence and reports of both the Freedmen's Bureau and the War Department, the three main sources of my investigation of property crimes in Louisiana rest on the State Attorney General reports for the years of 1867 to 1877, on State Penitentiary Reports for the years of 1865 to 1877 and on fifty state and local newspapers published in Louisiana between 1866 and 1876.[77]

Defining property crimes represents another important methodological problem. To get the most complete and accurate picture and patterns of the various forms of property offenses, I chose to include in my data set all cases of arson and other forms of destruction of property, breaking and entering and burglary, embezzlement, forgery and fraud, grand and small larceny, robbery and petty theft that were reported in Louisiana during these troubled years. To avoid duplication or repetition of cases, I included in my data set only cases for which there existed clear information about the name of the offender, the year, the place and the type of offenses. Consequently, the number of property offenses in Louisiana was much higher than the 2383 cases in our data set. The crosschecking of each case from a variety of sources has made it possible to diminish the deficiencies of some cases and to establish a relatively accurate data set that gives a comprehensive description of the nature and level of property crimes in rural Louisiana after the Civil War.

This data set, despite its limits, makes it possible both to look at local trends and to establish a global picture of property crimes in Louisiana after the War. Moreover, the statistics drawn from the present data set allows us to go beyond isolated cases, to establish various patterns and to examine property crimes in their broader social context. In the process, property offenses emerged as a social phenomenon that could be studied and interpreted in the particular mental and emotional context of post-Civil War Southern society, with all its fears and uncertainty. Finally, to complete my study and correct some deficiencies in this data set, I use qualitative information which has the advantage of providing specific information on particular trends and patterns.

ENDNOTES

1. *Lafayette Advertiser*, June 21, 1873.

2. 43rd Congress, 2nd sess., *House Report* no. 261, 196; *Opelousas Courrier*, Aug. 6, 1870; *New Orleans Republican*, Dec. 25, 1874, Dec. 24, 1875; *Shreveport Times*, Feb. 27, 1872, June 12, Oct. 27, 29, 1874, Jan. 31, June 18, 21, Sept. 21, Dec. 24, 1875; George C. Rable, *But There Was No Peace: The Role of Violence in the Politics of Reconstruction* (Athens, GA, 1984), 98.

3. Edward L. Ayers, *Vengeance and Justice: Crime and Punishment in the 19th-Century American South* (New York, 1984); Eric Foner, *Reconstruction: America's Unfinished Revolution, 1863–1877* (New York, 1988); Michael S. Hindus, *Prison and Plantation: Crime, Justice, and Authority in Massachussetts and South Carolina, 1767–1878* (Chapel Hill, 1980); Leon F. Litwack, *Been in the Storm So Long: The Aftermath of Slavery* (New York, 1979); Joe Gray Taylor, *Louisiana Reconstructed, 1863–1877* (Baton Rouge, 1974); Albert C. Smith, "'Southern Violence' Reconsidered: Arson as Protest in Black-Belt Georgia, 1865–1910," *Journal of Southern History* 51, 4 (Nov. 1985): 527–64; Ted Tunnell, *Crucible Reconstruction, War, Radicalism and Race Relations in Louisiana. 1862–1877* (Baton Rouge, 1984).

4. I have chosen to exclude the Parish of Orleans and to limit the present study to rural Louisiana for several reasons. Orleans Parish, including the city of New Orleans and its 200,000 inhabitants, represented a special case. With the exception of Shreveport (8,000) and Baton Rouge (7,000) there was no town or city outside of New Orleans in Louisiana that had more than 2,000 inhabitants. The state of Louisiana, outside of New Orleans, can therefore be considered rural. Finally, criminality did not follow the same pattern in New Orleans as in the countryside. New Orleans was better policed than the rural areas. Thus, to have included New Orleans in the study would have distorted the analysis. This general division of rural and urban area is largely supported by historians. J. M. Beattie, "The Patterns of Crime in England, 1660–1800," *Past and Present* no. 62 (Feb. 1974): 47–95; David Cohen and Eric A. Johnson, "French Criminality: Urban-Rural Differences in the Nineteenth Century," *Journal of Interdisciplinary History* XII, 3 (Winter 1982): 477–501; Harvey J. Graff, "Crime and Punishment in the Nineteenth Century: A New Look at the Criminal," *Journal of Interdisciplinary History* VII, 3 (Winter 1977): 477–491.

5. Angel J. Alloza, "Crime and Social Change in Eighteenth-Century Madrid," *International Association For The History of Crime and Criminal Justice* 19 (Spring 1994): 7–19; Beatty, "Patterns of Crimes," 95; J. S. Cockburn, "The Nature and Causes of Crime in England, 1559–1625" in Cockburn, *Crime in England 1500–1800* (Princeton, 1977), 49–71; V. A. C. Gattrell, Bruce Lenman and Geoffrey Parker ed., *Crime and the Law: The Social History of Crime in Western Europe Since 1500* (London, 1980); Barbara A. Hanawalt, *Crime and Conflict in English Communities* (Cambridge, MA. 1979); Robert A. Nye, "Crime and Modern Societies: Research Strategy for Historians," *Journal of Social History* 11, 4 (Summer 1978): 491–507.

6. D. S. Rivers and others to Major General W. L. Hancock, Civil Affairs, 5th Military Department, War Department, Micro 4588, 1867–70, New Orleans, Dec. 18, 1867;

PROPERTY OFFENSES 145

Petition to Major General W. L. Hancock, Opelousas, Dec. 27, 1867, Box 7, Book 61, Civil Affairs, 5th Military District, War Department; O. A. Violet to Lieut. J. M. Lee, Jan. 14, 1868, Bureau of Freedmen, Refugees and Abandoned Lands (BFRAL); *Baton Rouge Advocate*, Dec. 6, 1867, June 9, 1869; *Baton Rouge Gazette & Comet*, April 3, 1866; *Carroll Record*, April 4, 1868; *Donaldsonville Chief*, June 26, 1875; *Louisiana Democrat*, Nov. 2, 1868, May 10, 1871, Feb. 23, 1875; *New Iberia Sugar Bowl*, April 23, 1874, April 8, 1875; *New Orleans Picayune*, Nov. 25, 1869, Jan. 16, 25, Feb. 6, 1875; *New Orleans Times*, Jan. 11, 1875; *Courrier*, Nov. 14, 1873, July 22, 1875; *Thibodeaux Sentinel*, April 4, 1874, Nov. 6, 1875; Carl A. Brasseaux, *Acadian To Cajun, Transformation of a People* (Jackson, 1992), 75, 87; Taylor, *Louisiana Reconstructed*, 361, 422–23.

7. A planter in East Baton Rouge parish lost twenty-seven of his thirty-three hogs at the hands of thieves in early December 1867. His cows, goats and sheep disappeared in the same manner. Another planter saved sixty of his 110 hogs from theft by killing them himself. Cattle and even horses were often shot and killed during the night. There seemed to be no safety for stock of any kind. 44th Congress, 2nd Sess. *House Misc. Doc.* no 34, 169, 178, 179, 295; 43rd Congress, 2nd Sess., *House Report* no 261, 375; D. S. Rivers and others to Major General W. L. Hancock, Civil Affairs, 5th Military Department, War Department, Micro 4588, 1867–70, New Orleans, Dec. 18, 1867; Petition to Major General W. L. Hancock, Opelousas, Dec. 27, 1867, Box 7, Book 61, Civil Affairs, 5th Military District, War Department; Capt. F. A. Osborne to Lieut L. O. Parker, Aug. 10, 1867, Plaquemines, Letters Received, Box 4, Book 60, BFRAL; O. A. Violet to Lieut. J. M. Lee, Jan. 14, 1868, BFRAL; *Baton Rouge Advocate*, Dec. 6, 1867, June 9, 1869, May 9, 1870; *Baton Rouge Tri-Weekly Advocate*, Dec. 9, 1866; *Gazette & Comet*, April 3, 1866, Feb. 21, Dec. 5, 1867; *Bossier Banner*, Sept. 29, 1866; *Record*, April 4, June 13, 1868; *Democrat*, Nov. 2, 1868; *Sugar Bowl*, Aug. 12, 1872; *Picayune*, Sept. 12, Nov. 25, 1869; *Courrier*, Nov. 14, 1873; *Opelousas Journal*, Aug. 12, 1871; Brasseaux, *Acadian To Cajun*, 75; Taylor, *Louisiana Reconstructed*, 422–23.

8. 44th Congress, 2nd Sess., *House Misc. Doc.*, no 34, Part 3, 34, 35, 56, 58, 60; *Courrier*, March 24, 1866; *Baton Rouge Comet*, Dec. 5, 1867; Charles P. Roland, "Difficulties of Civil War Sugar Planting in Louisiana," *Louisiana Historical Quarterly*, 38, 4, (Oct. 1955): 45–46; Taylor, *Louisiana Reconstructed*, 422. In 1860, sheep were worth $3 a head, and a fat hog $7. Keith Fontenot, "Old Southwest Louisiana," *Attakapas Gazette* (June 1972), 83–84.

9. While an American mare was worth $50 and a stud $35, the demand for mules became so large by 1867 that their price rose to nearly $250 per head. *Democrat*, Dec. 4, 1872; *Sugar Bowl*, Aug. 12, 1872; *New Orleans Crescent*, Aug. 14, 1868; *Picayune*, July 31, 1868; *Courrier*, June 13, 1874; Fontenot, "Old Southwest Louisiana," 83–84; Brasseaux, *Acadian to Cajun*, 77; Taylor, *Louisiana Reconstructed*, 345.

10. *Carroll Watchman*, Aug. 12, 1875; *Picayune*, Feb. 20, 1875; *Democrat*, May 27, 1868; *Natchitoches Semi-Weekly Times*, Feb. 7, Sept. 26, 1866; *Journal*, Aug. 12, 1871.

11. *Advocate-Comet*, Feb. 13, 1866; *Gazette & Comet*, April 3, 1866, Dec. 5, 1867; *Tri-Weekly Advocate*, Feb. 6, 1866; *Watchman*, Aug. 12, 1875; *Chief*, Aug. 22, 1874; *Advertiser*, June 12, 1869; *Le Louisianais de St. Jacques*, June 11, July 15, 1871, Aug. 14, Dec. 4, 1875; *Democrat*, Aug. 16, 19, 1869, May 27, 1874; *People Vindicators*, Oct. 4, 1873, May 8, 1875; *Sugar Bowl*, Feb. 2, 1871, Aug. 7, 14, 1873, April 23, 1874, April 8, 1875; *Picayune*, Dec. 8, 1868, Oct. 20, 1869, Sept. 9, 1871; *Courrier*, Feb. 4, 1871; *Gazette*, Oct. 4, 1873; *Sentinel*, Aug. 14, 1869; Taylor, *Louisiana Reconstructed*, 91, 322.

12. *Sugar Bowl*, Aug. 29, 1872; *Picayune*, Aug. 24, Dec. 17, 1870, Jan. 20, 1872.

13. As the number of parishes, the political sub-units of Louisiana, increased from 48 to 58 between 1868 and 1877, any analysis based at the parish level is almost impossible and can bring only sketchy results. Therefore, we chose to create an intermediary level of

geographic and cultural areas between the parish and state levels. This approach gives us comparable data for each area for the whole period. The delineation of our sub-regions was done on the basis of the geographical and cultural characteristics of each region as reported by Daniel Dennett, *Louisiana As It Is* (New Orleans, 1876), Samuel Lockett, *Louisiana As It Is* (ed. by Laurence C. Post, Baton Rouge, 1969), and Alvin L. Bertrand, *The Many Louisianas: Rural Social Areas and Cultural Islands* (Baton Rouge, 1955). Lawrence E. Estaville, "The Louisiana French in 1900," *Journal of Historical Geography* 14, 4 (Jan. 1988): 342–359.

14. Gilles Vandal, " 'Bloody Caddo': White Violence against Blacks in a Louisiana Parish, 1865–1876," *Journal of Social History* 25, 2 (Winter 1991): 373–388; Gilles Vandal, "Black Violence in Post-Civil War Louisiana," *Journal of Interdisciplinary History* XXV, 1 (Summer 1994): 45–64.

15. *Tri-Weekly Advocate & Comet*, Feb. 6, 13, 1866; *Gazette & Comet*, April 3, 1866; *Advertiser*, June 21, Aug. 30, 1873; *Picayune*, Sept. 9, 1871; *Gazette*, Oct. 4, 1873.

16. *Democrat*, Nov. 2, 1868; *Le Louisianais*, July 15, 1871; Brasseaux, *Acadian to Cajun*, 130; Robert J. Haws and Michael V. Namorato, "Race, Property Rights and The Economic Consequences of Reconstruction: A Case Study," *Vanderbilt Law Review* 32 (1979): 305–26; Vandal, "Bloody Caddo," 373–388; Vandal, "Black Violence in Louisiana," 45–64.

17. In several instances, the quantity or value of the crops, farm animals or other goods taken away by whites were exorbitant if we look at the following example from Bossier parish. In 1868, a black who worked on shares on a plantation saw his former master steal nine head of his cattle. In 1870, Owen Ellis saw his cotton crop, ninety bushels of corn, two milk cows, and fifteen hogs stolen by whites. In 1874, a planter took from one of his field hands his horse, wagon and harness, all worth $500. Eleven blacks who worked on a plantation saw the owner of the plantation taken from them fifty-nine bales of cotton of five hundred pounds each and worth $0.25 a pound, and 4790 bushels of corn worth $1.50 a bushel for a total loss of $15,060. 44th Congress, 2nd Sess., *House Exec. Doc.* no 30, 165, 167, 173, 190, 191, 193, 204, 205, 211, 213, 223, 296, 408, 412, 424, 421, 424–427, 429, 431, 433, 435, 436, 442, 445, 448–50, 466–68, 471, 478, 482, 488–91, 493–94, 499, 500, 502, 504, 507, 517, 532, 533, 542–45.

18. On January 9, 1869, three blacks were shot and their throats cut by unknown parties in De Soto parish because they did not want to live under white control. Indeed, for whites, emancipation could only be conceived of in a very limited sense. The primary function of a black, they believed, was to work for a white man and take care of his family. *Republican*, Feb. 5, 1869, article from *Caddo Gazette*, Jan. 23, 1869.

19. 41st Congress, 2nd Sess., *House Misc. Doc.* no 154, 119, 132; 43rd Congress, 2nd Sess., *House Report* no 261, 143, 441; *Supplemental Report of the Joint Committee of the General Assembly on the Conduct of the Late Elections and the Condition of Peace and Order in the State* (New Orleans, 1869), 20; Nathaniel Burbank to Cunning Brown, Letters Sent, Aug. 27, 1867, Micro 4498, box 3, BFRAL; *Shreveport Southwestern*, Aug. 12, 1868; *Shrev. Times*, Oct. 19, 1875.

20. *Banner*, Aug. 29, Sept. 5, 12, 1868; *Picayune*, Sept. 4, 1868; *Courrier*, Sept. 12, 1868; *Southwestern*, Aug. 26, 1868, Dec. 7, 1870.

21. 43rd Congress, 2nd Sess., *House Report* no 261, 189–190; 43rd Congress, 2nd Sess., *Senate Exec. Doc.* no 17, 53; 46th Congress, 2nd Sess., *Senate Report* no 693, 172–73, 182; *Bulletin*, July 2, 1874; *Bee*, Jan. 20, 1875; *Picayune*, Oct. 20, 1874, Jan. 28, 1875; *N. O. Times*, Jan. 27, 1875; *Shrev. Times*, Jan. 18, 19, 21, 1875; Joseph G. Dawson, *Army Generals and Reconstruction Louisiana, 1862–1877*, (Baton Rouge, 1982), 189; Perry A. Snyder, "Shreveport During the Civil War and Reconstruction" (Ph. D. Dissertation,

PROPERTY OFFENSES 147

Florida State University, 1979), 214, 221–22, 227; Tunnell, *Crucible Reconstruction*, 203–4; Taylor, *Louisiana Reconstructed*, 299.

22. 43rd Congress, 2nd Sess., *House Report* no 261, 439, 440; *Advertiser*, July 12, 1873; *People Vindicators*, Dec. 30, 1870; *Sugar Bowl*, July 3, Aug. 14, 1873; *Bee*, May 23, 1874; *Crescent*, March 7, 1869; *Picayune*, March 3, Nov. 25, 1869; *N. O. Times*, April 2, 1873; *Gazette*, Nov. 29, 1873; *Beacon*, Feb. 26, 1875; *Shrev. Times*, Jan. 31, 1875.

23. When a black committed murder during a robbery, it was reported at length with all the sordid details particularly if the victim was a white. *Banner*, Sept. 29, 1866; *Advertiser*, June 21, 1873; *Le Louisianais*, May 20, July 22, 1871; *Sugar Bowl*, July 3, Sept. 4, 1873, Aug. 27, 1874; *Picayune*, Nov. 25, 1869; *N. O. Times*, Oct. 29, 1866, April 2, 1873; Horace V. Redfield, *Homicide, North and South*, (Philadelphia, 1880), 217; Taylor, *Louisiana Reconstructed*, 422.

24. *N. O. Times*, April 2, 1873; Vandal, "Bloody Caddo," 373–388; Vandal, "Black Violence in Louisiana," 45–64.

25. B. J. Ramage, "Homicides in the Southern States," *The Sewanee Review* IV (1995–1996): 217.

26. 44th Congress, 2nd Sess., *House Exec. Doc.* no 30, 254–55; 44th Congress, 2nd Sess., *House Misc. Doc.* no 34, Part 1, 5; *Tri-Weekly Advocate*, May 27, 1868; *Advertiser*, Sept. 18, 1869; *Sugar Bowl*, Aug. 14, 1873; *Bee*, Sept. 17, 1874; *Bulletin*, Oct. 15, 1875; *Picayune*, Sept. 3, 1868, Nov. 19, 1869, June 1, 1870, Sept. 9, 1871; *N. O. Times*, June 16, 1873; *West Baton Rouge Sugar Planter*, Dec. 22, 1866; Taylor, *Louisiana Reconstructed*, 423.

27. Blacks were charged with committing most crimes. "As the courts are now organized, they are in very little danger of either arrest or conviction no matter what may be the nature of the crimes they commit." 43rd Congress, 2nd sess., *House Report* no 261, 9–10, 375, 645; J. M. Keller to Capt M. H. Sterling, Franklin, Aug. 31, 1867, BFRAL, Box 1598, Vol 275, 53; *Gazette & Comet*, Dec. 5, 1867; *Banner*, May 26, Sept. 29, 1866; *Watchman*, Aug. 12, 1875; *Democrat*, May 27, Nov. 2, 1868, May 10, 1871, Feb. 23, 1875; *Sugar Bowl*, Aug. 31, 1869, Aug. 29, 1872, Aug. 21, 1873, April 23, Nov. 24, 1874; *Commercial Bulletin*, Sept. 11, 1869; *Picayune*, Jan. 16, 25, Feb. 6, 1875; *N. O. Times*, Jan. 11, 1875; *Courrier*, July 22, 1875; *Telegraph*, April 15, 1871; *St. Mary Planter's Banner*, Sept. 8, 1869, March 1, Sept. 8, 1871.

28. *Le Louisianais*, Aug. 14, 1875.

29. In October 1868, six blacks, armed with shot guns, muskets and pitstols, went to the house of the planter for whom they worked in West Feliciana parish and demanded an immediate settlement of their crop. In Dec. 1867, the black people of St. Mary were very agitated as they came into town fully armed and threatened to rescue some black horse thieves from St. Landry who had been put in jail in Franklin. Whites were ready to support the civil authorities. In Ouachita parish, William Smith, a black, was arraigned in Sept. 1872 on a charge of hog stealing. While on his way to Monroe to appear before the district judge, and under the guard of a constable, Smith was rescued by a band of thirteen armed blacks. *Planters' Banner*, Dec. 28, 1867; *Picayune*, Oct. 8, 1868; *Journal*, Jan. 4, 1868; *Telegram*, Sept. 21, 1872.

30. For example, two blacks burned a stable and a barn in 1868 in Baton Rouge. In May 1870, Joe Grim, who was working on the L'Argent Plantation in Tensas parish, was discharged by his employers for a trivial offense. On the same night, he set fire to their cabin and to the plantation stables which contained their corn, hay, and farming implements. 44th Congress, 2nd Sess., *House Exec. Doc.* no 30, 254–55; 44th Congress, 2nd Sess., *House Misc. Doc.* no 34, Part 1, 5; *Tri-Weekly Advocate*, May 27, 1868; *Advertiser*,

Sept. 18, 1869; *Sugar Bowl*, Aug. 14, 1873; *Bee*, Sept. 17, 1874; *Bulletin*, Oct. 15, 1875; *Picayune*, Sept. 3, 1868, Nov. 19, 1869, June 1, 1870, Sept. 9, 1871; *N. O. Times*, June 16, 1873; *Sugar Planter*, Dec. 22, 1866; Smith, "Arson as Protest," 527–64; Taylor, *Louisiana Reconstructed*, 423.

31.   The furniture of several freedmen was burned in De Soto parish in 1866. In April 1868, a black man and white woman who were living together were killed in Ouachita parish and their house burned. Three black cabins were burned in De Soto in 1868 by a group of fifty whites. Delos. W. White, a white Republican leader in Grant parish, was killed and his house, worth $10,000, was burned in September 1870. Two black churches in St. Martin parish and two other in Iberia parish were destroyed and burned in August 1874 by members of the White League. White regulators regularly burned the property of blacks in the parishes of East Baton Rouge, East and West Felicianas between 1874 and 1876. 44th Congress, 2nd Sess., *House Exec. Doc.* no 30, 159, 272, 325, 402–03, 408, 505; 44th Congress, 2nd Sess., *House Misc. Doc.* no 34, Part 1, 16, 26, 21, 353, 363; *Sugar Bowl*, Aug. 27, 1874.

32.   To determine whether or not any particular band really existed is almost impossible task. In some cases, bands pursued their predatory activity for months or years without ever being reported or detected. In other cases, the presence of a band of robbers in an area was often reported by newspapers on the basis of a few robberies by unknown people. Therefore, the present compiled data on bands are based on reports of the presence of a band of robbers and outlaws in particular regions or parishes. This approach must seem arbitrary at first, and yet it is revealing because it unveils the social tension that prevailed in each parish and region at the time.

33.   Many bands of thieves were not only well-organized but had leaders who were remarkably shrewd in their calculations, cautious in their movements and quick to accomplish their criminal projects. 44th Congress, 2nd Sess., *House Exec. Doc.* no 30, 171; *Advertiser*, July 12, 1873; *Sugar Bowl*, July 3, 1873, July 3, 1874; *Gazette*, Oct. 4, 1873; *Sentinel*, Aug. 14, 1869.

34.   *Advertiser*, June 2, Sept. 18, 1869, July 12, 1873; *Sugar Bowl*, May 13, 1873; *Picayune*, Sept. 3, 1868, Nov. 19, 1869, May 29, 1870; *Republican*, June 5, 1870; *Banner*, Sept. 29, 1866, Feb. 16, 1867; *Watchman*, Aug. 12, 1875; *Beacon*, June 26, 1875.

35.   44th Congress, 2nd Sess., *House Exec. Doc.* no 30, 231–232, 401–402; Capt. F. A. Osbourn to Lieut L. O. Parker, Aug. 10, 1867, Plaquemines, Letters Received, Box 4, Book 60, BFRAL; Scraps of newspapers, Sept. 1873, in United States Attorney General Correspondance with Louisiana, National Archives, RG 60; *People Vindicators*, Dec. 30, 1870, May 8, 1875; *Sugar Bowl*, July 3, Aug. 14, Sept. 4, 1873; *Picayune*, Sept. 12, 1869; *Republican*, Sept. 16, 1873; *New Orleans Weekly Louisianian*, June 15, 1872; *Courrier*, Feb. 4, 1871; *Journal*, June 8, 1872; Brasseaux, *Acadian to Cajun*, 127.

36.   The Lawson Kimball and John West band was typical of Louisiana post-Civil War bands of outlaws and robbers. These two notorious criminals had led guerrilla bands during the War, and after the War they formed a company to keep the country regulated. They operated during the late 1860s in Winn parish and made large incursions into the adjoining parishes. They were involved in the 1866 murder of Lieutenant Butts of the U.S. army. They rode and robbed throughout the countryside, killing blacks and stealing horses. The band was finally dismantled in April 1870 and its members were either killed or arrested by a vigilance committee. 43rd Congress, 2nd Sess., *House Report* no 261, 584; John Cromie to Governor Henry C. Warmoth, May 2, May 5, 1870, Letters Sent, *Warmoth Papers*, Archives of Tulane University; A. W. Ragan to Com. McFarlen, Sept. 5, 1866, Winn parish, no 1756, box 16, BFRAL; *Republican*, May 8, June 5, 1870. For information on other bands see 44th Congress, 2nd Sess., *House Exec. Doc.* no 30, 157, 178, 180–181, 224–225, 231–232, 250–252, 296–304, 381, 399, 401–402; 39th Congress, 2nd sess., *Senate Exec. Doc.* no 6, 86; Governor H. C. Warmoth to General

PROPERTY OFFENSES   149

Emory, Gulf Department, War Department, Micro 4501, Box 4, Oct. 26, 1869; Petition of Isaac Crawford and others to H. C. Warmoth, Micro 4501, Box 2, Sept. 68, Gulf Department, War Department; Scraps of newspapers, Sept. 1873, in U. S. Attorney General Correspondance with Louisiana, National Archives, RG 60; *Picayune*, Aug. 8, 1868; *Republican*, April 1, 1870, Sept. 16, 1873; Brasseaux, *Acadian to Cajun*, 127.

37.   39th Congress, 1st Sess., *House Report* no 30, 156; 39th Congress, 2nd Sess., *Senate Exec. Doc.* no 6, 86–87; *Picayune*, Aug. 8, 11, 12, 1868, Sept. 12, 1869; Brasseaux, *Acadian to Cajun*, 124–25; Dawson, *Army Generals*, 33–35; Taylor, *Louisiana Reconstructed*, 62–63, 68, 91–92, 317.

38.   *Banner*, Sept. 29, 1866, Feb. 16, 1867; *Watchman*, Aug. 12, 1875; *Advertiser*, June 2, Sept. 18, 1869, July 12, 1873; *Sugar Bowl*, May 13, 1873; *Picayune*, Sept. 3, 1868, Nov. 19, 1869, May 29, 1870; *Republican*, June 5, 1870; *Beacon*, June 26, 1875.

39.   44th Congress, 2nd Sess., *House Exec. Doc.* no 30, 383; Lockett, *Louisiana As It Is*, 58–59. The parishes of Lafourche, Terrebonne and Assumption, an area with numerous bayous and swamps, were particularly troubled by bands of robbers. *Advertiser*, Aug. 21, 1869; *Sugar Bowl*, Aug. 29, 1872, Nov. 13, 1873; *Courrier*, Feb. 4, 1871; *Sentinel*, Aug. 14, Sept. 18, 1869, Nov. 11, 18, 1872.

40.   For most of the Reconstruction period, the northern portion of Caddo parish known as the Black Bayou was infamous for the acts of violence and murders perpetrated against blacks there. In 1874 and 1875, in a locality commonly called "Hog Thief Point" about twelve miles south of Shreveport, a gang of outlaws known as the "Cicero Gang" committed numerous atrocious murders, several of which were extremely brutal. District Attorney Wm H. Wise to Wm P. Kellogg, July 16, 1875, *Kellogg Papers*, Louisiana State University Archives; *Chief*, May 29, 1875; 44th Congress, 2nd Sess., *House Exec. Doc.* no 30, 415; *N. O. Times*, Sept. 30, 1867; *Shrev. Times*, Aug. 27, 1874, May 8, 1875. R. Wilkinson to General J. A. Mower, May 28, 1869, Caddo parish, Record 4501, Box 4, BFRAL; see also Report of General J. A. Mower on Louisiana to the Secretary of War, Oct. 15, 1869, Report of the Secretary of War, 41st Congress, 2nd Sess., *House Exec. Doc.*, 1869–70; *N. O. Times*, July 17, 1870; *Southwestern*, March 10, 1869; Dawson, *Army Generals*, 101.

41.   And yet much of the lawlessness arose from white people who, as a rule, displayed too much sympathy for parties charged with criminal offenses and were willing to furnish arms to them. Great excitement prevailed in Terrebonne parish in September 1873, when the black parish sheriff proceeded to arrest a white coffee owner for having harbored a fugitive. The Fontenot were able to plunder the parish of St. Landry for three years because they had developed the support of local population and were well-connected to the locals by blood and marriage. 41st Congress, 2nd Sess., *House Misc. Doc.* no 154, Part 1, 154, 77; 43rd Congress, 2nd Sess., *House Report* no 261, 196, 227, 440; 44th Congress, 2nd Sess., *House Exec. Doc.* no 30, 231–232; *Banner*, Sept. 29, 1866; *Advertiser*, July 12, 1873; *People Vindicators*, Dec. 4, 1875; *Sugar Bowl*, Aug. 14, Oct. 2, 1873; *Republican*, June 5, 1870, Dec. 25, 1874, Dec. 24, 1875; *Beacon*, June 26, 1875; *Shrev. Times*, Feb. 27, 1872, June 12, Oct. 27, 29, 1874, Jan. 31, June 18, 21, Sept. 21, Dec. 24, 1875.

42.   A band of land pirates chose Labidieville, a small town close to New Orleans, as the center of its activities after the War. They regularly robbed the stores in the region. A gang of thieves extended its operations in 1868 from Louisiana into Mississippi. Meanwhile, a gang of horse thieves from Ascension, Lafourche and the surrounding parishes operated as far away as Texas. William Edwards to B. F. Flanders, Sept. 18, 1867, *Flanders Papers*, Archives of Louisiana State University; *Banner*, Sept. 29, 1866, Jan. 17, 1874; *Chief*, May 22, 1875; *Advertiser*, July 12, 1873; *Picayune*, Dec. 8, 1868, Aug. 1, 1869, Dec. 17, 1870; *Republican*, June 5, 1870; *Courrier*, Feb. 4, 1871.

43.   During Reconstruction, Northwestern Louisiana along the Texas line was greatly troubled by a gang of outlaws who came from Texas to steal horses, robbing and murdering

blacks in the process. A similar gang of forty Texans operated in Natchitoches parish in 1870, killing a white, destroying property and terrorizing blacks. 44th Congress, 2nd Sess., *House Exec. Doc.* no 30, 415; R. Wilkinson to General J. A. Mower, May 28, 1869, Caddo Parish, Record 4501, Box 4, BFRAL; Report of General J. A. Mower on Louisiana to the Secretary of War, Oct. 15, 1869, Report of the Secretary of War, 41st Congress, 2nd sess., *House Misc. Doc.*, 1869–70; District Attorney Wm H. Wise to Wm P. Kellogg, July 16, 1875, *Kellogg Papers*, Louisiana State University Archives; *Chief*, May 29, 1875; *People Vindicators*, Dec. 30, 1870; *N. O. Times*, Sept. 30, 1867, July 17, 1870; *Southwestern*, March 10, 1869; *Shrev. Times*, Aug. 27, 1874, May 8, 1875; Dawson, *Army Generals*, 101.

44.   In August 1869, a gang of robbers broke into the stores of Hilaire Charré and Louis Mouille and robbed some pieces of meat, soap and other bulky articles that reappeared a fews days later in the bayou. *Advertiser*, June 12, Sept. 18, 1869; *Sugar Bowl*, Aug. 29, 1872.

45.   43rd Congress, 2nd Sess., *House Report* no 261, 617; *Advertiser*, June 2, Sept. 18, 1869, July 12, 1873; *Sugar Bowl*, Feb. 2, 1871, March 13, May 13, July 3, Aug. 7, 14, Sept. 4, Oct. 7, 1873, April 8, 1875, May 11, 16, 1876; *Picayune*, Nov. 19, 1869, May 29, 1870, Jan. 20, 1872; *Sentinel*, Oct. 4, 1873; Brasseaux, *Acadian to Cajun*, 55; Fontenot, "Old Southwest Louisiana," 78–86.

46.   This illegal traffic was not new. Because slaves were not properly fed, planters had been careless before the War in ferreting out men who enticed their slaves to steal from them. Rather than blaming their slaves, planters blamed the merchants who bought the stolen corn, cotton, or anything else salvagable. But after suffering the effects of a terrible War, planters found it more difficult to tolerate bands of blacks who raided stores and plantations in searched of seed cotton. As a consequence, planters and blacks had nothing left at the end of the year. Black thieves were paid almost nothing by local merchants or storeowners for the cottonseed and those who worked on shares had, as a result of the thefts, only poor crops. 44th Congress, 2nd Sess., *House Misc. Doc.* no 34, 56, 58, 60, 75, 77, 87, 99, 192; *Gazette & Comet*, Jan. 6, 1859; *Banner*, Jan. 17, 1874; *Bulletin*, Oct. 15, 1875; *Picayune*, Jan. 17, 1874, Dec. 29, 1875, June 21, 1876; *N. O. Times*, Oct. 15, 1875; Floyd M. Clay, "Economic Survival of the Plantation System within the Feliciana Parish" (M.A. Thesis, Louisiana State University, 1962), 135; Taylor, *Louisiana Reconstructed*, 422–24.

47.   No horse-thief gangs were reported prior to 1860, however, the problem grew to become a social evil after the War with four gangs reported in 1867, one in 1868, two in 1869, one in 1873, one in 1874, one in 1875, two in 1876, six in 1877, one in 1878, three in 1880. Out of ninety-seven bands of thieves reported after the War, twenty-three were classed as horse thieves. Petition of White Citizens of St. Landry to Major General W. L. Hancock, Opelousas, Dec. 27, 1867, Box 7, Book 61, Civil Affairs, Gulf Department, War Department; *Advocate*, June 9, 1869, May 9, 1870; *Gazette & Comet*, Dec. 5, 1867; *Record*, June 13, 1868; *Chief*, May 22, 1875; *Picayune*, Aug. 1, 1869, Dec. 17, 1870.

48.   44th Congress, 2nd Sess., *House Exec. Doc.* no 30, 231–232, 401–402; Scraps of newspapers, Sept. 1873, in United States Attorney General Correspondance with Louisiana, RG 60, National Archives; *People Vindicators*, Dec. 30, 1870; *Sugar Bowl*, Aug. 14, Sept. 4, 1873; *Picayune*, Sept. 12, 1869; *Republican*, Sept. 16, 1873; *Weekly Louisianian*, June 15, 1872; *Journal*, June 8, 1872; Brasseaux, *Acadian to Cajun*, 127.

49.   Composed of planters and ex-guerillas, the "Black Horse Cavalry" terrorized Franklin parish for years and transformed that parish into a den of murderers and robbers. 39th Congress, 2nd sess., *Senate Exec. Doc.* no 6, 86; 43rd Congress, 2nd Sess., *House Report* no 261, 361; 44th Congress, 2nd Sess., *House Exec. Doc.* no 30, 280, 355; Governor H. C. Warmoth to General Emory, Gulf Department, War Department, Micro 4501, Box 4, Oct. 26, 1869; Petition of Isaac Crawford and Others to H. C. Warmoth, Micro 4501, Box 2, Sept. 68, Gulf Department, War Department; *Picayune*, Aug. 8, 1868; James G.

PROPERTY OFFENSES   151

Dauphine, "The Knights of the White Camelia and the Election of 1868: Louisiana's White Terrorists; a Benighting Legacy," *Louisiana History* XXX, 2 (Spring 1989): 173–90; Rable, *But There Was No Peace*, 16–32; Taylor, *Louisiana Reconstructed*, 61; Allie B. Windham, "Methods and Mechanisms Used to Restore White Supremacy in Louisiana" (M.A. Thesis, Louisiana State University, 1948), 54, 60.

50. In 1874 the New Orleans *Bulletin* reported that "For some five weeks past the people of St. Tammany residing in and around Mandeville have been in a state of great excitement in conveying of the advent and subsequent daring and outrageous proceeding of a herculean negro who had been in the wood … wanted to lynch him." *Banner*, Feb. 16, 1867; *Record*, March 6, 1869; *Le Louisianais*, June 11, July 15, 1871, Aug. 14, Dec. 4, 1875; *Democrat*, May 27, 1874; *Sugar Bowl*, Feb. 2, 1871, Aug. 29, 1872, Aug. 14, 1873, May 11, 1876; *Bulletin*, May 14, 1874, Jan. 18, 1876; *Picayune*, Oct. 20, 1869, Aug. 24, 1870.

51. *Watchman*, Aug. 12, 1875; *Beacon*, June 26, 1875.

52. In his 1869 report to the state attorney general, the district attorney of the Fifth District Court reported out of 206 criminal cases brought before the court 137(66.5%) that were classed as property offenses. These 137 cases were distributed as follows: five cases of burglary, two of arson, six of robbery, one hundred and seven of larceny, nine of horse stealing, five of receiving stolen goods, one of embezzelment, two of destroying property. Year after year, district attorneys across the state reported similar ratios of property crimes. See *Report of the Attorney General to General Assembly* for the years 1867 to 1877. See also *Chief*, July 3, 1875; *Sugar Planter*, Dec. 22, 1866; *Journal*, June 4, 1875.

53. *Record*, March 6, 1869; *Le Louisianais*, June 1, July 15, 1871, June 19, July 24, Aug. 14, Dec. 4, 1875; *People Vindicators*, May 8, 1875; *Sugar Bowl*, Feb. 2, 1871, Aug. 7, 1873, May 16, 1876; *Republican*, June 5, 1870, Sept. 16, 1873; *Courrier*, Nov. 14, 1873.

54. Ann P. Baenziger, "The Texas State Police During Reconstruction, A Reexamination," *Southwestern Historical Quarterly* LXXII (April 1969): 470–91; Dawson, *Army Generals*, 106, 148–49; Otis A. Singletary, *Negro Militia and Reconstruction* (Austin, 1957), 74–79; Otis A. Singletary, "The Texas Militia During Reconstruction," *Southwestern Historical Quarterly* LX (July 1956): 23–35; Taylor, *Louisiana Reconstructed*, 271, 274–75.

55. 40th Congress, 1st Sess., *Senate Exec. Doc.* no 14, 225; 43rd Congress, 2nd Sess., *Senate Exec. Doc.* no 17, 7; 43rd Congress, 2nd Sess., *House Report* no 261, 383; *Southwestern*, Jan. 28, 1871; *Shrev. Times*, June 18, 21, Sept. 21, 1875. *Picayune*, Jan. 28, 1875; *Republican*, Dec. 25, 1874; *N. O. Times*, Jan. 27, 1875; Snyder, "Shreveport During the Civil War and Reconstruction," 228.

56. *Banner*, Sept. 29, 1866; *Record*, June 13, 1868; *South*, Dec. 7, 1867; *Sugar Bowl*, Aug. 7, 1873; *Picayune*, Dec. 10, 1867, Dec. 15, 1868, Nov. 19, 1869, May 29, 1870; *Planter's Banner*, Sept. 8, 1869, March 1, 1871; *Shrev. Times*, Jan. 24, Sept. 21, 1875.

57. *Banner*, Feb. 16, 1867; *Record*, March 6, 1869; *South*, May 21, 1881; *Advertiser*, Aug. 30, 1873; *Sugar Bowl*, Feb. 2, 1871, Aug. 29, 1872, Aug. 14, 1873, May 11, 1876; *Bulletin*, Jan. 18, 1876; Richard Maxwell Brown, *Strain of Violence: Historical Study of American Violence and Vigilantism* (New York, 1975), 106–107, 124.

58. Bands of thieves made Northwestern Louisiana so insecure after the War that farmers in Bossier and Caddo parishes organized a convoy system to bring their agricultural products and other goods to towns. As a gang of murderous robbers ravaged the parish of East Baton Rouge during the Spring of 1868, a central committee, composed of the sheriff, the mayor of Baton Rouge and the members of the policy jury, coordinated the actions of a citizen association. In April 1870, a vigilance committee put an end to the operations of the Kimball and West band, in Winn parish. Property owners in Iberia parish organized

a similar protective association in August 1873. In 1874, citizens of Shreveport formed a volunteer police force of 250 men strong to put an end to a rash of robberies in the city. 43rd Congress, 2nd Sess., *House Report* no 261, 425–26, 435; John Cromie to Governor H. C. Warmoth, May 2, 5, 1870, Warmoth Papers; A. W. Ragan, to C. McFarlen, Sept. 5, 1866, Winn parish, No 1756, Box 16, BFRAL; *Tri-Weekly Advocate*, June 1, 1868; *Sugar Bowl*, Aug. 14, 1873; *Picayune*, March 3, 1869; *Republican*, May 8, June 5, 1870; Snyder, "Shreveport, During the Civil War and Reconstruction," 26–27, 32–34; Taylor, *Louisiana Reconstructed*, 317.

59. Minutes of the Police Jury, Lafayette Parish, Sept. 28, 1857, Sept. 30, 1860, Louisiana State University Archives; *Advocate*, July 11, 1854; *Gazette & Comet*, Oct. 6, 1858, May 7, 1860; Iberville *Southern Sentinel*, Dec. 27, 1856; *Bee*, April 14, 1852; *Picayune*, June 13, Aug. 10, 1853, Aug. 28, 1857; *Courrier*, Sept. 25, 1858, Feb. 18, 1860; *Pointe Coupee Democrat*, Oct. 2, 9, 1858; Brasseaux, *Acadian to Cajun*, 55–6, 114–118; Harvey Wish, "The Slave Insurrection Panic of 1856," *Journal of Southern History* 5 (1939): 217–219.

60. 44th Congress, 2nd Sess., *House Misc. Doc.* no 34, Part 1, 20, 21, 28, 35, 56, 60, 61, 75, 77, 86, 87, 98, 115, 179, 199, 268, 334, 369; *Bulletin*, Oct. 15, 1875; *Picayune*, Jan. 17, 1874, October 15, 19, Dec. 29, 1875, June 21, 1876; *N. O. Times*, Oct. 15, 1875; *Beacon*, Sept. 18, 1875; Clay, "Economic Survival in Feliciana Parish," 135; Rable, *But There Was No Peace*, 178–179; Taylor, *Louisiana Reconstructed*, 422–24.

61. In 1868, a committee of thirty men in Lafayette parish set a deadline of twenty-four hours for four black thieves to leave the state. Four blacks of Iberia parish received a similar notice in July 1874. 44th Congress, 2nd Sess., *House Exec. Doc.* no 30, 546; *Sugar Bowl*, July 20, 1874; Taylor, *Louisiana Reconstructed*, 284.

62. Alexandre DeClouet to Paul DeClouet, Sept. 13, 1859, DeClouet Collection, Louisiana Southwestern University Archives; *Courrier*, Sept. 25, 1858, May 21, Sept. 10, Oct. 14, 1859; *Pointe Coupée Democrat*, Aug. 21, Oct. 9, 1858; Brown, *Strain of Violence*, 109; H. L. Griffin, "The Vigilance Committees of the Attakapas Country; or Early Louisiana Justice," *Proceedings of the Mississippi Valley Historical Association* 8 (1914–1915): 155.

63. 44th Congress, 2nd Sess., *House Exec. Doc.* no 30, 399; *Natchi. Times*, Oct. 9, 1869; *Picayune*, Oct. 20, 1869; *Courrier*, Nov. 14, 1873.

64. For example, as horses and cows continued to be stolen in Iberia parish, committees of vigilance were formed in 1873, 1874 and 1876. 43rd Congress, 2nd Sess., *House Report* no 261, 617; *Sugar Bowl*, May 11, 1876.

65. Vermillion parish had for years been plagued by cattle and horse thieves. A committee of vigilantes was formed in the parish in late summer of 1873, as "thieves are getting more numerous and bolder than was ever known before in the parish." On September 5 and 10, 1873, twelve members of a band of cattle thieves were lynched. They had been previously advised to leave within a specified time, but instead of doing so, 150 of them armed themselves and threatened to destroy the town of Abbeville. The people of the town and of the adjoining country formed a commitee of vigilance three hundred men strong, caught twelve members of the band, and summarily lynched them. Other vigilance committees were formed in Vermillion parish in 1875 and 1876. *Cotton Ball*, Oct. 1, 1873; *Sugar Bowl*, Sept. 4, 11, 1873, Aug. 17, 1876; *Picayune*, Sept. 14, 1873; *Republican*, Sept. 16, Nov. 16, 1873, Aug. 19, 1876; *Courrier*, Nov. 14, 1873; *Beacon*, Sept. 20, Oct. 1, 1873; *Sentinel*, Oct. 4, 1873; Brown, *Strain of Violence*, 164; Donald J. Millet, "Cattle and Cattlemen of Southwest Louisiana, 1860–1900," *Louisiana History* 28, 3 (Summer 1987): 324–25; Taylor, *Louisiana Reconstructed*, 420.

66. According to the *Opelousas Journal*, the twelve cattle thieves lynched in September 1873 in Vermillion parish were "relatives of their executioners. In many cases it is hard to draw the line of demarcation between them, and to say how many cattle a man is justified

PROPERTY OFFENSES   153

in stealing before he becomes sufficiently respectable to join the vigilance committee."
The quote is taken from Millet, "Cattle and Cattlemen," 324–325; see also *Republican*,
Sept. 16, Nov. 16, 1873; *Courrier*, Nov. 14, 1873; Brown, *Strain of Violence*, 164.

67. The committees were described by some members of the press as groups of banditti
and outlaws, no better than the ones against whom they acted. *Republican*, Sept. 16, Nov.
16, 1873; *Courrier*, Nov. 14, 1873.

68. 41st Congress, 2nd Sess., *House Misc. Doc.* no 154, 36; 43rd Congress, 2nd Sess.,
House Report no 261, 439; *Republican*, Aug. 2, 1870, Dec. 25, 1874; *Shrev. Times*, May
8, June 18, 21, 1875; Ayers, *Vengeance & Justice*, 245, 249; Brown, *Strain of Violence*,
126–27, 146–147, 160–61.

69. 43rd Congress, 2nd Sess., *House Report* no 261, 169, 422, 782; 44th Congress, 2nd
Sess., *House Exec. Doc.* no 30, 218, 399, 482, 490, 511; *Republican*, Aug. 29, 1874.

70. In Aug. 1874, Jacques Boutte, alias Jack Jacob, was caught stealing a cow belonging
to Zeon Olivier, a black farmer of in St. Martin parish. Jacob, reputed to be a professional
cattle thief, was lynched after a summary trial by a jury composed of 200 citizens. 43rd
Congress, 2nd Sess., *House Report* no 261, 782; *Republican*, Aug. 29, 1874.

71. *Chief*, March 27, 1875; also *Picayune*, Aug. 8, 11, 12, 1868.

72. 43rd Congress, 2nd Sess., *House Report* no 261, 169; 44th Congress, 2nd Sess., *House
Exec. Doc.* no 30, 394, 434, 442, 443, 490, 494, 506, 542, 546; Brasseaux, *Acadian To
Cajun*, 130.

73. The presses and offices of the following Republican newspapers were destroyed by
white mobs: The *St. Landry Progress* on September 28, 1868, the *Attakapas Register* on
Oct. 19, 1868, the *Claiborne Republican* on Nov. 17, 1868, the *Marksville Register* on Dec.
30, 1868, and the *Shreveport Southwestern Telegram* on Dec. 23, 1874. 44th Congress, 2nd
Sess., *House Exec. Doc.* no 30, 170–71, 178, 179, 180, 184, 185, 187, 267; *Picayune*, Aug.
8, 1868; *Republican*, Aug. 9, 18, 1874.

74. *Chief*, June 26, 1875; *Sugar Bowl*, April 23, 1874; Taylor, *Louisiana Reconstructed*,
361, 422–23.

75. Ayers, *Crime and Punishment*, 111.

76. Donald J. Black, "Production of Crime Rates," *American Sociological Review*, XXXV,
4 (Aug. 1970): 733–747; V. A. Gatrell and T. B. Hadden, "Criminal Statistics and Their
Interpretation," in *19th Century Society: Essays in the Use of Quantitative Methods For the
Study of Social Data*, edited by E. A. Wrigley (Cambridge, 1972), 336–396; Roger Lane,
"Crime and Criminal Statistics in Nineteenth-Century Massachusetts," *Journal of Social
History* 22 (Winter 1968): 156–163; Michael D. Maltz, "Crime Statistics: A Historical
Perspective," *Crime and Delinquency* (Jan. 1977), 32–40; Eric Monkkonen, "Systematic
Criminal Justice History: Some Suggestions," *Journal of Interdisciplinary History* IX, 3
(Winter 1979): 451–464; Nye, "Crime in Modern Societies," 491–507; Samuel Walker,
"Counting Cops and Crime," *Review of American History* X, 2 (June 1982): 212-217.

77. Fuller documentation on these sources will be made available to anyone who forwards
such a request to the author.

[11]

THE CRIMINALITY OF WOMEN IN EIGHTEENTH-CENTURY ENGLAND

I

I propose in this essay to investigate the criminality of women in seventeenth- and eighteenth-century England by examining the judicial records of two southeastern counties, Surrey and Sussex. In particular, the essay rests on an examination of the cases dealt with in the principal courts of these counties in a total of sixty-two sample years between 1663 and 1802.[1] My aim has been mainly to uncover the patterns of offences charged against women and to suggest what they reveal about the place of women and the nature of crime in early modern England. I should emphasize immediately, however, that I have confined my attention in this initial investigation to the most common serious offences: crimes against the person, ranging from murder to assault; and crimes against property, by which I mean robbery, burglary, theft, and related offences. Women were, of course, charged with many other crimes (see Table 1). But the vast majority who came before the courts were up for some form of theft or personal violence.[2]

It is a common observation that in the modern world crime is overwhelmingly a male activity.[3] The records of the courts in Surrey and Sussex suggest that this was no less the case in early modern England. In Surrey, for example, 80 percent of those charged with felonies (taking all the sample years together) were men (Table 1). It is true that, apart from poaching and forgery, women participated in the same range of crimes as men and that the patterns of male and female crime were similar in the sense that for each, property offences accounted for roughly half of the charges laid and crimes against the person, roughly a third. But the numbers involved were markedly different. Except in some of the less common offences, like counterfeiting, men decisively outnumbered women in all crimes, predominating by more than three to one in the largest categories of property offences and personal violence. A strikingly lower level of criminality of women is clearly apparent.

These figures are derived from indictments, the formal charges laid against the accused. These documents survive by no means completely, but in consistent enough series to make the statistical study of crime possible in early modern England. But they have some limitations as sources for the historian of crime. In particular, because the charge had to be stated in terse and precise legal language, differences among crimes of the same type — differences, for example, in the degree of violence offered in a robbery or of injury done in an assault — were ignored if they did not affect the legal category in which

Table 1: Men and Women Accused of Major Offences in Surrey in years sampled between 1663 and 1802

Offence	Number of Persons Accused			Percent		Percent of Total		
	Total	Men	Women	Men	Women	Total	Men	Women
Property Offences	7,283	5,543	1,740	76.1	23.9	52.0	50.2	58.6
Dispossession and Trespass	406	367	39	90.4	9.6	2.9	3.3	1.3
Malicious Injury to Property	146	121	25	82.9	17.1	1.1	1.1	0.8
Game Offences	88	88	—	100.0	—	0.6	0.8	—
Forgery	33	32	1	97.0	3.0	0.2	0.3	—
Fraud	220	180	40	81.8	18.2	1.6	1.6	1.4
Coining	208	124	84	59.6	40.4	1.5	1.1	2.8
Offences against the Person	4,734	3,858	876	81.5	18.5	33.8	35.0	29.5
Offences against Public Justice	832	674	158	81.0	19.0	6.0	6.1	5.3
Offences against the State	66	59	7	89.4	10.6	0.5	0.5	0.2
Total	14,016	11,046	2,970	78.8	21.2			

the offence was to be placed. This makes the data derived from indictments especially limiting in the study of sex differences in crime, for it is one of the commonplaces of the literature on women's crime — a commonplace that it would be useful to test for a premodern period — that women not only commit fewer offences than men, but commit them less violently and less aggressively. Indictments alone do not offer much help with questions of that kind. In order to get behind the bare numbers of cases therefore, I have employed other kinds of evidence in the first two sections of this essay — accounts of trials when they are available,[4] examinations and depositions of prisoners and witnesses,[5] and, to a more limited extent, reports in the press — to attempt to characterize the types as well as the numbers of crimes against the person and against property committed by women.

The remainder of the essay offers an explanation of the patterns of women's crime addressed mainly to the question of levels of offences. This turns very largely on an examination of urban and rural differences in women's crime, made possible because more than half of the population of the county of Surrey lived in a large urban area — the borough of Southwark and several neighbouring parishes along the south bank of the Thames — that was in effect part of the metropolis of London. Women's crime, it is clear, was very much more extensive in the city than in the rural parishes and market towns of the rest of the county of Surrey or in the essentially rural county of Sussex. And women not only committed a larger number of offences in these urban parishes, but also accounted for a much higher proportion of the total crime in the city than in the countryside. These differences offer clues, I believe, that help to explain the level and nature of women's crime. For while they derive in part from the greater opportunities for theft in the city and to some extent from the age and sex structure of the urban population, they also more fundamentally can be seen to reflect the differing social and economic situations of women in London on the one hand and in rural Surrey and Sussex on the other. The contrasting urban and rural crime patterns, I shall argue, derive from and are evidence of differences in the nature of women's lives and work in these different settings, in the range of their social contacts and in their economic opportunities and difficulties. They thus provide clues to the effects of changes in women's social and economic position as well as to the nature of women's crime.

II

One of the explanations frequently offered for sex differences in criminality is the relative physical weakness of women compared to men. But in a society in which women were called upon to do a great deal of heavy labor this does not seem a very compelling explanation of why women constituted only 18 percent of those charged before the Surrey courts with crimes against the person. And it is not difficult, as we shall see, to find numerous examples of women whose physical strength and courage cannot be doubted.

Nor is it apparent that when women in the eighteenth century resorted to murder, to take the most serious of the crimes against the person, they turned naturally to devious methods, as has been suggested of their modern counterparts, or that they favored weapons, like poison, that compensated for lack of physical strength.[6] The Surrey cases at least do not suggest that women relied in their murderous attacks any more than did men on indirection, stealth, and excessive deception. Apart from three women accused of causing death by witchcraft, thirty-four other women were charged with murder, of whom fifteen were principals. Of these, three were accused of killing with knives; four had struck their victims on the head (with a club, poker, iron spit, and pewter drinking pot); one had used a pistol; two prostitutes were charged after throwing a client who objected too loudly to being robbed out of a second-floor window from which he was vainly trying to summon help; and at least two other women were accused of murder after the death of someone they had punched or kicked. In other years in Surrey not included in this sample, Mary Edmonson was convicted of cutting her aunt's throat and then, when this failed to kill her immediately, of dashing her head against the floor until she died.[7] And another woman was committed for trial in Southwark in 1774 for the murder of the man with whom she had lived for nineteen years and with whom she had had eleven children. "She cut his throat," it was reported, "in a fit of jealousy, and that not putting an immediate end to his life, she dashed out his brains with a poker."[8]

However characteristic of the methods used by women murderers, these two cases are typical in one important aspect: the victims were rarely strangers and were indeed often closely related to the accused. Though it is not always possible to identify victims precisely,[9] it is clear that most of the women indicted for murder or manslaughter were accused of killing someone within their own domestic circle or at least in their neighborhood. Their victims in Surrey included a husband, a daughter, and several children and servants. One woman was convicted of cutting her two-year-old son's throat and two others were alleged to have strangled younger children, one her own baby a few months old. Another, a widow in Kingston-upon-Thames, was charged in 1738 with the murder of a young girl left in her care by parish officials. Evidence was presented that the girl had been "in a lingering state of health" and had lost the use of her limbs. Indeed, Anne Barrett, the nurse, had beaten her because of this, thinking "she was sulky," though she was acquitted when an apothecary testified that he thought the beating had not in fact caused the death.[10] Such cases are related to more general cruelty to children and the mistreatment of servants and apprentices, both of which gave rise to numbers of assault charges and on occasion to murder and manslaughter cases.[11]

Violence in the home and towards neighbours was not of course confined to women and it is indeed probable that the majority of the victims of male

83

murderers were similarly wives, lovers, children, other relatives, and acquaintances. But men also became embroiled in disputes and fights with strangers in taverns and other public places, which on occasion gave rise to charges of murder and manslaughter. Women seem rarely to have been involved in squabbles of this kind. This reflects the narrower range of their social contacts and suggests one reason, though clearly not the only one, why women appear to have murdered so much less frequently than men: why, in the sixty-two years examined in Surrey between 1663 and 1802, only 37 of the 284 charges laid (13 percent) were against women (Table 2).

Though it is hardly a crime in the same sense, one form of killing (or, at least, an offence that presumed that violence had been done) was much more exclusive to women — infanticide. The illegal act was the killing of a newborn baby, but because of the difficulty of proving such a charge, the crime as established by statute made it a capital offence simply to conceal the birth of a bastard child born dead.[12] It was an offence unique in English law, for the usual presumption of innocence was entirely disregarded in favor of the opposite presumption, that if the mother concealed the birth of the child she must have killed it. The onus was on her to prove the contrary by the direct evidence of at least one witness. That was asking a great deal. A large number of those accused of infanticide were women for whom pregnancy and motherhood posed serious threats to their livelihood and indeed, to their survival — domestic servants, for example. It is hardly surprising that many of the women accused in Surrey and a majority of those tried at the Old Bailey were domestic servants, for women in service were, on the one hand, most commonly in their early child-bearing years and on the other, in close and constant contact with men, both members of the family they worked for and their fellow servants.[13] In addition, of course, a domestic servant was especially threatened by pregnancy, for apart from the ruinous blow it gave her character, it meant dismissal: if she had no family to turn to, an unmarried servant had little hope of keeping both her child and her job. Indeed, the pregnancy itself put her at risk and most of the women who came before the Surrey courts accused of infanticide had apparently managed to conceal their condition. Their children had been born unaided and under appalling conditions, in garrets, outhouses, and under stairs, which in themselves must have accounted for a large number of stillbirths. But though the pregnancy had been hidden, the birth itself was more difficult to conceal and the evidence difficult to hide. This again was especially true for domestic servants, surrounded as they were by their fellow servants as well as their employers.[14]

Judges and juries went out of their way in the eighteenth century to find evidence that would justify acquitaal and it was rare in Surrey for women to be found guilty of infanticide. The important question in court seems always to have been not whether she had concealed the birth, but whether she had intended to conceal it, and any evidence of preparation on the part

Table 2: Crimes Against the Person in Surrey

Offence	Number of Persons Accused			Percent	
	Total	Men	Women	Men	Women
Murder and Manslaughter	284	247	37	87.0	13.0
Infanticide	34	–	34	–	100.0
Assault and Wounding	3730	3016	714	80.9	19.1
Assault on Constables, etc.	375	312	63	83.2	16.8
Other Offences	311	283	28	91.0	9.0
Total	4734	3858	876	81.5	18.5

of the mother was seized on to justify acquittal, especially evidence that childbed linen had been prepared or other arrangements made. Failing that, the opinion of a midwife, however unsubstantiated by the apparent facts, that the child had probably been born dead, or even the absence of marks of violence on the body, were taken as sufficient evidence of innocence.[15] On one occasion in Surrey, a defence in effect of not guilty by reason of temporary insanity was successful.[16] And at the trial of another woman who insisted that she had not been delivered of a child, the judge in his summing up encouraged the jury to give her denial substantial importance. "As the Confession of a Prisoner is made use of to convict them," he told the jury, "so if they own anything which may be in their Favour, it ought to have some weight on the Trial." This is not a judicial sentiment that one encounters frequently in the eighteenth century and certainly not in trials of, say, shoplifters. In this case the jury took the hint and the woman was discharged.[17]

Infanticide was by its nature a woman's matter, though men were occasionally charged with complicity and occasionally indicted.[18] In all other categories of crimes against the person, men predominated overwhelmingly. This was true, we have seen, of murder and manslaughter. It was equally true of the large and general category of assault, an offence which covered a wide variety of actions from the merest threat of violence to an actual and serious beating. Only 20 percent of those so charged in the Surrey courts were women.

As in murder cases, it is my impression that a large proportion of the women who were brought to court on assault charges were accused of attacking or threatening a member of their own household or a neighbour or at least someone not entirely a stranger to them. Some of the charges against women, for example, arose from the mistreatment of servants, especially young girls. Sir William Brockman, a justice in Kent who kept a record of his judicial business over a long period at the end of the seventeenth century and the beginning of the eighteenth, records several complaints by servants against their mistresses. Mary Basset, a fifteen-year-old, told him how her mistress had not only called her "very opprobrious Names, as Bitch, Whore and the like," but also "beat her without provocation and beyond measure." Another young girl complained to him that she was regularly beaten by her mistress and that when her mother went to ask "why she so abused her daughter," her mistress, Mary Green, "fell upon her said mother and knocked her down." Several other parents complained to him about the mistreatment of their daughters in service.[19] Only a fraction of such cases must have been reported and of those only a handful prosecuted, but enough charges of mistreatment of servants did come to light to suggest that this kind of domestic bullying and abuse by women was not uncommon.[20] It seems clear, at any event, that the closeness and immediacy of family life made for a high degree of supervision over those who lived in as servants and apprentices. This was perhaps particularly true for young girls. And for them especially, surveillance and correction must very often have made the family something much less attractive than a "circle of affection" (life lived among "loved, familiar faces"), to quote a recent characterization of family life in England before the coming of industrialization.[21] For thousands of girls like Millicent Corick, who complained to the Surrey magistrates in 1703 that she was regularly beaten by her master and mistress and was so overworked that she was "as great a slave as any in Turky,"[22] the faces in the family must have been all too familiar but little loved.

The family was also frequently the scene of violence of a different kind, for the peace of the affectionate circle was all too often shattered by bitterness and conflict between husbands and wives. In this, no doubt, women were more often victims than aggressors. The common law, indeed, granted husbands the right to "correct" their wives' behaviour and restrict their movements, and though this right had been seriously challenged and modified in the courts in the seventeenth century, it was still thought by some to exist in the eighteenth and it was at any event clearly exercised.[23] Women were able to "pray the peace" against their husbands in the eighteenth century and were thereby able to get some protection from the courts, but it is clear that the ancient right of a husband to chastize his wife was still assumed and that there was still a great deal of wife beating. Defoe thought indeed that, with what he took to be an increase of drunkenness, it was getting worse.[24] On the other hand, the beating of husbands by their wives was not entirely unknown either, and magistrates were on occasion called upon to protect them. A shoemaker in Surrey told how his wife had stabbed him. Another man was beaten so severely by his wife that a magistrate committed

86

her to the house of correction for his protection. And in 1738 Susannah Hill was sent to the county gaol to be tried at the assizes because she had attacked and wounded her husband "with a hammer and hand whip in a most cruel manner" and because "he goes in danger of his life."[25]

Domestic violence was without doubt seriously underreported. And it is a fair presumption that abused husbands were especially reluctant to complain and to appeal for help from the courts, for this too openly and clearly reversed a husband and wife's expected relationship. In the natural order of things, women were subjects and dependents of their husbands, not their governors — a relationship not only preached in courtesy literature and legal guidebooks,[26] but clearly also popularly accepted as the proper state of affairs, for domineering women were frequently objects of demonstrations of community disapproval in charivaris.[27]

The subjection of wives not only contributed to the underreporting of domestic violence in which the woman was the aggressor. It also perhaps helps to explain why women were less frequently involved than men in violent confrontations outside the household. For a wife's dependence, it was widely believed, was matched by her husband's obligations towards her, one of which was to afford her protection in the community. The wife of a Wiltshire weaver expressed this expectation in petitioning the quarter sessions in 1662 for protection against two people in her village. Joanne Hobbs told the court that she had been assaulted by Thomas Smith, a husbandman, on Whitsun Eve, that he had "laid his hands on her and would have had his pleasure of her" had she not resisted him for half an hour; that further her husband had appeared while this was going on, "but did not help her or rebuke Smith." Later, she went on, she had been attacked by Elizabeth Whittle, the wife of a labourer, who not only assaulted her but threatened to kill her. She was afraid of both of them, especially because "it is well known that her husband will not protect her, that he neglects her and is insufferably bitter unto her, tho he had a sufficient porcon [portion] with her." Since her husband had failed in what she took to be his obligation towards her, she asked the court to bring Smith and Whittle to give securities so that she could "live without fear and dread of them."[28]

On the other hand, even if this popular expectation that a husband would protect his wife led inevitably to men being more involved in the kinds of disputes that gave rise to assault charges, it clearly did not remove women entirely from them. For many of the women who came before the Surrey courts had joined their husbands in assaults that arose out of conflicts with neighbours and involved the active defence of family interests. A number of charges involving women grew out of disputes over leases and the rightful possession of lands and buildings,[29] or out of disputes with other families in which the issue is less clear-cut than this.[30] Women can also be found defending the family's possessions with vigor — warding off thieves "with a great stick"; or, on one occasion in Southwark, chasing a burglar from a bedroom so rapidly that he fell downstairs, where the woman, a waterman's wife, "took him" with the aid of her servant girl.[31] A number of other assault charges against women, especially perhaps in London, appear to have arisen from their involvement in their husbands' (and the family's) business. Certainly this would help to explain why the wives of victuallers were so frequently accused of assault.

Occasionally the defence of family and personal interests included the defiance of authority. A number of women were brought to the Surrey courts for assaulting officers in the course of their duty — bailiffs distraining goods by court order or attempting to make arrests, for example.[32] Constables too got their share of violent treatment. The constable of the parish of Sutton told a familiar story of resistance to authority in reporting why he had been unable to serve a warrant on Rebecca Beecher, the wife of a laborer, for having assaulted Lucy Porter. When he came to her house, he reported, she attacked him, snatched the warrant from his hand and "tore it into several pieces some of which she put in her mouth and chewed them and then spit it out on the ground and immediately struck him . . . several times in the face."[33]

Women also came into conflict with officials in the eighteenth century over issues that were rather more general and public than the Beecher case seems to have been. They often took part in food riots; indeed women were often their instigators and leaders,[34] a reflection of the immediacy of their concern with the critical matter of the supply and price of food. And several of the disputes with officials that women in Surrey engaged in arose, as did food riots, out of conflicts over what women thought were their customary rights in matters that immediately touched the interests of their families. Gleaning and the collection of firewood, both critical to the families of rural laborers, were among rights increasingly denied in the slow transformation of rural society that accompanied the growth of commercial farming. But those rights were clung to tenaciously even as they became subject to criminal prosecution, and constables often found it difficult to enforce warrants to arrest offenders. Some women, like Ann Osborn of the parish of Egham in Surrey, simply confessed that she "did not know that there was any harm in it" when she was arrested for collecting some dry wood from Stephen Terrent's land two days before Christmas, 1762.[35] But others resisted more strenuously than this. In the same parish in the same year, Judith Marshe and Diana Hudson were arrested for being in Nicholas Hogflesh's grounds and picking up oak wood "severed from the trees" ("having nothing to burn at home," Judith explained), but as the constable of the parish was trying to take them away, Diana's mother attacked him and enabled them to escape.[36]

Women were thus charged in Surrey with a wide variety of offences involving some degree of violence, directed at members of their own households or arising from squabbles with neighbours or from actions taken in the defence of family interests. Of course women were also charged with assaults

88

that fit none of these categories: numerous examples could be cited of assaults made by one or more woman that have no apparent connection with immediate family interests, or at least in which family interest cannot be assumed. Other women came before the courts for violent crimes of a different kind — for false imprisonment (often linked with extortion) or, more rarely, for sexual offences.[37] And women were also charged, as we shall see, with violent acts committed in the course of robbery and similar offences.

But even though not all women's violence was thus immediately centered on the household and neighbourhood, it is my impression — and until more is known systematically about the identity of victims it must remain largely a matter of impression — that at least a higher proportion of the charges of violent behaviour brought against women sprang from domestic disputes, or from actions in which family interests were concerned, than was the case among those brought against men. If this is true, the narrower focus of women's actions will help to explain why men accused of some form of personal violence outnumbered women by more than four to one before the Surrey courts. Of course it is likely that women's offences were less well reported than men's, and especially assaults within the family. But if women had been involved as commonly as men in brawls in taverns or at work or in casual encounters elsewhere, underreporting would surely not have hidden it entirely. And it is worth remembering too that women were responsible for very few murders in Surrey and that sex differences in murder are not likely to have been much distorted by different reporting rates. The disparities in levels and types of violence between the sexes is too great to be fully explained by reporting. The principal reasons would seem to derive more from the restricted scope of women's lives and the training that shaped them to their social role. There is, I believe, persuasive evidence of this in the striking urban-rural differences in women's violence in Surrey to which we will return in a later section of the essay.

III

Women also committed fewer crimes against property than men, though they accounted for a larger proportion of such offences than of crimes against the person. Whereas around 18 percent of the assaults and other personal violence in Surrey were laid against women, they were charged with almost 24 percent of property offences. In addition, property cases dominated the list of female crime. Almost six out of ten women who appeared in Surrey courts for serious crimes were there for that reason, twice as many as were prosecuted for acts of violence (Table 1). For women even more than for men, it was theft and related offences that most often brought them into trouble with the law.

The patterns of male and female property crime differed significantly in a number of ways, however (see Table 3). In the first place, women were prosecuted relatively infrequently for robbery and other thefts in which force was used or threatened. Few women were ever reported for muggings in the streets of London and women highway robbers were even more rare. The essential requirements for successful highway robbery were good horseman-ship and skill with weapons, especially pistols, and neither were accomplish-ments that women acquired easily in their youth. Highway robbery by wo-men was unusual enough at any event for one victim of a lady robber in Essex to be able to pretend not to understand what she was about. The man, a butcher, was stopped near Rumford, in 1735 by "a Woman well mounted on a Side Saddle . . . who presented a Pistol to him and demanded his Money; he being amaz'd at her Behaviour told her, he did not know what she meant." This pose was cut short by a man who had been hiding nearby and who stepped out and told the butcher that "he was a Brute to deny the Lady's request, and that if he did not gratify her Desire immediately, he wou'd shoot him thro' the Head." The butcher gave up his watch and six guineas.[38]

When women actually did engage in robberies they were usually associ-ated with male robbers, sometimes, as in the Essex case, taking a direct part in crimes but more often acting as decoys and lookouts. Gangs of men and women travelled the country, the women giving a certain air of plausible respectability to the party and at the same time playing some role in their crimes. Women were even more commonly associated with robbers in Lon-don. Indeed, so sought after were women recruits that when Joseph Massie planned a refuge for penitent prostitutes near London in 1758 he thought that it would be necessary to hire three guards "to deter street robbers etc. from coming to that Reformatory to look for Female Associates."[39] Women accomplices were particularly useful in London because opportunities abounded for manoeuvring likely prospects into positions in which a robbery was easily accomplished. In a particularly nasty case in Southwark in 1785, for example, three women lured a pedlar into a house where they tried with-out success to get him to give them his money; this having failed, they called in their four male associates, one of whom "took out a knife, and ripped up the belly of the poor man."[40] Stories of that kind, or of prostitutes luring men into dark lanes where they were attacked and robbed by their bullies, were frequently reported. And it seems likely that a large number of women implicated in this way were never suspected or at least never taken and prose-cuted. And that being the case, though the proportions of men and women who appeared in the Surrey courts accused of robbery may well accurately represent sex differences in the actual commission of street and highway crimes, women were probably more seriously involved in robbery than the mere numbers of indictments suggest.

If women rarely committed robberies directly, the reason could not be entirely laid to their unwillingness to engage in crime that offered the possibil-ity of violence. Burglary and housebreaking did so too (though of course burglars rarely carried weapons) and women did not shy away from them

90

Table 3: Crimes Against Property in Surrey in Years Sampled Between 1663 and 1802

Offence	Number of Persons Accused			Percent		Percent of Total		
	Total	Men	Women	Men	Women	Total	Men	Women
Robbery	529	487	42	92.1	7.9	7.4	9.0	2.4
Burglary and Housebreaking	939	756	183	80.5	19.5	13.2	14.0	10.6
Theft from Dwelling-House	268	157	111	58.6	41.4	3.8	2.9	6.4
Shoplifting	86	63	23	73.3	26.7	1.2	1.2	1.3
Theft from Warehouse	38	37	1	97.4	2.6	0.5	0.7	0.1
Theft from Ship or Dock, etc.	55	53	2	96.4	3.6	0.8	1.0	0.1
Theft from Manufactury	37	33	4	89.2	10.8	0.5	0.6	0.2
Picking Pockets	30	16	14	53.3	46.7	0.4	0.3	0.8
Petty Larceny	930	659	271	70.9	29.1	13.0	12.2	15.7
Sheep-stealing	156	145	11	93.0	7.0	2.2	2.7	0.6
Cattle Theft	21	21	–	100.0	–	0.3	0.4	–
Horse Theft	205	202	3	98.5	1.5	2.9	3.7	0.2
Simple Grand Larceny	3,848	2,787	1,061	72.4	27.6	53.9	51.5	61.5
Total	7,142	5,416	1,726					
(Missing)	141	127	14					

nearly so much. Indeed, almost two hundred women were indicted for burglary and housebreaking in Surrey in the years sampled. Many of them had been associated with men. And as with robbery, it is likely that women were even more frequently involved than appears from the court records, for they were often in an excellent position to aid in burglaries without running any serious risk of being caught. Domestic servants, who knew both the contents of houses and the movements of the family, were especially valuable allies and the few cases that came to light of servants in league with burglars were undoubtedly only the visible tip of a large iceberg.[41] And laundrywomen, who often went to and from their work at night, as well as street sellers and basketwomen could all be usefully employed as accomplices in burglary, for they could carry tools and stolen goods about the streets without raising suspicion.[42] There was undoubtedly a wide range of such alliances. But many of the two hundred women indicted had operated without the support of men. In some cases it is true their crimes appear to have been very petty, the "house-breaking" having simply involved a woman slipping through an open door to snatch something and run. But there were also some genuine burglars among them, women who had broken into houses at night, like Isabella Simms, who entered a house in Southwark one evening in 1737 by taking out a pane of glass with a knife and slipping a bolt on the back door; or another woman, also in Southwark, who wrenched open a window shutter with an iron poker; or Mary Morgan, who got into a house by knocking a hole through a wall.[43]

Even though there was a growing revulsion in the eighteenth century against the execution of thieves and perhaps especially women, there was such public anxiety about burglary and similar crimes that the reporting rate is likely to have remained relatively high. It was certainly much higher than the reporting rate of a number of other crimes, many of them perhaps more typical of women's offences. One example was theft by domestic servants, a crime thought to be so common and at the same time so difficult to prevent that it was one of the first to be made subject to capital punishment when the right to claim benefit of clergy was extended to everyone, without regard to their literacy, in 1706.[44] Because, in the words of the statute, "wicked and ill-disposed servants and other persons" had been encouraged to pilfer from their masters now that they could claim benefit of clergy and so escape being hanged, theft from a dwelling house of goods over the value of forty shillings was made a capital offence in 1713.[45] But only one-hundred-and-fifty men and one hundred women were charged under that statute in the years examined in Surrey – a tiny fraction no doubt of those who pilfered, even of those caught, for it is likely that the harshness of the penalty as well as the trouble and expense of going to court discouraged prosecutions. It is a fair presumption that the real level of servants' pilfering was very high indeed and that it was encouraged in wealthy houses by the drudgery of the life, the lowness of the wages, and the abuse that was so frequently visited on servants, as well as by the constant and extreme contrast between the lives of servants and masters and the ready availability of saleable goods. But servants' theft was far more than simply a matter of the very poor stealing from the very rich. Servants and apprentices also lived with husbandmen and craftsmen and there are sufficient complaints from such men and their wives to suggest that petty pilfering affected more than just very comfortable households. Mary Bridgeman confessed, for example, to having taken soap, candles, a blanket, a pewter plate, and other things from John Clarke, a staymaker of Bermondsey, during the five years she had lived with him as his apprentice and to having given them to Margaret Price who kept a greengrocer's cellar next door.[46] And other craftsmen complained in Surrey about servants stealing clothes and tools from their houses. Many of the things reported stolen were of little value.

It was an undoubted encouragement to such petty pilfering that almost anything could find a buyer. Tiny scraps of iron, candle ends, a few old nails, a piece of silver, clothes, rags — everything could be turned to account. Not just pawnbrokers and old-clothes dealers, but craftsmen and tradesmen and publicans dealt in small tag ends of things, or at least numbers of them acquired reputations for being willing to buy without asking too many questions. It was not necessary for a servant to have arcane contacts or to steal only valuable objects to make occasional and petty theft a useful supplement to a tiny income. Receivers were undoubtedly easier to find in the city, as contemporaries concerned with what they took to be rising crime rates never tired of complaining.[47] But they could be found in the countryside too, many of them women and perhaps especially widows, reduced to scratching a living as best they could. Petty theft by servants was not unknown in rural parishes. Two women servants of a farmer in Wanborough in Surrey in 1762 confessed to taking one of the master's plowshares to the house of Mrs Daniel, a widow, "after sunset" where, having weighed it at 9 pounds she offered them 7-½d. "and said she could not offer more except in goods." The farmer complained that he had lost many bits of iron off his gates which he thought had gone the same route as his plowshare.[48] Two other women, servants of Thomas Burton Esq. of Windlesham, confessed to stealing clods from their master's shed and selling them to Sarah and Jane Burchett of Windlesham, "who received them knowing them to be stolen."[49] But servants' theft was overwhelmingly an urban phenomenon. Almost 90 percent of the women prosecuted under the 1713 statute were charged in Southwark or neighbouring urban parishes; in the county of Sussex only six women were charged altogether in the forty-five years sampled between 1713 and the end of the century.

If the true extent of petty theft by servants could be measured, the level of women's crime would be much higher than appears simply from the court records. But this does not necessarily mean that the difference between the sexes would be altered. In modern society it is possible to think that the

93

underreporting of thefts by servants largely means the underreporting of thefts by women because few men now live where they work. But in the eighteenth century this was not so obviously the case. Boys and men also lived with masters as apprentices and servants and there is no reason to think that their theft was any better reported. And of course if one were to add all the undetected thefts of everyone who worked for a master without necessarily living in his house, the weight would be overwhelmingly on the side of men.

It is however possible that the underreporting of two other offences, shoplifting and picking pockets, might have had relatively more effect on the apparent rate of women's crime than on men's. Neither was by any means exclusive to women, but clearly women engaged prominently in both. The numbers actually prosecuted in Surrey, however − a total of eighty-six shoplifters and thirty pickpockets − must represent only a tiny fraction of those caught, let alone of the total who committed such crimes. Certainly the frequency of reports suggests that both offences were very common (though, of course, one man or woman could have been responsible for a large number of offences). A lot of shoplifting was petty and occasional and many shoplifters, as a member of a Commons committee looking into crime suggested in 1819, were "not persons who are regular traders in thieving, but are persons in better circumstances, particularly the women." But, as another witness before the committee said, many shoplifters were "in the habitual practice of it," and it is clear that this also included many women.[50] Women frequently worked in pairs, for example, one distracting the attention of the shopkeeper while the other lifted something;[51] others contrived special pockets in their clothes (eighteenth-century women's fashions being already of course a godsend to the practised thief) and employed a great variety of ruses.[52] Examples of successful theft from shops over a long period are not lacking: Moll Flanders was not without real-life exemplars. According to the *Gentleman's Magazine*, when Sarah McCabe, alias Sarah Flood, alias Ridgely, alias Clarke, alias Brewit, appeared in court in 1764 numerous people came forward to prosecute her, for she had "for upwards of twenty years carried on the practice of shop-lifting."[53] Elizabeth Stevens, who was convicted in 1735, had a similar reputation, for her petition to be pardoned from a sentence of transportation was opposed by the Recorder of London because, as he told the Secretary of State, when "such people are set at liberty . . . they generally return to the same practices."[54]

Shoplifting by women was certainly very much more common than the mere number of cases suggests. Women were also prominent among pickpockets. It is difficult to know what sort of sample the thirty cases brought to the Surrey courts represents, but to judge from the number of reports in the press and the insistent warnings to travellers, it must be a very poor sample indeed. The harshness of the penalty (picking pockets and shoplifting were both capital offences when the sums stolen were more than one shilling and

94

five shillings respectively) and the relative ease with which a practised thief could make a hit and get away undetected together help explain the small numbers prosecuted. In addition many of the women charged with "stealing from the person" were prostitutes accused of robbing their clients. This clearly must have added to the reluctance of many victims to bring a prosecution, for in addition to trouble and expense, it involved a possibly embarrassing confession. It was also difficult to get evidence against the women involved, and judges, encouraged perhaps by the feeling that these men had brought their troubles on themselves, seem commonly to have examined the evidence closely and to have given the men a rough ride. Even when the women had male accomplices, the court often took a hard line with the prosecutor.[55] It seems a reasonable assumption not only that thefts of this kind were very much more common than the number of indictments reveals, but also that the sample of those charged with picking pockets that did come to the Surrey courts especially underrepresented women.

Overall, then, indictments suggest that there was a great difference not only in the numbers but also in the types of crimes against property committed by men and women. Far fewer women than men were indicted for the most serious offences: a total of 1445 men were charged in Surrey with robbery, burglary, and horsetheft, for example, as against 228 women; and together these offences accounted for almost 27 percent of all male property crime but only 13 percent of female. Similarly with other capital, though less common, thefts: virtually all indictments in Surrey for stealing from ships and barges, from warehouses and docks and places of manufacture, as well as for sheep stealing and cattle theft involved men. At the same time, theft by servants, stealing from shops, and picking pockets occupied a more prominent place among women's crimes than men's (8.5 percent vs. 4.4 percent). Women's crime tended, that is, to be rather less direct, less open, risking less of a confrontation with the victim. Though some women entered houses to steal, women robbers were much less common. If they engaged in street crime, it was more often as an associate or decoy, or they picked on children, for a number of women were indicted for enticing a child into an alley or house in order to take its clothes to sell or pawn. Further, thefts which after 1706 were judged not serious enough to demand the death penalty — simple grand larceny and petty larceny — accounted for a larger proportion of women's property crime than men's (77 percent as against 64 percent).

Given these broad tendencies it may be that women's crime was relatively less well reported than men's. The more minor the offence the more it was likely to have been ignored or dealt with outside the courts. Even more serious is the possibility that the number of married women are very seriously underrepresented because of the assumption — acted on by the courts — that a wife could not be held responsible for illegal acts done in the company of her husband: if she was subject to his will, she could only be assumed to have acted under coercion. This certainly led to numbers of married women being discharged by the courts.[56] But did it mean that married women caught with their husbands were not indicted in the first place? That is much less clear. Indeed it would be surprising if such women were not normally prosecuted, for it might be expressly proved in court that they had acted of their own free will — a possibility that the law allowed; or the husband might be found not guilty, in which case his wife was still liable to be convicted. Pending further evidence, I remain doubtful that many women escaped prosecution for this reason. We might still assume some tendency towards underreporting of women thieves, out of tenderness on the part of prosecutors,[57] or because women committed a larger proportion of minor offences. But the weight of extrajudicial evidence strongly suggests that there is no reason to think that any bias in the rate of prosecutions between the sexes was so massive as to change fundamentally the general picture derived from the indictments: that in Surrey something of the order of three crimes against property were committed by men for every one by a woman; and that, in addition, women's crimes were on the whole much less serious.

IV

There is obviously no simple explanation of the fact that women committed fewer crimes of violence and fewer crimes against property than men. Differences in sheer strength may have had some bearing on it, despite our earlier remarks, as may temperamental differences. But more fundamentally it must have resulted from contrasts in training and expected behaviour and in general from the place of women in society. Some characteristics of women's crime, as we have seen, appear to derive from women's place in the family. But the patterns and levels of women's crime also reflect their relationship to the wider community. This requires more elaboration than I am capable of providing here. But the subject can at least be explored and some evidence developed by looking at women's crime in urban and rural settings.

In fact more crimes were committed by both men and women in urban than in rural areas. Roughly seven out of ten cases that came before the Surrey courts had arisen in the Borough of Southwark and neighbouring parishes. Urban-rural differences in women's crime are even more striking. Almost 83 percent of crimes against the person committed by women occurred in the northern urban parishes and only 17 percent in the rest of the county, whereas for men the urban-rural distribution was 68 percent to 32 percent (see Table 4). In crimes against property a similar difference is apparent, for whereas 82 percent of women's offences were committed in the city, only 66 percent of men's were (Table 5). Looking at these figures another way, in the urban parishes the ratio of women to men accused of personal violence was 1:3.6 and for property crimes 1:2.5. In the rural parishes and market towns of Surrey, on the other hand, the ratios were 1:8.3 and 1:6 respectively. These rural Surrey figures are encouragingly confirmed by data

96

Table 4: Crimes Against the Person in Surrey (Urban and Rural Parishes)
and in Sussex Charged Against Men and Women

	Surrey Urban Parishes	Surrey Rural Parishes	Sussex	% in Urban Surrey	% in Rural Surrey
Men	2,604	1,254	1,457	67.5	32.5
Women	725	151	177	82.8	17.2
Total	3,329	1,405	1,634		
% Men	78.2	89.3	89.2		
% Women	21.8	10.7	10.8		

Table 5: Crimes Against Property in Surrey (Urban and Rural Parishes)
and in Sussex Charged Against Men and Women

	Surrey Urban Parishes	Surrey Rural Parishes	Sussex	% in Urban Surrey	% in Rural Surrey
Men	3,574	1,842	1627	66.0	34.0
Women	1,421	305	233	82.3	17.7
Total	4,995	2,147	1,860		
% Men	71.6	85.8	87.5		
% Women	28.4	14.2	12.5		

for Sussex, for in that essentially rural county the male-female ratios were
1:8.2 in crimes against the person and 1:7 in crimes against property. Women
in the city were thus much more likely to be accused of assault or theft than
women in the rural parishes and small towns of Surrey and Sussex and the
urban-rural disparity was much greater for women than for men.

To some extent these urban-rural differentials in Surrey are simply a reflection of population differences. The urban population not only grew more
rapidly over the period, but was both younger than that of the countryside
and more imbalanced in favour of women over men.[58] Unfortunately the
absence of data on the age and sex structure of the two parts of the county
(at any time, let alone on changes over time) makes it impossible to take these
factors into account in any precise way. Clearly the urban-rural differences

help to explain why 82 percent and 83 percent of the crimes against property and the person committed by women in Surrey were in London. But it seems reasonable to suppose that the urban population was neither so much larger than the rural[59] nor so overbalanced in favour of the young and of women that this in itself could account for so great a differential. What seems in fact more important than simply the numbers of women in the urban and rural populations is the difference in their lives and circumstances in the city as against the countryside.

For one thing, though life in urban parishes in London was not so anonymous as to prevent a sense of community being maintained,[60] a closer and greater degree of surveillance was undoubtedly achieved in the smaller and more personal community of a rural parish. In the countryside community pressures on those whose conduct threatened to disrupt village life were more insistent, and the figures of authority — the parson, and especially the magistrate — were more immediate and more formidable, for the rural justice in the eighteenth century still combined social and legal authority in a way that London justices did not. Rural society remained deeply deferential; and when the social authority of a landed gentleman of substance was combined with the legal powers that a magistrate had at his command to compel troublemakers to mend their ways, and when to this was added intimate local knowledge, the result was a degree of control over the lives especially of the young that could never be achieved in the different circumstances of a large urban parish.

Rural life was especially restrictive for women. Young girls were customarily bound into service during adolescence, either on farms where they were employed both in the house and, as needed, in the dairy and the fields, or as domestic servants or apprentices in market towns. Both at home and in service, young girls were hedged in by restraints that clearly had as one of their important objects the prevention of a pregnancy that would be an embarrassment to the girl's family and might in addition leave a bastard as a burden on the community. Such concerns are an aspect of the subjection of women to men and of the double standard that had existed in England for centuries by which the sexual relations of men before or outside marriage were judged to be of small account while being a matter of the greatest seriousness for women.[61] These deeply rooted ideas, which clearly derived from the fundamental assumption that men had a property in women, focused particularly on the training of girls in the critical years before marriage, during the transition from their subjection to a father to that of a husband. The author of a guidebook to the trades of London was voicing the common assumption that girls had to be more carefully watched and controlled than their brothers when he said in the middle of the eighteenth century that

> A Woman is always under Age till she comes (in the Law Phrase) to be under Cover. A Youth may be set a-float in the World as soon as he has

98

got a Trade in his Head, without much Danger of spoiling; but a Girl is
such a tender, ticklish Plant to rear, that there is no permitting her out of
leading-strings till she is bound to a Husband.62

How effective such controls were, especially among the lower classes, is
another matter. But the intention was universal that girls grow up with less
freedom of action than boys; and in the smaller and tighter rural community,
behaviour could be more closely scrutinized and courtship customs made
more binding than in the more impersonal world of a large urban parish.63

Even after marriage, women in rural society were not much less restricted
in their behaviour and range of social contacts. Not that they were bound to
housework: indeed it was expected that a wife, in both rural and urban
society, would contribute substantially to the family income.64 Her means
of contribution varied, depending in part on her social class and the extent to
which she could share in her husband's work. But most women in rural
society were limited to work they could do in and around their house, in
spinning or similar tasks or in managing a small plot of land, growing a few
crops, and keeping a few chickens, perhaps keeping a beast on the common
and supplementing the whole with field work at harvest time. The circles within which married women moved in rural society tended thus to be more narrowly restricted and circumscribed than their husbands', whose work,
whether as husbandmen, craftsmen, or even wage labourers, took them more
regularly into the world and who in addition were able to engage more freely
in whatever social life revolved around the local tavern, for the double standard extended to all forms of behaviour.65

In the populous urban parishes of northern Surrey, on the other hand,
women as well as men were thrown more regularly into contact with a wider
society and the checks imposed on them both by the community and the
authorities could only operate less effectively. It is this relative freedom that
lies behind the dismay at the evil effects of city life expressed by so many
commentators in the eighteenth century. Those who saw in the circumstances
of life in the city the encouragement of social disorder, rebelliousness, and
crime, especially condemned the freedom that life allowed to the young.
Poverty and crime and the weakening of the social bonds were the product,
in this view, of the licence that urban life granted to the poor to come and
go at will, to dress like their betters, to entertain themselves as they chose at
theatres and pleasure gardens, and to gamble and drink without restraint in
the thousands of taverns that catered to them.66 No matter what might be
thought about the validity of such analyses, they do contain a central truth —
that life in the city was on a different order from life in a village or even a
market town. It was a difference that changed entirely the tasks of constables
and magistrates — indeed that made regular and professional police forces
necessary — because in the large and complex urban environment neither the
family nor the community could any longer control its members. While this

relative freedom of the city made its impact on men, the contrast with the more closely ordered rural community must have been greater for women, married as well as single. For women the differences in the pattern of their lives must have been the more liberating.

The differences arose in part from the greater demands for women's labour in the city. London was the center of government, trade, and finance and the focal point of upper-class social life. As the population expanded in the seventeenth and eighteenth centuries and London spread gradually to the west, throwing up fashionable squares and residential quarters, and as a network of retailers to service this growing and wealthy population was gradually enlarged, there was an increasing demand for domestic servants, shop assistants, and the like. But beyond that, the demands of this population made London the greatest center of English industry in the eighteenth century, supporting a huge concentration of craftsmen and semiskilled and unskilled workers. The south bank of the Thames, especially the northern band of the county of Surrey, including the Borough of Southwark and neighbouring parishes like Lambeth, Rotherhithe, and Bermondsey, was among the most highly developed industrial areas in the metropolis.[67] Immediately surrounding this built-up area an intensive agriculture was practised, raising fruit and vegetables and producing meat, milk, and other food for the city market.[68]

Women participated in this economic activity extensively if not equally with men. Apart from their work in domestic service and in retail shops, women were employed in some of the larger-scale industries, and the clothing trades of the city depended on their work as semstresses and tailors, coatmakers and milliners. Women were also widely employed in the market gardens and dairies around the capital, working not only at hoeing and weeding and as dairy maids and cow keepers, but also as carriers, taking baskets of vegetables and other produce to the London markets. Large numbers of other women hawked fruit, vegetables, fish, and milk in the streets; and many wives of casual labourers struggled to add to the family budget by keeping a street barrow, or taking in washing or doing odd jobs that included work of the most menial kind.[69]

If the city provided work, it also created appalling working conditions and for many a merely marginal existence. The clothing trades were overstocked and poorly paid, especially for women. Their wages were assumed to be supplementary and women were fortunate to be paid at half the man's rate for the same work.[70] Apart from low wages, perhaps the greatest difficulties were created by the irregularity of employment. Work in the market gardens and the distribution network that depended on them was obviously seasonal, but so too were the clothing trades, for they entered a slack period when the summer season took the court and a large part of the "quality" out of London. Most of the women in the needlework trades worked either at home or in a small workshop, in a putting-out system in which they were dependent on small-scale employers who had to stop or reduce work when demand fell.[71]

100

Given the jobs open to them and the great irregularity of employment, the position of large numbers of women was precarious indeed. Married women, whose husbands also commonly suffered from the same irregularity of work, had difficulties enough. But the conditions of life and work bore particularly hard on single women, especially those who had come long distances to find work (and many did come from Ireland and Scotland) and who had no family or friends to fall back on; and with even greater security on widows with children and on women who had been deserted by their husbands and left to bring up families of their own, of whom it is clear there were a very large number.[72]

V

Such patterns of life and work in London – the relative freedom from the restraints that could be exercised by employers and the authorities, the availability of work, and the potential harshness of life – had a bearing on the level of crime in the city. But the crimes we have been considering did not all arise from the same circumstances. Whereas the level of property crime appears to be related mainly to economic conditions, for example, there is no similar connection with crimes of violence. Assault and other crimes against the person seem to have increased in Surrey very sharply indeed in the first third of the eighteenth century in urban parishes, less sharply in rural, and then, in general, to have declined in both areas through the rest of the century.[73] This trend is not related, at least in any direct way, to changes in economic circumstances as measured, say, by prices. Over the short term there are some brief periods in which there is some correspondence between a rising level of indictments for assault in the urban parishes of Surrey on the one hand, and rising prices and deepening unemployment in the city of London on the other. This is the case in the 1760s. But by no means all sharp fluctuations came at such times and it seems clear that the fact that 83 percent of the prosecutions for violence brought against women in Surrey were in urban parishes cannot be attributed in a simple way to the evil effects of city life. The urban environment may have produced a vast number of rootless and alienated women who out of their despair were driven to violence, but if so, their violence did not bring them into court in overwhelming numbers. For if this had been the root cause, one would expect not only a rise in indictments for violence in periods of dearth, but also that a disproportionate number of the women accused, especially in London, would have been single. In fact, however, the preponderance of women prosecuted for offences against the person were married. In Surrey the proportion of married women was even higher in the city than in the countryside, but in rural parishes, too, and in Sussex, married women were also more frequently prosecuted for assaults and other violence than were single women.[74] In addition many were women in settled and established positions in the community.

About 40 percent of the married women prosecuted for assault in the urban parishes of Surrey were married to men of some substance, mainly tradesmen, artisans, or yeoman; and they included twelve wives of gentlemen and one of an esquire. In rural Surrey almost 30 percent of the married women charged had husbands of a similar character.[75] A good part of the women's violence that came to the notice of the courts thus involved women who were not part of the dispossessed and rootless sections of society.

More married women were charged with assault and other violence in part because so many of the cases that came to court centered on the family and neighbourhood, and arose from the chastisement of children, brutality to servants and apprentices, and quarrels between husbands and wives and relatives and neighbours. And it is entirely possible that cases of the latter kind worked further to inflate the number of married women among the accused, for if the allegation of assault was part of a wider conflict between families, the charge of assault might even be fictitious; and to the extent that such charges were designed to extract damages, they would increase the number of accused, including married women, who could afford to pay. Such considerations help to explain why more than 60 percent of the women prosecuted for crimes against the person in Surrey and Sussex were married. But they do not explain the disparity in urban-rural ratios as between men and women, the fact that in urban Surrey 1 woman was accused for every 3.6 men, whereas in the rural parishes of the county and in Sussex the ratios were 1:8.3 and 1:8.2 respectively. The urban population, it is true, contained a higher proportion of women. But it was insufficiently large to explain this contrast between urban and rural areas. The explanation that seems most satisfactory is that in working more outside the home and in a social situation that made possible frequent and wider-ranging human contacts, women's lives changed relatively more sharply than men's in the transition from the countryside to the city. And the fact that in the city the influence of parents could only have been weakened, the control of masters over the personal lives of their servants less binding and the authority of magistrates less compelling also meant a greater contrast for women, even married women. It seems reasonable to think that it is the enlarged freedom of the city and the enlarged context of women's lives there that explains why women accounted for a much larger proportion of the prosecutions for personal violence in the urban parishes of Surrey than in the rest of the county or in Sussex. I am not yet able to say whether more women's violence arose in the city than in rural areas from casual encounters and disputes outside the immediate neighbourhood, but that seems a reasonable expectation.

If the offences in the general category of crimes against the person do not seem to be closely related to economic hardship, this is not the case with the other large group we are dealing with, crimes against property. Both in rural and urban parishes want and necessity seem to bear directly on levels of theft. That is not to say there were no "professional" thieves, if by that one

102

means men and women who might have earned a living legitimately but chose not to. Some women at least engaged in criminal activities that required skill and training, as members of coining gangs, for example, or in running a con game in a big or small way.[76] Others, like Mary Jones, alias Black Moll (whose husband turned in his former partners to save her life),[77] were associated with gangs of robbers, and some women, as we have seen, sustained a long criminal career by shoplifting or picking pockets. But the principal feature of crime against property was not its consistently high level, but its frequent and sizeable fluctuation. And this suggests that most theft was the work of people who chose to steal or not according to their circumstances and their ability to support themselves. Indeed the fluctuations in crimes against property seem clearly to be tied to economic conditions, and to two factors in particular — the prices of consumer goods, especially food, and the availability of work.

The fluctuation in the number of men and women accused of property offences in the years sampled are plotted in Graph 1 for the three areas we have been dealing with: (a) the urban parishes of Surrey; (b) the rural parishes and market towns of Surrey; (c) the county of Sussex.[78] Short-term variations in the number of prosecutions were greatest in the urban parishes of Surrey. They were especially striking for men, but the number of women accused of property crimes also occasionally varied sharply from year to year, if not on the same order of magnitude as men, at least with the same timing and direction.

It is striking how clear the relationship is in London between the number of prosecutions and years of war and peace. Virtually all of the low points in the eighteenth century in prosecutions in the urban parishes of Surrey, and certainly all of the deepest ones, came during wars; and conversely the greatest increases and the highest peaks came immediately after the conclusion of wars (Graph 1A). This points to a clear connection between the amount of theft in the city and the availability of work, for war absorbed some of the large pool of casually employed men in London into the army and navy and perhaps also into industries whose production was increased by the needs of the armed forces — rope and sailmaking, shipbuilding, brewing, and provisioning in general, and gunpowder production, a Surrey specialty. On the other hand, at the conclusion of wars a large number of soldiers and sailors were discharged over a short period and without any provision being made for their reentry into civilian life. Many were paid off in London or close enough that it was easy for large numbers to drift into the capital looking for work. The result was a huge glut of casual and unskilled labour in London soon after the ending of a war which, from at least the middle of the eighteenth century, was identified by many observers as the principal reason for the skyrocketing of crime at such times.[79] In some periods the problems of unemployment were compounded by a simultaneous rise in food prices. After 1780 and more especially in the 1790s, rising prices were apparently sufficient in themselves to encourage increases in theft even in war years, but in both cases crime

Graph 1 : Number of Men and Women Accused of Crimes Against Property

A : Surrey: Urban Parishes

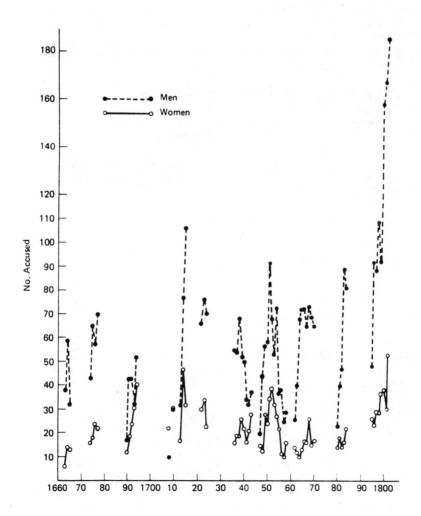

104

Graph 1:   B: Surrey: Rural Parishes

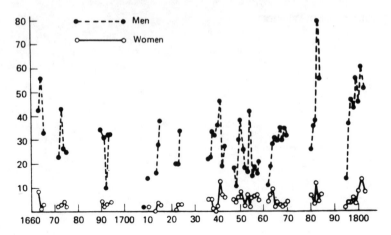

Graph 1:   C: Sussex

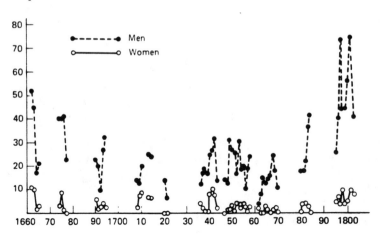

Graph 2: **Marital Status of Women Accused of Crimes Against Property in Urban Parishes of Surrey**

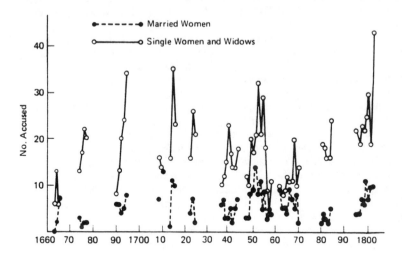

levels rose even further with the peace (in 1782 and 1802).

Though these patterns are most clearly evident in the graph of men's property crime in the city, theft by women in the urban parishes of Surrey seems to be similarly linked to changes in their economic circumstances, circumstances that were similarly governed by the price of necessities and the availability of work. Even at the best of times underemployment was the common situation for many women in the city. The clothing trades were severely overstocked and domestic service was glutted. Thousands of women came to the city every year looking for jobs and very large numbers of them, especially girls looking for domestic work, were disappointed: there was simply not enough work to go around.[80] There were thus many women in the city living in lodgings and earning a living as best they could for whom a sudden increase in prices or a shortage of work must have had the gravest consequences.

Though married women living with their husbands were not unaffected by such changes in the labour pool or in prices, other women must have felt their effects even more severely — especially young girls who had left their families

106

to come to the city, widows (more particularly widows with children, the
numbers of whom were enlarged by wars), and wives deserted by their husbands and left with families to raise. It is hardly surprising that it is thefts by
single women and widows that seem to have fluctuated the most violently in
periods of economic change (Graph 2). The striking feature of that graph
is not the revelation that married women stole less than single women and
widows, for that difference is in part at least simply a reflection of the numbers of such women in the urban population. Rather it is the much more
obvious volatility of thefts by unmarried women. In years of economic difficulty caused by high prices or unemployment it was mainly increased prosecutions of single women and widows that accounted for the sharpest changes
in the number of cases brought to the Surrey courts. This is the case, for
example, in the deepening economic crisis of the 1690s; following the Treaty
of Utrecht in 1713; again (after apparently reaching low levels during the war
in the 1740s), in the years following the peace in 1748; again, after further
very low points during the Seven Years' War, in the gradually worsening
economic circumstances of the 1760s; after the peace in 1783-84; and,
finally, in the 1790s. The latter case provides perhaps the clearest clue to the
economic pressures that encouraged theft in the city, for though the level of
property crimes committed by single women and widows rose in the last few
years of the century when prices climbed very steeply, it did not increase
with startling swiftness until 1802, the year of the peace, when it leapt
dramatically.

These fluctuations in women's property crime in London are less severe
than men's and in some periods changes in women's crime do not parallel
men's at all. This perhaps reflects the degree to which women in need could
turn to men for support or to prostitution. But the timing and direction of
short-term trends in women's theft, especially thefts by those women most
vulnerable to economic changes, nonetheless suggests that for women, as
much as for men, necessity provided the spur — the necessity of the woman
"forsaken by her husband at her lying in," of the "poor widdo woman that
have nothing for myselfe and child but what I can Git dayley," of the woman
who broke into a house two nights in one week to steal bread and cheese
from the kitchen.[81]

The patterns of women's crime against property in the rural parishes of
Surrey and in Sussex (Graphs 1B and 1C) are different from those of London,
for the levels were much lower and the fluctuations less extreme. Women
were only infrequently prosecuted for theft in the countryside and it seems
on this evidence that it took a very serious stimulus to encourage rural
women to steal. What movement there is in the patterns of prosecutions
(if levels that rarely got beyond a total of ten accused a year can be thought to
have movement) suggests that the stresses caused by rising food prices
sometimes led to higher levels of theft by women in rural areas. This is clearly
the case in 1740-41. But this response was not invariable and it is perhaps

especially revealing that women do not seem to have turned more to theft, as men apparently did, in the deepening economic crisis in the countryside in the last two decades of the century.

There are, furthermore, other clear differences between women's property crime in rural and urban areas. Not only were more than 80 percent of offences committed in the city; urban women were also responsible for almost all of the serious types of property crime. This is not true of burglary and housebreaking, for 28 percent of the women so accused had stolen from houses outside London. But well over 9 of 10 charged with such offences as robbery, shoplifting, and picking pockets had operated in the city. This is of course partly a measure of criminal opportunities. But it also perhaps reflects differences in attitudes and responses to economic adversity. This is further suggested by the apparent unwillingness of rural women to ally with others in the furtherance of theft. In the five years 1796-1800, for example, 149 women went on trial in Surrey for commiting crimes against property in London. Of these 69 percent were charged with having stolen on their own, 20 percent with having worked with other women (in groups of 2 to 4), and 11 percent with having been associated with men. At the same time only 14 rural women came before Surrey juries and all but 2 had been alone at the time of the theft. The 2 were accused with men.

Of course it is possible that rural offences were not vigorously prosecuted, that a larger proportion of women caught stealing in villages and small towns were dealt with informally by neighbours or employers or magistrates. (On the other hand, if the prosecution rate were lower in the countryside, the detection rate must have been considerably higher there than in the more congested and more anonymous urban parishes.) It also might be thought that the concentration on offences I have defined as crimes against property fails to reveal the full range of responses of rural women to economic troubles. But other forms of crime do not suggest a different picture to the one of relative passivity of rural women suggested by prosecutions for theft, robbery, and burglary. Women in rural parishes did not engage any more actively in malicious injury to property – arson, cattle-maiming, and similar acts of revenge – than in theft. Nor were they more prominent among those prosecuted for unlawful dispossession and detainer or for trespass, charges which usually stemmed from disputes over the ownership of land and buildings.[82]

A fuller investigation of the role of women in crimes committed by their husbands – and in general of the family in crime[83] – might modify to some extent the picture of the criminal activities of rural women derived from the judicial data. It is worth remembering, too, that a considerable distortion in the comparison of prosecutions against urban and rural women is introduced by the fact that women who found it difficult to survive in a rural parish or who rebelled against the constraints of rural life could and clearly did migrate to the city. This in itself helps to explain many of the rural-urban differences and only precise age- and sex-specific population information could

108

eliminate its effects. But even were that available, it is unlikely that all the problems of comparison would be eliminated, for it could be argued, for example, that a full understanding of the response of urban women to economic stresses would have to take into account the very large numbers who turned to prostitution, an alternative to theft that to all intents was not available to women in rural parishes.

Despite all the obvious difficulties of comparison, it seems clear that women were more likely to commit crimes against the person and against property in the city than in the countryside, and that this derives from vital differences in the circumstances of women's lives in these two settings. It reflects on the one hand the relative absence of restraints on the behaviour of women in the city, especially on the very large numbers who lived in lodgings, and it reflects too the difficulties that so many women experienced in the city. In a rural community paternalistic controls might restrict behaviour, but at the same time they also provided more cushions against adversity and more protections against extreme disaster. And for women living in their parishes of legal settlement, the poor-law system worked tolerably well so long as the problems of rural poverty remained occasional and manageable. In the city these protections were much less readily available. Women were thrown more directly into contact with a wider society; they were more regularly part of the work force and more dependent on working for wages and thus were more vulnerable to economic fluctuations; and they were less protected, sheltered, and restricted. It is such considerations as these that are likely to explain why the patterns and levels of women's crime in the city were much closer to those of men than in the rural parishes of Surrey and Sussex. And this points towards an explanation of women's crime and of differences in male and female crime which, while it might have to accommodate biological and emotional factors, will emphasize social realities, the relationships of men and women, and in general, the place of women in society.[84]

University of Toronto   J. M. Beattie

Notes

1.   It is not thought that Surrey and Sussex are "typical" counties or that their crime patterns will necessarily be duplicated elsewhere. They were chosen in part because of the quality of their records, for the assize files of the Home Circuit, of which they were part, are preserved in the Public Record Office from the reign of Elizabeth on. There are some gaps until the fourth decade of the eighteenth century, but it is still possible to get complete data for a reasonable number of years in the late seventeenth century and the early eighteenth. The quarter-sessions rolls of both Surrey and Sussex survive virtually intact, and in addition the records of the Southwark Borough quarter sessions survive, though not without gaps, in the London Record Office. These courts — the assizes and the county and borough quarter sessions — dealt with the bulk of the criminal business arising

in the county. On the work of the most important of these courts, see J. S.
   Cockburn, *A History of English Assizes, 1558-1714* (Cambridge, Eng., 1972).

2.   In addition to the felonies included in Table 1, women were also charged with a
   wide range of misdemeanors, including keeping a disorderly alehouse, selling
   underweight, keeping a bawdy house, etc., all of them of considerable interest in
   other contexts but not "crimes" in any straightforward sense. I have also excluded charges of riotous and unlawful assembly from consideration because they
   raise such wide-ranging issues that they require separate treatment.

3.   For some modern studies touching on the criminality of women, see John Cowie,
   Valerie Cowie, and Eliot Slater, *Delinquency in Girls* (Cambridge, Eng., 1968);
   Clyde B. Vedder and Dora B. Somerville, *The Delinquent Girl* (Springfield, Ill.,
   1970); T. C. N. Gibbens, "Female Offenders," *British Journal of Hospital Medicine* 6 (1971), pp. 279-286; Frances Heidensohn, "The Deviance of Women: a
   critique and an enquiry," *British Journal of Sociology* 19 (1968), pp. 160-175;
   and for two excellent summaries, Hermann Mannheim, *Comparative Criminology:
   A Text Book* (London, 1965), 2: ch. 26, and Nigel Walker, *Crime and Punishment
   in Britain: The Penal System in Theory, Law and Practice,* rev. ed. (Edinburgh,
   1968), ch. 14. Otto Pollak, who has made the most extensive study of women's
   crime, has disagreed in a fundamental way with the thrust of the modern literature. He has argued that the statistics of women's crime are particularly weak
   because women are psychologically and culturally predisposed towards dissimula-
   tion and that for this reason and because of their occupational and social roles,
   women commit a disproportionate number of petty crimes that are difficult to
   detect and are notoriously underreported. Pollak concludes that women's crime
   is peculiarly masked, therefore, and argues that if all women's infractions were
   reported the gap between male and female crime rates would be much less extreme (*The Criminality of Women* [New York, 1950]). But see Mabel A. Elliott,
   Crime in Modern Society, 2 vols. (N.Y., 1952), 2: ch. 8.

4.   Accounts of assize trials in Surrey were published occasionally in the eighteenth
   century under such titles as "The Proceedings at the Assizes for . . . Surrey" or
   "The Proceedings at the Sessions of Oyer and Terminer and General Gaol Delivery
   . . . " I have referred to them all simply as *Surrey Assize Proceedings.* Unlike the
   trials held at the Old Bailey, the Surrey assize proceedings do not appear to have
   been regularly published. I have found accounts of thirty-six sessions in the
   seventeenth and eighteenth centuries.

5.   In the Surrey Record Office: Quarter Sessions Bundles (QS2/6).

6.   Pollak, *The Criminality of Women,* ch. 3.

7.   *Surrey Assize Proceedings* (April 1759), pp. 4-9.

8.   *Gentleman's Magazine,* 44 (1774): 233.

9.   The indictment normally gives only the victim's name, but recognizances, in-
   formations, and examinations of prisoners when they are available often give
   additional information. Even more valuable are the accounts of trials at the
   assizes (see note 4 above).

10.   *Surrey Assize Proceedings* (March 1738), p. 20.

11.   One charge of manslaughter included in the Surrey sample arose from an accident
   in which a child in Rotherhithe in 1800 was held over a large copper of boiling
   water as a punishment for misbehaviour and slipped from the grasp of its nurse;
   "it died immediately," the *Gentleman's Magazine* reported, "in a most shocking
   state, the very skin coming off with the clothes when taken out" (88 [1800]:
   788). The mistreatment of a domestic servant also brought a Surrey woman into
   court on a murder charge in 1679 (*Surrey Assize Proceedings* [March 1679], p. 3).

12.   21 Jas I, c. 27 (1623).

13.   R. W. Malcolmson, "Infanticide in Eighteenth-Century England"(forthcoming in
   J. S. Cockburn, ed., *Crime in England, 1550-1800*).

110

14.   In March 1678, for example, at a trial of a servant for infanticide, the woman's mistress reported that she heard her "groan and make a great noise in the night," but "thinking it common sickness, took no notice of it" (*Surrey Assize* [March 1679], p. 6); in the following year another servant was tried who had concealed her pregnancy by "wearing loose garments." When she was delivered she cried out in the night but answered all enquiries by saying that she had an ache. A child was found hidden in her box the next morning. It had been strangled, and she was convicted (*Ibid.* [March 1679], p. 4).

15.   To take just one case of several, at the trial of Mary Martin in 1759, Sarah Rippon, a midwife, testified that she was brought to examine a dead infant found in the "hovel" where the prisoner, a servant, slept. It had been dead about a week. She was asked if there were any marks of violence upon it.

> *Rippon*: I saw none . . . she told me that the child was born dead; and I believe it was. *Question*: How come you to believe that? *Rippon*: It often happens, that children are born in appearance dead, which by outward application might recover, but I believe it was inevitable then . . . *Question*: How long have you practised midwifery? *Rippon*: Seven years, and in my opinion, I really believe, that if the child was not born dead, it died in the birth."

Mary Martin swore that she had prepared childbed linen (produced in court) and claimed that she had had an accident which caused the stillbirth. She was acquitted (*Ibid.* [March-April 1759], p. 11).

16.   A cook's maid at an inn in Guildford was indicted in 1751 when a baby was found with its throat cut hidden under the eaves of the inn. After denying it entirely at first her defence was that she had not known what she was doing. This was supported by the evidence of a woman who had nursed her after the birth and who testified that "there had been no sense in her for four of five days"; she was acquitted (*Ibid.* [August 1751], pp. 26-7).

17.   *Ibid.* (July 1741), p. 5.

18.   Malcolmson, "Infanticide."

19.   Add Mss 42598, fo. 76; Add Mss 42599, fos. 40, 40v.; Add Mss 42600, fo. 3.

20.   M. Dorothy George, *London Life in the Eighteenth Century* (London, 1925), pp. 231-4.

21.   Peter Laslett, *The World We Have Lost*, 2nd ed. (London, 1971), pp. 5, 22.

22.   QS2/6, 1705, no. 41.

23.   *A Treaty of Feme Coverts: or the Lady's Law* . . . (London, 1732), p. 81; C. S. Kenny, *The History of the Law of England as to the Effects of Marriage on Property and on the Wife's Legal Capacity* (London, 1879), pp. 153-4.

24.   Daniel Defoe, *The Behaviour of Servants in England* . . . (London, 1724), pp. 3-7.

25.   QS2/6, Michaelmas, 1742, no. 30; Michaelmas, 1721; Public Record Office: Assizes: Home Circuit indictment files, Assi 35/179/7: gaol calendar.

26.   Timothy Rogers, *The Character of a Good Woman* (London, 1697), pp. 9, 17-18; William Kenrick, *The Whole Duty of a Woman*, 13th ed. (London, 1792), p. 44; and see Wilfred Hooper, *The Englishwoman's Legal Guide* (London, 1713), pp. 93-4; *Laws Respecting Women as they Regard their Natural Rights or their Connections and Conduct* (London, 1777), p. 65.

27.   Edward P. Thompson, " 'Rough Music': le charivari anglais," *Annales, E.S.C.*, no. 2 (mars-avril, 1972): 285-312.

28.   Wiltshire Record Office, Q.S. Roll (April 1662).

29.   Dorothy L. Powell and Hilary Jenkinson, eds., *Surrey Quarter Sessions Records: Order Books and Sessions Rolls, 1661-1663* (Surrey County Council, 1935), 7: pp. 137-209; Powell and Jenkinson, eds., *Order Books and Sessions Rolls, 1663-1666* (Surrey Record Society, 1938), 16: 140.

30.   To take just two examples of many, two yeoman and their wives and another

111

yeoman were accused in Dorking in 1690 of assembling in a riotous manner and breaking into James Collin's house at night to assault him; and some years later James Stoddey, a cork cutter of Rotherhithe, was indicted with his wife, son, and daughter for assaulting Margaret Naylor (Surrey Q.S. roll, no. 115 [1691] ; Epiph. 1720). Very often such cases resulted in more than one indictment, for the injured parties frequently took direct revenge before the dispute got before the courts. Women were often among the victims as well as the accused in these assaults.

31. *Surrey Assize Proceedings* (March 1738), p. 18.
32. Elizabeth Harris, a widow living in Battersea, was joined for example by Grace Harris, spinster, and three Harris laborers (all presumably her children) and by two other laborers and their wives in assaulting a bailiff who was distraining her goods by court order; similarly, the wife of a butcher in Lambeth and her son forcibly prevented an overseer of the poor from distraining her goods for non-payment of poor rates (Surrey Q.S. Rolls [Xmas, 1752 (adjournment), and Xmas, 1784]).
33. QS2/6 (Midsummer 1751), no. 17.
34. E. P. Thompson, "The Moral Economy of the English Crowd in the Eighteenth Century," *Past and Present* no. 50 (Feb. 1971): 115-6.
35. QS2/6, Bundle I (1763), no. 37.
36. *Ibid.*, nos. 32, 35.
37. Eleanor Partridge was committed to the Surrey county gaol in 1720, for example, as an accessory to rape, for "assaulting and by force holding Isabell Powers whilst one Thomas Millener did against her will carnally know her" (*Ibid.*, [Jan. 1721], no. 37).
38. *Gentleman's Magazine* 5 (1735): 680.
39. Joseph Massie, *A Plan for the Establishment of Charity Houses for exposed or deserted Women and Girls and for Penitent Prostitutes* . . . (London, 1758), p. 40.
40. *Gentleman's Magazine* 55 (1785): 662.
41. See, for example, the case reported in the *Gentleman's Magazine* in 1782 in which two maids found tied to bedsteads in a house rifled of £500 worth of plate and other goods were eventually implicated when it was discovered that the mother of one had acted as the receiver (52: 403-4, 452).
42. *Ibid.*, 3 (1733): 267.
43. *Surrey Assize Proceedings* (March 1738), p. 7; *Ibid.* (March 1742), p. 9; *Ibid.* (April 1752), p. 15.
44. Benefit of clergy, which in effect excused a man's first conviction for felony, had originally extended to virtually all crimes, but had been granted only to those who could prove their literacy in court. In the course of two centuries, beginning in the sixteenth, the nature of clergy was changed entirely, for it was increasingly withdrawn from more and more offences, but at the same time extended to more people. In the seventeenth century, for example, it had been granted to women on the same basis as men — that is, to literate women. In 1706 the literacy requirement was withdrawn and clergy could henceforth be claimed by everyone. But in William III's reign and Anne's and through the eighteenth century a very large number of crimes were withdrawn from benefit of clergy. For a brief history of clergy see Sir William Blackstone, *Commentaries on the Laws of England*, 12th ed., 4 vols. (London, 1746), 4: 365-74 and Sir James Fitzjames Stephens, *A History of the Criminal Law of England*, 3 vols. (London, 1883), 1: 459-61.
45. 12 Anne, st. 1, c. 7.
46. QS2/6 (Easter 1764), no. 26.
47. See, for example, Henry Fielding, *An Enquiry into the Causes of the Great Increase of Robbers* (1751), in *The Works of Henry Fielding*, 10 vols. (London,

112

1806), 10: 411-12. and Patrick Colquhoun, *A Treatise on the Police of the Metropolis* (London, 1796), pp. 109-10.

48.   QS2/6 (Easter 1762), no. 57.
49.   QS2/6 (Michaelmas 1764), nos. 35, 36.
50.   *Report from the Select Committee on the Criminal Laws. Parliamentary Papers* (1819), 8: 27.
51.   QS2/6 (Christmas 1767), no. 59; QS2/6 (1712), no. 46.
52.   Perhaps the most unusual technique was that employed by Lydia Blackburn in an attempted theft from a pawnbroker in Southwark in 1752. She had come into his shop, he told a magistrate, and offered to sell him a pint copper pot, an iron candlestick, an iron heater, and an iron pin, all for a shilling, which he refused, he said, "suspecting them to be stolen." It was only when she had packed all her goods and left that he noticed that she had also packed up and taken a set of brass weights that belonged to him (QS2/6 [Easter 1752], no. 2).
53.   *Gentleman's Magazine* 34 (1764): 144.
54.   (P.R.O., State Papers) S.P. 36/37, fo. 23.
55.   See, for example, the vigorous cross-examination by the judge in the trial of Margaret Faulkner and Richard Sarnell in 1738. Thomas Ford testified that he had met Margaret Faulkner in an alehouse in Newington and that, after drinking with her, had gone to her room. Sarnell, he said, had come into the room and tried to put his hand in his pocket.

> *Court*: Where was his hand? *Ford*: By my pocket. I caught hold of his hand and he had got [my] Tobacco Box ... The Money [a guinea and a shilling] he had taken out, so I asked him for the money. *Court*: How do you know he had your money? Had it a particular mark on it? *Ford*: 'Twas a King George's guinea and a King William's shilling. *Court*: How many thousands are there more than yours do you think? What time was it when you went up with Faulkner? *Ford*: About 8 o'clock [the constable of the parish testified that Ford sent for him at eleven o'clock]. *Court*: So you were three hours with Faulkner.

Both prisoners were acquitted. (*Surrey Assize Proceedings* [March 1738], pp. 16-17).

56.   Hooper, *Englishwoman's Legal Guide*, pp. 93-4; Blackstone, *Commentaries*, 1: 27-8. The situation was described in 1777 as follows: "A Feme covert shall not be punished for committing any felony in company with her husband; the law supposing she did it by the coercion of her husband. But the bare command of her husband be no excuse for her committing a theft if he was not present; much less is she excused if she commit a theft of her own voluntary act" (*Laws respecting Women*, pp. 70-1). These rules seem to have been commonly applied in the eighteenth century. Anne Taylor of Newington, Surrey, was, for example, tried in 1738 for privately stealing from a house in which she was a lodger, but "it appearing [at her trial] ... that she acted under the Directions of her Husband, the jury acquitted her" (*Surrey Assize Proceedings* [Aug. 1738], p. 6).
57.   The attitude of the courts suggests that women were more leniently treated in the eighteenth century. In a sample of twenty-six years between 1663 and 1802, for example, 746 men were accused in Surrey of capital offences against property, of whom 159 (21.3 percent) were hanged; at the same time 203 women were accused, of whom only 11 (5.4 percent) were hanged.
58.   The population of London was sustained and enlarged mainly by the immigration of the young looking for work. It seems clear that the city attracted even more young women than men, partly because opportunities for work were relatively greater for them: a boy could apprentice nearer to home more readily than a girl could find domestic work. The population of England as a whole contained, in

113

any case, more women than men, but the metropolis was especially unbalanced in that direction. Gregory King calculated in 1695 that there were 1037 females for every 1000 males in the population of England and Wales. A sample of parishes in the City of London reveals at about the same time a population containing 1153 women for every 1000 men. On the size and structure of the London population, the growth of the city, and patterns of migration, see D. V. Glass, "Gregory King's Estimate of the Population of England and Wales, 1695," in D. V. Glass and D. C. Eversley, eds., *Population and History* (London, 1965); Glass, "Notes on the Demography of London at the end of the Seventeenth Century," *Daedalus* (1968): 581-92; E. A. Wrigley, "A Simple Model of London's Importance in Changing English Society and Economy, 1650-1750," *Past and Present* no. 37 (July 1967): 46-9; R. S. Schofield, "Age-specific mobility in an 18th century rural English parish," *Annales de démographie historique* (1970): 261-74.

59.   There are no precise population data for the county over this period, but (on the basis of the estimates adopted by Phyllis Deane and W. A. Cole, *British Economic Growth, 1688-1959* [Cambridge, 1964], p. 103; of the Hearth Tax returns of 1664 [for which see C. A. F. Meekings, ed., *Surrey Hearth Tax 1664* (Surrey Record Society Publications, vol.11)]; and the 1801 Census) I have estimated that the population of the county was about equally divided between "urban" and "rural" parishes in 1660 and that thereafter the urban share increased both because the influence of the "city" gradually widened and because the urban parishes received a constant flow of immigrants, many of course from the immediate rural hinterland (Wrigley: "A Simple Model of London's Importance," pp. 46-9). By the time of the first census in 1801 the population of the parishes that were part of the metropolis or clearly within its influence accounted for about 64 percent of the county total. It thus seems reasonable to think that over the whole period something under 60 percent of the Surrey population lived in "urban" parishes.

60.   One gets some sense of this, for example, in petitions from groups of inhabitants in Southwark and London parishes on behalf of men and women condemned to death; these very often refer to the convict as "an old resident" or "a well-known resident" of the parish.

61.   Keith Thomas, "The Double Standard," *Journal of the History of Ideas* 20 (1959): 195-216.

62.   R. Campbell, *The London Tradesman* (London, 1747), p. 228.

63.   Though it does not in this case involve a girl, the complaint of Mary Morris, a widow in a Kent village, illustrates the kind of influence a master could exercise over his apprentices (and also illustrates, incidently, a form of blackmail available to women). She threatened that "if ever she was with child agen without a Husband, she would lay it to Goodm[an] Tucker of Smeeth, Collar-maker, To be reveng'd of yt Rogue, Because he wou'd not let his Apprentice keep her Company" (Add Mss 42598, fo. 125).

64.   Ivy Pinchbeck, *Women Workers in the Industrial Revolution, 1750-1850* (London, 1969), pp. 1-2.

65.   Thomas, "Double Standard," p. 214.

66.   Fielding, *Great Increase of Robbers*, pp. 349-75; Colquhoun, *A Treatise on the Police*, pp. 33-49.

67.   The Borough of Southwark was a center of tanning and related industries in the eighteenth century. Brewing and distilling were similarly specialties south of the river; a directory of 1763 listed five brewers and sixteen distillers as established in Southwark and vicinity. Lambeth had become a center of the timber trade by the late seventeenth century; Rotherhithe had extensive shipbuilding as well as flour mills and bakeries. Away from the river, the northeast of Surrey had become a leading English center of bleaching and calico printing and along the river

Wandle, in the parish of Wandsworth in particular, bleaching grounds were numerous in the eighteenth century. In addition to such major enterprises, Southwark and neighbouring parishes sustained a variety of other industries and trades. Glassmaking and pottery were well established by the late seventeenth century and the south bank also included sugar refineries, wiremakers, dyers, sail and ropemakers, and a large number of textile and clothing-trade workers, most of whom worked at home or in small workshops (*Victoria County History of England: Surrey* vol. 2; J, Archer, "The Industrial History of London, 1603-43" [M.A. thesis, Univ. of London, 1934]; *Mortimer's Universal Directory* . . . [London, 1763]).

68. The parish of Bermondsey was typical of this northeast corner of Surrey, divided as it was in the mid-eighteenth century between an area with "middling sort of houses and such as have any ground to them . . . inhabited by tanners, fellmongers, woolstaplers etc." and the "outpart" of the parish, consisting "for the most part of garden and grazing ground," let to butchers, cowkeepers, and gardeners (QS2/6 [Midsummer 1756], no. 39).

69. Archer, "Industrial History of London," p. 142; Pinchbeck, *Women Workers*, pp. 287-290; George, *London Life*, ch. 4.

70. Campbell, *The London Tradesman*, pp. 149-50, 152-3, 170, 207, 210, 212-13, 218, 222, 225-7, 244, 246.

71. George, *London Life*, pp. 172-3.

72. The examinations of vagrants to be found among quarter-sessions records provide vivid evidence of the very large number of wives and children deserted because their husbands or fathers simply ran away or went into the army. Elizabeth Barnes, aged about twenty-six and with a child aged three, taken wandering by the constable of Croydon, declared before the justices who examined her that her husband "went away from her" soon after her child was born, that she had not seen him since nor knew where he was (QS2/6 [Easter 1743], no. 8). There are a very large number of mini-biographies of vagrants among the quarter-sessions papers and many tell similar stories of desertion by husbands. For more than a dozen examples from one parish see Blanche Berryman, ed., *Mitcham Settlement Examinations, 1784-1814* (Surrey Record Society, vol. 27 [1973], pp. 12, 36, 44, 80-82, 84-8, 90-91, 95, 104).

73. J. M. Beattie, "The Pattern of Crime in England 1660-1800," *Past and Present*, no. 62 (February 1974): 60-73.

74. Women Accused of Crimes Against the Person: Marital Status (%)

Location	Wife	Widow	Single Woman
Surrey Urban Parishes	63.3	9.3	27.4
Surrey Rural Parishes	56.6	13.3	30.1
Sussex	62.5	7.9	29.6

75. Status & Occupation of Husbands of Married Women Accused of Assault (%)

Location	Esquire. Gent; Yeoman	Tradesman Artisan	Unskilled Worker Laborer; Servant; Soldier
Surrey Urban Parishes	13.4	26.6	60.0
Surrey Rural Parishes	4.0	24.5	71.4

76. For the example of Sarah Wilson, alias Wilbraham, a "notorious imposter," see *Gentleman's Magazine* 38 (1768): 44; and see vol. 44 (1778): 329; vol. 53 (1783): 175; and QS2/6 (Christmas 1767), no. 56.

77. She had been convicted of returning from transportation prematurely and was sentenced to death (SP 36/137, fo. 113 [1757]).

78. The data in the graphs are simple totals of men and women accused of crimes against property They have not been corrected to take account of population changes because sex-specific data are not available; since I do not propose to discuss the possible significance of long-term trends it is not worth adopting a makeshift substitute. It is worth emphasizing, however, that the population of the county and especially of the urban parishes rose significantly over the eighteenth century and thus the long-term trends indicated in these graphs are meaningless. The short-term, and especially year-to-year changes, which are what I am interested in here, are not much affected by population changes.

79. Beattie, "Pattern of Crime," pp. 94-5; K. K. McNab, "Aspects of the History of Crime in England and Wales between 1805-1860" (Ph.D. diss., University of Sussex, 1965), p. 304.

80. Massie, *A Plan for the Establishment of Charity Houses . . .* (London, 1758), p. 54.

81. S.P. 36/56, fo. 255; QS2/6 (Christmas 1735); QS2/6 (Easter 1750), no. 60; necessity was ocasionally pleaded by women at their trials. Mary Howard tried a slight variation on this when she was tried at Surrey assizes for stealing a shoulder and a breast of mutton. When a constable deposed that he had found the shoulder under the bed in her lodgings and the breast on the fire, she told the judge that she had taken it because "she was big with child and long'd for the meat." She then went on to say, intriguingly, that "it would not have done her half so much good if it had been given to her, as if she had stole it." Whatever he made of this, the judge, Lord Chief Justice Raymond, was not moved by her appeal to nature for having noted that she was accused on another indictment of stealing a brass mortar "the judge desir'd to know if she'd long'd for that too" (*Surrey Assize Proceedings* [March-April 1726], p. 2).

82. Men and Women Accused of Malicious Damage, Unlawful Dispossession, and Trespass in Surrey and Sussex

Offence	Surrey Urban Parishes		Surrey Rural Parishes		Sussex	
	M	F	M	F	M	F
Malicious Damage to Property						
No.	61	20	58	6		
%	75.3	24.7	90.6	9.4		
Unlawful Dispossession and Detainer						
No.	151	14	78	3	61	9
%	91.5	8.5	96.3	3.7	87	13
Trespass; Unlawful Taking						
No.	72	25	84	6	214	21
%	74.2	25.8	93.3	6.7	91.2	8.8

83. For a discussion of some French evidence see Nicole Castan, "La Criminaltié familiale dans le ressort du Parlement de Toulouse, 1690-1730," in Abbiateci *et al, Crimes et Criminalité en France sous l'Ancien Regime, 17e-18e siècles*, Cahiers des Annales, no. 33 (Paris, 1971), pp. 91-107.

84. I would like to thank the county archivist of Surrey and the staff of the record office for their generous help; and the Canada Council for financial support. I am also grateful to James Cockburn, Natalie Davis, Robert Malcolmson, Michael Marrus, and Edward Shorter for their helpful comments on an earlier version of this essay.

116

[12]

THE VANISHING FEMALE: THE DECLINE OF WOMEN IN THE CRIMINAL PROCESS, 1687-1912

MALCOLM M. FEELEY
DEBORAH L. LITTLE

This article challenges the prevailing scholarly belief that women have always been at the periphery of crime and argues that a central issue for those studying the criminal process should be the decline over time of women as criminal offenders and defendants. Our argument rests on examination of criminal cases in the Old Bailey in London for 1687–1912, as well as of data drawn from English and some American courts for this period. For much of the eighteenth century women made up a substantial portion (over 45 percent at times) of all those indicted for felony offenses, in sharp contrast to contemporary levels of less that 15 percent. We conclude that the change is "real"—it cannot be explained away as an artifact of selective reporting, shifting jurisdiction, short-lived idiosyncratic enforcement policies, etc. We argue that these changes parallel and may be explained by significant shifts in the roles accorded women in the economy, the family, and society, and we conclude that the vanishing female in the criminal process may reflect a shift to more private forms of social control brought on by shifting social attitudes and the rise of industrialism.

[G]ender differences appear to be invariant over time and space.

—Gottfredson and Hirschi 1990:145

At the forefront of sociological interest at present are relatively short-term processes. . . . Long-term transformations of social structures . . . have by and large been lost to view.

—Elias 1968a:222

We wish to acknowledge the assistance of Teri Winter, Charles Lester, and David Johnson for coding; Shelly Messinger for careful reading of several drafts of this paper; John Langbein, David Lieberman, and David Sugarman for help in locating sources, supplying background material, and help in devising the code; Dan Rubinfeld, Richard Berk, and John Berecochea for technical advice on sampling and coding; Thomas Green and Pieter Spierenburg for comments on a previous draft; four anonymous readers for the *Review;* and Shari Diamond for several careful readings of the manuscript and many helpful suggestions. Above all we wish to thank John Beattie and Norma Landau for their careful readings of earlier drafts, extended discussions with us, and for sharing data from their own ongoing research. An earlier version of this paper was presented at the annual meeting of the Law and Society Association, Amsterdam, June 1991.

LAW & SOCIETY REVIEW, Volume 25, Number 4 (1991)

720   THE VANISHING FEMALE

Women's involvement in the criminal process has not always been marginal. Yet historians and criminologists have placed it at the periphery of study, highlighting distinctive female crimes or slight shifts in low rates of female criminal activity.[1] This article challenges the assumptions on which this neglect rests. We argue that one of the central puzzles for students of gender and crime should be the vanishing female participation in the criminal process.

Our contention that female criminal involvement changed over time rests upon an examination of criminal cases in London's Old Bailey between 1687 and 1912. We looked at "serious" crimes, felonies ranging from larceny to murder.[2] Although we will show that some of the decline in women's involvement in this court is more apparent than real, a strong pattern remains that reveals a high proportion of women defendants (by twentieth-century standards) in the early eighteenth century, followed by a decline over the next 150 years to near contemporary levels. To the extent that this pattern is general—and we consider additional evidence that suggests it is—a central mystery for both historians and criminologists is the marked decrease in women's criminal involvement that appears to have taken place over the course of the eighteenth and early nineteenth centuries.

Students of crime are well aware of the problems with "crime rates," particularly the lack of a reliable data base. Invariably research is based on some type of "reported" crime, but reporting systems have filters that encourage some and deter others from reporting. The situation is even worse in eighteenth-century England, for during that period there was no police force and no "official" record of persons picked up for questioning and charging by magistrates. Therefore, scholars of this period rely on court records as a measure of fluctuations in criminality (Beattie 1986), particularly in studies like ours of serious felonies (Sharpe

---

[1] An early exception is Bonger's 1916 study, *Criminality and Economic Conditions*, which examines male and female conviction rates in selected European countries during the latter part of the nineteenth century. Other early discussions (e.g., Lombroso and Ferrero 1895) are psychological or physiological studies, focusing on personality types rather than rates of crime in society. Since Carol Smart's 1977a critique challenging the male bias in such studies and Simon's 1975 and Adler's 1975 arguments about recent increases in female crime, there has been a significant increase in sociological research on women's criminality and involvement in the criminal process. For a good review of some of this newer literature, see Gottfredson and Hirschi 1990:144–49.

[2] In the eighteenth and nineteenth centuries, the Old Bailey heard the full range of serious felonies. The few misdemeanors we found were dropped from our study. We coded all crimes charged (over forty different crimes) and found that the vast majority of defendants until the mid-nineteenth century were charged with larceny. There were only a handful of petty larcenies in our sample; thus, when we refer to larcenies, we are referring to cases charged as simple grand larceny. Robbery, burglary, shoplifting, picking pockets, and murder also appeared regularly throughout the entire period.

1984:53–57).[3] We use the term "involvement" in the criminal process to emphasize that we do not and cannot examine criminality per se. However, insofar as we examine large historical changes in the patterns of female involvement in the criminal process, we are arguing that these records convey important information about shifts in official responses to women and crime.

Despite the recent upsurge in research about female criminality, little of this literature addresses our problem. Historians have shown a renewed interest in such "women's crimes" as witchcraft, infanticide, and prostitution and in women's roles in food riots, but have neglected shifts in the proportion of women involved in ordinary crime. Similarly feminist criminologists have begun a reexamination of theories of crime in light of women's generally low rate of involvement as offenders[4] but have neglected historical shifts in the proportion of women involved in the criminal process.[5]

This article suggests the need to reorient the attention of both historians and criminologists. We argue that a broader perspective is needed, one that places gender at the center of explorations of the criminal process as it considers broad shifts over time. Part I traces female criminal involvement over time, showing that it declines throughout the eighteenth and early part of the nineteenth centuries. Part II considers and largely rejects several hypotheses that treat this decline as more apparent than real. Part III outlines an argument that treats the declining involvement of women in the criminal justice system as part of a larger set of social processes that transformed social controls over women during this period.

I. PATTERNS OF FEMALE CRIMINALITY, 1687–1912

We begin with the remarkable shift in the presence of women in the Old Bailey,[6] as arrayed in Figure 1. This graph is based on a 25 percent sample of indicted defendants—taken at roughly

---

[3] Some have argued for the value of indictment records as a measure of overall criminal patterns, suggesting that insofar as forces affecting prosecution did not change wildly from year to year, the indictments may be interpreted as reflective of changes in offense rates (see, e.g., Emsley 1987; Sharpe 1984; Beattie 1986; Hay 1982).

[4] See, e.g., Smart 1979, 1977a; Simon 1975; Adler 1975; Leonard 1982; Box 1983; Heidensohn 1985; Naffine 1987; Hagan, Simpson, and Gillis 1989, 1979; Chesney-Lind 1989; Gottfredson and Hirschi 1990; and Zedner 1988, 1991. Mainstream criminologists have been slower to incorporate gender into their analyses (Heidensohn 1989).

[5] An important exception is Boritch and Hagan 1990, which examines female arrests in Toronto between 1859 and 1955.

[6] The Old Bailey is the popular name for London's criminal court, established by charter from Henry I early in the twelfth century. Beginning in the late Middle Ages, its jurisdiction was roughly equivalent to that of courts of assizes elsewhere in England. These courts handled indictable offenses—felonies punishable by death. The Old Bailey was in effect a special court for inner London, a densely populated area at the confluence of several counties. In 1834

722   THE VANISHING FEMALE

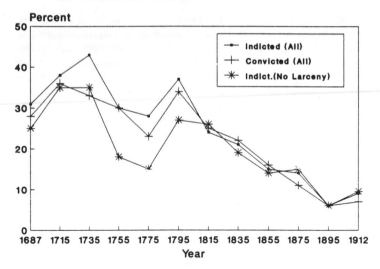

Figure 1. Female defendants, by year

SOURCE: *Old Bailey Sessions Papers* 25 percent sample; Appendix Table A1 presents these data

twenty-year intervals and reported in the *Old Bailey Sessions Papers* (*OBSP*).[7] It depicts three indicators of shifts in female involvement in the criminal process over time: women defendants as a proportion of (1) all indictments brought; (2) indictments with larcenies (the most numerous and least serious group of offenses) excluded; and (3) all convictions. At the outset, we note their substantial similarity.

To the contemporary student of the criminal process, two features of Figure 1 stand out: first, the high proportion of women in the early part of the eighteenth century, and second, their steady decline to a low of under 10 percent toward the end of the nineteenth century (a level that has remained throughout most of the twentieth century for courts in England). In short, during the first half of the eighteenth century women constituted roughly three to four times the proportion of felony defendants that they have in the twentieth century.

We double-checked the pattern found in the sample displayed

---

the City of London, all of Middlesex County, and parts of Essex, Kent, and Surrey were designated a single venue for the purpose of indictments and criminal trials, and the Old Bailey was given a new name, the Central Criminal Court. See Beattie 1988 regarding the development of the Old Bailey's jurisdiction.

[7] The year 1687 was selected as the beginning date because that was the first year for which a nearly complete set of records was available (we were able to review records for seven of the eight sessions in that year, and substituted the first session of the following year in order to have a sample of eight sessions), and 1912 was the last year of publication of the *OBSP*. All sample years after 1687 had complete records.

in Figure 1 by examining 100 percent of all those indicted at five-year intervals from 1715 to 1912, using names (sex indicated by first names) listed in the indexes of the annual *OBSP* reports (see Appendix Table A2).[8] We found that the percentage of males and females brought before the Old Bailey during these years closely tracks the trend in the 25 percent sample. For this reason the remainder of the article is based on a discussion of the smaller sample for which more information is available.

To test the trend, we first dropped all larcenies, the single largest and least serious (although still felony) set of cases, to see if the pattern of high and then declining involvement by women held for the remaining, most serious cases. Figure 1 suggests that it does. (We will show below the importance of larcenies in the shifting jurisdiction of the court.)

In an effort to determine how "deep" this involvement was, we calculated women as a proportion of all those convicted of felonies at the Old Bailey. Figure 1 indicates that the same pattern of high involvement followed by decline occurs here too. In short, all indicators point to the same conclusion, that in the early eighteenth century women represented a high proportion of defendants involved in the criminal process, followed by a steady decline.

These findings pose a substantial challenge to conventional historical and sociological treatments of crime, which proceed as if criminal activity is and always has been a male phenomenon.[9] Indeed the scholarly belief that women are marginal in the criminal process and that gender is invariant with respect to crime is so pervasive that our first reaction was to see whether the patterns we

---

[8] An obvious issue is the reliability of the *OBSP*. In particular, we considered the possibility that shifts in the proportion of women in this court could be a function of shifts in reporting practices. For more than 250 years, from the mid-seventeenth century to the early twentieth century, the Old Bailey cases were published by reporters who used shorthand to summarize the proceedings. Until the early 1710s cases seem to have been reported somewhat selectively, with an emphasis on sensational cases. However, with the appointment of a new reporting service, coverage was expanded and standardized. Langbein (1983) compared details of cases reported in the *OBSP* with the detailed shorthand notes of one of the judges who sat at the Old Bailey in the mid-eighteenth century, Sir Dudley Ryder, and found no significant differences between the two sets of records. He concluded that, at least for the period he was examining, the *OBSP* provided a generally accurate record of adjudicated cases. Landsman (1990), however, speculates that there was selective reporting until the 1740s. In either case there is no evidence to suggest that reporters selectively over- or underrepresented women or the types of cases women were involved in ways that would account for variation over time.

[9] The few exceptions have done little more than puzzle over the high rates of female criminality in eighteenth- and nineteenth-century England. For example, Philips (1977), who examined figures from records in the Black Country from 1835 to 1850, observed, "This general male-female ratio of 3:1 is of interest, differing markedly from the situation today, where this sex ratio in indictable offenses is about 7:1" (148). Similarly Sharpe (1984) and Langbein (1983) note the larger proportion of women defendants in the mid-eighteenth century but do not focus on the issue. Cf. Zedner 1988, 1991, discussed in the text below.

uncovered were an artifact of processes that "overrepresented" women in some ways. The next section considers several hypotheses.

II. SEARCHING FOR AN EXPLANATION

Here we consider several explanations that might lead us to conclude that the patterns in Figure 1 are more apparent than real: First, it is possible that changes in court jurisdiction were responsible for the declining percentage of females in the criminal process. Second, demographic changes in London might account for the shift. Third, we considered the possibility that a handful of "women's offenses" for a period were vigorously enforced in ways that skewed the pattern of the remaining criminal offenses (just as during Prohibition tax evasion skewed the percentage of "normal" offenses and during the Vietnam War "draft evasion" skewed the overall pattern of criminal offenses). Fourth, the high proportion of female defendants during the early eighteenth century might be a function of women's involvement with a man who was primarily responsible for precipitating the charge. Finally, women might be "overrepresented" during times of war, when men were absent, engaged in the war effort, and subject to an alternative military sanctioning system.

Some of these possibilities suggest that change in the proportion of women is nothing more than a statistical artifact that dissolves on closer inspection. Others suggest more complicated social processes that affect institutions of control in ways that have a variable effect on women brought into court. The first possibility—that jurisdictional shifts affected the patterns—receives considerable support. But it still fails to account for most of the variation. The other factors complicate but certainly do not "explain away" the pattern of greater involvement by women in the eighteenth century.

Shifting Jurisdiction

It may be that jurisdictional changes removed offenses that disproportionately involved women from the Old Bailey and into the lower courts, so that the changes depicted in Figure 1 reflect this shift rather than changes in gender and criminal involvement. As we will show, these jurisdictional changes account for much of the reduction in women at the Old Bailey throughout the second half of the nineteenth century. Indeed, they account for the very substantial absolute reduction in the size of the court's caseload between 1835 and 1900. However, jurisdictional shifts do not so easily account for the decline in the proportion of women throughout the eighteenth century, and it is this shift that is of particular interest to us.

During the period under consideration in this study, the an-

FEELEY AND LITTLE   725

Table 1. Five Principal Crimes Charged in Old Bailey, by Year, 1687–1912
(Percent)

	1687	1715	1735	1755	1775	1795	1815	1835	1855	1875	1895	1912
Larceny	28	41	52	50	59	57	52	58	31	13	10	13
Burglary	22	19	6	7	9	8	7	6	10	7	16	9
Theft DH*	11	6	—	7	5	9	8	4	—	—	—	—
Shoplifting	7	6	10	5	—	3	6	—	—	—	—	—
Murder	6	7	6	—	—	—	—	—	—	—	—	—
Sheep theft	—	—	—	5	—	—	—	—	—	—	—	—
Receiving	—	—	—	5	4	—	—	4	—	—	—	—
Coining	—	—	—	—	—	3	—	—	19	12	—	8
Forgery	—	—	—	—	—	—	—	—	8	9	11	8
Pickpocketing	—	—	—	—	—	—	8	13	5	—	—	—
Sexual assault	—	—	—	—	—	—	—	—	—	—	9	—
Robbery	—	7	8	—	7	—	—	—	—	—	8	—
Fraud	—	—	—	—	—	—	—	—	—	9	12	10

SOURCE: *Old Bailey Sessions Papers* 25 percent sample.
Theft DH: theft from a dwelling house, a crime usually committed by servants.

nual number of cases adjudicated at the Old Bailey grew steadily from 1687 to 1835 when it reached a high of more than 2,000 cases. Over the next seventy years, and particularly after 1850, its caseload plummeted by over 300 percent, reaching a low of 627 in 1900 (see figures in the 100 percent sample in Appendix Table A2). This reduction occurred in spite of a substantial increase in the population within the Old Bailey's jurisdiction. It was largely a result of nineteenth-century acts of Parliament, which culminated in the Summary Jurisdiction Act of 1879. These reforms downgraded offenses, both in severity and sentence, abolished capital punishment for selected offenses, and shifted lesser property offenses away from crown courts, expanding the summary jurisdiction of the magistrates.

These nineteenth-century shifts affected both the size and the composition of the caseload of the Old Bailey and are reflected in our data. Throughout the eighteenth century the major types of cases tried at the Old Bailey remained steady (see Table 1), and it was only in the nineteenth century, as many of the less serious cases were shunted off to the lower courts, that the *mix* of cases changed substantially. These jurisdictional changes reduced the overall percentage of cases accounted for by property offenses—as lesser offenses (like larceny, shoplifting, pickpocketing) were transferred to lower courts, the range and accompanying percentage of offenses charged at the Old Bailey shifted.

The percentage of larcenies charged dropped dramatically as a result of nineteenth-century jusdictional changes. For instance, in 1835 larcenies accounted for 58 percent of all crimes charged and 62 percent of the crimes charged to females—figures that are more or less representative of the court's workload for the entire eighteenth century. But by 1855, only 31 percent of all defendants, and 38 percent of the women, in our sample were charged with larcenies. These figures were reduced still further; between 1875 and

1912, such cases accounted for only 10–13 percent of Old Bailey defendants in our sample. Since throughout the nineteenth century women were more likely to be charged with larcenies than men, wholesale shifts of such cases from one court to another clearly disproportionately affected women and contributed to their decline as a proportion of all defendants at the Old Bailey.

In addition, the number of violent offenses charged at the Old Bailey increased in the late nineteenth century (more than doubling in our sample between 1855 and 1875). At the same time the numbers of those charged with property crimes decreased, rising again after 1875, although not as dramatically (see Table 3 below).[10] This increase in defendants charged with violent crimes, coupled with the shift of lesser property offenses away from the Old Bailey and the smaller increase in the numbers charged with remaining property crimes, contributed to the dramatic decline in the proportion of female defendants at the end of the nineteenth century.

The eighteenth century appears to produce a different story; it was a period of expanding, not contracting, jurisdiction for the Old Bailey (and equivalent courts elsewhere) as a vast array of new capital crimes were created (see, e.g., Thompson 1975a; Hay 1975; Radzinowicz and Hood 1986; and Beattie 1975, 1986). Although these newly created offenses added substantially to the numbers of cases heard by the courts, their greatest impact was on those living in rural areas. They had only minimal impact on the Old Bailey's caseload.[11] Nevertheless, we wondered whether informal jurisdictional shifts in the eighteenth century might have transferred female defendants from the Old Bailey to lower courts.

Although it was beyond the scope of this research to conduct a full review of the combined caseloads of the courts of quarter sessions of Middlesex, London, and Westminster which had overlapping jurisdiction with the Old Bailey, we were able to test the effect of shifting jurisdiction is other ways. These efforts all support the patterns suggested in Figure 1, that there was a substantial decline in women's involvement in the late eighteenth and early nineteenth centuries.

---

[10] There were only 15 defendants charged with violent crimes in 1855, equaling 7 percent of crimes charged in that year (see Table 3). In 1875, 37 defendants were so charged; this increased to 40 in 1895 and 49 in 1912. Women were seldom charged with violent offenses. The number of those charged with property offenses dropped dramatically between 1835 and 1875, after the legislative changes of the 1850s, from 515 in 1835 to 185 in 1855 to 117 in 1875. Thereafter, the numbers of those so charged at Old Bailey increased to 161 defendants by 1912.

[11] The famous "Black Acts" were directed at poaching, stealing firewood, and other activities of rural commoners (Thompson 1975a). A handful of other new offenses, such as theft of lead (1731), theft from a ship (1753), theft from a post office (1765), and embezzlement (1795) affected people (and especially males) in urban areas (Hay 1982; Hall 1935; Radzinowicz and Hood 1986), but only a few such cases appeared in our sample.

Since larcenies constituted the single largest group of "hybrid" cases that could most easily be brought in either quarter sessions or the Old Bailey, we examined the mix of these charges in relation to other charges. In particular we wanted to see if larcenies declined as a percentage of the total caseload in the mid-eighteenth century, when women's presence began to decrease, as in the nineteenth, when formal jurisdictional changes substantially reduced the total number of cases heard at the Old Bailey as well as the proportion of larcenies.

Table 1 indicates that no major shift occurred until 1855. Throughout the first 150 years under consideration, larcenies accounted for the single largest group of crimes charged, and they remained a relatively constant proportion of the court's caseload. From the mid-1800s, however, other crimes shared the spotlight. This suggests that shifts in the types of cases handled by the Old Bailey cannot account for the decline in women defendants that took place in the eighteenth century.

We examined the possibility of informal jurisdictional shifts, particularly of larcenies and other types of property offenses, in other ways. As a second test, we dropped from our analysis *all* larceny cases (that is, those cases most likely to be candidates for shifting from one court to another) and examined only those cases remaining. Figure 1 shows that while the female percentage is dampened somewhat when larcenies are excluded, the trend is *not* eliminated. Indeed it follows closely the pattern for all indictments and for convictions.

Third, we tried to examine caseload shifts in the lower criminal courts to see how they may have affected business at the Old Bailey. Throughout the eighteenth century, jurisdictional lines between assizes (and in London the Old Bailey) and quarter sessions were not firmly fixed. The result was that judicial practices were based on practical considerations and varied by county and over time.[12] Although the judges sitting at the Old Bailey did not ride circuit and held eight sessions per year (as opposed to less frequent sittings of equivalent judges elsewhere), they too might have informally shifted some of their work to quarter sessions, either by allowing lower court judges to hear the lesser offenses or by encouraging victims to bring lesser charges at less trouble and expense to themselves in the sessions. One way to assess this would be to consider changes in the workloads of the two levels of courts in combination. Although we have been unable to do this directly, we were able to take "soundings" from several sources.

Certainly substantial informal changes in jurisdiction occurred in at least some assizes and sessions. For instance, Beattie

[12] Throughout England, assizes justices rode circuit and were scheduled for a limited period of time at each location. If they did not complete their docket before leaving, it was not uncommon for them to charge the quarter sessions with handling their remaining business.

(1986:284), who examined the workload of the sessions and assizes in Surrey and Sussex from 1660 to 1800, found major shifts in the ways larcenies were handled in the Surrey parishes. Between 1660 and 1749 Surrey quarter sessions heard only 18 percent of the cases involving simple larcenies (i.e., noncapital grand and petty larceny cases), and the remaining 82 percent were tried at assizes. But from 1750 to 1800, the pattern was reversed; 71 percent were tried at quarter sessions and only 29 percent at assizes. Beattie shows that a similar, although dampened, shift occurred for rural Sussex.[13] Although we were unable to relate this shift to the proportion of women defendants in these two courts, if women were disproportionately charged with larcenies, their decline in assizes could be a function of these jurisdictional changes.

However, in his earlier study of women in the criminal process, Beattie (1975) considered the *combined* caseloads of both the assizes and quarter sessions. His goal there was to compare differences in the proportion of women in cases heard in urban areas with those heard in rural parishes. We have recomputed his data so that they emphasize the proportion of cases involving women over time. Figure 2 indicates that the proportion of female defendants charged with indictable property offenses in the combined urban Surrey courts of assizes and quarter sessions increased in the late 1600s but began to decline some time after 1710[14] (see also Appendix Table A3). By the end of the eighteenth century, women constituted less than half the proportion of defendants that they had at the outset of the century. Thus, it appears that the shift in the proportion of women in the Surrey courts in the eighteenth century is not simply an artifact of jurisdictional changes. Although the downward trend in Figure 2 is not steady and the slope is not steep, the general pattern parallels the one we found for the Old Bailey. Even if we set aside the large increase at the outset of the eighteenth century, Beattie's data reveal a substantial decline in the proportion of women defendants.

Second, we were able to examine selected cases for the Middlesex quarter sessions during the eighteenth century. As part of her ongoing study of the Middlesex sessions records, Norma Landau recorded the sex of individuals in two samples of sets of cases from the early, middle, and late eighteenth century. The first sam-

---

[13] We are indebted to Professor Beattie for calling our attention to the table in his book (1986) that shows this shift.

[14] We are limited by the lack of reliable records for the Old Bailey prior to the 1680s. Thus the beginning date of our study is somewhat artificial and does not represent some "natural" time shift. Although this limit is common to much historical research, it is especially frustrating to us, since both Beattie's and our own figures indicate an increase in the percentage of women in the late seventeenth and early eighteenth centuries. A review of cases extending back into the seventeenth century would allow us to determine whether these increases were part of a long term pattern or constituted an unusual spike.

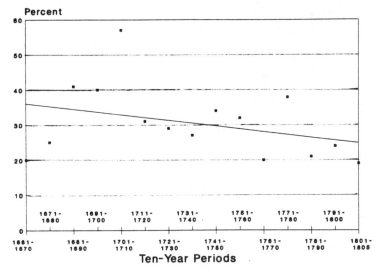

Figure 2. Women as a percentage of all property crimes charged, Surrey urban parishes, 1661–1805

SOURCE: Adapted from Beattie (1975), Graph I, pp. 225. We are deeply indebted to Professor Beattie for providing us with raw numbers to facilitate the reconstruction of his graph.

ple included all *individuals* against whom an indictment was brought; the second consisted of all those *cases* in which an indictment was brought. Her findings are described in Table 2.

Columns (1) and (2) in Table 2 describe the total number of persons against whom indictments were brought and the proportion of them who were female.[15] Two features of these columns stand out. First, there was no increase over time in the numbers of indictments brought. Indeed there was a decrease, at least when the 170½ sittings are compared with the later years. Second, although women as a percentage of people against whom an indictment was brought ranges from 23 to 37 percent, there is no identifiable shift over time. Columns (3) and (4) reinforce this interpretation.[16] Although there was an increase in the numbers of

---

[15] The number refers to the number of persons against whom a bill was brought before the grand jury and not the total number of persons whom the grand jury indicted.

[16] The number refers to the number of cases in which a bill was brought to the grand jury and not the total number of cases in which the grand jury declared that the bill was true. Since some portion of these cases involved multiple defendants, the figure understates the actual numbers of individuals involved. The accompanying percentages of females are somewhat misleading since they refer to the percentage of cases in which a female was involved and not the percentage of those indicted who were female. They no doubt over-represent women as a proportion of all persons involved in these cases. Data for individuals were not readily available to us. Nevertheless, in light of the lack of fluctuation in cols. (1) and (2), the lack of fluctuation (i.e., the averages of 41, 42, and 40 percent) in col. (4), can probably safely be interpreted to indi-

730   THE VANISHING FEMALE

Table 2. Charges Preferred to the Grand Jury of the Middlesex Court of Quarter
Sessions

	Indictments Brought		Fraudulent Taking/ Receiving Sought	
	No. of Individuals (1)	% Female (2)	No. of Cases (3)	% Female (4)
Oct. 1701	210	33	11	36
Dec. 1701	143	28	9	67
Jan. 1702	75	27	5	20
Feb. 1702	130	28	12	50
Ap. 1702	252	31	11	55
Average per session	(162)	(30)	(9.6)	(41)
Oct. 1733	141	23	1	100
Nov. 1733	118	29	17	29
Jan. 1734	67	37	6	67
Average per session	(109)	(38)	(8)	(42)
Oct. 1753	114	28	18	44
Dec. 1753	64	27	16	44
Jan. 1754	122	24	21	33
Average per session	(100)	(26)	(18)	(40)
Oct. 1795	108	28	18	33

SOURCE: These data were graciously supplied by, and reprinted with the permission of, Professor Norma Landau of the University of California at Davis. We deeply appreciate her help.

indictments brought for these types of larcenies, even at their most
numerous there was a mere handful of such cases. Most important
for our purposes, the proportion of cases involving women remained constant, between 40 and 42 percent. Thus, there is nothing here to suggest a shift of cases and/or of cases involving women away from the Old Bailey to the Middlesex sessions.

We would have expected to see a decline in the presence of
women and this is somewhat puzzling. However, we don't see an
increase, which the "shifting jurisdiction" hypothesis would have
suggested. Admittedly Middlesex quarter sessions was not the only
lower court connected with the Old Bailey (we were unable to obtain data from the other courts, London and Westminster quarter
sessions), and admittedly these data constitute only a small
number of the many sittings of this Middlesex court. Nevertheless,
there is nothing in these data to suggest that the decline of women
at the Old Bailey was the result of an informal shift in jurisdiction
that redirected cases disproportionately involving women to the
lower courts.

Other available figures that report on women as a proportion
of the *combined* totals of assizes and quarter sessions support an
interpretation that women constituted a larger proportion of the

cate that there was no significant variation in the proportion of women among
all persons against whom an indictment was brought, at least for these types
of larcenies.

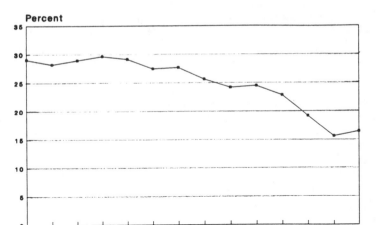

Figure 3. Women as a percentage of all indicated in assizes and quarter sessions, England and Wales, 1805–1818

SOURCE: "A Statement on the Number of Persons Charged with Criminal Offenses Who Were Committed to the Different Gaols in England and Wales for Trial at the Assizes and Sessions Held for the Several Countries for the Years 1805 to the Year 1818," 16 *British Parliamentary Papers*, 18 Feb. 1819.

business in the criminal courts in the eighteenth and early nineteenth centuries and that the figure began to decrease in the early nineteenth century. An 1810 Parliamentary report (14 *British Parliamentary Papers* 549–51) summarized figures by sex on all offenses brought in both assizes and quarter sessions in England and Wales during the four-year period, 1805–8. Overall, 18,114 charges were brought, of which 5,246, or 29 percent, were against women. Roughly half of all these charges were larcenies, and women accounted for 32 percent of them. However, when larcenies are excluded (but other male-dominated offenses such as rape, dealing livestock, and other violent offenses are included), women still constituted 18 percent of all remaining cases.

Still another set of nationwide indictment figures for combined quarter sessions and assizes from 1805 to 1818 (presented in Fig. 3) reveals a decline in the proportion of women, from 29 percent in 1805 to 17 percent in 1818 (16 *British Parliamentary Papers* 295–99).

Several features of these figures should be emphasized. First, they are indictable offenses brought in the *combined* courts of quarter sessions and assizes. Second, they are for the nation as a whole. If they were broken down by region, the proportion of women in urban areas might be higher than the national figures. Third, the higher levels (relative to contemporary figures) of women's involvement are not restricted to a narrow set of lesser offenses. They include a wide variety of types and, and as measured

732   THE VANISHING FEMALE

by both indictments and convictions, levels of seriousness of offenses. Obviously more detailed figures from a longer run of cases
would be useful as a basis for comparison. Still these limited
figures do closely parallel the data for the Old Bailey during
roughly the same years.

Only a few historians of crime in the eighteenth and nineteenth centuries have focused on gender and crime in any detail.
However, some report findings similar to ours. For instance,
Zedner (1988, 1991), who reviewed nineteenth-century court
records for England and Wales, concluded: "Surveying the extent
and nature of crime over the nineteenth century indicates the relatively high rates of participation by women compared with today"
(Zedner 1991:317). She reports that in 1857 women accounted for
27 percent of those against whom indictments were brought. By
1892, this figure had dropped to 19 percent. As in the eighteenth
century, patterns of crime by men and women were broadly similar to one another with the exception of a number of sex-specific
offenses, most notably relating to prostitution.

Similarly, in her study of women charged with serious felonies
in colonial Massachusetts, Hull (1987) found that women in colonial times had a much higher (three to five times) rate of participation in serious felonies than women do today and that colonial
women constituted a substantially larger proportion of defendants.
Furthermore, she found a steady and significant decline in females
as a percentage of the total number of defendants for serious crime
in Massachusetts between 1673 and 1774 (ibid., p. 67). Spierenburg
(1984:116) found a mixed but generally declining trend in the proportion of women who were sentenced for serious offenses in Amsterdam between 1651 and 1750, and Faber (1983:253–54) found a
steady decline in the proportion of Dutch women sentenced for serious offenses in the eighteenth and early nineteenth centuries.
And Boritch and Hagan (1990) reported a steady and significant
decline in the arrests of women in Toronto between 1859 and 1955.

Our purpose in this section has been to determine if the decline in the proportion of women at the Old Bailey might have
been an artifact of jurisdictional changes rather than actual
changes in women's criminal involvement. We have controlled for
the influence of larcenies, reviewed evidence that combines figures
for both courts with overlapping jurisdictions, and reviewed evidence from a number of other studies. The evidence all points in
the same direction, suggesting that in the past women were more
heavily involved as defendants in the criminal process than they
are today and that some time in the eighteenth and early nineteenth centuries there was a real decline in the proportion of women involved in the criminal courts.

Demography

A second possible explanation for the higher proportion of women brought before the Old Bailey in the eighteenth century is
the demography of London. Certainly there is an immense and
long-standing literature on London that emphasizes its distinctive-
ness, if not uniqueness, in terms of size, population, worldwide importance and the like (see, e.g., Mayhew 1900). And Beattie (1975)
argues that there is something distinctive about urban settings and
women's criminality more generally. In comparing cases between
1660 and 1800 in urban and rural parishes near London, he found
that women were more likely to commit crimes against the person
and against property in the city than in the countryside,[17] and concludes that women in urban areas were more dependent on working for wages and less restricted and sheltered than women in rural areas. Thus his explanation for the higher proportion of
women in the urban courts rests on a thesis that the courts compensated for weaker forms of social control over women in urban
areas. This is an intriguing hypothesis, and one to which we will
return. However, Beattie used it to account for different proportions of female involvement in urban and rural areas, and it cannot easily account for changes in proportions *within* the same area
across time.

We considered whether the high proportion of women in the
early eighteenth century was a consequence of a disproportionate
number of women in the city during this period. In short, we
asked whether there were shifts in the *rates* of women's and men's
involvement, or whether the shift in the proportion of women was
a result of changes in the numbers of men and women in the city.
This is easier said than done for this period. As demographers well
know, since no censuses were taken before the nineteenth century,
it is difficult to obtain accurate population figures (Wrigley and
Schofield 1981; Mitchell and Deane 1962). As a result, figures on
the rates of male and female defendants (expressed in terms of
numbers of defendants per 100,000 population) are at best only
crude estimates. Our problem was compounded still further since
the Old Bailey's jurisdiction was something of an artificial unit
within the larger metropolitan area and its daytime population
consisted of a large number of nonresidents. In short, it is not clear
what its "base" population should be: the London area, the jurisdiction's residents, or its daytime population.

Available estimates of the population of England indicate that

---

[17] The urban-rural differences existed in the late 1600s and after 1800.
Shoemaker (1991) compared defendants in urban and rural Middlesex and
Westminster quarter sessions for the period 1660–1725, finding a larger proportion of female defendants in urban areas. Rude (1985) examined nineteenth-
century data for the Old Bailey, Gloucestershire, and Sussex. He concluded
that women not only accounted for a higher percentage of defendants in the
urban areas but that they committed a greater range of criminal acts.

in the eighteenth century there were more women than men in the overall population, and this was even more pronounced in London (Law 1967; Tranter 1985). Finlay (1981) reports a decline in the proportion of men in London over the course of the seventeenth century, so that by 1700 there were more women than men in London.[18] However, the ratio of women to men appears to have been relatively stable between 1695 and 1851 (Glass 1969). While the available statistics may explain the higher proportion of female urban crime (relative to rural crime), there is no evidence of significant shifts in the ratio of men to women in greater London during the period we examined. Thus, the shifts in the proportions of men and women defendants would not disappear if they were expressed in terms of rates. Indeed, using available population estimates for London, we have attempted to determine rates. Appendix Figure A1 depicts shifts in rates (per 100,000 population) of men and women defendants at the Old Bailey. It reveals the same pattern suggested by the percentages, and certainly cannot account for the downward trend in the proportions of women defendants.[19]

Female Offenses

We considered as a third hypothesis the possibility that the higher percentage of women in the early eighteenth century was a function of distinctively female offenses such as witchcraft and infanticide which for periods were vigorously enforced and then declined. This possibility was suggested by research that has focused on distinctive features of female criminal activity, for example, food riots (Thompson 1971), witchcraft (Larner 1980), prostitution (Walkowitz 1980), and infanticide (Hull 1987).[20]

Following such leads, we sought to control for these and other distinctively "female offenses." However, prostitution was never a felony offense during the period under consideration, witchcraft had all but died out as an offense by the end of the seventeenth century, and there were far too few cases involving riots and infanticide to have any measurable impact on the pattern we found.

Table 3 indicates that property offenses constituted the vast bulk of all cases across the entire period, a continuation of an earlier trend in all parts of England (Sharpe 1984:55), and one that

---

[18] These demographic changes may explain some of the increase in the proportion of female defendants in the late seventeenth century but do not easily account for shifts in the 1800s.

[19] Since demographic estimates are that the ratio of males to females was relatively stable during the period we examined (and given the problems of trying to calculate the population base for the Old Bailey jurisdiction), the discussion that follows is based on proportions rather than rates.

[20] See also the discussion of food riots in Hay 1975 and Thompson 1975b. Other studies of witchcraft include Trevor-Roper 1969; Keickhefer 1976; Macfarlane 1970; and Boyer and Nissenbaum 1974. And see Sharpe's (1984:60–62) discussion of the "infanticide wave" which took place in England in the seventeenth century.

Table 3. Type of Crimes Charged by Year, All Defendants

	% Violent	% Robbery	% Burglary	% Property	% Other	Total
1687	12	2	22	62	2	100
1715	8	7	19	65	1	100
1735	8	8	6	76	1	100
1755	5	4	7	80	4	100
1775	1	7	9	81	1	100
1795	2	3	8	84	2	100
1815	3	5	7	83	2	100
1835	3	2	6	87	1	100
1855	7	3	10	76	4	100
1875	22	4	7	60	7	100
1895	20	8	16	51	5	100
1912	21	6	9	55	9	100
N	(217)	(117)	(240)	(1,884)	(87)	(2,545)

SOURCE: *Old Bailey Sessions Papers* 25 percent sample.

has remained since.[21] We found some differences between men and women: most notably men were more frequently charged with violent offenses, and women were usually involved in nonviolent property offenses.[22] However, the high proportion of female defendants in the early eighteenth century is not a result of greater female involvement in distinctively female crime.

Although we developed a detailed code for all offenses charged at the Old Bailey, here we grouped them into more general categories to facilitate comparison across time. "Violent" crimes include acts like homicide, rape, infanticide, assault, arson and riot. The "robbery" category includes robbery, attempted robbery, and robbery with violence (a crime added in the nineteenth century). "Burglary" includes both entering a dwelling at night (burglary) and entering a dwelling during the day (housebreaking). "Property" includes nonclergyable offenses ranging from shoplifting and theft from a dwelling house to larceny, coining,

---

[21] In his study of female crime in England between 1660 and 1800, Beattie (1975) found that property crimes predominated. Rude (1985) examined nineteenth-century cases at the Old Bailey and in Gloucester and Sussex courts and concluded that larceny dominated the criminal charges for both men and women. He found no evidence of large numbers of infanticide cases. Sharpe (1984) looked at felony indictments for the sixteenth and seventeenth centuries and found that property offenses constituted between 74 and 93 percent of all indictments in nine counties. Typically, and frustrating to us, he grouped the cases in 100–150-year periods and failed to look at gender or changes over time.

[22] Beattie (1986:238) reports that while women were accused of only 13 percent of the robberies and 16 percent of the burglaries over the period 1660–1800, they were charged with 40 percent of the housebreaking offenses, 36 percent of the nonclergyable (crimes in which the defendant was not permitted to avoid the death penalty by reading from the Bible "under benefit of clergy") larcenies and 29 percent of the simple grand larcenies. Using Beattie's criteria, we found women charged with 29 percent of the robberies, 15 percent of burglaries, 19 percent of housebreaking offenses, 35 percent of nonclergyable larcenies, and 43 percent of all simple grand larcenies between 1687 and 1800.

736   THE VANISHING FEMALE

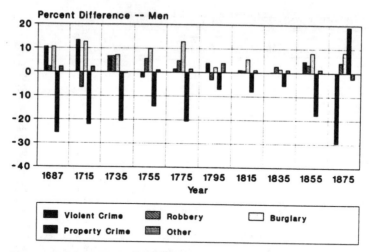

Figure 4. Male/female percentage differences by types of crime charged. Bars
          above zero axis indicate greater involvement of men; bars below the axis
          indicate greater involvement of women.

SOURCE: *Old Bailey Sessions Papers* 25 percent sample.

and receiving. "Other" is a category in which few defendants were
charged; it covers things like bigamy and perjury.

The importance of property offenses in accounting for women's criminal involvement is seen in Figure 4, which compares
differences in the percentages of male and female indictments by
type of offense. In all years but 1875 (after formal jurisdictional
changes altered the court's caseload) men were overrepresented in
violent crimes and women were overrepresented in property
crimes. What stands out most clearly is that the high proportion of
female defendants in the early eighteenth century was due in large
part to their "overrepresentation" in property offenses (i.e., larceny, shoplifting, pickpocketing, theft from a dwelling house, receiving stolen goods, and uttering counterfeit coins). Although
these offenses are not sex-specific, traditionally women have been
charged much more often with these types of offenses and less
often with violent offenses.

We considered whether additions to the category of property
crimes might have led to increased male involvement in the Old
Bailey, thus decreasing the proportion of women. In particular we
considered whether the expansion in the numbers of capital offenses during the eighteenth century might have contributed to an
increase in male defendants at the Old Bailey. But as noted earlier,
the overwhelming majority of these new offenses were directed at
rural folk, and their impact on the Old Bailey's caseload was min-
iscule. Indeed some of the new offenses dealing with passing
forged currency were, if anything, likely to disproportionately im-

Table 4. Proportion of Females Charged Alone or with Co-defendant

	Alone	With Codefendant	Total	N
1687	68	32	100	(40)
1715	78	22	100	(55)
1735	71	29	100	(66)
1755	68	32	100	(31)
1775	56	44	100	(54)
1795	63	37	100	(60)
1815	64	36	100	(75)
1835	69	31	100	(112)
1855	69	31	100	(32)
1875	74	26	100	(23)
1895	38	62	100	(13)
1912	85	15	100	(20)
Total	67 (392)	33 (189)	100	(581)

SOURCE: *Old Bailey Sessions Papers* 25 percent sample.

pact on women. Thus, expanded criminalization of distinctively "male" offenses cannot account for the declining percentage of female defendants.

Women Following Men

A fourth possibility was that the high percentage of women defendants in the eighteenth century was due to women following men into crime.[23] Such an explanation is not a statistical artifact like shifting jurisdiction. Indeed it could reveal important shifts in social processes. It suggests that apparent shifts in women's criminal involvement might be explained in terms of shifts in prosecutorial policies regarding accomplices and the like, and so we consider it here. To explore this issue we divided the sample into cases involving persons singly accused and cases involving co-defendants, and considered each separately. Throughout the entire period approximately two thirds of the women defendants were charged singly (see Table 4); an equivalent table for men would show roughly the same picture. We then considered women as a proportion of *all* cases, and contrasted this with the proportion of women in cases that did not involve a male co-defendant (i.e., we dropped all women in our sample who had a man as a co-defendant). If the higher proportion of women during the early part of the eighteenth century was a result of their following men into crime as accomplices, we would expect to find a gap between these two sets of figures during periods when women constituted the greatest proportion of defendants. Nothing of the kind is suggested in Figure 5; the two lines—representing all women and women in

23 Contemporary criminologists have found that delinquency is in large a group phenomena and that a substantial portion of girls involved in crime are associated with boys who are likely to have been the initiators in criminal activity. See, e.g., Gottfredson and Hirschi 1990:154–68.

738   THE VANISHING FEMALE

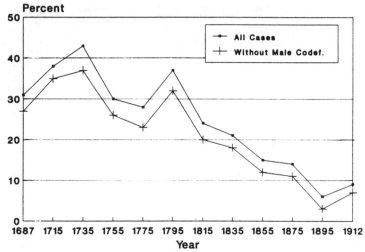

Figure 5. Percentage of women in Old Bailey, 1687–1912

SOURCE: *Old Bailey Sessions Papers* 25 percent sample.

cases without male codefendants—track each other nearly perfectly.[24]

War and Peace

Finally, we examined the influence of war and peace as it
might have affected men's and women's criminal involvement.
From John Howard onward, historians and government officials
have noted that during periods of war the crime rate declines and
that immediately following cessation of war, the crime rate increases (Sharpe 1984; Beattie 1986). These observers have not generally explored how crime rates during periods of war and peace
might differentially affect men and women.

However, the hypothesis is clear: The proportion of cases involving women increases during periods of war and decreases during peace time. Under this hypothesis the variation in women's
participation would be a function of shifts in male involvement.
During periods of war, men would be subject to alternative forms

---

[24] When we divided men into "spouses" and others, we found that between 1687 and 1775 spouses constituted between 30 and 40 percent of all
"mixed" co-defendants, while the average after 1775 was around 20 percent.
Thus, while men and women appeared as co-defendants in roughly the same
proportions through the entire period, the men with whom women were involved changed somewhat. During the earlier period, they were more likely to
be involved with their husbands. (Although the *OBSP* are not consistent in
identifying the marital status of defendants, they do seem to be consistent in
reporting the marital status of husband and wife co-defendants. This may have
been because wives could (and sometimes did) claim coverture (feme coverte)
as a defense when they were charged with their husbands. The few coverture
cases were not concentrated in the early eighteenth century.)

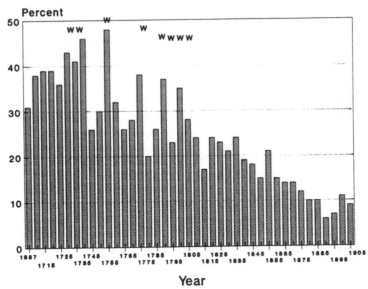

Figure 6. Percentage of women charged in Old Bailey, 1687–1912

SOURCE: Old Bailey Index.

of control and absorbed in military affairs. Immediately following wars, large numbers of men would be released from military service and be dislocated. Some would turn to crime and thus increase the crime rate (and decrease the proportion of women offenders).

Douglas Hay (1982) reports such a finding in his study of Staffordshire crime in the eighteenth century.[25] We found no such pattern; while indictments increased in the aftermath of war, it is not clear that war and peace are linked to the pattern of women's involvement in the Old Bailey. The early years in the eighteenth century, when women constituted the highest proportion of criminal defendants, were primarily years of peace.

Still we do not want to wholly discount war as a factor, and we suspect that wars may have had something to do with the erratic upsurges in the proportion of women during certain years after 1735. We have indicated eighteenth-century war years with a "W" on Figure 6. During war years, there would have been fewer men in London; thus, these upward jumps, which deviate from the

---

[25] Hay 1982 looked briefly at female crime rates during war years and found that women's rates of property crime, especially noncapital thefts, were higher during the war years in which prices were high. He concludes that women resorted to petty theft as the "appalling pressure of dearth reached more and more families"; in the alternative, he postulates that prosecutors might have been more willing to prosecute women when general theft levels were high or that in war years an increased number of abandoned wives and mothers were left to fend for themselves. Cf. Beattie 1975, who reports less fluctuation in female than male property crime rates in London as prices rose. However, he did not systematically compare war and peace years.

overall downward trend, may in part be the result of periods of war. Beattie's data show similar upward leaps at roughly the same periods of time. In short, although wars may affect involvement, they do not account for the long decline in women's involvement in the criminal process.

Discussion

Earlier we presented figures that revealed women's involvement in the criminal process to have been substantially higher in the eighteenth century than in the twentieth century or even the late nineteenth century. They also revealed a precipitous decline in the rate of this involvement throughout the eighteenth and early nineteenth centuries. The discussion in the several sections of Part II suggests that this higher level of involvement and subsequent decline was real. Although shifting jurisdiction appeared to have amplified the pattern of decline, this alone cannot completely account for the downward trend in the proportion of females at the Old Bailey. The other factors we examined—women following men, demographic shifts, the possibility of distinctive female offenses, and war and peace—bore no meaningful relation to the trend.

Thus our question remains: Why, in the first half of the eighteenth century, did women constitute such a large proportion of those charged with felonies, and what accounts for the decline over the next hundred or so years? It is worth remembering that throughout the entire period under consideration, the crimes tried at the Old Bailey were viewed as extremely serious, unlike shoplifting today. Like other more serious and violent offenses, property crimes—including larcenies—were punishable by severe sanctions, up to and including death (although transportation was in fact the usual punishment).[26]

Below we offer an exploratory analysis of some other explanations grounded in criminological theories of social control and in historical studies of shifting roles of women in the eighteenth century.

III. THE VANISHING FEMALE: AN EXPLORATORY ANALYSIS

At the outset we suggested that criminologists have generally focused on short-term processes and tended to ignore broad-scale transformations. One result is the belief that gender is stable and invariant with respect to crime. The discussion above challenges this belief in a central way. In this section we suggest that the pat-

---

[26] We note that both men and women were sentenced to death for larceny during the eighteenth century. The records do not always indicate whether sentences were in fact carried out, but here we merely want to emphasize that all the offenses—even the larcencies—at the Old Bailey were regarded as serious crimes.

tern during at least the first half of the period we have explored
was the consequence of social and structural changes that affected
the place of women in society generally. This was a period in
which women's lives, and more particularly forms of social control
of women, were substantially altered. This transformation took
many forms: women became less inclined and able than men to engage in activity defined as criminal, and women were less subject
to the criminal sanction as other forms of more private control
emerged.

We are guided by criminologists who have explored different
"roles" or opportunity structures for the two genders, or looked at
social control mechanisms that may differ qualitatively for men
and women in the twentieth century. Some suggest that the relative lack of criminal behavior by women is due to female "socialization" that stresses conformity (Adler 1975). Others point to such
structural factors as women's labor force participation, suggesting
that women have had fewer opportunities to engage in illegal activity (Simon 1975; Box 1983). Several criminologists argue that
women's lesser criminality can be explained by different types of
social control for men and women, including familial restraints on
girls (Hagan et al. 1989), occupational segregation, and women's
limited participation in the "public" spheres of the state and the
military (Heidensohn 1989). We explore changes in social controls
of women over the course of the eighteenth and early nineteenth
centuries in the discussion that follows.

Our discussion is also informed by Norbert Elias's (1968a,
1968b) monumental work of historical sociology, first published in
1939, which traces a "civilizing process," or changes in a variety of
norms and behaviors since the late medieval period. By "civilization" Elias means a *process* by which behavioral norms are internalized and sensibilities changed. Once accepted, he argues, they
lead to behavioral changes (Elias 1968a:308 ff.). Two recent studies
have used his work to illuminate the rise of modern penal policies.
In *The Spectacle of Suffering*, whose title brilliantly announces its
thesis, Pieter Spierenburg (1984) traces the disappearance of public
executions and the evolution away from executions to imprisonment. David Garland (1990) uses Elias's theory to explore shifts in
sentiments—and policies—about punishment. He marshals considerable evidence to show that in the eighteenth and nineteenth centuries attitudes toward violence shifted significantly. With this
shift came both a decline in violent criminal conduct and the substitution of less violent (and more private) forms of punishment as
capital punishment was largely abolished, corporal punishment
was curtailed, and imprisonment expanded.

In the text below we suggest that sensibilities about the role
of women in society as well as the forms of their control and punishment changed. Just as there was a transformation in and a low-
ering of tolerance for violence, by both citizens and officials, so too

742   THE VANISHING FEMALE

we suggest there was a transformation in the acceptability of women in the criminal process that resulted in a decline in the use of
the public criminal justice system as a form of social control of women.

The eighteenth century is generally known as the time of the
"Bloody Codes," a period when more than two hundred crimes
were legally punishable by death. Rising commercial classes called
for deterrents against property crimes (Hay 1975; Thompson
1975a). Criminal control mechanisms were primarily informal—
there was no organized system of police and prosecution depended
on private initiative. This initiative was promoted through a system of rewards for successful prosecutions and pardons for defendants turned informant (Phillips 1983; Rock 1983). Some have argued that the severity of punishment coupled with private and/or
official leniency after indictment or conviction reinforced the dependence and deference of the lower classes who were the primary
objects of criminal prosecution (Hay 1975).[27]

The pressures to criminality were similar to those of the twentieth century—unemployment, underemployment, destitution.
Much of the workforce in London was dependent on casual, often
seasonal labor (Beattie 1986; George 1965). We were not able to
systematically gather occupational data for the Old Bailey defendants. However, our reading of the cases reveals that almost all of
them were poor. Some worked as laborers, apprentices, servants;
others were unemployed. For most lower-class workers such
events as war, increases in food prices, interruptions in export
trades, seasonal layoffs, and the movement of upper-class families
out of the city meant the difference between employment and unemployment. In fact, many defendants, especially in the eighteenth century, claimed hunger or poverty as a defense. This was
the general context in which crime occurred in London.

Our concern within this context is what might account for the
decline of female defendants in the eighteenth century. Below we
review two schools of social history, both of which support a view
that the decline was due to a shift in public sensibilities and social
controls over women during this period. One school emphasizes
shifts in the modes of production and their effects on women's
roles and economic opportunities. The other emphasizes shifts in
social relations and sensibilities independent of economic conditions. Although these schools of thought are quite different and
their advocates often antagonistic, the types of factors they emphasize are in fact those identified as important in contemporary criminological control theories that examine women's criminality. The
discussion that follows is put forward as a hypothesis in need of
further exploration and refinement rather than a test of either a

---

[27] See also Haagen's (1983) discussion of the ways in which the debtor
laws produced similar effects.

theory of female criminality or a developed historical analysis of the role of women in crime.

Both economic and social historians point to major changes in social relations between men and women during the eighteenth and nineteenth centuries. In the broadest terms, there was a redefinition of the female, and a shift and perhaps intensification of private patriarchal control of women within the household. In the earlier period women were more or less equal participants in household production. As a subsistence economy gave way to a market economy, women were excluded from much of developing industry or segregated in fewer and fewer low-wage occupations. With the development of the male breadwinner ideal came a stricter sexual division of labor (Belchem 1990). Women's time was increasingly devoted to child care, as children also were removed from productive work. A number of these changes are regarded by some historians as having been harmful to women's status (see, e.g., Belchem 1990; Charles and Duffin 1985; Clark 1919; Hill 1989; Pinchbeck 1930). The loss of their economic functions led to a decline in women's power and autonomy within the family; male head-of-household authority was solidified. By the end of the nineteenth century, there was a separation of home and work, a firmer sexual division of labor, the exclusion of women from the public sphere and from much of productive work, and an intensification of cultural ideals of woman as wife and mother. Our data indicate that there was also a decline in female criminal court involvement during this period.[28]

Although economic and social changes did not occur in a uniform or linear manner, it is striking that the decline in women in the criminal process occurred during a period of shifting gender roles and controls. Shifts in cultural ideals undoubtedly had more to do with bourgeois women than with those at the bottom rung of the economic ladder, whose lives may not have been touched directly by the shifting sensibilities of the middle classes. However, our argument hinges less on the actual behavior of women and more on the sensibilities of those who were able to bring charges or administer justice. New conceptions of the roles of women may have led those in a position to bring criminal charges to eschew public prosecutions for other more private responses. Our goal here is to link two trends, identified by economic and social his-

---

[28] Boritch and Hagan (1990:587) point to similar developments in their study of declining female arrests for public order offenses in Toronto between 1859 and 1955:

> The sexual stratification of social control is linked to the separation of public and private spheres, which was intensified during the early stages of industrialization. Men's participation in the labor force and public sphere made them increasingly subject to official legal regulation, while the exclusion of most women from wage labor left them more liable to informal controls operating in the private domestic sphere.

744   THE VANISHING FEMALE

torians, with the decline of women's involvement in the criminal
process we have identified here. The connection between these
two trends is reinforced by the themes of contemporary control
theorists who see the low rate of female criminal involvement in
crime as a consequence of highly developed forms of social control
of women.

Economic Changes

A number of economic historians following Clark (1919) argue
that the period of the family economy in the seventeenth and early
eighteenth centuries was a period of significant economic participation by women. At the same time, some argue that men were more
occupied in domestic activities (Clark 1919; Medick 1976). All this
changed with industrial capitalism, "which broke away from the
family system, and dealt directly with individuals, the first fruit of
individualism being shown by the exclusion of women from the
journeyman's associations" (Clark 1919:301).

Marriage in much of the eighteenth century was an economic
partnership (Tilly and Scott 1978). Everyone worked, including
women and children. In rural areas women farmed, engaged in
dairy work, and sold home-manufactured products in the market.
In urban areas, where much of the production of food and clothing
had moved outside of the home, women spent more time in consumption activities to meet the subsistence needs of their families.
Women in families of craftsmen or shopkeepers assisted in the
craft or shop. While occupational designations were male, when
husbands died, guild memberships passed to the wives. Some women practiced independent trades—as bakers, grocers, innkeepers,
milliners, butchers, etc. When their husbands were unskilled laborers, women worked in the informal economy as petty traders
and hawkers or sold their labor, carting goods or water, sewing, or
doing laundry. In London, where the widest range of occupations
was practiced, women engaged in the full range of productive activities (George 1965). Widows who didn't inherit a guild membership had a difficult time, and many had to send children to charities, being unable to support them with low-wage work. However,
that many widowers had similar problems provides evidence that
two adults were necessary for the economic well-being of a family
(Tilly and Scott 1978). As work moved out of the household, this
changed, for both men and women.

In industry after industry—textiles, the domestic industries,
the mines, crafts, and business—the range of employment for women shrank dramatically throughout the eighteenth and nineteenth centuries (Pinchbeck 1930). For example, up until the mid-
eighteenth century, women and children pursued work alongside
their husbands and fathers in textile production, combining spinning and the like with housework. With the rise of wage labor

these jobs were transferred out of the house into the factory. By 1830 the textile industry had been entirely removed from the cottage into the factory, where it was performed by skilled workmen on complicated machinery. In the case of London, the movement from a putting-out system to the factory meant that silk winding and silk throwing, occupations that employed large numbers of women, disappeared as production moved to textile factories outside of London (George 1965). More generally, new forms of production required specialized knowledge and training, which men had already begun to monopolize (Clark 1919; Pinchbeck 1930; Hill 1989; Middleton 1985). Thus, women were squeezed out of many aspects of economic participation. With this came the development of what Clark called the "doctrine of the subjugation of women to their husbands" (Clark 1919). Men were "freed" from economic dependence on their wives and a Victorian ideal of the subjection of women to their husbands gradually developed. The result, in Clark's and others' view, was that industrial capitalism exerted a "momentous influence" on the economic position of women that contributed to a substantial decline in their economic well-being and opportunities.

Historians do not suggest that women were "equal" to men in the eighteenth century. Women were low-waged labor, paid much less than men even before industrialization (Rose 1988). They were denied membership in many guilds so long as their husbands lived (Tilly and Scott 1978). Additionally, husbands were the legal heads of the household, with rights to physically chastise wives and children. However, the fact that women had greater participation in the household economy and control over certain aspects of production indicates that social controls in the family and economy may have been less than they were in the nineteenth century. One historian even argues that not only did men and women share productive work during this period, but that there was almost "sex-role reversal" in the sharing of household tasks (Medick 1976). Control theorists posit that controls over female labor and the restriction of women to domestic work leads to lesser female deviance; the greater participation of women in economic production in the eighteenth century may mean that they were less controlled, more able to engage in criminal activity, and more subject of formal legal controls.

Along with changes in the mode of production came a growing view about gender and work. Exclusionary provisions were justified on the grounds that certain work was unsuitable and unfeminine or would lead women into immoral habits because it required being in close proximity to men (Hill 1989). When women worked, only occupations that coincided with their "natural sphere" were encouraged (Alexander 1983). Hill (1989:263) observes, "Far from industrialization meaning the emancipation of women, for many the first phase must have meant a greater servi-

746   THE VANISHING FEMALE

tude and conditions where they had no defence against the arbitrary wielding of patriarchal power."

Even without exclusionary provisions against women, the transition to a family wage economy in which households needed cash and not labor meant that women's capacity to make a productive contribution was now limited by their domestic, child-bearing and child-rearing duties (Tilly and Scott 1978). All this was reinforced by accompanying theories of femininity, which further restricted the range of socially acceptable behavior permitted to women.

The restriction of women's participation in industry continued throughout the nineteenth century. Trade unions used exclusionary practices to keep women out of some areas of employment.[29] The development of the "family wage" and protective legislation further restricted female employment. Accompanying these restrictions was the rise of the "Cult of Domesticity" in the middle classes, an ideology that portrayed women's proper role as a subservient, virtuous, and pious wife and mother. This Victorian ideology changed broader cultural norms about the relations and roles of both men and women, affecting individuals in all classes ultimately.

In London, the economic changes were both less dramatic and more gradual. In an urban area in which trades, crafts, and casual employment predominated, women did not experience the rapid transitions from putting out to factory work detailed for agricultural workers by Pinchbeck (1930). Some women continued to work in their husbands' trades well into the nineteenth century; however, probably less than 10 percent of London women were married to tradesmen (Alexander 1983). Moreover, as work moved from the home to workshops and male tradesmen acquired capital, they began to hire larger numbers of male journeymen and apprentices, excluding their wives from participation in the trade (George 1965).

In London, as in the rest of the country, the gradual separation of home and work meant reduced opportunities for women to learn skills or contribute equally to their family's economic wellbeing. Women's trades passed into male hands. In addition, although new industries were created, women were excluded from them. Alexander (1983) details a host of occupations in which by the 1820s London women did not work.[30] When women did work, they participated in "women's" jobs like domestic and household

---

[29] See Hartmann 1979; Rose 1988. There is substantial debate over the reasons male unionists tried to exclude women and the participation/agreement of working-class women in these struggles. However, the fact of their increasing exclusion from production remains.

[30] These included shipping industries, public utilities, transport, semi-processing and extractive industries (i.e., London's factory trades), professions, civil service, clerical work, scientific trades, and the old craft guilds (Alexander 1983).

labor, child care and training, the distribution and retail of food and other articles of regular consumption, and manufacturing skills based on the sexual division of labor in the household (ibid.). Industrial work was primarily "slopwork" in which a division of labor broke jobs into semi- and unskilled tasks and then exploited cheap labor. Women were especially exploited here with long hours and extremely low wages; in addition, slopwork contributed to the demise of women's occupations since it occurred in trades that had previously been occupied by skilled women, trades like dressmaking and needlework. Overall, then, the rise of slopwork, the increase in out-of-home work, the exclusion of women from new trades and occupations, and the competition of slopwork with traditional women's trades led to both declining wages for women and an overall reduction in the range of work available to women in London.

Thus, it appears that from a situation of marital partnership in a household economy, women gradually moved to a weaker economic partnership working out of the household and finally to no economic partnership and economic dependence on men. It is always difficult to directly link macro-structural changes to micro data like ours. However, some control theorists suggest that lower rates of female criminality can be explained by restrictions and controls on women's economic participation.[31] Beattie (1975) suggests that women committed more crime in urban areas because they were both less restricted in work and less protected than women in rural areas. Economic historians point us to the possibility that economic opportunities and social controls *changed* over the course of the eighteenth and early nineteenth centuries. Women were increasingly restricted in their work and in their ability to contribute to the household income. This transition coincided with a decline in female criminal court involvement and suggests that women had fewer opportunities to commit crimes and were subject to increased private informal controls rather than public legal controls.

Social and Cultural Changes

Social historians point to changes in the family and in ideologies that affected both the relations between men and women and the nature of social controls over women. For instance, Stone (1977) notes that the eighteenth century witnessed the acceptance of the idea of the "companionate marriage," in which marriage

---

[31] We do not argue here, like Adler 1975 and Simon 1975, that female economic participation per se leads to greater female criminality. These claims have been challenged by many (see, e.g., Steffensmeier 1989, 1980, 1978; Box and Hale 1983; Giordano and Cernkovich 1979; Smart 1979). Rather, our discussion looks at changes in female economic participation and changing social controls over women within a specific historical context, the transition from precapitalist household production to capitalist forms of production.

748   THE VANISHING FEMALE

came to be regarded as a decision to be made by the couple in accord with their own feelings. More generally, he identifies other
changes in sexual relations. Pointing to the collapse of the Puritan
movement and the weakening of kin protections as causes, he reports a rise in the illegitimacy and premarital pregnancy rates after 1700. "This was caused by the weakening of the social controls
over the seducer previously exercised by the neighbors, the parish
clergy and the local community, caused in part by the isolation of
migrant and propertyless young people in the big cities" (Stone
1977:646).

Hill (1989) discusses courtship relations among the laboring
classes in the eighteenth century, concluding that women in the
lower classes seem to have enjoyed a good deal of freedom in
choosing a mate. A real period of courtship occurred in which
couples evaluated each other's character and ability to contribute
economically to the marriage. Because there was no property to be
inherited, however, the laboring classes had a more tolerant view
of premarital sex than did the propertied classes, and thus had
higher illegitimacy rates, as reported by Stone.

Over the course of the nineteenth century, however, with the
rise of Victorian ideology, sexual controls over women tightened.[32]
Ideological links were made between female crime and sexual morality. Indeed, Zedner (1991) has detailed the effect of this ideology
on views of female criminals and the resulting policy decisions
about treatment of female prison inmates. Women, who were supposed to be the moralizing force in society, especially among the
lower classes, caused tremendous anxiety when they engaged in
criminal deviance. Female criminals were the opposite of virtuous
Victorian womanhood; they were "shameless," "more dangerous to
society than the other sex," and comparable to beasts (Zedner
1991:321, quoting from various journalists). The result was a penal
system geared to moral regeneration and the highest levels of control over all aspects of women's prison life and conduct.

Other historians have examined long-term declines in interpersonal violence in England (and other countries), arguing that
the last two to three hundred years have seen a "civilizing process"
(Elias 1978), in which interpersonal violence has been increasingly
prohibited and subject to sanction (Gurr 1980; Gurr, Grabosky, and
Hula 1977; Gatrell 1980; Garland 1990). They suggest that people
have been socialized to control anger and find nonviolent means of
resolving conflict. These cultural changes and the decline in interpersonal violence roughly parallel our own downward trend in female criminal involvement. It seems possible that these "civilizing
processes" affected women first, insofar as they were viewed as the

---

[32] Sexual controls in general increased during the Victorian era. In our
data we saw a rise in prosecutions for sexual offenses, especially sexual assaults of minor girls and homosexuality in the late nineteenth century.

moralizing influence in society.[33] They may also help to explain our findings.

A brief look at the situation in London and more specific social control efforts indicates that eighteenth-century London reformers and members of the governing classes tried to cope with the problems of the poor and working classes in ways that especially affected women in these classes. Concerns about infant mortality and the quality of mothering led to the opening of increased numbers of lying-in hospitals, regular hospitals, and dispensary health centers throughout the mid- to late eighteenth century. These facilities provided midwifery services and advice about hygiene. In addition, they focused on educating poor women about proper child rearing. During the early part of the century legislators enacted a number of bills that limited the consumption of alcohol by the laboring classes; of major concern was the effect of gin on women's performance of their maternal responsibilities, as well as fears that it led women into prostitution (George 1965). (These concerns resurfaced in the late nineteenth century when social reformers blamed drunken mothers for irresponsibility and failure to fulfill maternal duties; Zedner 1991.) In essence, there were increased efforts to both protect and control women in their maternal duties.

Legislative efforts to reduce the number of individuals, primarily wage earners, imprisoned for debt may have reduced the numbers of women and children left destitute (and perhaps driven to crime) by the imprisonment or desertion of a spouse confronting debts. Other efforts throughout the eighteenth century to deal with the problems of orphaned infants, apprentices, and those needing poor law assistance may also have had the effect of both restricting and protecting women (George 1965).

Our purpose here is not to provide a detailed historical analysis. Rather, we only suggest directions for future study. Macro social changes in the economy, in sexual relations within the family, in the roles of both men and women, and in cultural values during the eighteenth and nineteenth centuries all lead in the same direction—that is, toward a greater range of social controls that restricted women to domestic life, controls that may at the same time have provided some protections for women against the economic uncertainties of life in London. Further research into the specifics of the lives of women in London is necessary to point to the ways in which macro and local-level social changes and reforms led to changes in the informal and formal controls over women, contributing to the decline in their criminal involvement.

---

[33] Cf. Foucault (1979, 1980) who has a very different interpretation of the rise of imprisonment and of sexual controls. While he does not focus on gender, his study of sexuality certainly elaborates on nineteenth-century controls directed at female sexual behavior.

750   THE VANISHING FEMALE

CONCLUSION

The research reported in this article reveals the high rate of female involvement in the criminal process in the early eighteenth century and its decline over the next century. We have suggested that social and economic changes that took place during the same period may help explain the decline. While we recognize that we have not solved the mystery, we have identified a significant problem and suggested several explanations for it.

This exploration suggests still other avenues for study. The decline in women's involvement in the criminal process throughout the eighteenth century took place on the eve of the establishment of the modern criminal justice system and during a period of decreasing criminal violence. This decline coincides with the widespread embrace of new and more "civilized" forms of punishment, the creation of stipendiary magistrates in London, the creation of the first professional police force, and a significant expansion of prosecution societies. All these and related reforms undoubtedly had a significant effect on the operations of the criminal justice system.

Although there is debate as to whether these innovations had any appreciable affect on the rates of crime per se, they clearly had an impact on *who* was subject to criminal control. Debates about the subjects of the administration of an increasingly rational system of criminal justice took place at a time when women's roles and places in society were being redefined. Most certainly these issues were joined, and joined in ways that diverted women from the criminal process. The nature of the control was shifted to the male as husband and to other institutions increasingly defined as suited to "distinctively female problems."[34] As Zedner (1991:312) correctly comments: "Criminal men were, indeed, the primary target of the development of formal policing and the proliferation of prisons—and the histories have reflected this."

In concluding, we acknowledge that we end with more questions than answers and an even longer research agenda than we started with. A fuller examination of the shifts we have uncovered requires attention to these additional factors. More generally, the rise of public criminal justice institutions must be related to the sorts of social and economic developments we have considered. We have noted what we believe is an important and little-addressed problem, the decline of women in the criminal process, and con-

---

[34] There is of course a huge literature on the construction of femininity in the Victorian era (see, e.g., Showalter 1987), some of which relates it to public social control. A number of students of Victorian crime have noted that throughout the nineteenth century women constituted a declining portion of the prison population and correspondingly a growing portion of the population in insane asylums. More generally there was a shift of views of female deviants who came to be seen as "mad not bad" (Zedner 1991) Our data suggest that such a shift occurred but was set in motion in the eighteenth century, predating the Victorian era by several decades.

nected it to large-scale shifts in the controls over women. The connection is certainly strong enough to warrant additional sustained attention by both social scientists and historians.

REFERENCES

ADLER, Freda (1975) *Sisters in Crime: The Rise of the New Female Criminal.* New York: McGraw-Hill.

ALEXANDER, Sally (1983) *Women's Work in Nineteenth Century London: A Study of the Years 1820–1850.* London: Journeyman Press and London History Workshop Centre.

BEATTIE, J. M. (1982 [1975]) "The Criminality of Women in Eighteenth Century England," in D. K. Weisberg (ed.), 1 *Women and the Law: A Social Historical Perspective.* Cambridge, MA: Schenkman Publishing Co.

—— (1986) *Crime and the Courts in England 1660–1800.* Princeton, NJ: Princeton University Press.

—— (1988) "London Juries in the 1690s," in J. S. Cockburn and T. A. Green (eds.), *Twelve Good Men and True: The Criminal Trial Jury in England, 1200–1800.* Princeton, NJ: Princeton University Press.

BELCHEM, John (1990) *Industrialization and the Working Class: The English Experience, 1750–1900.* Aldershot, Eng.: Scholar Press.

BONGER, William A. (1916) *Criminality and Economic Conditions.* Boston: Little, Brown.

BORITCH, Helen, and John HAGAN (1990) "A Century of Crime in Toronto: Gender, Class, and Patterns of Social Control, 1859 to 1955," 28 *Criminology* 567.

BOX, Steven (1983) *Power, Crime, and Mystification.* London: Tavistock Publications.

BOX, Steven, and Chris HALE (1983) "Liberation and Female Criminality in England and Wales," 23 *British Journal of Criminology* 35.

BOYER, Paul, and Stephen NISSENBAUM (1974) *Salem Possessed: The Social Origins of Witchcraft.* Cambridge, MA: Harvard University Press.

CHARLES, Lindsey, and Lorna DUFFIN (eds.) (1985) *Women and Work in Pre-industrial England.* London: Croom Helm.

CHESNEY-LIND, Meda (1989) "Girl's Crime and Woman's Place: Toward a Feminist Model of Female Delinquency," 35 *Crime and Delinquency* 5.

CLARK, Alice (1919) *Working Life of Women in the Seventeenth Century.* London: Routledge & Kegan Paul; reprinted 1982.

ELIAS, Norbert (1968a [1939]) *The Civilizing Process:* Vol. 1, *The History of Manners.* New York: Pantheon.

—— (1968b [1939]) *The Civilizing Process:* Vol. 2, *Power and Civility.* New York: Pantheon.

EMSLEY, Clive (1987) *Crime and Society in England, 1750–1900.* London: Longman.

FABER, Sjoerd (1983) "Strafrechlspeging en Criminaliteit te Amsterdam, 1680–1811." Ph.D. dissertation, Vrije Universiteit te Amsterdam.

FINLAY, Roger (1981) *Population and Metropolis: The Demography of London 1580–1650.* Cambridge: Cambridge University Press.

FOUCAULT, Michel (1979) *Discipline and Punish: The Birth of the Prison.* New York: Vintage Books.

—— (1980) *The History of Sexuality:* Vol. 1, *An Introduction.* New York: Vintage Books.

GARLAND, David (1990) *Punishment and Modern Society.* Chicago: University of Chicago Press.

GATRELL, V. A. C. (1980) "The Decline of Theft in Victorian and Edwardian England," in V. A. C. Gatrell, B. Lenman, and G. Parker (eds.), *Crime and Law: The Social History of Crime in Western Europe since 1500.* London: Europa Publications.

GEORGE, M. Dorothy (1965) *London Life in the Eighteenth Century.* New York: Capricorn Books Edition.

GIORDANO, Peggy C., and Stephen A. CERNKOVICH (1979) "On Complicat-

752   THE VANISHING FEMALE

ing the Relationship between Liberation and Delinquency," 26 *Social Problems* 467.

GLASS, D. V. (1969) "Socio-economic Status and Occupations in the City of London at the End of the Seventeenth Century," in A. E. J. Hollander and W. Kellaway (eds.), *Studies in London History*. London: Hodder & Stoughton.

GOTTFREDSON, Michael R., and Travis HIRSCHI (1990) *A General Theory of Crime*. Stanford, CA: Stanford University Press.

GURR, Ted Robert (1980) "Historical Trends in Violent Crime," in N. Morris and M. Tonry (eds.), 2 *Crime and Justice: An Annual Review of Research*. Chicago: University of Chicago Press.

GURR, Ted Robert, Peter N. GRABOSKY, and Ricarhd C. HULA (1970) *The Politics of Crime and Conflict: A Comparative History of Four Cities*. Beverly Hills, CA: Sage Publications.

HAAGEN, Paul (1983) "Eighteenth-Century English Society and the Debt Law," in S. Cohen and A. Scull (eds.), *Social Control and the State*. Oxford: Basil Blackwell.

HAGAN, John, John SIMPSON, and A. R. GILLIS (1979) "The Sexual Stratification of Social Control: A Gender-based Perspective on Crime and Delinquency," 30 *British Journal of Sociology* 25.

——— (1989) "Feminist Scholarship, Relational and Instrumental Control, and a Power-Control Theory of Gender and Delinquency," 39 *British Journal of Sociology* 301.

HALL, Jerome (1935) *Theft, Law and Society*. Boston: Little, Brown.

HARTMANN, Heidi (1983) "Capitalism, Patriarchy and Job Segregation by Sex," in E. Abel and E. K. Abel (eds.), *The Signs Reader: Women, Gender & Scholarship*. Chicago: University of Chicago Press.

HAY, Douglas (1975) "Property, Authority, and the Criminal Law," in D. Hay, P. Linebaugh, J. G. Rule, E. P. Thompson, and C. Winslow (eds.), *Albion's Fatal Tree: Crime and Society in Eighteenth-Century England*. New York: Pantheon Books.

——— (1982) "War, Death and Theft in the Eighteenth Century: The Record of the English Courts," 95 *Past and Present* 117.

HEIDENSOHN, Frances M. (1985) *Women and Crime*. New York: New York University Press.

——— (1989) *Crime and Society*. London: MacMillan Education Ltd.

HILL, Bridget (1989) *Women, Work, and Sexual Politics in Eighteenth-Century England*. Oxford: Basil Blackwell.

HULL, N. E. H. (1987) *Female Felons: Women and Serious Crime in Colonial Massachusetts*. Urbana: University of Illinois Press.

KEICKEHEFER, Richard (1976) *European Witch Trials*. Berkeley: University of California Press.

LANDSMAN, Stephan (1990) "The Rise of the Contentious Spirit: Adversary Procedure in Eighteenth Century England," 75 *Cornell Law Review* 497.

LANGBEIN, John H. (1983) "Shaping the Eighteenth-Century Criminal Trial: A View from the Ryder Sources," 50 *University of Chicago Law Review* 1.

LARNER, Christina (1980) "Crimen Exceptum? The Crime of Witchcraft in Europe," in V. A. C. Gatrell, B. Lenman, and G. Parker (eds.), *Crime and the Law: The Social History of Crime in Western Europe since 1500*. London: Europa Publications.

LAW, C. M. (1967) "Local Censuses in the Eighteenth Century," *Population Studies* 23 (1).

LEONARD, Eileen B. (1982) *Women, Crime and Society: A Critique of Theoretical Criminology*. New York: Longman Group.

LOMBROSO, Caesar, and William FERRERO (1895) *The Female Offender*. New York: D. Appleton.

MACFARLANE, Alan (1970) *Witchcraft in Tudor and Stuart England*. New York: Harper & Row.

MAYHEW, Henry (1900) *London Labour and the London Poor*. New York: D. Appleton.

MEDICK, H. (1976) "The Proto-industrial Family Economy: The Structural Function of Household and Family during the Transition from Peasant Society to Industrial Capitalism," 1 *Social History* 311.

MIDDLETON, Chris (1985) "Women's Labour and the Transition to Pre-industrial Capitalism," in L. Charles and L. Duffin (eds.), *Women and Work in Pre-industrial England*. London: Croom Helm.

MITCHELL, B. R., and Phyllis DEANE (1962) *Abstract of British Historical Statistics*. Cambridge: Cambridge University Press.

NAFFINE, Ngire (1987) *Female Crime: The Construction of Women in Criminology*. Sydney: Allen & Unwin.

PHILLIPS, David (1983) " 'A Just Measure of Crime, Authority, Hunters and Blue Locusts': The 'Revisionist' Social History of Crime and the Law in Britain, 1780–1850," in S. Cohen and A. Scull (eds.), *Social Control and the State*. Oxford: Basil Blackwell.

——— (1977) *Crime and Authority in Victorian England*. London: Croom Helm.

PINCHBECK, Ivy (1930) *Women Workers and the Industrial Revolution 1750–1850*. London: Virago Press. Reprinted 1969.

RADZINOWICZ, Leon (1948) 1 *A History of English Criminal Law and Its Administration from 1750*. London: Heinemann.

——— (1956a) 2 *A History of English Criminal Law and Its Administration from 1750*. London: Heinemann.

——— (1956b) 3 *A History of English Criminal Law and Its Administration from 1750*. London: Heinemann.

——— (1968) 4 *A History of English Criminal Law and Its Administration from 1750*. London: Heinemann.

RADZINOWICZ, Leon, and Roger HOOD (1986) 5 *A History of English Criminal Law*. London: Stevens.

ROCK, Paul (1983) "Law, Order and Power in Late Seventeenth- and Early Eighteenth-Century England," in S. Cohen and A. Scull (eds.), *Social Control and the State*. Oxford: Basil Blackwell.

ROSE, Sonya O. (1988) "Gender Antagonism and Class Conflict: Exclusionary Strategies of Male Trade Unionists in Nineteenth Century Britain," 13 *Social History* 191.

RUDE, George (1985) *Criminal and Victim: Crime and Society in Early Nineteenth-Century England*. Oxford: Clarendon Press.

SHARPE, J. A. (1984) *Crime in Early Modern England 1550–1750*. London: Longman.

——— (1988) "The History of Crime in England 1300–1914: An Overview of Recent Publications," 28 *Britist Journal of Criminology* 254.

SHOEMAKER, Robert B. (1991) *Prosecution and Punishment: Petty Crime and the Law in London and Rural Middlesex, c. 1660–1725*. Cambridge: Cambridge University Press.

SHOWALTER, Elaine (1987) *The Female Malady: Women, Madness, and English Culture, 1830–1980*. London: Virago.

SIMON, Rita James (1975) *Women and Crime*. Lexington, MA: Lexington Books.

SMART, Carol (1977a) *Women, Crime and Criminology: A Feminist Critique*. London: Routledge & Kegan Paul.

——— (1977b) "Criminological Theory: Its Ideology and Implications Concerning Women," 28 *British Journal of Sociology* 89.

——— (1979) "The New Female Criminal: Reality or Myth?" 19 *British Journal of Criminology* 50.

SPIERENBURG, Pieter (1984) *The Spectacle of Suffering*. Cambridge: Cambridge University Press.

STEFFENSMEIER, Darrell J. (1978) "Crime and the Contemporary Woman: An Analysis of Changing Levels of Female Property Crime, 1960–75," 57 *Social Forces* 566.

——— (1980) "Sex Differences in Patterns of Adult Crime, 1964–77: A Review and Assessment," 58 *Social Forces* 1081.

——— (1989) "Development and Female Crime: A Cross-national Test of Alternative Explanations," 68 *Social Forces* 262.

STONE, Lawrence (1977) *The Family, Sex and Marriage in England 1500–1800*. New York: Harper & Row.

THOMAS, W. I. (1907) *Sex and Society*. Boston: Little, Brown.

——— (1967) *The Unadjusted Girl*. New York: Harper & Row.

THOMPSON, E. P. (1971) "The Moral Economy of the English Crowd in the Eighteenth Century," 50 *Past and Present* 76.

754   THE VANISHING FEMALE

—— (1975a) *Whigs and Hunters: The Origins of the Black Act.* New York: Pantheon Books.

—— (1975b) "The Crime of Anonymity," in D. Hay, P. Linebaugh, J. G. Rule, E. P. Thompson, and C. Winslow (eds.), *Albion's Fatal Tree: Crime and Society in Eighteenth-Century England.* New York: Pantheon Books.

TILLY, Louise A., and Joan W. SCOTT (1978) *Women, Work and Family.* New York: Holt, Rinhart, & Winston.

TRANTER, N. L. (1985) *Population and Society 1750–1940: Contrasts in Population Growth.* London: Longman.

TREVOR-ROPER, H. R. (1969) *The European Witch Craze of the 16th and 17th Centuries.* London: Harmondsworth.

WALKOWITZ, Judith (1980) *Prostitution and Victorian Society: Women, Class and the State.* Cambridge: Cambridge University Press.

WRIGLEY, E. A., and R. S. SCHOFIELD (1981) *The Population History of England, 1541-1871.* Cambridge, MA: Harvard University Press.

ZEDNER, Lucia Helen (1988) "The Criminality of Women and Its Control in England 1850–1914." Ph.D. diss., University of Oxford.

—— (1991) "Women, Crime, and Penal Responses: A Historical Account," in M. Tonry (ed.), 14 *Crime and Justice: A Review of Research.* Chicago: University of Chicago Press.

APPENDIX

Appendix Table A1. Sex of Indicted Defendants, Indicted Defendants (Larcenies Excluded), and Convicted Felons by Year, All Crimes Charged

	Indicted Defendants, All Crimes Charged			Indicted Defendants (Larcenies Excluded)			Convicted Felons		
	Males	Females	N	Males	Females	N	Males	Females	N
1687	69%	31%	130	75%	25%	93	72%	28%	79
1715	62	38	144	64	35	85	64	36	92
1735	57	43	155	65	35	75	67	33	76
1755	70	30	102	82	18	51	70	30	63
1775	72	28	194	85	15	79	77	23	109
1795	63	37	162	73	27	70	66	34	99
1815	76	24	317	74	26	152	75	25	229
1835	79	21	535	81	19	224	78	22	417
1855	85	15	209	86	14	145	84	16	170
1875	86	14	165	85	15	144	89	11	116
1895	94	6	201	94	6	180	94	6	165
1912	91	9	231	90.5	9.5	200	93	7	183
Total	77%	23%		82	18		79	21	
N	(1,964)	(581)	(2,545)	(1,225)	(273)	(1,498)	(1,426)	(372)	(1,798)

SOURCE: *Old Bailey Sessions Papers* 25 percent sample.

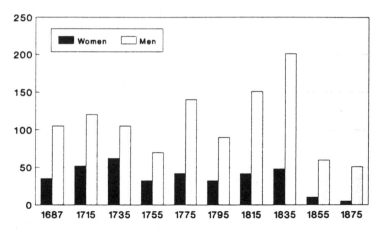

Appendix Figure A1. Charge rates for Old Bailey, 1687–1875

SOURCE: Based on estimated population counts for London population and index counts for Old Bailey.

756   THE VANISHING FEMALE

Appendix Table A2. Sex of Indicted Defendants, by Year (All Crimes Charged)

	Males	Females	Total	*N*
1687	**69**	**31**	**100**	**130**
1715	**62**	**38**	**100**	**144**
1720	61	39	100	444
1725	61	39	100	690
1730	64	36	100	614
1735	**57**	**43**	**100**	**155**
1740	59	41	100	494
1745	54	46	100	382
1750	74	26	100	599
1755	**70**	**30**	**100**	**102**
1760	52	48	100	293
1765	68	32	99	473
1770	74	26	100	669
1775	**72**	**28**	**100**	**194**
1780	62	38	99	557
1785	80	20	99	1,105
1790	74	26	99	872
1795	**63**	**37**	**100**	**162**
1800	77	23	100	901
1805	65	35	100	832
1810	72	28	100	975
1815	**76**	**24**	**100**	**317**
1820	83	17	94	1,820
1825	76	24	96	1,991
1830	77	23	96	2,119
1835	**79**	**21**	**100**	**535**
1840	76	24	100	1,875
1845	81	19	100	1,597
1850	82	18	100	1,599
1855	**85**	**15**	**100**	**209**
1860	79	21	100	715
1865	85	15	100	836
1870	86	14	100	883
1875	**86**	**14**	**100**	**165**
1880	88	12	100	730
1885	90	10	100	873
1890	90	10	100	727
1895	**94**	**6**	**100**	**201**
1900	93	7	100	627
1905	89	11	100	694
1912	**91**	**9**	**100**	**231**

SOURCE: *Old Bailey Sessions Papers* 100 percent sample and 25 percent sample. All years taken from indexes except those in boldface type, which were taken from sample data. A few defendants in some indexes had only an initial given for their first names, and thus we were unable to determine their sex. Missing information never accounted for more than 6 percent of all defendants in a given year. Also, some indexes in the eighteenth century did not always indicate when the same individual had been brought up twice, in separate cases. This did not occur often enough to cause us to lose confidence in the indexes as rough indicators of trends. Moreover, men were generally involved in multiple cases, and thus our counts would, if anything, underrepresent the proportion of women.

Appendix Table A3. Men and Women Accused of Property Crimes in Surrey Urban
Parishes, 1661–1805

Period	No. of Men	No. of Women	Total	% Women	No. of Years
1661–70	129	33	162	20	(3)
1671–80	235	80	315	25	(4)
1681–90	17	12	29	41	(1)
1691–1700	170	115	285	40	(4)
1701–10	40	53	93	57	(2)
1711–20	215	96	311	31	(3)
1721–30	212	87	299	29	(3)
1731–40	279	102	381	27	(5)
1741–50	283	146	429	34	(7)
1751–60	415	192	607	32	(8)
1761–70	550	140	690	20	(9)
1771–80	23	14	37	38	(1)
1781–90	257	70	327	21	(4)
1791–1800	587	182	769	24	(6)
1801–5	352	83	435	19	(2)

SOURCE: Beattie (1975), Graph I, p. 225. We are deeply indebted to Professor
Beattie for providing us with these figures which were reported only in graph form
in his 1975 article.

NOTE: Beattie's data have been grouped in ten-year periods to assess the trend in
the percentage of women involved in property crime. Surrey was part (about one-
sixth according to Beattie) of the greater London metropolis.

Part III
Policing and Prosecution

[13]

The Contours of Crime and Justice in Massachusetts and South Carolina, 1767-1878

by MICHAEL STEPHEN HINDUS[1]

The criminal law has a unique position in the legal system. It catalogs in great detail what behavior is so strongly proscribed that society's general resources will be employed to punish and prevent it. Moreover, it specifies what acts are so threatening to the social order that they cannot be left to the informal structures of authority provided by such institutions as church, family or neighborhood. The criminal prosecution exists at a crucial junction between law and society, between values (embodied into law) and behavior. The study of crime and justice in history is critical to understanding the relationship between law, values and behavior and serves as an important indicator of the role of formal, legal authority in society. Because crime is a behavioral phenomenon which comes to the historian's attention only after proscription and prosecution, the history of crime is not simply social history but an important component of legal history.

The present study is concerned with only one aspect of criminal law and procedure — the pattern of prosecutions.[2] It represents an attempt to demonstrate the close correlation between crime and the social and economic bases of society. To highlight this correlation, this study concentrates on two extremely diverse jurisdictions: Massachusetts and South Carolina. Both places were seventeenth-century colonies and their patterns of crime, authority and justice were more or less indigeneously established by the end of the eighteenth century. In addition, each state had an important commercial city which was also a regional cultural capital. Thus,

---

1. Ph. D. in History, University of California at Berkeley, now studying law at Harvard.

2. Some of the issues raised in this article are discussed in greater detail in the larger study of which this is a part. Michael Stephen Hindus, *Prison and Plantation: Crime, Justice and Authority in Massachusetts and South Carolina, 1767-1878* (Ph. D. dissertation, University of California, Berkeley, 1975).

differences between the two states were not simply a matter of frontier versus established settlement or urban versus rural. But there the similarities end. Massachusetts was in many ways the prototype for the economic and demographic development of the Northeast in the nineteenth century. The first state to undergo large-scale industrialization. Massachusetts also absorbed a huge immigrant population, spurring the growth of its numerous secondary urban centers. Hand in hand with this transformation, Massachusetts was one of the first states forced to confront and grapple with the new problems of crime and disorder which accompanied the transition.

South Carolina, by contrast, represented a second regional prototype. This was the aristocratic, coastal, South, highly dependent on the slave labor which worked the huge plantations. South Carolina had no cities to speak of except for Charleston, little industry, and indeed, virtually no free non-agrarian workforce to maintain any industry. In the same decades in which Boston was flooded with immigrants — the 1840's and 1850's — the most salient fact about South Carolina's demography was native white outmigration. The most striking characteristic of the state's population was its blacks, who comprised 59 percent of the population, a proportion significantly higher than that in any other state.

This study examines the patterns of criminal prosecutions from the earliest reliable records up to the Civil War. By the nineteenth century, the patterns of offenses prosecuted in the two states were distinctly correlated with economic, social, and cultural characteristics. Massachusetts' prosecution of crimes against property and propriety well served the needs of its urbanizing, industrializing society but also reflected the severe dislocations which both accompanied these processes and in turn stimulated deviant behavior. In South Carolina, by contrast, the absence of a distinct predatory class of whites and the strength of the cult of honor resulted in an overwhelming emphasis on crimes of violence, with little concern for crimes against property and propriety.

There are numerous conceptual and methodological problems associated with any statistical study of crime. All historians of crime have wrestled with them, but most have ended up using statistical material to some degree. I will not repeat the litany — both of difficulty and utility — except to add that my use of this data conforms to most of the caveats in the existing literature. Only long-term, large-scale differences are accorded significant explanatory value. Rates generated by the data are not taken literally, but are used comparatively, both over time and cross-sectionally whenever changes in reporting and collection do not invalidate the results. These problems are discussed very well and convincingly by the scholars cited.[3]

One central question can never be fully resolved, given the lack of available data. This is the extent of correlation between officially recorded crime and actual levels of criminal behavior. Of course, official crime statistics do not mirror behavior. But rather than reject all use of this material, we can recognize, as a matter of common sense, that crime statistics are not totally divorced from reality, just as they are not totally reflective of it. Moreover, there is another reason for looking at the official data collected in the past — namely, that this information frequently served as the basis of popular perception and attitudes and thereby influenced public policy.

---

3. There have been several recent studies in the history of crime which have used statistics. Despite individual reservations about the validity of the data, all the scholars (except Tobias) have used criminal statistics. Some, such as John Beattie, are satisfied that the "dark figure," or crimes which will never be known to the historian, is a fairly constant multiple of reported crimes. Therefore, he implies, statistics do register significant changes in criminality over time. Gatrell and Hadden maintain that if the jurisdiction is sufficiently large and the timespan sufficiently long, then local changes in police manpower and policy will not interfere with analysis of the trends. Tobias, however, disagrees, and, in the only statistical part of his monograph, shows reported crime is affected by policy matters. The most significant works on the history of crime are J. M. Beattie, "The Pattern of Crime in England," *Past and Present* v.62, p.47 (1974); Beattie, "Towards a Study of Crime in 18th Century England: A Note on Indictments," in Paul Fritz and David Williams, eds., *The Triumph of Culture: 18th Century Perspectives* (1972) p.299; V. A. C. Gatrell and T. B. Hadden, "Criminal Statistics and Their Interpretation," in Anthony Wrigley, ed., *Nineteenth Century Society* (1972) p.336; Joel Samaha, *Law and Order in Historical Perspective: The Case of Elizabethan Essex* (1973); and Abdul Quaiyum Lodhi and Charles Tilly "Urbanization, Crime, and Collective Violence in Nineteenth Century France," 79 *Amer. J. of Sociology* (1973) p.296. An earlier attempt to deal with American crime statistics can be found in Roger Lane, "Crime and Criminal Statistics in Nineteenth Century Massachusetts," 2 *J. Soc. Hist.* (1968) p.156. One scholar who rejected crime statistics (while using a statistical argument) is J. J. Tobias, *Crime and Industrial Society in the Nineteenth Century* (1967). Perhaps the most elaborate statistical study of criminality in America is Eric Monkkonen's *The Dangerous Class.* (1975) Monkkonen uses matching techniques to identify the criminal class of Columbus, Ohio. Concerned with offenders, not offenses, Monkkonen successfully avoids the problem of the dark figure. A good statistical overview of female criminality in this period can be found in Estelle Brenda Freedman, *Their Sisters' Keepers: The Origins of Female Corrections in America* (Ph. D. dissertation, Columbia University, 1976) 6-39.

Comparing the incidence and type of crime in Massachusetts and South Carolina presents some problems. First of all, there was slavery. Slaves and free balcks were subjected to an entirely different penal code and mode of trial (I have analyzed elsewhere their experiences in the criminal justice system).[4] But whites could be prosecuted for crimes involving slaves and such crimes have no counterpart in the Bay State. Secondly, there is the problem of jurisdiction. Both states had two levels of criminal proceedings. The first was summary or trial without jury. In South Carolina, these trials were conducted by a justice of the peace or magistrate. Some town councils also heard minor cases. In Massachusetts, summary proceedings were conducted by a peace justice, trial justice or police court. Since complete records of summary jurisdiction do not exist, such cases are excluded from the comparison. Only the second type of proceeding — cases originally presented to the grand jury and (if brought to trial) heard by a petit jury — are considered.

But even this limitation poses complications. The jurisdiction of trial courts in the two states was not equivalent. Assaults and larcenies were almost invariably tried before a jury in South Carolina while in Massachusetts they could be heard by both justices and juries. Including summary jurisdiciton when known in Massachusetts changes the absolute incidence of offenses, of course, but does not significantly alter the general pattern.[5] Summary jurisdiction was less important in South Carolina (because the types of cases which could be heard in that manner were limited) so that the absence of such records is not crucial.

It would be possible to avoid these problems by studying only felonies, but even that solution would leave two problems unsolved. First of all, the reports of the attorney general in Massachusetts usually made no distinction between felonies and misdemeanors for such crimes as larceny. More significantly, felonies were an extremely small part of the total crime picture. To understand the concern about crime, to appreciate the impetus for building penitentiaries and correction houses and for establishing police forces, one must look at the entire spectrum of criminal behavior.

---

4. On slave justice see Michael Stephen Hindus, "Black Justice under White Law: Criminal Prosecutions of Blacks in Antebellum South Carolina, 62 *J. Amer. Hist.* 575 (1976).

5. The pattern remains similar because liquor-related offenses were the most significant in either jurisdiction. For summary jurisdiction, drunkenness was the most common offense. For jury trials, it was violations of the license law. Arrests for these offenses varied with the passage of liquor legislation.

There are also problems concerning the completeness of the data. Consistent with the manner in which justice in South Carolina was administered, there are no centralized judicial statistics, and many court records have not survived. In 1838, in an attempt to justify the state's need for a penitentiary, Benjamin F. Perry asked each district to prepare summaries of criminal trials since 1800.[6] If the district complied, and if the compilation has survived, those figures have been incorporated here. Other sources include court journals and grand jury findings. A fragment of the records of the Charleston court has survived so this vital urban district can be included.

The Massachusetts data are more complete. The attorney general's reports are a major source, but the method of reporting was not always consistent throughout the period. Moreover, the office was abolished from 1843 to 1848; for these reasons, only summaries for the 1830s and 1850s are reliable. The most consistent source — and the one, therefore, used to document changes over time in Massachusetts — is the annual report of the commitments to the jails and houses of correction. Since there is no counterpart in South Carolina, this material is not used comparatively. The advantage of the commitment reports is that they include all jurisdictions, even summary modes, as well as all institutions to which people were committed.[7] However, they only include people who were incarcerated at some stage between arrest and punishment. This is a more comprehensive group than obtainable from any other data source except arrest records, but the omissions are not randomly distributed but rather are influenced by such class-based factors as ability to make bail.

Now we can turn to the data itself. The first striking difference in the two states is the pattern of crime. A simple frequency distribution by category and offense illustrates the types of crime dominant in each state independent of rates of incidence. In South Carolina, in both the eighteenth and nineteenth centuries, assault cases dominated the dockets. (Tables 1-2) In Massachusetts, crimes against morality dominated in the colonial era. In the nineteenth century, property crimes — particularly those involving theft —

---

6. Benjamin F. Perry, *Report of the Special Committee . . . on the Subject of the Penitentiary System* (1839) p.18.

7. The returns for the jails and houses of correction include the commitments to the Massachusetts State Prison since convicts were placed in jail after arrest, while awaiting trial, and before removal to the prison. Statistics on removals from jails to other institutions are found in the later years. The reports of the Attorney General include trials heard in the Supreme Judicial Court, Court of Common Pleas, and Boston Municipal Court (which had the equivalent jurisdiction of Common Pleas, but for Suffolk County only).

Table 1. *Colonial Crime Patterns, Massachusetts and South Carolina (Percentage of total prosecutions by category)*

| | Location | | |
| | Essex County, Massachusetts 1651-1680 | Middlesex Co., Massachusetts 1760-1774 | South Carolina (Charleston) 1769-1776 |
Crime			
Murder		1.2	5.1
Assault		n.a.	48.3
Rape		n.a.	.2
Total, Crimes Against Persons	20.8	10.4	53.6
Larceny		13.9	28.8
Arson		.3	.4
Other Crimes Against Property		n.a.	8.6
Total, Crimes Against Property		14.2	37.8
Bastardy, Fornication	16.8	63.0	1.6
Riot, Vagrancy	6.8	n.a.	1.6
Total Crimes Against Order And Morals	23.4	63.0	3.2
Forgery, Fraud, Conterfeit	n.a.	1.2	2.4
Slave-related	n.a.	n.a.	3.1
Crimes Against The Church	32.7	8.0	—
Contempt of Authority	23.1	2.3	—
Total	100.0	10.0	100.1*
Number of Cases		370 (includes 31 misc.)	597 (includes 48 misc.)

* Rounding error

Sources: Essex County: Kai Erikson, *Wayward Puritans: A Study in the Sociology of Deviance* (New York, 1966), recomputed from data on p. 175. Middlesex County: William E. .Nelson, *Emerging Notions*, pp. 452-453. South Carolina: South Carolina Court of General Sessions, Journal (Charleston Sitting) 1769-1776 (Ms.), South Carolina Archives.

218   THE AMERICAN JOURNAL OF LEGAL HISTORY   Vol. XXI

Table 2. *Criminal Prosecutions in Nineteenth-Century*
Massachusetts and South Carolina

Crime	Massachusetts Prosecutions, 1833-58[a]		South Carolina Prosecutions, 1800-60[b]	
	Number	Per cent	Number	Per cent
Murder	103	.5	107	1.9
Assault	3768	16.8	3311	59.2
Rape	34	.2	21	.4
Total, Crimes Against Persons	3905	17.4	3439	61.5
Theft, Receiving	6639	29.6	872	15.6
Arson	174	.8	33	.6
Total, Crimes Against Property	6813	30.4	905	16.2
Nuisance, Riot, Vagrancy	1221	5.4	320	5.7
Drunkenness	365	1.6	—	—
License Law	7841	35.0	195	3.5
Sexual Offenses	1284	5.7	176	3.1
Other	—	—	7	.1
Total, Offenses Against Order and Morals	10,741	47.9	698	12.5
White Collar	970	4.3	55	1.0
Slave Related	—	—	497	8.9
Total	22,429	100.0	5594	100.0
Other	2299		552	
Grand Total	25,228		6146	

NOTE: Percentages may be subject to rounding error.

a. 1833-1838, 1849, 1851-1852, 1855, 1858

b. Spartanburg (1800-1860), Horry (1800-1835), Richland (1800-1835), York (1800-1860), Lexington (1810-1824), Laurens (1806-1835), Charleston (1857-1859), Chester (1806-1835). Complete statewide returns unavailable.

Sources: Massachusetts: *Annual Reports of the Attorney General,* Legislative Documents. South Carolina: Richland County Grand Jury Findings, York Cases, Spartanburg Sessions Index, Charleston Sessions Journal, South Carolina Archives; Lexington, Horry, Chester, Laurens, miscellaneous manuscripts, South Caroliniana Library.

became significant. White collar, financial crimes also increased in importance. But the single largest category in nineteenth-century Massachusetts was liquor-related offenses. This general description includes both violations of the licensing laws (the offense prosecuted most frequently in trial courts) and drunkenness (the offense for which the largest number of people were committed to jails and correction houses).

The South Carolina pattern shows a striking absence of crimes against property; the incidence of assaults conforms to the stereotype of Southern violence. The most serious crimes of violence — murder and rape — were proportionally more significant in South Carolina than in Massachusetts. The decline in the relative importance of crimes against property in South Carolina in the nineteenth century was a result of an expansion of the court system. In the period from 1769 to 1776, South Carolina had only two courts. In the nineteenth century, courts met twice a year in every district. Therefore, it became easier to instigate assault prosecutions. In South Carolina, then, the pattern of crime changed little over two centuries. In Massachusetts, however, there was considerable change, suggesting an inverse relation between crimes against morality and crimes against property. What are we to make of this transition?

One recent and widely-known interpretation of the historical evolution of crime in Massachusetts is by William E. Nelson. Using criminal prosecutions from 1760-1830, Nelson stresses a transition from crime as sin to crime as theft, or from morality to property. From 1760-1774, 38 percent of all prosecutions were for violations of sexual morality. Offenses against morality and religion together constituted 51 percent of all prosecutions. Only 13 percent were for crimes against property and 15 percent for crimes of violence. The revolutionary era represents something of a turning point. From 1790 to 1830, by contrast, 41 percent of all prosecutions were for crimes against property and only seven percent for crimes of morality.[8] Nelson relates this shift to a more general and simultaneous change in the Massachusetts legal system from ethical concerns (i.e., morals) in the colonial period to the protection of the bases of the commercial economy in the early nineteenth century (i.e., property). The data presented in this study certainly offer some support for Nelson's interpretation. But a more sensitive analysis shows that Nelson's explanation, while not incorrect, is an oversimplification. The nature, timing, and degree

---

8. William E. Nelson, *The Americanization of the Common Law: The Impact of Legal Change on Massachusetts Society, 1760-1830* (1975) pp.37-39, 118.

of this shift all become questionable when the data is examined in more detail.

First of all, let us consider crimes against morality. By the second half of the eighteenth century, when Nelson picks up the story, the concern of the legal system in prosecuting sexual offenses had already shifted from moral disapproval to economic interest. In the seventeenth century, courts prosecuted even the most minor, unthreatening deviations from moral norms. Of the prosecutions for sexual crimes in seventeenth-century Essex county, for example, 37.9 percent involved married couples with an early birth. Only 12.3 percent were bastardy cases.[9] Thus, in the seventeenth century control of behavior, not economic interest, was the primary motive for these prosecutions.

By contrast, in eighteenth-century Middlesex County, all but ten of 210 fornication prosecutions involved illegitimate births.[10] Since the economic interest of the town was at stake in such proceedings, seeing them strictly as prosecutions for sin is misleading. Prosecutions for bastardy continued well into the late nineteenth century. In short, the shift away from prosecutions for unambiguous crimes against morality happened earlier than Nelson describes.

There is an additional factor which must be considered. Nelson tends to divorce behavior from prosecution. That is, he implies that the shift from crime as sin to crime as theft occurs within the legal system, which changes its emphasis as reflected by prosecutions. But in the case of sexual behavior, we do have a rare opportunity to observe behaviorial changes and their impact on the legal system. Premarital pregnancy ratios are indicative of changes in sexual behavior. In the seventeenth century, for example, prosecutions increased as the ratio increased. In the eighteenth century, prosecution peaks also conform to peaks in the ratio. Unknowingly Nelson finds high rates of prosecution for sexual misconduct during something of a sexual revolution in Massachusetts, with nearly half of all brides pregnant at marriage. When Nelson finds a decline in prosecutions, the sexual practices were also changing. The year Nelson begins his research, 1760, was a demographically importune time to use for a major interpretation of legal change. In fact, the pattern of prosecutions for sexual offenses in eighteenth-century Middlesex County shows a greater peak on 1731-1735 than

9. Daniel Scott Smith and Michael S. Hindus, "Premarital Pregnancy in America, 1640-1971: An Overview and Interpretation," 5 *J. Interdisciplinary Hist.* 554 (1975).

10. William E. Nelson, "Emerging Notions of Modern Criminal Law in the Revolutionary Era: An Historical Perspective," 42 *N. Y. U. L. Rev.* 453n (1967).

that observed by Nelson for 1760-1774. Moreover, the interim decades show a significant decline in fornication prosecutions. Thus, looking over the entire eighteenth century, it is difficult to conclude that the period 1760-1774 was typical of the colonial pattern.[11]

These comments are not intended to invalidate Nelson's general findings, but rather to challenge the nature and timing of that shift, and to try to suggest ways in which it was linked to changes in proscribed behavior.

One part of Nelson's paradigm is clearly true. Offenses against morality were not pursued as vigorously in the nineteenth century as in the seventeenth and early eighteenth centuries. The routine, nonthreatening offenses were ignored by the nineteenth century, in part because they were now viewed differently by the general society, and in part, simply because the previous efforts at prosecution had failed. Despite rigorous efforts to ferret out all fornicators, premarital pregnancy ratios rose dramatically in the eighteenth century. Continued prosecution of this minor offense would have only served to undermine the law, rather than to control behavior.

While there was a gradual shift from crime as sin to crime as theft, it was quite different from that described by Nelson. First of all, the shift took two centuries, not a few decades. Secondly, it was related in part to evolving concerns in the legal system, but also to shifting patterns in behavior and society. Sexual behavior changed, as did the conditions which gave rise to crimes against property.

In a larger sense, crimes against morality never ceased to be a central concern of the legal system. What changed was the type of morality proscribed and prosecuted. Instead of premarital fornication, in the late eighteenth and nineteenth centuries, only the more serious and threatening sexual offenses were prosecuted, such as bastardy, incest, polygamy, bigamy, adultery and sodomy. The nature of offenses which were prosecuted shifted from private to public — almost literally from indoor to outdoor. The drunk, vagrant, prostitute or purveyor of spirits became far more important than the unwed parent or pregnant bride. These new "crimes" were certainly crimes against morality as much as they were crimes against the public order. Commitments for drunkenness and violations of the license law climbed steeply with the passage of restrictive liquor legislation; in effect, such legislation criminalized a common habit of a major segment of the population. The object of punishment for such crimes was not so much to cure behavior, but

---

11. Smith and Hindus, *ibid.* pp.537-539: George Elliott Howard, *A History of Matrimonial Institutions* (1904) v.2, p.193.

merely to rid the streets of the offensive presence of such people. Long-term confinement for such convictions was both unjust and prohibitively expensive. As an expedient compromise, drunks were arrested, released after a small fine and perhaps a night or two in jail, and then picked up again. Multiple arrests for drunkenness became the expectation.[12] One set of victimless crimes simply replaced another; morality prosecutions did not decline, but their focus and emphasis shifted.

In the context of the social history of Anglo-American law, seventeenth-century Massachusetts was somewhat unique in its insistence on prosecuting relatively minor sexual offenses in secular courts. South Carolina prosecuted no sexual offenses at all except bastardy — where the sexual politics of eighteenth-century child care was the main concern. Studies in early modern England indicate that morality prosecutions were insignificant in the civil courts and that crimes against property were dominant from 1550 on. Vigorous prosecution of crimes against morals was a product of the intentional fusion of church and state, not only in Massachusetts, but in such southern colonies as Maryland and Virginia as well, where sexual prosecutions were also common.[13] In early modern England, prosecutions for fornication were conducted by the church. This was also true in many colonies in the New World, but, unlike England, when the various religious sanctions proved insufficient, the state intervened as well.

In nineteenth-century Massachusetts, crimes against property — particularly theft-related offenses — sharply increased as a percentage of all prosecutions. This was in part the result of increasing social stratification and population concentration. Although geographic segregation by economic class was beginning to occur, cities and towns were still sufficiently compact so that

---

12. The *Annual Reports* of the Massachusetts Board of State Charities were filled with stories of people arrested literally dozens of times for drunkenness. See especially the *Sixth Annual Report* (1870) p.20. Note also that convictions and cases in trial courts for liquor-related offenses were dominated by violations of the license law while commitments to jails and correction houses were dominated by arrests for drunkenness. The difference, of course, is that drunkenness was tried summarily. Common Pleas and the Boston Municipal Court heard only cases involving common drunkards, or multiple offenders.

13. Samaha, *op. cit. supra*, note 3, p.19-20; Beattie, *op. cit. supra*, note 3, p.68-83; Gatrell and Hadden, *op. cit. supra*, note 3, p.365; David Flaherty, "Law and the Enforcement of Morals in Early America," *Perspectives in American History* v.5, p.203, see also Arthur P. Scott, *Criminal Law in Colonial Virginia* (1930) p.239 and Raphael Semmes, *Crime and Punishment in Early Maryland* (1938) p.174.

criminal and victim lived or worked in some proximity.[14] Many places experienced geographic specialization by economic function. Thus, large areas of port cities were predominantly commercial and provided opportunity for thefts.[15] Certain crimes, as nineteenth-century observers realized, were associated with advances in technology and with an increasingly complex commercial economy.[16] These were the white collar crimes — forgery, counterfeiting, extortion, embezzlement, and fraud. In contrast with Massachusetts, and indicative of the relative status of economic development, white collar crimes were virtually insignificant in nineteenth-century South Carolina.

What about the incidence of crime itself? Although one historian contends that crime declined in Massachusetts from the mid-nineteenth century on, the only consistent figures show the decline occurring after 1880.[17] What about the previous half-century? The total commitment rate to Massachusetts penal institutions fluctuated throughout the period with a peak in the mid-1850's. (Figure 1) If only offenses against persons and property are measured, however, then there was one substantial increase between 1837 and 1855, with no significant trend thereafter.[18] Therefore, there is no evidence of a decline in serious crime before 1880, but some evidence for a decline in minor crime.

From this data, one can see that the crime wave which followed the Mexican War was only part of a long-term upward swing which peaked well after the crime wave itself was popularized. Similarly, the celebrated post-Civil War crime wave was serious only in relation to the abnormally low rates during the war itself, with many men away at war and others given a choice between prison

14. Samuel Bass Warner describes Boston as a "walking city" in this period, *Streetcar Suburbs* (1962) p.16.

15. Roger Lane points out that the simultaneous growth of both cities and industry was somewhat unique to America; "Crime and the Industrial Revolution: British and American Views," 7 *J. Soc. Hist.* p.287 (1974); Richard D. Brown discusses urbanization in Massachusetts outside of Boston during this crucial period, "The Emergence of Urban Society in Rural Massachusetts, 1760-1820," 61 *J. Amer. Hist.* p.29 (1974).

16. Francis Lieber, *Remarks on the Relation Between Education and Crime in a Letter to the Rev. William White, D.D.* (1835) p.5.

17. Lane, "Crime and Criminal Statistics," Theodore N. Ferdinand, "The Criminal Patterns of Boston Since 1849," 72 *Amer. J. Sociology* p.87 (1967). Ferdinand uses police arrest records.

18. Commitments were not affected (in any way that can be determined) by the capacity of the institutions or by economic fluctuations. Correlations between commitment rates for property crimes and the Pearson-Warren Price Series and correlations between actual commitments and several different variables related to capacity yielded nothing of significance.

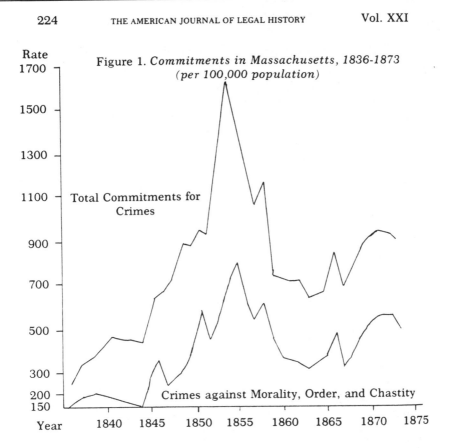

Figure 1. *Commitments in Massachusetts, 1836-1873 (per 100,000 population)*

and the army.[19] This crime wave sorely strained the capacity of penal facilities, caused substantial changes in pardoning and sentencing policies, and inspired the construction of a new state penitentiary. Therefore, it is noteworthy that it did not represent a substantial change in observed criminal behavior, particularly when one considers only commitments for serious crimes against persons and property.

What is the relationship between urbanization and the pattern and incidence of crime? The popular stereotype of cities as places in which crimes and sin are centered has been borne out to some extent for eighteenth-century Britain and nineteenth-century

---

19. As is shown below (Figure 2), female commitment rates rose during the Civil War as women were forced to support families. The increase in the commitment rate for females did not, however, offset the overall decline.

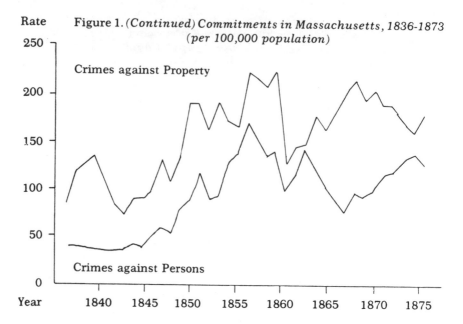

Figure 1. *(Continued) Commitments in Massachusetts, 1836-1873*
(per 100,000 population)

France.[20] Roger Lane, however, credits urbanization with reducing the rates of serious crime in nineteenth-century Massachusetts. But Lane reached his conclusion on the basis of statewide data only; he did not study crime within cities. Urbanization as the cause was strictly an ecological inference, since the decline in crime rates and the growth of cities occured simultaneously.[21]

Urban crime in Massachusetts was distinctive in two ways: its pattern and its incidence. Suffolk County, which consisted solely of Boston and Chelsea and is therefore a pure urban example, had from 13 to 18.2 percent of the state's population throughout this period. But from 24.9 to 51.4 percent of the commitments to the state's jails and houses of correction were in Suffolk County and from 31.4 to 43.7 percent of the verdicts in criminal cases were in Suffolk. Commitment rates were from 2.2 to 3.7 times as high as for the state as a whole. Of course, rates cannot reflect the fact that the number of people in a city at any given time may exceed its resident

---

20. Beattie, *op. cit. supra*, note 3, p.81; Lodhi and Tilly, *op. cit. supra*, note 3, p.306.

21. Lane, *op. cit. supra*, note 17: Monkkonen also finds certain crimes more closely correlated with urbanism, *The Dangerous Class*, p.34. Crimes of theft are highly correlated; crimes of violence much less so.

population. But these figures predate extensive daily commuting from "streetcar suburbs." To see urban crime simply as the result of such factors as high-density housing, high levels of transiency, and ethnic heterogeneity is tautological, since these features characterized life in nineteenth-century cities.

Both the commitment rates and the distribution of verdicts (Tables 3, 4) for Suffolk County point to a distinctive urban pattern of crime. Suffolk County had a disproportionate amount of theft; the rate in 1849-51 was eight and one-half times the state rate. Consistent with Boston's position as a major financial center, frauds, forgery, and counterfeiting proliferated. Ethnic tensions and street brawls account for the high proportion of assault and battery cases (showing that this was not strictly a rural phenomenon as anticipated from the South Carolina data). On the other hand, crimes of public order were less of a uniquely urban concern, although the rate of commitments was extremely high. The most salient fact about urban crime—and one which calls sharply into

Table 3. *Suffolk County Commitment Rates, 1839-1870*
(commitments per 100,000 population)

Crime	1839-1841	1849-1851	1859-1861	1869-1870
Murder	2.1	3.4	3.1	7.0
Assault	78.3	328.7	282.7	292.8
Rape	2.0	6.2	1.7	5.2
Total, crimes against persons	82.4	338.3	287.5	305.0
All theft	431.2	691.7	432.5	478.9
White Collar	23.0	14.9	3.0	28.8
All serious crimes	536.6	1044.9	723.0	812.7
Drunkenness, License Law	567.0	1034.8	701.0	1046.9
Sexual Offenses	128.4	137.5	39.3	49.1
Total, crimes against morals and order	695.4	1172.3	740.3	1096.0
Other	614.0	1236.5	181.5	213.3
Total	1846.0	3453.7	1644.8	2122.0

Sources: Computed from the annual *Abstracts of Returns from the Jails and Houses of Correction, 1833-1863*, Massachusetts Legislative Documents (none published for 1840). Data for 1869-1871 are from the Massachusetts Board of State Charities, *Annual Report*, 1869-1871, Massachusetts Public Documents.

Table 4. *Urban Crime Patterns: Percentage of Massachusetts*
Verdicts from Suffolk County, 1833-1858

Crime Total	1833-1839 31.4	1849-1858[a] 43.7
Above Average		
Assault (all)	39.1	49.5
Theft (all)	33.4	52.4
Brothels, Sexual Misconduct	34.4	61.0
Forgery, Counterfeit, Fraud	50.3	51.3
Arson	36.0	
Rape		50.0
About Average		
Murder, Manslaughter	27.3	42.9
Below Average		
Rape	0.0	
Arson		8.3
Nuisance, Vagrant	11.1	28.5
Drunkenness, License Law	26.4	34.4
N	3049	4271

[a] 1849, 1851-1852, 1855, 1858
Sources: *Attorney General Reports.*

question Lane's hypothesis about the civilizing effect of cities—is that Suffolk commitment rates were higher than those of the entire state for every crime and for every decade in the period.

This pattern was not universal to major commercial port cities. Charleston, South Carolina experienced a pattern similar to that of the state at large. In fact, the proportion of property convictions was lower than for the state as a whole. (Table 5) Did Charleston, like Boston, experience an inordinate share of the state's crime? Evidence is scanty and the criminal court handled cases from the entire Charleston district (including rural and outlying areas). But for 1859, Charleston's prosecution rate was 1417 per 100,000, or more than four times the state-wide maximum and very close to Suffolk's commitment rate for the same period (1645 per 100,000 in 1859-1861). While Charleston did not share Boston's tendency toward higher rates of crimes against property and white collar crime, the city did conform to the urban pattern of increased crime.[22]

---

22. One author reaches this conclusion using a slightly different calculation and also found that Charleston had a higher rate of larceny; Jack Kenny Williams, *Vogues in Villainy: Crime and Retribution in Ante-Bellum South Carolina* (1959) 2. In all likelihood, the difference involves categori-

228   THE AMERICAN JOURNAL OF LEGAL HISTORY   Vol. XXI

Table 5. *Urban Crime in South Carolina*

Crime	Distribution of Cases	
	South Carolina (excl. Charleston)	Charleston
Murder	2.1	1.2
Assault	59.1	57.1
Rape	.4	.1
Total, Crimes Against Persons	61.6	58.3
Theft	15.6	12.3
Arson	.5	.6
Total, Crimes Against Property	16.1	12.9
License Law	4.0	2.2
Sexual Offenses	3.5	1.2
Nuisance, Vagrant, riot	6.7	2.3
Total, Crimes Against Order and Morals	14.3	5.7
Forgery, Counterfeit, Fraud	1.0	.8
Liquor to Slaves		17.0
Slavery-related	6.8	5.3
Total, Slave-related	6.8	22.3
Total number above	4739	853
Other	522	32
Grand Total	5261	885

Source: Same as Table 2.

The most distinct divergence between the crime pattern in South Carolina in general and that in Charleston was in the slave-related offenses. Southern cities faced peculiar problems in slave control, as the Vesey Rebellion in Charleston had shown over three

zation; I have lumped together all animal thefts with larcenies. These, of course, are more common in agricultural and rural districts.

decades earlier. One of the specific justifications for establishing a police force in 1857 was to halt the sale of liquor to slaves, a commerce in which the old city Guard was alleged to have had a financial interest. The court records indicate the new police took this function seriously. While only seven of 1249 surviving indictments from 1800-1842 were for selling liquor to slaves, this offense accounted for almost one-sixth of all bills presented to the grand jury from 1857 to 1859.[23]

Although the crime patterns varied greatly in the two states, the total prosecution rates were comparable. Such a measure must be used with extreme caution, given the differences in jurisdictions. Nevertheless the data show that rates of criminal prosecutions in the two states were similar (Table 6). South Carolina had a slightly higher rate in the 1830's; this pattern was reversed in the 1850's.

Certainly there was concern about lawlessness in South Carolina, but it was largely a concern about violence. Grand jury presentments, the most reliable source of public sentiment about crime in the state, complained about assaults, duelling, and carrying concealed weapons.[24] Other major problems included violations of race control (such as trading with blacks), violations of morals (which were not indictable because they were not legally proscribed) and attacks on slave property (the wanton killing, beating, and stealing of slaves).

The complaints which did exist about crimes against property fell into two categories. The first decried the periodic raids and visits of robber gangs, horsethieves and swindlers. The second group dealt with local theft, and was viewed almost exclusively as the work of blacks.[25] Slave thefts were cited as the rationale for

---

23. There are two sets of criminal records for Charleston. Both are in the South Carolina Archives. The more reliable of the two is the Sessions Journal for 1857-1860 (although 1860 is not complete and is therefore, excluded). This is the source used in tables 2 and 7. Indictment rolls survive for the earlier period (1800-1842) but they are incomplete. They are used here to indicate changes over time in Charleston (where they are sufficiently indicative of trends) but not for the statewide calculations.

24. Presentments are comments to judge and legislature about the state of legal affairs in the districts. They are distinct from bills, which are indictments for crimes. Grand juries regularly issued presentments at the beginning of each court term. The presentments are in the Legal System Papers, South Carolina Archives. Each presentment contained from one to several dozen complaints; since they were issued twice annually in every district, the sum total amounts to several thousand comments on law, crime, politics, and social affairs. See also Richard Younger, *The People's Panel: The Grand Jury in the United States, 1634-1941* (1963).

25. Hindus, *op. cit. supra*, note 4.

stronger laws against trading with and hiring out slaves. Such petty thievery was rarely seen as the work of whites. With a ready pool of slave suspects, and the fact that thefts rarely occurred in a witness's presence, the cultural stereotype of slave thievery precluded acknowledgment of a white predatory class, and therefore contributed to the low rate of white prosecution for property crimes. Although the difficulty of discovering thieves in rural areas might account for the low rate of prosecutions, that would not explain Charleston's similar pattern or the lack of serious concern about white theft in thousands of presentments.

Table 6. *Rates of Criminal Prosecutions, Massachusetts and South Carolina (per 100,000 per year)*

Year	Massachusetts	South Carolina [a]
1800-1810		208
1811-1820		227
1821-1830		302
1831-1840		217
1834	180	
1835	168	
1836	153	
1837	148	
1838	198	
1841-1850		220
1849	277	
1851-1860		278
1851	275	
1852	250	
1855	311	
1858	223	

[a] 1800-1810: York, Spartanburg, Richland Districts.
  1811-1820: Same as 1800-1810, with Lexington added.
  1821-1830: Same, extrapolating Lexington from 1821-1824.
  1831-1840: Spartanburg, Richland (extrapolating from 1831-1835).
          York (extrapolating from 1831-1838).
  1841-1860: Spartanburg.
  Rates based on white population only.
  Sources: Same as Table 2.
  Annual population estimates compiled using compound interest table.

Finally, there is one more area in which cultural patterns and crime patterns converge. This concerns the sex of those who were prosecuted. One durable stereotype in southern history has been the idealization of white womanhood in the antebellum period. In Charleston, at least, women got off their pedestals to assault both sexes. Women accounted for 10.9 percent of all assault defendants from 1800 to 1842. In 41 percent of the cases, men were the alleged victims. The image of female virtue may have strengthened toward the end of the period. By 1857-1859 women had dropped to eight percent of assault cases and only 7.3 percent of all prosecutions. The comparable rate in Massachusetts was nearly twice as high (14.8 percent for 1866-1872). To the courts, however, women were still pristine. Few females ever went to trial. Only six out of 105 named for assault in the earlier period were tried. From 1857 to 1859 only 20 percent of females named in grand jury bills were tried for any crime, less than half of the rate for men (43.7 percent).

The pattern of female crime differed from that of Charleston as a whole in three respects. First of all, obviously the level of female crime was significantly lower. Secondly, females were under-represented in those crimes which depended either on participation in the economy or on positions of authority and dominance (Table 7). No females were indicted for forgery or retailing liquor without a license. Women were also underrepresented in selling liquor to slaves (frequently a crime committed by small merchants and tavern owners) and in slave-related offenses where the authority of the male as master was frequently at issue. Lastly, women were under-represented in crimes against morals and order. In Charleston, however, where crimes against morality were rarely prosecuted, this category was dominated by rioting and liquor-related offenses. The sex-related offenses for which Massachusetts women were so regularly committed had no counterpart in Charleston. Seven people were accused of maintaining a disorderly or bawdy house; only one was a woman, and her case was dropped.

In the Bay state, female defendants were seen primarily as sexual miscreants. Except during the Civil War, female commitment rates generally paralleled the total pattern (Figure 2), but at a lower level.[26] The percentage of female commitments for each crime

---

26. The two lines in figure 2 are not completely comparable. For the sake of consistency, the total commitment rate is the same as in figure one. The female commitment rate is based on all commitments, not those only for crime. Unfortunately, this is the only data available for females before 1866, when detailed breakdowns by offense are possible. The only difference is that the data used in figure one includes commitments for debt and examination, a negligible amount compared to commitments for crime. Nevertheless the female rates are slightly inflated.

Table 7. *Female Crime in Charleston, 1857-1859*

Crime	Females #	%	All #	%	Per Cent Female
Murder	3	4.6	9	1.1	33.3
Assault	39	60.0	487	57.1	8.0
Rape	0	0	1	1.1	0
Total, Crimes Against Persons	42	64.6	498	58.3	8.5
Theft	13	20.0	105	12.3	12.4
Arson	0	0	5	.6	0
Total Crimes Against Property	13	20.0	110	12.9	11.8
Nuisance, Riot, Vagrant	0	0	20	2.3	0
License Law	0	0	19	2.2	0
Sexual Offenses	1	1.5	10	1.2	10.0
Total, Crimes Against Order and Morals	1	1.5	49	5.7	2.0
Liquor to Slaves	6	9.2	145	17.0	4.1
Trading with slave	2	2.1	17	2.0	11.8
Other Slave-related	1	1.5	28	3.3	3.6
Total, Slave-related	9	13.8	190	22.3	4.7
White Collar (forgery)	0	0	7	.8	0
Total (above)	65	100.0	853	100.0	7.6
Other	0	—	32	—	0
Grand Total	65	—	885	—	7.3

Source: Charleston District General Sessions Journal, 1857-1859, South Carolina Archives.

Figure 2. *Female Commitment Rates in Massachusetts, 1840-1865*

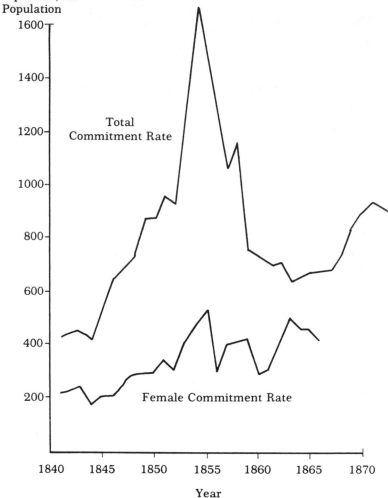

Rate per 100,000 Population

(Table 8) does reveal a pattern. Since only 15.3 percent of all commitments were female, one can assume that any crime for which at least 25 percent of those committed were female can be considered a significant offense for women. This was the case for 24 crimes in this period. With only two exceptions, female crimes

Table 8. *Female Commitments to Jails and Houses of Correction as Percent of All Commitments, Massachusetts, 1866-1873*

Crime	1866	1867	1868	1869	1870	1871	1872	1873
Murder	7.4	27.6	15.2	11.1	14.0	8.1	5.9	5.9
Manslaughter	0	22.2	30.0	16.7	0	6.7	0	0
Assault	12.3	12.5	9.6	9.5	9.2	7.5	8.2	7.3
Vagrancy, nuisance	26.0	23.8	28.1	27.1	24.2	21.4	25.4	24.4
Drunkenness	11.5	18.6	15.1	13.1	11.9	11.8	10.1	13.0
Larceny	23.8	20.2	21.1	18.4	16.5	14.6	15.2	13.2
Lewdness	18.3	31.3	27.3	21.2	21.2	15.6	23.0	31.8
Arson	7.1	8.3	15.5	4.3	22.6	23.7	19.0	9.7
Burglary	0	3.6	1.7	2.0	1.8	0	1.7	0
Forgery, counterfeit	7.2	3.3	8.3	2.8	7.9	0	2.6	0
Brothel	67.9	72.3	72.3	77.5	20.8	77.4	32.0	75.8
License law violation	19.7	19.0	23.4	18.9	13.5	12.6	9.8	8.8
Robbery	4.1	7.8	1.0	1.6	1.7	0	1.9	2.4
Fraud	4.7	4.5	8.7	12.5	9.4	10.1	4.3	8.5
Adultry	26.7	33.0	29.8	33.3	27.4	24.7	34.0	35.0
Breaking and entering	3.1	4.0	1.8	3.4	.9	1.7	.5	1.0
Other	28.0	29.3	27.3	32.7	29.9	18.8	19.7	21.6
Total	20.9	18.9	16.9	16.0	14.4	13.0	12.4	12.9

Source: Massachusetts Board of State Charities, *Annual Reports* 1865-1873.

were crimes of sexual misconduct.[27] Thus in each state, female criminality had a pattern distinct from the state as a whole, but conforming to regional cultural stereotypes about women.

The prosecution data point to two distinct contrasts. First of all, in Massachusetts there was a temporal shift from crimes against morality (and recall that even this category had some subtle changes within it) to crimes against public order and property. This change was linked to the rise of the urban-industrial order and also reflected new ideas about class inspired by the influx of immigrants. In South Carolina, where no such transformation occurred between the Revolutionary Era and the Civil War, there was no substantial variation in prosecutions. Secondly, in diametric opposition to the Massachusetts pattern, South Carolina criminal prosecutions were marked by a high level of personal violence and considerable anxiety about slave control.

There are three possible ways of interpreting this material. First of all, one can see the pattern of prosecutions as reflective of actual patterns of proscribed behavior, discounted by the "dark figure," which, for convenience, we take to be a constant. This would be a gross oversimplification. But we must bear in mind the changes in Massachusetts society which made crimes against property and propriety both more common and a likely response to new problems of poverty and anomie. Similarly, the societal underpinnings for a high level of crimes involving slaves and crimes against the person in South Carolina are also clear. While there is no exact correlation between behavior and prosecutions, there is a logical connection between social change and behavior.

Another way of viewing these patterns is to conceive of the legal system not as a mirror, passively reflecting behavior, but as an active intervenor, selecting certain types of proscribed behavior for special concern. This resembles the sociological maxim that prosecutions will reflect challenges to society's most important values.[28] Thus a commercial society, fearful of its unacculturated

---

27. Vagrancy was the charge for which prostitutes were arrested. For another discussion of this aspect of female criminality, see Freedman, *Their Sisters' Keepers*, 6, 34-36. The proportion of female criminality in eighteenth-century England was similar to that in nineteenth-century Massachusetts. See J. M. Beattie, "the Criminality of Women in Eighteenth-Century England," 8 *J. Soc. Hist.* 81 (1975). The pattern cannot easily be compared with the data here, since Beattie used serious offenses only. Monkkonen finds an increase in the proportion of female defendants during the Civil War in Columbus, Ohio, but the postwar levels are about half those observed here, *The Dangerous Class*, 62.

28. This concept appears in Kai T. Erikson, *Wayward Puritans: A Study in the Sociology of Deviance* (1966), ch.1.

236 THE AMERICAN JOURNAL OF LEGAL HISTORY Vol. XXI

immigrants, will place a heavy emphasis on prosecuting offenses against propriety and order, just as their Puritan antecedents were compelled to ferret out the fornicator. This compelling argument is insufficient, because it assumes there is no relationship between behavior and prosecutions, while such a relationship is clear with respect to sexual prosecutions in colonial Massachusetts.

To see prosecution patterns as the product both of actual behavior and of concern generated by the legal and social orders is the best interpretation. Thus, in nineteenth-century Massachusetts, crimes against property and order were prosecuted because they were both frequent and threatening. Similarly, in South Carolina, crimes involving slaves were endemic to a society which had a majority of slaves. In both states, these were the crimes most threatening to the social order.

But there are two more factors which need to be discussed before the picture is complete: slave prosecutions and criminal procedure. Prosecutions of white South Carolinians showed a noteworthy absence of crimes against property. Yet prosecutions of slave offenders show a concentration of crimes against property and order which is remarkably similar to that for Massachusetts. This suggests that South Carolina was neither free from nor ignorant of crimes against property, but believed them to be primarily the work of slaves. At the same time, in the mid-nineteenth century, Massachusetts was beginning to ascribe its crime problem to some not yet defined criminal class. At some risk of divorcing behavior from prosecutions, this comparison suggests similar social ascriptions for groups in similar positions in society.

Finally, as one looks at the three systems of law and justice—that of Massachusetts, that for slaves, and that for white South Carolinians—one finds that the meaning of prosecution varies. Criminal procedure is the key to understanding these differences. In Massachusetts, indictment was virtually tantamount to trial and conviction. Only 18 percent of those indicted were never tried and only 12 percent of those tried were acquitted. In South Carolina 37 percent were not tried and 29 percent were acquitted.[29] But South Carolina prosecuted its slaves much more seriously, with conviction rates similar to those of Massachusetts.[30]

These figures represent not simply the contours of crime, but also those of justice. Discretionary factors within the legal and criminal justice systems acted as a filter through which we see crime and the criminal. The patterns of prosecutions in the two

---

29. For a discussion of the meaning and significance of those figures, see Hindus, *op. cit. supra*, note 2, ch.5.

30. Hindus, *op. cit. supra*, note 4, p.586.

states indicate not merely different social values and behavioral patterns, but also contrasting conceptions of criminal law and public justice.

In the larger context, the explanation of these patterns of crime and justice can be found in the views on the role of formal law and authority held in each state. When one looks at authority as it operated on all levels—formal and informal, legal and extra-legal, traditional and bureaucratic—one finds that, by the nineteenth century, Massachusetts relied on formal legal authority for the orderly functioning of society. That state envisioned (and, indeed, strove to create) a legal system based on certainty, predictability and rationality. Such a legal system was deemed essential for the prosperity of the new economic order. Furthermore, in a society where immigration, outmigration, secularism and urbanization had effectively destroyed the old communitarian modes of life, legal, formal authority seemed to provide the only universally legitimized means of enforcing widely held values.

In South Carolina, by contrast, the powerful, entrenched slaveholding aristocracy reduced the role of the political and legal orders to a minimum. That elite consciously subordinated the legal system to a host of informal and extralegal arrangements, some of which were accorded official sanction. Only when issues of race relations and slave control proved too problematical for the informal network of authority did the legal system come to life. Where law in Massachusetts represented some notion of the popular will, in South Carolina the legal system was frequently used simply to legitimate informal, extralegal arrangements. Thus, criminal prosecutions represent more than the confluence of norms and behavior: they are important clues to the role of law in society.

[14]

POLICE AUTHORITY IN LONDON AND NEW YORK CITY 1830-1870

Policemen are a familiar feature of modern urban life, the most conspicuous representatives of the political and social order. However, until American society seemed to be falling apart in the mid-1960s, social historians on this side of the Atlantic gave only a passing nod to the cop on the beat.[1] Like other institutions which people have taken for granted, the police are products of distinct historical circumstances, the complex process of social discipline and resistance fostered by the industrial revolution. As Allan Silver points out, the police represented an unprecedented extension of the government into the lives of ordinary citizens.[2] Some people welcomed and others resented this extension, while at the same time its nature and degree varied in different societies. A comparison of the mid-nineteenth-century London police — the first modern full-time patrol force, created in 1829 — and the New York City police — the second such force outside of the British Empire, created in 1845 — reveals how different political and social developments influenced the principles and practices of police authority.

I

The statutes which established London and New York's police forces provided only a skeleton around which a definition of authority and a public image of the police could develop. Consequently London's Metropolitan Police owed much to Charles Rowan and Richard Mayne, the army officer and lawyer whom Sir Robert Peel appointed to head his new force, while the New York police were formed and reformed by a succession of elected and appointed officials throughout the mid-nineteenth century.[3] However much individuals may be credited or blamed for various aspects of the police, they worked within a social context which encouraged some responses and discouraged others. To understand the nature of police authority one must examine the societies which produced the forces.

Although the British metropolis was a much larger city than the "metropolis of the New World," both were heterogeneous cities marked by gulfs between wealth and poverty and recurrent social conflict. Michael Banton, to whom I am indebted for much of the conceptualization later in this article, argues that police authority reflects the degree of heterogeneity in modern societies. He finds that the stability of Scottish police authority reflects a culturally homogeneous society with widely shared expectations, while the instability of American police authority reflects a culturally heterogeneous society with few shared expectations.[4] However, it is difficult to maintain that nineteenth-century London was more homogeneous than contemporary New York. Disraeli spoke of England's "two nations, the rich and the poor" despite their ethnic homogeneity, and social conflict in London had more serious political implications than ethnic squabbles in New York. An examination of the *quality* of conflict in the two cities seems more promising for understanding the nature of police authority than an effort to measure their relative degrees of heterogeneity.

Formed in response to political violence and ordinary crimes against property,[5] the London force took to the streets amidst England's constitutional crisis over parliamentary representation for disenfranchised middle-class citizens. The politically-dominant landed aristocracy met the challenge from the industrial and commercial middle classes, backed by a reserve of working-class anger and violent protest, by tying them to the existing order through the electoral reform of 1832. The next challenge, fended off rather than co-opted, arose from various working-class groups dissatisfied with selecting "one or two wealthy men to carry out the schemes of one or two wealthy associations," the political parties under the new system of representation.[6] Culminating in Chartism, which included demands for universal suffrage, annually elected Parliaments and abolition of the property qualifications for M.P.s among its demands, working-class protest was defeated largely by the middle-class commitment to the social order. After a lull during the prosperous fifties and early sixties, working-class groups again demanded the franchise. Reflecting the increased economic power of workers organized into trade unions, the reform of 1867, another co-optive measure, gave urban workers the vote without altering the balance of social and economic power.[7]

Recurrent political crises were of profound importance to the police force charged with upholding the social order and controlling a turbulent population in the national capital, to which people looked with hope or apprehension in difficult times. Since disenfranchised protestors could have impact on Parliament only "out of doors" — demonstrations in the streets — policemen inevitable collided with them. Would these confrontations feed the fire of social conflict? Would the police be identified as the cutting edge of the ruling minority's oppression? Since their role was fundamentally political amidst challenges to the legitimacy of the government, the commanders of the force had to devise a strategy for containing conflict if they expected the new police to survive the Tory government which created them.

The New York police worked within a different context than their London brethren. New York was not a metropolis in the European sense, the seat of national government as well as center of culture and commerce. Except in the spectacular draft riots of 1863, Americans did not look to New York for the nation's political fate as Englishmen looked to London.[8]

New York did have its own local disorder, the ethnic conflicts which punctuated the era. While not as portentious as London's political disturbances, they did have consequences for the nature of police authority. The presence of large groups of immigrants in American cities gave a distinct tone

82

to class conflict. Antagonism between skilled and unskilled urban workers increased with the filling of the unskilled ranks by immigrants, especially Irish, in the mid-nineteenth century. Native-born workers, concerned about the degradation of their trades by industrialization, regarded the unskilled Irishman, willing to work for longer hours and lower wages, as an economic and social threat. This rivalry between elements of the working class undercut their sense of common interest against the employers. In fact, the native-born skilled workers who dominated American trade unions accepted the existing political system of representative democracy, believing that it gave all men an equal chance to rise in the world. The rowdy Irishman threatened to disrupt cherished institutions. Organized labor joined the propertied classes in denouncing the Irish draft rioters. While George T. Strong "would like to see war made on Irish scum as in 1688," the leading labor newspaper pictured them as "thieving rascals . . . who have never done a day's work in their lives."[9] The paper remarked, "The people have too much at stake to tolerate any action beyond the pale of the law. . . . No improvement can be made by popular outbursts upon the great superstructure created by the wisdom of our fathers."[10] In England such rhetoric was rarely embraced by working-men; America's propertied and working classes alike saw a political order they valued threatened by irresponsible foreigners who did not appreciate democracy.

Since the New York police upheld the political institutions of representative democracy which most Americans valued, there was little pressure for them to transcend social conflict to ensure their own survival. Instead of supporting the rule of a small elite which was challenged by the majority of London's population, the police supported a political order threatened by an alien minority. Thus to a great extent the police were free to treat a large group of the community as outsiders with little fear for the consequences as long as their actions coincided with most people's expectations.

What sort of police authority emerged from the different social circumstances of London and New York? In both cities pure repression was unacceptable, in London because of past failures and tendency to promote more violence, and in New York because it was unacceptable to American democracy.[11] In societies with representative governments, whether aristocratic like England or democratic like America, the police ultimately depend on the voluntary compliance of most citizens with their authority. As Edwin Chadwick said, "A police force . . . must owe its real efficiency to the sympathies and concurrent action of the great body of the people."[12] The commanders of the two forces had to define the institution to win this public support.

London's Police Commissioners, Rowan and Mayne, had an especially difficult task: they had to develop a force sufficiently strong to maintain order but also restrained enough to soothe widespread fears of police oppression. The combination of strength and restraint became the foundation of the

83

London Bobby's public image. To achieve acceptance the Commissioners
sought to identify the police force with the legal system, which embodied the
strength of national sovereignty and the restraint of procedural regularity and
guarantees of civil liberties. While the laws of England were hardly a pure
realm of justice above contemporary social inequality, they were the broadest
available source of external legitimation for the police.

Definition of the force as agents of the legal system made their authority
impersonal, derived from legal powers and restraints instead of from the local
community's informal expectations or the directives of the dominant political
party.[13] Amid social conflict the Commissioners, in their own words,
"endeavoured to prevent the slightest practical feeling or bias, being shewn or
felt by the police."[14] With varying levels of success during their long terms of
office Rowan and Mayne determined that "the force should not only be, in
fact, but be believed to be impartial in action, and should act on principle."[15]

Behind this commitment to impersonal authority was the strength the
police gained from being an independent agency of the national government.
The Metropolitan Police, created by Act of Parliament, had no links with
London's local government, and the Commissioners, appointed for life, were
responsible to the Home Secretary who exercised only a broad authority over
them. As a national institution the police could draw upon a reservoir of
symbolic as well as physical power. "Power derived from Parliament," said a
contemporary observer, " . . . carries with it a weight and energy that can
never be infused by parish legislation; and in respect of an establishment for
general security, it is doubly advantageous, by striking terror into the depred-
ator, and arming the officer with augmented confidence and authority."[16]
Similarly, "the mob quails before the simple baton of the police officer, and
flies before it, well knowing the moral as well as physical force of the Nation,
whose will, as embodied in law, it represents."[17] Although both the strength
and moral authority of the police required several years to develop, impersonal authority proved to be a secure foundation of police legitimacy.

Rowan and Mayne's notion of impersonality extended into many aspects
of their force's structure and practice. They made the police into a tightly-
disciplined body of professionals divorced from the localities they served.
The men were kept out of partisan politics (Bobbies could not vote until
1885) and were often recruited from outside of London. They wore a blue
uniform which further separated them from ordinary citizens. The Commissioners inculcated loyalty and obedience, enforced by quick dismissal for
infractions, expecting the men to be models of good conduct by subordinat-
ing their impulses to the requirements of discipline and the legal system they
represented. An observer of the 1850s vividly captured the police image:
"P.C. X 59 stalks along, an *institution* rather than a man. We seem to have no
more hold of his personality than we could possibly get of his coat buttoned
up to the throttling point."[18]

The New York policeman was less thoroughly molded than his London brother, but he did embody a distinct image which reflected conscious efforts as well as circumstantial results. His authority was *personal*, resting on closeness to the citizens and their informal expectations of his power instead of formal bureaucratic or legal standards.[19] Instead of having to rise above social conflict by indentification with the legal system, New York officials created a force which conformed to pre-existing, widely accepted patterns of democratic government. Survival of the new police depended originally on its ability to incorporate ideals of democracy in which authority was not only supposed to serve the people but also be the people. Until 1857, when the state government took over the force, it was directly controlled by popularly-elected local officials and policemen were recruited from the population of the district they patrolled. They did not wear a distinguishing blue uniform until 1853. As representatives of municipal instead of national government, the New York policeman did not have the symbolic authority his London colleague could invoke. Nor did he have the same reserve of physical force to back up his power: he was much more alone on the streets than his London colleague (New York always had fewer patrolmen in proportion to the citizens than London) and his effectiveness depended more on his personal strength than on broader institutional authority.[20]

New Yorkers rejected many important features of the London police as too authoritarian for democratic America. In the late fifties, the *Times* and Mayor Fernando Wood agreed that New York policemen were not as disciplined and efficient as their London brethren, but this was a necessary price of America's healthy social mobility and its citizens' independent spirit.[21] The New York patrolman was more a man than an institution because democracy suspected formal institutional power and professional public officials.[22] Paradoxically, lack of institutional power also meant lack of institutional restraints, and the personal New York policeman often ended up with more awesome power than his impersonal London counterpart.

II

The most important element of the distinction between the impersonal and personal approach is the amount of discretionary authority the patrolman exercised. Every policeman has to exercise personal discretion in his duties — decisions about when and how to act, whom to suspect and whom to arrest. Such choices are the most important part of his work, distinguishing the policeman from the soldier who does not act without direct orders.[23] Nevertheless, the commanders of the force and the judiciary set wide or narrow boundaries to discretion, and various public reactions to the police often center around the degree of discretion people think patrolmen should exercise. Consistent with his image of impersonal authority derived from the powers and restraints of the legal system, the London Bobby's personal discretion was more regulated than that of his New York colleague. Not as closely bound by the legal system, the New York patrolman often acted in the context of official and public toleration of unchecked discretionary power. The London policeman upholding an aristocratic, hierarchical society had more limits on his personal power than the democratic New York policeman.

The patrolman's most formidable discretionary power is his ability to use force to maintain his authority. The commanders of both the London and New York police warned their men to use lethal violence only for self-defense and prescribed punishments for violators of this essential principle.[24] In practice, however, the New York policeman's use of force was much less carefully monitored than in London.

As is well known, the London Commissioners carefully supervised Bobbies' use of force. They inculcated coolness and restraint, restricting the police arsenal to the truncheon. Except in unusually dangerous circumstances, London patrolmen never carried firearms. The Peelers could rely on muscle and blunt weapons partly because their antagonists were not usually more formidably armed, although revolvers seemed to be spreading in the underworld in the late sixties. There was some escalation of weaponry and incidents of unwarranted police violence did occur, but the Commissioners punished men who flouted their rule that restraint was the best way to win public acceptance of the force.[35]

New York's locally-controlled Municipal Police carried only clubs, but when the state government took over the force in 1857 — prompted by a mixture of reform and partisan motives — many New Yorkers violently expressed their hostility to the new Metropolitan force and the police replied in kind. Individual Captains encouraged their men to carry revolvers for self-protection against a heavily-armed underworld.[26] By the end of the 1860s, revolvers were standard equipment, although they were never formally authorized.[27] Guns seemed to be popping throughout the city, the civilians uncontrolled by effective legislation and the police unchecked by their superiors. The New York *Times* complained that shooting was becoming a substitute for arrest and described the patrolman as "an absolute monarch, within his beat, with complete power of life and death over all within his range . . . without the forms of trial or legal inquiry of any kind."[28] Amidst a vicious cycle of criminal and police violence, the patrolman was free to exercise much greater physical force than his London colleague.

Whether he made his arrest violently or quietly the New York patrolman consistently exercised broader personal discretion than the London Bobby. In both cities policemen had wide power to arrest people on suspicion of criminal intent, from stopping and searching people in the street to taking them to a magistrate for examination. Such arrests were more carefully scrutinized by police and judicial officials in London than in New York.

The London Commissioners reduced (although they did not eliminate) complaints of arbitrary arrest by warning their men to be extremely careful about whom they detained, directing that they pay attention to external

86

indicators of social class as a guide to their suspicions.[29] These guidelines did not lift police scrutiny from workers in middle- and upper-class neighborhoods and Parliament endorsed this use of police authority and later expanded stop-and-search and arrest powers.[30] However, the judiciary contributed to control of police discretion by carefully checking patrolmen's grounds for arrest, and higher courts directed that people could be detained without formal trial and charges for only five days in normal circumstances or a maximum of two weeks in unusual cases.[31] Generally magistrates' committals of suspects for jury trial did not keep pace with London's population growth during the 1830-70 period, possibly reflecting declining crime or the shift of many petty offenses to Justice of the Peace's summary jurisdiction from 1847 to 1861.[32] However, since the conviction rate in higher courts in proportion to magistrates' committals *increased* during the period, and higher court convictions in proportion to policemens' arrests also increased, it is quite likely that policemen were arresting and magistrates committing people on grounds that were increasingly firm over the years.[33]

Contemporary American observers testified to London's cautious use of arrest on suspicion when they mistakenly reported that Bobbies could arrest only for overt acts.[34] George W. Walling, who joined the New York force in 1848, said that "A New York police officer knows he has been sworn in to 'keep the peace,' and he keeps it. There's no 'shilly-shallying' with him; he doesn't consider himself half-patrolman and half Supreme Court judge." He did not hesitate to arrest on suspicion even if it were "often a case of 'giving a dog a bad name and then hanging him,' — men being arrested merely because they are know to have been lawbreakers or persons of bad character."[35] Moreover, the Police Justices (elected Justices of the Peace) did not check this aggressiveness. Judges in over-crowded courts did not take time to investigate police charges, tacitly encouraging hasty or arbitrary arrests on suspicion by accepting police testimony without oath or corroboration, refusing prisoners the opportunity of defending themselves, and failing to inform them of their rights or frightening them into confessions.[36] People arrested on suspicion were usually held in the Tombs, but the magistrates also allowed the police to confine them in the station house while they "worked up a case" against them.[37] There was no time limit for detention on suspicion until a reforming judge instituted the English practice in the early 1850s. This seems to have satisfied the New York Prison Association, which had led a public outcry against abuses of detention on suspicion, but it did not attempt to change other practices.[38]

Discretion played an important part in arrests for overt acts as well as on suspicion. Checks could help prevent arbitrary arrests because sometimes both London and New York patrolmen charged people with disorderly conduct when their offense was merely unruliness or disrespect for the officer's authority.[39]

Rowan and Mayne warned Bobbies that "No Constable is justified in

87

depriving any one of his liberty for words only and language however violent towards the P.C. himself is not to be noticed . . .; a Constable who allows himself to be irritated by any language whatsoever shows that he has not a command of his temper which is absolutely necessary in an officer invested with such extensive powers by the law."[40] They put teeth into the warning by forbidding desk officers to discharge people arrested for disorderly conduct who promised to behave in the future. Thus they prevented policemen from using the disorderly conduct charge to scare people into respecting them without having to bring a weak case before the magistrate. The only grounds for station house discharge was false arrest, which had to be reported immediately to Scotland Yard.[41] Although they never eliminated arbitrary disorderly conduct arrests (an epidemic of them broke out in the sixties), the Commissioners kept them in check.[42]

The commanders of the New York force also expected their men to be calm under provocation, and a high official said that disorderly conduct arrests were covered by "a good many rules."[43] However, there is little to suggest that such arrests were limited in practice. A journalist contended that they usually depended "exclusively upon the fancy of the policeman," who had "a discretionary power that few use discreetly."[44] New York patrolmen made many more disorderly conduct arrests than their London brethren. In 1851 they made one for each 109 people; London officers made one for each 380 people. In 1868-69, New York's absolute number of disorderly conduct arrests was greater than London's: 14,935 compared to only 2,616 in the much larger British metropolis.[45] Although there is plenty of evidence that New York was more rowdy than London,[46] the great discrepancy probably reflects London's discouragement of disorderly conduct charges. The heads of the New York force left disposition of patrolmen's charges, without any special checks on disorderly conduct arrests, up to station-house desk officers.[47]

New York patrolmen's free hand for disorderly conduct arrest may illustrate the use of personal action to compensate for lack of institutional authority. Patrolmen could not arrest for assault without a warrant unless they had seen the attack or the victim was visibly wounded. London policemen labored under a similar restriction until they were granted full powers in 1839. In New York, arrests for disorderly conduct may have compensated for limitations of arrest for assault.[48]

After arrest and lock-up came police interrogation and evidence-gathering. Earlier discussion of arrest on suspicion revealed that in New York there was little regulation of these practices. Judges readily accepted police evidence with little concern about how they obtained it. Moreover, the police had no scruples about obtaining confessions by entrapment or "strategem."[49]

In London all levels of the criminal justice system scrutinized interrogation and evidence-collection. With judges and high officials looking over their shoulders, the Commissioners reiterated warnings against false incrimination or distortion of evidence in the courtroom.[50] Repetition of such warnings suggests that policemen engaged in improper practices, but the men at the top were determined to keep them in line.

Until the 1850s, English courts were extremely sensitive about police interrogation, especially inducement of prisoners' confessions by promises or threats. Their concern may have been a carry-over from the days of a harsh penal code when confession of even minor crimes brought death or transportation for life.[51] The Commissioners' directives to their men reflected this sensitivity.[52] Sometimes Bobbies took such cautiousness too much to heart, preventing voluntary confessions because they feared criticism from judges and defense counsel.[53] Following a Court of Queens' Bench decision in 1852, judges began to relax their restrictions on confessions, increasingly accepting prisoners' statements as evidence against them. Nevertheless the Attorney General of England and the Police Commissioners were concerned that patrolmen not carry this too far by presenting all incriminating statements as confessions.[54] The courts seem to have returned to earlier strict interpretations in a case of 1865, and the police fell into line.[55]

Official concern was important because of the power of the police within the criminal justice system of England — they served as public prosecutors, taking charge of serious cases in the higher courts with jury trial as well as petty cases before magistrates. In New York, serious cases left police hands after arrest and became the popularly-elected District Attorney's responsibility. He decided whom to prosecute and how to conduct the case. Critics charged that he was lenient towards his constituents and abused "plea bargaining," which allowed criminals to escape deserved punishment by pleading guilty to lesser offenses.[56] New York policemen, with greater leeway in arrest and interrogation practices than their London brethren, had less power over the outcome of serious cases. Because of the police role in the courtroom, the London Commissioners realized that suspicion of deceit or prosecutorial bias would undermine public acceptance of the force. Watchfulness at all levels of the criminal justice system satisfied a Parliamentary inquiry that England did not need a public prosecutor like the American District Attorney.[57]

The trial is the last stage of police participation in the administration of criminal justice. Police-judicial relations are important for understanding patrolmen's attitudes toward discretionary power and procedural regularity. From their viewpoint, their most significant relationship with judges is how many arrests are rewarded with convictions. A vital element of the policeman's psychology, convictions make the officer feel that his job is worthwhile, giving meaning to his work by validating his judgment to arrest a person. Having made a quick decision, he finds it hard to admit error.[58] Low convictions in proportion to arrests can make policemen into frustrated antagonists of the judiciary, ready to substitute street-corner justice for procedural regularity.

89

London Bobbies often criticized judicial decisions, but the Commissioners insisted that they keep their comments to themselves and required strict decorum and impartiality in the courtroom.[59] Perhaps more significant, convictions for all crimes in the higher and lower courts increased relative to arrests during the mid-nineteenth century. Averaging about 45 percent of arrests during the 1830s and 1840s, convictions rose to around 55 percent of arrests during the 1860s.[60] Bad in the early years of the force, police-judicial relations improved after 1839, with settlement of a jurisdictional dispute between the Commissioners and magistrates.[61] Increasing convictions suggest that police and judicial standards of proper procedure were moving toward each other.

Although judges in New York made few procedural demands on policemen, from the early days of the force and increasingly after state takeover of the police in 1857, police officials complained of bad relations with the judiciary and charged judges with leniency toward major and minor offenders alike.[62] Lacking statistics comparable to those of London, it is difficult to evaluate these accusations. Available information indicates high conviction rates for drunkenness and vagrancy, slightly fewer convictions for petty larceny compared to arrests than in London, very few assault and battery convictions and in more serious crimes during the 1860s about one conviction for every three arrests.[63] Judges seem to have been more lenient toward serious than petty offenders, whereas in London conviction rates were generally higher for serious crimes.[64] Paradoxically, judges seemed to have overlooked arbitrary arrest practices but let many offenders off. This may have been a last-minute effort to regulate the police — Police Justice Michael Connolly was a crusader against brutality[65] — but the absence of clear guidelines for the police made patrolmen and judges into adversaries.[66] They never moved toward a single standard of conduct.

III

Looking back over the survey of police practices, we have seen the London patrolman's impersonal authority resting on control of discretionary power through the legal system and the directives of the judiciary and heads of the force. In contrast, the New York policeman's personal authority rested on unregulated discretion and less concern for working within legal restraints. The two forces did not develop their images in isolation. As part of the societies which created them, public perceptions of crime and the role of the police were important underpinnings of their authority.

Recognizing that various classes or groups would react differntially to the police, the London Commissioners hoped that the new force had "conciliated the populace and obtained the goodwill of all respectable persons."[67] On the whole they achieved this goal, although antagonism to the force remained in 1870.

"Respectable persons" were not always middle-class, but the Victorian middle classes did see themselves as custodians of respectability. Although hardly united in interest and outlook, the groups composing the middle classes would have shared suspicion of a police too closely linked to the landed aristocracy. They accepted aristocratic domination of politics as long as it was not oppressive. They were always ready to criticize arbitrary policemen, but as their own political influence consolidated over the years, they came to see Bobbies mainly as useful servants for coping with the various unpleasantries of urban life. Rowan and Mayne noticed that predominantly middle-class complaints against the police shifted from oppressiveness to inefficiency during the 1830s. They had to remind complainants that policemen lacked legal power to do many of the things that were expected of them.[68]

The middle classes came to depend for protection and peace and quiet upon an institution which fostered social stability by the restrained exercise of power. Karl Polanyi's argument that the fragility of the industrial and commercial economy tied to the stock market made riotous disorder intolerable in the nineteenth century applies to repressive violence as well. "A shooting affray in the streets of the metropolis might destroy a substantial part of the nominal national capital . . . , stocks collapsed and there was no bottom in prices."[69] In England the military, not the mob, had done the shooting in the past. A police force which contained disorder with a minimum of violence increased people's sense of security and contributed to economic stability. Generally, London's propertied classes believed that public order was steadily improving in the metropolis. Commentators recognized that police restraint as well as power contributed to this orderliness.[70] In the Sunday trading riots of 1855 in Hyde Park, when policemen got out of hand and brutalized innocent spectators as well as participants, the London *Times* joined radical working-class papers in condemning police excesses. The lesson was clear: respectable citizens as well as the populace expected restraint.[71] The middle classes, seeing themselves as the repository of such virtues, usually took pride in a police force with a reputation for respectability and "habitual discretion and moderation of conduct."[72]

During the sixties, a period of economic uncertainty and working-class unrest, "respectable" fear of crime and disorder mounted. The garotting or mugging scare of 1862, the reform riot of 1866 and increasingly violent robberies along with hunger riots in the winters of the late sixties made Londoners question police efficiency. Significantly complaints focused on lack of manpower and the declining quality of recruits, poor administrative methods and excessive bureaucratization and militarization, instead of demands for arming the police or allowing them broader discretion than the law defined.[73] Parliament's response was tougher laws for the police to enforce rather than a redefinition of the force's impersonal authority. Alan Harding is right in calling some of the harsher provisions of the Habitual Criminals Act of 1869 (aimed at the paroled convicts whom most people

91

blamed for the crime wave) "positively medieval," but the act was a precise
administrative control which judges interpreted strictly, continuing to
monitor police discretionary power.[74] The new law expanded authority but
also defined its limits. The police themselves recruited more men, reformed
administrative procedures and after Mayne's death in 1868, expanded the
detective division which he had always distrusted.[75] They did not resort to
violence or unregulated discretionary power. Although strained by a crime
wave, impersonal authority was still viable.

Having obtained and retained the "good will" of at least most "respectable
persons," could the police achieve the more formidable goal of conciliating
"the populace?" Although working-class reaction to the police was as varied
as the often conflicting and competing groups which made up the proletariat,
generally a working man or woman was more likely to see the police (whom
they preferred to call "crushers" instead of "Bobbies") as masters instead of
servants. Subordination of the force to the legal system simply meant that it
was part of the apparatus which upheld "one law for the rich, another law for
the poor." This view that the scales of justice were weighted in favor of the
rich and powerful, and only slightly less so toward the middle classes, was the
most common theme of working-class social criticism.[76] The Commissioners'
concern for the rights of "respectable" Londoners meant that social class was
often the basis of police treatment of citizens. Although the Bobby was
expected to be polite to "all people of every rank and class," a writer friendly
to the police could say, "although well-dressed people always meet with
civility . . . it is possible that the ragged and the outcaste may occasionally
meet with the hasty word or unnecessary force from the constable, who is for
them the despot of the streets."[77] The other side of the coin is that some
workers felt that the police were ignoring their neighborhoods, allowing disorder they would not tolerate in "respectable" areas.[78] This partly reflected
the dangerousness of some rookeries and dockland slums, but also the
Commissioners' policy of "watching St. James's while watching St. Giles's"
— patrolling slum areas not to protect the inhabitants from each other, but to
keep them from infiltrating nearby prosperous neighborhoods.[79] Workers
could complain of both too much and too little police power. Their feelings
came out in the popular music-hall songs of the sixties, such as "The Model
Peeler," an off-color account of police oppression and dereliction. "Oh, I'm
the chap to make a hit,/No matter where I goes it," runs the chorus; "I'm
quite a credit to the force,/And jolly well they knows it./I take folks up,
knock others down,/None do the thing genteeler,/I'm number 14, double X,
And called the Model Peeler."[80] Impersonal authority, like so much else in
Victorian England, seemed reserved for "respectable" people.

Nevertheless, the force does seem to have worked toward conciliating "the
populace." Except among persistently antagonistic groups like the costermongers,[81] the police did achieve at least a grumbling working-class acquiescence to their authority. By the 1860s, there was more violence against

92

them in the music halls than on the streets.[82] Partly this acquiescence reflected the clearly-established power of the force — "People feel that
resistance is useless," Mayne declared. However, the police also made some
effort to reduce working-class antagonism. Their concern for restraint in
handling political demonstrations was one (imperfectly achieved) aspect.
They also deliberately stayed as much as possible away from the enforcement of Sunday blue laws, which working-class Londoners bitterly resented
as middle-class dictation of their life style. This was not a case of failure to
enforce existing laws, for that would undermine police subordination to the
legal system, but of successfully lobbying in Parliament against new measures
which evangelical Sabbatarians sought in the Victorian era.[83] Upholding a
hierarchical social order, the police never won the "good will" of the working
classes, but because they rejected pure repression the Commissioners achieved
at least acquiescence to police authority. The force had authority, not mere
power.

Across the Atlantic the reactions of both middle- and working-class New
Yorkers to the police were more ambivalent than in London. By limiting the
force's institutional power but tolerating broad personal discretion, New
York's officials revealed a distrust of institutions but great trust in men.
Alexis de Tocqueville argued that democratic Americans impowered their
officials with broad discretion because they elected them, being able to
remove them if they were dissatisfied. In aristocracies like England, on the
other hand, appointed officials independent of both rulers and ruled had to
have more formal checks on their discretion to prevent oppression.[84] Although New York policemen were never themselves elected, they were at first
directly and after 1853 indirectly accountable to elected officials and the
broad directives of public opinion remained their guidelines instead of formal
limitations of their personal power.

Turning from theory to public reactions to the police, Tocqueville's
notion is complicated by the institutional rivalry of the police and judiciary.
"Respectable" New Yorkers, although they criticized democracy's immersion
of the force in partisan politics and sought to move it closer to London's
independent professionalism,[85] usually sided with the police in their controversy with the judiciary, which often owed its position to local, in many
cases working-class Irish, constituencies. This taking of sides was most pronounced after state (Republican) take-over of the police in 1857, while the
Police Justices remained in the unclean (Democratic) hands of local politicians who courted the votes of ignorant and impoverished immigrants. Thus,
to a great extent, the propertied classes formed the constituency of the police
force, while the propertyless made up the support of the lower levels of the
judiciary, the Police Justices. Recurrent quarrels between police officials and
judges were contests, to some extent before but especially after 1857,
between representatives of different class and ethnic constituencies. Such
battle lines had been occasionally drawn in the early years of the London

93

force, but rarely later on.

Since respectable citizens did not expect justice from the courts, they turned to policemen, tolerating their broad personal authority in the war against crime. Although one's view of the police often depended on one's politics, this toleration frequently transcended partisanship. If to put down crime, said the Democratic *Herald* in 1856,"it were necessary for us to have a Turk as Chief of Police, we, for our own parts, would go for the Turk, turban, Koran and all."[86]

A later journalist remarked of John A. Kennedy, the tough Republican General Superintendent of the Metropolitan Police, that although called "king Kennedy" among "the masses," respectable citizens regarded him more highly. "He has often exceeded his power, and has committed acts that smack strongly of petty tyranny; but there can be no doubt of the fact that he has earnestly and faithfully labored for the cause of law and order."[87] A little petty tyranny was acceptable in the interests of law and order, especially in light of "a general, and perfectly natural feeling in the community, that it is a postive godsend to get rid of one of the many scoundrels who infest our streets, by any means and through any agency possible" when people lacked faith in "the capacity or common honesty of our legal tribunals."[88] New York was a violent city, whose disorder seemed to be steadily outstripping a police force plagued with manpower shortages and disciplinary problems. Citizens worried about the well-armed politically influential lumpenproletarian "volcano under the city."[89] Violence and distrust of the courts placed a premium on physical force and personal authority instead of London's restrained impersonal authority. Democratic ideology and disorder combined to create a policeman who often seemed more authoritarian than aristocratic England's London policeman.

How did New York's largely Irish immigrant "masses" view the police? James Richardson suggests that they had fewer grievances against the locally-controlled Municipal Police than the state-controlled Metropolitan Police. Nevertheless, the large number of Irish patrolmen in Irish wards, because of the Municipal force's local residency requirement, did not guarantee smooth relations with the working-class Irish public. Irish officers often arrested their countrymen for petty offenses, and complaints of violence or improper arrest, averaging some 29 a year between 1846 and 1854, were not much fewer when Irish officers confronted their countrymen than when WASP policemen dealt with Irish citizens.[90] Common ethnicity may not have been sufficient to overcome class antagonism — policemen seem to have been recruited from skilled workers while the people they arrested were predominantly unskilled laborers.[91] Relations worsened under the state-controlled Metropolitan Police, despite a proportion of Irish patrolmen similar to the levels of the old force.[92] Hatred of the new force, often politically motivated, underlay much of the draft rioters' ferocity, to which Irish policemen replied, in kind, earning the gratitude of respectable New Yorkers.[93] Irish Democrats'

94

antagonism to the Republican state force, roused by judicial and journalistic champions, resembled London radicals' hatred of the police in the 1830s. The anger was as much against whom the police represented as what they did.

The Metropolitan Police do not seem to have made efforts to reduce Irish working-class hostility. Their enforcement of Sunday laws, as bitterly resented by immigrants in New York as by London workers, increased hostility to the force. The old Municipal Police had ignored blue laws except under sporadic Sabbatarian pressures; the Metropolitans, responding to sustained Sabbatarian influence, enforced strict new measures which roused the opposition and evasion of normally peaceful Germans as well as the volatile Irish. The police could not claim impartiality when they enforced laws passed by one group against another's customs and amusements. Eventually enforcement of the blue laws broke down, becoming a convenient tool for Boss Tweed to keep saloon keepers in line and a lucrative source of pay-offs for all levels of the police force. Such corruption seems only to have increased "respectable" criticism without significantly improving relations with the working classes.[94]

IV

Although she wrote before the creation of New York's force, Harriet Martineau captured the difference between London and New York's police. She identified the English police as "agents of a representative government, appointed by responsible rulers for the public good," and the American police as "servants of a self-governing people, chosen by those among whom their work lies."[95] The London policeman represented the "public good" as defined by the governing classes' concern to maintain an unequal social order with a minimum of violence and oppression. The result was impersonal authority. The New York policeman represented "a self-governing people" as a product of that self-government's conceptions of power and the ethnic conflicts which divided that people. The result was personal authority.

Wilbur R. Miller
Princeton University.

This article is a revised and enlarged version of a paper presented at the American Historical Association convention in New York, December 1971.

NOTES

1.   Notable exceptions are Selden D. Bacon's unpublished Ph.D. dissertation (Yale, 1939), "The Early Development of American Municipal Police," and James F. Richardson's dissertation (New York University, 1961), "The History of Police Protection in New York City, 1800-1870," which was not published until 1970 as part of his book, *The New York Police: Colonial Times to 1901* (New York, 1970).
2.   Allan Silver, "The Demand for Order in Civil Society: A Review of Some Themes in the History of Urban Crime, Police and Riot," in David J. Bordua, ed., *The Police: Six Sociological Essays* (New York, c. 1967), 12-14.
3.   For Rowan and Mayne, see Charles Reith, *A New Study of Police History* (Edinburgh, 1956) and Belton Cobb, *The First Detectives and the Early Career of Richard Mayne, Commissioner of Police* (London, 1957), both *passim*. Rowan served 20 years (1829-50), Mayne almost 40 years (1829-68). For the administrative history of the New York Police, see Richardson, *N. Y. Police*, chs. 2-7.
4.   Michael Banton, *The Policeman in the Community* (New York, 1964), esp. ch. 8.
5.   For background on the London police, see Charles Reith, *The Police Idea: Its History and Evolution in England in the Eighteenth Century and After* (London, 1938) and Leon Radzinowicz, *A History of English Criminal Law and its Administration from 1750*, 4 vols. (London, 1948-68), vol. IV.
6.   Walter Bagehot, *The English Constitution* (New York, n.d., first pub. 1868), 14 (quotation).
7.   For English political history see, e.g., Asa Briggs, *The Making of Modern England, 1784-1867: the Age of Improvement* (New York, 1965), chs. 5-10.
8.   For the significance of America's federal system in violence and its control, see David J. Bordua, "Police," in David L. Sills, ed., *International Encyclopedia of the Social Sciences*, 17 vols. (New York, c. 1968), XI, 175-76; Richard Hofstadter, "Reflections on Violence in the United States," in Hofstadter and Michael Wallace, eds., *American Violence* (New York, 1971), 10.
9.   George Templeton Strong, *Diary*, quoted by Richardson, *N. Y. Police*, 141-42; *Fincher's Trades Review*, July 25, 1863, quoted by David Montgomery, *Beyond Equality: Labor and the Radical Republicans 1862-1872* (New York, 1967), 106-07.
10.   *Fincher's Trades Review, loc. cit.*
11.   F. C. Mather, *Public Order in the Age of the Chartists* (Manchester, c. 1959), chs. I, III; Richardson, *N. Y. Police*, ch. 2.
12.   Edwin Chadwick, "On the Consolidation of the Police Force, and the Prevention of Crime," *Fraser's Magazine* 67 (Jan., 1868), 16. Full discussion of the consensual basis of police power is in Silver, "Demand for Order," 6-15.
13.   My contrast between impersonal and personal authority (discussed below) is my distillation of several writers' ideas, most importantly from Banton, *Policeman in the Community*. See also James Q. Wilson, *Varieties of Police Behavior: the Management of Law and Order in Eight Communities* (Cambridge, Mass., 1968), chs. 4-6, and Jerome Skolnick, *Justice without Trial: Law Enforcement in Democratic Society* (New York, c. 1966), 42-70. The impersonal and personal models are meant to be a rough guide, not precise definitions.
14.   Commissioners to J. Scanlon, March 2, 1842, Metropolitan Police Records, Public

96

Record Office 1/41, letter 88301 (hereafter cited as Mepol).

15.   Parliamentary Papers 1839, XIX, First Report, Constabulary Force Commissioners (hereafter cited as PP), 324. Rowan was one of the authors.

16.   Anon., "Principles of Police, and Their Application to the Metropolis," *Fraser's Magazine* 16 (Aug., 1837), 170.

17.   Anon., "The Police of London," *London Quarterly Review* (July 1870), 48, quoted by Silver, "Demand for Order," 14.

18.   A. Wynter, "The Police and the Thieves," *Quarterly Review* 99 (June 1856), 171; also quoted by Silver, "Demand for Order," 13-14. The writer goes on to say that off-duty, one sees the men as human beings: their public and private roles are separated. For the various features of the London police mentioned in this paragraph, see, e.g., Reith, *New Study*, chs. X-XIII.

19.   See note 13 above.

20.   In 1856, New York had one policeman per 812 citizens, London one per 351 (N. Y. City Board of Aldermen Documents, 1856, XXIII no. 10, Mayor's Annual Message, 35) (hereafter cited as BAD). For later complaints of shortages, see N. Y. State Assembly Documents, 1859, II no. 63, Metro Police Annual Report 1858, 6-7 (hereafter cited as AD), and Edward Crapsey, *The Netherside of New York: or, the Vice, Crime, and Poverty of the Great Metropolis* (New York, 1872), 12. For the features of the police mentioned in this paragraph, see Richardson, *N. Y. Police*, chs. 3-5.

21.   N. Y. *Times*, Dec. 9, 1857, 4; BAD 1856, XXIII no. 10, Mayor's Annual Message, 33-34.

22.   For the general mid-nineteenth-century suspicion of expertise, see Daniel Calhoun *Professional Lives in America: Structure and Aspiration 1750-1850* (Cambridge. Mass., 1965), 4-15, 193-94; also Andrew Jackson's famous fears that professional officials would lose touch with the people and threaten the democracy in which "the duties of public officers are, or at least admit of being made, so plain and simple that men of intelligence may readily qualify themselves for their performance" (James D. Richardson, comp., *A Compilation of the Messages and Papers of the Presidents*, 22 vols. [New York, c. 1897, ed. of 1915], III, 1012).

23.   Among the most important discussions of police discretion are Banton, *Policeman*, 127-46; Skolnick, *Justice*, ch. 4; Wayne R. LaFave, *Arrest: the Decision to Take a Suspect into Custody* (Boston, 1965), *passim*; and Joseph Goldstein, "Police Discretion not to Invoke the Legal Process: Low-Visibility Decisions in the Administration of Justice," *Yale Law Journal* 69 (1960), 543-94.

24.   Wynter, "Police and Thieves," 170; Police Orders (London) Sept. 6, 1832 (hereafter cited as PO), Mepol 7/2, folio 93; Aug. 21, 1830, Mepol 7/1, ff. 95-96. For New York, *Rules and Regulations for Day and Night Police of the City of New-York; with Instructions as to the Legal Powers and Duties of Policemen* (New York, 1846), 6; *Ibid.*, 1851, 6-7; *Manual for the Government of the Police Force of the Metropolitan Police District of the State of New York* (in AD 1860, II no. 88), 90.

25.   Charles Reith, *British Police and the Democratic Ideal* (London, 1943), 36; PP 1834, XVI, Metro. Police, test. Rowan, 12, q. 180; Kellow Chesney, *The Victorian Underworld* (London, 1970), 111, 119; [Thomas Wontner], *Old Bailey Experience* (London, 1833), 338; *Lloyd's Weekly Newspaper*, May 10, 1868, 6.

26.   Richardson, "History of Police Protection," 305-08; N. Y. *Herald*, July 14, 1857, 1; July 15, 1857, 1. Apparently some Municipal Policemen had carried pistols on dangerous assignments. William Bell, ms. *Journal* 1850-51 (New York Historical Society) describes an all-out battle with some rescuers of his prisoner. He intimidated them with his pistol, but in the ensuing affray the gun miraculously never went off. In 1857 one Captain told a reporter that George W. Matsell, Chief of the Municipal Police, had "made it a standing rule to look upon every man as a coward and unfit to be put a second time on duty, where he had descended to the use of a pistol" (*Herald*, July 15, 1857, 1).

27.   James D. MacCabe, *The Secrets of the Great City: A Work Descriptive of the Virtues and the Vices, the Mysteries, Miseries and Crimes of New York City* (Philadelphia, 1868), 72.

28.   *Times*, May 10, 1867, 4; Nov. 18, 1858, 4 (quotation).

29.   PO March 8, 1830, Mepol 7/1, f. 243; April 9, 1831, *Ibid.*, f. 193; Aug. 4, 1831, Mepol 7/2, f. 20; PP 1837, Third Report, Criminal Law Commissioners, App. I, test. Mayne, 20.

30.   In the Metropolitan Police Act of 1839, and the Habitual Criminals Act of 1869. There were enough fears of police power, however, that the 1839 Act's stop-and-search provisions were not adopted outside of London. See Delmar Karlen, Geoffrey Sawer, Edward M. Wise, *Anglo-American Criminal Justice* (New York, 1967), 116.

31.   PO March 1, 1843, Mepol 7/8, f. 259; PP 1871, XXVIII, Metro. Police Annual Report 1870, 8; N. Y. State Senate Documents, 1856, II no. 97, Police Investigation (hereafter cited as SD) test. J. W. Edmonds, 166.

32.   J. J. Tobias, *Crime and Industrial Society in the 19th Century* (London, 1967), 227-28. Contemporaries often used declining committals to verify their belief in declining crime, but modern students agree with Edwin Chadwick that committals reflect the reporting and prosecution of crime more than its actual occurrence. Chadwick, "Preventive Police," *London Review* 1 (Feb. 1829), 260-62.

33.   The basis of this conclusion is the committal and conviction figures in the Parliamentary *Returns of Criminal Offenders* before 1855 and the *Judicial Statistics*, 1856 on. See also sources cited in note 60 below.

34.   M. H. Smith, *Sunshine and Shadow in New York* (Hartford, 1868), 180-81; George W. Walling, *Recollections of a New York Chief of Police* (New York, 1887), 196.

35.   Walling, *loc. cit.*

36.   SD 1856, II no. 97, Police Investigation Report, 3; test. Abraham Beal, General Agent New York Prison Association, 103-04; test. Police Justice Daniel Clark, 43; AD 1849, VI no. 243, Annual Report, N.Y. Prison Association 1848, 59 (hereafter cited as NYPA); AD 1850, VIII no. 198, NYPA 1849, 25-26.

37.   SD 1856, II no. 97, Police Investigation, test. Police Justice G. W. Pearcey, 15, 23-24; test. Capt. G. W. Walling, 91-92; test. ex-Police Justice W.J. Roome, 34; SD 1861, II no. 71, test. Metro. Police Supt. J. A. Kennedy, 6-9.

38.   For criticisms see AD 1849, VI no. 243, NYPA 1848, 44; AD 1850, VIII no. 198, NYPA 1849, 25-26. The NYPA dropped its attacks after the early fifties.

39.   "Necessity is the mother of invention," *Punch* quipped, "so when you find it necessary to make a charge against somebody you have locked up, invent one." *Punch's Almanack for 1854*, 4, in *Punch's 20 Almanacks 1842-1861* (London, 1862?). Paul Chevigny, *Police Power: Police Abuses in New York City* (New York, c. 1969), ch. 8, discusses "cover charges" like disorderly conduct in the modern context.

40.   PO June 3, 1830, Mepol 7/1, ff. 63-64.

41.   PO July 13, 1833, Mepol 7/2, f. 152.

42.   See PO Jan 4, 1863, Mepol 7/24, 12; Sept. 30, 1865, Mepol 7/26, 275; Sept. 12, 1866, Mepol 7/27, 287.

43.   *Rules and Regulations*, 1851, 38; *Manual*, 1860, 90; SD 1861, II no. 71, Police Investigation, test. Metro. Comm. T. C. Acton, 29 (quotation).

44.   Crapsey, *Netherside*, 27; SD 1861, II no. 71, Police Investigation, test. Police Justice J. H. Welch, 14.

45.   1851 figures: PP 1852-53, LXXXI, Arrest Statistics, 290; BAD 1856, XIII no. 16, Chief's Semi-Annual Report, 12-13. I computed the ratios from London's estimated population, 1851, in the above source and New York's 1851 population in Joseph Shannon, comp., *Mannual of the Corporation of the City of New York* 1868 (New York, 1869), 215. London 1869 figures are in PP 1870, XXXVI, Metro. Police Annual Report 1869, table 5, 18 (listing "disorderly characters" which I have assumed to be the same as disorderly conduct). N. Y. figures are in AD 1870, II no. 16, Metro. Police

Annual Report 1869, 74. The disparity of these latter figures is all the more impressive considering that London was over twice as populous as New York.

46. See below, note 89.

47. SD 1861, II no. 71, Police Investigation, test. Comm. T. C. Acton, 25.

48. The policy is set forth in *Rules and Regulations*, 1846, 39; and *Ibid.*, 1851, 55. The phrasing is verbatim from London's PO June 25, 1833, Mepol 7/2, f. 14. The *Manual*, 1860 is silent on assault powers.

49. SD 1856, II no. 97, Police Investigation, test. Capt. J. Dowling, 149; Walling, *Recollections*, 38-39.

50. PO July 26, 1851, Mepol 7/15, f. 290; Feb 26, 1869, Mepol 7/31, 58; Memo of 1854 by Mayne, Mepol 2/28, loose.

51. For judicial sensitivity, see the case of *Regina v. Furley*, Central Criminal Court 1844, in *1 Cox's Criminal Law Cases* 76. The court construed the policeman's traditional warning to suspects that what they say may be held against them as a threat or inducement to confession. For possible impact of old harsh laws, see PP 1845, XIV, Eighth Report, Criminal Law Commissioners, App. A, letter of H. W. Woolrych, 281.

52. PO Nov. 3, 1837, Mepol 7/5, f. 284.

53. PO May 15, 1844, Mepol 7/9, f. 245; PP 1845, XIV, Eighth Report, Criminal Law Commissioners, App. A, letter of Lord Chief Justice Denman, 211; William Forsyth, "Criminal Procedure in Scotland and England" (1851) in *Essays Critical and Narrative* (London, 1874), 41-42.

54. The case is *Regina v. Baldry*, Court of Queen's Bench 1852, in *2 Dennison's Crown Cases Reserved* 430. See also James Fitzjames Stephen, *A History of the Criminal Law of England*, 3 vols. (London, 1883), I, 447. For Commissioners' views, Mayne's 1854 memo, Mepol 2/28; the views of Attorney General A. J. A. Cockburn are in PP 1854-55, XII. Public Prosecutors, 186, q. 2396.

55. PO Sept. 22, 1865, Mepol 7/26, 268; Jan. 2, 1866, Mepol 7/27, 13.

56. AD 1866, III no. 50, NYPA 1865, 128, 134, 150; AD 1865, III no 62, NYPA 1864, 222; Alexander Callow, *The Tweed Ring* (New York, c. 1965), 148.

57. See PP 1854-55, XII, Public Prosecutors, report and testimony.

58. William A. Westley, *Violence and the Police: A Sociological Study of Law, Custom, and Morality* (Cambridge, Mass., c. 1970), 81-82; Albert J. Reiss, Jr., *The Police and the Public* (New Haven, 1971), 134-38.

59. PP 1837-38, XV, Police Offices, test. Rowan, 101, q. 1078; PO Nov 29, 1829, Mepol 7/1, f. 241; Nov 5, 1830, Mepol 7/1, f. 130; July 9, 1834, Mepol 7/3, f. 45; Sept 27, 1837, Mepol 7/5, f. 279; July 26, 1851, Mepol 7/15, f. 290; Memo of 1854, Mepol 2/28, loose; PO May 13, 1865, Mepol 7/26, 138.

60. I have computed these approximate percentages from statistics in Anon., "The Police System of London," *Edinburgh Review* 96 (July 1852), 22 (1831-41); Joseph Fletcher, "Statistical Account of the Police of the Metropolis," *Journal of the Statistical Society* 13 (1850), 258 (1842-48); PP 1871, XXVIII, Metro. Police Ann. Report 1870, 21 (1850-70).

61. See Reith, *New Study*, 150-51; Radzinowicz, English *Criminal Law*, IV, 172ff.

62. BAD 1852, XIX pt 1 no. 7, Chief's Semi-Annual Report, 107; SD 1856, II no. 97, test. Capt. J. W. Hartt, 101; Capt. J. Dowling, 157; AD 1861, I no. 27, Metro. Police Ann. Report 1860, 6; AD 1867, VII no. 220, Metro. Police Ann. Report 1866, 11-12.

63. Tenth Precinct Blotter, May 25-Aug. 27, 1855; July 27-Aug. 26, 1856, Ms, N. Y. City Municipal Archives; SD 1861, II no. 71, Police Investigation, test. Comm. T. C. Acton, 27; J.W. Edmonds, 163-64. Arrest figures for assault and battery and petty larceny are found in the police annual reports. They can be compared with convictions for these offenses in the Court of Special Sessions published in Shannon, comp., *Manual* 1868, 178. Convictions for "simple larceny" in London were 54 percent of arrests in 1868; for petty larceny in New York 29 percent of arrests in 1868-69. Convictions for

99

"common assault" in London in 1869 were 55 percent of arrests compared to New York's 8 percent for assault and battery in 1868-69. (See AD 1870, II no. 17, Metro. Police Ann. Report 1869, 24 [arrests] ; AD 1870, VI no. 108, Ann. Report of the Secretary of State on Criminal Statistics 1869, 144-46 [convictions] ; PP 1870, XXXVI, Metro. Police Annual Report 1869, table 5, 18). Comparison of N. Y. felony arrests and convictions is in AD 1867, VII no. 20, Metro. Police Annual Report, 1866, 11-12.

64.   This is based on a comparison of the proportion of convictions in indictable offenses and offenses summarily tried by a magistrate in the Parliamentary *Judicial Statistics*, 1856-70.

65.   See N. Y. *Times*, April 14, 1867, 5; N. Y. *World*, Feb. 11, 1867, 4.

66.   For this remark I am indebted to a letter from James Richardson, commenting on an earlier draft of this paper.

67.   PO Oct. 15, 1831, Mepol 7/2, f. 41.

68.   See statement (of which I could not locate the original) quoted in Reith, *British Police*, 183, and Comms. to Home Office Jan 6, 1835, Mepol 1/17, letter 27751. By 1835 complaints in the Mepol letter books are overwhelmingly of alleged neglect of duty. Later Mayne wrote to H. Fitzroy, Sept. 29, 1853: "The public now expect to see a constable at all places at every moment that he may be required." (Mepol 1/46, n.p.).

69.   Karl Polanyi, *The Great Transformation* (New York, 1944), 186-87, phrase order rearranged.

70.   Some contemporary comment on orderliness in the 1850s includes Charles Dickens, "The Sunday Screw," *Household Words* 1 (June 22, 1850), 291-92; *Illustrated London News* 18 (May 31, 1851), 501 and June 28, 1851, 606, on working-class orderliness at the Great Exhibition; Wynter, "Police and Thieves," 173. On the police role, see Frederic Hill, *Crime: Its Amount, Causes, and Remedies* (London, 1853), 6-7; Anon., *The Great Metropolis*, 2 vols., 2nd ed. (London, 1837), I, 11; PP 1837-38, XV, Police Offices, test. Rowan and Mayne, 183-85, qq. 2091, 2094, 2102; PP 1854-55, X, Sale of Beer, test. Mayne, 86, q. 1138. See also Silver, "Demand for Order," 5.

71.   London *Times*, July 3, 1855, 8; *Reynolds's Newspaper*, July 29, 1855, 8; *Lloyd's Weekly Newspaper*, July 8, 1855, 6. According to the *Times*, July 16, 1855, 12, overt antagonism to the police was short-lived. The riots are discussed by Brian Harrison, "The Sunday Trading Riots of 1855," *Historical Journal* 7 (1965), 219-45.

72.   Anon., "The Metropolitan Police and What Is Paid Them," *Chambers's Magazine* 41 (July 2, 1864), 424.

73.   Good accounts of complaints and the state of the force are in the *Times*, Dec 29. 1868, and in "Custos," *The Police Force of the Metropolis in 1868* (London, 1868).

74.   Alan Harding, *A Social History of English Law* (Baltimore, 1966), 366; W. L. Burn, *The Age of Equipoise: A Study of the Mid-Victorian Generation* (New York, c. 1965), 176-94.

75.   J. F. Moylan, *Scotland Yard and the Metropolitan Police* (London, 1929) 150-57. For Mayne's distrust of detectives, see, e.g., Memo to Superintendents, Jan. 23, 1854, Mepol 2/28, loose. Mayne did turn more to detection in the sixties than earlier, but his successor as Commissioner, Col. E. Y. W. Henderson, considerably expanded the detective force. See PP 1870, XXXVI, Metro. Police Ann. Report 1869, 3-4.

76.   For expressions of this grievance, see *Illustrated London News* 3 (Dec. 23, 1843), 406; see also *Reynolds's Newspaper*, May 2, 1852, 8; July 25, 1858, 9; Aug. 17, 1862, 4; April 5, 1863, 4; Feb.9, 1868, 4; *Lloyd's Weekly Newspaper*, July 5, 1863, 1; Thomas Wright, *Our New Masters* (London, 1969, first pub. 1873), 155-56.

77.   PP 1830, XXIII, Instructions to Metro. Police, 11; Anon., "Metropolitan Police," 426. Cf. Mrs J. C. Byrne, *Undercurrents Overlooked*, 2 vols. (London, 1860), I, 51, 54-55.

78.   *East London Observer*, June 6, 1868, 5; July 4, 1868, 4; Dec. 5, 1868, 4.

79.   For danger, Chesney, *Victorian Underworld*, 92-93; Byrne, *Undercurrents*, I,

78-79; James Greenwood, *The Wilds of London* (London, 1874), 1, 56. For police policy, PP 1834, XVI, Metro. Police, test. Rowan, 11, qq. 165-67; *Hansard's Parliamentary Debates* 1830, n.s. vol. 25, col. 358; and Anon., "Police System of London" (1852), 9. Study of the distribution of the London police reveals the most policemen usually in neighborhoods where poverty rubbed shoulders with wealth.

80.   "The Model Peeler" by C. P. Cove, *Diprose's Music-Hall Song-Book* (London, 1862), 50. Cf. the number Mrs Byrne heard in 1860 in *Undercurrents*, I, 256-57.

81.   For the costermongers, see Henry Mayhew, *London Labour and the London Poor*, 4 vols. (2nd. ed., 1862-64), I, 22.

82.   For workers as leaders of the early opposition, see *Hansard's Parliamentary Debates* 1833, 3rd. ser. vol. 16, col. 1139; PP 1833, Cold Bath Fields Meeting, test. Supt. Baker, C Division, 159, qq. 3914, 3917; J. Grant, *Sketches in London* (London, 1838), 391.

83.   Mayne states his outlook on this problem succinctly in PP 1867-68, XIV, Sunday Closing, 8, qq. 127-28.

84.   Alexis de Tocqueville in Francis Bowen, ed., *Democracy in America*, 2 vols. (2nd ed., Cambridge, Mass., 1863; first pub. in U.S. 1835-40), I, 265-68.

85.   See Richardson, *N. Y. Police*, chs. 3-5, 7.

86.   N. Y. *Herald*, March 25, 1856, 4.

87.   MacCabe, *Secrets*, 70-71. The *Herald*, however, did not like the Republican Superintendent, calling him "Mr. Fouche' Kennedy" (Dec. 22, 1860, 6).

88.   *Times*, Nov. 18, 1858, 4, editorializing on the first killing of an offender by a patrolman.

89.   William O. Stoddard's *The Volcano under the City* (New York, 1887) is an account of the draft riots which reminds its readers that the volcano is still simmering. For similar imagery see Samuel B. Halliday, *The Lost and Found: or, Life among the Poor* (New York, 1860), 332; and Junius Henri Browne, *The Great Metropolis: A Mirror of New York* (Hartford, 1869), 74. On New York's violence, see Richardson, "History," 393ff.; *Times*, May 10, 1855, 4; AD 1859, II no. 63, Metro. Police Ann. Report 1858, 14; AD 1865, II no. 35, Metro. Police Ann. Report 1864, 11-13; Crapsey, *Netherside*, 29-30; and especially Charles Loring Brace, *The Dangerous Classes of New York, and Twenty Years' Work among Them* (New York, 1872), arguing that New York could claim "elements of the population even more dangerous than the worst of London" (p. 25).

90.   The figures are rough calculations based on the surnames of officers and complainants in the Complaints against Policemen, 1846-1854, City Clerk Papers, N. Y. C. Municipal Archives.

91.   This conclusion rests on fragmentary records, the Applications for Positions as Policemen 1855, Boxes 3209-10, City Clerk Papers, N. Y. C. Municipal Archives. Of 43 successful applicants, only 3 were unskilled laborers and 7 drivers or other transport workers. Twenty-two were various sorts of skilled workers, one a mechanic, five shopkeepers, five clerks or other white-collar workers. The arrest statistics in the police reports reveal the overwhelming preponderance of unskilled offenders.

92.   For the increase of Irish officers in the Metropolitan Police after a decline in 1857-58, I counted Irish surnames in the lists in D. T. Valentine, comp., *Manual of the Corporation of the City of New York* (New York, 1848-68) for 1856 (last year of the old force), 1858 and 1861 (the last year policemen's names are listed).

93.   See AD 1864, III no. 28, Metro. Police Ann. Report 1863, 13. Joel Tyler Headley, *The Great Riots of New York 1712-1873* (New York, 1873), 305-06, and MacCabe, *Secrets*, 70-71, praise the Irish policemen.

94.   See Richardson, *N. Y. Police*, 52, 57, 110, 154-56, 182-85.

95.   Harriet Martineau, *Morals and Manners* (Philadelphia, 1838), 192. Here "police" refers to the old constabulary and night watch system which preceded modern forces in America.

101

[15]

The Historical Journal, 29, 1 (1986), pp. 87–107
Printed in Great Britain

PRIVATE DETECTIVE AGENCIES AND LABOUR DISCIPLINE IN THE UNITED STATES, 1855–1946*

ROBERT P. WEISS

State University of New York: Plattsburgh

As a professional and bureaucratically organized institution of social control, the police in the United States originated less than 150 years ago. Traditionally, this development has been explained as an inevitable response to a dramatic rise in felonious crime.[1] According to this type of account, a criminal reaction was a natural by-product of such factors as urbanization, immigration, and industrialization. Other investigators have disputed this interpretation, arguing that there is little evidence to support the occurrence of a crime wave. Rather, the municipal police in America originated as part of a larger class control apparatus designed to regulate working class social and political activities, including 'subversive' speeches, strikes, riots, and daily breaches of the 'public order'.[2] Those who argue that the 'new police' developed as a crime fighter typically neglect to discuss one of the oldest forms of professional policing in the nation, the private detective agency.

From the mid-nineteenth century private detective businesses policed on behalf of corporations, and in doing so they had a considerable impact on industrial relations for over seventy years. This paper investigates the origin, development, and major transformations of private detective industrial policing in the United States. The early development of the private detective agency was largely concerned with helping provide a disciplined supply of labour to power capitalist industrialization, and its transformation was a result of changes in the nature of the political economy as these affected the 'labour question'.

Our analysis will begin with a historical sketch of the origin and early labour discipline activities of the nation's most prominent policing business, the Pinkerton National Detective Agency. Successive sections will delineate major

---

* This is a revised version of a paper prepared for the Past and Present Society Colloquium on 'Police and Policing', History Faculty Library, Oxford, 8 July 1983.

[1] Roger Lane, 'Urban police and crime in nineteenth-century America', in *Crime and justice: an annual review of research*, vol. 2, ed. N. Morris and M. Tonry (Chicago, 1980); Roger Lane, *Violent death in the city: suicide, accident, and murder in nineteenth-century Philadelphia* (Cambridge, Mass., 1979); James F. Richardson, *The New York police, colonial times to 1901* (New York, 1970); E. H. Monkkonen, 'A disorderly people? urban order in nineteenth and twentieth centuries', *Journal of American History*, LXVIII (December 1981), 536–59.

[2] T. Platt et al., *The iron fist and the velvet glove* (Berkeley, 1982); E. Parks, 'From constabulary to police society', *Catalyst*, v (1970), 76–96; S. L. Harring, 'Class conflict and the suppression of tramps in Buffalo, 1892–1894', *Law and Society Review* no. 11 (1977), 873–911.

developments in the history of private detective agency labour work. Altogether, one can discern three distinct phases or periods in the development of labour policing. These phases reflect developments of the state and economy in relation to labour discipline, and their demarcation will provide a basic structure for this paper. First, the continous policing of labour was almost the sole responsibility of private detectives until the First World War. This was followed by a period during which a war-bolstered Federal Bureau of Investigation joined the effort, forming with private police a two-front assault that helped thwart progressive unionizing efforts until the Great Depression. Thirdly, a major transformation in private policing occurred when, at the time of the La Follette Senate investigations in the late 1930s, the bulk of labour discipline was shifted from private detective agencies (and corporate security divisions) to representatives of big labour unions, with an assist from the FBI and the underworld. Labour bureaucrats then assumed many of the duties of the detective agency.

The final recognition of trade unionism was contingent upon changes in the nature of capitalism, that is, with changes in the way privately owned productive enterprises related to the state and by the values and beliefs of the period. This is a difference between laissez-faire and liberal corporate capitalism. The New Deal brought a new discipline under corporate liberalism. The importance of the labour contract under these different forms of capitalism was pivotal, and we will sketch its changing significance.

I

Born in Scotland in 1819, Allan Pinkerton immigrated to Chicago, Illinois in 1842 to escape imprisonment for Chartist activities. After serving as a deputy sheriff for Kane and then Cook counties, he accepted an appointment in 1850 as Chicago's first city detective. In the same year he established his own detective agency, and from then until emancipation was largely engaged in the escape of slaves. Whilst Pinkerton was busy with the Underground Railroad, he initiated in 1855 the first labour spy service in the United States by providing 'spotters' to detect thieving and lazy employees for his earliest and most lucrative client, the transportation industry. Later, in one of the most infamous ethnic betrayals, he was to expand his espionage service and employ an Irishman to expose the purported leaders of a 'secret labour society', the 'Mollie Maguires'.

Mr Pinkerton developed his expertise in organizational espionage during service for the Union during the Civil War. As the first Chief of the United States Secret Service, he dispatched Agency detectives to infiltrate Confederate ranks to obtain information on troop movements and enemy strength. 'Secret operatives' also served in Washington as counter-intelligence agents. This detective force was the federal government's earliest intelligence agency. Though as an intelligence agent Pinkerton showed imagination and daring,

PRIVATE DETECTIVES AND LABOUR DISCIPLINE 89

and developed a remarkable organization, he was a miscast. The problem was that he was *too* imaginative and consistently overestimated enemy troop strength.[3] The detective's sharpened capacity to persuasively exaggerate would better serve his Agency on another battle front – the labour movement. Begun in 1855, Pinkerton's employee 'testing' service expanded in the 1860s along with the rapid growth of railroads, express companies, and city transit systems. In his 1870 publication, *Tests on passenger conductors made by the National Police Agency*, Pinkerton claimed that railroads were losing from 40 to 60 per cent of their ticket revenues because of conductor dishonesty.[4]

Pinkerton's business thrived in the wake of Civil War industrial expansion. As informal and personal labour controls began to erode, employers increasingly paid to know about their employees' work performance and their attitudes toward management. Throughout the 1860s there were fears of unionizing and the danger of strikes. Because of periodic depressions and intense industrial competition in many productive sectors, sweating of the labour force was essential for sustained profits. Wages during the Civil War were high, but post-war conditions of periodic recession and unemployment fostered bitter fights over pay.[5] Along with control over production, the wage and hour contract became focal points of intense struggle during this period.

By the early 1870s, Pinkerton's 'testing' programmes had been implemented in Chicago, Philadelphia, and New York City. Operatives were instructed to make detailed reports on the daily conduct of employees, noting *expressions of discontent* as well as dishonesty. *In moving beyond the detection of criminal behaviour*, Pinkerton was able to greatly expand his business. This new service of revealing 'dissatisfied' workers, and more importantly, those who were recruiting members for 'secret labour societies', was explained in a circular addressed to a variety of fearful employers by the 'Pinkerton Preventative Patrol, connected with Pinkerton's National Detective Agency'.[6] Shortly after the Paris Commune, Allan Pinkerton added a second espionage service. This one went beyond the shop-floor. His secret operatives could gather damaging legal information by infiltrating radical political groups and the 'inner circle' of labour organizations, an especially helpful service during strikes.[7]

In the face of increased labour unrest during the 1870s,[8] Pinkerton offered property owners a powerful new tactic with which to fight back. The use of detectives for the internal surveillance of a union, though not unheard of, was

[3] Bruce Catton, *Mr Lincoln's army* (Garden City, N.Y., 1962), p. 122. See also, pp. 119–23, 129.

[4] Allan Pinkerton, *Tests on passenger conductors made by the national police agency* (Chicago, 1870).

[5] Norman J. Ware, *The labor movement in the United States: 1860–1895* (New York, 1964), p. 9.

[6] U.S. congress, senate committee on labor and education, 'Investigation in relation to the employment for private purposes of armed bodies of men, or detectives, in connection with differences between workmen and employers', Senate report 1280, 52d congress, 2nd sess. (Washington, D.C., 1893), pp. 61–2.

[7] Allan Pinkerton, *Strikers, communists, tramps and detectives* (New York, 1878).

[8] For instance, nearly 100,000 workers in the New York building and mechanical trades participated in a strike in 1872 for the eight-hour day. Brecher, *Strike!*, p. 70.

on an unprecedented scale in a case that was to catapult the Agency to new heights of fame, that of the 'Mollie Maguires'.[9]

Although Pinkerton's business prospered throughout the 1860s, shortly after the turn of the decade his Agency was in serious financial trouble.[10] In 1871 the great Chicago fire destroyed his home office. Additionally, wide public exposure of his 'spotter' programme resulted from several celebrated embezzlement trials.[11] This put the recently formed Order of Railway Conductors on the aggressive in publicizing the spy system. These setbacks were compounded by a general business decline throughout industry that culminated in one of the nation's most severe depressions.

The failure of Jay Cooke's bank and the 'crash of 1873' also brought increased labour agitation in the rail and coal industries; hence, new business opportunities for the Pinkerton family (Allan's two sons, Robert and William, had recently joined the Agency). Allan sent operative George Bangs to visit his acquaintance, Franklin B. Gowan, president of the Philadelphia and Reading Railroad, to 'suggest something to Mr Gowan about one thing or another'. This led to the dispatch of two secret operatives into the anthracite coal region of eastern Pennsylvania, one of the nation's most economically depressed and volatile mining areas.[12] Their mission was to infiltrate an Irish immigrant 'terrorist society' accused of the vandalism of company property and violence against German, English, and Welsh mine superintendents. This was the setting for what Bimba called 'the first major battle in American labour history'.[13]

In October of 1873, Allan Pinkerton visited Gowan to discuss plans. What was Gowan's motive? And was he concerned about more than criminal behaviour? Pinkerton described part of their interchange in his book, *The Mollie Maguires and the detectives*, and reports Gowan as saying:[14]

...the Mollie Maguire...wields with deadly effect his two powerful levers: secrecy – combination. Men having their capital locked up in the coal-beds are as obedient puppets in his hands. They have felt for sometime that they were fast losing sway over that which by right should be their own to command.

[9] This incident has been well-covered by labour historians, including A. Bimba, *The Mollie Maguires* (New York, 1931); Broehl, *The Mollie Maguires*; R. O. Boyer and H. Morais, *Labor's untold story* (New York, 1971); and H. W. Aurand, *From the Mollie Maguires to the united mine workers* (Philadelphia, 1971).

[10] Allan Pinkerton to George Bangs, 15 Aug., 1872, *Allan Pinkerton letter books, 1872–1875*, in Pinkerton MSS, Library of Congress; Allan Pinkerton to Robert Pinkerton, 26 May 1875, *Letter books*.

[11] The trial of 1855 of Oscar Caldwell, one of the rail conductors nabbed by the Pinkertons, drew considerable publicity. Considered a 'test case' by the rail companies, this was also one of the nation's first embezzlement trials (in fact, there was as yet no such legal statute). Numerous fellow conductors and railworkers came to Caldwell's defence with attorney's fees and moral support. See Morn, *The eye that never sleeps*, pp. 17–18. Did fellow workers not define Caldwell's actions as criminal, but rather as wage-in-kind?

[12] Marvin W. Schlegel, 'The workingmen's benevolent association: first union of anthracite miners', *Pennsylvania History*, x, 4 (Oct. 1943), 245.

[13] Bimba, *The Mollie Maguires*, p. 24.

[14] Allan Pinkerton, *The Mollie Maguires and the detectives* (London, 1877), p. 15.

PRIVATE DETECTIVES AND LABOUR DISCIPLINE 91

Despite the high sounding laissez-faire principles, 'secrecy–combination' were just what Gowan was up to in his effort at regulating prices in concert with competitors, as well as his circumvention of legal restrictions on the purchase of coal lands by the Reading. Using a pseudonym, he bought more coal lands than all competitors put together and, having a near monopoly over both rail and coal transportation in the Schuykill region, the only remaining impediment to complete control of production was the strength of the Workingmen's Benevolent Association (WBA).[15]

For this important assignment the former Chartist fugitive went outside of his Agency to select someone special, James McParlan, an Irish Catholic from Ulster.[16] McParlan, alias James McKenna, spent two and a half difficult years in his investigation of the Schuykill region. During that time he exemplified detective role playing at its best. He worked, fought, drank, sang, danced, and conspired with his countrymen, and eventually was elected secretary of the Shenandoah Lodge of the Ancient Order of Hibernians. From that position he was able to gather incriminating evidence with the help of another Pinkerton operative, P. M. Cummings, a member of the district committee of the WBA.

Scores of suspected Mollies were rounded up by the Coal and Iron Police, who were simply deputized Pinkerton operatives.[17] On the basis of testimony of McParlan and an informer, Jim Kerrigan, who was granted immunity, the suspects were charged with various offences including murder. In trials during 1876 and 1877, Benjamin Gowan, acting as special state prosecutor, won a conviction that sent nineteen accused Mollies to the gallows. The disastrous 'Long Strike' of 1875, in the resistance to which Gowan played a prominent part, starved the miners into submission, destroying the WBA. The Mollie Maguire trials crushed the Ancient Order of Hibernians, which had been at the centre of the guerrilla warfare resistance since the strike.

In Pinkerton's book, *The Mollie Maguires and the detectives*, there is an engraving of a scene at the West Shenandoah Colliery, 3 June 1875, depicting an encounter between rioting Irishmen and armed police. On one side stands Pinkerton detective Robert J. Linden, in charge of the Coal and Iron Police. On the other side, in the front ranks of the miners with his bulldog, stands McParlan, brandishing a club. That plate depicts the first known instance when private spies coordinated with private police to effect a *system* designed to crush a union, and the practice became widespread in succeeding years. Harold Aurand comments on the significance of this peculiar arrangement. The handling of the Mollie Maguire affair was:[18]

---

[15] Marvin W. Schlegel, 'America's first cartel', *Pennsylvania History*, XIII, 1 (Jan. 1946), 5, 1–16.

[16] James McParlan to Allan Pinkerton, 10 Oct. 1873, vol. II, binder 14, Pinkerton national detective agency papers, Pinkerton's, Inc. archives, New York City; Allan Pinkerton, *The Mollie Maguires and the detectives*, pp. 22–3.

[17] For a discussion of the origin and employment of Pennsylvania's Coal and Iron police commissions, see J. D. Shalloo, *Private police, with special reference to Pennsylvania* (Philadelphia, 1933), pp. 58–134.

[18] H. W. Aurand, *From the Mollie Maguires to the united mine workers* (Philadelphia, 1971), p. 25.

one of the most astounding surrenders of sovereignty in American history. A private corporation initiated the investigation through a private detective agency; a private police force arrested the alleged offenders; the coal company attorneys prosecuted them. The state only provided the courtroom and the hangman.

The Mollie Maguire affair bolstered the image of the Pinkertons in the eyes of corporations, and the money it received saved the Agency financially.

In the aftermath of Gowan's victory, Pennsylvania's railroads and industrial corporations were adopting the Coal and Iron Police commission as a device to build up their own formidable private armies. Appearing first in the anthracite coal fields of eastern Pennsylvania in 1866, commissions under the Coal and Iron Police Act merely required a petition to the governor with a list of names for appointment. After 1871 there was a fee charged. Between then and 1929 for one dollar the state sold police power to railroads and mining companies. The contract, according to Shalloo, involved 'no investigation, no regulation, no supervision, no responsibility' on the part of the state, 'which had literally created 'islands' of police power which were free to float as the employers saw fit'.[19]

In the two decades after the Mollie case, the Pinkerton agency used Coal and Iron Police commissions in their armed guard work, most notably for Henry Frick, chairman of the Carnegie Steel Company. The last quarter of the nineteenth century witnessed increased ethnic tensions in the coalfields as the composition of the Pennsylvania mining population changed, from immigrants of North European origin, to East European – mainly Hungarian and Slavic – and Italian immigrants. For instance, in 1884 Frick hired the Pinkertons to guard his coal fields and to protect the Hungarians and Slavs he imported to displace the North Europeans. Then in 1891 when the Hungarians and Slavs revolted, Frick hired the Pinkertons to protect the Italian strikebreakers. Frick's next assignment for the Pinkerton agency would result in a scandal of such proportion that William and Robert decided to temporarily abandon labour espionage work, and eliminate altogether its armed guard strike service.

Perhaps of all the controversial situations involving private detective agency policing of labour, reaction to the Homestead 'riot' tells us the most about congressional and public opinion concerning the rights of labour, private property protection, and the duties of the state. This was the first time that detective agencies like the Pinkerton company were seriously questioned by Congress, and they would be challenged only one other time, almost a half century later.

The conflict at this rural industrial town highlighted the disparity between the economic reality of corporate capitalism and the traditional rural understanding of property. The development of corporations had made the old laissez-faire principle of the unrestrained use of one's possessions untenable, yet at Homestead that meaning of private property was being applied to the changed situation.

[19] Shalloo, *Private police*, p. 59.

PRIVATE DETECTIVES AND LABOUR DISCIPLINE 93

In 1892, the contract expired between the management of the Carnegie Steel Company at Homestead, Pennsylvania, and the 750 members of the highly skilled Amalgamated Association of Iron and Steel Workers. Henry Frick, chairman of Carnegie, had been determined to break the power of the Amalgamated men since the previous contract negotiations in 1889. Because of their skill, the union men had a fairly strong control over the production process. They had control over most of the details of production such as the apportioning of work and productivity of workers, and could use their monopoly of skill to strong advantage during contract negotiations.

Aided by sympathetic strikes against other Carnegie plants, the union succeeded in making the company back down on its 1889 contract demands for a 25 per cent wage reduction and individual contracts for workers. This time Frick was even more determined to eliminate the union, and issued what he knew to be impossible demands. The contract Frick proposed included a reduction in tonnage rates, because 'new and improved machinery gradually being installed in the plant would enable the workers to increase their output'[20] by simplifying the production process. Furthermore, Frick proposed to abolish many of the crucial job rules which the union had used to prevent speedups. This was one of the first times that labour in the United States collectively tried to resist deskilling and, when they ignored an ultimatum issued by the company, Frick ordered a lockout. All 3,800 of the workmen, skilled, semi-skilled, and unskilled alike, responded by calling a strike.

Frick immediately requested the 300 armed Pinkerton men whom he had contracted *prior* to the negotiations and in anticipation of the union's intransigence. As Frick noted in a subsequent congressional inquiry,[21] local deputies were not hired because of past experience with the sheriff of Allegheny County, where citizens had refused to join him as deputies for service against labour.

Recruited from Chicago, New York and Philadelphia, the Pinkerton guards were placed in heavily armoured barges and were instructed to seize the plant from a vantage on the bank of the Monogahela River. The Pinkertons had to surrender after a 12-hour siege, complicated by the mutiny of those who had been hired under false pretenses and shipped to Homestead under gun point. The battle left 12 dead, 10 of whom were strikers. Finally, the National Guard was called in to end the 'riot'. The state moved swiftly to mete out justice to workers who had violated the twin rights of private property and individual 'freedom' of contract. On this rare occasion when labour won a battle, 167 strike leaders were arrested, and Chief Justice Paxson of the Pennsylvania Supreme Court asked the grand jury to indict them for treason! The workers had the legal right to refuse to work, Judge Paxon reasoned, but they became rioters 'the moment they attempted to control the works, and to prevent by violence, other laborers from going to work'.[22]

[20] Horan, *The Pinkertons*, p. 339.
[21] 'The employment of Pinkerton detectives', House report no. 2447, 52nd congress, 2nd. session (Washington, D.C., 1893), pp. 56-7.   [22] Quoted in Horan, *The Pinkertons*, p. 355.

Newspapers, labour leaders, and Congress[23] all agreed that the incident was abhorrent and that the use of the Pinkertons was irresponsible and led to violence. But for most observers the issue was not the right of capital to protect its property, nor even Frick's attempt to regain his plant by force; rather, the complaint was that this work should have been the business of the government. From the press came strong criticism of the use of private armies. A *Harper's Weekly* editorial observed: 'A truly civilized community would not have to look to a Pinkerton force to do under private pay that which is obviously the business of the regularly constituted authority'. The force of laissez-faire notions concerning private property protection can be seen in the opinion of elements of organized labour, too. Among others, Terrence V. Powderly of the Knights of Labor, while denouncing the character of the men hired by Pinkertons, could think of no other remedy than to suggest that law and order be maintained by the 'legally constituted authorities'.[24] Powderly did not question the need for policing of private property; rather, for him only the *manner* of its protection was at issue.

The Senate investigation objected to the Pinkertons on the grounds that they were usurping the state's authority.[25] The previous congressional investigation in 1887–8 and all of the 28 subsequent investigations of labour/police conflicts raised the same objection.[26]

Whether assumedly or not, the employment of armed bodies of men for private purposes, either by employers or employees, is to be deprecated and should not be resorted to. Such use of private armed men is an assumption of the State's authority by private citizens.

Both House and Senate stated that Federal legislation against the use of the Pinkertons would be unconstitutional, and urged individual states to legislate.[27] However, the minority report claimed that Congress had the authority to prevent the use of private police by persons in interstate commerce.[28]

But Congress did not appear to be much interested in passing legislation anyway. As the La Follette Senate subcommittee investigating the strike-breaking business 47 years later observed, previous congresses were more concerned with the 'evils of the practice of using professional strikebreakers and strikeguards than with its causes and objectives'.[29] They deplored the method, but found its objective both legal and ethical.

---

[23] House report no. 2447; senate report no. 1280; see also B. J. Hogg, 'Public reaction to Pinkertonism and the labor question', *Pennsylvania History*, XI (July 1944), 171–99.

[24] *Journal of the knights of labor*, 14 July, 1892.   [25] Senate report no. 1280, 1893: xv.

[26] Senate report no. 1280, 1893: xv, for a summary of these congressional investigations.

[27] 'The States have undoubted authority to legislate against the employment of armed bodies of men for private purposes, as many of them are doing. As to the power of Congress to legislate, this is not so clear, though it would seem that Congress ought not to be powerless to prevent the movement of bodies of private citizens from one State to another for the purpose of taking part, with arms in hands, in the settlement of disputes between employers and their workmen' (Senate report no. 1280: xv).

[28] House report no. 2447, 1893: xxviii, lxviii.

[29] U.S. senate, committee on education and labor, 'Strike-breaking services'. Report no. 6, part I. 76th congress, 1st session (Washington, D.C., 1939), p. 13.

PRIVATE DETECTIVES AND LABOUR DISCIPLINE 95

In the decade following the controversy at Homestead, some state governments chose to exercise their constitutional power to enact reform measures in the form of 'anti-Pinkertonism' laws, but they were ambiguous, very restricted and riddled with loopholes. For instance, many states prohibited the importation of armed guards from other states, so many agencies transported the two separately. Some states even prohibited the importation of strikebreakers, so numerous branch offices were established to recruit locally.[30]

Pennsylvania officials tried to avoid exasperating capital/labour conflicts by having companies deputize local men as Coal and Iron Police. This, of course, had little success in tempering violence. The state legislature responded by 1905 to sustained violence by creating the nation's first state police. Now, officials reasoned, capital would have an easily mobilized, cheap, and efficient police force, an official representative of the state that hopefully would avoid inflaming workers. Theodore Roosevelt noted that this new police force eliminated the situation, as under the Coal and Iron Police, in which the state sold 'her power to one of the contending parties, that of the vested interests'.[31] The new mounted State Police soon proved to workers whose side the state was on, and the 'American Cossacks' were especially odious during the Bethlehem Steel strike of 1910.[32]

Despite the loss of its 'watchmen' service, the Pinkerton agency prospered during the Progressive era. Beefing up its labour espionage work, the Agency established 15 new branch offices from 1892 to 1910 to recruit labour spies locally. Eight new offices were added between 1903 and 1906 alone.[33] The Agency boasted an unmatched capacity to break established union locals, and their participation on the Western Front in battles against the Industrial Workers of the World (IWW) and the Western Federation of Miners (WFM) illustrates some of their tactics.[34]

In Colorado Pinkerton worked in close association with state authorities in the 'Thirty Years War' of strikes and violence. They frequently participated in coordinated attacks on members of the WFM, a syndicalist union that was the most militant and powerful in the West. State officials seemed genuinely confused as to the difference between public and private power, and treated the corporate interest as if it were the public interest. For example, the 1903 Cripple Creek strike involved National Guard troops under the direction of Governor James Peabody, but paid for by the Mine Owners' Association and housed on company property. Just as at Telluride, the Pinkertons were

---

[30] For a summary of these laws, see 29 above, appendix B, pp. 149–50. Also, see 'Sixteenth annual report of the commissioner of labor', House of Representatives (1901), vol. XVI.

[31] Theodore Roosevelt in K. Mayo, *Justice for all* (Boston, 1920), p. 9.

[32] Pennsylvania state federation of labor, *The American cossack* (Washington, D.C., 1915).

[33] Friedman, *Pinkerton labor spy*, p. 4.

[34] Melvyn Dubofsky, *We shall be all* (New York, 1969); Friedman, *The Pinkerton*. The internal organization and typical operations of one of Pinkerton's regional offices have been provided for the public by Friedman, a disgruntled stenographer who absconded with some financial ledgers and secret information about the Denver office.

employed as spies by the state but paid and supervised by the Mine Owners Association.[35]

Detective agencies specializing in the provision of strike services proliferated during the Progressive era.[36] Many agencies provided strikebreakers in addition to armed guards: Jim Farley, known as the 'King of Strikebreakers'; Pearl Bergoff, who in the second decade of the new century commanded a veritable army of thugs; Corporations' Auxiliary Company; Baldwin-Felts, and old timers like Gus Thiel, who expanded from the St Louis area to the coalfields of the Northwest. By the turn of the century the character of those who were recruited as strikebreakers changed. At first they were chosen from among the honest but destitute and gullible newer immigrant groups, and were usually brought to the scene of a strike under false pretenses. Now, these 'finks' were recruited from a *class* of professional strikebreakers, a lumpenproletariat with long criminal records who made a profession of their work.[37]

The suppression of strikes reached an unprecedented ferocity later in the Progressive era, with the years 1911 to 1916 especially notable. Frightening confrontations occurred between municipal, state and private police on the one side, and on the other side unskilled, newer immigrants in the garment, textile, and mining industries. The increasing organization of these workers by the Wobblies and the Socialist party raised the spectre of revolution. It was this same fear of the masses that was behind the Red Scare of 1919 and 1920. The First World War brought some respite, however, with a temporary reconciliation of conservative trade unions, the federal government, and enlightened elements of capital.

II

The advent of the First World War gave labour a new strength which temporarily altered the attitudes of business and government to trade unionism. The war created an enormous need for commodity production, and with immigration terminated, employers were faced with a scarcity of labour. Under these circumstances strikes were extremely potent, endangering corporate profits and threatening critical war production. With the unavailability of a mass of unemployed, employers could no longer use the old strategy of tolerating strikes until a body of strikebreakers was recruited.

These circumstances prompted a new strategy to keep workers under control: engage union leaders in labour discipline. Employers and government struck a bargain with the American Federation of Labor (AFL), in which the union was permitted to organize unmolested in government contract work for a pledge not to strike. 'As a result', Brecker observes, 'union membership increased by about two million during the war. Both the AFL and the war

[35] Dubofsky, *We shall be all*, p. 53.
[36] E. Levinson, *I break strikes!* (New York, 1935).
[37] Levinson, *I break strikes!*, also, Senate report no. 6, part I, 1939, p. 16; pp. 187–99, provides a job record and a criminal and arrest record for 150 strikeguards and strikebreakers.

PRIVATE DETECTIVES AND LABOUR DISCIPLINE 97

employers agreed that wages were to be set, for the duration of the war, by boards composed of business, labor, and government'.[38]

Whilst big business and the federal government were stressing 'conciliation' through the medium of conservative trade unions like the AFL, which were concerned merely with wage and hour concessions, they expanded their brutal suppression of the IWW, which was trying to organize the semi-skilled and unskilled majority for the avowed purpose of effecting workers' ownership of industry (syndicalism). On 5 September 1917, agents from the Department of Justice and local police ransacked the homes and offices of 'Wobblies' in every city where the IWW was established, herding hundreds into jails throughout the nation.[39]

Once the war was over and the federal government no longer needed labour's support for the effort, even the philosophy of 'conciliation' between capital and trade unionism was abandoned. Additionally,[40]

Real wages had risen considerably during the war as a result of the enormous demand for labor; with the end of the great wartime industrial expansion and the return to 'normalcy', it was widely felt necessary to reduce wages if profits were to be maintained. As John Maynard Keynes once pointed out, this can be done with less resistance by inflation than by direct wage cuts. So in 1919, the government simultaneously ended wartime price controls and allowed corporations to resume their traditional union breaking policies.

So the post-war period was one of a resurgence of violent, state-sanctioned private repression in the service of capital. 'Throughout the twenties, industrial employers developed new tactics or refined old ones to deter labor organization and to avoid genuine collective bargaining. Their tactics ranged from the so-called American Plan, which entailed the use of every hostile technique of anti-unionism, to the paternalism of welfare capitalism'.[41] To implement this American Plan, the decade saw the proliferation of private agencies devoted exclusively and unabashedly to strikebreaking. These agencies and corporations stockpiled huge arsenals of weapons, including millions of dollars' worth of machine and hand guns, sickening gas, tear gas and deadly chloropicrin.[42] Literally the war was brought home. Whilst most hostile tactics of employers were legal – there was no federal legislation prohibiting espionage or violent strikebreaking, and private police agencies went largely unregulated by state and federal law – the activities of labour groups were frustrated by court injunctions and antitrust prosecution. *It was only labour's use of force which was illegitimate.*

Besides a sympathetic legislature and judiciary, capital was assisted in its war against organized labour by a government with a repressive apparatus of

[38] J. Brecker, *Strike!* (Boston, 1977), p. 103.
[39] Dubofsky, *We shall be all*, p. 406.
[40] Brecker, *Strike!*, p. 104.
[41] J. S. Auerback, *Labor and liberty* (Indianapolis, 1966), p. 22.
[42] Senate report no. 6, part I, 1939.

unprecedented strength. After WWI the federal government had a greatly expanded administrative bureaucracy and a large military; it was able to manipulate patriotic and anticommunist sentiment into a fervent anti-labour movement. Under the liberal Wilson administration the federal government began using this new power to assume more of the responsibility for labour discipline. Wilson appointed J. Edgar Hoover as the head of the Justice Department's Radical Division and, in conjunction with the Immigration Department, the government conducted the infamous 'red raids' against steel and railroad workers participating in the 1919 mass strike. Thousands of aliens suspected of radicalism were arrested, and hundreds jailed and deported.[43] The U.S. Army also was mobilized to restore 'order' when the National Guard proved insufficient to suppress strikes and demonstrations. The post-war period marked the end of federalist hesitation to develop a national secret police, and the federal campaign against 'reds' and unionization continued with a new 'private' twist under the Warren G. Harding administration.

President Harding's new attorney general, Harry M. Daugherty, replaced William J. Flynn as chief of the Bureau of Investigation with a fellow member of the 'Ohio gang' – William J. Burns. Like Flynn, he was a former head of the Secret Service, and upon retirement in 1909 established his own private detective agency. After some notorious incidents involving jury tampering, office break-ins and wiretapping, 'Colonel' Burns was recalled to federal service in 1921. Ostensibly leaving direction of the William J. Burns International Detective Agency to his two sons, Raymond and Sherman, the new chief embarked on a three-year tenure that was to take the Bureau to new depths of unethical and illegal activity.

Ever since Allan Pinkerton's service during the Civil War, private detectives spent time at federal secret service jobs. During the Harding administration the flow of personnel and influence from the private sector reached an apogee, with most newly appointed agents having been at one time private detectives.[44] Strengthened by the war, the Justice Department became partners with private detective agencies (and corporate security divisions) in labour discipline. In a two-pronged assault, the Bureau's General Intelligence Division (GID) became the nation's political police, whilst private detective agencies specialized in shop-floor spying and picket slugging. The Bureau's participation in the post-war 'open shop' campaign was an example of the most flagrant collusion of public and private power, and from that period one can date the beginning of an 'old boy network' between private and federal police to effect mutual influence, facilitate the sharing of information, organize 'joint operations', and arrange for the 'moonlighting' of government agents at private detective agencies.

The 1922 railroad shopmen's strike was the first big assignment for the Bureau in its effort to enforce the Lever Act, and it provided the opportunity to develop many of the types of collusion identified above. The Lever Act was

[43] W. Preston, *Aliens and dissenters* (New York, 1963), passim.
[44] Max Lowenthal, *The federal bureau of investigation* (New York, 1950).

PRIVATE DETECTIVES AND LABOUR DISCIPLINE   99

a war-time measure to prevent price increases, and was often the basis on which, perversely, courts issued strike injunctions. The Bureau of Investigation argued that, because strikes curtailed production, they raised prices, although union officials argued that they were merely attempting to regain their 'real' wages in the face of post-war cost of living increases. When the Lever Act was revoked in 1922, the Sherman Anti-trust Act was appealed to on the basis that labour unions were guilty of establishing a monopoly over labour.[45]

The state of the economy after the war was favourable to an all out anti-union effort, as the unemployment resulting from the depression of 1922 fostered a plentiful supply of strikebreakers. With anti-radical sentiment reaching a fevered state, even the conservative AFL was branded 'Bolshevik', despite Samuel Gomper's inflated patriotism during the war. When the government's Railway Labor Board ordered a pay cut of $12\frac{1}{2}$ per cent, hundreds of thousands of AFL union workers rebelled. Management hired 'replacement men', and Daugherty obtained a federal district court injunction that, amazingly, prohibited 'acts or words' that would interfere with rail operations.[46] The Bureau then got to work.

To enforce the injunction the Bureau dispatched agents throughout the country to espionage work, to infiltrate strikers' ranks, to attend meetings undercover, and to search for violations.[47] The scenario was reminiscent of private detective agency strike work. Indeed, special agents worked closely with the security divisions of the railroad companies.[48] Back in Washington, the Bureau of Investigation coordinated all of the information, projections were made on strike activity for employers, and reports were made to the Department of War.[49] When all was over, some 1,200 employees were arrested for contempt of court.[50] And the strike had been broken.

The Bureau's next endeavour involved nearly all of the possible types of private/public interpenetration and collusion. In the spring and early summer of 1923 an association of Arizona copper mine operators hired the Burns Detective Agency to infiltrate the ranks of workers to expose union organizers. Not wanting to be merely reactive, Burns agents seized the opportunity themselves by acting as IWW organizers. To back up the Burns private detectives in case of trouble were Burns G-men. Chief Burns used the Bureau of Investigation to help build up his private detective agency. In March of 1924, *Industrial Solidarity*, the IWW news weekly published a number of documents

[45] Lowenthal, *The federal bureau*, pp. 269–81.

[46] 'Lawless disorders and their suppression'. Appendix to the annual report of the attorney general for the fiscal year of 1922, containing the correspondence relating to the action of the government with reference to the interruption by force of interstate commerce, the carriage of the mails, etc. in the year 1922. Printed pursuant to concurrent resolution of March 3, 1923, p. v

[47] Lowenthal, *The federal bureau*. See hearings. House appropriations committee on department of justice appropriations for 1924, p. 71.

[48] 'Lawless disorders and their suppression', pp. 8, 76, 80, 288, 349, 371, 431, 452.

[49] Hearings. House appropriations committee on department of justice appropriations for 1924, pp. 71, 78.

[50] H. A. Millis and R. E. Montgomery, *Organized labor* (New York, 1945), p. 638.

stolen from the Los Angeles office of the Burns Detective Agency.[51] These materials revealed that the Bureau of Investigation had transferred federal agents from other parts of the country to work with Burns private detectives in the Arizona operations; employed private detectives; assembled 'blacklists' of suspected agitators, distributing the names to employers; and, in the ultimate contravention of the duties of office, acted as *agent provocateur*.

Among the materials published by *Industrial Solidarity* were letters of correspondence between managers of the Los Angeles and New York offices of Burns Detective Agency, and copper company officials, sheriffs, police commissioners, and Justice Department officials, including Bureau Director Burns. Additionally, the Wobblies published photographed copies of espionage contracts with a mining company, and an itemized financial statement.[52]

The first letter was written 19 May 1923 by G. P. Pross, manager of the Los Angeles office of Burns, to William Garvin, manager of the New York office. Pross enclosed reports from agents in the Arizona mining camps, and after discussing how time and expenses were to be pro-rated among 30 different mining companies, remarks:[53]

All the arrangements on this operation were made while the Governor was here in Los Angeles. I am also sending copies of each report to him so that the Department of Justice will have full records of all going on; and, in fact, the agent in charge of the Department of Justice in Arizona is to work in conjunction with our investigation so that should anything come up, that would need immediate attention, the agent in charge will be able to go with us.

The 'Governor' is, of course, William J. Burns, and on 23 May 1923 he responded about the arrangements in a letter written on government stationery, and signed 'Director':[54]

I have just received a letter from Mr Dowell in which he suggests that we have two of our Agents in Arizona call on Frank Carlock, Special Agent of the Old Dominion Copper Company, located in Globe, Arizona, so that they together might be able to suppress some of the activities of I.W.W. radicals.

'Mr Dowell', a former Thiel Detective Agency Manager, is the paymaster for the mining companies undercover work. Arrangements were not long in coming, and on 23 June Pross wrote a letter to Mr R. J. Burns, President, at the New York office, stating that the Arizona investigators are in 'direct touch with the Department of Justice Agent, whom the Governor transferred from Butte, Montana to Arizona, and he is a real fellow and knows the game...also well thought of by the Mine Managers...'.[55]

The Ruthenberg case provides an instance of how well the private and public

[51] 'I.W.W. exposes Burns', *Industrial Solidarity* (no. 281), 22 March 1924; 'Burns incited violence', *Industrial Solidarity* (no. 282), 29 March 1924; see also, Sidney Howard, *The labor spy* (New York, 1924), pp. 128–56.

[52] *Industrial Solidarity*, 22 March 1924.

[53] 'Burns used United States office to build up agency', Industrial Solidarity, 22 March 1924.

[54] *Industrial Solidarity*, p. 1. Letter photographed and reproduced in its entirety.

[55] *Industrial Solidarity*, p. 3.

sectors could work for mutual benefit. In April of 1923 Charles Ruthenberg went to trial on criminal syndicalism charges for possessing Communist party documents, and for participating in a party convention in northern Michigan.[56] According to testimony, the impetus behind the convention was provided by A. C. Myers, head of the Radical Bureau of the Burns Detective Agency. Acting undercover, he infiltrated the Central Committee, and as *agent provocateur*, also 'planted' radical documents in Ruthenberg's luggage, according to defence attorney Frank Walsh. Then, Mr Myers changed hats, and with credentials as a special agent of the Department of Justice, took part in directing the state police raid (no federal laws had been violated).[57] Apparently, here was an example of another 'joint operation', this time for political rather than industrial espionage.

During the trial defence witness Albert Balanow, who in 1917 was a Department of Justice agent, accused Jacob Spolansky, head of the Radical Bureau of the Department of Justice, of selling documents to the Thiel Agency for $25.00 per day. 'Spolansky, he swore, had a cousin in the Thiel Agency and another relative on the Chicago Police Bomb Squad "and they all worked together"'.[58] We do not know if the sale of information actually occurred, but it was well-known that the Bureau *gave away* privileged information. For instance, Mr Burns handed over information obtained under search warrant in the Michigan case *before* the trial to R. M. Whitney of the American Defense Society.

Mr Burns frequently worked in conjunction with 'patriotic societies', especially in providing them with information from radical investigations.[59] Sidney Howard, in a 1924 *New Republic* editorial, observed: 'The militant patriots were publicity agents for Mr. Burns when he didn't have evidence to convict these 'so-called liberals' and worse, he turned the patriots loose in his treasure house of rumours and portentous subversive documents'.[60] Burns had an especially close relationship with Mr Ralph Easely of the National Civic Federation, and that organization's annual Survey of Progress made special note of the Bureau's assistance. This cooperation, some have surmised, provided 'a convenient link between sworn enemies, Mr. Burns and Easely's pal Sam Gompers; provided, too, a convenient source of A.F. of L. propaganda against renegade unions'.[61]

[56] 'Accuse Burns in red trial', *New York Times*, 21 April 1923; 'Links Ruthenberg to reds!', *New York Times*, 24 April 1923.
[57] *New York Times*, 24 April 1923. The Bureau frequently spent time helping enforce laws of the individual states.
[58] *New York Times*, 'Charges inciting of red outrages!', 13 February 1923.
[59] Preston, *Aliens and dissenters*, p. 242.
[60] Sidney Howard, 'Our professional patriots', *The New Republic*, 10 September 1924, p. 40.
[61] *The New Republic*, 10 September 1924. See also, Norman Hapgood, *Professional patriots* (New York, 1927), p. 99. 'Mr Samuel Gompers, though long opposed to Mr. Burns as a labor spy and the representative of anti-union employers, had a common interest with him while he was in the Department. Both were fighting Reds – Mr. Gompers in the unions, Mr. Burns, anywhere. Mr. Easley was the friend of both. So there was, in effect, a most extraordinary alliance – the secret service, organized labor, and big business, all united in a patriotic effort to down radicalism'.

The mounting scandal surrounding the Department of Justice, especially in regard to the Teapot Dome corruption, finally led to Attorney General Daugherty's dismissal by President Coolidge.[62] About one month later, 9 May 1924, William J. Burns resigned.[63] Apparently, the final straw was when Burns tried to discredit the Department's congressional critics, especially Senator Burton K. Wheeler. Burns had his agents spy on Wheeler from the bushes of his home, ransack his Capitol Hill office, and attempt to entice him into sexual compromise.[64] Political intrigue of this kind was just what Congress most feared when, back in 1908, it soundly defeated Attorney General Charles Bonaparte's proposal to create a federal bureau of investigation.[65]

The new Attorney General, Harlan Fiske Stone, promoted J. Edgar Hoover to Director of the Bureau, and pledged that thereafter the Bureau would be 'a fact-gathering organization' whose 'activities would be limited strictly to investigations of violations of federal laws'. This was easy enough to say, as the union movement had been smashed. But, the Bureau would re-emerge as a red-hunter and labour suppressor in the late 1930s and 1940s, when Mr Easely's view of conservative trade unionism finally prevailed, and such unionizing was given federal protection.[66] The AFL and CIO leadership would cooperate with the renamed Federal Bureau of Investigation (FBI) in ferreting-out Communists from within their ranks.

Meanwhile, private detectives like Mr Burns left government service with valuable connections. FBI agents in the following decades would become well-trained at public expense to perform after retirement labour discipline work for corporations. They would learn more sophisticated methods than those employed by the usual union-busting detective agencies.

III

Throughout the twenties, a period of great capital expansion, strikes were largely unsuccessful, union membership declined, and industrial violence remained low. However, with the onset of the Great Depression, workers lost patience with the trade union movement and thousands resorted to direct action. Self-help movements of workers and the unemployed assumed various forms – mass demonstrations, coal bootlegging, spontaneous strikes, anti-eviction 'riots', and so on. By the end of 1931 more than fifteen million workers were unemployed, and many feared a revolutionary movement.

To meet the general crisis of the Depression, Franklin Roosevelt established the National Recovery Administration in 1933. To gain labour's support for this emergency measure, Section 7A gave employees the right to organize and

[62] 'Daugherty ousted by Coolidge; turns on president and accusers', *New York Times*, 29 May 1924.

[63] 'W. J. Burns quits fed service; long under fire', *New York Times*, 10 May 1924.

[64] 'Burns sent agents to help build case against Wheeler', *New York Times*, 11 April 1924; S. J. Ungar, *The FBI* (Boston, 1976), p. 46.

[65] Lowenthal, *The federal bureau of investigation*, pp. 3–9.

[66] See G. Kolko, *The triumph of conservatism* (Chicago, 1963) and J. Weinstein, *The corporate ideal and the liberal state* (Boston, 1968).

PRIVATE DETECTIVES AND LABOUR DISCIPLINE   103

bargain collectively, free from employer interference. This was a relatively safe move for the government, as socialist unionism was dead by the 1930s. Trade unionism itself had nearly disappeared as union officials failed to deal with wage cuts and lay-offs. But following passage of Section 7A there was a rush to trade unionism.

Whilst the giant U.S. Steel Corporation accepted collective bargaining, the 'little steel' companies such as Republic Steel and Bethlehem Steel Corporation resisted vigorously. There was no means of enforcing Section 7A (that had to await 1935 and the Wagner Act), and small and middle level manufacturers organized in the National Association of Manufacturers (NAM) and the National Trade Association (NTA) helped precipitate an alarming number of strikes. By 1935 social unrest had spread over all regions of the country, evoking memories of the 1890s. Again, the state was faced with twin dangers, this time by fascism on the Right and socialism on the Left. Socialist ideas gained new vitality after a long period of decline, and for the first time explicitly fascist groups began to organize successfully.

At this point Roosevelt encouraged a congressional investigation into violations of free speech and rights of labour and the role that 'citizens committees' and private police played in frustrating those rights.[67] The Senate Committee on Education and Labor formed an investigatory subcommittee chaired by Robert M. La Follette, Jr. The Committee's target was the 'intransigent minority of powerful corporations' organized in NAM. Such 'economic royalists' and 'anarchists', including old family corporations like Ford, were endangering the existence of capitalism in the long run by their selfish robber-baron behaviour. If Roosevelt and like-minded progressives were to save capitalism, they had to defeat NAM's short-run, interest-conscious position, to uphold the interests of the capitalist class as a whole.

The New Deal saw the fruition of the National Civic Federation's teachings during the Progressive era. With the recognition of conservative trade unions, labour discipline could be shifted from management to union officials. Once a contract was negotiated (with specified limits) union officials would pledge worker efficiency, no strikes and noninterference with the basic prerogatives of management. The recognition of unions 'left the subordinate position of workers intact, but provided a mechanism for eliminating those grievances which could be rectified without undermining the profit-making of the employer'.[68]

The ability of certain industrialists to bargain with trade unions was based on developments in the mode of production since the turn of the century. The growing merger movement and monopolization meant that the added costs represented by wage increases could be passed on to the consumer. This left small industry at a competitive disadvantage, adding to the monopoly

---

[67] See U.S. senate committee on education and labor, 'The "little steel" strike and citizens' committees'. Report no. 151 (1941). Also, see: Auerbach, *Labor and liberty*; L. G. Silverberg, 'Citizen's committees: their role in industrial conflict', *Public Opinion Quarterly*, v (March, 1941).
[68] Brecker, *Strike!*, p. 252.

tendency. Furthermore, with new technology and 'scientific management', which was rapidly de-skilling workers, management gained greater control of output rates. Also, increasing industrial efficiency meant a shift in the labour force, with factory wage earners decreasing in numbers so that higher relative wages could be paid to a shrinking proportion of workers.[69] In turn, trade union officials would attempt to guarantee uninterrupted production.

A test of how effective the union hierarchy might be in controlling its rank and file came suddenly with the onset of the Second World War. By the start of the war unions were recognized by many large industrial corporations. As in the First World War, big union bosses once again pledged no strikes or walkouts, and the leadership of the AFL and the Congress of Industrial Organizations (CIO) got busy disciplining their rapidly increasing membership.[70] As a consequence, during a time of labour scarcity and burgeoning profits, those unions failed to make wage gains. Communist-led unions were no exception, and according to *Business Week*, they had 'perhaps the best no-strike record of any section of organized labor', and were 'the most vigorous proponents of labor–management cooperation'.[71] Wartime working conditions were so bad, however, that despite the union and management co-operative effort to discipline workers and prevent 'wildcat' strikes, there were $14\frac{1}{2}$ thousand strikes involving millions of people, more strikes 'than during any period of comparable length in United States history'.[72]

So, with the end of the war unions faced a serious crisis. How would they keep their membership now that the government-backed maintenance-of-membership provisions were no longer in effect?[73] Moreover, the massive lay-offs following 'reconversion' further depleted union ranks. Five million displaced war workers joined three million discharged military personnel on unemployment. Just after the war the federal government, recognizing the ineffectiveness of wartime controls, dropped the wage freeze in which wages were held at their 1942 level. Economists expected 'deflationary forces' to begin to come into play soon.[74] And so they did. In contrast to the 1918–20 post-war rise in wages, weekly earnings in 1946 were expected to experience a 20 per cent decrease because of the reduction of work hours alone.[75] With the prospect of such a drop in income in 1946, combined with continually rising prices, strikes were certain. The question was, would they be 'wildcat' or union-led?

There followed a rash of union-backed demands for higher wages, with a 30 per cent increase being the CIO standard.[76] How was management to deal

[69] Harry Braverman, *Labor and monopoly capital* (New York, 1974), p. 150.
[70] 'In exchange for enforcing the no-strike pledge, unions had their hands upheld by being granted rights that greatly aided their growth, while making them less vulnerable to pressure from their own rank and file', Brecker, *Strike!*, p. 222.
[71] 'Bridges' setback', *Business Week*, 18 March 1944, pp. 83–4.
[72] Brecker, *Strike!*, p. 226.
[73] 'For labor: readjustments', *Business Week*, 18 August 1945.
[74] 'U.S. takes brakes off wages', *Business Week*, 25 August 1945; 'Auto union forces showdown', *Business Week*, 22 September 1945.
[75] *Business Week*, 25 August 1945.

PRIVATE DETECTIVES AND LABOUR DISCIPLINE   105

with this? Try to repeat the post-First World War strategy of smashing unions? The example of Ford Motor Company is very instructive, for here was a case of a corporation moving immediately from the most 'feudal' approach to organized labour to the most advanced. The Ford leadership definitely turned liberal in its attitude toward unions. This turnaround coincided with the transfer of leadership from Henry Ford to his grandson, Henry II, who put forth a new labour philosophy and strategy.

Henry Ford Senior took a hard line toward unions, and in 1941 his company was the last of the big automakers to come to an agreement with the United Auto Workers (UAW), an affiliate of the CIO. The company's labour philosophy was a paragon of Social Darwinism. Mr Ford would do with his property just as he pleased. To help enforce his prerogatives, Ford employed a large number of police – he preferred his own to those of private detective agencies. The company's Service Department was headed by ex-navy boxer Harry H. Bennett, and at its height, consisted of 3,500 thugs, including former boxers, ex-cops, bouncers, football players and ex-FBI agents, many of whom were associated with the underworld.[77] With this private army Ford resisted New Deal reforms.

Henry Ford II, grandson of the 88-year-old founder, took over as president in September of 1945. Within a week of assuming office he made major executive changes that announced an important shift in corporate philosophy. The first top official to go was Harry Bennett, personnel director. Various of Bennett's confidants and assistants promptly resigned or were transferred – a signal that 'Ford Runs Ford', in the words of *Business Week*. To help him wrest control of the company from Bennett and his gangsters Ford elicited the help of James J. Bugas, Bennett's recently appointed assistant. He promoted Bugas to head of 'industrial relations', a new Ford title.[78]

Mr Bugas came to his job well-prepared to deal with the new labour situation. He came to the attention of Ford officials whilst he was chief of the Detroit office of the Federal Bureau of Investigation, one of the nation's 'hot spots', and where recently he supervised raids against 'communists'. According to *Business Week*, Bugas joined Ford in 1944 only 'on the company's plea to Edgar Hoover that his experience concentrated at Ford would help win the war'.[79] The changing of the guard at Ford, from gangsters to ex-G-men, brought a 'new style' to Ford's labour relations effort, involving 'subtle' tactics rather than the slugging offensive of Bennett. 'J. Edgar Hoover boasts that under his technique the G-men never have to use rubber-hose or other physical persuaders'.[80] Bugas' approach was not timid, however, but direct and 'frank', a strategy designed to control the situation. Unions would be recognized, but

---

[76] *Business Week*, 22 September 1945, pp. 99–100.

[77] Huw Beynon, *Working for Ford*, (London 1973), pp. 29–30; Frank Pierce, *Crimes of the powerful* (London, 1976), pp. 134–45; K. Sward, *The legend of Henry Ford* (New York, 1968).

[78] 'Ford runs Ford', *Business Week*, 8 October 1945, pp. 18–19; 'Ford brings more', *Business Week*, 29 September 1945.

[79] 'Ford employs new strategy', *Business Week*, 20 July 1946, pp. 96–8.

[80] 'BI's old grads', *Business Week*, 20 July 1946, pp. 19–20.

their leadership would be put on the defensive and held accountable to the *company's* demands.

Bugas' assistant, Mel B. Lindquest, also came to Ford well-equipped to help implement the company's new labour philosophy. His position as super-intendent of labour relations put him on 'the direct firing line in the Ford relationship to labor'. An ex-boxer? No, Lindquest came from the 'labor relations' department of the Murray Corporation, where the 'company evolved its program for training union members as time study experts, so the union would have its own advocates in any dispute on timing of operations'.[81] This fitted in well with Ford's new strategy which, succinctly put by Henry II, was 'company security' should equal 'union security'. The company was willing to grant generous wage and hour concessions, but insisted on rank-and-file discipline. Henry Ford II majored in sociology at Yale, and that is where he may have learned that labour would be better disciplined by its own institutions.

At the start of the 1945 contract negotiations Bugas advanced 31 demands of the union in exchange for the 'union security' of a union shop and dues checkoff. Bugas put the UAW on the defensive with these counterproposals to ensure worker efficiency and continuity, and suggested $5.00 a day per worker fines on the local treasury for wildcat strikes.[82] Moreover, there were certain matters that were off limits; the company would not consider negotiation over profits, for one. Another company demand excluded from UAW membership certain classes of personnel, such as supervisors and clerical workers.[83]

So, a half century after Homestead, the fundamental principles of capitalism were unaffected. Property owners have since retained complete control, with the basic prerogatives of management uncompromised. Big business and big labour bosses work together and the working class gets disciplined by its own institutions. Unions have come to employ against labour itself the very same methods of discipline as the employers used: espionage, blacklisting, use of strikebreakers during 'outlaw' or 'wildcat' strikes, fines, intimidation, red baiting, etc. Once a contract is accepted, the very existence of the union and the jobs of its officials will depend on its enforcement.

[81] *Business Week*, 8 December 1945; 'Union time study', *Business Week*, 29 August 1942.

[82] As an example of how effective Bugas' new offensive tactics were, and how far the grounds of dispute had shifted, union bargainers countered Ford with an offer to bring unauthorised strikers up before a union trial board. 'The union was kept so busy answering the company demands that it was not until a few days ago that it was able to inject its own call for 30 per cent in the discussion at all', observed *Business Week*, 8 December 1945.

[83] 'Two-way bargaining demand', *Business Week*, 24 November 1945; 'Clerical revolt', *Business Week*, 15 September 1945; 'White collared', *Business Week*, 22 September 1945. White-collar workers were becoming increasingly discontent, and willing to show it in organizational activity. The September 1945 strike at Westinghouse dramatized the 'revolt of the white-collar worker'. The close integration of plant and office idled 30,000 non-striking production workers, with the prospect of soon idling 60,000 more. This, one of the biggest strikes of white-collar workers, revealed the power that office employees possessed to stop manufacturing operations cold. Undermining unionization of the 'new working class' would provide a new area of 'labour relations' work for private detective agencies. See Huberman, *The labor spy racket* (New York, 1966, rev. edn).

PRIVATE DETECTIVES AND LABOUR DISCIPLINE 107

IV

This study has traced aspects of the origin, development, and transformation in the United States of private detective agency labour policing. We discussed its early development during the period of rapid industrialization under very competitive conditions. Policing of labour was largely the direct responsibililty of employers until the First World War. Various turning points in private detective agency development were identified, and one of these was when the federal government's Justice Department joined private detectives as partners in labour control (although officials of individual states had been doing so all along). This marked the beginning of a 'new state', a period when federalist hesitation was overcome. The example of the FBI since the First World War indicates the permeability of the membrane separating the private and public realms of policing. From the standpoint of a theory of the state, the private detective agency occupies an interesting space between the private and public realms of power. Although under private direction, the close association that private detective agencies have enjoyed with state and federal authorities, including the circulation of personnel, suggests that they have been *more* than civilian in nature. Further study of the origin and development of private policing in this regard could suggest something about the changing parameters of the state in the United States.

A major transformation of private policing occurred when the nation's economy moved from a period of competitive, laissez-faire capitalism to the liberal corporate variety. This had particular significance for the wage contract, and once capital was able to accept the more effective labour discipline of conservative trade unions, the coercion of private detectives became unnecessary and undesirable. In dealing with union leadership, management after the Second World War had the help of former FBI agents. This was especially useful in dealing with 'subversives' (and thus in helping to keep union demands 'reasonable'). 'The FBI training and practice develop unusual qualities that are being sought by various business concerns', *Business Week* observed in a 20 July 1946 article on the occupational market for ex-G-men. After retirement, many former FBI officers continued on to personnel and labour relations departments of major corporations or private detective agencies that had labour services. The area of labour discipline was 'natural' for old grads, *Business Week* continued, 'FBI experience has taught them not only how to handle personnel but to know what is going on within groups, with special reference to communistic and other subversive activities'.[84]

---

[84] To 'keep alive their old bonds, the ex-stalwarts of the FBI have created their own association', the Society of Former Special Agents of the FBI, Inc., whose president at the time was a personnel executive of American Airlines, observed a 20 July 1946 *Business Week* article. The Society is a formal institutionalization of the 'old boy network' begun under Mr Burns. This fraternity serves as a recruitment and placement service for graduates, and *Business Week* continued, 'relations with the old chief are cordial, almost reverent'. See also, 'Post to FBI ex-agent', *New York Times*, 25 September 1947, p. 44.

[16]

FROM COSSACK TO TROOPER:
MANLINESS, POLICE REFORM, AND THE STATE

By Gerda W. Ray   University of Missouri-St. Louis

"A distinctively American type of men" was sought by the first Superintendent of the New York State Police to fill the ranks of his controversial new force. To Superintendent George F. Chandler, "distinctively American" evoked an "Anglo-Saxon" ideal—tall, square jawed, broad shouldered. Looking for men who were "physically perfect," Superintendent Chandler also demanded a demeanor and manners which could qualify a man as a "soldier and a gentleman."[1] Chandler was well suited to enforce his preference. A physician, Chandler personally examined each applicant, a practice continued throughout his six years as Superintendent. Photographs of the troopers confirm his success in creating a certain image for the state police by attending to the personal appearance of his men, much as a couturier selects models with the "right" look.

Chandler knew that the survival of his new force was at stake. The bill establishing the State Police had passed by only one vote in 1917 and had been signed by Governor Charles Whitman over the objections of trade unionists, farmers, and Civil Service reformers. No Democrats had voted for the measure, and the Democratic platform in 1918 called for abolishing the force. It had taken a four-year campaign to win state police for New York, and a similar campaign in New Jersey had failed. The Pennsylvania State Police, the only other mounted, regularly patrolling state police in the country, faced regular efforts to abolish it, and it had just won in 1917 its first increase in size and salary in six years. Chandler knew that his success or failure in New York would have important repercussions for the state police movement as a whole.

Today it is hard to imagine controversy over creating a police force. Police are ubiquitous in contemporary U.S. life and culture. The relative weakness of the police in the nineteenth century, however, was one aspect of what historians have called a state of "courts and parties."[2] Introducing public police before the Civil War had excited much opposition, as did uniforming them. Persistent corruption, inefficiency, and other problems defined the police as part of the "Shame of the Cities" throughout the late nineteenth century, and the Keystone Cops were among the most popular comedies in the new motion picture industry in the 1910s.[3] Policing was mired in what Alan Dawley has called the "imbalance of state and society," a weak state unable to contain rapidly escalating social conflict.[4]

The relationship between the police and society, however, changed dramatically in the twentieth century. The best-known aspects of this transformation are the professionalization of the urban police and the creation of the Bureau of Investigation, later called the Federal Bureau of Investigation. The controversy over creating state police forces, however, has gone unstudied, despite the fact that state-level police are arguably the most dramatic institutional innovation

566   journal of social history   spring 1995

of the period. Prior to the twentieth century, most policing in the United States was local in scope and reactive in nature. When disorder exceeded the capability of the police, the militia or the army was called. State-level policing ran counter to the popular association of democracy with local control and evoked the traditional fear of standing armies.[5]

Chandler's concern with his men's appearance reflected the need to win popular acceptance for the new force. Why, however, did he believe that physical appearance would be decisive in the force's acceptance? Why did the opponents of the state police similarly emphasize the intimidating demeanor and crude violence of the men on horseback, the "Black Cossacks"? This essay argues that conflicting images of manliness provided a language for both contesting and asserting the legitimacy of the new force. Analyzing the gendered character of this debate provides a window on what Joan Scott has called the "reciprocal nature of gender and society."[6] Most of the important new work on the history of masculinity has addressed the variety of ways in which "society" constructs masculinities.[7] My effort here is to look at how the proponents of the new force invoked elite definitions of masculine authority in an increasingly self-conscious effort to legitimate a controversial extension of the state's coercive power.[8] Opposition to the state police was similarly structured within an alternative conception of manliness. Understanding the gendered character of the debate over the state police suggests new ways of analyzing the interrelationship of gender and the state in the early twentieth century.[9] The essay focuses on the campaign for state police in New York because it was there that the debate first assumed its characteristic shape.

Creating state police in Pennsylvania had not been controversial because "the matter was intentionally kept as quiet as possible" in order to avoid opposition.[10] The high level of labor conflict in Pennsylvania's mines throughout the last quarter of the nineteenth century had meant that the state's militia saw strike duty so frequently that one historian called them the "policemen of industry."[11] Using the militia for strikes, however, was expensive and required on-going service from men who had volunteered to serve only part-time. Strike duty, moreover, undermined the National Guard's readiness for the military service which the country's new international role demanded. From 1876 on, advocates of a professional National Guard called for the creation of a specialized police force which would relieve the militia from strike duty.[12] Spurred by the huge anthracite mine strike of 1902, the Republican governor of Pennsylvania moved to push a state police bill quickly through the mineowner-dominated legislature. Popular with financiers, manufacturers, and the editors of progressive journals such as the *Nation* and the *Outlook*, the Pennsylvania force was hated by labor throughout the country.[13]

Following Pennsylvania's example, the Chamber of Commerce of the State of New York proposed the state police for New York in 1913. To them, the need for a specialized strike control force which could free up the National Guard for military purposes was almost obvious. Strike duty in New York, while not as arduous as that in Pennsylvania, nevertheless contradicted military reformers' goal of a militia ready to function as the expansion force of a professional army.

The Chamber created a Committee for State Police which set up its office on Wall Street and expected quick cooperation from a Republican governor.[14]

Trade union and socialist spokesmen were outraged. Unlike Colorado or Pennsylvania, where there was open conflict between the mine owners and workers, organized labor in New York saw itself as having a voice in state policy.[15] By 1914 they were on the defensive, trying to preserve the reforms of earlier years and stave off the advance of Preparedness agitation, but they had not expected that Seth Low, President of the National Civic Federation and one of the most important advocates of labor-management cooperation in the country, would propose Cossacks for New York. Socialist objections lacked this sense of betrayal, but both labor and socialist condemnation of the state police sounded the same theme: manly, law-abiding, American workmen should not be subjected to the violent, foreign, illegal, mounted constabulary. Within days of the first announcement, the Central Federated Union of Greater New York protested to Low that "the members of organized labor are law abiding, ... we perceive in this project an attempt to class members of labor unions as law breakers unworthy of consideration or recognition."[16]

The trade union opposition expressed a conception of manliness and the state which asserted both the self-control and citizenship of the worker and the legitimacy of striking to protect his manly independence, "to insure us a respectful living for ourselves, our wives and children."[17] The Socialist *Call* condemned the Pennsylvania Cossacks for clubbing and shooting "workingmen who demanded more bread for their babies."[18] New York could not permit itself to become like Pennsylvania, "where nearly all the manhood of the workers had been crushed out by the murderous tactics of the constabulary."[19] "We instruct our men in the unions to perform their work peacefully," insisted the head of the Buffalo labor council.[20] As "an industrious, civilized, law abiding people," workers had no need for "any such Russianized system."[21]

If the workers were manly, law-abiding, patriotic Americans, the state police were, by contrast, violent, foreign, illegal strikebreakers. Trade unionists and socialists called the force "Black Cossacks" or "Black Hussars," run by the czars of industry, and they claimed that the police was "a strike breaking institution ... a cross between the Irish Constabulary and the Russian Cossack."[22] They objected to modeling a force on the "most uncivilized force in the most uncivilized country in the world."[23] Arguing that the force established a "rough riders escort for strike breakers at state's expense," they objected to the usurpation of local authority.[24] "Seek to Use State as Strikebreaker" summarized the headline of the *Legislative Labor News*, while the *Call* argued "they are neither soldiers nor police, nor minions of the law in any manner, but mercenaries."[25] Violating the rights of citizens and distorting the purpose of the state added up to "un-Americanism."[26] Trade union and socialist spokesmen supported the concept of an active state, but in the spirit of the *Albany Federationist's* gibe: "If they need constabulary, why not train them to compel employers to deal fairly with men?"[27]

Opponents of the state police bolstered their charge of "un-Americanism" with the examples of brutal and illegal tactics of the Pennsylvania State Police collected in a pamphlet, *The American Cossack*, by James Maurer. Head of both the Pennsylvania State Federation of Labor and the Socialist Party in that state, as well as a state legislator, Maurer made opposition to the constabulary a hallmark of his career. Each year the *American Cossack* was reprinted with more examples from Congressional investigations and personal testimony. The *American Cossack* was widely quoted in the labor and socialist press, and Maurer addressed the New York Federation of Labor's 1916 annual meeting and numerous smaller meetings.[28] The *American Cossack* documented instances in which the state police beat, trampled, and even shot strikers. They infiltrated strike crowds in plainclothes and pulled down American flags carried in striker parades. They provided bail and legal advice to strikebreakers who had been arrested by local authorities.

Labor's strongest condemnation, however, was reserved for two constabulary practices which in their view contravened justice and manliness: arresting without a warrant and attacking women and children. Arresting without a warrant was "viciously un-American legislation" which allowed the state body to "supersede local police authority."[29] If state police arrests violated labor norms of legality, the attacks on women and children both insulted labor's manliness and provided proof positive of the Cossacks' brutal cowardice. The Pennsylvania constabulary was nothing but "a band of Cossacks tearing up and down the state overriding local authorities and intimidating women ... The women and children of the Toilers are not safe in a state where hounds of vandals ... operate under sanction of law."[30] A huge drawing of a mounted state police officer trampling a woman with a child clutched to her breast illustrated the *Call's* special issue "Black Cossacks at Work."[31]

The trade unions and socialist locals mounted an impressive campaign of resolutions, petitions, and delegations. But they exerted little influence in the legislature. The Chamber of Commerce and its Committee failed to enact the state police measure quickly because they lacked the support of the Republican governor and legislators.[32] A constabulary required a significant appropriation from a Republican administration which was pledged to lower taxes, an administration whose constituency was based on rural voters who were opposed to government spending in general and opposed to this measure "on the ground that the rural districts do not need it and it is purely for the protection of manufacturing plants and the railroads."[33] The governor and legislators agreed that "there is little rural crime" and "the necessity of relieving the National Guard from police duty ... [is not] great enough to justify the expenditure of the sum required for a state police."[34] The measure failed in 1915 and again in 1916.

Ironically, it was the labor and socialist opposition which provided the key to the successful marketing of the state police. To convince the recalcitrant Republicans, the Committee initiated a public relations blitz designed to create middle-class pressure on the legislature in favor of the state police. Two women, the writer Katherine Mayo and her companion, the heiress M. Moyca Newell, reorganized the crusade and became so closely identified with it that the new force formally acknowledged them as the "Mothers of the State Police." Mayo wrote the publicity materials for the campaign while Newell concentrated on fund raising and lobbying. They never mentioned rural opposition to the new force and focused their propaganda on two simple ideas: first, the people who opposed the state police were lawless and violent, and two, the Pennsylvania force was made up of heroic and disciplined men.

Mayo and Newell worked closely with John C. Groome, Superintendent of the Pennsylvania State Police. He was a wealthy Philadelphia merchant who had led that city's elite First Cavalry against numerous strikes and in the Puerto Rico campaign of the Spanish-American War. Handsome and commanding, Groome came to symbolize in Mayo's writings the virility of the state police. Subjected to criticism from legislative investigations, sections of the press, trade unionists and socialists, Groome was very motivated to make common cause with the Committee for State Police in New York. He spoke at their meetings, answered endless requests for information, and provided contacts who would praise the force. Working directly with Mayo and Newell in the making of the film "Trooper 44," he deployed an entire troop for weeks at a time to shoot both the film and photographs for the publicity materials.[35]

In the new publicity materials, the state police was portrayed as the living embodiment of state authority against the onslaught of rural crime perpetrated by violent immigrants and blacks.[36] This fantastic imagery, worked and reworked in publicity photos, a movie, articles and editorials supplied to rural newspapers, was most fully elaborated in Mayo's book, *Justice to All: The Story of the Pennsylvania State Police*. No longer could critics complain, as a writer in the *New York Call* had in 1915, that ten out of the twelve photos illustrating a state police brochure showed the constabulary at strikes.[37] Written to promote the state police proposal in New York and to support the Pennsylvania force's demand for increased appropriations, *Justice to All* was launched with favorable reviews in influential newspapers, wide distribution of illustrated excerpts to smaller newspapers, and advertisements featuring former president Theodore Roosevelt's introduction to the book. The first edition sold out within a month.[38] The book went through at least five editions in three years. Roosevelt had copies sent to each member of the New York State legislature, along with a facsimile of his handwritten note, "This is the force which New York should adopt—without delay," and Groome paid for copies to be sent "from the author" to the Pennsylvania legislature.[39]

Justice to All reflected the same preoccupation with masculinity and state power which had been apparent in Mayo's earlier short stories about Surinam, a Dutch colony in South America.[40] The daughter of a mining engineer who had never struck it rich, Mayo had lived in Surinam for eight years and drew on her own experience in fashioning stories which reveled in the exoticism of the East Indian Hindu and the black laborers while celebrating the civilization wrenched from the jungle by the civilized white men.[41] In developing these themes of sexually unrestrained inferiors, the beneficent influence of European colonialism, and the necessity of a strong state power to protect the lower orders from themselves, Mayo was working within a vigorous literary tradition which located Victorian conceptions of masculinity within a political context.[42] Ten years after the publication of *Justice to All*, Mayo would hit the high point of her career with the publication of *Mother India* in 1927.[43] Purportedly an impartial examination of British rule in India, *Mother India* attributed all of India's problems to the sexual obsessions of Hindu men. Mayo relied on information and assistance from the British government in conducting her research, and the book was published during an intense period of independence agitation in 1927. Gandhi condemned the book, and it was publicly burned in New Delhi, Calcutta, San Francisco, and New York.[44] *Mother India* brought the themes of

570   journal of social history   spring 1995

race, masculinity and the state which were present in *Justice to All* to bear on the explosive issue of British colonialism.

Justice to All emphasized the individual men of the state police in a manner calculated to set them apart from the contemporary stereotypes of the Keystone Cops, brutal city police, or the Pennsylvania Cossacks. This imagery, new to American police but common in contemporary descriptions of the Northwest Mounted Police, the Trooper Police of Australia, and other colonial forces, portrayed the state police as brave men defending a majestic yet threatened state.[45] Coded female, the state's virtue is its commitment to the rule of law, its insistence on neutrality despite provocation. In his introduction, Roosevelt asserted that the Pennsylvania force had originated as a replacement for the private Coal and Iron Police, rescuing the state from prostituting its authority:

> ... when the laboring masses rocked in mortal combat with the vested interests, the State stepped in to prove her impartial justice *by selling her authority into the vested interests' hands!* ... whenever the miners elected to go out on strike ... they invariably found the power of the State bought, paid for, and fighting as a partisan on their employers' side. Nor was there any attempt made to do this monstrous thing under mask of decency.[46]

Fortunately for the mine owners, the "mask of decency" provided by the state police did not mean the end of the Coal and Iron Police whose numbers continued to increase until the 1930s.[47] Ignoring the on-going cooperation between the private and state police, Mayo portrayed the force as policemen-soldiers serving to enforce the laws of an impartial State. Opposition to the state police, then, became by definition un-American.

State police had not been needed when "the mass of the people came from generations of law-revering stock," but to the new immigrants "liberty had no meaning other than gross licence." Seeing "no *gendarmerie*, no *carabinieri*," they "joyfully drew an invitation to make of the Decalogue a daily sacrifice."[48] Not seeing the "sword of the King," Slavs and Italians "looked in vain for outward evidence of authority and law." Poles and Hungarians were little better than animals: "A simple, mercurial people, easily victimized, easily infuriated to serve the will of others, they were scarcely guiltier in their fury, ... than the bull in the ring."[49] One of the bill's sponsors distributed an open letter to rural newspapers arguing for the state police as a defense against the "farm labor problem," men who " ... differ by education, training, and character from our forebears. They are not moved by the same ideals, not are they amenable to the same control of public opinion or public morality. No longer is the country free from elements which our fathers would speedily have eliminated as vile and un-American."[50] Reversing the language of the unionists, state police propaganda called the workers "un-American."

State police propaganda hammered relentlessly on the alleged crisis of rural crime. Never convincing the farmers, whose organizations opposed or remained silent on the issue, Committee press releases and targeted mass mailings created a barrage of letters and postcards to legislators from middle-class businessmen and professionals in urban and rural areas alike. Eschewing images of the police as strike breakers, the canned articles supplied to rural newspapers featured staged photographs of the police capturing bootleggers, kidnappers and auto-

FROM COSSACK TO TROOPER   571

mobile thieves, protecting rural women, and tracking down check forgers.[51] A mailing to about four thousand doctors warned of "many unpunished crimes, thousands of homes open to attack."[52] Totally unaccustomed to "any form of self-government," the immigrants and "Negroes" were especially prone to rape, the "one sin above all other in which the State Police is pledged to mortal war." Rapes brought forth some of the force's most heroic deeds. An attack on an eight-year-old girl so horrible that "when they had found her dead under the drifted leaves, they were glad she had died," spurred a Sergeant to a three-day pursuit, "never once taking off his clothes, never once lying down, never once catching a moment's sleep."[53]

Anglo-Saxon women needed protection, but the lasciviousness and degradation of black and immigrant women confirmed the disorder of their communities. The state police were Anglo-Saxon heroes standing up against the immigrant and black hordes. Both personally brave and part of a disciplined whole, these soldiers were not an aggressive invading force.[54] They were the patriotic defenders of a way of life and system of government which were threatened by foreigners who were themselves the invaders. Like the real soldiers, sailors and marines who were being dispatched to fulfill the United States' new "international police power," the state police were not conquering nations or peoples. "Wars with uncivilized powers," according to Roosevelt, were not really wars, but rather "mere matters of international police duty."[55] They were combatting crime and disorder, using force in the interests of both the policing and the policed. The State police enabled the "rudimentary minds" of the immigrants and African Americans to learn "obedience to the State." Describing the Force's impact as "magical," Mayo described how the "stern, somber, silent horsemen" made the immigrants understand "that this new power was power indeed—the Power of the State, till now unseen; they understood that it was inexorable, impersonal, calm as death; that it must be obeyed."[56] Unlike "Clubber Williams," the New York City policeman immortalized for his brutality by Lincoln Steffens, the state police were supposed to control their anger and use force only when necessary. The new state power was, moreover, impartial and fair: "*The State Police has no purpose save to execute the laws of the State.*"[57]

State police propaganda emphasized the enforcement of criminal law and the necessity of neutrality in strike policing. The Committee's profound contempt for unions and strikes was never far from the surface. Mayo herself had proposed *Black Hussars* as the title for her book, and the publicity film "Trooper 44" took its title from the identifying number of the Pennsylvania trooper who had killed a Hungarian bystander during the 1910 strike at the Bethlehem Steel plant. Impartiality was important, but the real problem was worker violence, especially from ignorant Slavs or members of the criminal IWW. There the military training of the police, who "had sharpened their wits all over the world, against the wits of yellow men, brown men, and white," was invaluable.[58] A veteran of infantry and marine corps service in the Philippines, China, Japan, and Panama, Private Hershey "had been trained in a school where wounds and broken bones are supposed to deflect neither a man's wits nor his trigger finger."[59] If the conquest of the Indians, Filipinos and Colombians was essential to realizing the national destiny, then so too was the taming of the unions.[60] Mayo invoked Greek mythology to express the ferocious beauty of the new force entering a

572   journal of social history   spring 1995

strike scene: " ... Looking neither to right nor to left, not a flicker of nervous tension on their strong, stern faces, the men followed pair on pair, lean, lithe, panther-built, perfect specimens of the finest physical type, each one, sitting their horses like the centaurs they were."[61] The state police were more than disciplined, well trained and brave, they were handsome and heroic, willing to lay down their lives for a principle of justice. As the "unchallengeable figure of the State wielding in majesty her Arm of Law,"[62] the state police possessed "an inward and spiritual force that could not be bought, bent, confused, alarmed or exhausted."[63]

Calling the state police a "sword in the hand of Justice," Mayo described the force as the embodiment of a protective masculinity.[64] Militarism became transmuted into an idealized middle-class masculinity which included both bodily perfection and a "spiritual force." Distinct from the lazy, corrupt, frequently Irish city police, the state police are described as meeting a masculine ideal of working without sleep, without food, without thought for themselves.[65] Unlike the lustful blacks and immigrants and the sexually vulnerable women, the men of the Pennsylvania State Police were strong in part because of what Mayo implied was an ideal of celibacy. Unmarried, the men revelled in clean, wholesome male camaraderie, bonded together through military discipline and personal devotion. The "splendid manhood" of this "close-knit brotherhood" was due to its leader, Major John Groome: "by the sheer, bare beauty of an austere and selfless ideal, he has drawn the very flower of the young men to him, eager to live, or to die if need be, for the simple love of The Finest Thing in the World."[66] Giving his life "as knight crusaders died for the Grail," Private Timothy Kelleher, veteran of the Boer army and Philippines, was killed while stopping a rape by two Italians.[67] The "bond between man and man, man and officer" was so close, that when asked about it, a "captain turned slowly white, even to his lips: 'I don't think I could speak about that,' said he, almost unsteadily—nor were words needed."[68] Strengthened by devotion to their leaders, the men enjoyed a high level of *esprit de corps* and male camaraderie, "knitted together by the free-masonry of the past, and now allied by a common exalted purpose ... to make of the little brotherhood the 'finest thing in the world.'"[69] Defending a Negro rapist from a lynch mob, a Sergeant thought: "A little hard, perhaps, to give his life for the life of that inconceivable wretch ... But—was it hard to die for the 'finest thing in the world'? A smile lighted the Sergeant's eyes."[70] Self-restrained by nature and discipline, state police only used force when the violence of others required it.

Justice to All infuriated the trade union and socialist opponents of the state police, but it was not, after all, aimed at them. The political problem had been to win over the upstate Republican legislators who would have to defend their votes to rural and small town constituencies. For them, the state police propaganda provided the perfect language for impugning the manliness and lawfulness of all state police opponents. Senator Elon Brown's response to one of the hundreds of labor memorials against the state police was published—with the Committee's urging—in newspapers throughout the state. Implying that the unionists wanted violence at strikes, he fumed "Is it possible that men of the intelligence and position of railroad trainmen think so lightly of maintaining order and security in the community that they are opposed to an effective police force? Or is there some particular kind of disorder which you are unwilling to have restrained?"[71]

Union men could choose between defending their "intelligence and position" or their right to strike. Rapidly escalating preparations for American entrance into World War I caused conflict between the Socialists and the State Federation of Labor in the last weeks of the campaign, but both persisted in their opposition to the state police. James Holland, President of the Federation, cited the Federation's immediate support for breaking relations with Germany to argue that unionists needed "no lessons in patriotism," and that precisely because of the war emergency no money should be spent for state police.[72] His arguments were to no avail. The bill passed by one vote in March 1917.

"Well, women are supermen, after all," chortled the Chancellor of the University of Buffalo to Newell and Mayo.[73] Enactment of the legislation, however, did not put to rest the controversy over the state police. Farmers expressed disappointment and bewilderment that their opinions counted for so little, and the state Democratic platform called for abolishing the force. Mayo, Newell, and the Committee for State Police, however, were determined to make the new force a success and to win adoption of similar bodies in other states. Mayo wrote two more books and twenty-five articles about the state police, and despite its patent exaggeration, her work was cited with approval by the academic police experts of the 1920s and 1930s.[74] Members of the Committee kept a close watch on the new body, spurred the campaigns of local Chambers of Commerce to build barracks, and began agitating for increasing the number of state police.[75]

Chandler's approach to shaping the New York State Police developed out of both his own experience as a physician and National Guard officer and his close, on-going contact with Mayo and Newell, after whom he named the first training camp "Newayo".[76] Both sets of influences converged to shape his preoccupation with the image and public perception of the new force. Seeking to recruit a "distinctively American type of men," Chandler worked to weld them into a force not only of soldiers, but of gentlemen, a force whose manliness would command respect in areas which had not before been subject to routine policing.

Chandler directed his attention first to uniform design, personally devising a distinctive grey cloth set off with a purple tie and purple band in a Stetson hat.[77] Training emphasized appearance, personality, and courtesy as much as horsemanship and target practice. "Always be a gentleman, courteous, kind, gentle, fair, keep yourself clean and neat, you and your horse equally well groomed, stand erect, put snap and vigor into your movements," commanded Chandler.[78] The training manual included chapters on Telephone Courtesy, Police and the Press, Police and Character, as well as the usual units on firearms, riots, and traffic. Chandler condemned any trooper who "makes a noise over the soup, or eats with his knife, or covers his knife and fork with his great big hands, or takes a piece of bread and wipes it all around his plate and mops up everything."[79] He chose the huge state fair in Syracuse for the force's debut, guaranteeing that they could make an impressive ceremonial appearance.[80] Although the force's official title, as in Pennsylvania, was State Police, Chandler used the title State Troopers on signs and stationery and urged the newspapers to utilize the term.[81] As "troopers," Chandler hoped to avoid the two terms used most commonly

574 journal of social history spring 1995

in Pennsylvania, constabulary by supporters and cossacks by critics. Chandler attempted to shape both the self image and the public perception of the force.

In his annual reports, published jointly with the Committee for State Police until 1921, photographs told the story of a manly force protecting rural womanhood. The 1918 report started with a photo of Chandler and his second in command standing at attention with riding crops in hand. The second image showed the State Police apprehending a man about to commit "the worst danger that country women have to face ... the danger worse than death." A trooper helping a farmer get a car carrying milk cans out of a ditch is the third photo. In the last photo, an elderly black man is caught with a gunny sack of chickens saying "I ain't never stole no chicken in all my life." The images became even more fantastic in the report for 1919. For a year in which over half the force's time was spent in strike work, the photos show troopers finding a lost child, returning a strayed calf, and demanding to see a hunter's license.

Although the photographs were posed, there was truth to Chandler's claim to building strong bodies and character. Good health was a prime requirement for recruitment, and Chandler excluded many urban working-class men with the requirement that a man know how to ride a horse.[82] Discipline was strict, and unlike the city police, the men had no Civil Service protection and were discharged immediately for offenses such as drinking and insubordination.[83] Like Groome, Chandler fostered the image of the state police as a selective body, a place where a worthy man could prove himself. Starting pay was less than that of city police, but since most of the men were single and had their housing, food and clothing paid by the force, it was substantial. The training and opportunity to meet people provided by the patrol system meant that most men were able to move on to better paying work within a few years. When not on patrol, the men spent much of their time in barracks improving their horsemanship and engaging in athletic contests. Trick riding exhibits at country fairs enabled the young men to show off skills such as riding a horse in a three-man pyramid and guiding their mounts on jumps through flaming hoops.[84] The entire rank and file belonged to a secret society called the Ancient Order of Fleas.[85] Despite, or perhaps because of, barracks life, the state police was a desirable job, and after the war Chandler was able to limit his recruitment to ex-service men.

Chandler sought out a variety of tasks from other state government departments in order to render the force indispensable and shape its image of manly helpfulness. State Police worked with the Department of Education on "Safety First" and "Obedience to Law and Order" educational campaigns. The Agriculture Department enlisted their help in enforcing the quarantine against rabies. They made temporary repairs and tracked stolen equipment for the Highway Department.[86] During the war, the force worked extensively with Military Intelligence, and after the war it conducted some of the infamous Lusk Committee's raids on alleged subversives. A commendation from the War Department for the Troopers' work with Military Intelligence was featured on the cover of the Committee for State Police's second report. Effective work against radicals enhanced the force's manly image.

It was the postwar strike wave, however, which put the severest strain on the force's public image. Democratic Governor Alfred E. Smith had been elected on a platform vowing the dismantling of the force, and he was subjected to on-going union pressure to carry out his inaugural pledge. After the first time he called the state police for strike work, however, he changed his mind. Working closely with Smith, Chandler was determined to create an appearance of neutrality in strike work and to minimize the public perception of the troopers as a strike control force. Since the state police spent most of its time in strike work in 1919, 1921, and 1922, this was not an easy task.[87]

Chandler, however, took much greater care than his counterpart in Pennsylvania to create the appearance of neutrality in strike work. Troopers were not housed on company property, and designated spokesmen for the force were careful in how they described its role in strikes. In the 1919 Olean trolley strike, where the State Police were protecting the strikebreakers and assisting in the prosecution of strikers, Lieutenant E. Joseph Sheehan boasted to a reporter: "We're neutral all the way. We don't know anyone connected with the strike, and we don't want to. We don't know any grievances, and we don't want to. We are here to put down disorder. Both sides in the strike look alike to us."[88] Neutrality was determined by perceptions. During a huge streetcar strike in Buffalo in 1922, Chandler assured the trolley company that it could run cars with strikebreakers by sending a message with the Chief of Police. Reporting to Governor Miller, he congratulated himself for having had no meeting with either the employers or the strikers, "we only being here to maintain law and order without regard to the merits of the strike."[89]

In addition to asserting his force's neutrality, Chandler justified harsh tactics as a defense against lawless and subversive radicals. During the troopers' first large-scale strike intervention in Rome in 1919, a house-by-house search of the Italian district uncovered a home with IWW literature. Working with the Committee for State Police, Chandler issued press releases asserting that a dangerous conspiracy by Italian and other foreigners to incite a general strike had been narrowly averted.[90] He dismissed criticism of his men for violence in the steel strike of 1919 and during 1921 and 1922 as emanating from lawless immigrants rather than American workers who welcomed the presence of the state police.[91] Immigrant women strikers required not chivalry, but a special kind of horseman. Explaining his tactics during the 1921 Albany strike, Chandler told the governor that " ... women sympathizers endeavored to start a riot. They had sticks and stones, and one woman in particular was armed with a piece of brass gas pipe and she was very vicious. The language of the women was indescribable and when ordered to move on they refused and showed fight."[92] The problem, Chandler averred, is that "it is hard for any kind of man to fight a woman. The horse solves the problem for the policeman ... "[93] For women, Chandler argued, "the use of the horse is invaluable. Women are instinctively afraid of horses and will run before the horsemen reach them."[94]

Seeking to maintain his public relations capacity when Mayo and Newell turned increasingly to international interests, Chandler teamed up with society writer Frederic F. Van de Water to form the private Publicity Bureau of State Police which published the *State Troopers Magazine*. Making Van de Water an "honorary trooper," Chandler gave him full access to the force in order to write *Grey Riders: The Story of the New York State Troopers*. With an endorsement from Governor Smith and a forward by Chandler himself, *Grey Riders* was modelled closely on *Justice to All*. Van de Water made clear that the purpose of the book was countering the negative image of state police: "Say 'State Police' to the average citizen and straightway he will conjure up the picture of an iron-faced man on a rearing horse, surging into a mob of strikers with flailing night stick or smoking gun."[95] Van de Water's approach was even more nativist and racist than Mayo's. Describing isolated rural areas full of "native born aliens" who had returned to savagery, "redskins," and cities full of Italians, Poles, Hungarians and other aliens, Van de Water argued that the troopers had rescued the state from almost certain ruin. Going beyond Chandler's earlier claims of sedition in Rome, for example, Van de Water claimed that "captured correspondence" proved that the metalworkers' strike was directed by "Communistic and I.W.W. leaders" who saw the conflict as the opening salvo for revolution throughout the eastern United States.[96] "Persistent savagery" marked the 1921 Albany streetcar strike because of "strange new doctrines from Russia."[97] Like Mayo, Van de Water countered the barbarism of immigrant men with the achieved manliness of the state police: "The ordeals through which they had passed not only served notice on the world that they had come to man's estate. They disclosed, as well, that this maturity was well tempered, sane, and courageous."[98] This manliness, moreover, could serve as a model for America's youth. The state police "heroes ... are not supermen. Except for their training and a certain physical excellence bred by the nature of their work, they are counterparts of eight out of every dozen young men of America." Recruit and train properly, and "in ninety-nine cases out of hundred you evolve a soldier or policeman almost as invincible as Achilles."[99]

Despite Chandler's attention to public relations, however, trade unionists routinely protested state police intervention in strikes and succeeded in getting legislation restricting the use of the State Police introduced in the legislature in 1923 and 1924.[100] Senator William E. Martin protested on behalf of his constituents in terms reminiscent of Maurer's *American Cossack*: "the people of my district ... call them the 'Cossacks.' They are extremely cruel and apparently have forgotten the first principles of manhood, to take proper care of women and children."[101] The bills barely made it out of committee. Both four-term Governor Smith and the Republican Governor Nathan L. Miller whose election in 1920 kept Smith out of office for two years, strongly supported Chandler. The only state police legislation which passed was that increasing the size and salaries of the force.

The *New York Times* editorialized in 1926 that the State Police "are not called 'Cossacks' anything like so often as they used to be."[102] The effort to transform "Cossacks" into "Troopers" had been at least partially successful. This transformation had taken place on two levels, through real changes in police training and practice coupled with an unrelenting effort to shape public perceptions of the force. The battle of perceptions had begun during the campaign to create the force. There the two contending visions of masculinity collided. One asserted the claim of working-class men to be treated with respect and to have the opportunity to protect their economic interests through successful strikes. Its advocates denounced the state police as armed strikebreakers, state-paid agents of the corporations, who in their willingness to attack women acted more like beasts than men. The opposing viewpoint claimed to stand above class conflict and

FROM COSSACK TO TROOPER   577

to advance the common interest in a strong state as a protection against crime and violence. By publicizing the state police as a chivalric force dedicated to the maintenance of order and the protection of white womanhood, proponents of the state police identified their cause with the interests of respectability.[103] Using gendered language to promote police reform, they identified new forms of state coercion with familiar assumptions of racial and gender hierarchy. These assumptions were shared in large measure by many of the working-class opponents of the state police who found themselves unable to oppose the expansion of state power without undermining their own commitment to respectability.

Racial and gender assumptions remained central to the new state police force. Like the larger police professionalization movement of which it was a part, the state police embedded these prejudices into its core identity. The numerous crime commission surveys of the 1920s and 1930s lacked the vivid imagery of Mayo and Van de Water, but they expressed the same values. No longer a potentially anti-democratic standing army, the state police were the last defense against lawless un-Americans and a possible source of personal pride. Writing in the wake of the state police's 1919 strike work, one supporter beamed: "no man can hear the record of these soldiers of mercy and right without feeling the stir of true manhood within him."[104] "True manhood" precluded the recruitment of blacks, women, or members of certain ethnic groups, and the state police forces would remain bastions of "distinctively American type of men" for decades.

Nor was concern with the manly image of the police in the early decades of the twentieth century limited to state-level forces. Everywhere the reformers associated with the police professionalization movement, from police chiefs to "police science" academics, exhorted the men to dress neatly, exhibit a manly demeanor, and overcome popular prejudices against the police. Taking over the Bureau of Investigation in 1924, J. Edgar Hoover would turn this emphasis on image into a veritable obsession. Professional policing was rooted in the same claim of superior men devoted to the policing of inferior men that Mayo had used to explain the necessary sternness of the Pennsylvania constabulary. The expansion of the coercive apparatus of the state in twentieth-century America was legitimized through frequent invocations of commonly held assumptions about the superior masculinity of the "Anglo-Saxon" middle class.

Department of History
St. Louis, MO 63121-4499

ENDNOTES

An earlier version of this article was presented at the Annual Meeting of the Organization of American Historians in April, 1993. Commentators Mark C. Carnes and Wilbur R. Miller and chair Alan Dawley made useful challenges. I appreciate help from Martha Kohl, Dana Frank and Jonathan D. March and the critiques on a related aspect of the argument developed here provided by Paula Baker, Geraldine H. Forbes, Estelle B. Freedman, Sidney L. Harring, Marilynn S. Johnson, Eric H. Monkkonen, Tony Platt, and Bill Preston.

1.   New York State Police, *Second Annual Report for the Year 1919* (Albany, 1920), p. 20.

2.   By state, I mean the whole complex of governmental, legislative, and judicial insti-

tutions which structure political life and are in turn transformed by political and social change. The term state police refers to police organized at the state level of government. There is a growing literature on the weakness of the American state in the nineteenth century. A few of the most useful works are Morton Keller, *Affairs of State: Public Life in Late Nineteenth Century America* (Cambridge, MA, 1977); L. Ray Gunn, *The Decline of Authority: Public Economic Policy and Political Development in New York, 1800–1860* (Ithaca, 1988); Amy Bridges, *A City in the Republic: Antebellum New York and the Origins of Machine Politics* (New York, 1984); Stephen Skowronek, *Building a New American State: The Expansion of National Administrative Capacities, 1877–1920* (New York, 1982); Richard Franklin Bensel, *Yankee Leviathan: The Origins of Central State Authority in America, 1859–1877* (New York, 1990).

3.   On the problems of policing in nineteenth-century America, see Roger Lane, *Policing the City: Boston, 1822–1885* (Cambridge, MA, 1967); James Richardson, *The New York City Police: Colonial Times to 1901* (New York, 1970); Wilbur R. Miller, *Cops and Bobbies: Police Authority in New York and London, 1830–1870* (Chicago, 1977); Robert M. Fogelson, *Big-City Police* (Cambridge, MA, 1977); Samuel Walker, *A Critical History of Police Reform: The Emergence of Professionalism* (Lexington, MA, 1977); Eric H. Monkkonen, *Police in Urban America, 1860–1920* (New York, 1981); Sidney L. Harring, *Policing a Class Society: The Experience of American Cities, 1865–1915* (New Brunswick, 1983).

4.   Alan Dawley, *Struggles for Justice: Social Responsibility and the Liberal State* (Cambridge, MA, 1991), pp. 1–13, 139–71.

5.   On the opposition to a standing army and the use of the militia, see Russell F. Weigley, *History of the United States Army* (New York, 1967); Barton C. Hacker, "The United States Army as a National Police Force: The Federal Policing of Labor Disputes, 1877–1898," *Military Affairs* 33 (April 1969): 255–64; Jerry M. Cooper, *The Army and Civil Disorder: Federal Military Intervention in Labor Disputes, 1877–1900* (Westport, CT, 1980); Richard H. Kohn, ed., *The United States Military Under the Constitution of the United States, 1789–1989* (New York, 1991).

6.   Joan Wallach Scott, "Gender: A Useful Category of Historical Analysis," in *Gender and the Politics of History* (New York, 1988), p. 46.

7.   Most recent work on the historical construction of masculinity focuses on "Anglo-Saxon" middle-class men and argues that the decline of Victorian certainties around 1900 caused a crisis of self identification to which men responded with a reassertion of "traditional masculinity." This approach has been developed in Jeffrey P. Hantover, "The Boy Scouts and the Validation of Masculinity," *Journal of Social Issues* 34 (1978): 184–95; Joe L. Dubbert, *A Man's Place: Masculinity in Transition* (Englewood Cliffs, NJ, 1979); E. Anthony Rotundo, "Body and Soul: Changing Ideals of American Middle-Class Manhood, 1770–1920," *Journal of Social History* 16 (1983): 23–38; Peter Filene, "Between a Rock and a Soft Place: A Century of American Manhood," *South Atlantic Quarterly* 84 (Autumn 1985): 339–55; J.A. Mangan and James Walvin, eds. *Manliness and Morality: Middle-Class Masculinity in Britain and America, 1800–1940* (New York, 1987); Gail Bederman, " 'The Women Have Had Charge of the Church Work Long Enough': The Men and Religion Forward Movement of 1911–1912 and the Masculinization of Middle-Class Protestantism," *American Quarterly* 41 (1989): 432–65; Gail Bederman, " 'Civilization,' The Decline of Middle-Class Maleness, and Ida B. Wells's Antilynching Campaign (1892–94)," *Radical History Review* 52 (1992): 5–30; Peter G. Filene, *Him/her/self: Sex Roles in Modern America,* 2nd ed. (Baltimore, 1986); Michael S. Kimmel, "Baseball and the Reconstitution of American Masculinity, 1880–1920," Peter Levine, ed., *Baseball History* 3 (Westport, CT, 1990): 98–112; Melvin L. Adelman, *Sporting Time: New York City and the Rise of Modern Athletics, 1820–1870* (Urbana, 1986); Michael S. Kimmel, "The Contemporary 'Crisis' of Masculinity in Historical Perspective," in Harry Brod, ed., *The Making of Masculinities: The New Men's Studies* (Boston, 1987).

The crisis interpretations help account for the prominence of gender in social debate at the turn of the century, but other historians have argued that change took place over a longer period of time and that there was a variety of masculine styles available to both middle- and working-class men. Peter N. Stearns, *Be a Man! Males in Modern Society* (New York, 1990); Mark C. Carnes and Clyde Griffen, eds., *Meanings for Manhood: Constructions of Masculinity in Victorian America* (Chicago, 1990).

8.   Carnes and Griffin note that the essays in their collection analyze how social change "led to shifts in the way men and women understood masculinity. Less frequently expressed is the possibility that causation also worked the other way—that changing conceptions of masculinity influenced broader social, economic, and political processes." Carnes and Griffin, *Meanings for Manhood*, p. 7. The controversy over the state police reflected the changing conceptions of masculinity in the period and the effective use of an elite ideology of masculinity in propaganda. I am using the distinction between ideology and propaganda developed in Barbara Jeanne Fields, "Slavery, Race and Ideology in the United States of America," *New Left Review* 181 (April 1990): 95–118, especially p. 111: "The most successful propagandist is one who thoroughly understands the ideology of those to be propagandized." For a more recent example of masculinity as ideology and propaganda, see Joshua B. Freeman, "Hardhats: Construction Workers, Manliness, and the 1970 Pro-War Demonstrations," *Journal of Social History* 26 (Summer 1993): 725–44.

9.   The recent surge of interest in gender and the state has focussed primarily on women and the state. Paula Baker, "The Domestication of Politics: Women and American Political Society, 1780–1920," *American Historical Review* 89 (June 1984): 620–47; Suzanne Lebsock, "Women and American Politics, 1880–1920," in Louise A. Tilly and Patricia Gurin, eds., *Women, Politics, and Change* (New York, 1990); Linda Gordon, ed., *Women, the State and Welfare* (Madison, 1990); Noralee Frankel and Nancy S. Dye, eds., *Gender, Class, Race and Reform in the Progressive Era* (Lexington, KY, 1991); Theda Skocpol, *Protecting Soldiers and Mothers: The Political Origins of Social Policy in the United States* (Cambridge, MA, 1992).

An important work which deals with both men and women and the state is Paula Baker, *The Moral Frameworks of Public Life: Gender, Politics, and the State in Rural New York, 1870–1930* (New York, 1991).

10.   Thomas S. Crago to Katherine Mayo, June 2, 1916, Katherine Mayo Papers, Manuscripts and Archives, Yale University Library (hereafter Mayo Papers).

11.   Joseph John Holmes, "The National Guard of Pennsylvania: Policemen of Industry, 1865–1905," Ph.D. diss., University of Connecticut, 1970.

12.   Hyman Kuritz, "The Pennsylvania State Government and Labor Control From 1865 to 1922," Ph.D. diss., Columbia University, 1953, p. 248.

13.   The killing of Joseph Szambo, a bystander, by the Pennsylvania State Police during a strike at the Bethlehem Steel Works in 1910 was documented in a government report and received wide publicity. U.S. Senate, "Report on Strike at Bethlehem Steel Works," Doc. No. 521, 61st Congress, 2nd Session (1910), pp. 1–136. The 1915–1916 hearings of Frank P. Walsh's Commission of Industrial Relations included extensive testimony on the excesses of the Pennsylvania State Police which was in turn widely reprinted in both the labor and city press. The Commission concluded that the Pennsylvania force was "an extremely efficient force for crushing strikes" and that "it seems desirable rather to leave the State policing of industrial disputes to the sheriff and the militia." U.S. Senate, *Industrial Relations: Final Report and Testimony Submitted to Congress by the Commission on Industrial Relations Created by the Act of Aug. 23, 1912*, Doc. No. 415, 64th Congress, 1st Session (1916), 11 vols. Quotes on pp. 97–98; testimony on state police, pp. 10550–11024.

14. Chamber of Commerce of the State of New York, *Fifty-sixth Annual Report* (New York, 1914), p. 114.

15. Two key works on New York State politics are Richard L. McCormick, *From Realignment to Reform: Political Change in New York State, 1893–1910* (Ithaca, 1981) and Robert F. Wesser, *A Response to Progressivism: The Democratic Party and New York Politics, 1902–1918* (New York, 1986). Important works on the political role of labor in this period include Irwin Yellowitz, *Labor and the Progressive Movement in New York State, 1897–1916* (Ithaca, 1965) and Melvyn Dubofsky, *When Workers Organize, New York City in the Progressive Era* (Amherst, 1968).

16. Ernest Bohm [Corresponding Secretary of the Central Federated Union of Greater New York and Vicinity] to Hon. Seth Low, Dec. 27, 1913, Seth Low Papers, Rare Book and Manuscript Library, Butler Library, Columbia University.

17. Letter from Citizens of Madison to James H. Maurer, Feb. 22, 1911, in The Pennsylvania State Federation of Labor (PSFL), *The American Cossack* (Harrisburg, 1912; repr. New York, 1971), quoted in *New York Call*, Feb. 14, 1915 and throughout trade union and socialist propaganda. Opposition to the state police was an extension of what David Montgomery has analyzed as the "workers' own code of ethical behavior." David Montgomery, *The Fall of the House of Labor: The Workplace, the State, and American Labor Activism, 1865–1925* (New York, 1987). On the connection between conceptions of working-class manliness and the ability to support a family, see Stearns, *Be a Man!*, pp. 128, 139; Ava Baron, "An 'Other' Side of Gender Antagonism at Work: Men, Boys, and the Remasculinization of Printers' Work, 1830–1920"; Mary H. Blewett, "Manhood and the Market: The Politics of Gender and Class Among the Textile Workers of Fall River, Massachusetts, 1870–1880"; Nancy A. Hewitt, " 'The Voice of Virile Labor': Labor Militancy, Community Solidarity, and Gender Identity among Tampa's Latin Workers, 1880–1921"; and Ileen A. DeVault, " 'Give the Boys a Trade:' Gender and Job Choice in the 1890s," in Ava Baron, ed., *Work Engendered: Toward a New History of American Labor* (Ithaca, 1991); Colleen McDannell, " 'True Men as We Need Them:' Catholicism and the Irish-American Male," *American Studies* 27 (Fall 1986): 19–36; Steven Maynard, "Rough Work and Rugged Men: The Social Construction of Masculinity in Working-Class History," *Labour/Le Travail* 23 (Spring 1989): 159–69; Gunther Peck, "Manly Gambles: The Politics of Risk on the Comstock Lode, 1860–1880," *Journal of Social History* 26 (Summer 1993): 701–23.

18. *New York Call*, Feb. 8, 1915.

19. Editorial, *New York Call*, Dec. 7, 1914.

20. *Legislative Labor News*, Apr. 3, 1916.

21. D.V. Linneham, B.J. Gardephe, and A. St. Clair, [Resolutions from Glens Falls mass meeting], Feb. 28, 1917, Abraham I. Shiplacoff Papers, Tamiment Library, Bobst Library, New York University. Many of *Labor Herald's* articles on the state police started with Cossacks in the headline, including "Cossack Craze Strikes Ohio." *Rochester Labor Herald*, Feb. 15, 1917. See also "Cossacks are Blamed," May 4, 1916 on the rioting in Wilkes-Barre, Pennsylvania and "No Cossacks for New York" on the trade union opposition; "Labor Men Pan Cossack Bill at Albany," Feb. 22, 1917 on the legislative hearing.

Terming the state police bill "the most infamous legislation ever presented to the Empire State Legislature," and "patterned after the Pennsylvania State Constabulary," the *Albany Federationist* denounced the "Cossack system" because "the intention is to use the mounted police as strikebreakers." *Albany Federationist*, May 3, 1916.

The *Albany Federationist* joined the *Rochester Labor Herald* and other New York State trade union newspapers in blaming the violence in the Wilkes-Barre streetcar strike of

FROM COSSACK TO TROOPER   581

1916 on the "lawless Cossacks," "a horde of irresponsible chaps who wear the badge of the state and go about armed to the teeth looking for and provoking trouble." *Albany Federationist*, June 7, 1916.

22. *Auburn Advertiser*, Jan. 22, 1917; PSFL, *The American Cossack*, pp. 63, 84; Wagaman [Pennsylvania Federation of Labor Vice President], "The American Cossack is a Strike Breaking Institution," *American Federationist* (June 1916): 467–69, reprinted in *Albany Federationist*, July 5, 1916 and throughout trade union and socialist press.
   Several historians have taken at face value the claim that the Pennsylvania force was modelled on the Irish constabulary, but I have found no evidence. Mike Brogden, "The Emergence of the Police—The Colonial Dimension," *British Journal of Criminology* 27 (Winter 1987): 4–14.

23. *New York Call*, Apr. 14, 1915.

24. Editorial, *Rochester Labor Herald*, Jan. 18, 1917.

25. *Legislative Labor News*, Feb. 12, 19 & 26, 1917; Alexander R. Golder, "We Want No State Constabulary," *New York Call*, Dec. 5, 1914.

26. *New York Call*, Feb. 14, 1915; *Legislative Labor News*, Feb. 12, 1917; *Rochester Labor Herald*, Apr. 19, 1917.

27. *Albany Federationist*, May 3, 1916.

28. James Maurer, *It Can Be Done* (New York, 1938).

29. PSFL, *American Cossack*; *Rochester Labor Herald*, May 4, 1916; *Legislative Labor News*, Feb. 12, 1917.

30. *Minnesota Labor Review*, quoted in *Rochester Labor Herald*, Feb. 15, 1917.

31. *New York Call*, Feb. 14, 1915.

32. Gerda W. Ray, "Contested Legitimacy: Creation of the State Police in New York, 1890–1930," Ph.D. diss., University of California, Berkeley, 1990, pp. 109–218.

33. *Watertown Times*, Feb. 10, 1917. On the fiscal conservatism of rural voters, see Wesser, *A Response to Progressivism*; Paula Baker, "The Culture of Politics in the Late Nineteenth Century: Community and Political Behavior in Rural New York," *Journal of Social History* 18 (1984): 176–93.

34. Helen Hoy Greeley, "Report to Committee for State Police," n.d. [Apr. 1916], Mayo Papers.

35. John C. Groome to Mayo, Feb. 17, 1914; Jan. 15, 1916; June 12, 1916; July 31, 1916; Jan. 8, 1917; Lynn G. Adams to Mayo, Jan. 18, 1917, Mayo Papers. The company which made the movie recognized its client's exacting demands: "It is obvious that an immense amount of mental as well as physical effort will have to be expended before these pictures shall have passed the censorship of Major Groome." (Pathescope Exchange of Philadelphia to Mayo, Mar. 18, 1916.)

36. Stanley Coben, *Rebellion Against Victorianism: The Impetus for Cultural Change in 1920s America* (New York, 1991), pp. 4, 23–24, 27–28, 32–34 locates racism and nativism as central to the Victorian worldview.

37. *New York Call*, Feb. 14, 1915.

38. Katherine Mayo, *Justice to All: The Story of the Pennsylvania State Police*, with an introduction by Theodore Roosevelt (New York, 1917). At least thirty newspapers reviewed *Justice to All* in January 1917. By the end of May there had been eighty reviews. Mayo Engagement Book, May 26, 1917; Katherine Mayo Diary, Jan. 31, 1917, Mayo Papers.

39. Groome had asked Roosevelt to write and then revise the introduction. Groome to Roosevelt, Oct. 30, Nov. 1, Nov. 4, Nov. 22, 1916; Roosevelt to Groome, Nov. 1, Nov. 4, Nov. 9, Nov. 22, Nov. 24, 1916, Theodore Roosevelt Papers, Microfilm Edition, Library of Congress (hereafter Roosevelt Papers); Groome to Mayo, Nov. 25, 1916, Mayo Papers. Roosevelt to Groome, Nov. 28, 1916, enclosed in Groome to Mayo, Nov. 29, 1917, Mayo Papers.

40. Katherine Mayo, "Big Mary," *Atlantic* 107 (Jan. 1911): 112–17; "Bushed," *Scribner's* 49 (June 1911): 754–61; "My Law and Thine," *Atlantic* 109 (Feb. 1912): 239–44; "Sissa and the Bakru," *Atlantic* 110 (Oct. 1912): 497–503; "The Devil-Hen," *Scribner's* 54 (Dec. 1913): 756–64.

41. The biographical information here is based on Mayo's Papers and Mary E. Handlin, s.v. "Mayo, Katherine," in Edward T. James, Janet Wilson James, and Paul S. Boyer, eds., *Notable American Women* (Cambridge, MA, 1971); *Current Biography 1940*, s.v. "Mayo, Katherine"; *National Cyclopedia of American Biography*, s.v. "Mayo, Katherine."

42. On the interrelationship of gender, race, and colonialism, see Edward W. Said, "Kim, The Pleasures of Imperialism," *Raritan* 7 (Fall 1976): 27–64; Mrinalini Sinha, "Gender and Imperialism: Colonial Policy and the Ideology of Moral Imperialism in Late Nineteenth Century Bengal," in Michael S. Kimmel, ed., *Changing Men: New Directions in Research on Men and Masculinity* (Newbury Park, CA, 1987), pp. 217–31; Cynthia Enloe, *Bananas, Beaches & Bases: Making Feminist Sense of International Politics* (Berkeley, 1990; orig. 1989), esp. chap. 3, "Nationalism and Masculinity," pp. 42–64; Nupur Chaudhuri and Margaret Strobel, *Western Women and Imperialism: Complicity and Resistance* (Bloomington, 1992); Vron Ware, *Beyond the Pale: White Women, Racism and History* (London, 1992), esp. part 3, "Britannia's Other Daughters: Feminism in the Age of Imperialism," pp. 117–66.

43. Katherine Mayo, *Mother India* (New York, 1927).

44. Mahatma Gandhi, "Drain Inspector's Report," *Nation* 124 (Nov. 2, 1927): 488–90. At least eight books were written to refute *Mother India*, as well as several to defend it. The political impact of *Mother India* in the United States is analyzed in Manoranjan Jha, *Civil Disobedience and After: The American Reaction to Political Developments in India during 1930 and 1935* (Meerut, 1973), pp. 29–31, 182, 209. Manoranjan Jha, *Katherine Mayo and India* (New Delhi, 1971) documents British direction of Mayo's research and writing.

45. William Carman Roberts, "Guardians of the Northwest," *Munsey's Magazine* 29 (Sept. 1903): 933–36; L.R. Freeman, "The Northwest Mounted Police: The Splendid Force on the Canadian Frontier," *Overland Monthly*, n.s. 43 (Mar. 1904): 217–22; Aubrey Fullerton, "The Soldier-Policeman of the Plains," *World To-Day* 8 (July 1905): 725–30; Lawrence Mott, "A Day's Work in the Mounted Police," *Outing Magazine* 48 (Apr. 1906): 96–100; W. G. Fitz-Gerald, "Policing the Wilderness," *Outlook* 87 (Oct. 26, 1907): 431–39; Agnes Deans Cameron, "Sentinels of the Silence," *Century Magazine* 79 (Dec. 1909): 289–99; Arthur L. Haydon, *The Riders of the Plains: A Record of the Royal Northwest Mounted Police of Canada, 1873–1910* (Toronto, 1910); Elmer E. Ferris, "A Land of Law and Order," *Outlook* 98 (July 22, 1911): 685–93; Alan Sullivan, "The Last Patrol," *Harper's Weekly* 56 (Oct. 12, 1912): 11–12; "Defying the Canadian Mounted," *Literary Digest* 46 (May 31, 1913): 1244–46; Agnes Deans Cameron, "The Riders of the Plains," *Living Age* 276 (Mar. 15, 1913): 656–63; J.A. Dimock, "True Tales of the Northern Frontier," *Country*

FROM COSSACK TO TROOPER   583

Life 25 (Apr. 1914); 43–45; Max McDonald, "Northwest Mounted Police: The Men Who Do Not Fail," *Overland Monthly*, n.s. 64 (Oct. 1914): 413–16; Arthur L. Haydon, *The Trooper Police of Australia* (Chicago, 1912).

46. Mayo, *Justice to All*, p. 2. Emphasis in the original.

47. J.P. Shalloo, *Private Police with Special Reference to Pennsylvania* (Philadelphia, 1933).

48. Mayo, *Justice to All*, p. 7. She might have added "no slave patrol," for although she considered African Americans to be as violent and criminal as the immigrants, and quite possibly more depraved, she offered no explanation of why their long years in the United States had failed to accustom them to ordered liberty.

49. Mayo, *Justice to All*, pp. 32, 135.

50. Louis H. Wells, "Open Letter to the Farmers of New York," Mar. 28, 1917. Mayo Papers.

51. "State Police Contemplated for New York," "State Police for Protection of Country," Mats, American Press Association, Mar. 29, 1917, Mayo Papers.

52. Committee for State Police to 3,900 Doctors in New York State, Mailing, Mar. 5, 1917, Mayo Papers. The Committee was also able to send out mailings under the mastheads of organizations in which its members were prominent. The Audubon Society wrote to its New York membership urging support for a force to prevent the slaughter of song birds. Committee for State Police to Audubon Society, Mailing, Mar. 27, 1917, Mayo Papers. *Outlook* magazine wrote to its 15,400 subscribers to ask support for the bill to "prevent crime and safeguard property in districts now unprotected." *Outlook* to Subscribers, Mar. 28, 1917, Mayo Papers.

53. Mayo, *Justice to All*; pp. 32, 88–92.

54. Several historians have seen the popularity of Theodore Roosevelt's invocations of a war spirit as a throwback to earlier notions of masculinity. Kimmel, "The Contemporary Crisis of Masculinity"; T. Jackson Lears, *No Place of Grace: Anti-Modernism and the Transformation of American Culture, 1800–1920* (New York, 1982). The militarism of the state police campaign, and its vitality throughout the 1920s, suggests that it resonated with newer conceptions of the military as well. On manliness and modernization within the military, see David Axeen, " 'Heroes of the Engine Room': American 'Civilization' and the War with Spain," *American Quarterly* 36 (Fall 1984): 481–502; Amy Kaplan, "Romancing the Empire: The Embodiment of American Masculinity in the Popular Historical Novel of the 1890s," *American Literary History* 2 (1990): 659–90.

55. Theodore Roosevelt, "Second Annual Message," in Herman Hagedorn, ed., *The Works of Theodore Roosevelt* (New York, 1925), vol. XVII, p. 175. The army which suppressed the fight for independence in the Philippines, for example, was called a "constabulary," as was the force led by the Marines in Nicaragua.

56. Mayo, *Justice to All*, pp. 46–48.

57. Mayo, *Justice to All*, p. 33. Emphasis in the original. On anger control and the masculine ideal, see Carol Zisowitz Stearns and Peter N. Stearns, *Anger: The Struggle for Emotional Control in America's History* (Chicago, 1986).

58. Mayo, *Justice to All*, p. 59.

59. Mayo, *Justice to All*, p. 70.

60. Mayo echoed a theme of military control of labor which dated back to the railroad strike of 1877. See Richard Slotkin, "The Indian War Comes Home: The Great Strike of 1877" in *The Fatal Environment: The Myth of the Frontier in the Age of Industrialization, 1800–1890* (New York, 1985), pp. 477–98; Ronald Takaki, *Iron Cages: Race and Culture in 19th-Century America* (New York, 1990).

61. Mayo, *Justice to All*, p. 177.

62. Mayo, *Justice to All*, p. 52.

63. Mayo, *Justice to All*, p. 35.

64. Mayo, *Justice to All*, p. 210. Mayo advocated the creation of armed bodies which could protect the social order rather than the inculcation of a masculine ideal among the non-elite. Contrast John Springhill, "Building Character in the British Boy: The Attempt to Extend Christian Manliness to Working-Class Adolescents, 1880 to 1914," in Mangan and Walvin, eds., *Manliness and Morality*.

65. The importance of physical strength to early twentieth-century concepts of masculinity is discussed in E. Anthony Rotundo, "Body and Soul: Changing Ideal of American Middle-Class Manhood, 1770–1920;" Donald J. Mrozek, "The Habit of Victory" in Mangan and Walvin, eds. *Manliness and Morality*, pp. 220–39.

66. Mayo, *Justice to All*, p. 242.

67. On the chivalric ideal in early-twentieth-century conceptions of masculinity, see George Mosse, *Nationalism and Sexuality: Respectability and Abnormal Sexuality in Modern Europe* (New York, 1989), pp. 7–8, 23–24; Rotundo, "Body and Soul," p. 27. Axeen, "'Heroes of the Engine Room,'" argues for the compatibility between the chivalric and professional ideals.

68. Mayo, *Justice to All*, pp. 329–33.

69. Mayo, *Justice to All*, p. 59. This brotherhood ideal resembles the notion of "Christian brotherhood" promoted by the clergymen working with sailors analyzed in George Chauncey, Jr., "Christian Brotherhood or Sexual Perversion? Homosexual Identities and the Construction of Sexual Boundaries in the World War One Era," *Journal of Social History* 19 (Winter 1985): 189–211.

70. Mayo, *Justice to All*, pp. 97–98.

71. *New York Times*, Feb. 13, 1917; *Syracuse Journal*, Feb. 13, 1917; *Buffalo Courier*, Feb. 14, 1917; *New York Evening Sun*, Feb. 14, 1917; *New York Tribune*, Feb. 15, 1917; *Rochester Union and Advertiser*, Feb. 16, 1917; *Rochester Democrat*, Feb. 16, 1917, *Jamestown Journal*, Feb. 16, 1917.

72. *Legislative Labor News*, Feb. 19, 1917.

73. Charles P. Norton to Newell, Apr. 5, 1917, Mayo Papers.

74. P.O. Ray, "Metropolitan and State Police," Report of Committee "I" of the Institute, *Journal of Criminal Law and Criminology* 10 (Nov. 1919): 351–55 and 11 (Nov. 1920): 453–67; Margaret Mary Corcoran, "State Police in the United States: A Bibliography," *Journal of the American Institute of Criminal Law and Criminology* 14 (Feb. 1924): 544–56; Bruce Smith, *The State Police: Organization and Administration* (New York, 1925); Bruce Smith, *Police Systems in the United States* (New York, 1940); August Vollmer and Alfred E. Parker, *Crime and the State Police* (Berkeley, 1935); Kansas Legislative Council Research Department, *State Police: Analysis of Existing Laws and of the Experience of Other States*

with Special Application to Kansas(1934); Oklahoma State Planning Board, *A State Police for Oklahoma* (Oklahoma City, 1936).

75. William Church Osborn to Lewis Morris, May 2, 1917, Mayo Papers. The first cooperative pamphlet was Committee for State Police, "The New York State Troopers," n.d. [Oct. 1917], Mayo Papers. Lewis R. Morris signed the Committee statement, but Mayo wrote it. Lewis R. Morris to M. Moyca Newell, Aug. 19, 1917. The second pamphlet, Committee for State Police, "Powers and Territory of the New York State Troopers," Feb. 1918, published five months after the troops went on duty, was called "First report for the year 1918." The next two annual CSP reports, "Annual Report," Feb. 1919; "The State Speaks," Feb. 1920; included the text of the Department of State Police's first two annual reports to the Governor. Percy E. Barbour to Mayo, Aug. 7, 1917; Feb. 9, 1918, Mayo Papers; "The Governors Speak," Jan. 1921 was the last joint report.

76. In writing to Mayo and Newell to request permission, Chandler noted, "The only objection might be that it sounds like an Indian name and I am sure there is no Indian blood in your family, despite your good fighting qualities." Chandler to Moyea [sic] Newell, June 14, 1917; Chandler to Mayo, June 14, 1917, Mayo Papers.

77. He explained that he decided on purple because it was the trim color of the togas worn by the Caesars' Praetorian Guard when not in military clothes. Sgt. Pamela T. Shelton, *History of the New York State Police, 1917–1987* (Albany, 1987), p. 23.

78. George F. Chandler, Bulletin, Nov. 1, 1917, quoted in Committee for State Police *Annual Report*, 1919, p. 8.

79. George F. Chandler, *The Policeman's Art As Taught in the New York State School for Police* (New York, 1922; repr. New York, 1974), p. 32.

80. The *Syracuse Post-Standard* cooperated with a full-page feature spread headlined "Because a woman wanted it, We now have a state mounted constabulary." Sept. 2, 1917.

81. George F. Chandler, *Dawn Days of the State Police* (Troy, 1928), p. 15.

82. The five foot, six inch height requirement, increased in 1924 to five foot, eight inches, also worked to exclude first and second generation immigrants. Unfortunately, detailed quantitative analysis of state police recruits is impossible because all of the early personnel records were destroyed in a 1925 fire.

83. NYSP, Annual Reports, 1918–1930.

84. Shelton, *History of the New York State Police*, pp. 32–33.

85. Frederick F. Van de Water, *Grey Riders: The Story of the New York State Troopers* (New York, 1922), p. 60.

86. Chandler listed co-operation with each department in NYSP, *Annual Report*, 1918, p. 9. The first three joint NYSP and CSP pamphlets included endorsements from the heads of various departments. Bruce Smith, *The State Police: Organization and Administration*, pp. 66–67, noted that it was characteristic of a state police force under criticism from organized labor to take on numerous administrative functions.

87. Gerda W. Ray, " 'We Can Stay Until Hell Freezes Over': Strike Control and the State Police in New York, 1919–1923," *Labor History*, forthcoming.

88. *Olean Evening Times*, Aug. 21, 1919.

89. George F. Chandler to Gov. Nathan L. Miller, July 21, 1922, Box 14, File 150–

642, Nathan L. Miller, Governor's Subject and Correspondence Files, New York State Archives, Albany (hereafter Miller Papers).

90. *Rome Daily Sentinel*, July 15, 16, 19 & 30 , 1919; *Utica Observer*, July 16, 18 & 19, 1919; *New York Times*, July 15, 16 & 17, 1919; Chandler, *Dawn Days*, pp. 18–19.

91. Committee for State Police, "The State Speaks," p. 4; J. M. O'Hanlon to John Fitzpatrick, Mar. 22, 1924, Victor A. Olander Papers, University of Illinois Library at Chicago Circle.

92. George F. Chandler to W. Ward Smith [Secretary to the Governor], Feb. 26, 1921, File 150–141, Miller Papers.

93. Chandler, *Dawn Days*, p. 20.

94. Chandler, *The Policeman's Art*, p. 53.

95. Van de Water, *Grey Riders*, p. 12.

96. Van de Water, *Grey Riders*, pp. 285–97.

97. Van de Water, *Grey Riders*, p. 335.

98. Van de Water, *Grey Riders*, p. 357.

99. Van de Water, *Grey Riders*, pp. 367–69.

100. Ray, "Contested Legitimacy," pp. 313–18.

101. William E. Martin [Senator 49th District] to Gov. Miller, July 24, 1922, Box 14, File 150–642, Miller Papers. New York City Assemblyman Thomas F. Burchill and Councilman Frank C. Perkins also called for an investigation. Thomas F. Burchill to Gov. Nathan L. Miller, Aug. 30, 1922, Box 14, File 150–642, Miller Papers; *Albany Times-Union*, July 25, 1922.

102. *New York Times*, Jan. 27, 1926.

103. On the significance of "respectability" to nationalism in Europe, see Mosse, *Nationalism and Sexuality*.

104. Committee for State Police, "The Governors Speak," pp. 3–4.

Part IV
Social Histories of Punishment

[17]

CRIME AND PUNISHMENT AS HISTORICAL PROBLEM

> The criminal produces not only crimes but also criminal law, and with it, the professor who gives lectures on criminal law, and in addition to this, the inevitable compendium in which the professor throws his lectures on the general market as "commodities." This brings with it the augmentation of the national wealth, quite apart from the personal enjoyment which . . . the manuscript of the compendium brings to the originator himself.[1]

There has been of late a considerable augmentation in the wealth of literature on crime and punishment in the modern period. Historians like E.P. Thompson and Michel Foucault, who have distinguished themselves by the significance of their contributions in other areas of historical work, are now bringing their talents to bear on this problem. Their achievements have been momentous.[2] Yet the theoretical tools used and devised by the many researchers in the field are still at a primitive level of development. The "commodities" of which Marx spoke so ironically continue to lack either a self-conscious social theory or a consistently applied and adequate theoretical approach to the problem of crime and punishment.

This article proposes to map out some of the problems that historians of crime and punishment now face by reference to particular recent work and to propose some ways in which we can move toward a more adequate social theory of crime and punishment as an historical problem.

*   *   *

European countries after 1750 witnessed the development of new institutions to deal with the problems of law and order. A bureaucracy of interlocking penal, policing, and legal institutions was erected throughout western Europe. Although the rate of development varied from country to country, the phenomenon itself was general. The modern penitentiary was established in the 19th century: it was based on the structurally new institutional aim of the separation of prisoners from one another. The purpose of the system, as the original utilitarian reformers described it, was to prevent crime and to rehabilitate the criminal. At about the same time as the creation of prisons, the French police (1800) and the English metropolitan force (1829) became the models for the creation of modern police systems throughout Europe. Modern in this sense meant the appearance of a uniformed, neutral, civilian force, the rhetoric of which was based on the concepts of prevention as well as repression.[3] This rationalization of the function of peace-keeping placed the police between the public and a body of law. The law itself was rationalized, codified. In France, the principles of equality before law and the protection of property were embodied in the Napoleonic code and a centralized legal system was created.

0022-4529-78-0601-0508–$1.00. ©1978. Peter N. Stearns

Codification and legal reform that emphasized prevention were processes not confined to France. Indeed, one can speak of a fundamental transformation in the forces of law and repression in 19th-century Europe.

The very nature of crime, its definition and incidence, also underwent important transformations. Crime was said to be increasing at unprecedented rates.[4] Nineteenth-century reformers, either apocalyptic or prescriptive in their observations, explained the mounting crime rate most frequently in terms of urbanization and industrialization. Friedrich Engels was not atypical in recognizing the localization of crime in one class, the working class. Crime, like alcoholism, was a form of demoralization among workers. Engels spoke of "social war of all against all," "the threat of social upheaval," which manifested itself symptomatically in the form of crime.[5] Honoré Frégier, a French police official, saw the dividing line between laboring classes and dangerous classes as one that was easily crossed.[6] The working class was increasing; hence, crime increased. The criminal whom this new system spoke of reforming was a worker without religion, without morals, and without a job.

Probably the most startling statistical proof of the deteriorating situation was the perceived phenomenal increase in the rate of recidivism.[7] The habitual and chronic relapse into crime by the multiple offender constituted an irrefutable indictment of the failure of the penal system to rehabilitate the criminal. It is certainly true that recidivism is a phenomenon that the system itself created: perception of recidivism was dependent on a centralized information and coding system; it was dependent on a new technology that could identify one criminal among all other criminals; and it was dependent on a bureaucratic system that could control and integrate data. There is also the self-fulfillingly prophetic aspect of the institutions themselves creating a class of hardened criminals by their methods of isolation, separation, and rehabilitation. These assumptions were built into the penal system. Even reformers like Tocqueville and Beaumont, who advocated reforms in France based on their observations of the system in the United States, spoke of a "little nation" of criminals that threatened the safety and well-being of society-at-large.[8] The fear of a criminal nation within a larger national community was statistically verified by the end of the 19th century.

The concept of the hardened criminal detected in changing patterns of criminality was at the base of a whole new ideological apparatus, the science of criminality known as criminology. By the end of the century, with Cesar Lombroso heading the Italian school and Gabriel Tarde the French, criminology and the social sciences in general became legitimizing and conservative mechanisms for a new system of self-conscious social control.

As the fear of crime and the threat of criminality increased, the system saw itself as moving toward a more humane attitude to the criminal. Michel Foucault very ably captures the flavor of this change in the opening pages of *Surveiller et punir*. He juxtaposes two incidents as a means of describing the differences between 18th- and 19th-century forms of repression. A parricide condemned in 1757, Foucault tells us, was tortured on a public square, covered with boiling oil, dismembered by four horses, and in the course of the spectacle, was expected to cry out for pity to his Maker. Finally his body was reduced to ashes and these ashes were thrown to the winds for the edification of all there assembled. Retribution, not rehabilitation, was the obvious object of such punishment. In contrast, Foucault describes without comment the rules governing juvenile offenders in 1838. Punishment in this case, "less than a century later," was based on a carefully detailed daily schedule that prescribed the hours to rise, to eat, and to sleep. Work and schooling, as the bases of rehabilitation, were the center of the schedule. Separation, silence, and discipline in a rigidly controlled system had replaced the physical torture and public spectacle of punishment of the earlier period.[9]

These are, in the most general and descriptive way possible, the facts of what happened to the structure of crime and punishment in the 19th century. New categories of crime were created and they were punished in new ways. Criminal behavior itself was changing with an evolution of patterns and changing rates within given categories. Yet how are these facts to be interpreted? How are the transformations to be explained? What are the important questions to be asked by the historian and what are the analytic tools to be used? There are a variety of ways in which historians have sought to deal with the historical problem of crime and punishment: it is worth considering some of those approaches here.

There is the liberal historical approach that argues that institutional forms in the 19th century represent progress over the earlier period. As the interpretation goes, a more humane system evolved with the recognition of the efficacy of institutions for bettering the human condition.[10] The self-conscious aim repeatedly emphasized in the rhetoric of 19th-century reformers is taken at its face value or at least imbued with the validity of good intentions in this liberal analysis. Yet Foucault plainly states in his work that what took place in the 19th century was not progress at all. He argues that the target of power ceased to be the body of the condemned and became at a certain historical point the prisoner's mind and spirit. The forms of repression had changed: what emerged in the modern period was a new disciplinary society. Foucault's basically romantic analysis is opposed here to the liberal interpretation of institutional development: the clear implication is that, instead of getting better, things are getting worse. These are moral judgments on the nature of change — opposing moral judgments — that in this form offer no possibility of explaining why the change took place.

On the other hand, Karl Marx did try to explain the reasons for the change — yet without providing the necessary analytical tools. Classical Marxian analysis relegated crime to a "parasitic and politically insignificant" state.[11] It is in this context that Marx's concept of the lumpenproletariat must be understood. For Marx, unlike Engels, the lumpenproletariat is more than a criminal and demoralized sector of the work force: the lumpens are the riff-raff, scum, social degenerates, and marginal types found on all levels of society.[12] They are class traitors who become the tools of the ruling elite against the proletariat. Marx does not use this term with any rigor and is very similar to his morally outraged Victorian contemporaries who saw crime basically as moral transgressions. Marx's lumpens were the dangerous classes and he expressed the same kind of moral outrage toward them as did any good bourgeois. Marx's condemnation had the added feature of seeing in the existence of crime the weakening of the class

CRIME AND PUNISHMENT   511

struggle. In *The Eighteenth Brumaire of Louis Bonaparte*, Marx is clear in this regard: "The French bourgeoisie offered resistance to the domination of the working proletariat; it has brought the lumpenproletariat to domination."[13] In other writings Marx seems to be arguing that crime and punishment exist because it is in the bourgeois interest that they exist.[14] Marx does not provide a theoretical apparatus for dealing with the state and his inadequacy in analyzing repression in the modern period is related to this. Furthermore, in Marx, there is the absence of any sense of process between economic conditions and individual actions. In other words, in distinction to Engels, Marx is not concerned with why people become criminals: Marx instead makes a case for the utility of crime to the dominance of a particular class. For Marx criminal activity was a false, prepolitical form of consciousness. Although it may be difficult to contend that Marx is a functionalist in depicting crime as sustaining capitalist social relations, it is not so difficult to make a case that Marx is a true 19th-century moralist in his treatment of crime and criminality in the dangerous classes. Lumpen-proletariat, as a basically criminal group, becomes a sloppy term of derision applied by Marx to unacceptable types from the peasant "swamp flowers" of the French military to the head of state himself, Louis Napoleon. In short, Marx is of little help in constructing a social theory of crime and punishment in the modern period.[15]

Marxists after Marx usually take one of two positions in treating crime and punishment as historical problem. Some Marxists concern themselves with the question of consciousness and look at crime from the bottom up as a form of individual protest. Other Marxists compensate for the absence of an adequate theory of that state and view the phenomenon of repression from the top down.

Those concerned with the relationship between consciousness and crime generally distinguish between collective and individual protest and label phenomena as political or prepolitical. Some Marxists like Hobsbawm consider social crime as prepolitical protest that can serve only short-term ends and that will disappear with the abolition of capitalism.[16] Others, like E.P. Thompson and his collaborators, speak of social crime, in spite of good intentions, as something distinct from a deviant subculture.[17] This approach falls heir to the crowd studies led by George Rudé. Rudé's main concern in cleaning the crowd up and making it respectable was to show that collective and revolutionary protest was something altogether distinct from criminal activity. The accomplishments of the crowd studies are now potential vices when certain theoretical assumptions are applied to understanding crime as protest. Indeed, Rudé in a recent review of *Albion's Fatal Tree* and *Whigs and Hunters* registers a generally applicable form of praise: "Through such explorations as this . . . we may perhaps one day be able to draw a more generally acceptable dividing line between the criminal and the protester."[18] Why this should be the aim at all is not clear. The political implications of such an approach are, however, obvious. Cleaning up the crowd falls into the trap of accepting the rhetoric of the 19th century at its face value and leaves unquestioned how that dividing line, of which Rudé speaks, between normal and abnormal was created.

Those who are not working within a Marxist framework have been most helpful in obscuring the dividing line between normality and abnormality.

Although he doesn't make any theoretical headway, Richard Cobb has managed to avoid the demarcation in his work on the revolutionary period.[19] Cobb implies a pecular kind of relationship between individual protest and collective action, without arguing that there is a direct relationship between crime and impoverishment. As collective and political action becomes less likely, deviant activity increases. Frantz Fanon makes exactly the opposite case for 20th-century liberation movements.[20] His fundamental assumption is the same as Cobb's: there is something authentic in individual forms of protest, madness, and crime. In *The Wretched of the Earth*, however, he asserts that individual deviance is proof of alienation and oppression and that it constitutes the potential base of collective violence in Third-World countries. For Fanon, deviants are the building blocks of collective action; for Cobb they are the irreducible fragments of the human condition.

The other main branch of Marxists are those who understand a theory of the state as the basis for understanding repression in modern society. They are concerned with the institutions, not the criminals. The tendency here is to make a determinist argument that the links between the mode of production (industrial capitalism) and the institutional forms of repression are direct. The self-consciousness of the ruling elite is also an important component in understanding the development of those forms. A classic statement of this analysis appears in Rusche and Kirchheimer's *Punishment and Social Structures,* which first appeared in 1939.[21] These authors explain different punitive regimes by different systems of production. In a servile economy punitive mechanisms constitute a civil slavery alongside that which is assured by war and commerce. In feudalism, where money and production are not developed, so the argument goes, there would be a high incidence of corporal punishments because the body is most accessible. In the 19th century with the free market of manufacture in the industrial system, the mechanisms of punishment increase as the role of obligatory feudal labor decreases.

The determinist equation between economy and institutions is now being self-consciously rejected by those working on the problem of crime and punishment in the modern period because the argument sees no dialectical relationship between the superstructure and the infra-structure. Nevertheless it continues to be an approach treated with seriousness by radical social scientists.[22]

The single work that breaks new ground in rejecting existing approaches to the problem of crime and punishment is Michel Foucault's *Surveiller et punir: naissance de la prison.* This is the most important study yet to be done on prisons in the modern period. In developing a social theory of crime and punishment, Foucault follows four methodological rules. 1) He does not view punishment solely according to its repressive effects but also considers it as a "complex social mechanism." His purpose here is to understand punishment according to a series of positive effects that it may induce. 2) He does not see punitive methods as simple consequences of social structures. He is concerned with punishments as techniques in a more general field where power and political tactics take on a particular meaning. 3) Foucault looks for a common matrix in the history of penal law and the human sciences — what he calls the "technology of power." 4) By far his most mystical methodological rule is to examine the introduction of

CRIME AND PUNISHMENT   513

the body-mind dichotomy into the arena of penal justice. His concern is to see how with the introduction of scientific knowledge into judicial practice, the body itself is invested in relation to power. Here he is concerned with the political technology of the body and how it changes with the metamorphosis of punitive methods in the modern period.[23]

As a basis for this method, Foucault presents certain postulates that, he accurately claims, call into question all work done by the Left in the area of crime and punishment.[24] Foucault begins by postulating that power is not the attribute of a class that has conquered it. As against Marxist determinists, he contends that power is less a charactertistic than a strategy. Foucault does not deny the class struggle but he fairly well ignores it. For him the effects of power are not attributable to appropriation but to functions (dispositions, maneuvers, tactics, techniques). In arguing that power is the combined effect of *positions stratégiques,* Foucault is replacing economic determinism with "this new functionalism."[25]

Foucault further denies that power is the power of the state, localized in the apparatus of the state. In fact, Foucault has no theory of the state. He argues that the state itself is the effect of a multiplicity of movements (*rouages,* as in machinery) on another plane. Modern societies are disciplinary societies but this discipline cannot be defined by or contained in a particular apparatus, such as the prison or the factory. Discipline is a technology, a way of exercising power that is similar for various apparatuses, institutions.

In a more explicit way and building on these two postulates, Foucault denies that power as it is exercised in the apparatus of the state will be subordinated to the mode of production. He denounces economic determinism for relating everything back to the economy and he returns to a familiar argument that there is no centralization, only serial space.

A fourth postulate, which is at the base of the most important and positive contribution of the book, is the replacement of repression by a concept of normalization. Ideology does not necessarily operate by violence or repression. Law is the chief concern here. Unlike Douglas Hay or E.P. Thompson who see law as a state of peace and stability in a war won by the strongest,[26] Foucault argues that law is the war itself. His argument is developed by undermining the polarity between law and illegality so important to Thompson and by replacing it with a correlation between "illegalisms" and law.[27] It is, of course, a difference in emphasis in regard to the same phenomenon, the shift in the modern period (earlier for England than France) in law toward property rather than persons. Disciplinary powers through law define, indeed create, deviance. Deviance does not exist in some natural or arbitrary state: it exists by virtue of law. The shift in emphasis is an important one: the dividing line between the criminal and the political-social that Rudé is eager to discover, is chimerical in this approach. The question here is by what strategy of power abnormality is created, and by what strategy the normal is created as well.

Foucault is avowedly offering us a new theory of crime and punishment in modern society. He rejects mechanistic Marxism, radical moralism, conflict and consensus models, and structural reductionism: he gives us "a new functionalism." Foucault does not consider class and a theory of the state as fundamentally important: the dialectic is not its own justification. Instead Foucault choses to replace a dialectical analysis by juxtaposing differences according to different systems. The main problem with Foucault's theory is not in what it explains but in what it fails to explain. This approach does not explain the transformation from one system to another, it does not explain conflict within systems, it does not explain how institutions develop. Foucault recognizes that strategies of power differentiate groups from one another and operate in a system of conflict, which may at base be stable. Yet he does not explain why differentiation takes the form it does or what the process of normalization is. Juxtaposition becomes the chief method in this new functionalism and hence provides a static model.

There is an additional difficulty in Foucault's theory that results from the ambiguity between his analysis of individual action and his functionalism. Although he sees deviance as a product of power, he enshrines individual criminal action. Authenticity of action is introduced here, creating important methodological problems. The problems are most apparent in a book edited by Foucault and appearing just before his prison study, *I, Pierre Rivière, Having Slaughtered My Mother, My Sister, and My Brother. . . .* A long memoir by the murderer himself, a twenty-year-old peasant, is accompanied by the legal and medical documents concerning the case and an analysis of them in essays by Foucault and his students at the Collège de France. The commentators are fastidious in their avoidance of the Rivière memoir itself for this reason:

> Its beauty alone is sufficient justification for it today. We can hardly help feeling that it has needed a century and a half of accumulated and reconstituted knowledge to enable us at last not perhaps so much to understand it as to read it — and, even so, to read it none too well and to grasp so little of it. How much less, then, could the doctors, lawyers, and jury make of it when they had merely a preliminary investigation and court hearing to enable them to determine the grounds for deciding between madness and death in the 1830's?[28]

The beauty of the text implies its underlying authenticity and historical transcendence. In looking at the conflict within discourses, the discourse of the madman is exempted from the process. Foucault spells out the method most clearly in the foreword of the book:

> As to Rivière's discourse, we decided not to interpret it and not to subject it to any psychiatric or psychoanalytic commentary. In the first place because it was what we used as the zero benchmark to gauge the distance between the other discourses and the relations arising among them. Secondly, because we could hardly speak of it without involving it in one of the discourses (medical, legal, psychological, criminological) which we wished to use as our starting point in talking about it. If we had done so, we should have brought it within the power relation whose reductive effort we wished to show, and we ourselves should have fallen into the trap it set.[29]

The implication is that there is a validity to the document that exists someplace outside the power relationship. The avoidance of the "trap" is based upon a mystical sense, a terror, of the inviolability of the document.

In his critique of the capitalist system, Foucault glorifies those who are defined as outside the system. His critique is part of a "post-structuralist anarchism,"[30] that sees the sources of tension and possible revolution not restricted to the proletariat as such but to the oppressed in general. This is because the strategies of power are pervasive and are not confined to the economic sphere. The excluded assume a privileged position in Foucault's theory. This may not constitute a theoretical inconsistency, but the revolutionary possibilities of the oppressed remain at best ambiguous in Foucault's static model. Nevertheless, it is here that Foucault goes beyond the Marxists in his analysis of structures: class is no longer the crucial analytical tool for understanding how a system works or how it changes. The pervasiveness of oppression means that the sources of revolutionary action are not necessarily or primarily rooted in class exploitation. How revolution is possible in this new functionalist theory remains to be answered.

Both Thompson and Foucault are in agreement about the need for a self-conscious social theory of crime and punishment and both make important contributions in that direction. Although Thompson is not always able to break as free of a confirmation of "the class-bound and mystifying functions of law," as he would like, his conclusion recognizes the necessity of "rejecting ulterior reductionism and modifying the typology of superior and inferior (but determining) structures."[31] Thompson's conclusions echo Foucault's general postulates, although with very different ideological implications. Law must be regarded as a process: for Thompson this means looking at law as the social control of the rich as well as the poor. It also means looking at law as a battleground on which the conflict between classes is mediated.

The theoretical emphasis on process in both works is an important one. The three British sociologists, Taylor, Walton, and Young, arrived at a similar kind of emphasis in their Marxist critique, *The New Criminology*. With a respect for Durkheim and his method, the three authors affirm the need for a theory of deviance that is fully social.[32] This means an emphasis on the process of social interaction in institutional development. For the historian undertaking a study of crime and punishment in the 19th century, without question it means rejecting a social theory of the state as a sufficient means of understanding the development of law and order in modern society. It also means rejecting the isolation of police, prisons, and law courts as serial institutions and instead attempting to discover the mediations between these institutions and other social phenomena. Such a study has yet to be undertaken. In light of work already done, it seems that the most likely areas in the search for mediations include: class, family, and ideology.

Class. Class analysis should not only mean the relationship between classes but also the conflict and interaction within classes. The historian's concern should be less exclusively the relationship between the criminal groups and the dominant groups (or the lumpens and the bourgeoisie) and more the relationship between the working class and the criminal group. An important twin concern should be an examination of the efficacy of a class analysis for understanding the criminal group itself. Why people commit crimes and why people do not are important issues that the analytical tool of class may help to illuminate. Clearly more empirical work is needed. What is at stake here is the internalization of values: the concept of an absolute dividing line only impedes attempts to penetrate the strategy of normalization. Is the historian able to talk about a sense of difference or consciousness of workers against deviants at a particular historic moment or is deviance a category that is created by institutional response and at some point internalized by the working population? This is not asking if social control is a cause or an effect; it is emphasizing the importance of interaction with an economic base from a different perspective. For the historian of the 18th and 19th centuries this means looking at such phenomena as riots of workers against prisons, the treatment of criminals as class enemies by revolutionary groups, and the community response to a growing criminal presence. Instances of these phenomena predate institutional and ideological developments. More must be done with the perhaps isolated cases of workers invading prisons that they recognize as competition in the workplace. The question of riots within prisons in the 19th century deserves more careful study.* The penitentiary with its vocational training and production for the market was quite literally a workplace and as such exploited the prisoner as worker. This may figure into the equation of the ideological separation of normal from abnormal. In spite of Foucault's critique, therefore, the concept of class is useful, but only if it is widened to include a broader range of social interactions than the bourgeoisie versus the proletariat, which traditional Marxist studies perpetuate.

Family. This is another structural mediation worth considering. It is more than an oversight that Foucault can study disciplinary society and the consequences of normalization without ever considering the links with the changing role of the family as a socializing institution. His focus is the exclusive relationship between the individual and the institution. Yet men, women, and children as inmates of institutions were separated from each other for the first time in 19th-century prisons. Separation was determined on the basis of sex, age, offense, and ultimately on the individual basis; each prisoner came to be isolated from every other prisoner. Sex remained the basis for the difference in institutional response for most of the 19th century. The sequence of isolation and the nature of rehabilitation were different for men and for women. These differences, which Foucault for the most part ignores, occurred in a system where all prisoners were treated and legally considered as minors. For example, the young, as well as the working class, were perceived as a criminal and immoral group — especially working-class youths. Recent work on juvenile delinquency has emphasized the necessity of a generational and family-based approach to the problems of crime and punishment in a modernizing and urbanizing society.[33] One way that sense can be made of the differences in criminal patterns and institutional response is by relating these differences to the changing functions of the family in modern society. The groundwork has been laid but much remains to be done in this area. Generational distinctions for crimes and punishments could prove to be valuable in the search for structural mediations.

Distinctions according to sex must also be examined. Michelle Perrot has recently made some valuable observations about the relationship between repression and sexuality in the penitentiary system and has suggested some useful

*Since the writing of this article, work by Michelle Perrot on the relation between prisons and revolution has appeared. Perrot is concerned with both riots in prisons and the attitudes of the popular classes toward the prison, while recognizing the problems of evidence in such an endeavor. Michelle Perrot, "1848. Révolution et prisons," *Annales Historiques de la Révolution Française* (July-September, 1977), pp. 306-338.

guidelines for future research.[34] Pursuing this mediation can only highlight the tensions within the system. The different aims of institutional rehabilitation according to sex were grounded in the dominant social values. For most of the century, men in groups were regarded as dangerous; women were not. In contrast to the treatment of men, homosexuality among prison women, although recognized, created little administrative concern. The rehabilitation of women did not primarily emphasize vocational training; instead the importance of religion and an autonomous moral sense were recognized as indispensable. Women were regarded as the more malleable and impressionable by reformers and administrators. Yet the principles of rehabilitation and isolation were enforced against the more resistant male population. This, of course, changed at a certain point. The change itself is important and makes sense only in relation to the changing role of women in the family and the workplace. These inter-relations deserve careful delineation. We need not talk here about institutions mirroring each other; we must talk about mediations by which values come to be dominant on different institutional levels and how these values interact and reinforce one another.

Ideology. The important transformation in the modern system of law can be reduced to one principle: the previous classical emphasis on the mathematical equation between crimes and punishments gave way to a new positivist emphasis on the relationship between the criminal and punishment. The shift belied an evolution in the system of repression and prevention. What is involved here is a basic tension and even institutional and intra-institutional conflict that func-tionalist analysis completely overlooks. The intra-institutional dynamic in the formation of ideology has not yet been adequately studied, nor have the contradictions between the ideology of the system and its mode of operation been mapped out. Ideology certainly is a battleground, as Thompson suggests. It should be examined as something both determining and determined and that is only possible by considering ideology in the social context. The concept of recidivism, for example, which was an important ideological force in institu-tional development, itself was heavily influenced by dominant social attitudes toward the laboring classes. The treatment of the multiple offender was deter-mined by a theory of the hardened — and hence irredeemable — criminal, which in turn gave way to the concept of the scientifically verifiable born criminal. At the point, therefore, at which the institutions of repression and prevention were becoming most highly articulated, the ideology came to absolve the institutions of responsibility in a system of social control. Concentrating on the tensions between ideology and institutions replaces the juxtaposition of forms with a history of institutions that is interwoven with the social history of a period.

Recent scholarship has been successful in mining new areas of the historical problem of crime and punishment in the modern period. Howard Zehr's com-parative studies of France and Germany question conventional wisdom by showing the relationship between patterns of criminality and modernization.[35] In his work he calls for case studies and a closer examination of individual groups. The problem continues to offer a rich and virtually untouched lode of research possibilities of which the mediations with class, family, and ideology seem to be especially rich veins. What is needed is a directing social theory that

journal of social history

does not see institutions as divorced from other social phenomena and that offers a more complex and satisfying analysis of social conflict. Foucault has helped provide historical studies with a "new cartography"[36] for approaching these problems. It remains an incomplete cartography for territory yet to be discovered.

University of California, Irvine Patricia O'Brien

FOOTNOTES

1. Karl Marx, *Theories of Surplus Value,* Part 1 (London, 1964), 375.

2. E. P. Thompson, *Whigs and Hunters: The Origin of the Black Act* (New York, 1975); Douglas Hay, Peter Linebaugh, John G. Rule, E.P. Thompson, Cal Winslow, *Albion's Fatal Tree: Crime and Society in Eighteenth-Century England* (New York, 1975); Michel Foucault, *Surveiller et punir: naissance de la prison* (Paris, 1975).

3. Allan Silver provides a fine analysis of this transformation: "The Demand for Order in Civil Society: A Review of Some of the Themes in the History of Urban Crime, Police, and Riot," in *The Police: Six Sociological Essays,* edited by D.J. Bordua (New York, 1967), 1-24.

4. Works to consult for the changing image of crime in the 19th century include J.J. Tobias, *Urban Crime in Victorian England* (New York, 1972); and Louis Chevalier, *Laboring Classes and Dangerous Classes in Paris During the First Half of the Nineteenth Century* (New York, 1973).

5. Friedrich Engels, *The Condition of the Working Class in England in 1844* (Stanford, 1968), 149.

6. Honoré Antoine Frégier, *Des classes dangereuses de la population dans les grandes villes, et des moyens de les rendre meilleures* (Paris, 1840).

7. In France after mid-century, for example, fear of the increasing recidivism rate was the cause of major legal and penal reforms. A report made to the Chamber of Deputies in January of 1885 showed that in 1850 20% of all prisoners were recidivists: the figure had grown steadily to 44% in 1882. Archives Nationales – F^7 12704. Documents parlémentaires.

8. Alexis de Tocqueville and Gustave de Beaumont, *Le système pénitentiaire aux États Unis* (Paris, 1845), 392-393. The notion of "a little nation" is not totally new but rather an adaptation of a traditional urban view. See Chevalier, *Laboring Classes.*

9. Foucault, *Surveiller et punir,* 9-13.

10. The best historical analysis of this phenomenon is found in Ian Taylor, Paul Walton, and Jock Young, *The New Criminology: For a Social Theory of Deviance* (New York, 1973).

11. In an excellent review of the Taylor, Walton, and Young book, John Ainlay clarifies some of the problems of Marx's analysis. See *Telos,* 26 (Winter, 1975-1976), 213-225.

12. Karl Marx, *Class Struggles in France, 1848-1850* (New York, 1964), 50-51; and *The Eighteenth Brumaire of Louis Bonaparte* (New York, 1967), 75.

13. Marx, *Eighteenth Brumaire,* 118.

14. Marx makes this case in *Theories of Surplus Value,* "The apologist conception of the productivity of all professions." Taylor *et al.* in the *New Criminology* counter a liberal interpretation of this and other sections on crime by showing the irony of Marx's remarks (209-221).

15. Marxists Taylor, Walton, and Young find Marx's treatment of criminal motivation to be "extremely truncated," *Ibid,* 217.

16. Eric Hobsbawm, *Primitive Rebels* (New York, 1959).

17. Hay *et al., Albion's Fatal Tree.* The weighting toward social crime is acknowledged in the preface (14).

18. George Rudé, "Poachers and Protestors," *Times Literary Supplement,* January 30, 1976, 104.

19. Richard Cobb, *The Police and the People: French Popular Protest,* 1789-1820 (New York, 1970); and *Reactions to the French Revolution* (New York, 1972).

20. Frantz Fanon, *The Wretched of the Earth* (New York, 1963).

21. Georg Rusche and Otto Kirchheimer, *Punishment and Social Structures* (New York, 1939).

22. Rusche and Kirchheimer's influence, for example, pervades a recent collection of works in radical criminology. Charles E. Reasons, ed., *The Criminologist: Crime and the Criminal* (Pacific Palisades, 1974). The contribution of Mark C. Kennedy, "Beyond Incrimination," (106-135) relies explicitly on Rusche and Kirchheimer's theory of the state.

23. Foucault, *Surveiller et punir,* 28-29.

24. Foucault "in revenge" listed these postulates himself in his course taught in 1973 at the Collège de France. Gilles Deleuze enumerates and discusses the postulates in "Ecrivain non: un nouveau cartographie," *Critique* (December, 1975), 1207-1227.

25. Deleuze uses the term in his highly favorable review of the book, *Ibid.,* 1209. It is likely that Foucault finds the term a congenial one.

26. D. Hay, "Property, Authority, and the Criminal Law," *Albion's Fatal Tree,* 52: "The private manipulation of the law by the wealthy and powerful was in truth a ruling-class conspiracy, in the most exacting meaning of the word." In spite of the fact that in *Whigs and Hunters* Thompson spends almost the entire book showing how this "hard lot of men," the Hanoverian Whigs, triumph as a class over the hunters, he devotes the last section of his book (258-269) to a warning against the equation of the rule of law with the rule of a class.

27. Foucault, *Surveiller et punir,* 261-299.

28. Michel Foucault, ed., *I, Pierre Riviere, Having Slaughtered My Mother, My Sister, My Brother . . .: A Case of Parricide in the Nineteenth Century* (New York, 1975), 199.

29. *Ibid.,* xiii.

30. I am indebted to my colleague Mark Poster for this term, which he sees as applicable to the work of Michel Foucault, Jean Baudrillard, Gilles Deleuze, Felix Guattari, and J.F. Lyotard.

31. Thompson, *Whigs and Hunters,* 260.

32. Taylor, Walton, Young, *The New Criminology*, 268.

33. John R. Gillis, *Youth and History: Traditions and Change in European Relations, 1770-Present* (New York, 1974).

34. Michelle Perrot, "Délinquance et système pénitentiaire en France au XIXe siècle," *Annales: Économies, Sociétés, Civilisations* (February, 1975), 67-90.

35. Howard Zehr, "The Modernization of Crime in Germany and France, 1830-1913," *The Journal of Social History*, VIII (1975), 117-141; and *Crime and the Development of Modern Society* (London, 1976).

36. Deleuze, "Écrivain non: un nouveau cartographie."

[18]

Journal of African History, **27** (1986), pp. 481–495
Printed in Great Britain

THE PEDAGOGY OF PORTER: THE ORIGINS OF THE REFORMATORY IN THE CAPE COLONY, 1882–1910

BY LINDA CHISHOLM

DURING the past decade a considerable literature has emerged examining the birth of the prison and asylum. Based primarily on the European and American experience, this has investigated the economic, social and intellectual roots of such institutions, their repressive internal characteristics, techniques and ideologies of punishment and their relationship to the wider society.[1] To a large extent, debate has revolved around the relationship between their hidden 'internal' character and their public 'external' character, while the ways in which the imprisoned have responded to the new controls has constituted an important ancillary theme.[2] From these studies it would appear that, in Europe, the process of criminalizing newly-formed proletarians and the emergence of new forms of punishment took place over three centuries. The workhouse, prison and similar institutions were the products of new economic and social relationships forged during the process of transition from feudalism to capitalism. These new institutions constituted an attempt to blunt the impact of a radically counterposed popular culture which combined forms of the old peasant way of life with new methods of resistance called into being by changed conditions. They also sought, through habituating inmates to work, to inculcate new values. By the late eighteenth century, their basic forms had been established. In the United States, the institutionalization of criminals, the insane and the delinquent was similarly confirmed as a method for rehabilitation by the 1870s.

In South Africa the development of two sociologically-related institutions, the prison and the compound, show significant divergences from the pattern sketched above. To a large extent this is attributable to South Africa's relatively late industrialization, fuelled by the discovery of diamonds in 1867

---

[1] David J. Rothman, *The Discovery of the Asylum, Social Order and Disorder in the New Republic* (Boston and Toronto, 1971); Michel Foucault, *Discipline and Punish: The Birth of the Prison* (London, 1977); Michael Ignatieff, *A Just Measure of Pain: The Penitentiary in the Industrial Revolution, 1750–1850* (London, 1978); Patricia O'Brien, *The Promise of Punishment* (Princeton, 1982); Douglas Hay, Peter Linebaugh, E. P. Thompson, John G. Rule and Cal Winslow, *Albion's Fatal Tree: Crime and Society in Eighteenth Century England* (London, 1975); Mike Fitzgerald, Gregor McLennan and Jennie Pawson (eds), *Crime and Society: Readings in History and Theory* (London, 1981); Dario Melossi and Massimo Pavarini, *The Prison and the Factory: Origins of the Penitentiary System* (London, 1981); Erving Goffman, *Asylums: Essays on the Social Situation of Mental Patients and other Inmates* (London, 1961); Stephen Humphries, *Hooligans or Rebels: An Oral History of Working Class Childhood and Youth 1889–1939* (Oxford, 1981); M. A. Crowther, *The Workhouse System 1834–1929: The History of an English Social Institution* (London, 1981). See also, Colin Sumner (ed.), *Crime, Justice and Underdevelopment* (London, 1982); David Williams, 'The role of prisons in Tanzania: an historical perspective', *Crime and Social Justice*, Summer (1980) and Megan Vaughan, 'Idioms of madness: Zomba lunatic asylum, Nyasaland, in the colonial period', *J. Southern African Studies*, IX, 2 (April 1983), 218–38.

[2] P. Tyor and J. S. Zanaildin, 'Asylum and society: an approach to institutional change', *J. Social History*, XIII, 1 (1979), 23–48.

and gold in 1886. Not only was South Africa a relatively late industrial starter, but its form of industrialization was very different from that of the metropole. Unlike the United Kingdom, where industrial capitalism was initially largely based on textiles, industrial capitalism in South Africa was founded on primary extractive industries. It relied not so much on a labour force entirely dispossessed from the land and with a large female and juvenile component, but on a labour force partially separated from the land and entirely male and adult. Its industrial revolution was built on workers differentiated by colour, gender and age from that of the European and American pattern. In the burgeoning industrial centres of Kimberley and the Witwatersrand, this predominantly black, migrant proletariat was housed, regimented and controlled in an institution showing marked similarities to the prison: the compound. The prison itself supplemented the compound, since a large majority of the Rand's black male workers passed through it at one point or another during their sojourn there: attempts by the gold mining industry to restrict the movement of this labour included the introduction of pass laws, under which many were convicted. Thus the population of both compounds and prisons consisted not of criminals in any ordinary sense, but of a new labouring population criminalized by laws and controlled in new institutions.[3]

The first reformatory in South Africa, Porter Reformatory, was founded in 1882; not in the industrial heartland of the Northern Cape or Witwatersrand, but in the commercial and agricultural hinterland of the Cape Colony. This was no accident. It emerged in a region where colonial conquest and attendant processes of dispossession and proletarianization had already been under way for several generations. In the Western Cape, in particular, a labouring population had been created by the disruption of colonial conquest by the beginning of the nineteenth century. The reproduction of this working class had become a matter of serious concern to merchant capital and local agricultural interests some time before the advent of industrial capitalism. In this sense the origins of the reformatory were different from that of the prison and compound. Its establishment, and formative period, however, also coincided with the emergence of industrial capitalism in South Africa. It thus emerged in the interstices of the transition from merchant to industrial capitalism, effectively straddling two distinct phases in South African history. It is the argument of this article that although Porter Reformatory was based on the British model, it was rapidly transformed in the local context to take

[3] Charles van Onselen, *Chibaro : African Mine Labour in Southern Rhodesia 1900–1933* (Johannesburg, 1980); Charles van Onselen, 'The regiment of the hills – Umkosi Wezintaba: the Witwatersrand's lumpenproletarian army, 1890–1920', *Studies in the Social and Economic history of the Witwatersrand 1886–1914*, II: *New Nineveh* (Johannesburg, 1982); R. V. Turrell, 'Capital, class and monopoly: the Kimberley diamond fields 1871–1880' (Ph.D. thesis, University of London, 1982), ch. 7; Martin Legassick, 'Gold, agriculture and secondary industry in South Africa, 1885–1970: from periphery to sub-metropole as a forced labour system', in Robin Palmer and Neil Parsons (eds), *The Roots of Rural Poverty in Central and Southern Africa* (London, 1977); Dirk van Zyl Smit, 'Public policy and the punishment of crime in a divided society: a historical perspective on the Southern African penal system', *Crime and Social Justice*, 21–22, special double issue (1984); Charles van Onselen, 'Crime and total institutions in the making of modern South Africa: the life of Nongoloza Mathebula, 1867–1948', *History Workshop Journal*, 19 (Spring 1985).

on a rather different character. Whilst its growing segregationist practice reflected local colonial social policy, the emphasis on apprenticeship in the curriculum of the reformatory was designed to meet the needs of commercial agriculture in the Western Cape.

The historical moment of the emergence of the reformatory in the Cape Colony was that of a dramatic 'spatial shift' in the core of the regional economy of Southern Africa.[4] This shift from the south-western Cape to the north was prefigured in the boom years of the 1870s by intensified rural production and the discovery of diamonds in Griqualand West in 1867. Investment in sheep farming and an increasing concentration on ostrich-farming led to the growth of colonial trade and the strengthening of merchant capital in Cape Town. Kimberley was propelled into pre-eminence in the colonial economy in the latter years of the boom by the diversion of capital from Cape Town to its diamond diggings. It rapidly became the centre of large-scale industrialized production in the Colony. Here new forms of labour control were developed. The social and spatial separation of black from white workers, and the development of the closed compound system after 1884 for the tighter control of workers characterized the response of employers to heightened labour tensions on the mines.

The pattern of economic development in the Cape, following the northward redirection of capital, was highly uneven. On the one hand, Cape Town's increasing involvement in a wider capitalist revolution was reflected in its population which doubled between 1865 and 1891.[5] These numbers were considerably augmented by the dispossession of Xhosa-speakers in the last frontier wars of 1877–9 and their entry to the wage-labour market of the Western Cape. All the same, the Cape's manufacturing capacity remained limited, and the mineral discoveries on the Witwatersrand in 1886 caused a further efflux of capital to the goldfields: the Cape concentrated on conducting the commercial and carrying trade of the north rather than developing its own industry. Investment in existing manufactures, which included confection-eries, breweries, match factories, steam mills and leather factories, remained low.[6] Commercial agriculture continued to be the major, albeit struggling, enterprise of the south-western and eastern regions. First thrown into insolvency by the recession of the early 1880s, many farmers suffered a further setback in the early 1890s as wool prices fell. To their chagrin, diamond, gold and railway employers were also recruiting from their sources of labour, and by the middle 1890s the demands of Cape farmers for the control and adequate distribution of labour became urgent.

A key by-product of the transition to industrial capitalism was the institutionalization of juvenile offenders in the Cape Colony. Before the reformatory was established in 1882, there had been no special institutional provision for the confinement of juvenile offenders in the Colony. Generally,

[4] Alan Mabin, 'The making of colonial capitalism: intensification and expansion in the economic geography of the Cape Colony, South Africa 1854–1899' (Ph.D. thesis, Simon Fraser University, 1984), 248; see also Vivian Bickford-Smith, 'The economic and demographic growth of Cape Town: 1880–1910', paper presented at South African Historical Association Conference, Cape Town, January 1984.

[5] Mabin, 'Making of colonial capitalism', Appendix.

[6] *Ibid.*, ch. 6.

484   LINDA CHISHOLM

if convicted of pilfering or stock-theft, juveniles were whipped or fined; in rare cases they were incarcerated with adult prisoners.[7] In the mid-1850s, colonial officials could confidently declare that 'juvenile delinquency...in this Colony, as a class of crime may be said not to exist'.[8] Thirty years later its prevalence had necessitated the construction of a reformatory.

By this stage, the structural changes in Cape economy and society had brought into being a new class of impoverished whites and proletarianized blacks in the smaller towns of the Eastern Cape, where vagrancy, begging and crime had become the shared fate of white and black, juvenile and adult.[9] The Western Cape, and in particular Cape Town, witnessed similar developments. In the first case, the recession of the late 1870s and the accelerated conquest of African societies hastened the entry of large numbers of unemployed and recently proletarianized people into Cape Town. After 1879 several thousand 'rebel' Xhosa-speaking men, women and children were brought to the Western Cape as convicts or to be indentured. Once freed, they occupied the present-day industrial and residential areas of Woodstock and Salt River from which they were removed to Cape Town's sixth district during the 1890s.[10] District Six, one of the areas of most rapid growth during this period, was also the home of domestic servants, unskilled labourers, casual workers at the docks and the unemployed. In addition, District Six was also gradually filled with farm workers leaving the country during the 1880s and 1890s.[11]

Amongst these were considerable numbers of children. In the first half of the century, the most important means of controlling juvenile labour was apprenticeship. A proclamation in 1812 had empowered farmers to apprentice children reared on their farms for ten years, from the age of eight. In 1819 the power of apprenticeship was extended to cover orphans and deserted children. Ordinance 50(1828), in stipulating that children could no longer be apprenticed without parental consent, merely reformed and did not abolish child apprenticeship. In 1841 the first Masters and Servants Act extended the period of indenture until the apprenticed reached the age of twenty-one. However, from the middle of the nineteenth century, as growing numbers left the countryside, apprenticeship appears to have exercised less control over the children's futures. Nor was there any compulsory schooling for either white or black children in the Cape Colony before 1905. What schooling there was for the popular classes was mainly provided by missionary societies. Evidence submitted to the Labour Commission of 1894 suggests, moreover, that access to mission education was enjoyed by the more settled labouring communities rather than by those thrust onto the labour market

[7] A. F. Hattersley, *The Convict Crisis and the Growth of Unity: Resistance to Transportation in South Africa and Australia, 1848–53* (Pietermaritzburg, 1965).

[8] M. van Wyk, 'Die Ontwikkeling van die Gevangeniswese in die Kaapkolonie vanaf 1906 tot 1910' (Ph.D. thesis, University of South Africa, 1964), 371.

[9] Colin Bundy, 'Vagabond Hollanders and runaway Englishmen: white poverty in the Cape before poor whiteism', Carnegie Conference Paper no. 247: University of Cape Town, Second Carnegie Inquiry into Poverty in South Africa, 1984.

[10] B. H. Kinkead-Weekes, 'A history of vagrancy in Cape Town', Carnegie Conference paper no. 11, *ibid.*; Christopher Saunders, 'Segregation in Cape Town: the creation of Ndabeni', Centre for African Studies, University of Cape Town, *Africa Seminar: Collected papers*, 1 (1978).

[11] Bickford-Smith, 'Growth of Cape Town', 12.

during the 1880s and 1890s.[12] It is thus not surprising that by 1910 a large proportion of Porter Reformatory's inmates were drawn from the District Six community.

None of the social developments accompanying the movement of people to the towns were welcomed by the Cape Colony's merchant bourgeoisie. Increasingly rich and self-assured, this governing class set about fashioning new forms of control for the poor.[13] William Porter, Attorney-General of the Cape Colony and member of the Legislative Council, was one of these.[14] Along with English social reformers and philanthropists, he strongly believed that character was shaped by environmental influences rather than being an innate attribute.[15] Placed within the correct disciplinary context, he believed, delinquents could be exposed to different, more positive influences than those which had been responsible for their conviction or which were exercised over them by adult criminals with whom they were incarcerated. Through a reformatory, based on the English model, the state could intervene to restructure social attitudes.

Porter's bequest of £20,000 provided the means to achieve these goals. His will stipulated that the reformatories to be established should be based on similar English institutions. In its daily routine Porter Reformatory was indeed modelled almost precisely on that of Redhill and Parkhurst, reformatories established to train convicted youths in agricultural work 'suitable for colonial life'.[16] Work and schooling were separated by meal times; lights out, when inmates were locked into reformatories for the night, was shortly after nightfall; warders mounted guard over juveniles, imparting a penal rather than an educational and reformative character to the institutions. School work was elementary. There was a basic form of grading and classification of 'hard core' youths from newcomers, and a rudimentary system of rewards for good conduct governed aspects of the system. These reformatories facilitated the transportation and emigration of 'undesirables' from England. The fate of youths living and working in Canada under these circumstances has been well documented by Joy Parr.[17] A few children so disposed of were sent to the Cape Colony, but partly as a result of ill-treatment and partly because they mixed with black farm workers and thus antagonized their employers, the practice was discontinued at the Cape.[18] At Porter Reformatory, apprenticeship was an integral part of the operation of the institution. Through it juvenile convict labour became an important source of domestic and agricultural labour for local dignitaries and farmers.

[12] Evidence submitted to Labour Commission, Cape Town, 1894.

[13] Bundy, 'Poor whiteism', op. cit. for elaboration.

[14] Born at Artikelly, near Newtownlimavady, Co. Derry, on 15 Sept. 1805 into a Nonconformist family, William Porter was appointed Attorney-General of the Cape of Good Hope in 1839 and held office until 31 August 1865. In conjunction with this office, he was a member of the Legislative Council and held a seat in both Houses of Parliament. He left the Cape in 1876 and died in Ireland in 1880.

[15] See 'On infant schools', where Porter elaborates on his ideas about education for the poor, *The Porter Speeches: speeches delivered by the Hon. William Porter during the years 1839–45 inclusive* (Cape Town, 1886); see also *Cape Times*, 27 June 1891.

[16] Alex G. Scholes, *Education for Empire Settlement: A Study of Juvenile Migration* (London, 1932).

[17] Joy Parr, *Labouring Children: British Immigration Apprentices to Canada 1869–1924* (London, 1980).

[18] Scholes, *Empire Settlement*, op. cit., and Parr, *ibid.*

The establishment of a reformatory was seen by its administrators as having a dual purpose. First, it was felt that juvenile offenders should be removed from 'degrading surroundings, fraught with many temptations' where, 'if left to their fate they would in all probability become Hooligans and later on would (go) amongst the criminal classes'.[19] Secondly, it was argued that by separating juveniles from adult criminals they could be 'brought within the ranks of wage-earners and become a valuable asset to the Colony'.[20] It was to their re-formation as 'truthful, honest and to an extent trustworthy servants and mechanics'[21] that their guardians looked. As such, a liberal Parliamentarian, Gordon Sprigg, felt that 'little material advantage is to be gained by anything beyond industrial training. And the government is of opinion that this should be accepted as an axiom in the future management of the reformatory.'[22] Significantly, however, the Act of 1879 which provided for the establishment and management of reformatories for youthful offenders empowered the resident magistrate of the district within which the reformatory was situated to 'bind any such inmate as apprentice to any useful calling or occupation as he may think fit, in the same manner in which destitute children are now authorized to be bound by the law of this colony'.

In this context it is noteworthy, too, that Porter Reformatory had as its immediate aim the inculcation of the discipline of work into a generation that was unlikely to receive much schooling. This purpose, as expressed by a Management Board comprising lawyers, merchants and a representative from the Church, was to break down 'wild and reckless' habits and to build up values considered appropriate for an emergent working or labouring class: obedience and willingness to work, honesty and cleanliness. Its constituency, as revealed in the reformatory's Description Registers for the period between 1894 and 1897, was the urban and rural labouring poor.[23] Juveniles were drawn not only from the urban environs of Cape Town and Kimberley but also from the rural towns and districts of Graaff Reinet, King Williams Town, Queenstown and Victoria West, towns whose population had grown considerably during the 1860s and 1870s. Over the years many of the smaller villages in the Cape also contributed a number of inmates. Apart from a tiny fraction which was school-going, all the boys detained in the reformatory had previously been employed as messengers, attendants, shepherds, domestic servants or labourers.[24]

Not all the youths convicted of crimes were sentenced to a period in the reformatory. It appears that the great majority of male juvenile offenders who committed crimes of violence ended up in gaols. To the reformatory, however, were sent boys who were apprehended for a variety of crimes against property, such as stock-theft on farms, house-breaking, theft and pilfering. Boys convicted of such crimes were seen as 'reformable', whereas those guilty of murder were assumed to have an innate criminal disposition. Girls of a similar age-group were sentenced not only for theft and 'female crimes'

[19] Colonial Office (C.O.), Cape Archives Depot, vol. 1966, Folio 233 (Documents in this series are hereafter referred to in the form C.O. 1966).

[20] *Ibid.*

[21] House of Assembly (H.A.) 203, ref. 386, Report of Board of Porter Reformatory for 1882.

[22] C.O. 6451; C.C.P. (Cape Archives) 1/2/2/1/33, Appendix C.

[23] C.O. 6971, Description Register of Juvenile Offenders.

[24] *Ibid.*

such as concealment of childbirth and prostitution, but also for crimes considered 'unnatural' to the female sex – assault, culpable homicide, poisoning and murder.[25] In the case of both boys and girls, assumptions about what constituted 'natural' behaviour influenced decisions as to whether they went to gaol or reformatory. Separate provision was also made for girls. Not until 1897 was a dormitory set aside in the Female House of Correction, a part of the Cape Town gaol, for seven girls between the ages of thirteen and twenty-one.[26]

Although Porter Reformatory's constituency was class- and sex-specific, no distinctions were initially made between black and white. The inmates included 'Coloured Afrikanders' and 'Hottentots', who constituted the majority, as well as Africans from the Eastern Cape Transkeian regions, 'Mozambiques' generally employed on the docks in Cape Town, Malays and Europeans, who together comprised the remaining quarter of the reformatory population. This was entirely in keeping with broader penal policy which at this stage did not legally differentiate between white and black prisoners inside gaols.

Methods for the control and discipline of reformatory inmates changed dramatically during the 1890s. At first, under the direction of a Managing Board and Superintendent drawn from the Church, the institution lay open to the fields and the boys, undifferentiated by colour, enjoyed a relatively free existence within its confines. Little control was exercised over them. Warders and supervisors were few in number, and the Superintendent's powers were limited by those of the magistrate to whom all major decisions regarding punishment had to be referred. Time was unstructured. A strict time-table did not exist, although boys did spend a few hours of each day in industrial training and clearing the farm grounds. Few heeded what punitive controls there were. Sentences were no longer than two years on average, and the reformatory was treated with contempt rather than fear. In 1889 the colonial government took over control. This inaugurated a new era: the reformatory was reorganized and different means of 'character reformation' were introduced.

The punitive aspect of Porter Reformatory was symbolised in its location.[27] Originally situated on the farm Valkenberg, the reformatory was moved to the Tokai Estate in 1889 when the farm was taken over for use as a mental hospital. Located some miles outside Cape Town and surrounded by forest, the reformatory was secluded from the common concourse of society. The isolation and enclosure of inmates was secured by thick wire fencing around the grounds, barred dormitory, school and hospital windows, enclosed yards serving as playgrounds and several isolation cells for the solitary confinement of recalcitrant offenders.[28] At first, two dormitories were flanked by the Superintendent and warders' rooms which overlooked the yard. In this confined space the boys spent two hours of each day under conditions of sun and rain. Here they had their meals and spent their leisure time.

[25] C.O. 6972, Description Registers of Female Prisoners; see also Carol Smart, *Women, Crime and Criminology: A Critique* (London, 1976).

[26] van Wyk, 'Gevangeniswese', op. cit. 475.

[27] C.O. 6414 and 6485, ref. 134/93; C.O. 6521, ref. 271/95; C.O. 6504, refs. 148/94 and 153/94.

[28] C.O. 6436, refs. 138/90, 194/90; C.O. 6504, ref. 143/94; C.O. 6533, ref. 1396. Also see *Cape Times*, 27 June 1891.

Life in the reformatory was rigidly structured and tightly controlled. To the same unyielding routine of work and socialization were subjected boys of profoundly varying origins, few of whom had previous experience of institutional life. Many had for years led lives largely free of control, either by families or the state. Those from towns had received their most significant socialization in what the Superintendent chose to call 'gangs of young thieves'.[29] To eradicate such independence and autonomy as there was, they were drilled into docility by a time-table characterized by military discipline:

5.30	Rise. Muster. Wash. Make up beds.
6.00	Muster for work.
8.00	Breakfast. Prayers. Play.
8.30	Muster. One half the number of boys in the institution to attend school – the other half to work.
11.30	School dismissed. Working parties brought in.
12.00	Dinner. Play.
1.00	Muster for work and school. The boys who attended school in the forenoon now take up work. Those who worked earlier now attend school.
4.00	School dismissed. Scholars to work.
5.00	Muster. Wash. Supper. Prayers. Play.
6.00	Muster. March to dormitories. Lock-up.
8.30	Visit by warden. Remove lights.[30]

Except when the boys themselves subverted or disrupted the daily routine, it was interrupted only when the institution demanded the labour of all boys: during the planting and harvesting seasons all other activities, including schooling, were abandoned.[31] At these times, the institution's capacity to remain self-sufficient took predecence over its disciplinary function; economic imperatives alone broke the social-psychological regimen.

Productive labour was clearly the most important aspect of disciplinary training. Through work, it was believed, boys would become disciplined wage-earners. Non-productive labour was strongly discouraged by the Colonial Office. It argued that forms of punishment characteristic of the precapitalist epoch and discarded in Britain, 'including all purely mechanical work on cranks and treadmills should, except as prison punishment, be entirely abolished wherever possible'.[32] Instead, but also in line with the imperative to be self-supporting, farm work and varieties of craft labour were advised and put into practice. Through dairy-farming, market-gardening and fruit cultivation an agricultural surplus for sale to other penal institutions was produced, while boys were simultaneously trained in largely unskilled manual farm labour.

Industrial training, which involved tailoring, carpentry and blacksmithing, was intended to teach boys 'some useful handicraft by which they can earn their living after their release'.[33] For a number of reasons, it did not succeed in achieving this aim. No consistent training was provided; only a handful of boys were employed for short periods in each activity. In practice,

---

[29] C.O. 6451, ref. 384/95 and C.O. 6533, no page ref.
[30] C.O. 6451, ref. 44/91.
[31] *Ibid.*, refs. 131/91 and 217/91; C.O. 6465, ref. 280/92.
[32] H. A. Annexures, vol. 383, *Report on the Management and Discipline of Prisons and Convict Stations for the year 1894*, 23.
[33] *Ibid.*

industrial training meant that they made the uniforms for their fellow-inmates and did the necessary repairs to the reformatory buildings and equipment. Their training was directed by warders, themselves untrained and ill-equipped to teach. In tailoring, each boy cut and sewed an entire article, a labour process already superseded in the light clothing industries of Cape Town. Industrial training achieved little more than the transmission of forms of de-skilled work.

Both skills and products manufactured at the reformatory were unmarketable. Very early on, in the late 1880s, as the reformatory regime became established, production became geared to the needs of other penal institutions. Apart from producing commodities in a way that made them uncompetitive, there is also some evidence to suggest that pressure had been exerted by craft unions, which by the 1890s had become racially exclusive, for the colonial government stressed that by confining production in prisons and reformatories to the supply of government institutions, it had 'ensured that the government does not enter into competition with private enterprise or business'.[34] By 1896, all basket-ware for the General Post Office, hospitals, Robben Island leper colony and other government institutions was made at the reformatory.

The schooling, such as there was of it, was a travesty of what is usually understood by the notion of education. The hours assigned to school work, for at least one group, were those when boys were least alert, and then only for two to three hours every day. Most boys arrived at the reformatory illiterate; few possessed even rudimentary skills of literacy and numeracy.[35] At first, irrespective of age or educational level, all boys were crowded into one room. Here they received religious instruction and elementary skills in the three Rs. Religious instruction on weekdays was provided in the precepts of the Church of England, even though most boys with a religious affiliation belonged to the Dutch Reformed Church.[36] Only on Sundays were the latter catered to by the Visiting Chaplain, J. Roos, of the Dutch Reformed Church. At first the Superintendent and the warders, the latter barely literate themselves, supervised this instruction, but when the institution was taken over by the colonial government, a schoolmaster was appointed. In order to control the large number of boys crammed into the schoolroom, he used a monitorial system.[37] While this might have been an effective method for controlling large numbers of untutored boys, it did not significantly advance their education.

As in all other similar establishments – prisons, compounds or boarding schools – it was inevitable that the boys would respond by creating a distinctive sub-culture. It was a sub-culture brought into being by the integrating effects of institutional life and mediated by the boys' experiences outside the reformatory. Through it they established their own, autonomous spheres of authority in and through which they attempted to reject the authority of the state and sought to assert their right to control their own lives. Through it they demonstrated a degree of cohesion and solidarity which could be contained but not always controlled. The other side of this was a violence amongst one another, an aspect of the sub-culture which can only be

[34] Cited in van Wyk, 'Gevangeniswese', 50–1.
[35] C.O. 6436, ref. 30a/90.
[36] C.O. 6465, ref. 292/92; C.O. 6971, Description Registers of Juvenile Offenders.
[37] C.O. 6451, ref. 172/91; C.O. 6521, ref. 384/95; C.O. 6533, no page ref.

understood in terms of the brutalizing effects of institutional life and by reference to the alternatives open to them.[38]

Hierarchies of age and strength amongst the boys replicated the hierarchical structure of authority in the reformatory. Initiation into the 'under-life' of the reformatory could be through homosexual rape, while younger boys were soon drafted into service, sexual and otherwise, for older boys. Masturbation and homosexuality were common,[39] while fagging, a common boarding school phenomenon, also appears to have been in practice, as is indicated by the following warder's report:

On Saturday afternoon last, after play, I fell in the stable party for the purpose of milking, bedding down the animals, etc. The boy Mposwana whose duty it was to feed the pigs, did not do so, but sent a little one to do it, whilst he played marbles....[40]

The time and place that boys were most powerless and vulnerable was at night, in the dormitories, after lock-up. Locked in and largely shorn of all external control, they seem to have used this opportunity to weld hierarchies of authority and plan various forms of opposition, including the most powerful response – attempts at escape.

In 1891 the first schoolmaster at Porter, Herbert Armitage, drawing on his knowledge of Dr Barnardo's home for Destitute Boys in Stepney, London, located the origins of unruliness in the reformatory: 'I believe', he observed, 'that all the serious offences that have been committed here have had their *rise* [sic] in the dormitories'.[41] To 'remedy the evil', in order to 'raise the tone among the boys and make them a credit to the institution',[42] Armitage recommended a series of privileges and rewards to supplement punishments. Stripes and badges should reward good conduct: these would carry extra privileges and power. Forfeiture of these privileges could be used as punishment for bad conduct. The boys could be graded hierarchically, the 'good conduct boys' acting as local authority and 'spies' for the Superintendent in the dormitories at night. Armitage also recommended simpler prayer services than the recital of catechisms, more time and equipment for recreation, larger playgrounds and a prize-giving ceremony. His report was forwarded to the Secretary of the Law Department, John J. Graham, who rejected almost all his suggestions, probably on the grounds of their cost to the state, except for those involving the division of boys through privilege and punishment. Graham gained his formative experience in the courts of the Eastern Districts and rose to become Secretary of the Law Department in 1882, a post he held for more than twenty years. He introduced far-reaching changes in the prison-service, such as those concerning the separation of black and white prisoners at all levels. He felt particularly strongly about this, 'whether regarded from the moral or economical point of view'.[43] With reference to Porter, he argued that in the future management of the

---

[38] See Paul Corrigan, *Schooling the Smash Street Kids* (London, 1979) and Don Pinnock, *The Brotherhoods: Street Gangs and State control in Cape Town* (Cape Town, 1984).

[39] C.O. 6521, ref. 89/92.   [40] C.O. 6504, ref. 279/94.

[41] C.O. 6483, ref. 238/93.   [42] C.O. 6451, ref. 31/91.

[43] H.A. Annexures, 383, ref. 401, *Report on the Management and Discipline of Convict Stations for the year 1894*, Minute by Secretary to the Law Department, 17 Sept. 1895.

reformatory, if there was to be any material change, it should be in the separation of black and white. This, he felt, should be effected not only as regards sleeping arrangements, but also as regards education.[44] Accordingly, a ward for white boys was completed at the end of 1892 and at the end of 1894 it was noted that 'still further classification seems to be necessary'.[45]

During the 1880s and 1890s, the provision of housing, poor relief and formal schooling in Cape Town was increasingly administered on a racially differential basis. In 1891 the Superintendent General of Education, Langham Dale, affirmed a particular direction for black education:

In a few institutions handicrafts have been taught and general industrial habits have been created and cultivated for many years. What the Department wants is to make all the principal Day-schools places of manual instruction, as well as of book instruction. It is not expected that all the boys will become expert tradesmen; but it is something to train them to use the spade and the hoe, the plane and the saw, the mason's trowel and the plumb line.[46]

This trend began to be reflected in the workings of Porter Reformatory from the early to mid-1890s. White boys were channelled into industrial training and blacks into manual labour: 'gardening, milking, tending cows, working with horses...and general farm labour'.[47] White boys were also granted extra privileges. From 1893 they could remain in the dining room up to 8.00 p.m. (instead of being locked up at 6.00 p.m. as the black boys continued to be) and were allowed to play games such as draughts and dominoes. A small library of books was made available to them. Whether any of these were read is highly doubtful, as they were selected by the Superintendent whose notion of what would be appropriate reading was derived from the British context. Amongst the books, for a group of mainly Afrikaans-speaking boys, were Dr Barnardo's *Child's Treasury, Little Folks, Boys' Own Annual, Chatterbox, Child's Companion, The Prince, Sunshine, Children's Own Magazine* and *Christian Friend*.[48]

The segregation of boys in Porter Reformatory began as an attempt to control and weaken the informal culture cutting across colour lines that had begun to appear in the institution. That classification became interpreted as a means of segregating boys along racial lines which reflected broader social policy in the Cape Colony during the 1890s. It was no doubt related to the way in which colonial officials reinterpreted imperialist ideas relating to the poor in a colonial context.[49] It was possibly also a reflection of the changing ideology of a ruling class that increasingly took its cues from the developing racial division of labour in the mining industry in Kimberley and on the Witwatersrand.

Classification was based not only on race, but also on age and conduct. To this end, an exhaustive examination of Porter was undertaken at the beginning of 1895 by the Inspector of Prisons. Structural alterations to the building were recommended and two additional dormitories were built to separate the

[44] C.O. 6451, ref. 32/91.
[45] H.A. 292, no page ref.
[46] South African Library, Cape of Good Hope Publications, *Report of the Superintendent General of Education for 1891*, 12.
[47] C.O. 6504, ref. 198/94.
[48] *Ibid.*, ref. 330/94.
[49] Bundy, 'Poor whiteism'.

'incorrigibles' from the newest and youngest arrivals. For reformatory authorities this was a victory; for at least the younger boys it meant some form of protection. The introduction of a system of privileges and rewards was similarly double-edged. It divided, protected and rewarded boys who conformed to the rules of the reformatory; it gave the smaller, younger boys, who consciously aimed at good conduct marks, some bargaining power over bullies in the dormitories.[50] It was a bargaining power, however, that could easily be subverted and undermined. Rewards for good conduct were at the same time a privilege and a potential punishment, at once carrot and stick. Whenever a privilege was conceded – such as attendance at the monthly Magic Lantern slide shows, football on Saturday afternoons, puddings for Sunday lunch, wearing a distinctive stripe-less dress on Sundays which would become the boy's property on his release, or monthly outings to the beach with the Superintendent – it was understood that it could be withdrawn for bad behaviour.[51]

By the end of 1896 the Superintendent was singing the praises of classification according to conduct. 'Classification', he exulted, 'strict discipline and supervision, both by day and night, works wonders. Boys of the most pronounced physical types, who were considered as completely incorrigible, have...become...decent characters.'[52] By 1909 the dormitories had been classified according to age, conduct and colour. The eight dormitories were divided as follows: No. 1, coloured, 9–12 years; no. 2, coloured, 15–16 years; no. 3, coloured, incorrigible; no. 4, coloured, 12–15 years; no. 5, coloured, good conduct boys; no. 6, European, 13–16 years; no. 7, European, 9–13 years; no. 8, coloured, smaller, good conduct boys.[53] In order to assess the efficacy of his strategy, all convict stations were circularized to discover whether any of their convicts had served a period in the reformatory. Perhaps it was too early to tell in 1895 and 1896, but both years produced evidence of recidivism. It was later estimated that of all the boys released between 1882 and 1896, there was a 14·4 per cent rate of recidivism.[54] These figures, small and imprecise though they might be, nonetheless begin to cast some light on the role of the reformatory in reproducing rather than stemming delinquency.

A close and changing relationship existed between the reformatory and the labour market of the Western Cape during this period. Boys were apprenticed to local Cape farmers and dignitaries on a regular basis. The reformatory does not seem to have been a major source of labour: no more than 800 a year passed through its doors. Nevertheless, the steady trickle of apprentices swelled during periods of labour shortage in the Cape. Numbers were at their highest, for example, during the farm labour shortage of the mid-1890s. Again, during the South African War (1899–1902), when many adult workers were drawn into military service, numbers in the reformatory expanded and contracted according to the demands made on the institution.[55]

[50] C.O. 6504, ref. 146/94.
[51] C.O. 6465, refs. 98/92, 104/92 and 106/92; C.O. 6504, ref. 139/94.
[52] H.A. 292, no page ref.
[53] van Wyk, 'Gevangeniswese', 552.
[54] *Ibid.*, 555; Department of Justice Annual Report for 1911; *Transvaal Leader*, 11 Apr. 1911.
[55] See W. R. Nasson, 'Black society in the Cape Colony and the South African War 1899–1902, a social history' (Ph.D. thesis, University of Cambridge, 1983).

Apprenticeship was a key index of the role the reformatory played in training and disciplining boys for farm labour. The extension of apprenticeship was explicitly linked to employers' demands for indentured labour.[56] The practice of apprenticeship in the reformatory built on and modified modes of forcible apprenticeship in existence since the beginning of the century in the Cape Colony. In 1879 legislative provision had been made for the apprenticeship of juvenile offenders during their detention at the reformatory provided that prior parental consent had been obtained. In practice, those boys whose parents could not be traced and whose consent was unobtainable were singled out for indenture. Since in many cases parents lived in remote rural districts or had died or had difficulty in communicating with their children, it was a relatively easy matter for the state to take possession of these youths and apprentice them during their term of sentence at the reformatory. In other cases, if the state judged parents to be of 'dissolute' or degenerate character, generally a synonym for the labouring poor, they lost their claim to their son.

A contract of apprenticeship does appear to have been signed by the 'Master', i.e. the employer, who was accountable only to the local magistrate of Wynberg. It stipulated the length of apprenticeship – generally two years – and the 'Master's' responsibilities. These included instructing the apprentice in a calling or trade, providing for his education and religious instruction, clothing, lodging and food. The employer had to pay a certain sum to the Superintendent as wages for the boy, until termination of the contract, when the youth was returned to the reformatory. Clearly this was part of the process of accustoming inmates to wage-labour on farms.

No record was kept of the boys either during or after their apprenticeship. No provision was made for inspection of the conditions under which they laboured.[57] The reason for this was given by John Graham in 1891. He admitted that some of the clauses, such as those dealing with education and religious instruction, were unenforceable.[58] Proper inspection would have exposed the fact that they were not enforced, and such exposure would have conflicted with employers' interests in the labour of the boys. There is thus no evidence of the working conditions of the apprentices, but it is clear that reformatory boys did not relish the prospect of being apprenticed for almost half their sentence. Superintendent Johnston reported as early as 1885 that '...the little boys do not respond very cheerily.... They get attached to their comrades in the institution. Most of them have just left farming work and they certainly know that they are better treated (in the reformatory).[59] If treatment in the reformatory was preferable to treatment on farms, some indication of the arduous work enforced on boys is provided. Of the older boys Johnston also indicated that there was a 'general objection.... If left to themselves, I believe not one boy would go...excepting perhaps in the case of relations where they are claimed.'[60] A few boys did use the opportunity to leave the reformatory to join family or friends.[61] Damon Jonker, for

---

[56] Department of Justice, vol. 56, Annual Report for Porter Reformatory for 1911.
[57] C.C.P. 1/2/2/1/33, Report of Select Committee on Porter Reformatory, 1885.
[58] C.O. 6451, Notes made by Secretary, 29 June 1891.
[59] C.C.P. 1/2/2/1/33, Report of Select Committee, 12.
[60] Ibid.
[61] C.O. 6485, ref. 17093; C.C.P. 1/2/2/1/33: Johnston's evidence ran as follows, 'frequently if a lad has a friend he gets him out by having him apprenticed'.

example, who was due for discharge in 1893, asked to be apprenticed on a farm where his brother had been apprenticed.

It was not unusual for boys to abscond from their employers. Anthonie Klerck, apprenticed to the liberal Cape M.P., John X. Merriman, absconded after three years.[62] Another apprentice, Stephanus Jonker, fled the farm for the reformatory, stating that he had been severely beaten by his master and his master's sons.[63] It is not clear whether such boys were returned to the original employer, re-apprenticed to another or kept at the reformatory for the remainder of their sentence. There was certainly no guarantee that they would be dealt with sympathetically, and absconding apprentices took a considerable risk.

There is little information about the lives of boys once they left Porter. Some found their way back into prison as adults; others, defined as destitute by the state, were drafted into farm labour. A few sought employment in the environs of the reformatory. It is about these that we have most information. It seems that they chose this option for a variety of reasons: to maintain friendships forged during the period of incarceration or to use this as a time for negotiating re-entry into the wider world. When boys were discharged, the marks of the outcast were removed and new symbols of incorporation were introduced. They were given 1–5 shillings (depending on their conduct inside), a suit of discharge clothing made at the reformatory and their fare to the railway station nearest to their ultimate destination.

By the end of the century, as the Cape increasingly 'became a commercial partner for an industrial hinterland',[64] the focus on juvenile crime also shifted northwards. In 1900 provision was made in Porter for the detention of juvenile offenders from the Orange River Colony and the Transvaal, but this was clearly merely an interim measure until the Rand had developed its own thrust in penal policy and its own network of penal institutions. Here, as ideologists such as de Villiers Roos, Minister of Justice after 1910, began to consider the question of crime control in the context of industrialization, they turned their eyes towards the United States of America, more and more in the forefront of international penal policy. New explanations and methods of rehabilitation were discussed. Positivist criminology and psycho-pathological models of delinquency became dominant. Some of these began to filter through to Porter. After the South African War, greater interest was bestowed on the social environment and especially the family background of the offender. Hitherto, Description Registers had simply recorded details about the crime and sentence, the occupations of parents and their ability to maintain the offender; they now elicited reports on the 'environment of the offender previous to the conviction', the traceability of the crime 'to any known cause', the character and condition in life of the parents and whether the parents had a criminal record themselves.[65] Knowledge about the offender begins to assume a new status. Much more intimate information regarding the family and social background of the inmate was required.[66] The recom-mendations of the 1909 Inquiry into Porter stressed the need for re-

[62] C.O. 6533, ref. 105/96.
[63] C.O. 6485, ref. 36/93.
[64] Mabin, 'Making of colonial capitalism', 248.
[65] C.O. 2736, no page ref.
[66] *Ibid.*

organization of Porter 'upon the same basis as similar modern institutions elsewhere and introducing higher reformative principles'.[67] Accordingly, it also made recommendations for the further classification of boys according to the nature of the crime committed and control over boys after discharge. Crucially, however, the patterns established in Porter were incorporated into the new framework. Apprenticeship was retained as the major aspect of reformatory life and the state's hand was strengthened even further over the boys in that it was now given the power to apprentice boys after expiration of sentence without having to obtain the consent of parents or guardians. The *de facto* situation was thus legitimated. Secondly, whereas segregation had been introduced within the institution of Porter as far as accommodation and education were concerned, separate institutions were now to be built for 'Europeans, Africans and Coloureds'.

SUMMARY

This article explores the origins and nature of the reformatory in Cape colonial society between 1882 and 1910. Born in a period of economic transition, its concern was with the reproduction of a labouring population precipitated by colonial conquest. Unlike the prison and compound, which gained their distinctive character from the way in which they were articulated to an emerging industrial capitalist society, the reformatory was shaped by the imperatives of merchant capital and commercial agriculture. Although based on the English model, local social realities quickly began to mould the particular nature of the reformatory in the Cape Colony. Firstly, classification for the purposes of control came to mean segregation in a colonial context. Secondly, the needs of commercial agriculture meant that in Porter there was a much greater stress on the apprenticing of inmates than there was in the internal operations of the British reformatory.

[67] C.O. 1883.

[19]

Journal of Interdisciplinary History, XXIII:2 (Autumn 1992), 279–299.

Ricardo D. Salvatore

Criminology, Prison Reform, and the Buenos Aires Working Class

Between 1900 and 1920, positivist criminologists introduced important reforms into the Argentine prison system. Influenced by the work of José Ingenieros, who redefined crime as a moral-social-psychological pathology that could be treated and cured, a new group of experts and prison administrators organized the transformation of old repressive prisons into experimental clinics for the rehabilitation of inmates. Their finest achievement—the National Penitentiary of Buenos Aires—hosted a new disciplinary system that combined the most current trends in the science of punishment: the humanist positivism of the "Italian School," and the methods of rehabilitation of leading penitentiaries and reformatories in the United States. Central to this disciplinary strategy was the use of confinement, redemptive work, elementary education, and religious instruction. Other methods borrowed from Europe and the United States, such as "grading" and the modification of sentences according to inmates' behavior, added to the novelty of the reform.

The impetus of reform reached various institutions of the justice system in the capital—the police, the prison for indicted felons, the juvenile reformatories, and the courts—and swept the old, classical penology from university chairs and academic circles. In modifying the criminal code, the reform proved less impressive. The revised Criminal Code of 1920 supported positivist principles without completely eliminating the penalties advocated by the old penology. Similarly, prison facilities in the

Ricardo D. Salvatore is Research Fellow, Instituto Torcuato Di Tella, Buenos Aires.

He is the author of "Modes of Labor Control in Cattle-Ranching Economies: California, Southern Brazil, and Argentina, 1800–1870," *Journal of Economic History*, LI (1991), 441–451; "The Old Problem of Gauchos and Rural Society," *Hispanic American Historical Review*, LXIX (1989), 733–745.

The author thanks Monica Gomez for helping with the tabulation of censuses and Carla Feldpausch for helping to locate bibliographical sources. He also thanks Jonathan C. Brown, Donna J. Guy, Joan W. Scott, Wilfred Spohn, Peter Linebaugh, Harry Cleaver, and an anonymous reviewer for their helpful comments. He is grateful for funds from CONICOR (Council for Scientific Research of the Province of Cordoba, Argentina).

interior provinces lagged behind the establishments in the nation's capital in adopting the new methods. Despite these limitations, the reforms produced long-lasting effects on the Argentine prison system.

A profound change in the city's working class, triggered by the arrival of a massive number of European immigrants at the turn of the century, provided both the context and the impetus for prison reform. In the eyes of policymakers, mass immigration brought about problems of housing, unemployment, and crime. Another disturbing attribute of the immigrant workers was their capacity for organization and struggle. The foreign-born proletariat of the city led the way in the rapid unionization drive of the late 1890s, participated in the strikes that paralyzed export production in 1901–02, and organized the first socialist- and anarchist-led labor confederations. Less visible changes also affected the composition of the city's working class. The seasonality of export agriculture, the nature of domestic demand, and periodic economic crises caused the increase of temporary and unskilled jobs in number and in proportion to the total amount of employment, forcing newly arrived immigrants to move constantly in search of jobs. This "casualization" of the urban labor market was contemporaneous with the "feminization" of some segments of this market. In services and manufacturing particularly, underpaid women and children were hired instead of men, experiencing the insecurity of a highly fluctuating labor demand with them.

This article examines the connections between the new criminology, the prison reform movement, and the changed composition of Buenos Aires' working class. These three phenomena are linked by the perceptions of positivist criminologists about the city's emerging "social problems." The spread of positivist criminology contributed more than new methods of rehabilitation of inmates. It provided the rhetorical devices and the images within which the newly formed working class could be comprehended, classified, and ordered. At a time of great occupational mobility and social conflict, prison reformers produced novel interpretations of the urgent "social problems" facing the ruling class. New conceptions about crime and criminals centered around work habits and attitudes served to divide the new working class into an honest core, an endangered middle ground, and an irredeemable margin—the "criminal class." Constructing social

PRISON REFORM IN BUENOS AIRES | **281**

problems as the summation of individual anomalies (moral, vo-
litional, and intellectual), criminologists were able to provide "explanations" for questions of immigration policy, working-class
culture, and work discipline. In particular, criminologists' emphasis on the relationship between crime and the refusal to work
brought to public attention an issue insufficiently articulated by
private sector employers: labor discipline. Often viewed as isolated reformers swimming against the current of the *república
conservadora*, positivists contributed important ideological and disciplinary instruments for the renovation and continuity of the
oligarchy's rule.

As in every construction, positivists' perceptions of crime
and class obscured as much as they revealed. Unable to perceive
the changes operating in the sexual composition of the city's work
force and incapable of separating work from manhood, criminologists concentrated their reform efforts on male offenders. The
question of women and crime—and the possible implications for
issues of gender, class, and social control—received little or no
attention. In their writings about crime, prison reform, and the
"social question," reformers relegated the political, collective
struggles of workers to a second plane. Collapsing the manifestations of workers' protests with other "anomalies" resulting from
individuals' "struggles for subsistence," criminologists failed to
appreciate the importance of class struggle in the formation of the
new Buenos Aires working class.

CASUAL LABOR, WOMEN, AND LABOR DISCIPLINE   Changes in the
composition of the work force during the period 1880–1910 provided the context for the experimentation with modern reformatory practices. Mass immigration transformed the character of
the Buenos Aires working class. Between 1900 and 1908, 1.9
million immigrants entered the port; by 1914 foreigners constituted 46 percent of the total work force.[1] Several authors have
underlined the impact of mass immigration on government policy, elite perceptions, and working-class culture. Other important
aspects of the recomposition of the work force—the casualization

---

1   Ronaldo Munck, *Argentina from Anarchism to Peronism* (London, 1987), 43; Ernesto
Kritz, "La formación de la fuerza de trabajo en la Argentina, 1890–1914," *Cuaderno del
CENEP*, (Centro de Estudios de la Población) (Buenos Aires, 1985), 18.

282 | RICARDO D. SALVATORE

and the feminization of a large portion of the jobs created during this period—are less known.

Casual laborers—engaged for short periods of time in activities requiring no previous training or particular skills—constituted an important and growing segment of the city's work force. In the censuses of 1895 and 1914, categories such as "peons," "day laborers," (*jornaleros*), and "workers without fixed occupation" constituted between 10 to 18 percent of the economically active population of Buenos Aires. As much as 45 percent of the new jobs created during this period fell under these categories.[2] Other groups of workers shared some of the characteristics of casual laborers. Occupations requiring no initial skills (such as domestic servant, messenger, gardener, stevedore, charcoalman, cart-driver, waiter, clothes-washer, and ironer) and those (due to their low wage and irregularity) constituting disguised unemployment (witch doctor, street artist, boxer, flower vendor, bottle peddler, paper boy, street vendor, shoe shiner, and stable boy) comprised at least another 11 to 12 percent of the new jobs created between 1895 and 1914.

Unskilled labor pervaded the employment structure of the city. In a survey of 544 firms by the National Department of Labor in 1913, 50 percent of the work force was classified as *obreros sin oficio* (unskilled workers). Railroads, construction firms, and manufacturing plants ancillary to construction showed the highest proportion of unskilled workers (76, 61, and 58 percent respectively). Labor contracts tended to be temporary; seasonal and cyclical fluctuations limited the duration of employment. For the country as a whole, Kritz estimates that 44 percent of the average growth in employment between 1895 and 1914 was temporary in nature. In Buenos Aires, where employment was more influenced by seasonal variations in key economic activities (for example, the shipping, handling, and storage of exports, and the manufacturing of clothing), the proportion of temporary employment must have been higher. Cyclical economic crises created additional unemployment. The crisis of 1899–1902, which coincided with one of the peaks in immigration, generated tens of

2   Edgardo Bilsky, *La F.O.R.A. y el movimiento obrero* (Buenos Aires, 1985), I, 37–39. Calculation based on data provided by the national population censuses of 1895 and 1914. República Argentina, *Segundo Censo de la República Argentina, mayo de 1895* (Buenos Aires, 1898), II, 47–50; *Tercer Censo Nacional, junio de 1914* (Buenos Aires, 1917), IV, 201–212.

PRISON REFORM IN BUENOS AIRES | **283**

thousands of unemployed people, particularly affecting the situation of casual laborers.[3]

The seasonal nature of labor demand in the countryside added to the occupational and spatial mobility of the city's work force. Production directly related to the export sector—grains, livestock, sheep shearing, and the transportation and shipment of these products—demanded large numbers of workers only in late spring and summer. Temporary workers hired by the task or by the day comprised approximately 30 percent of the active male population of the major cereal-growing provinces. Part of this seasonal demand was filled with *golondrina* ("swallow") immigrants who came only to work in the grain harvest—close to 50,000 a year in the 1890s and over 100,000 a year in the 1900s. When the harvest was over, these workers had to return to the city and work temporarily until their scheduled departure for Europe. Urban workers joined recent immigrants in their journey to the countryside. Workshop and factory workers as well as construction and railroad laborers usually abandoned their jobs temporarily in order to earn better wages shearing wool, threshing wheat, or harvesting corn.[4]

Casual labor, temporary employment, and high occupational mobility became constant realities for many immigrants. An increasing proportion of them had to accept unskilled engagements upon their arrival at Buenos Aires and, in order to get these jobs, more declared themselves as unskilled. Although in time immigrants managed to save enough to return to Italy or Spain, or to install a shop in Argentina; they spent the first years in a constant search for employment and were ready to accept, temporarily, occupations not in accordance with their expectations nor their skills. Not surprisingly, for the few immigrants who wrote about their experiences, life in Argentina was presented as a long journey through many places and occupations.[5]

3 "Grado de ocupación obrera en la Capital Federal," *Boletín del Departamento Nacional del Trabajo*, XXX (1915), 158–161; Kritz, "La formación," 35; Guido Di Tella and Manuel Zymelman, *Ciclos económicos en la Argentina* (Buenos Aires, 1973), 62–86.
4 Hilda Sábato, "La formación del mercado de trabajo en Buenos Aires, 1850–1880," *Desarrollo Económico*, XXIV (1985), 570–574; Ofelia Pianetto, "Mercado de trabajo y acción sindical en la Argentina, 1890–1922," *Desarrollo Económico*, XXIV (1984), 300–302; Roberto. Cortés Conde, *El progreso argentino, 1880–1914* (Buenos Aires, 1979), 200, 207; James Scobie, *Buenos Aires; Plaza to Suburb* (New York, 1974), 136.
5 See, e.g., the story of Félix Serret, a French immigrant, in Guy Bourdé, *Urbanisation*

284 | RICARDO D. SALVATORE

Another characteristic of the city's labor market was the feminization of the lowest tier of the work force. In the first decade of the century women entered occupations that could be characterized as low-paying, unstable, and unskilled. They comprised an important proportion of the work force in four sectors of the urban economy: personal and social services, manufacturing, commerce, and "not well specified activities"—a category including those without a fixed employment. By 1914, 30 percent of manufacturing workers, 39 percent of finance and insurance employees, 53 percent of workers in personal services, and 66 percent of those without a fixed occupation were women.[6]

Women made significant gains in employment between 1895 and 1909 vis-à-vis their male counterparts, gains that concentrated precisely in services, manufacturing, and commerce. The most impressive growth in female employment corresponded to the residual categories identified with casual labor. If, in 1895, women represented 68 percent of the category "workers without a fixed occupation," in 1909 that proportion rose to 88 percent. Between 1895 and 1914 five of the ten fastest growing occupational categories were dominated by women. Casual workers topped the list; domestic servants, dressmakers, and cooks came fifth to seventh; and commercial employees occupied the ninth rank.

As factories, workshops, and domestic work opened opportunities for partial or temporary employment, women began to switch back and forth between paid and unpaid work. Among female out-workers (women working at home for a distant boss providing the raw materials) of the "needle trades," for example, the intermittency of work was pervasive. Work loads could be excessive or insufficient according to the season's demand for a particular kind of clothing. A survey of domestic industry taken by the Department of Labor in 1913 showed that only 45 percent of the women interviewed worked year-round.[7] These women

---

et immigration en Amerique Latine (Paris, 1974), 233–234; the account of Oreste Sola, an Italian immigrant, in Samuel Baily et al. (eds.), *One Family, Two Worlds* (New Brunswick, 1988), 33–71. Similar stories are told in the interviews with Roberto Rojas and Victor Elmez, Chileans detained at the Viedma prison, Rufino Marin, *Hablan desde la cárcel los hijos de Martín Fierro* (Buenos Aires, 1934), 43–56, 91–134.

6 Calculation based on data provided by the *Tercer Censo Nacional*, IV, 201–212.

7 "El trabajo a domicilio en la Capital Federal," *Boletín del Departamento Nacional del Trabajo*, XXX (1915), 75–126.

PRISON REFORM IN BUENOS AIRES | 285

were in a similar situation to that of casual male laborers, except for one difference: their wages were half those of men.

Conditions of labor markets in the city (casual labor, temporary engagements, and constant spatial and occupational mobility) made it difficult for employers to instill regular, industrial work habits in their workers. Moreover, except for large workshops demanding skilled and semiskilled labor, most work places did not confront this problem; market mechanisms and authoritarian bosses were sufficient to maintain work discipline.

Four forms of organizing labor power—the factory, the artisan shop, the putting-out system, and the work-gang—served to mobilize most of the city's work force. Craftsmen, motivated by the desire to move upward in the social ladder and pressed by foreign and local competitors, disciplined themselves into the ethic of hard work and productivity. They needed no other stimulation than the market. On the other hand, factories—medium or large workshops employing skilled workers and apprentices in a largely manual process—experienced bitter struggles over the imposition of work discipline. Manufacturers' introduction of reglamentos internos (internal rules) which were aimed at the imposition of greater regularity of work, better compliance with schedules, and stricter control of the labor process, faced fierce opposition from workers organized in craft unions.

In these confrontations, however, manufacturers dealt directly with their workers, often resisting state intrusion in what they considered matters of private business.[8] The factories of the 1990s—larger establishments using machinery and employing mainly children and women—also resisted state intervention. Women and children, perceived as a docile work force which adapted more easily to new work conditions, also provided a way of reducing the costs of production at a time of acute competition from imports. The authority of fathers, husbands, and foremen, combined with the threat of dismissal, was deemed sufficient to keep these workers under control.

Among male casual laborers, the work-gang served as the principal form of recruitment. Contratistas (labor contractors), or

---

8 Ricardo Falcón, El mundo del trabajo urbano, 1890–1914 (Buenos Aires, 1986), 102–105, 108; Hobart Spalding, La clase trabajadora argentina (Buenos Aires, 1970), 18–19; Juan Alsina, El obrero en la República Argentina (Buenos Aires, 1905), II, 112–113.

foremen, arbitrarily selected, day-to-day, a group of laborers for the performance of a specific task. This method of organizing labor left little room for the infusion of work discipline. Most of these workers were not confined to a closed work place—they wandered through dockyards, municipal markets, railroad stations, and construction sites—and did not stay long enough to learn norms of punctuality, regularity, and sobriety. As a result, employers found little incentive to teach them new attitudes toward work; they relied instead on authoritarian foremen and on dismissals. Similarly, employers of women working at home did not need to concern themselves with issues of labor discipline. The piecework system, under conditions of ample reserves of family labor, worked well enough to expand or contract production according to market demand.

Except for large workshops using semiskilled labor, entrepreneurs expressed little concern for the question of work habits and work discipline. Leaving aside periods of exceptional harvests or of financial crises, the functioning of an international market for labor provided a sufficient supply of labor power. Mobilization of the labor force, however, was not a guarantee of productivity and much less of the industriousness, punctuality, responsibility, and loyalty ideally attributed to European workers. Unstable labor markets and the work-gang could not provide for the adequate socialization of casual laborers. Instilling the work ethic into the mass of often unemployed, itinerant, and unskilled laborers required either the mediation of disciplinary institutions or a new model of economic development based on the factory system. Unlike private employers, criminologists put the question of labor discipline at the center of their conceptions of crime and reformation.

PERCEPTIONS OF CRIME AND CLASS   At first, Argentine positivist criminology embraced uncritically the theories and methodologies developed by the Italian *Scuola Positiva*. The founders of the Association for Juridical Anthropology who introduced the new discipline in the 1880s replicated the principles sustained by the Italian school: the experimental method applied to the study of crime and punishment; crime as both a natural and a social phenomenon; social defense as the criterion for imposing penalties; and the penalty as a means of rehabilitation, not of punishment.

PRISON REFORM IN BUENOS AIRES | **287**

Considering the existing Criminal Code—enacted in 1887—as the embodiment of these outmoded principles of classical penology, these early positivists fought for the enactment of new legislation that would extend the use of therapeutical labor within prisons, abolish brutal punishment, and implement new methods for the identification of delinquents.[9]

Under the influence of José Ingenieros, criminological positivism grew in popularity and complexity during the first decade of the century. Ingenieros' research at the *Instituto de Criminología* into the new model penitentiary, his editorial work at the journal *Archivos de Psiquiatría y Criminología*, and his teaching at the Universidad de Buenos Aires gave a definite impulse to a doctrine that, while upholding positivist notions, abandoned earlier notions of atavism and socially-determined criminals. A psychological dimension was added to existing interpretations of crime. Each delinquent presented a combination of "moral," "intellectual," and "volitive" anomalies reflecting the influence of environment, inheritance, and personal psychological development.[10] Social "problems" like unemployment, drinking, gambling, homosexuality, and mental illness turned into individual pathologies subject to medical scrutiny and treatment.

9 The *Scuola Positiva*, built around the pioneer work of Cesare Lombrosso, Rafael Garofalo, and Enrico Ferri, had the greatest impact on Italy and France and had little influence in England and the United States. For a summary of the schools' achievements, see Edwin Seligman (ed.), *Encyclopedia of the Social Sciences* (New York, 1930), III, 584–587; Christopher Hibbert, *The Roots of Evil* (Boston, 1963), 185–197; David A. Jones, *History of Criminology* (Westport, 1986), 81–125. Some of the works of these early positivists are: Norberto Piñeiro, *Problemas de criminalidad* (Buenos Aires, 1888); Luis M. Drago, *Los hombres de presa* (Buenos Aires, 1888); Antonio Dellepiane, *El idioma del delito y diccionario lunfardo* (Buenos Aires, 1894). For their collective contribution, see Abelardo Levaggi, *Historia del Derecho Penal Argentino* (Buenos Aires, 1978), 151–155.

10 Enrique Hernández, "Positivismo y cientificismo en la Argentina," *Cuadernos Universitarios (Bariloche)*, V (1975); M.J. Bustamante, "La Escuela Positiva y sus aplicaciones," *Archivos de Psiquiatría y Criminología*, X (1911), 288–418; Aníbal Ponce, "Para una historia de Ingenieros," in José Ingenieros, *Obras Completas* (Buenos Aires, 1939), I; José L. Damis, "José Ingenieros (1877–1925)," in *El movimiento positivista argentino* (Buenos Aires, 1985), 527–538; Oscar Terán, *Positivismo y nación en la Argentina* (Buenos Aires, 1987), 45–53. In general, habitual delinquents suffered from "moral anomalies," the inability to internalize social norms and perform accordingly. Permanent or constitutional "madness" tended to impair individuals' resistance to crime, a condition Ingenieros called "intellectual anomaly." Epileptics, chronic alcoholics, and passionate criminals—those unable to control their wills—were included among those suffering from "volitive anomalies." Ingenieros, "Nueva clasificación de los delincuentes fundada en la psicopatología," *Revista de Derecho, Historia y Letras*, XXIV (1906), 18–27.

The new psychological approach expanded the role of medical science in the treatment of delinquents and changed the nature of penitentiary discipline. Penitentiaries and reformatories could help delinquents to internalize norms of discipline only if administrators relied on the principles of indeterminate sentence and individualized treatment.[11] Prisoners' clinical and criminal records at any given moment were the best indicators to determine the duration of sentences and the modalities of treatment. Work, religious instruction, and education were the preferred means for enacting the transformation of criminals. Confinement, no longer the center of prison discipline, was now part of a system of incentives and penalties designed to cause inmates to internalize the social norms that they lacked.

The impact of positivist criminology reached beyond the walls of the penitentiary, affecting ruling-class perceptions of crime, immigrant labor, and work discipline. With its emphasis on observation and experimentation, the new discipline gave impetus to the collection of data about crime and criminals—statistics, clinical records, and anthropometric studies—opening novel avenues for detecting and analyzing problems of social and labor control. Police stations, prisons, reformatories, and courtrooms became sites for observing crime and reflecting about its social/psychological context. Prisons, in particular, turned into clinics where specialists, through the observation of individual cases, were able to perceive current social problems (immigration, deviance, alcoholism, unemployment, child labor), diagnose the causes of society's illnesses, and recommend remedies. Disciplinary institutions generated useful class perceptions: constructs about the tensions between ideal and actual society that abstracted from class confrontations. These constructs privileged the opposition between work and crime over other systems of reference. Indeed, work became central to positivists' representations of crime and criminals and informed most of their discussions about other social problems.

The writings of Veyga illustrate the centrality of work in positivist discussions about crime. In his study about professional

---

11   The duration of the sentence had to depend upon an inmate's progress toward rehabilitation, not upon fixed statutory limits. Similarly, disciplinary practices within the prison had to vary in proportion to an inmate's "dangerousness" and potential for reform. *Idem, Criminología* (Buenos Aires, 1919), 258.

delinquents, Veyga made ample use of the metaphor of work. At the root of the problem of professional delinquency was the "absolute lack of work discipline" of many criminals. Theft appeared as an "elementary activity," requiring little physical or intellectual effort; like unskilled and repetitive work, it could be easily learned by individuals lacking moral resources in the struggle for subsistence. The constitutional weakness of occasional offenders related to their preindustrial habits; nomads of the city, *lunfardos* (thieves) showed no sense of thrift or concern for the future. The passage from occasional to professional theft entailed a process of "apprenticeship"; the street and the prison served as "schools" providing delinquents with the "skills" of their trade. Due to their "absolute incapacity for reflexive labor," professional thieves rarely changed specialization or branch of work during their lifetime.[12]

In a second book devoted to the "auxiliaries" of crime (for example, liquor salesmen, prostitutes and their bosses, gambling impresarios, loan sharks, and pawners of stolen goods), Veyga explored the connections between delinquents and the working class. The auxiliaries of crime constituted an incipient, amoral entrepreneurial class ("industrialists of defective morality") the activities of which represented "an aberrant form of work, like that of the beggar or of the prostitute, though not a delinquent form like that of the thief." The auxiliaries possessed good aptitudes for the struggle for subsistence—audacity, tenacity, and profit motivation—but were engaged in a socially dangerous business, one that contributed to the reproduction of the "criminal class." In their bordellos, bars, cafes, hostels, and race-tracks, professional delinquents came into contact with honest workers, pulling them into a career of crime.[13]

Positivist interpretations of crime reflected a concern for the erosion of the boundary separating the world of crime from the world of work. Veyga's auxiliaries stood in a nebulous area between the honest working class and the criminal class, pulling the two closer together. Different manifestations of crime indicated the existence of problems in the formation of work habits among

---

12 Francisco de Veyga, *Los Lunfardos. Psicología de los delincuentes profesionales* (Buenos Aires, 1910), 10–11, 16–21, 24.
13 *Idem, Los auxiliares de la delincuencia* (Buenos Aires, 1910), 14–19, 26–29, 49–50.

vast sectors of the urban working class. Statistics showing rising crime rates, the visible presence of abandoned children in the streets, and the existence of marginal neighborhoods where thieves, vagrants, and casual laborers lived together preoccupied reformers. With insistent frequency, positivists expressed concern about the existence of two pernicious circuits in the reproduction of the Buenos Aires working class: one turning abandoned children into juvenile delinquents; the other turning unemployed or casual laborers into occasional, and later, professional criminals.

Criminologists' concentration on the study of juvenile delinquents, vagrants, and recidivists underscores this preoccupation. Under the clinical eye of the new criminology, the maladaptation to the discipline of wage labor became a predisposition to delinquent behavior. Discouraged job seekers, the unemployed, and those who disliked wage labor were considered socially maladjusted and, hence, potential criminals. Abandoned children, in daily contact with the world of crime, also presented a latent danger to society. Recidivist delinquents, as a class of workers who had learned to live without working, were particularly threatening.

Positivists presented vagrancy as a mental illness of persons who, due to their relative weakness in the struggle for subsistence, were unable to habituate themselves to the rhythm and conditions of wage labor. Consiglio, for example, defined vagabonds as "a multitude of abnormals" characterized by "the incomplete state or the actual lack of nervous energy and of psychic potential." They were individuals "less active, less complete, less disciplined" than the rest. Vagrancy led almost inevitably to crime. "Professional criminality," wrote Moreno, "generally enlists proselytes from vagrants, the unemployed, and beggars, inconvenient and antisocial elements always ready to transform themselves into subjects threatening society's stability."[14]

The abandoned children working on the streets of Buenos Aires were also in peril of falling into the trap of crime. Criminologists saw the streets as schools where the criminal class re-

14 Pedro Consiglio, "Los vagabundos," *Archivos de Psiquiatría y Criminología*, X (1911), 436–437, 444–447; Rodolfo Moreno, *Legislación Penal y Carcelaria* (Buenos Aires, 1912), 202. On the role of vagrancy in police discourse, see Beatriz C. Ruibal, "El control social y la policía de Buenos Aires," *Boletín del Instituto de Historia Argentina y Americana*, II (1990), 79–80.

cruited its young elements. "The professional criminal," wrote Veyga, "inept for social life since childhood and protected against all culture and all discipline, begins his criminal career as a vagabond minor and then graduates as a professional within the prison, living afterwards from street to prison for the rest of his life." Concerned about abandoned minors, Ingenieros conducted a survey on children distributing the city's newspapers. Expectedly, paperboys' predisposition for crime was inversely correlated with their acceptance of the work ethic. This street occupation predisposed children to the habits of leisure and vagrancy: "They learn necessarily to detest work in workshops." As a result, 90 percent of those children took the road of vagrancy and delinquency after entering adolescence.[15]

Besides vagrants, abandoned children, and recidivist delinquents, reformers also were concerned with the growing numbers of adult casual workers in the city. Ingenieros examined the cases of two immigrant workers who, having circulated through many unstable employments, fell into the world of crime. The first was an Italian immigrant who had served several terms in prison, the last time on charges of fraud. At age 15 he dropped out of school and abandoned his home in order to follow a prostitute. Circumstances led him to robbery and swindling and later, already related to *malvivientes* (criminal elements), he became a habitual delinquent. Then Ingenieros added to the file: "Strong inclinations towards vagrancy and lack of love for work. Neuropathic temperament, unstable behavior, personality maladjusted to his social environment."[16]

The second case was a Spanish immigrant accused of killing a ranch owner in southern Buenos Aires. At the age of sixteen, he arrived in the country at the invitation of his brother José, who found him employment as peon of an *estancia* in General Lamadrid. After the agricultural season was over, he took another job at a brick kiln in Azul, then moved to another town doing the same work. Six months later, he returned to the ranch to dig ditches by the day; when this work was done, he moved to

---

15 Veyga, "Los lunfardos," *Archivos de Psiquiatría y Criminología*, IX (1910), 522. See also Ruibal, "El control social," 84–90; Ingenieros, "Los niños vendedores de diarios y la delincuencia precoz," *Archivos de Psiquiatría, Criminología y Medicina Legal*, VII (1908), 329–346.

16 Ingenieros, *Criminología*, 134.

another ranch to work as sheepshearer. He returned to his brother's farm, worked there for a year, then moved back to the ranch and tended a herd of horses. After so many occupations, Ingenieros tells us, this man lost his incentive to work and, with it, his sanity: "He becomes kind of lazy, . . . little by little he loses his love of work, . . . he begins to talk foolishness, he subordinates his conduct to incorrect facts," and "his mind does not work well."[17]

In contrast to the growing concern about the socialization of male workers, the rising proportion of women in the city's labor force had little impact on positivist writings about crime. Adult women, viewed as daughters, wives, and mothers rather than as workers, presented no specific threat to the social order. In fact, when reformers spoke of thieves, vagrants, and juvenile delinquents, it was understood that they referred to male offenders. The only exclusively female "problem" was prostitution, one important channel through which working-class women abandoned the sphere of family and of socially accepted labor. Since prostitution remained legal between 1875 and 1934—hence, practitioners were not subject to incarceration—prostitutes were not considered delinquents, only auxiliary agents of crime. Their "weakness" derived both from their "innate incapacity" for holding stable jobs and from the "inability" of working-class families to "control the sexuality" of young women. Whereas in theory positivists favored the confinement of immoral and lazy women, in practice the reformation of "fallen women" was taken over by private, semireligious benevolent associations, most of them run by middle-class women.[18]

In the perception of positivist criminologists, the criminal class was composed of those workers who, because of their psychic makeup or of the influences of the environment, were unable to adapt to the discipline of work. The transition from normal to pathological behavior resulted, in most cases, from the loss of work motivation. Discouraged job seekers, the unem-

17   *Ibid.*, 16.
18   Donna J. Guy, "Prostitution and Female Criminality in Buenos Aires, 1875–1937," in Lyman L. Johnson (ed.), *The Problem of Order in Changing Societies* (Albuquerque, 1990), 89–113; Veyga, *Los auxiliares,* 33; Ricardo González, "Caridad y filantropía en la ciudad de Buenos Aires durante la segunda mitad del siglo XIX," in Diego Armus (ed.), *Sectores populares y vida urbana* (Buenos Aires, 1984), 252–257; Alsina, *El obrero,* 92, 131.

ployed, and those unskilled workers who constantly changed occupations were considered a population at risk of joining the ranks of the criminal class. A second group, subject to the same risk, was the abandoned children and adolescents who frequented certain social environments where the contact with adult, professional delinquents was almost certain.

Work, not gender or national origin, informed most discussions by positivists about crime and social problems. Work helped to organize workers' experiences into two mutually exclusive and attracting worlds: work and crime. Images of work provided powerful metaphors to understand the criminal class, and the latter, by opposition, defined the working class. Within the penitentiary, work represented the means of rehabilitation and the measure of reform. In society at large, the lack of a work ethic gave meaning to a multiplicity of social problems associated with the recomposition of the work force. A growing criminal class promised the likelihood of alarming social upheaval. As a subculture within the city, the *mala vida* (bad life) exhibited its own sociability codes, its own dialect (*lunfardo*), and a remarkable degree of specialization. More importantly, it pointed to an alternative method of subsistence. Having replaced theft for work in everyday life—a fact reflected in their professional jargon in which *trabajo* (work) meant theft—professional delinquents presented negative examples for the diffusion of favorable attitudes toward work to be successful.[19]

Although a literary construction within positivist discourse, the term "criminal class" also emerged in reference to a particular type based on the collection and analysis of statistical data gathered at police stations. Data on police arrests tended to confirm the fears and alarmist opinions of positivist reformers. Between 1911 and 1915, the city's police rounded up nearly 1,500 minors for vagrancy, just a sample of the estimated 10,000 who wandered through the streets of Buenos Aires. The number of offenders less than sixteen years old increased fivefold between 1887 and 1912. By 1915, one-fourth of all police arrests were of minors. The number of recidivists was also staggering by contemporary standards: they constituted 4,768 of the 8,233 arrested between

---

19 Veyga, *Los lunfardos*; Antonio Dellepiane, *El idioma del delito y diccionario lunfardo* (Buenos Aires, 1894).

294 | RICARDO D. SALVATORE

1892 and 1899. By 1912, a "true colony" numbering 20,000 people regularly involved in theft was said to reside in Buenos Aires. Most police arrests during the period 1902–1913 were of day laborers. They comprised 89 to 98 percent of those arrested for drunkenness, 85 to 96 percent of those apprehended for disturbing the peace, and between 67 and 83 percent of those indicted for criminal behavior. As to the types of crime and the nationality of offenders, Blackwelder is conclusive: "Most arrests were for public drunkenness or disturbing the peace and most were of persons judged by the police not to be of Argentine origin." Apparently, the police targeted immigrants as the source of public disorder.[20]

The prison population, however, differed significantly from the one subject to police arrests. Day laborers comprised only 38 percent of the penitentiary's inmates; 40 percent were craftsmen; 15 percent commercial and clerical policemen, waiters, and servants; the rest were industrialists and merchants. Whereas an overwhelming proportion of police arrests were due to minor violations of the public order (drunkenness and disturbances accounted for 80 percent of the arrests during 1900–1909), pentitentiary inmates accused of crimes against morality and public order constituted a minority (4 percent during the same period). Most were prosecuted for more serious crimes: 36 percent for crimes against persons, 31 percent for crimes against property, and the remaining 29 percent were detained without causes. This group consisted almost entirely of political prisoners, most of them having entered the penitentiary during the tumultuous years of 1900–1903, when waves of labor protest disrupted the calm of the city.[21]

The idea of a criminal class found little confirmation within the walls of the pentitentiary. True, recidivists were numerous

20 As Veyga acknowledged, the evidence came from the files of the police's *Depósito de Contraventores*, Veyga, *Los lunfardos*, 9; República Argentina, Ministerio de Justicia, *Memoria 1916* (Buenos Aires, 1917), 580, 248; Miguel A. Lancelotti, *La criminalidad en Buenos Aires al margen de la estadística, 1887–1912* (Buenos Aires, 1914), 16–17, 25–29, 55–56; Julia K. Blackwelder and Lyman Johnson, "Changing Criminal Patterns in Buenos Aires, 1890–1914," *Journal of Latin American Studies*, XIV (1984), 369; Blackwelder, "Urbanization, Crime, and Policing: Buenos Aires, 1880–1914," in Johnson, *The Problem of Order*, 73.
21 Foreigners constituted the majority of inmates at the penitentiary. Of those entered in 1901, 62% were foreigners, in 1909, 65%. (Among police arrests the proportion was 65% for the period 1882–1901.) *Anuario Estadístico de la Ciudad de Buenos Aires* (Buenos Aires, 1901); *Censo de la Ciudad de Buenos Aires, 1909*, II, 302; Alsina, *El obrero*, 265.

Table 1 Prisoners Admitted to Men's and Women's Prisons by Type of Crime, 1900–1909

CRIMES	NATIONAL PENITENTIARY		WOMEN'S CORRECTIONAL[a]	
Against Persons	5,380	(35.9)	904	(35.7)
Against Property	4,620	(30.8)	1,293	(51.1)
Against Morality	114	(0.8)	187	(7.4)
Against Public Order	480	(3.2)	148	(5.8)
Unknown Cause	4,401	(29.3)	—	—
Total	14,995	(100.0)	2,532	(100.0)

Only adult women considered.
SOURCE   Censo de Población de la Ciudad de Buenos Aires, 1909.

but the majority of the urban "dangerous class"—thieves, pick-pockets, vagrants, racketeers, and pimps—stayed out of the penitentiary. Instead, the penitentiary held authors of violent crimes, most of them workers, over half of them immigrants. A significantly larger proportion of craftsmen and factory operatives in the penitentiary, compared with police arrests, reflected the social tensions of an epoch marked by general strikes and an anarchist-dominated labor movement. These inmates were already specialized in a trade and politically active.

Women constituted a small minority of prison inmates throughout the period. At the time of the first national census of prisons (1906), only 4 percent of the inmates of the city's prisons were women, most of them confined to the Asilo Correccional de Mujeres.[22] As most offenses committed by women were classified as misdemeanors and handled by the police, few went to prison. Poor women under age 20 frequently entered houses of correction, asylums, and workshops administered by charitable and religious institutions. In fact, the Asilo Correccional itself had three to four times more *menores depositadas* (minors in custody) than *detenidas* (adult offenders). Of the latter, few were factory operatives, most held traditional roles for poor women at the time—maid, cook, washerwoman, seamstress, ironer, midwife, or nurse—or had no occupations. Injury, homicide, infanticide,

22 Republica Argentina, Minesterio de Justicia, *Primer censo carcelario de la Republica, 1906* (Buenos Aires, 1909), 55–56.

and theft represented the most common causes for imprisoning women.

The prison reform and positivist discussions on crime were an interpretive moment about the encounter between the Argentine ruling class and the new, immigrant working class. Positivist criminology contributed in different ways to the redefinition of class relations in early twentieth-century Buenos Aires. Responding to the changing composition of the city's work force, criminologists furnished categories, relationships, and metaphors that helped to interpret the problems posed by immigrant workers. From their privileged positions, the police and the prison reformers were able to observe, statistically and clinically, some preoccupying features of the new working class. If police statistics provided a vision of the city's dangerous class, then the penitentiary served as a clinic for the observation, experimentation, and treatment of the dropouts of a highly mobile and unstable labor market.

By connecting the definition of crime to the work ethic, criminologists were able to articulate ruling-class fears of the blurring of boundaries between crime and work in the new metropolis. The fact that immigrants tended to change jobs all too often or to remain unemployed for long periods of time—a situation that reflected the condition of labor markets for unskilled labor—presented a problem. Discouraged job seekers and the unemployed tended to lose the "love of work" and this facilitated their entry into the "world of crime."

The importance that positivists attributed to work as both a reform therapy and as an ordering principle for the definition of criminal behavior, underscored the problem of instilling work habits on the new proletariat. Just at a time when the regime began to confront the radical manifestations of the immigrant working class (under the form of general strikes, street violence, and anarchist and socialist labor organizations), positivists presented immigrants as individuals lacking the work ethic or the morality that the ruling class had imagined. This revelation was particularly disquieting since private capitalists seemed unable or unwilling to take the responsibility for teaching the love of work to their workers.

PRISON REFORM IN BUENOS AIRES | **297**

Concerning labor discipline, positivist constructs revealed greater insight and less pragmatism than the programs of private capitalists. Their insistence on the connection between casual labor, unemployment, and crime showed a greater awareness of the problems posed by the export economy for the project of modernization and nation building. At the same time, the penitentiary/factory stood as an ideal, distant model in contradiction with the actual employment structure of the country (dominated by semiartisan workshops, domestic work, temporary and unskilled laborers, and an overgrown commercial and service sector).

The question of female industrial labor—raised by many labor organizers and socialist leaders—preoccupied positivist reformers less than prostitution. As long as male-dominated families could keep guard of young women's morality, their incorporation into paid labor through the putting-out system was not problematic. Women entering factories and large workshops were neglected by criminologists. The solution to women's "moral anomalies," on the other hand, could not be achieved in the penitentiary. The rehabilitation of fallen women and the seclusion of those at risk was the task of semireligious benevolent associations not under the control of positivist reformers.[23]

Positivists' studies and essays on the world of crime presented the ruling class with a fuller and more exact image of working-class life. The interest of reformers in abandoned children, drinking, prostitution, theft, and vagrancy provided new information about how difficult it was for immigrants to be assimilated into the elite's project of export-led development. Depictions by the positivists of the criminal class, a social territory of fuzzy and shifting boundaries, reinforced existing beliefs that unchecked immigration threatened the peace and stability of the nation. The explanation of social problems as the result of individual anomalies strengthened the view that "progress" would be possible without class struggle.

The search for clear frontiers within the city—honest worker/delinquent, criminal class/working class—was an expression of the elite's need for new organizing dualities that would replace

---

23 Donna J. Guy, University of Arizona, suggested this explanation in a personal communication.

298 | RICARDO D. SALVATORE

those eliminated along with the Indian frontier—civilization/bar-
barism, urban/rural, and immigrant/creole worker. The general
formula, *hacer la América* (the myth of immigrants' rapid upward
social mobility), could not explain the social problems—crime
and protest—created by immigrant labor; a new social imagery
was needed to redefine and to reinterpret class relations. Positivists
contributed this imagery: a pernicious social milieu within the
city (the *mala vida*), a swelling number of abandoned children in
danger of contamination, an unskilled and mobile proletariat lacking industrial work habits, and an army of intermediaries pulling
the two worlds into contact.

The penitentiary affirmed the necessity of a nonrepressive,
humanistic solution to the problem of immigrants' maladjustment
in terms of work habits and social behavior. But it did not constitute a general solution. Obviously, positivists did not intend to
reshape the work attitudes of the whole casual proletariat, only
those who fell into the prison system. Other functions of the new
disciplinary institution were more salient. The penitentiary served
as a means of controlling ideological representations of poverty,
unemployment, and crime; that is, it provided a means of presenting the working poor with different explanations of their fate
than those provided by anarchists and socialists. As an instrument
of social control, the penitentiary competed with other methods:
the infamous "law of residence," police harassment of labor leaders, elementary public education, obligatory military conscrip-
tion, protective labor legislation, and the promotion of benevolent
societies. The penitentiary played, however, an important role in
this complex disciplinary grid because it attempted to illuminate
a problem left unsolved by the private sector: how to adapt
immigrant workers to the new conditions of work required by
the urban, export economy. By focusing the elite's attention on
the relationship between work and crime, criminologists brought
into public debate the issue of labor discipline.

Positivist reformers were more concerned about the reformation of male, rather than female, offenders. Despite a growing
presence in the worlds of labor and politics, women did not draw
much attention among prison reformers. The small incidence of
women in criminal statistics together with the belief that other
institutions (family, charitable societies, and public health authorities) could better discipline poor women, led positivists to see

PRISON REFORM IN BUENOS AIRES| **299**

female offenders as less threatening to the reproduction of the city's work force. To this extent, the penitentiary reflected the gender-biased perspective of the reformers.

Bound by a theory that de-emphasized the political aspects of workers' struggles, criminologists also failed to address the question of social protest. When casual laborers joined factory workers in a collective refusal to work in demand for social, political, and economic reforms, they confronted not the humanism of the new criminologists but police brutality, ideological persecution, and the extradition or impressment of their leaders.

As the male participants of these strikes and demonstrations filled the cells of the National Penitentiary of Buenos Aires, they found a new mode of discipline in operation, one that relied upon the redemptive power of work, moral suasion, and education to prepare convicts for their reinsertion into the world of capitalist work.

[20]

Contemporary Crises 6 (1982) 315–331
Elsevier Scientific Publishing Company, Amsterdam – Printed in The Netherlands

SOCIAL CONTROL FOR LABOR IN NINETEENTH-CENTURY PERNAMBUCO, BRAZIL

MARTHA HUGGINS

Between 1850 and 1880, Pernambuco's [1] slave population was in decline, while the sugar economy expanded. The intersection of those events made it inevitable that planters would have to find a new work force. Most students of the transition [2] claim that the shift from slave to free labor was relatively easy, because of the presence of large numbers of free rural poor in a region where the absence of "free soil left [squatters] with nowhere else to go and [where] they consequently found themselves in a position of complete dependence and submission vis-à-vis the sugar planters who monopolized the land" [3]. Jaime Reis adds that, owing to those conditions, employers did not have to resort to anything but voluntary methods of recruitment, and "harsh methods were ill-advised" [4].

Reis and others have correctly noted that there was a large surplus of potential workers in the sugar zone on the eve of the abolition of slavery; they incorrectly assumed that workers who had been underutilized in the export sector could be freely substituted for slaves. Herbert Gutman [5] and E.P. Thompson [6] have shown in their studies of the North American and English working classes that sheer numbers of workers do not make labor transitions easy. The lesson of Gutman and Thompson is that men and women bring more to the job than their physical presence. Laborers bring relevant skills acquired in the process of working, a useful attitude toward work, and a concept of time commensurate with the form of work organization [7] – all attributes Marx called labor power (i.e., the capacity to labor).

Another problematic assumption is that the powerlessness of the rural poor made it easy to incorporate them into the work force. While it is true that the squatters' individual power was both much less and far more vulnerable than that of the landowners, the troublemaking potential of the rural free lay in many of them retaining squatting rights while landowners were trying to mold such free workers into a rural proletariat. Workers with land had a survival alternative to wages and were slow to become the kind of labor force planters demanded.

Union College, Schenectady, New York 12308, USA

0378–1100/82/0000–0000/$02.75 © 1982 Elsevier Scientific Publishing Company

316

The claims that the transition to free labor occurred without a struggle contradict other reports that police and legislative action was taken against unwilling free workers. This contradiction provided the focus for this study. If Pernambucan officials, in fact, helped landowners obtain a work force by criminalizing the free people's marginality, then the labor transition was not as conflict-free as some historians have suggested. Furthermore, if two ingredients for social conflict, namely social control and crime, can be shown to have played a role in the labor transition, then we will be able to cast new light on some traditional research problems in economic development and social change.

The Material Roots of Deviance and Control

The "deviant" label usually applies to acts threatening to someone or something. It is essential to determine why some acts pose a threat and others do not. Steven Spitzer maintains that groups are defined as deviant ("problem populations") when they threaten the social relations of production in a particular system. Spitzer's dictum need not imply that deviants are motivated by revolutionary objectives, only that people are labelled deviant when their behavior and/or personal qualities represent a "significant impediment to the maintenance and growth of a system" [8]. A population becomes a problem and a "social expense" when it undermines wealth accumulation.

By refusing to participate in Pernambuco's export sector as slavery declined, free people contributed to the erosion of planters' resources; without a large work force, production could not expand to compensate for low sugar prices. Those conditions turned the free population into a social expense. However, it is essential to recognize that the free population was not always a cost; in fact, before the end of the slave trade in 1850, free men and women, as a surplus population, were part of the planters' resources, for they provided cheap back-up services for slave-powered sugar plantations. Free people became an expense when the slave population declined and the free refused (directly and indirectly) to fill slave vacancies in the export sector. In Pernambuco, the threat to wealth accumulation was resolved by repressive social control; repression effected the transition to free labor and turned the social debts back into assets.

Let us now turn to the conditions in the plantation zone and see whether Spitzer's ideas fit them. Pernambuco's pre-1850 rural labor structure consisted of two separate but interrelated work systems: slaves produced the cash crop, while a surplus population of feudally organized free producers provided a number of extra-economic support services. As long as slaves were plentiful, free squatters were marginal to the profit-producing sector of the economy.

317

According to a source cited by Prado [9], forty to fifty percent of the Pernambucan population in the nineteenth century was marginal to the sugar economy. However, by all accounts [10], the erratic work habits and nomadic life style of the dependent poor were neither major social problems nor criminal problems requiring formal outside intervention. At most, squatters were an inconvenience to landowners, and usually the problems they caused could be handled within the confines of the plantation. A squatter who did not produce the required amount of food or failed to supply supplementary labor was expelled from the property and his house and crops burned [11]. State intervention against the free rural poor was minimal, serving to supplement rather than supplant plantation-based social control. When it did come, state intervention was represented by national guard recruiters, who swept through the countryside impressing idlers into the passing military units.

So long as slaves were plentiful, there was no need to correct the undesirable qualities of the rural poor. But, as the slave population declined, planters began to look in an entirely new light upon free people's unwillingness to work. It was a simple fact that, with the slave population depleted, landowners could not afford to see free people engaged in non-wealth-producing activities. Consequently, after 1850, being free and without work, having irregular work habits, or simply moving around too much became problems for the planters and, ultimately, for the police and lawmakers.

The Moral Passage Against Marginality

The shift in stance toward the free population's marginality illustrates what Gusfield [12] calls a "moral passage," or period of re-definition in which once-tolerated behavior comes to be seen as immoral and treated as deviant or criminal. A moral passage facilitated the transition by providing an ideological justification for increased repression against the free population.

The transition's moral passage had two stages, each involving different definitions of the labor crisis and ways of coping with it. *Labor scarcity* was the planters' primary worry during the first phase, kicked off by the forced cessation of the African slave trade. At that time, "labor scarcity" was equated with an insufficiency of slaves rather than a shortage of free labor. During this phase of the transition, traditional mechanisms of labor recruitment predominated; state intervention was generally not concerned with repression, being directed instead at limiting the slave drain and concentrating the remaining slaves in the export sector. The latter was accomplished by regulating planters' utilization of their bondsmen.

As the period progressed and planters incorporated more free people into

318

the work force, the issue of labor scarcity was replaced by talk of the *labor problem*. That definition of the situation emerged because free workers failed to come forth in sufficient numbers to fill slave vacancies and because their job performance was well below planters' expectations. Planters wanted to make free labor equivalent to slave labor; with that attitude, any deviation from the master–slave relationship was intolerable. In order to achieve their objectives, in this phase planters set aside many of the traditional mechanisms of control in favor of broader repressive strategies.

The Material Roots of the Moral Passage

Several developments joined after the seventies to increase repression against the free population. The price of sugar on the international market broke from an average of $87.42 per ton in the seventies to an average price in the eighties of $69.25; in the decade of the nineties, prices fell still further, to an average of $48.92. Price averages thereafter remained at about that level (Table I). The falling prices, starting in the eighties, meant that some drastic adjustments had to be made if planters were to maintain their previous profits.

Planters' first adjustment to falling prices was to raise output; the average annual output of the 1880s was almost double that of the seventies, and it rose still more in the nineties (Table II). Furthermore, these substantial increases cannot be attributed to technological improvements, since the first central mills (largely failures anyway) did not begin operation until the 1885–1886 harvest, and the really big sugar refineries did not take hold until the turn of the century. Consequently, higher total output was due principally to larger labor inputs, which, from the eighties onward, could have come only from the free population.

TABLE I

Average of Annual Recife Sugar Price Index and Range by Period, 1860–1914

Period	Average annual Recife price index (Dollars* per ton)	Range of annual average price (Dollars* per ton) per decade
1860–1869	87.09	77.22– 97.99
1870–1879	87.42	74.43–101.64
1880–1889	69.25	43.66– 84.77
1890–1899	48.92	34.10– 69.93
1900–1909	45.84	27.40– 83.85
1910–1914**	49.25	33.45– 60.92

*Prices in United States gold dollars.
**Figures were not available for the entire decade.
Source: Calculated from Denslow [13].

TABLE II

Average Annual Sugar Production in Pernambuco, and Range by Period, 1850–1915

Period	Annual average output (Tons)	Range of annual average output (Tons) per decade
1850–1859	63,630	47,630– 82,830
1860–1869	58,880	42,240– 77,880
1870–1879	89,520	45,540–141,900
1880–1889	150,740	101,300–205,700
1890–1899	159,610	119,900–228,800
1900–1909	144,780	97,570–216,700
1910–1915*	154,660	132,000–176,000

*Figures were not available for the entire decade.
Source: Calculated from Denslow [14].

In the absence of technology to increase productivity, there were three broad strategies to extract greater amounts of labor from free workers: planters could raise wages to give the free population a greater work incentive; landowners could evict squatters to force them into wage dependence; and/or they could use the repressive agencies of the state to coerce the free into working for the planters for next to nothing.

Wages could have provided a noncoercive inducement for the free population to work in the export sector, but wages in the eighties and nineties were too low to reward free workers for doing what they had always avoided. Table III shows that both real and nominal wages began declining in the 1870s and plummeted in the eighties, to hit rock bottom in 1890 [15]. Although nominal wages then climbed steeply in the nineties, real wages crept up slowly, because of high inflation.

The free rural poor were unmotivated by low wages and lived up to their reputation of only working "long enough to obtain the most basic necessities" and behaving as if "to be free is to have the liberty not to work" [16]. Planters had to face the inescapable fact that as long as free men and women retained the right to squat, low wages would not lure them to the export sector.

These conditions left the sugar barons with two general alternatives for securing more work from the free population. They could marginalize the free by evicting squatters and forcing on them wage dependency for survival, or they could make greater use of the legislative and law enforcement agencies to pull squatters and other free persons into the plantation work force [17].

With respect to marginalization, the central question is: why would landowners force squatters off the soil and introduce a wage system, however inadequate, when their revenues were so poor and they could already secure

320

TABLE III

Minimum Daily Wages of Unskilled Rural Labor in Pernambuco for Selected Year, 1855–1910

Year	Wages	
	Nominal (Reis)	Real (Reis) (1852=100)
1855	580	330
1862	1,043	756
1874	1,000	625
1880	640	358
1882	600	345
1884	800	415
1886	500	319
1888	560	418
1889	600	255
1895	1,200	283
1897	1,500	291
1900	1,200	396
1902	800	333
1910	1,030	N/A

Source: Eisenberg [18]

labor in exchange for granting squatting rights? The answer is that under prevailing conditions landowners needed a greater amount of labor than they previously had: with production expanding, planters required six to seven work days a week from their squatters rather than the customary three or four.

Planters could gain much tighter control (e.g., more work days and greater productivity) over squatters by separating them from their means of support and forcing wage dependence as the only way to avoid starvation. The problem is clarified by Marx's story of "Mr. Peel," who took 3,000 "persons of the working class — men, women, and children — to Australia expecting them to work on his plantation. But with land available for the taking, laborers preferred to start their own farms and Mr. Peel was left without a labor force" [19].

It is not easy to determine whether marginalization was used by the planters. Data on evictions during the nineteenth century are difficult to obtain because planters' informal expulsion of squatters was not recorded and travelers did not mention large-scale evictions. There is evidence for marginalization during the twentieth century [20], and the careful researcher might be able to find it for an earlier period as well. However, because of insufficiency of data, the question of squatter evictions must be set aside and attention given instead to the role of state-initiated social control in the transition to free labor.

Stages of the Moral Passage

"LABOR SCARCITY" PHASE, 1850–1880

The cessation of the African slave trade posed more of a threat to the labor supply than any other factor; even high slave mortality could be offset so long as nothing prohibited importation. Once the slave trade ended, however, planters began to think of alternative labor sources, but the emphasis was on supplementing rather than replacing slave labor. Planters began using free workers, although with great reluctance. As one powerful figure observed, slave labor still persisted, and "we are not accustomed to free labor . . . so we are like a man who has old habits and does not know how to adapt himself to new circumstances" [21].

Prices for slaves rose as their numbers declined, encouraging many landowners to divest themselves of slaves in order to pay their debts. A regular slave trade developed between Northeast Brazil and the Brazilian Center–South because coffee planters were hungry for slaves and ready to buy all whom the sugar barons could supply.

It may seem contradictory to claim that planters worried about a shortage of slaves when they were busily selling them to the Center–South. Indeed, not everyone supported the slave drain; two years after the interprovincial trade began, Pernambuco imposed an exit tax on slaves leaving the Province [22].

Furthermore, some planters did not sell their slaves (after 1873, only approximately 4/10 of one percent of the slave population was sold annually) [23], and even fewer planters divested themselves of their entire slave force. It is reasonable to assume that each landowner had a rough calculation of how many slaves he could sell (allowing for deaths) and still produce sugar with supplementary free labor.

Provincial and municipal taxes provided additional insurance that slaves would be used in the most efficient way: concentrated in agriculture rather than employed in urban occupations. Taxation was used as early as the fifties to discourage slave owners from using their captives in urban occupations. In 1852, a tax was imposed on slaves working as artisans and mehanics in the provincial capital [24].

During the labor scarcity phase of the moral passage, landowners could come up with a number of good reasons for clinging to slaves, not the least of which was their perception of the free population as lazy, unreliable, and totally lacking the "readiness and continuity" of slaves [25]. Even when

322

planters could find enough free people who would perform plantation agriculture, they reported that they could not get a good day's work out of these hired hands, because free workers only remained in the fields "long enough to obtain the most basic necessities" [26].

However, the elite adopted a more generous attitude toward the free population as the slave shortage became acute, conceding that not all free people were a loss to the sugar economy — only a portion of them. Provincial President Cavalcante de Albuquerque even rejected the often-heard claim that "our people are lazy [and] incapable of agricultural labor" [27], preferring to believe instead that even though a segment of the population was "profoundly demoralized, even lost," planters could obtain useful labor from the majority of free workers. In order to realize that objective, the president recommended in 1871 that the state establish agricultural schools to teach free workers the "sacred skills" of agriculture, with the Beggars' Asylum and the Orphans' School annexed to agricultural compounds so that destitute beggards and orphans could be "regenerated" through work.

The Beggars' Asylum and Orphans' School are illustrative of the first state-funded "retraining" programs directed at the free population. The Beggars' Asylum was established to "correct and regenerate the unhappy victims of misery" [28]. The state's rehabilitation program could not have been a smashing success, since the first asylum was simply a room in Recife's Pedro II Hospital, with a capacity for twenty beggars. In the late 1870s, a permanent facility was completed (capacity 100), after a series of financial setbacks.

The Orphans' School (*Colonia Orphanologico Isabel*) was established in 1874 to provide "abandoned orphans and free children of slave women an opportunity to become peaceful and moral citizens, useful to themselves and their country" [29]. In the Colonia Isabel, children would study the arts, industry, and "above all," agriculture [30].

In 1874, Provincial President Pereira de Lucena voiced his support for the Orphans' School: "From an infancy that is miserable, ignorant, and abandoned come, sooner or later, a whole class of no-goods. . . . " The Provincial President stressed his commitment to elementary education and reminded his constituents that "a society must educate its children" because moral and religious instruction along with elementary and professional education "clarify and elevate the spirit and give [orphans] the means to work." And "work," the President added, "in all cases removes crime" [31] For Pereira de Lucena, therefore, the Orphans' Colony offered great promise, since it would mount a frontal attack on crime by teaching orphans a trade. If we cut through the laudable objectives of the Orphans' School and examine its goals more pragmatically, we can see that the Colony offered a means of securing labor and creating work discipline.

In 1871, Provincial President Cavalcante de Albuquerque pointed to the value of cooperation between institutions for indigents and business concerns. He reasoned that such cooperation would provide agriculture with an infusion of trained, disciplined free workers while rehabilitating the "unhappy victims of misery" [32]. The partnership between business and institutions for indigents was in full swing by 1874 when Provincial President Pereira de Lucena reported, for example, that "in conformity with contractual arrangements. . . sixteen students of this . . . school were delivered to the owner of a factory in order to learn the principles of milling" [33].

Thus, during the first decades of the labor transition, planters were worried about labor shortages because of the disappearance of slaves. Talk of abolition was met with laws to insure that it proceed gradually, and the slave drain was attacked by taxation. Landowners could not imagine free workers as the dominant labor force in the export sector and warned that abolition would result in a "dramatic reduction in the production and export of our sugar, with fatal consequences for private and public wealth" [34].

Planters complained bitterly about the indiscipline of free labor, but, so long as free workers were merely supplementary to slaves, state action against free labor tended to have an educational focus and was directed at only a fraction of the free population. Broad-based repression would not appear until the eighties, when the scarcity of slaves began to make it clear that planters would have to do their work with the free population.

"LABOR PROBLEMS" PHASE, 1880–1900

The first Recife Agricultural Congress, in 1878, can be used to mark the beginning of the "labor problems" phase of the transition to free labor. At that convention, planters articulated what was to be the dominant social control strategy in the years surrounding abolition. One participant made the strategy abundantly clear in his call for a "severe police regime . . . , to which all individuals without trade or craft will be subjected" [35]. Another urged authorities to "oblige the lazy to work [because] the agglomeration of idle men in the large population centers is an imminent danger, a postponed and brutal revolution" [36].

By the eighties, the war was against the men and women who thought that "to be free is to have the liberty not to work" [37]. Once the enemy had been identified, the battle strategy was clear: a planter–state alliance would orchestrate the transition while repression propelled it.

The crisis atmosphere of the labor problems phase of the moral passage was fueled by a decline in the international price of sugar and by planter hysteria over the presumed inadequacies of free labor. With sugar prices low and dropping, planters needed an abundant supply of cheap labor, and free

324

men and women were not filling the bill. One worried planter at the 1884 Recife Agricultural Congress warned his fellow-delegates that abolition would result in a "dramatic reduction in the production and export of our sugar, with fatal consequences to private and public wealth" [38].

Planters proposed to avert that tragedy by advocating work contract laws. The sugar barons wanted work contracts because "there is no persistent work without force, and that is what the free worker presently needs" [39]. An 1882 newspaper editorialist reasoned that the best place to implement such a work contract proposal was in the capital city, where the initial indiscipline of free labor would not seriously threaten export production [40].

Police officials, however, did not have to wait for work contract legislation to begin their war against the undutiful free population. The vagrancy statute had long since been enacted. Its *termo de bem viver* [41] provided a means of extracting labor from unwilling workers. According to the Brazilian Penal Code of 1830 [42], a vagrant was any person lacking a fixed residence and an "honest" occupation, not offensive to public morals or custom. An individual adjudged vagrant was required to sign a *termo de bem viver* (kept by the local Justice of the Peace) obliging the lawbreaker to secure "honest employment" within fifteen days. Failure to do so, or re-arrest for vagrancy, would result in three years' imprisonment. Vagrant children were to be sent to disciplinary industrial establishments until they reached twenty-one.

Vagabonds were not the only ones required to sign a *termo*. It was also designed for habitual drunks, beggars, and "turbulent" individuals who "offend good customs by words or acts [or who] offend the public peace or the peace of families" [43]. The latter stipulation was sufficiently vague to be used to cover a wide range of behavior. In so doing, the statute could provide a quick solution for labor shortages.

The vagrancy law and *termo* were part of the planters' arsenal of weapons against the free marginals; it remains to be shown that these laws were in fact used to secure a labor force. Statistics on entries to the state House of Detention are used here to examine the assumption that some arrests were used as mechanisms of labor recruitment [44].

Table IV gives the combined percentages of arrests punishable under the vagrancy statute and the *termo*. Arrests legitimated by these mechanisms will be labeled "labor recruitment arrests," in recognition of their association with legal mechanisms that have such potential for labor recruitment.

Labor recruitment arrests constituted five percent of all referrals to the House of Detention in 1860. They had increased to thirty-five percent of the referral total by 1870 in the middle of the labor scarcity phase of the transition. By contrast, in the first period of the labor problems phase, labor recruitment arrests had already increased to over one-half of all referrals;

TABLE IV

Percentage of Arrests Punishable under the Vagrancy Statute and Termo of all Referrals to the Recife House of Detention, for Selected Years, 1860–1922 (Weighted Sample)

Year	Percentage
1860	5
1870	35
1880	51
1885	51
1890	2
1900	54
1910	25
1922	35

Source: *Livros de Entradas e Sahidas da Casa de Detenção de Recife.*

in 1885 these arrests continued to constitute one-half of all violations. In the middle of the moral passage (1890), labor recruitment arrests fell to only two percent of all referrals, but in the last period of the labor problems phase, such arrests again rose to over fifty percent of all referrals. In the two years sampled after the moral passage (1910, 1922), labor recruitment arrests had fallen to twenty-five and thirty-five percent of all referrals respectively.

Additional evidence that arrests served as labor recruitment mechanisms comes from the increase in free people arrested for vagrancy offenses during the labor problems phase of the moral passage. Free people were increasingly the target of social control mechanisms as the transition progressed. However, the most critical point of comparison is between the slave and free arrests for vagrancy offenses in the labor scarcity phase (1860, 1870) and the labor problems phase before abolition (1880, 1885). Between 1860 and 1870, there was a fifty-nine percent increase in the number of free people sent to the House of Detention for the vagrancy offenses, and, by 1880, free persons arrested for such crimes had increased another eighty-seven percent. The percentage of all slaves arrested for vagrancy actually remained constant between 1860 and 1870 and then increased by only twenty percent in the critical period between 1870 and 1880.

As the moral passage progressed, referrals of free people for vagrancy offenses continued to climb steeply. In 1885, the last year for which a free-slave comparison can be made, 1,745 free men and women were sent to the House of Detention for vagrancy offenses: a seventy-four percent increase over 1880. That increase is even more striking when we realize that at the same time, referrals of slaves for public order violations decreased by two percent [45]. (See Table V.)

326

TABLE V

Numbers, Proportions, and Proportional Changes in Numbers Arrested for Public Order Crimes of All Slave and of All Free Detainees, Recife House of Detention, for Selected Years, 1860–1885 (Weighted Sample)

Year	Slave			Free		
	N	Change* (%)	Proportion** (%)	N	Change* (%)	Proportion** (%)
1860	100	NA	50	340	NA	37
1870	99	−1.0	66	539	+58.5	39
1880	120	+20.2	77	1006	+86.6	56
1885	118	−1.7	61	1745	+73.5	67

*Percentage change from number detained for that crime in previous selected year.
**Percentage of public order arrests among detainees of a given status.
NA: Data not available.
Source: *Livros de Entrados e Sahidas de Casa de Detenção de Recife.*

Labor Problems: Instilling Work Discipline

The vagrancy statute and the *termo* provided quick solutions to labor shortages but lacked provisions to mold the newly recruited workers into a dependable labor force. As the need for cheap, dependable labor increased, programs to impress free laborers into the work force proliferated. In the year of abolition (1888), the Recife Chief of Police called for an agricultural penal colony for recidivist vagrants; two years later, the head of one of the major banks demanded additional poorhouses and asylums, and "strict penalties for vagabonds and beggars who did not enter such institutions" [46].

Apparently these proposals reached the Governor's ear, because in 1890 he recommended that the state establish a disciplinary agricultural colony for "all individuals who did not dedicate themselves to work, or who do not look for it, or for being vagrants" [47]. The Governor added that idlers would be incarcerated whether they were out of work because "they can't find it" or because of "personal vice." The Governor reminded law enforcement officials that they could begin immediately "regenerating" the idle through forced work by sending idlers to one of the abandoned drought relocation camps now reopened for this purpose. The Governor's choice for the first agricultural colony was the Fazenda Suassana drought camp, conveniently located in a rich sugar municipality near Recife [48].

Besides founding new correctional facilities to house idlers, politicians of the 1890s expanded the definition of vagrancy. Changing definitions of the problem population can be seen in the target population of the agricultural

327

colony proposed in 1890. It would house, in addition to vagrants, two new categories of deviants: "people not dedicating themselves to work" or "not looking for it" [49]. Thus, in 1890 the able-bodied who could work but elected not to had joined traditional vagrants to become the problem population.

In the nineties, the most popular strategies of labor recruitment continued to be coercive legislation and punitive arrests. Politicians wanted forced labor laws, while police officials called for institutions to make existing statutes enforceable. However, it appears that planters in the 1890s did not find additional penal colonies the answer to their labor problems. In 1893, Pernambucan politicians drew up the long-awaited forced labor law entitled "Project Seven" [50]. Project Seven would have required agricultural workers to sign work contracts with landowners, and forbidden workers to seek employment outside their municipality of birth without a travel voucher from the Justice of the Peace. Any agricultural worker caught without a contract and a travel voucher was to be subject to punishment for vagrancy.

Landowners would literally have had the rural poor both coming and going with Project Seven: if agricultural workers did not sign a work contract, they were to be subject to arrest as vagrants, and the only way someone caught without a contract would be able to defer punishment would be to sign a *termo* obliging the lawbreaker to secure "honest employment" within fifteen days. And, if they traveled looking for work, they had to have permission from the landowners' Justices.

In spite of its obvious utility to landowners, Project Seven was never passed. Eisenberg [51] argues that such proposals did not become law because men who had just abolished slavery were not disposed toward new forms of coerced labor. Perhaps it would be satisfying to believe Eisenberg's interpretation, but everything in the present study suggests the contrary. In fact, planters and politicians began searching for ways to force free people to work as soon as slaves became scarce. A more plausible argument than Eisenberg's is that only when labor-saving technology and the loss of the world market had reduced the industry's need for labor in the early twentieth century would state-initiated coercion become unnecessary to secure a work force.

However, during the nineties, politicians clearly declared their intention to use state power to regulate the undisciplined labor force. Governor Correa de Araújo [52] was for even more expansion of state power than previous officials had suggested, in arguing that nothing short of a reorganization of the state's punishment apparatus could solve the vagrancy problem. The Governor's program included: "Penitentiaries. . . ; asylums for beggars; correctional schools for minors; [and] penal colonies for recidivists . . . "

328

He justified his proposal with the warning that "without those endowments you can expect the black army of crime, and ex-convicts returning to society without work habits, to return to their criminal careers" [53].

Reorganization of the state's punishment apparatus was in full swing as the nineties drew to a close. Next on the agenda was State Law 370 [54], which budgeted an additional agricultural disciplinary colony for adults and an industrial school for minors. Most past proposals for additional correctional facilities had bogged down because the police had to await construction of appropriate facilities before enforcing the vagrancy laws. This time the lawmakers had been farsighted enough to include in Law 370 a clause that made it possible to take more immediate action against the problem population. Article Five stipulated that individuals or associations could set up agricultural penal colonies. That gave landowners the go-ahead to turn their plantations into agricultural colonies to rehabilitate idlers; it also gave them a steady supply of cheap labor. The state also benefitted from that arrangement because it was spared the expense of maintaining a large inmate population.

Material Changes and the Deceleration of Repression

Lawmaking directed at pulling the free population into the export sector decelerated after the turn of the century. It was not until 1923 that a Governor's annual report again spoke of the criminal problem posed by idlers and vagrants. However, by that time the sugar industry's labor dependence had been reduced by technological developments and the loss of foreign markets. The highest state official, therefore, could afford a more benevolent posture toward the poor, though not toward idlers. Governor Sergio Loreto [55] affirmed that vagrants, drunkards, beggars, and *capoeiras** were the state's "social parasites," but he recommended that police officials overlook the "legitimate paupers" among the population. Governor Loreto explained that legitimate paupers were those who "don't have the ability to work," as well as those with "the ability, but not the means" [56]. However, no pressure was to be spared against those who have "the ability and the means [to work] but lack the desire"; they were, he said, "a stratum of dangerous indigents against whom preventive and repressive measures are necessary," a familiar litany from the late nineteenth century.

Summary: the Political Economy of Repression

The best sociohistorical studies of the material roots of social control are by William Chambliss [57] and by Georg Rusche and Otto Kirchheimer

---

*public dancers trained in a type of Martial Art.

[58]. Chambliss shows how shifts in labor supply and demand influenced the focus and content of vagrancy laws in Europe and North America, while Rusche and Kirchheimer relate the changing types of penal punishment to such material factors as labor supply and the degree of impoverishment of the population.

Changing levels of material resources also influenced the amount and type of social control during Pernambuco's labor transition. Gusfield's concept of a moral passage captures the impact of this resource depletion on social control during the transition.

There were, in fact, two stages in Pernambuco's nineteenth-century moral passage, each associated with a different state of resource depletion and different ways of coping with it. The labor scarcity phase of the moral passage began with the cessation of the African slave trade. At that time, planters equated labor scarcity with a shortage of slaves, not an insufficiency of free workers. During this phase, informal plantation-based strategies of labor recruitment predominated. When state intervention appeared, it was directed at limiting the slave drain rather than pulling the free population into cash crop production. In order to guarantee a sufficient number of slaves for the plantation sector, the provincial government imposed taxes on slaves sold to the Center–South of Brazil and applied pressure on slave owners to use their bondsmen in plantation agriculture rather than in urban occupations.

So long as slaves were still relatively plentiful, there was no need to pull the free marginal population into plantation agriculture. However, with the simultaneous decline of the slave population and fall in world sugar prices in the 1880s, planters could no longer afford to have free workers engage in activity that did not produce wealth for the planters. Consequently, people being free, yet without work, having irregular work habits, or simply moving around too much, became problems for the planters and, therefore, for the lawmakers and police.

Thus, it was the combination of falling sugar prices and an insufficiency of cheap labor that created the labor problems phase of the moral passage. During this period, state-initiated repression replaced many of the traditional means of labor recruitment and regulation. Punitive arrests became a central mechanism of labor recruitment, while beggars' asylums and agricultural correctional facilities enforced work discipline.

The shift from planter self-reliance to state assistance and from non-repression to repression illustrates Stanley Diamond's argument that law arises in the breach of prior customary order and increases with the conflicts that divide political societies. The Pernambucan transition seems to lend support to Diamond's claim that "law and order is the historical illusion, law *versus* order the historical reality" [59].

330

Notes

1   Pernambuco is one of eight states in the Brazilian Northeast. Its capital, Recife, is in the coastal plantation zone. Until the abolition of slavery in 1888, Europeans grew rich while their slaves died producing sugar for the international market.

2   Peter L. Eisenberg (1974), *The Sugar Industry in Pernambuco: Modernization without Change, 1840–1910,* Berkeley, Calif.: University of California Press; Robert Levine (1979), *Pernambuco in the Brazilian Federation, 1889–1945,* Palo Alto, Calif.: Stanford University Press; Jaime Reis, "From Bangue to Usina," Unpublished paper, no date.

3   Jaime Reis (1974), "Abolition and economics of slaveholding in North East Brazil," *Boletin de Estudios Latinoamericanos y del Caribe* 17: 6.

4   Reis, "From Bangue to Usina," op. cit.

5   Herbert G. Gutman (1977), *Work, Culture, and Society in Industrializing America,* New York: Vintage.

6   E.P. Thompson (1966), *The Making of the English Working Class,* New York: Vintage.

7   E.P. Thompson's argument is that the concept of time that is compatible with agriculture is different from that of the modern factory and that agricultural workers cannot become effective in the industrial sector until they have internalized its unique rhythms.

8   Steven Spitzer (1975), "Toward a Marxian theory of deviance," *Social Problems* 22 (June): 641–651.

9   Caio Prado, Jr. (1967), *The Colonial Background of Modern Brazil,* Berkeley, Calif.: University of California Press.

10   Ibid.; Stuart Schwartz (1973), "Free Labor in a Slave Economy: The Lavradores de Cana of Colonial Bahia," in D. Alden (ed.), *Colonial Roots of Modern Brazil,* Berkeley, Calif.: University of California Press; Levine, op. cit.

11   Levine, op. cit.

12   Joseph R. Gusfield (1976), "Moral passage: the symbolic process in public designations of deviance," *Social Problems* (Fall), 175–188.

13   David Denslow, *Sugar Production in Northeastern Brazil and Cuba, 1858–1908,* New Haven, Conn.: Ph.D. Dissertation, Yale University, pp. 17–18.

14   Ibid., pp. 9–10.

15   The low wages could have been used to coerce laborers to work long hours just to secure sufficient income to survive. However, such coercion is less effective when workers retain squatting rights.

16   *Falla com que o Excellentissimo Sr. Pereira de Lucena abrio a Assembleia Legislativa Provincial de Pernambuco,* Recife, 1874.

17   Some combination of the first and second strategies is most likely.

18   Eisenberg, op. cit., p. 190.

19   Karl Marx (1906), *Capital (I: The Process of Capital Production),* Chicago: Kerr, 1906 (reprint New York: Random House).

20   Cynthia N. Hewitt (1969), "Brazil: The Peasant Movement of Pernambuco, 1961–1964," in Henry A. Landsberger (ed.), *Latin American Peasant Movements,* Ithaca, New York: Cornell University Press, pp. 374–398; Kit Sims Taylor (1969), "Brazil's northeast sugar and surplus value," *Monthly Review* 20 (March).

21   *Falla com que o Excellentissimo Sr. Pereira de Lucena,* op. cit.

22   Eisenberg, op. cit., p. 156.

23   Reis, "Abolition and the Economics of Slaveholding," op. cit., p. 11.

24   Manual Diegues Junior, "Escravo em Pernambuco no Tempo de Joaquim Nabuco," *Revista do Arquivo Publico de Recife,* 1952–1956, p. 50.

25   Reis, "Abolition and the Economics of Slaveholding," op. cit., p. 9.

26   *Diario de Pernambuco,* Recife, 1882.

27   *Falla com que o Excellentissimo Sr. Cavalcante de Albuquerque abrio a Assembleia Legislativa Provincial de Pernambuco,* Recife; 1871.

331

28 *Falla com que o Excellentissimo Sr. Castello Branco abrio a Assembleia Legislativa Provincial de Pernambuco,* Recife, 1865.
29 *Falla com que o Excellentissimo Sr. Cavalcante de Albuquerque,* op. cit.
30 *Falla com que o Excellentissimo Sr. Pereira de Lucena,* op. cit.
31 Ibid.
32 *Falla com que o Excellentissimo Sr. Cavalcante de Albuquerque,* op. cit.
33 *Falla com que o Excellentissimo Sr. Pereira de Lucena,* op. cit.
34 Quoted in Reis, "Abolition and the Economics of Slaveholding," op. cit., p. 8.
35 Quoted in Eisenberg, op. cit., p. 196.
36 Ibid., pp. 196–197.
37 Ibid., p. 195.
38 Reis, "Abolition and the Economics of Slaveholding," op. cit., p. 8.
39 *Diario de Pernambuco,* op. cit.
40 Ibid.
41 "Terms of good behavior," a written promise between the vagrant and the police to secure honest employment.
42 *Codigo Penal do Brazil* (1830).
43 Ibid.
44 The inmate population includes all people recorded in the Pernambucan logs of 1860, 1870, 1880, 1885, 1890, 1900, 1910, and 1922. A fifteen percent systematic sample of the free inmates was drawn from each log, whereas the small number of slaves in the House of Detention made it possible to secure information on all of them. Information was recorded on 2,848 inmates. However, because of unequal sampling proportion, the data could not be analyzed until the free sample was made comparable to the slave universe through the following procedure: the fifteen percent sample of free inmates was multiplied by 6.66%. This procedure created a free inmate population estimate for the years sampled. When the slave inmate population for the four sample years before abolition and the free inmate estimate for all eight periods are combined, using the corrective weighting described, the total number of inmates for the sampled years becomes 14,975.
45 Further credibility is added to the labor recruitment argument by the evidence that sixty percent of those arrested for the vagrancy offenses had left the House of Detention (and conceivably were at work) within three days of arrival, as compared with only twenty-three percent of those arrested for theft, thirty-five percent of those detained for interpersonal violence, and seven percent of those charged with murder.
46 Eisenberg, op. cit., p. 197.
47 *Relatorios e Mensagems dos Governadores do Estado de Pernambuco, 1890,* Recife: Arquivo Publico Estadual de Pernambuco, 1890.
48 Ibid.
49 Ibid.
50 *Journal do Recife,* April 7, 1893.
51 Eisenberg, op. cit.
52 *Relatorios e Mensagems dos Governadores do Estado de Pernambuco,* Recife: Arquivo Publico Estadual de Pernambuco, 1898.
53 Ibid.
54 *Collecção dos Leis do Estado de Pernambuco,* Recife, 1899.
55 *Relatorios e Mensagems dos Governadores do Estado de Pernambuco,* Recife: Arquivo Publico Estadual de Pernambuco, 1923.
56 Ibid.
57 William Chambliss (1964), "A sociological analysis of the law of vagrancy," *Social Problems* 12: 67–77.
58 Georg Rusche and Otto Kirchheimer (1968), *Punishment and Social Structure* New York: Russell and Russell.
59 Stanley Diamond (1971), "The rule of law versus the order of custom," *Social Problems* 38.

[21]

PRISONS, PRODUCTION, AND PROFIT: RECONSIDERING THE IMPORTANCE OF PRISON INDUSTRIES

Introduction

Work has been an important feature of prison systems in the United States from the colonial period until today. Historians have documented that prison labor was initiated for disciplinary reasons in the seventeenth and eighteenth centuries,[1] extended and expanded for financial profit with the development of the industrial prison in the nineteenth,[2] and maintained in the twentieth for its alleged therapeutic and educational value.[3] Yet in spite of all this documentation, there is very little historical analysis of the role work played in the general growth of penal systems and in their daily operations, or on the impact that external social and economic forces had on penal industries. Historians have been blinded by their concentration on intellectual history, particularly their focus on the reformers' differing philosophies of rehabilitation. An important result of this approach to penal history is that work and prison industries are studied for their contribution to rehabilitating the offender, rather than studied on their own merits. One is left with the conclusion that prison industries were subservient to the punitive and rehabilitative goals of penal systems.

A recent example of the impact of this research perspective is found in David Rothman's challenging work, *The Discovery of the Asylum: Social Order and Disorder in the New Republic* In discussing the debate between the Pennsylvania and Auburn systems, he argues that the "point of dispute was whether convicts should work silently in large groups or individually within solitary cells."[4] An equally plausible and more pragmatic explanation of the debate is that the true point of disupte was the type of industry that the new penitentiaries would encourage. The question was whether the prisons should organize their structures and processes to facilitate individual, craft-oriented labor or to facilitate congregate, factory-oriented labor. The reason that the Pennsylvania system lost out to the Auburn model was not only because of the latter's lower cost of construction, but also because Pennsylvania had embraced a labor system that was outdated. The Auburn model was in line with the new demands and challenges of factory production that would provide the state with a means of exploiting the labor of inmates to defray the expenses of the institution, and possibly earn a profit for the state.

This study is a modest attempt to place the industrial prison in a fresh light. The thesis is that prison industries were a central feature of penal development in the United States, and that production and profit were the cornerstones of penal policy. Changes in the physical structure, administrative processes, and disciplinary methods were directly related to the desire among state officials and private businessmen to exploit inmate labor for profit. A sub-theme is that prison industries did not fade out as a result of the emergence of the rehabilitative thrust of penal reformers at the turn of the century; prison industries were alive, if not well, and they dominated the concerns of state officials and prison administrators well into the twentieth century.

258 journal of social history

Material for this article was taken from a larger study of the origin and development of the penal system in Oklahoma.[5] Oklahoma is used as an ideal example of the general prison movement in the United States in the twentieth century.[6] It modeled its prison, as did other states, after the Auburn system, and it made a heavy political and financial investment in carrying on the Auburn tradition of using prison industries as the central feature of its penal system. Further, because Oklahoma's penal system was created within two years after achieving statehood, it provides an opportunity to study the social, political, and economic forces that influenced decisions about the role of the penitentiary.

The Political and Economic Context of the Penal System

The establishment of one state from the consolidation of two culturally distinct territories was unprecedented.[7] Other states had been created through territorial organization with most of the governmental improvements in existence, but Oklahoma "was wholly unorganized — no county organization, no school districts, no townships, no bridges, no roads, and little experience in local government." From these desperate beginnings leaders of the new state believed that they could create a new economic climate, and a government that not only would encourage that climate, but would actually reflect it through its daily operations.[8]

The new economic order envisioned by the public and the state's leaders included governmental control of industrial growth in order to improve the economic stability of small farmers and businessmen. The Populist, and later the Socialist, proposals for social change were not lost on the new settlers. Some of these people had been relatively successful in other parts of the country prior to their migration to Oklahoma, while others had suffered severe economic losses during the depression of 1890. But they all had one common ambition; they wanted to prosper. They were individualistic and competitive, but they recognized that the extravagances of individual competition had to be controlled if they were to share in the benefits of economic growth. They looked to the government to encourage industrial growth and, at the same time, to control its abuses. Governor Charles N. Haskell (1907-1911) summarized that ideal in his inaugural address:

> "Our great state and the surrounding states are full of production of great value. We have some manufacturing interests and we want them increased many fold to the end that our raw materials may be made a source of profit and that we may furnish labor and create a demand for the commerce and products of the mill and the factory. We have great mining and oil interests and we want them expanded . . . We want those corporations in our midst not as monopolies, but as means to compete with trusts and monopolies."[9]

This did not mean that the agricultural economy of Oklahoma was going to be replaced by factories and industry. Oklahoma saw the need to maintain a high level of agricultural production, but on an efficient and profitable basis and not to forestall industrial growth in the state. The bond envisioned as a link between these competing elements was a recognition that they were all businessmen. Governor Haskell made this clear in his inaugural speech:

> "The farmer is a business man. The laborer is a business man. Those engaged in financial, commerce, manufacturing, mining, or transportation, are business men, each and all; and in the aggregate they must, for stability and prosperity, depend on their government. Clearly, then we agree that government itself is a business proposition, requiring business experience, of (sic) business sense, or (sic) business judgment, as absolutely free of (sic) as possible from petty politics and political intrigue."[10]

The message was clear; Oklahoma would encourage industrial growth within the state. The government of Oklahoma would operate itself along business lines; the best price would receive state contracts and the state would operate its agencies, including the penitentiary, for a profit whenever possible. The new state government did not see its primary role as providing social services to the general community, but saw itself as a facilitator of economic growth and a protector of the small farmer and businessman. Humanitarian issues such as convict rehabilitation were secondary to the dominant concern for economics. It is within this climate of concern for economical government and the encouragement of industrial growth that Oklahoma's prison system emerged in 1909.

The Importance of the Economic Role of the Penitentiary

Construction of the penitentiary began in May of 1909, two years after statehood. The penitentiary followed the Auburn (N.Y.) model with a massive wall 625 feet by 615 feet surrounding ten acres of land. Inside the walled area the two cell wings extended 200 feet from a central rotunda, like spokes from the hub of a wheel, and each wing had a capacity of housing 640 inmates. These cell houses rose four stories high, and each floor had 80 cells divided into two rows. The remaining area of ten acres inside the wall was reserved for industrial buildings similar to the factory-style found in the Auburn prison; additional factories were planned for the 2000 acres outside the prison.[11]

The new penitentiary was no ordinary construction project. Even accounting for the generally accepted characteristics of size and strength, the Oklahoma penitentiary required additional construction effort not found in any other state institution except the state capital building. Not only did the state erect the massive compound, it also moved man and land to accomplish its objective. The land was hilly with many sloping grades, gullies, and ravines that required massive amounts of land fill; at some points along the wall the concrete piles go as deep as 35 feet below the grade to the foundation. The state also had to relocate a large number of families. The 2000 acres surrounding the initial 120 acres had many mining camps of all sizes. The state moved "nearly 200 families with their improvements, including buildings, fencing, bag and baggage, and including three graveyards."[12]

The state had made a major commitment in its construction of the state prison. This massive fortress on the north side of the city of McAlester represented the best in design and construction of prison facilities at that time. It also had the latest electrical equipment for opening and closing cell doors and corridor entryways. One political observer of the period editorialized that the penitentiary would always be second to the state capitol building in its importance and its cost of maintenance, but it represented the state's "heaviest investment in permanent improvement."[13]

Did all this gigantic movement of man and nature mean that Oklahoma had made a firm commitment to the rehabilitation of the convicted inmate? Was this institution designed to achieve the humanitarian goals of training, moral reform, and social reintegration of the inmates so fervently articulated by Kate Barnard, the Oklahoma Commissioner of Charities and Correction? The answer is no. There was never any serious discussion of the rehabilitative objectives of the penal system during this early period of construction or later in its development. The penitentiary stood as a symbol not of modern corrections, but of a new economic order in Oklahoma.

The penitentiary was to serve as a model for industrial growth. Thus, the first attempt at industrialization in Oklahoma occurred in its prison. It was to play a

260   journal of social history

major role in the state's plan to provide efficient government and to serve as the catalyst for industrial expansion. First, through their commitment to an industrial prison, state officials assumed that they could show that governmental agencies could be self-supporting and, in some cases, even earn a profit. They believed that the inmates could and would work for the benefit of the state; inmates helped build the institution, and now they would work in prison factories to pay for the cost of their incarceration. Second, if the state could operate income-producing industrial prisons, the message to the general community would be that the manufacturing potential for the state was without limit.

The state's leaders believed that prison industries could be operated on the same basis as factories or small businesses. If properly administered these industries would reap sizeable profits, and they would eliminate prisoner idleness and help maintain order because "the greatest aid to discipline is regular employment."[14] Thus, the industrial prison served two goals: first, it was a model of manufacturing to be duplicated in the private sector; second, the prison industries would relieve the problem of inmate idleness and ease the taxpayer's burden, and the public sale of prison-made goods at low prices would contribute to the general welfare of the community.[15] Although the tax relief and the sale of prison-made products were secondary goals, they illustrated that general benefits to the community could be derived from an economic system that controlled profits. This possibility appealed to the anti-monopolistic attitude of Oklahomans.

The Warden's primary function as head of the state penitentiary was to earn a profit for the state treasury. By placing the emphasis on the industrial nature of the prison and the goal of earning a profit, the state defined the Warden's role as one similar to a chief executive officer of a private corporation rather than a public official with expertise in correctional administration. Governor Robert L. Williams (1915-1919), discussing the type of person he would select for the position and the importance of that position, said that the Warden was as "big as the Governor" in state government. The person he selected as Warden would be able to handle men, but he would also be a businessman who would efficiently use "these convicts to . . . bring in an income for the state." Governor James B. Robertson (1919-1923), said in 1923 that the Warden's responsibility was "to extend and enlarge the industries by reinvesting the profits so that we may run the institution without an appropriation."[16] Ideally the difference between the results of the warden's efforts and the efforts of a corporation president was that the profits generated by the prison industries contributed to the general welfare of the community, whereas the profits generated by a private company benefited only a few stockholders.

Prison Industries and the Private Sector

If the industrial penitentiary was to serve as a model for the business community then it had to function as a business. Like any cautious businessman, the state did not invest all its funds in a single market or in a single method of production. Oklahoma used a combination of the contract, state account, and state-use systems of prison production and sales.[17] During the 1920s Oklahoma had a heavy and profitable involvement with the contract system. Warden W.S. Key noted that three contract industries — overalls, shirts, and brooms — used more than 600 men during peak production and earned a handsome profit for the state. The contractor provided materials, supervision, instruction, and paid the state a specified amount for each completed unit of production. The state in turn rented the contractor's equipment, but it also made large capital investments by constructing factory buildings and warehouses inside the prison walls, with inmate labor, for the contractor's use at no cost.[18] The state's desire to build an industrial climate was a contractor's dream come true.

In order for the prison to make a profit it had to develop industries that would produce goods for a ready market. The industries closest to the industrial ideal set by the early chief executives were the twine and brick factories. They were also the real money makers for the penitentiary because the state controlled all aspects of production and sold the products on the open market on a cash basis. Twine production was first mentioned as a possible industry as early as 1912 when Warden Dick proposed that the state purchase a used loom for $85,000 and authorize him to build a factory. Governor Lee Cruce (1911-1915) had collected data from prisons in other states showing that the twine industry in a prison was profitable. He urged the legislature to support the industry because 1500 inmates were idle most of the time when a good number of them could be producing a product needed by the farmer. He claimed that Oklahoma farmers were forced to pay "tribute to the twine trusts in the form of exorbitant prices for twine used in harvesting their crops." Although his arguments were sound, the legislature did not immediately support the project.[19]

The twine factory represented some financial risk because the state had to deposit about $200,000 in a New York bank for the purchase of the raw material (sisal) needed to make the rope. Governor Robert L. Williams (1915-1919), however, continued to exert pressure for this industry and cited letters he had received from other Wardens which detailed their success in making a profit from twine production. With strong support from the Farmer's Union he was successful, and the legislature funded the twine plant and deposited $165,000 for the purchase of raw material in a New York bank.[20]

Meanwhile, in order to build the twine factory the penitentiary arranged with the financially crippled Choctaw Brick Company in McAlester to use convict labor to manufacture the brick necessary for the construction of the factory. In return the brick company received 25% of all the brick produced for that project, had its factory completely rebuilt with convict labor, and had their plant "turned back to them in first class condition." Shortly after this the state bought machinery for manufacturing bricks in the penitentiary and sold them to various supply companies and construction firms throughout the state.[21]

The twine business grew quickly and within three years the state had sold directly to Oklahoma farmers more than three million pounds, about one-third of the total amount of twine sold in the state. The state's policy to expand the industrial capability of the prison was a success, if the warden's reports are to be believed. In the 1918 penitentiary report the warden indicated that the industries earned $202,161 for the year which represented two-thirds of the cost of maintaining the institution. The warden credited the twine factory's net earnings of $85,600 as contributing the largest share of the profits. The competition from the prison's twine production also had an impact on the twine market. During the 1919-1920 fiscal year the price of twine sold in the state from external private corporations dropped two to six cents per pound depending on the grade. Governor James B. Robertson claimed that the penitentiary twine factory had brought the "trust twine down in price" with a saving of at least $500,000 to Oklahoma's farmers.[22]

The interdependence of prison and private industry was the overriding characteristic of the successful industrial prison. The state's success in these early attempts to earn profits from the production of prison-made goods could not have journal of social history

occurred without the close cooperation of private industry.

The state's commitment to the industrial prison encouraged prison administrators and the private sector to join forces. Factory construction, marketing strategies, and production methods in one way or another used convict labor to generate profits for private entrepreneurs, private companies, and the prison. This intial flurry of cooperation from the private sector was a direct result of the huge profits they received from prison production.

Internal Problems Associated With The Industrial Model

The success of the industrial prison, however, was short-lived. Problems that eventually crippled the prison industries and deflated the idea of using the industrial prison as a model for the state revolved around the prison's inability to maintain a profit, to achieve full employment of inmates, to resolve the issue of prison goods competing with private firms, and to meet effectively the political threat posed by the emerging coalition of business and labor interests opposed to the prison industries.

Because of the state's commitment to make the penitentiary profitable, prison administrators were under intense pressure to show a profit in their annual reports. Whether the prison made significant profits during these early years is open to question. The pressure was so intense that most prison administrators manipulated production figures, sales, and labor costs in their financial reports in order to show a profit for the prison industries. That may explain why so many annual reports indicated a profit, yet the institutions constantly applied for emergency deficiency funding by the middle of the following year. Wardens conveniently used shoddy accounting practices. Warden Switzer noted that "in previous reports it has not been customary to show the cost of labor employed." When that expense was added to the cost of production, many industries shifted from the profit to the loss columns. In addition sales were recorded at higher prices than actually sold in order to show larger profits on the books. The prison also used the revolving funds as working checkbooks to purchase raw materials, construct buildings, buy and repair equipment, and to record sales of the prison products, including sales from one prison department to another. As a result the revolving funds were inflated by the amount of business conducted within the institution. In showing these profits and high balances in the revolving fund the administrators hurt their own budgetary requests because the legislature viewed them as assets and adjusted the appropriation downward. This resulted in a cyclical pattern where inflated profits brought less and less financial support for necessary institutional needs and capital investment.[23]

A second problem of the industrial prison was that it could not maintain full employment of the inmates. The evidence indicates that the state never achieved its goal "to employ profitably all the inmates . . . for their benefit as well as for discipline, and to make the institution self-sustaining."[24] The various industries did make brooms, mattresses and other assorted items used by the institution, but the glaring inefficiencies of production and management probably resulted in higher costs to the state. All these industries, however, were not capable of absorbing the inmate population. Warden Switzer probably was correct when he claimed that 200 men worked on the general maintenance of the prison, 250 were trusties, and another 250 worked on the farms, but he hedged when he said the 750 remaining members of the population worked in the factories. Many of these industries were seasonal, and the average work force in any one factory was from 10 to 20 inmates. Under the best of conditions no more than 600 inmates, less than half the population, worked in the prison factories. If prison discipline was maintained, it was not because the inmates were fully employed.[25]

A third problem, and the most critical for the survival of the industrial prison, was that the business and labor communities no longer saw the industrial prison as a valuable asset to their particular interests. Although the prison industries operated inefficiently, they did produce various goods in various quantities. As a result, private firms saw the prison output as a threat to their share of the market, and labor assumed that convict production stole jobs from free labor. Even while Oklahoma officials were constructing their prison and planning their factories the national debate about prison goods competing with free labor and the free market had begun to have a practical effect through federal and state regulatory laws. In 1924 the United States Department of Commerce, pressured by the furniture, boot and shoe, garment, textile, and cordage industries, held a national conference to discuss the practical problems raised by the selling of prison-made goods on the open market at lower prices. As a result of these meetings the House considered legislation which would ban the interstate shipment of prison-made goods and would require that the goods be labeled, "made in prison." A protest from the states, including Oklahoma, delayed passage of the legislation for a while, but the coalition of labor and commercial interests was too strong and the Hawes-Cooper bill became law in 1929.[29]

While the battle between the state prisons and the coalition of manufacturers and labor was fought at the national level, Oklahoma's prison industries came under sharp attack from similar quarters within the state. Labor unions had been disturbed for a long time by the state's attempt to employ convicts on large-scale industrial enterprises. In January 1918 the United Mine Workers of Oklahoma, Arkansas, and Texas called a regional meeting and passed a resolution condemning Oklahoma for its plan to purchase the mineral rights to the McAlester coal mines on the penitentiary grounds for mining by convict labor. When Warden W.S. Key journeyed to Washington in 1926 to protest the pending labeling legislation, the Oklahoma State Federation of Labor wrote a critical letter to Governor Trapp demanding to know who authorized a state employee to protest a federal law similar to one already on the books in Oklahoma that was not obeyed.[27]

The law in question was the 1910 Oklahoma Statue that required the labeling of all prison-made goods; later it was amended to limit their sales only to state agencies. The state's manufacturers had supported the labeling law and, with the help of the labor unions, succeeded in getting it passed. The Oklahoma Employers Association also took an active stand in support of the bill and lobbied for its passage, but not all private businesses favored the legislation. The Oklahoma Grocers Association, whose members were also members of the employer's group, chastised the Employers Association Secretary for not polling its membership on this issue. The Grocers opposed the labeling bill because they bought canned goods from the prison for retail at a sizeable profit. Because of conflict and confusion surrounding the issue, Governor Trapp was successful in getting the labeling section of the law repealed in 1925, but Governor-elect Henry S. Johnston (1927-1929) indicated his support for the labeling of prison goods and the law was amended again.[28]

This on-again-off-again situation illustrated the confusion surrounding the issue, but it also indicated the relative political weakness of the manufacturers in Oklahoma. It was not until the labor unions joined forces with the manufacturers that legislation designed to limit the amount of prison industrial production became law. Labor leaders, manufacturers, and state officials were no longer concerned about the success of the initial plan to create a partnership between the state and private industry. These long-range social issues gave way to the immediate concerns of economic self-interest. At the slightest sign of competition from the prison industries, vested economic interests, that earlier had supported the prison's industrialization efforts, lobbied hard and strong for limiting its industrial capacity.[29]

Oklahoma's business community was not willing to rely solely on the legal process to achieve their objective; they also used political power to limit competition from prison production. Industry after industry in the private sector made known their desires through informal but powerful political channels. For example, in response to political pressure from newspaper publishers, Governor Robertson abolished the prison printing plant and divided public printing among the newspapers throughout the state. The Board of Public Affairs, with obvious delight, notified the Governor that "within the past 12 months the Board has revised the method of handling public printing, and has distributed among the county editors a greater patronage than ever before in the history of the state." Governor Trapp tried to reinstitute the printing plant two years later to help employ inmates. Even though he planned to limit production to state printing needs, the county publishers made their protest known to the Governor through a letter signed by the President of the Oklahoma Press Association. The local publishers had received the state's printing business during the previous four years and did not want to lose it. The plan to reopen the prison printing plant was dropped.[30]

Another example of the shift away from support of the industrial prison and the use of political power to protest particular economic interests involved the brick industry. In the 1920's the brick companies in the state supported the penitentiary's effort to develop a capacity to produce bricks. At that time, the brick industry opposed a labelling bill designed to limit generally the prison's production of a variety of products, including bricks. The brick companies did not have a manufacturing capacity of their own, and they bought all their bricks from the prison. The companies then sold these inexpensive bricks at retail for sizeable profits. By 1940 the brick industry had developed its own production capacity, and through its lobby group, the Brick and Tile Association, protested any production or sale of bricks by the prison. Pressure generated by the Association on the Board of Public Affairs resulted in the firing of a competent superintendent of the prison's brick production because of a sale of 250,000 bricks to a private contractor. The brick industry also proposed that the state increase its construction of brick roads. This would keep the prison plant busy all year, and it would keep prison brick out of the construction industry because at that time private companies were not involved in road building.[31]

The state's ability to maintain its prison industries was inversely related to the private sector's ability to produce these same goods. The private sector supported the development of the industrial prison because it would produce goods crucial to their economic growth. Private companies purchased retail and manufacturing goods from the prison at a significantly lower cost than if they purchased these same products from wholesalers. This arrangement increased the profit margin of the private industries. As soon as these private industries developed their own capacity to meet market demands, however, they turned their backs on the industrial prison, and successfully used their economic and political power to curtail or stop production by the prison.

External Contradictory Pressures for Change

Idleness became an outstanding feature of state prisons during the 1930s be-

PRISONS, PRODUCTION, AND PROFIT   265

cause of the depression, the increase in prison population, and the crippling impact of the federal regulatory legislation that outlawed the sale of prison goods in interstate commerce and required the labeling of all prison-made products. Because of its massive investment in prison industries, Oklahoma was hard hit by these economic and political forces, as well as the natural forces of long droughts which played havoc with the state's agricultural economy. The penitentiary was overcrowded from the start, and the bulk of the inmates were idle or employed at make-work tasks. In the late 1920s, a warden had recommended doubling the penitentiary's cell space from 640 to 1700 two-man units because of the press of increasing population.

In an attempt to solve the idleness problem and to stem the downward spiral of production, the state sought advice from federal penal experts during the 1930s. A 1937 study noted that 70 percent of the total value of goods produced by the penitentiary in 1923 was through the contract system. By 1935, this method of production had represented less than 38 percent of the goods produced and was declining rapidly. Unemployment and under employment were chronic problems; more than 40 percent of the prisoners performed menial maintenance functions, less than 40 percent of the inmates worked in short-run production projects with high levels of idleness, the remaining inmates were either sick or unemployed. The study team recommended that the prison expand its small-scale industries, increase the use of road camps, and initiate public work projects such as conservation and forestry programs to "keep the prisoners busy." These suggestions did not evoke a sense of commitment to the industrial prison concept or to training or rehabilitation; they were designed to reduce idleness. Overpopulation was critical and the main concern of officials was how to get the prisoners busy to alleviate boredom and mischief in order to ease the control problems of prison administrators. The state had no power over the external forces that were crippling its industrial prison, but it could have changed the type and scale of the industries and developed alternative objectives such as building public parks to more effectively use inmate labor. The state took no action, however, and the penal system limped along without direction.[32]

With the outbreak of World War II conditions at the penitentiary changed dramatically. Initially the war's impact on the prison's industries was negative because the War Production Board placed restrictions on all penal industries regarding the purchase of raw materials and the sale of prison goods. These regulations further decreased the industry operations and added to the problem of inmate idleness. Oklahoma attempted unsuccessfully to locate a new market by mailing sales inquiries to institutions in other states that did not have a large industrial capacity. But war-related contracts from the federal government began to trickle into the prison after a loosening of federal restrictions, and they quickly became the foundation for shoring up the weakened prison industries. A representative of the War Production Board visited the penitentiary in the fall of 1942 after many requests from state officials and finally at the urging of the Oklahoma congressional delegation. The representative said later that he had hesitated to visit Oklahoma because he and the Board did not expect to find any large industrial capacity in penitentiaries this far west. He was surprised at the production capacity of the McAlester institution, however, and he "not only wired . . . Washington, but he wrote them" a detailed letter informing his superiors that Oklahoma "had one of the best industrial set-ups of any prison in the country." The representative probably overstated the case, but the military contracts began to flow to the penitentiary. In October, 1942 the penitentiary accepted a quarter of a million dollars in contracts for Navy clothing, furniture, rope and bricks. In January and February of 1943 the prison received an additional $107,000 worth of contracts, and by the end of 1943 the Board of Public Affairs reported to the Governor that it had accepted well over a half-million dollars worth of military contracts for the year. The prison industries had received a new lease on life and were operating on a full-time basis.[33]

From 1930 to 1950 the state's prison industries had experienced a wide range of conflicting pressures that suggested that the industrial prison was anachronistic, while also suggesting that it was a viable and profitable enterprise. Wartime military contracts helped revive the prison industries, but they also delayed any serious and concentrated search for a fundamental role for the Oklahoma penal system. During this period more than 1,000 inmates worked full-time in the prison factories with slightly less than 600 working at non-productive or maintenance tasks.[34] These shifting pressures occurred when the state was cooling to the idea of an industrial prison, but officials had no alternative model in mind and the upsurge in production during the 1940s lulled them into a false sense of security. As a result, they ignored the lingering problems of overcrowding, the inefficient and disorganized factories, and the larger question of penal reform in general. The question of what role the penitentiary should play in Oklahoma's criminal justice process never surfaced.

The Ambivalent Search For Alternatives

The post World War II era brought a tightening of the restrictions on the sale of prison-made goods, rising inmate populations, and further economic troubles for state penitentiaries, particularly those that relied heavily on the industrial model. The only outlet remaining for the sale of prison-made goods was the state-use system which limited sales to state and local government agencies. The Oklahoma penitentiary had sold its products to other state institutions from the beginning, but these industries were small and seasonal. Few of the early Governors believed in the state-use system because they felt that production orders would not employ all the prisoners and forced idleness would result. Another argument against the state-use system was that it was not economically feasible because such a limited market would not support the industrial model envisioned by the state's leaders. The state institutions simply could not order enough products to sustain large-scale prison industries. In order to supply these institutions the penitentiary would need to operate many small factories and still have most convicts unemployed. But the problem of inmate idleness and its threat to security forced the state to look for alternative markets to keep the prison industries functioning. State officials were encouraged by a federal study that showed the prison could increase its annual sales by one million dollars if all state institutions bought their supplies from the prison, and it could add another million in sales if city and county governments followed suit. Unwilling to face the reality that the industrial prison was a bankrupt concept, Oklahoma officials attempted to save it by embracing the state-use system of production.[35]

Other state institutions did not cooperate, however, and the state-use system had little beneficial impact on the prison. Opposition from state institutions and local officials convinced the legislature not to pass a law that required these agencies and officials to buy prison goods. Without such a law these agencies merely tolerated and by-passed, whenever possible, the state-use system. State institutions delayed their requisitions until after the state purchasing agent had issued his quarterly orders to the suppliers, including the prison. They would then submit their orders on an emergency basis and force the purchasing agent to buy

PRISONS, PRODUCTION, AND PROFIT 267

from private suppliers, sometimes at a higher cost, and thus by-pass the normal state production schedule. Some institutions purposely ordered goods with specifications not available from the penal industries. For example, the penitentiary listed canned dried beets, but the State Hospital at Taft or the Central State Hospital consistently ordered sliced beets. One institution administrator flatly said that he preferred to buy from a Vermont firm rather than the penitentiary. State institutions obviously went to great lengths to avoid buying their supplies from the penal industries.[36]

These institutions had good reason to avoid buying prison-made goods. The quality of the products of the penal industries had deteriorated, and the production schedules were inefficient and unreliable. The Griffin Memorial Hospital in Norman complained that the canned fancy yellow corn had "white corn in with the yellow . . . and a large portion of the hull is still on the kernels," and that the vegetables had a very starchy taste.[37] Forty gallons of syrup shipped to the Whitaker State Home soured immediately after opening. During the early 1940s at least one-third of all brick delivered was useless. In addition to the quality of the product, customers also complained about poor delivery. Central Oklahoma Hospital ordered 100 dozen ladies' shoes and six months later they had received only two dozen. Even the chairman of the Board of Public Affairs suffered at the hands of the penitentiary industries. He had ordered a pair of leather boots, but they were two sizes too small. He said he didn't think his feet had grown because he had "passed the growing stage some 40 years ago." In a serious observation he also noted that "the failure to properly manufacture goods has been our greatest drawback in the sale of products from that institution."[38] The issue of quality and delivery schedules were only symptomatic of a larger, more pervasive problem of prison industries. Prison administrators and state officials attempted to apply a free-market perspective to prison industries that had a captive employee force without incentive, outmoded and inefficient equipment, and a limited and closed market.

Finally, the prison had weak pricing practices throughout its history. Penitentiary goods from socks to rope to bricks were priced higher than private industry. At one point prison shirts sold for $2.40 a dozen while private industry sold the same item for $2.00. Steel buckets sold for $4.00 each on the open market, yet the prison listed them at $7.00. Prices on prison goods were educated guesses. Prison administrators summed the cost of materials and salaries, but did not calculate overhead or inmate labor; they simply added a rough 20 percent to their estimated cost. The prison industries had no cost accounting system and as a result about half their price bids were slightly higher than private companies. The state purchasing agent constantly lowered the bids from the prisons in order to meet the bids of private companies. When prison officials were asked by a legislative investigating committee how private firms underbid the prison price when the latter had no labor or depreciation costs, no one knew the answer.[39]

Because of the deplorable state of the prison industries, constantly rising populations, and massive idleness of inmates, Oklahoma officials attempted after World War II to develop more prison farms because they absorbed a greater number of personnel. Unlike its southern sister states, Oklahoma had not placed much emphasis on penal farms during its early years of development. The penitentiary had over 1,920 acres of rolling land under its control, but only 1200 acres were cultivated and this land was of poor quality. The Stringtown facility, a sub-prison opened in the 1930s, had 7,897 acres, but only 300 were cultivated and the balance was timber and grazing land. Although the farms were listed as an industry in the annual reports, prison administrators were content if farm production relieved some of the hugh financial burden generated by the annual grocery bill of the institution. The early wardens were not enthusiastic about prison farms and they cautioned the state about relying too heavily on farm production for profit. Warden Fred P. Switzer said in 1923 that "contrary to popular belief, farming is not profitable to a prison." He said that the production rate and market prices cannot compensate for the high cost of farm gangs requiring guards, and the only reason farms looked profitable was because excess grain was fed to livestock which was then sold on the open market. He also noted the condition of the Texas prison system "which at this time showed a deficit of two million dollars" because they relied solely on the farm to the exclusion of industry. Clearly the rural state of Oklahoma saw itself as different from its southern sister states. That difference was a firm, if miscalculated, commitment to see industrial development as the key to a self-sustaining penal system.[40]

But the post World War II era saw a shift within the penal system from an emphasis on industry to a half-hearted attempt to follow the farm plantation model of the south. The impact of the regulatory acts limiting the sale and shipment of prison goods brought the penal industries to a state of collapse. Out of pure frustration one Warden argued for the expansion of the agricultural industry to employ inmates and help cut expenses; he cited Texas, Mississippi, and Georgia as examples of success. A House Investigating Committee, after visiting penal farms in Tennessee and Texas in 1957 and uncritically accepting their hosts' portrayal of economic success and the lack of sexual perversion and gambling, recommended that Oklahoma begin a long-range plan to expand their farm operations.[41]

The state looked at these suggestions, but it never developed them into a major policy. In the early 1950s the legislature authorized the purchase of a large farm near McAlester, but never funded the project. A consultant had been hired by the penitentiary to evaluate land purchases for their farming potential. He worked about ten days a month for a monthly salary of $400, but a Legislative Committee found that he did very little work and terminated the arrangement. These weak attempts to develop more penal farms resulted from the pressures generated by the increasing inmate population. In 1955 the prison warden claimed that he could place 700 more men on trusty status if he had the place, such as a farm, to send them.[42]

The major problem of the institution was that it had too many men for the available jobs. Wardens complained that even with new farm land they would have to work two men on one-man jobs simply to get the inmates out of their cells. They also cautioned the state officials about the limited benefit to be derived from an expanded farm program. Warden C.P. Burford, an ex-administrator of a federal prison farm, warned that most of the inmates came from towns and cities and that less than 10 percent were interested in agriculture. He said, "You cannot take a fellow who has lived in town all his life and interest him and teach him anything by milking cows or doing other farm work." A citizens group studying the problem said that instead of purchasing more farm land the state should "extend the vocational program." The legislature took no action on either program, yet Governor Raymond D. Garey (1955-1959) told the legislature at the end of his four-year term that expanded farm operations at the penal institutions had "kept the per capita appropriations down to a minimum." The facts indicate there was no substance to that claim, yet no one rose to challenge it. In Oklahoma, when public policy decisions were delayed and critical problems ignored, an unsubstantiated reference to the economical operation of government provided a soothing effect that seemed to make the problem disappear.[43]

Conclusion

Like most states during the post civil war period, Oklahoma made a firm political and economic commitment to the industrial prison.[44] All decisions regarding appropriations, daily management, and the measurement of the prison's effectiveness were based on production output and profit margins. The early successes bolstered the state's commitment, and encouraged it to expand the prison's productive capacity. As long as the prison supplied products that were needed in the state and were not produced by private companies in the state, the industrial prison received political and financial support from the community. As soon as the economic situation and the private manufacturing capacity of the new state improved to the point where private businesses competed with the prison, however, these private interests exercised their political muscle and succeeded in crippling the industrial prison. The impact these economic and social changes had on the prison industries was severe and long lasting.

After the initial financial support for buildings and machinery during the first three decades of the twentieth century, the legislature succumbed to the pressures it received from vested economic interests and began a long period of decreasing capital investment in the industrial prison. After 1930 the legislature never sufficiently funded any new industry so that it would have qualified foremen or adequate equipment. Most of the machinery was purchased second hand during the 1930s and never replaced. As late as 1958 the second hand equipment of the tag plant, the cannery, the soap and paint factory, and the brick factory was still being used even though it was falling apart. A legislative committee investigating the penitentiary in 1957 concluded that the "quality of work cannot be improved until new and better equipment is provided." The Chairman of the Board of Public Affairs echoed this sentiment when he testified that the prison had "time and labor," what it needed was machinery. Oklahoma would not abandon the industrial model.[45]

The early commitment to detailed planning of the physical structure in order to facilitate industrial production and expansion also suffered as a result of the impact of external economic forces on the decision-making process. The physical plant of the institution and the layout of its factories quickly worked against any possible success for industrialization. A study conducted in 1966 said that "the penitentiary is in worse shape than many institutions built 50 years earlier; evidence of neglect of plant and equipment is seen at every hand." Added to this neglect by prison administrators was the disorganized layout of the factory buildings. Additions to the physical structure of the institution over the years were placed because of space convenience, not for ease of operation. The result was a hodgepodge of buildings that exacerbated custody and order maintenance problems and worked against efficient production. One Board member, possibly foretelling the future, urged the movement of the prison factories to a location outside the walls "in case of a riot or anything like that."[46]

The uncontrolled and uncontrollable size of the inmate population also frustrated any serious attempt to become fully industrialized. The constant turnover of the inmate population created havoc in the factories. In 1953, 66 percent of the inmates had sentences of three years or less. Foremen did not know from one week to the next how many inmates they would have available in the factories or how long they would be assigned to any particular plant. Obviously very little quality and consistency in production could be expected under these conditions. In addition men received assignments to industries whether there was work or not; the objective was to get them out of the cells. Good training or good work habits could not be learned when tasks were given to twice the number of men necessary to accomplish them or when half the work force was kept idle. For example, the book bindery shop that repaired school books for the state employed from 300 to 700 inmates during the summer months, but except for the dozen or more men who worked the bindery machinery, the only task performed by the inmates was to erase pencil marks from the pages of the school books.[47]

Finally, the state refused to recognize that the original concept of the industrial prison based on the idea of exploiting convict labor for profit was not a viable policy. It assumed that the inmates would work in a forced working environment without incentives to produce products for which they received little or no remuneration, but which made large profits for the state and its partners in the private sector. The concerns over product quality, production schedules, delivery problems, accounting procedures, and prison farms did not deal with the substantive problems inherent in the industrial prison.

The importance of prison industries to the development of penal systems in the United States is substantiated by this study. Production and profit outweighed any other penological concern of prison administrators and state officials. The emphasis of the administrators of the Oklahoma prisons was identical to that found by David Lewis in his study of nineteenth-century prisons in New York.[48] The emphasis was on profit, and that emphasis shaped the prison structure, prison processes, and prison policies. When economic and political changes in the larger community shifted, the impact of those shifts were directly and immediately felt by the industrial prison.

From the beginning Oklahoma's prison system was cast as a model for industrialization. The prison would operate efficiently and on a business-like basis in order to limit the taxpayer's burden and to make a profit for its investors. The prison's various functions would be evaluated on their potential for profit and their ability to decrease operating costs. When the evidence clearly indicated that the industrial prison was not a viable policy, the state was frozen by its refusal to reject it, and by its failure to move away from the concept of a self-sustaining prison. With economic indicators no longer a valid means of measuring the effectiveness of the prison and with no commitment to rehabilitation or any other alternative model, the state had no philosophical base upon which to evaluate the prison. With the collapse of the industrial prison after World War II, Oklahoma's penitentiary simply existed without any direction. As a result the penitentiary provided a custodial service for the courts, and its primary objective was to maintain order within its walls.

University of Wisconsin — Milwaukee   John A. Conley

FOOTNOTES

* An earlier version of this paper was presented at the Annual Meeting of the American Society of Criminology (1978). The author wishes to thank Mark Haller (Temple University), Sam Walker (University of Nebraska-Omaha), and Ellen Hochstedler (University of Wisconsin-Milwaukee) for their critical comments on an earlier draft of this paper.

1. For pioneering studies, see Johan Thorsten Sellin, *Pioneering in Penology: The Amsterdam Houses of Correction in the Sixteenth and Seventeenth Century* (Philadelphia, 1944); Harry E. Barnes, *A History of Penal, Reformatory, and Correctional Institutions of the State of New Jersey:*

PRISONS, PRODUCTION, AND PROFIT 271

Analytical and Documentary (1918; reprinted New York, 1974), *Repression of Crime: Studies in Historical Penology* (1926; reprinted Montclair, N.J., 1969), and *The Story of Punishment: A Record of Man's Inhumanity to Man* 2nd edition revised (1930; reprinted Montclair, N.J., 1972); Orlando F. Lewis, *The Development of American Prisons and Prison Customs, 1776-1845* (1922; reprinted Montclair, N.J., 1967); Negley K. Teeters, *The Cradle of the Penitentiary: The Walnut Street Jail* (Philadelphia, 1953), *The Prison at Philadelphia Cherryhill: The Separate System of Penal Discipline, 1829-1913* (New York, 1957).

2. Harry E. Barnes, "The Economics of American Penology as Illustrated by the Experience of the State of Pennsylvania," *Journal of Political Economy* 29 (Oct., 1921): 618-638; Blake McKelvey, *American Prisons: A Study in American Social History Prior to 1915* (Chicago, 1936); David Lewis, *From Newgate to Dannemora: The Rise of the Penitentiary in New York, 1795-1848* (Ithaca, 1965); David J. Rothman, *The Discovery of the Asylum: Social Order and Disorder in the New Republic* (Boston, 1971).

3. Blake McKelvey, *American Prisons: A History of Good Intentions* (Montclair, N.J., 1977), Chaps. 10-14; Gordon Hawkins, *The Prison: Policy and Practice* (Chicago, 1976); James B. Jacobs, *Stateville: The Penitentiary in Mass Society*, (Chicago, 1977); Elmer H. Johnson, "Prison Industry," *Crime, Correction, and Society* (Homewood, Ill., 1968), 558-566. For a critical study of the Federal Prison industry see Robert Mintz, "Federal Prison Industry — 'The Green Monster' — Part One: History and Background," *Crime and Social Justice*, 6 (Fall/Winter, 1976): 41-48.

4. Rothman, *Discovery of the Asylum*, 82.

5. John A. Conley, *A History of the Oklahoma Penal System, 1907-1967* (Michigan State University: Unpublished Ph.D. Dissertation, 1977).

6. Unlike the prisons of the nineteenth century, the twentieth-century prison has generated very little interest among social historians. Yet the competing philosophies of rehabilitation, industry, and punishment that dominated the nineteenth century were played out during the next century. For an overview that suggests the importance of these issues, but which is an inadequate analysis, see McKelvey, *American Prisons*, 234-348. For examples of studies of state penal systems that illustrate that Oklahoma's prison experience was not unique, see Mark T. Carleton, *Politics and Punishment: The History of the State Penal System* (Baton Rouge, 1971) and Harvey R. Hougen, "The Impact of Politics and Prison Industry on the General Management of the Kansas State Penitentiary, 1883-1909," *The Kansas Historical Quarterly* XLIII (1977): 297-318.

7. For histories of the rapid settlement of the Oklahoma and Indian Territories, see Luther B. Hill, *A History of the State of Oklahoma*, 2 vols. (Chicago, 1909), 205-267; Roy Gittinger, *The Formation of the State of Oklahoma, 1803-1906*, (Norman, 1939), 184-235; Grant Foreman, *A History of Oklahoma* (Norman, 1942), 238-272.

8. *First Message of the Governor to Extraordinary Session of the State Legislature, 1910*, 2. Governor's Messages hereafter cited as *Governor's Message, 19--*.

9. Inaugural Address of Governor C.N. Haskell, November 16, 1907, University of Oklahoma Archives, Haskell Collection; also see Philip S. Foner, *American Socialism and Black Americans From the Age of Jackson to World War II* (Westport, 1977), 233, and H. Wayne Morgan and Ann Hodges Morgan, *Oklahoma: A Bicentennial History* (New York, 1977), 95-97.

10. Haskell, Inaugural Address, 1907.

11. Robert Park, *History of the Oklahoma State Penitentiary, Located at McAlester* (McAlester, Okla., 1914), 5-6; Percey R. Parnell, *The Joint* (San Antonio, 1976), 4-6; *Harlow's Weekly*

(Oklahoma City, Oklahoma), October 19, 1912, 14-15; Commissioner of Charities and Corrections, *Second Annual Report, 1910* (Oklahoma City, 1910), 28. Commissioner's Reports hereafter cited as *C & C Report 19--; Harlow's Weekly*, October 19, 1912, 15-16. For a description of Auburn Prison, see Lewis, *From Newgate to Dannemora*, 116-118.

12. The additional land which also had coal deposits was purchased from the Choctaw and Chickasaw Nations for about $10 an acre. Because of an unclear title to the 120 acres the state was forced to pay an additional $3,000 plus interest in 1915 to the original owners. *Governor's Message, 1910*, 13; Quote from *Harlow's Weekly*, October 19, 1912, 14; *Harlow's Weekly*, February 2, 1915, 30; Oscar P. Fowler, *The Haskell Regime: The Intimate Life of Charles Nathanial Haskell* (Oklahoma City, 1933), 168.

13. *Harlow's Weekly*, October 19, 1912, 121.

14. Oklahoma State Penitentiary, *Annual Report, 1925*, 24-25, hereafter cited as *O.S.P. Annual Report, 19--*.

15. Letter, Governor Martin E. Trapp to William M. Franklin, October 3, 1925, State Archives Governor Trapp Records: *Governor's Message, 1927*, 45.

16. Letter, Governor Robert L. Williams to Ben F. Johnson, November 16, 1914, State Archives Governor Williams Records, Appointments; *Governor's Message, 1923*, 123.

17. The prison industries of most states used four open-market systems during this period and one closed-market system after 1940. Under the lease system the state relinquished all responsibility for the care of inmates and received a stipulated sum for their labor. This was the most abused system and reform groups effectively forced the states to abandon it by the end of the 1920s. Oklahoma never used this form of production. The contract system allowed the state to retain control over the prisoners, but sold their labor to private firms or individuals for a specified daily fee per inmate. This system resulted in much graft and corruption and prisoners were still abused by the contractors. The piece-price method of production was a variation of the contract system where the contractor supplied the materials and paid the state a stipulated price for each unit of production. Under the state account system the state went completely into the manufacturing business, buying all raw materials, setting up factories, marketing the product, and assuming all financial risks. The closed-market system relied on the state-use method which limited the sale of prison goods to state and local government agencies and non-profit organizations. For abuses related to the use of prison labor, see Thomas L. Baxley, "Prison Reforms During the Donaghy Administration," *Arkansas History Quarterly* 22 (1963): 76-84; Jane Zimmerman, "The Convict Lease System in Arkansas and the Fight for Abolition," *Arkansas History Quarterly* 8 (1949): 171-188; A.C. Hutson, Jr., "The Overthrow of the Convict Lease System in Tennessee," *East Tennessee Historical Society* 8 (1936): 82-103; Blake McKelvey, "A Half Century of Southern Penal Exploitation," *Social Forces* 13 (1934): 112-123; Harry Elmer Barnes and Negley K. Teeters, *New Horizons in Criminology* (New York, 1943, with revisions, 1945), 685-716.

18. Letter, Warden W.S. Key to Governor A.W. McLean (North Carolina), June 3, 1925, State Archives Governor Trapp Records, Subject File; *O.S.P. Annual Report, 1921*, 1-3.

19. Minutes, Board of Control of State Penal Institutions, November 11, 1912; *O.S.P. Annual Report, 1919*, 2; *Governor's Message*, 1913; 89-90.

20. Letter, Board of Public Affairs to Governor Robert L. Williams, March 23, 1918, State Archives Governor Williams Records; *Governor's Message, 1915*, 23-30 and *1917*, 273.

21. *Governor's Message, 1923*, 123. Prior to this time the state had contracted with the brick plant to manufacture bricks necessary to build the various prison buildings. See *Harlow's Weekly*, July 12, 1914, 393.

PRISONS, PRODUCTION, AND PROFIT 273

22. Quote from *Governor's Message, 1923*, 122. Also see *O.S.P. Annual Report, 1921*, 2, and *Harlow's Weekly*, November 13, 1918, 6-7.

23. *Governor's Message, 1923*, 127, quotes from *Governor's Message, 1927*, n.p. *O.S.P. Annual Report, 1926*, n.p. Financial Reports for 1919 showed most of the 11 industries including the farms, the brick, broom, canning, dairy, and tag factories in the loss column with the highest profit of $8,000 shown by the license tag plant, *O.S.P. Annual Report, 1919*, 1; also see financial reports in *O.S.P. Annual Report, 1922* and *1925* and Testimony Joint Committee, 1910, 74-75, State Archives Legislature, Joint Committee Records. Interdepartmental sales were a necessary part of the prison's operations and continued for many years to inflate the institution's assets; see Testimony, Investigation of State Penitentiary, February 4, 1957, 41, hereafter cited as Testimony, 1957, State Archives Legislature, House Committee Records.

24. *O.S.P. Annual Report, 1922*, 2.

25. *O.S.P. Annual Report, 1922*, 2; Letter, Warden Fred C. Switzer to Senator G. Williams (Texas), March 21, 1921, State Archives Governor Robertson Records; *Governor's Message, 1923*, 127-128.

26. Copies of the federal bills and the Commerce Department's news release dated December 3, 1924 announcing the meeting are in State Archives Governor Trapp Records, Subject File; Warden W.S. Key testified before a Congressional Committee in opposition to the proposed legislation, see Letter, Warden W.S. Key to Carl L. Rice, Board of Public Affairs, April 6, 1926, States Archives Governor Trapp Records, Subject File. The Hawes-Cooper law divested "prisonmade goods of their interstate character" which made them subject to the receiving state's law, see 49 *U.S.C.A.* sec. 60. In 1935 Congress passed the Ashurst-Summers law which required that all prison-made goods be labeled "made in prison," see 49 *U.S.C.A.* sec. 61-64. This law was repealed and replaced in 1948 by 18 *U.S.C.A.* sec. 1761 and 1762 which tightened the language of the original sections and incorporated them into the federal criminal code.

27. *Harlow's Weekly*, January 16, 1918, 1; Letter, Joe C. Campbell, President Oklahoma Federation of Labor to Governor M.E. Trapp, April 9, 1926, and Letter, Warden W.S. Key to E.B. Howard, December 30, 1924, State Archives Governor Trapp Records, Subject File. The union official was referring to the 1910 law that required all prison-made goods be labeled "convict-made goods," see *Session Laws of Oklahoma, 1910*, 6.

28. Letters, John M. Hammong to H.V. Kahle, May 23, 1925, to J.T. Griffith, May 25, 1925, to Governor M.E. Trapp May 25, 1925, State Archives Governor Trapp Records, Subject File; *Governor's Message, 1927*, 45; Platform, Henry S. Johnston Democratic Candidate for Governor, n.d. (1926), State Archives, Governor Johnston Records.

29. The issue of prison-made goods being sold on the open-market surfaced again and again over the next four decades and organized labor never changed its position; see for example, Testimony, 1957, 38, State Archives Legislature, House Committee Records; *Oklahoma Compiled Statutes 1921*, sec. 11015, 11016; *Oklahoma Session Laws 1925*, 304 and *1937*, 114-115.

30. Letter, State Board of Affairs to Governor J.B. Robertson, n.d., State Archives Governor Robertson Records, Correspondence; letters, Clyde E. Muchmore to Carl Rice, Board of Affairs, September 10, 1925 and Vice Versa, September 12, 1925, State Archives Governor Trapp Records, Subject File.

31. Letter, Board of Public Affairs to Warden C.P. Burford, January 1, 1948; State Archives Governor Turner Records, Penitentiary File; Letters, Brick and Tile Association to E.W. Smart, Chairman Board of Public Affairs, July 2, August 1, and September 5, 1940, State

Archives Board of Public Affairs Records, Correspondence State Institution; 10, 1940, State Archives Board of Public Affairs Records, Correspondence Penitentiary. Letters, H.C. Rice to Harry V. Kahle, May 5, 1925 and J.G. Puterbaugh to Governor M.E. Trapp, May 1, 1925, State Archives Governor Trapp Records, Subject File.

32. *Governor's Message, 1926*, n.p.; Frank T. Flynn, "The Federal Government and the Prison Labor Problem in the States," *Social Service Review 24*, (1950) 21-22. Quotes from U.S. Prison Industries Reorganization Administration, *The Prison Labor Problem in Oklahoma: A Survey* (Washington, D.C., 1937), 4, 10-11, 20-26. Except for the pathbreaking article by Flynn there has been no study of the New Deal's impact on state penal systems or criminal justice generally. This obtains in spite of the fact that President Roosevelt had renowned experts on the subject as his key advisors.

33. Letter, Warden Fred Hunt to Board of Public Affairs, October 23, 1942, Monthly Report of Contracts Accepted for War Production, December, 1942 and January and February, 1943, State Archives Board of Public Affairs, Correspondence Penitentiary. For Oklahoma's attempt to develop a market with other states and for a list of the type and amount of military contracts, see generally Letters, Board of Public Affairs to various state penal institutions for 1942-44 and Memo, Virgil Brown, Chairman, Board of Public Affairs to Governor's Office, November 15, 1943, State Archives, Board of Public Affairs, Correspondence Prison Industries.

34. Letter, Warden Fred Hunt to Board of Public Affairs, March 3, 1943, State Archives, Board of Public Affairs, Correspondence Penitentiary.

35. *Governor's Message, 1915*, 23, *1923*, 125, *1927*, 45; Letter, Warden Fred C. Switzer to American Prison Association, August 20, 1919, State Archives Governor Robertson Records, General Correspondence; PIRA, *Prison Labor Problem*, 15, 18; James J. Waters (Warden) *Additional Information for the Committee Studying Rehabilitation Programs at State Institutions, 1954*, 12, State Archives Penitentiary Records, hereafter cited as Waters, *Additional Information, 1954*.

36. Report, General Investigating Committee of Oklahoma State Penitentiary, February 4. 1957, 8, hereafter cited as Report, 1957 and Testimony taken by same, 43, 54-55, State Archives Legislature, House Committee Records; Transcript of Proceedings of Investigation at Oklahoma Reformatory, March 1949, Vol. II, 22 State Archives Governor Turner Records, Reformatory File, hereafter cited as Transcript, 1949.

37. Letter, Central State Memorial Hospital to Mrs. N.M. Bedingfield, Superintendent of Industries, *O.S.P.*, November 23, 1956, State Archives Legislature, House Committee Records.

38. Quote from Letter, E.W. Smart, Chairman Board of Public Affairs to J.C. Reddin, Plant Superintendent *O.S.P.*, October 19, 1939, also see Letter, Board of Public Affairs to Warden Jess F. Dunn, January 1, 1940, Letters to various machinery manufacturers, January, 1940, Letters, Board of Public Affairs to J.C. Reddin, Plant Superintendent *O.S.P.*, January 2, 1940 and to Warden Jess F. Dunn, December 13, 1939, State Archives Board of Public Affairs, Correspondence Penitentiary; Internal Memo, Board of Public Affairs, November, 1965 in Testimony, 1957, 45, State Archives Legislature, House Committee Records.

39. Testimony, 1957, 40-50, State Archives Legislature, House Committee Records; Letters, Board of Public Affairs to Warden Jess F. Dunn, January 4, 1940; J.C. Reddin, Superintendent of Prison Industries to Board of Public Affairs, January 23, 1940, State Archives Board of Public Affairs, Correspondence Prison Industries.

40. *Governor's Message, 1923*, 124-125 and *1926* n.p. PIRA, *The Prison Labor Problem*, 4; For a discussion of southern penal farms see Blake McKelvey, "A Half Century of Southern

PRISONS, PRODUCTION, AND PROFIT   275

Penal Exploitation," *Social Forces* 13 (1934): 112-123 and "Penal Slavery and Southern Reconstruction," *Journal of Negro History* 20 (1935): 153-179 and *American Prisons*, 172-189.

41. *O.S.P. Annual Report, 1954*, 6, State Archives, Penitentiary Records; Report, House Committee Visiting Prison Farms in Tennessee and Texas 1957, State Archives Legislature, House Committee Records.

42. Testimony, 1955, 321-322 and Report, 1955, 2, and Report, 1957, 12, State Archives Legislature, House Committee Records.

43. Burford's quote in Transcript, 1949, Vol, II, 10, 25, State Archives Governor Turner Records, Reformatory File; Testimony, 1955, 311-313, State Archives Legislature, House Committee Records; Citizens Group Recommendation in Oklahoma Citizens Committee on Delinquency and Crime, *Apathy or Action: A Survey* (Oklahoma City, 1958), 76-77; Quote of Governor Garey in *Governor's Message, 1959*, 15.

44. Historians have largely ignored the importance of prison industries to Penal Development in this country. For solid, but rare, examples see Lewis, *From Newgate to Dannemora*, 179-200, 260-267; Carleton, *Politics and Punishment*, generally; Hougen, "The Impact of Politics," 297-318, Martin B. Miller, "At Hard Labor: Rediscovering the Nineteenth Century Prison," *Issues in Criminology* 9 (1974).

45. Transcript, 1949 Vol. II, 9, 19, State Archives Governor Turner Records, Reformatory File; Oklahoma Citizens Committee on Delinquency and Crime, *Apathy or Action: A Survey* (1958), 7.5; Quotes from Testimony, 1957, 5, 35, and Report, 1957, 10, State Archives Legislature, House Committee Records.

46. Testimony Investigation of Oklahoma State Penitentiary, February 4—5, 1955, 77-78, hereafter cited as Testimony, 1955, and Testimony, 1957, 5 (Board Member's quote), State Archives Legislatue, House Committee Records; National Council on Crime and Delinquency, *Correction in Oklahoma: A Survey* (Washington, D.C.: NCCD, 1966), 13, for quote and condition of prison. The Penitentiary suffered a massive riot on July 27, 1973 that destroyed the majority of workshops and factories on the prison grounds.

47. Waters, *Additional Information, 1954*, 2, 17-18, State Archives Penitentiary Records; Testimony, 1955, 84-85, and Testimony, 1957, 96, State Archives Legislature, House Committee Records; NCCD, *Correction in Oklahoma*, 29.

48. Lewis, *From Newgate to Dannemora*, 181 and 178-200 generally.

[22]

SOCIAL PROBLEMS, Vol. 30, No. 5, June 1983

PUNISHMENT AFTER SLAVERY: SOUTHERN STATE PENAL SYSTEMS, 1865-1890*

CHRISTOPHER R. ADAMSON
York University

This paper identifies and analyzes the political and economic functions of the state penal systems in the southern United States after the Civil War. The system of prison administration, discipline, and labor which emerged after 1865—known as the convict lease system—was a functional replacement for slavery. Like the Black Codes, vagrancy laws, and sharecropping arrangements, the convict lease system was a mechanism of race control used to prevent ex-slaves from obtaining the status and rights enjoyed by wage workers. The organization and philosophy of crime control both before and after the Civil War reflected the fact that both slaves and ex-slaves were problem populations. As such, they were a threat to the existing system of class rule but also a useful resource—economically as a pool of cheap labor for southern industrialization, and politically or symbolically as a means to consolidate white supremacy.

Changes in criminal law and punishment have been traced to wider political and economic developments (Conley, 1982; Rusche and Kirchheimer, 1968; Scull, 1977; Sellin, 1976). This can easily be demonstrated with reference to the southern United States which evolved a distinct penological outlook based on brutal discipline and hard labor. This paper analyzes the complex political and economic functions of the state penal systems which emerged in the southern states after the Civil War of 1861-1865.

Tannenbaum (1924:82) noted that the southern prison system in the early 20th century in fact consisted of three separate systems: state prison buildings which resembled those in the North; the county chain gang; and the state prison farm. During the 19th century, the state prison system consisted of a number of prison buildings, several of which had been built prior to the Civil War to house white offenders, and a wide variety of huts or lean-to shelters within stockades built on plantations, near coal mines and pine forests where turpentine was extracted, as well as rolling cages that could be pushed along the railroad tracks laid down by black prisoners. In addition to these settlements or camps operated by private companies which leased state convicts, punishment in the post-Civil War South also included a county system of hiring out vagrants and petty offenders to local farmers.

The focus of this paper, however, is restricted to an examination of the state penal systems. The analysis is based mainly on secondary sources. In reading the major studies of the social and economic history of blacks during the late 19th century, I was struck by how few references there were to the prison system. In my search through the sociological and historical journals, I also found very little written about punishment in the South. This article draws extensively on a small number of published studies of the prison systems in certain states, and on several master's theses and Ph.D. dissertations on southern penology.

To understand the political and economic forces which shaped the post-Civil War approach to crime control and punishment, it is necessary to keep in mind that plantation justice tended to siphon blacks out of the state punishment system in the pre-Civil War period. Slaves were punished according to slave codes, so that the criminal justice system which emerged prior to the Civil War was for whites only. Although the abolition of slavery led to a number of important changes in state criminal justice systems, there was also considerable continuity in how white and black offenders were treated and controlled. Certainly the locus of criminal prosecutions

---

* Correspondence to: Box 1006, Station A, Toronto, Ontario, Canada M5W 1G5.

and punishment changed when slavery ended. But the infliction of "separate but unequal" measures of pain on white and black felons remained, for slavery continued to haunt just about every aspect of social and economic organization in the post-Civil War South.

Many historians point to the fiscal insolvency of the southern state governments during Reconstruction to explain why the convict lease system was popular (Green, 1969). Although states on both sides of the Mason–Dixon line had experimented with leasing out prison buildings and the labor of prisoners to private contractors, most adopted some form of the contract system whereby prisoners worked for outside employers and labored under the supervision of outside foremen but remained under the disciplinary control of a warden and guards.[1] The practice of leasing state prisoners to private companies and relinquishing responsibility for supervising and disciplining them became widely entrenched in the South after the Civil War. Many of the prisons built before the war were destroyed during it and because there was no money to erect new penitentiary buildings, leasing was adopted.[2] This arrangement had considerable fiscal appeal, since state governments were paid hundreds of thousands of dollars by the companies leasing convicts.

However, convict leasing appealed to governments not simply because of its fiscal utility. Hiring out convicts to planters, mining companies, and railroad contractors on a long-term basis was not designed solely to rid the state of a prison problem. In a real sense, the convict lease system was a functional replacement for slavery; it provided an economic source of cheap labor and a political means to re-establish white supremacy in the South.

The system of plantation justice prior to the Civil War and the state penal systems after the war were the principal mechanisms whereby black crime was punished in the southern United States during the 19th century. One way of accounting for the functional similarity between the two systems is to realize that both slaves and ex-slaves were "problem populations," and one of the paradoxes which characterize problem populations is that they represent both a potential threat to the existing system of government and class rule, and a potential resource. Plantation slavery was an important cause of economic growth (North, 1961:189). In addition to being valuable economic resources, however, slaves were a problem population, or rather a troublesome property.

Similarly, slaves freed legally by the 13th Amendment in 1865 were both a threat to social relations and a useful resource, a dangerous population which stood in need of control but also a welcome source of manpower. In this respect, the ex-slaves can be analyzed as a surplus population which, according to Marxist theory, "is both useful and menacing to the accumulation of capital" (Spitzer, 1975:643). The fact that the emancipated slaves represented both a dangerous class and, in the words Marx used to describe the reserve army of labor, "a mass of human material always ready for exploitation" (Marx, 1967:631), helps to explain the rise of the convict lease system.

---

1. In 1798 the wardens of the houses of correction in Massachusetts were permitted to hire out prisoners to anyone who would furnish employment (Zimmerman, 1947:23). The state of Kentucky leased both its prison building and prisoners in 1825 (Sneed, 1860:182). Officials in Alabama and Louisiana resorted to leasing when prison industries failed in the 1840s. In Louisiana, however, the government stipulated that convicts had to be employed within the walls of the Baton Rouge penitentiary (Carleton, 1971:9).

2. Southern prisons were a prime target for the invading Union armies. In 1863 General Sherman ordered his troops to destroy the Mississippi State Prison—a munitions factory. Sherman's men also burned Georgia's penitentiary. When Nashville was besieged by Union troops, the guards at the penitentiary fled, and 240 inmates destroyed the building and fled to the countryside. A similar situation arose in Virginia where prison inmates ransacked the buildings after the guards left. Union armies burned Alabama's prison and partially destroyed the Arkansas prison. The Baton Rouge penitentiary was so dilapidated that convicts were removed to the New Orleans workhouse and military stockades. With the exception of the Texas penitentiary, every southern prison was extensively damaged during the Civil War, either by the Union Army or as a result of misuse by confederate authorities (Carter, 1964:29; Zimmerman, 1947:50).

PUNISHMENT UNDER SLAVERY

The existence of slavery made two separate systems of punishment necessary. Through plantation justice, masters sought to impose an absolute system of authority on their bondsmen. Like monarchical law, the slave codes prescribed barbaric and public punishments. The heads of 16 rebels in Louisiana were "stuck upon poles along the Mississippi River as a grim warning to other slaves" (Stampp, 1956:135). The northern prison reformer, Matthew Carey, was sickened to learn that South Carolina had enacted a law "for burning alive slaves who murder their masters" (Carey, 1831:12).

By turning punishment into a public spectacle, rulers are able to legitimate an absolute control over their subjects (Foucault, 1977). At public executions in monarchical Europe, the bodies of the condemned were visibly destroyed in front of the social body. In a similar fashion, plantation slaves were made to witness the awesome force of their white masters at public hangings and whippings. The most widely used plantation punishment was whipping: "no other penalty carried the same meaning or so embodied the social relations of the peculiar institution. The lash in the white hand on the black back was a symbol of bondage recognized by both races" (Wade, 1964:186).

In the cities where slavery posed a more complex problem of control, runaway slaves and hirelings caught without travel passes were detained in local jails and houses of correction. For a fee, masters could send disobedient bondsmen to municipal jails for a whipping. But penal custody was not suitable, since it deprived slave owners of labor. The very idea of imprisonment as a punishment for crimes committed by slaves was a contradiction. The African slave was already a prisoner. Whereas the white felon was punished for violating norms of freedom, slaves were punished for rejecting the rules of bondage. Any idea of rehabilitative confinement for slaves threatened the philosophical basis of the peculiar institution.[3]

The existence of slavery also "made it ideologically difficult to acknowledge the existence of a white criminal class and to legislate for its control" (Hindus, 1980:xix). The South was a closed society in which, ideally, all whites belonged to the master class and all blacks were slaves. Perceptions of class in South Carolina, as Hindus has shown, permitted only black and white, and the pattern of class relationships was threatened by groups which exhibited status inconsistency: poor whites, white criminals, and free blacks. The equation between race and class was legitimated by the existence of separate systems of law and punishment but also different conceptions of the kinds of illegality of which whites and blacks were capable.

White criminality was linked to an inability to control passion. This conception, as Hindus (1980:243) has pointed out, led to a philosophy of punishment that stressed vengeance; since crimes of passion were deemed unavoidable, reformation of the criminal was also considered difficult. If only a small number of whites committed crimes of passion, and if slaves were punished on the plantation, then it would seem that the region had no need for the penitentiary. Nevertheless, with the exception of Florida and the Carolinas, every southern state had erected an Auburn-type prison by 1850.[4] However, these institutions were not as large as their counterparts in the North, and the utopian impulse which gave rise to pentitentiary construction in Jacksonian

---

3. Barnes (1972), Lewis (1965), Rothman (1971), and others have illuminated parts of the process whereby northern prison reform drew inspiration from and served to legitimate an emerging moral and political community founded on the philosophical principles of liberal democracy. Southern political culture was aristocratic and ascriptive, and so there was not the same need to rationalize the legal and penal systems. Also, southern leaders could not ignore the fact that northern prison reformers were abolitionists and critics of the methods used to discipline slaves (Carleton, 1971:5).

4. The Baton Rouge penitentiary had 240 cells, the Texas penitentiary, 225 cells, and prisons in Alabama and Mississippi, 208 and 150 cells respectively (McKelvey, 1977:47).

New York and Pennsylvania was missing. Plantation owners were prone to see northern penology as an "impractical scheme for the amelioration of the world" (Stampp, 1956:420).

Southern states were more likely than northern ones to rely on extra-legal and informal systems of authority: vigilantism instead of professional police forces, dueling as an alternative for litigation, the lash and the noose as much cheaper expedients than regular prison discipline (Hindus, 1980:33). The penchant for business rather than institutional solutions for crime also persisted after the Civil War. The southern reliance on custom and informal authority to settle disputes arising between whites and to control its slave population helps to explain why after the Civil War there was no opposition to the brutal convict lease, itself a highly informal system of repression. State governments in the 1870s and 1880s abdicated responsibility for overseeing discipline at the prison camps. State officials had no legal power to supervise the work done at the camps, or to regulate health conditions. It was not just prison labor that was leased, but full responsibility for custody was signed over to private companies, so that the nature of confinement hinged totally on whatever informal structures the lessees decided to implement. Working and living conditions were left to the discretion of the private lessees.

Crime control in the antebellum South was subordinated to race control. With the abolition of slavery, alternative forms of race control had to be found, and race control naturally became a major aim in crime control. Indeed, the system of crime control — the convict lease — resembled slavery in many respects, in the political and economic functions it performed, of course, but also in its organization, terminology, and relationship to the wider society. Neither slavery nor the convict lease were subjected to close public scrutiny.

EX-SLAVES: A PROBLEM POPULATION

The 13th and 14th Amendments to the U.S. Constitution, ratified by Congress in 1865 and 1868 created a new class of offenders.[5] Blacks, who comprised more than 50 percent of the population of Louisiana, Mississippi, and South Carolina, were now to be punished as free men (Carleton, 1971:44). The size of the population punishable by some form of custody also increased in the late 1860s when state governments ratified constitutions which reduced the scope of offenses punishable by death (Stampp, 1965:172). Although the Republicans who had taken over the instruments of government in the Confederate states by 1867 promised fair trials and equal treatment for black offenders, political and economic realities were such that, although the rights of black defendants and prisoners were acknowledged *de jure,* these rights could not be recognized *de facto,* without posing a challenge to the economic superiority of the white race.

Following President Lincoln's Emancipation Proclamation, thousands of slaves fled from the plantations, wandered through the countryside, and flocked to the cities where they lived in crowded tenements. Refugee slaves rejoiced in freedom and "for a time many of them took special pleasure in making use of one of its chief prerogatives: the right to move from place to place without the consent of any white man" (Stampp, 1965:121). Union armies had to deal with the problems of vagrancy and destitution amongst the freedmen. Able-bodied men and boys were conscripted, arrested, and put to work loading and unloading military supplies, and placed on abandoned plantations. During the period of presidential reconstruction which lasted until

---

5. On January 1, 1863, President Lincoln as commander-in-chief of the United States armies issued the Emancipation Proclamation which declared free those slaves still in rebel hands, but not slaves in the Border states. The importance of this declaration was mainly symbolic, since for those blacks still in the Confederacy, freedom depended on the progress of the Union armies. Legally and practically speaking, it was the 13th Amendment, approved by Congress in February and ratified in December 1865, which freed the slaves. But the 14th Amendment, ratified by Congress in July 1868, was the real piece of enabling legislation that accorded blacks the rights of citizenship. They were no longer property, but guaranteed all the legal rights of citizens of the United States, including equal protection of the laws (Stampp, 1965:135).

1867, when the radical Republicans took control of the southern state governments, the Johnsonian legislatures introduced the Black Codes. More than just vagrancy laws, their purpose was "to keep the Negro exactly what he was: a propertyless rural laborer under strict controls, without political rights, and with inferior legal rights" (Stampp, 1965:79).

In effect, the Black Codes brought back a form of the hiring-out system that had existed under slavery. Blacks without visible means of support were obliged by law to hire themselves out during the first 10 days of January. Those without labor contracts or who broke their contracts were prosecuted as vagrants and sentenced to hard labor on local plantations. Blacks in South Carolina had to obtain special licenses for non-agricultural employment. Mississippi prevented freedmen from renting land. Local communities restricted the movement of the ex-slave population by requiring them to obtain travel passes (Novak, 1978:1;Stampp, 1965:80).

Although the radical Republicans in Congress proclaimed that blacks would be granted basic political freedoms, such freedoms were meaningless given their economic destitution. Both political and economic stability in Reconstruction years depended on the continued participation of the black population in agricultural labor.[6] Economic assistance was not provided, and the Freedman's Bureau, although empowered to regulate labor contracts, ended up enforcing regulations which tied the freedmen to the land. The number of blacks working as artisans, mechanics, and shopkeepers declined rapidly after 1865. Ex-slaves formed a large pool of landless labor.

Nothing less than sweeping land reform would have ended the plantation system. Southern planters and northern adventurers leased many of the plantations which had been confiscated by the federal government. Freedmen were forced to work on them for extremely low wages or payment in the form of food, shelter, and clothing. Sharecropping arrangements, whereby the ex-slave, instead of working for a wage, rented plots of land and paid to the landowner a proportion of the crop, sprang up throughout the region. The advantage of sharecropping over wage payments was that it gave planters superior control over their labor force. Croppers were compelled to purchase food, clothing, and tools from the plantation owners at high prices, and they frequently discovered that their crops failed to pay for their purchases. A system of debt peonage arose whereby "insolvent croppers unable to repay debts from one year to another were required by law to work indefinitely for the same unscrupulous planter" (Meier and Rudwick, 1966:141).

The Black Codes, sharecropping, and both the county and state systems of hiring out vagrants and felons to agricultural or industrial employers aimed to achieve the same objective: to prevent the ex-slaves from obtaining the status and the rights enjoyed by wage workers. Plantation owners stressed that ex-bondsmen needed compulsory labor. Former masters bewailed the fact that old hands were passing away, and fewer laborers were, in the words of an Arkansas planter "trained from childhood to hard labor" (cited in Litwack, 1979:344). Even the Freedman's Bureau emphasized that the transient black population needed discipline and control.

A THREAT AND A RESOURCE

Given the complete destitution of the freedman, it is not surprising that the ex-slaves were viewed as a dangerous class. Their powerlessness explains why state governments had no second thoughts about implementing a brutal system of forced labor outside the walls of prisons or jails. However, one of the paradoxes which characterize "problem populations" is that they can represent both a potential threat to the existing system of government and class rule, but also a potential resource. To account for the profitability and brutality of the state systems after

---

6. The Civil War is viewed as a turning point in U.S. economic history, signalling the end of plantation agriculture and the rise of industrial capitalist culture. However, this shift was extremely gradual. Certainly slaves were employed in industry and construction, while after the war blacks were still tied to the land (Starobin, 1970).

1865, it is important to keep in mind that the ex-slaves were a threat to social and economic organization, but also an economic resource—a pool of cheap labor.

The system of leasing on the county level was a dragnet for sharecroppers who left their plots. Most states prescribed criminal punishments for failure to fulfill labor contracts. Vagrants, debtors, and petty thieves tried in county courts were released to planters who paid their fines. Since the planter typically charged for feeding and sheltering offenders, it took the average county misdemeanant many years to work off his or her debt. In one county in Georgia, officials sentenced blacks to long stretches of hard labor for what amounted to improper demeanour — spitting, swearing and trespassing (Novak, 1978:35). County courts were virtual employment bureaus. Company agents travelled from county court to county court to pick up men and women. Often offenders who had worked off their debt were arrested while returning home, prosecuted as vagrants, and returned for another stint of unpaid toil (Carter, 1964:95).

Both male and female state convicts were an important resource. Under slavery black women did field labor as well as domestic work. They also worked as sharecroppers and tenant farmers alongside men in the post-slavery period. Moreover, as Angela Davis (1981:89) has stated, men and women "were frequently housed together in the same stockade and were yoked together during the workday." More men were leased out than women: 34 black females — less than three percent of the black prison population — were detained by the state of Georgia in 1878 (Green, 1969:282). Although crime control both during and after slavery fell more heavily on black males, women felons could be found in state lease camps, and most black female misdemeanants were farmed out as field hands and domestics. In spite of the larger number of male prisoners at railroad building sites and on plantations, the fact that some women were sent there as well reveals that the system of punishment aimed to achieve more than simply crime control.

Demand for cheap labor was urgent on the railroads. In the first years of Reconstruction, prisoners in Georgia, Louisiana, and North Carolina were leased to a variety of railroad companies (Zimmerman, 1947:62). Although little data on crime rates and patterns of sentencing are available in secondary source materials, it is still possible to conclude that the mobilization of cheap labor was a key element in crime control on the state level. The convict lease was designed both to punish and deter crime and to mobilize cheap labor.

In the first instance, the decision to lease state convicts to private employers occurred because the radical state governments lacked the financial resources to build new facilities. But the acceptance of a policy which failed to guarantee adequate treatment or discipline for the felon must be seen in relation to the failure of the radical Reconstruction governments to prevent the white landholders and businessmen from implementing new forms of economic control over the black laboring population. Ultimately, the economic mechanisms used to extract a surplus from the landless blacks were buttressed by the criminal justice system. Before resorting to vigilante action, ex-planters and local officials used the penal system to control unruly blacks who withheld their labor.

Southern landowners, who believed the gap between themselves and the laboring class to be permanent and unbridgeable (Wagstaff, 1970:4), also feared an uprising from below. No wonder they were unwilling to relax traditional controls over the black labor force. The very terminology of slavery was retained under the convict lease system. Employers used the slaveholders' classification of laborers, according to their ability to work, into first, second, third, fourth, and fifth class hands (Carter, 1964:63). Able-bodied males were referred to as 'full hands'; women and children prisoners were known as 'half-hands.' Company employers were reluctant to rent 'dead hands'—prisoners too old or too sick to work (McKelvey, 1977:213).

Camp discipline was repressive. It mirrored plantation discipline insofar as prisoners were whipped for poor work. The lease system perpetuated the tradition of slavery in another respect: it did not discriminate between male and female labor. Men and women were often housed together in the same stockade. A resolution passed by the Texas State Convention of Negroes in 1883 condemned "the practice of yoking or chaining male and female convicts together" (cited in Davis, 1981:89). Women were given the same punishments as men. Several witnesses—guards and overseers—testified before a legislative committee in Georgia in 1870 that the women convicts who worked on the railroads were "whipped on their bare rumps in the presence of men" (Zimmerman, 1947:100).

While leasing was less brutal in the early years of Reconstruction than after the Democrats gained power, it was impossible to prevent abuses, since convicts were scattered throughout the region, and state officials usually yielded all disciplinary rights and responsibilities to the company overseers. Although some states had penitentiary boards, their members either sided with company officials, or lacked the power to do anything about inhuman conditions. As a result, black convicts throughout the South were starved, chained to each other at night in overcrowded, dirty stockades, overworked and forced to continue working while sick, and whipped, occasionally to death.

Legislatures pressured by landowners and businessmen to do something about the unreliability of their labor supply agreed to expand leasing, as long as the prisoners rented out were ex-slaves. In 1866 there were 300 black and only 25 white convicts in Georgia, and there were 212 black and 85 white felons detained at the dilapidated penitentiary in Baton Rouge, Louisiana in 1868. Mississippi locked up 259 blacks and 105 whites in 1869, and in 1870 the combined population of the penitentiary, city prison, and county jails in South Carolina included 584 black and 148 white offenders (Carleton, 1971:15; Taylor, 1924:18; Wharton, 1965:240; Zimmerman, 1947:62).

The radical Republicans failed to eradicate the repressive system of agriculture. By the early 1870s, railroad promoters, industrialists, and entrepreneurs with connections in New York or Boston began to exert greater influence on political affairs in the region. The average period of radical Republican state rule was under three-and-a-half years. No radical government remained in office more than a decade (Woodward, 1971:22). The defeat of the radical Republican regimes was inevitable, since they comprised a very unstable alliance of so-called 'carpetbaggers' from the North, southern collaborators or 'scalawags', and emancipated slaves. Success at election time depended upon black voter turn-out, which was high in those states which still had federal troops, but declined markedly in other states as a result of the vigilante tactics of the conservative Democrats. Opposition to radical Reconstruction existed from the outset amongst the ex-slaveholders and ex-Confederate soldiers drawn to the Democrats. Yet their ability to oust the Republican governments varied by state. Whereas the Democrats, or Redeemers as they are often called, took over in Georgia and Tennessee before 1872, other states were not redeemed until 1877. The struggle for 'Home' rule, as the Democrats put it, produced violent incidents throughout the South. Victory was assured, however, when the northern ruling class realized that "the southern conservatives did not represent the pre-Civil War ruling class but rather the self-same socioeconomic forces as itself" (Camejo, 1976:128).

The Democratic state regimes were business-based and allied with northern railway and mining interests. Ties between northern businessmen with resource interests in the South and southern legislators help to account for the tremendous expansion of the state prison populations in the late 1870s, and the transformation of leasing from a temporary expedient into an established means of providing cheap labor. In addition to being sent to plantations and railroad camps, state convicts worked in mines, in factories, and in turpentine woods. Unskilled, labor-intensive work was the rule. The idea of giving black felons skilled work, such as cabinetmaking, shoemaking, and iron manufacturing, never crossed the minds of the politicians and businessmen who shaped the convict lease system. Guards in the camps had no trade skills. They were paid meagre wages, and were often replaced by trusted prisoners.

The extent to which the Democrats used the state penal systems to exploit the labor of the ex-slave population is revealed by the growth in the number of prisoners. Criminal laws were enacted which increased the number of serious crimes. Democrats in Mississippi secured passage of that state's "pig" law which defined the theft of property worth more than $10—including cattle and swine—as grand larceny, punishable by up to five years of hard labor (Wharton, 1965:237). In 1875 a similar law in Georgia made stealing hogs a felony. North Carolina courts did not distinguish between petty and grand larceny, so that a person could get three to 10 years for stealing a couple of chickens (Logan, 1964:193). These laws increased the size of the prison labor pool. In Mississippi it increased nearly 300 percent in less than four years, from 272 convicts in 1874 to 1,072 by the end of 1877. Two years after Georgia's new law was enacted, the size of the convict population had more than tripled, from 432 to 1,441 (Novak, 1978:32; Wharton, 1965:237; Woodward, 1971:213).

The black criminal population represented a threat to the economic supremacy of the white race, but also a resource that could be easily exploited. Crime control and economic oppression were one and the same thing in the South after the Democrats seized power. The pig laws were designed to eliminate the threat posed by a wandering army of propertyless blacks, but also to channel their labor into socially productive use.

THE LESSEES AND SOUTHERN INDUSTRIALIZATION

If Reconstruction is considered a later phase of "the victory of industrial capitalism over the fetters of the plantation economy" (Moore, 1967:151), it can be argued that the restoration of conservative Democratic rule represented the final phase in the reconstruction of U.S. society as a unified, industrial, capitalist civilization. Neither increasing fear of a dangerous class nor the fiscal self-interest of the state governments can entirely account for the growth of prison populations in the 1880s. Economic modernization of the South depended on the mobilization of cheap convict labor. As Woodward (1971) has shown, it was the Redeemers, not the radicals, who laid the foundation for an industrial order. They guaranteed northern financial and industrial interests unprecedented economic freedom. Southern politicians introduced laws which made it quite profitable for the northern corporate octopus to thrust its tentacles south of the Potomac.

The outfits leasing state convicts were northern subsidiaries. Yet, company directors held public office themselves, or knew their way around state capitols.[7] The virtual identity of interest between business and government helps to explain the fact that the South kept pace industrially with the rest of the country (Woodward, 1971:140). The region's untouched natural resources drew lumber syndicates, mining companies, and railroad interests from the North. Convicts supplied the labor needed for mining and lumbering, as slaves had done in the antebellum period.

Railroad companies employed large numbers of convicts. During the 1870s, 2,650 miles of track were laid in the states east of the Mississippi, and over 14,000 miles were added to this network in the following decade.[8] In 1884 more than 5,000 convicts worked on southern railroad building. In North Carolina alone, more than 1,800 miles of track were laid by prisoners between 1873 and 1893 (Carter, 1964:76). In 1886 Mississippi's penitentiary was leased to the Gulf and Ship Island Railroad Company. The first two Redeemer governors in this state were both railroad attorneys (Camejo, 1976:194). In the Carolinas, the Cape Fear and Yadkin Valley, and the Greenwood and Augusta were the principal railroad companies employing prisoners. Elsewhere,

---

7. Joseph E. Brown and Alfred H. Colquitt in Georgia participated in many northern ventures. Tennessee Governor James D. Porter was a director of the Tennessee Coal and Iron Company (Camejo, 1976:190).
8. One hundred and eighty new railroads were incorporated in the 1880s. More than $150 million was invested in railroads—excluding those in the trans-Mississippi states—between 1879 and 1881 (Woodward, 1971:120).

there were myriad others: the New Orleans and Pacific; the Mississippi Valley Railroad Company; the Alabama Railroad Company; and, of course, the Tennessee Coal Iron and Railroad Company (Zimmerman, 1947:123).

Leasing served the interests of Redeemer politicians. Colonel Arthur S. Colyar was leader of the pro-industrial Whig wing of the Democratic party in Tennessee, and general counsel for the Tennessee Coal Iron and Railroad Company. He arranged for this company to lease the entire convict population in the state for $101,000 a year (Woodward, 1971:215). "Penitentiary rings" were formed in almost every state. Georgia's Civil War governor, Joseph E. Brown, who became a prominent Democrat, amassed a fortune by using convicts in his coal mining operations in Dade County (Stampp, 1965:161). He cannily offered the legislature a dollar more per convict than anyone else. Beginning with 100 men at $11 each in 1874, his companies took on more and more prisoners (Roberts, 1960:400; Taylor, 1942).

Another man who got rich from convict labor was Edmund Richardson, a Mississippi speculator and one of the richest cotton planters in the world. Several businessmen made money just by subleasing prisoners. Jones S. Hamilton was a southern-style robber baron. In addition to his interests in race tracks, gas works, and real estate, he made a fortune from subleasing convicts to railroads and plantations in Mississippi (Wharton, 1965:239). The growth of monopolies in the country at large was reflected in the consolidation of the convict business in the South. Georgia leased its prisoners to three interconnected companies. Tennessee leased its prison population to one lessee in 1884. By the mid-1880s both the number of convicts and the length of prison sentences had risen considerably (McKelvey, 1977:200).

Political Foundations of Penal Repression

The restoration of Home rule, which occurred with the victory of the Democrats at the polls, was made possible because extra-legal means of coercion were used to intimidate black voters. Terrorism was one way to redeem the South; using the machinery of crime control was another. Thus, state penal policies whereby more and more blacks were subjected to perpetual hard labor helped to increase the cohesion of a white South.

Erikson (1966) and Kanter (1972) have shown that real or imaginary threats to community order will give rise, on the one hand, to harsher treatment of those individuals or groups singled out as threats, and, on the other hand, will increase group solidarity. One of the ideological techniques used by the Democrats to gain control over southern legislatures in the 1870s was to brand the radical Republicans as traitors. The Redeemers played on the fears of the southern white population, describing the alliance of carpetbaggers, scalawags, and blacks, who were exercising their newly acquired right to vote and thereby keeping the Republicans in power, as a corrupt plot. The very foundations of southern civilization were allegedly threatened by the radical Republican state governments.

Charges of corruption and treason were brought against the so-called carpetbaggers and scalawags. Finally, the Democrats resorted to vigilante action to intimidate the black population. Groups of armed men calling themselves the White Line or the Red Shirts organized attacks on Republican meetings. The White League of New Orleans, which boasted more than 2,000 members, most of them ex-Confederate soldiers, represented the "military arm of the Democratic counterrevolution" (Camejo, 1976:151) in Louisiana. Radical Republican candidates were beaten up and threatened with death unless they withdrew. Vigilantes prevented blacks from getting to the polls on election day; white employers dismissed blacks who attended political meetings. The ultimate weapon was physical intimidation: between 40 and 80 black militant leaders were massacred at Vicksburg, Mississippi, in 1875 (Camejo, 1976:152). Against this background of extra-legal flogging and lynching, it is possible to understand why the brutality in the convict lease camps far exceeded the level needed to keep prisoners working. The ex-slaves represented a problem in crime control, and an opportunity to redefine the South as a white man's community.

The use of penal repression to consolidate white power can be demonstrated by contrasting the lease system under radical Republican rule and under Home rule. Whereas the Reconstruction governments adopted leasing by default, the Redeemers promoted leasing as the ideal policy for handling the black criminal population. As pointed out, the decision to lease convicts to companies in the private sector was adopted during Reconstruction when state treasuries were in financial collapse. But leasing was entrenched in the 1870s and 1880s after the Democrats returned to power.

Reconstruction governments in Louisiana, Mississppi, Alabama, and Arkansas lacked the capital necessary to rebuild prisons destroyed during the Civil War. The cost of financing penitentiary construction in North and South Carolina was one of the reasons why leasing was adopted in the first years of Reconstruction (Oliphant, 1916:4; Zimmerman, 1947:56). Moreover, leasing was thought to be a temporary measure that would be discontinued if the money could be found to build prison cell blocks.

The radical governments realized that convict labor could be profitably exploited, but did not feel justified sharing in the spoils. In looking at the financial agreements between the radical Republicans and the private lessees, it is evident that profit was *not* always the foremost consideration. Georgia and North Carolina received no money from railroad contractors employing convicts; Arkansas and Mississippi in the early years of Reconstruction actually compensated contractors for taking felons off their hands (Carter, 1964:45; Zimmerman, 1947:61). The man who leased the Chattahoochi prison-arsenal in Florida received bonuses amounting to $30,000 from the state (Zimmerman, 1947:54).

Although leasing was conceived as a temporary solution for overcrowding, the money needed to build prisons could not be found. The recession of 1873 increased the treasury debts of the radical governments still in power. The Democrats accused the radical regimes of extravagant spending and corrupt business practices. Their central election promise was economical administration.

Penitentiary policies were singled out to illustrate that radical Republicans sought to loot the state treasury. Wade Hampton, the Governor of South Carolina and a conservative *par excellence,* vowed to make the penitentiary self-supporting by sending 500 able-bodied convicts to railroad chain gangs. The Democrats in North Carolina shelved plans to build a penitentiary and sent the prisoners who had been confined in log huts at the building site to railroad camps throughout the state (McKelvey, 1977:204).

Criminal code revision and prison reform following the American Revolution of 1775 served in part to legitimate the political boundaries of the new states, especially Pennsylvania and New York (Barnes, 1972; Lewis, 1965; Rothman, 1971). In contrast, punishment in the South following the Civil War helped to reaffirm the boundaries of the South as a white community. Thus, the transition to Home rule was symbolically legitimated by harsher punishment for the black felon. Increased severity was reflected in a total philosophical acceptance of leasing and a deliberate commitment to profit from punishment. Whereas the radical Republicans had attempted to save money by leasing prisoners, the Democrats in Mississippi, Georgia, Tennessee, and Florida received anywhere from $40,000 to $100,000 annually from leasing convicts (Zimmerman, 1947:66,123,151,155). Texas' governor announced that a lease signed in 1878 put "more cash into the treasury in one year than has been paid from the establishment of the penitentiary" (Zimmerman, 1947:140).

The ex-slaves were singled out as a threat to the stability of a social order based on white supremacy. Hence, punitive arrangements had to be extraordinarily severe. The Democrats discontinued state supervision of the prison camps. Inspections were infrequent or perfunctory. The whereabouts of many stockades was unknown, since convicts were subleased. In 1874 the president of Louisiana's penitentiary board declared "the convicts may be in Plaquemine, Iberville, or at the bottom of the Mississippi for all I know" (cited in Carter, 1964:43).

RACE CONTROL AND CLASS STRUCTURE

Southern state penal systems were themselves instruments of social stratification. Blacks comprised over 95 percent of most prison populations. In Georgia in 1878, 1,122 of the 1,239 convicts were black (Green, 1969:282). In addition to its economic function, leasing represented an effective method of segregating white and black offenders, and thereby reaffirming the age-old equation between race and class which emancipation threatened to dissolve. In most states, black felons toiled outside, while efforts were made to keep white felons employed within penitentiary walls. Officials justified this policy on the grounds that special security measures were necessary to ensure that white prisoners did not escape. No doubt this view can be traced to the antebellum stereotype of the white criminal as someone predisposed to commit violent and desperate acts.

There was almost complete segregation of white and black prisoners. While black felons in Mississippi worked on plantations and railroads, not a single white left the penitentiary (Wharton, 1965:240). No white convicts worked in the Tennessee mines (Carter, 1964:54). It was rare for a jury in Florida to send a white man to one of the convict camps (Powell, 1970:332). After all, the philosophical justification for the convict lease system, certainly after the Democrats returned to power, lay in the view that blacks needed compulsory labor. Contractors in Alabama were forbidden to mix white and black prisoners (Novak, 1978:32). Local sheriffs in Mississippi made sure that whites were never put in chain gangs (Wharton, 1965:235). In Florida black convicts outnumbered whites 20 to 1. "It was possible," a camp overseer wrote, "to send a negro to prison on almost any pretext, but difficult to get a white man there unless he committed some very heinous crime" (Powell, 1970:332).

Crime control in the antebellum South meant race control. Slaves were punished on the plantation, and harsh measures were necessary to legitimate the absolute authority of the white master. With the end of slavery, alternative forms of race control were introduced, and the system of criminal justice became a key element in keeping blacks politically and economically subservient. Whereas prior to the Civil War crime control was a problem in slavery, one of the consequences of abolition was that race control became the central aim of crime control, and measures of punishment were brutal in the extreme.

The notion that criminal slaves could be rehabilitated was a contradiction in terms. Like exconvicts and ex-mental patients, the freedmen were rarely allowed to forget that they had once been the property of their white masters. Thus, southern penology was characterized by racist theories of black criminality, and no attempt was made to offer any rehabilitative, theoretical justification for forced labor. There was no rhetoric of reform behind which to disguise the brutality of living arrangements. The convict camps were dispersed throughout the rural South so that the public ignored them. George Cable, (1969) a man who eventually left the South to settle in Massachusetts, provided the only liberal attack on the convict lease system. In the mid-1880s he attempted to gain admission to various camps. He was turned away at the gates, and told to direct his inquiries to the government, but his letters to state officials were unanswered. Whereas inmates in the North produced several interesting memoirs about life behind bars, there are no prisoners' accounts of southern prison life during this period.

In the South no one apologized for what was done to prisoners, and no one wrote that black felons were being hurt rather than helped, or suggested that they spend time reading Bibles or in vocational training workshops. Part of criminal justice strategy in the northern states, certainly during the Jacksonian period, was to erect penitentiaries that would inspire awe and dread in the hearts of whoever passed by them. The penitentiary at Cherry Hill in Philadelphia, which had cost $775,000 by 1835, was the most expensive building of any kind in the United States (Teeters and Shearer, 1957:74). In contrast, the southern camps consisted of make-shift huts in which convicts slept chained together on wooden benches. Rolling cages were used on the railroads. Dogs and armed patrols, rather than granite and stone walls, maintained security. Runaways were shot on sight, or brought back and punished by being strung up by the thumbs or shut in airtight boxes — a punishment known as sweating — which caused the body to swell and bleed (Powell, 1970:8).

Living conditions for the predominantly black convict populations were inhuman. This is demonstrated by the high mortality rates. In 1883 a physician in Alabama estimated that most convicts died within three years. In that year 36 percent of the men working at the Milner coal mine died. The annual death rate at the camps run by the Greenwood and Augusta Railroad reached 53 percent (Zimmerman, 1947:160). Mortality rates were also high in Louisiana. The editor of the New Orleans *Daily Picayne* suggested quite seriously that execution would be more humane than a prison sentence (Cited in Carleton, 1971:37).

Although disease and accidents contributed to the high death rates, one cannot ignore the effects which deliberate cruelty and neglect had on prisoners. Convicts at the Inman mines in Tennessee worked all day in the mud and at night slept in wet clothes (Zimmerman, 1947:163). The prisoners who laid down the track through the Canay swamps in Mississippi suffered from malaria and pneumonia. According to a report in the Raymond *Gazette* on March 8, 1885, convicts were "placed in water ranging to their knees, and in almost nude state they spaded rooty ground, their bare feet chained together. They were compelled to attend to the calls of nature as they stood, their thirst compelling them to drink water in which they deposit their excrement" (cited in Foreman and Tatum, 1938:263).

In Florida, the work of "chipping" trees at the turpentine camps was dangerous. Prisoners stooping continuously to hack at the trunks of the pine trees had to contend with heat, mosquitoes, and snakes (Powell, 1970:29). According to a report on conditions at the Dade Coal Company, tabled in Georgia's House of Representatives, prisoners had to "lie in mud and water to get out the daily amount of coal that will save them from the whipping boss" (cited in Taylor, 1942:126).

Living conditions in the lease camps were far worse than on the average plantation, and convicts were not as well protected from hazardous and dangerous work as industrial slaves had been. Job safety was a concern of the mining and tunnelling contractors who hired bondsmen, for if a slave were killed or injured as a result of a cave-in, explosion, fire, or flood, the employer had to compensate the slave's owner (Starobin, 1970:45). There was no such incentive to protect the black convict. A machinist from Wilmington, North Carolina explained that a convict "works in the worst places, because if he dies it is a small loss" (cited in Logan, 1964:192). South Carolina's prison warden admitted in 1880 that "casualties would have been far less frequent if convicts were property having a value to preserve" (cited in Oliphant, 1916:6).

CONCLUSION

Both criminal justice procedure and penology in the southern United States between 1865 and 1890 were shaped by local economic and political conditions, rather than by the assumptions, theories, and methods embodied in policing, prosecutorial, and penal practice elsewhere in the country. The 13th Amendment created a wandering army of ex-slaves, and an immediate crisis in crime control. It was not just that crime rates rose, but that the size of the population punishable by some form of custody doubled. The crisis was partly solved by leasing convicts out to private companies engaged in labor-intensive economic projects.

But the convict lease system also served a more explicit economic function: it was one of several instruments used to prevent the ex-slaves from obtaining the status and rights enjoyed by wage workers. The demand for cheap labor by companies engaged in railroad building, mining, agriculture, and other businesses helps to explain why leasing was so profitable. No one opposed the cruel and inhumane conditions which existed in the convict camps because both the state governments as lessors and the companies as lessees profited from the arrangement. Moreover, the harsh and unequal treatment which was accorded to blacks as a result of the leasing system symbolically reinforced the age-old equation between race and class in the wider society.

During the 1880s, the contract system of convict labor was abolished in the northern states, and replaced by a piece-price system, partly as a result of strenuous lobbying by the labor movement.[9] In the still predominantly rural Cotton Belt, unions restricted entry to blacks, and only objected to leasing when their interests were directly affected—if prisoners were used as strikebreakers, for example (Bloch, 1965; Grob, 1960; Mandel, 1955). Southern legislatures would not have listened to union protests anyway, since profits from the convict business made up more than 10 percent of government revenues in some states (Carter, 1964:92).

The convict lease system was an economic substitute for slavery, but also a political replacement, insofar as it helped to redefine the boundaries of the South on the basis of color. Attempts to provide the freedmen with civil and political rights during Reconstruction failed; the Redeemer governments systematically deprived the freedmen of economic opportunities, and through vagrancy laws, sharecropping arrangements, and disenfranchisement, enforced a new kind of class rule on what was, after all, a problem population. The convict lease system was an ultimate but very effective mechanism for keeping blacks politically and economically subservient.

REFERENCES

Adamson, Christopher R.
    1982   "Hard Labor: The form and function of imprisonment in 19th century America." Unpublished Ph.D. dissertation, Princeton University.
Barnes, Harry E.
    1972   The Story of Punishment. Montclair, N.J.: Patterson Smith.
    [1930]
Bloch, Herman D.
    1965   "Labor and the Negro, 1866–1910." Journal of Negro History 50 (July):163–184.
Cable, George W.
    1969   The Silent South. Montclair, N.J.: Patterson Smith.
    [1889]
Camejo, Peter
    1976   Racism, Revolution, and Reaction: The Rise and Fall of Radical Reconstruction. New York: Monad Press.
Carey, Matthew
    1831   Thoughts on Penitentiaries and Prison Discipline. Philadelphia: Clark and Raser.
Carleton, Mark T.
    1971   Politics and Punishment: The History of the Louisiana State Penal System. Baton Rouge: Louisiana State University Press.
Carter, Dan T.
    1964   "Politics and business: The convict lease system in the post-Civil War South." Master's thesis, University of Wisconsin.
Conley, John A.
    1982   "Economics and the social reality of prisons." Journal of Criminal Justice 10(1):25–35.

---

9. During the 1880s northern state legislatures somewhat reluctantly enacted laws restricting the market for prison goods. Both manufacturers and organized labor objected to the contract system whereby private businesses produced and sold convict-made shoes, brooms, chairs, and so on. One way to get around the anti-contract laws was to adopt the so-called piece-price system whereby contractors were prohibited entry into the prison, but the products of convict labor were turned over to outside firms at a specific price per item. In effect the piece-price system represented a return to the system of manufacturing under public account which had been popular in the early decades of the nineteenth century (Adamson, 1982:186).

568   ADAMSON

Davis, Angela Y.
    1981   Women, Race and Class. New York: Random House.
Erikson, Kai T.
    1966   Wayward Puritans: A Study in the Sociology of Deviance N.Y.: John Wiley and Sons.
Foreman, Paul B., and Tatum, Julian R.
    1938   "A short history of Mississippi's state penal system." Mississippi Law Journal 10 (April):
            255–277.
Foucault, Michel
    1977   Discipline and Punish. N.Y.: Pantheon Books.
Green, Fletcher M.
    1969   "Some aspects of the convict lease system in the southern states." Pp. 271–287 in J. Isaac Cope-
            land (ed.) Democracy in the Old South and Other Essays. Nashville: Vanderbilt University Press.
Grob, Gerald N.
    1960   "Organized labor and the Negro worker, 1865–1900." Labor History 1 (Spring):164–176.
Hindus, Michael S.
    1980   Prison and Plantation: Crime, Justice, and Authority in Massachusetts and South Carolina,
            1767–1878. Chapel Hill: University of North Carolina Press.
Kanter, Rosabeth M.
    1972   Commitment and Community. Cambridge, Mass.: Harvard University Press.
Lewis, W. David
    1965   From Newgate to Dannemora: The Rise of the Penitentiary in New York. Ithaca, N.Y.: Cornell
            University Press.
Litwack, Leon F.
    1979   Been in the Storm So Long: The Aftermath of Slavery. N.Y.: Alfred A. Knopf.
Logan, Frenise A.
    1964   The Negro in North Carolina, 1876–1894. Chapel Hill: University of North Carolina Press.
McKelvey, Blake
    1977   American Prisons: A History of Good Intentions. Montclair, N.J.: Patterson Smith.
    [1936]
Mandel, Bernard
    1955   "Samuel Gompers and the Negro workers, 1886–1914." Journal of Negro History 40 (January):
            34–60.
Marx, Karl
    1967   Capital. Volume 1. New York: International Publishers.
    [1867]
Meier, August, and Rudwick, Elliott M.
    1966   From Plantation to Ghetto. N.Y.: Hill and Wang.
Moore, Barrington, Jr.
    1967   Social Origins of Dictatorship and Democracy. London: Penguin.
North, Douglass C.
    1961   The Economic Growth of the United States, 1790–1860. Englewood Cliffs, N.J.: Prentice Hall.
Novak, Daniel A.
    1978   The Wheel of Servitude: Black Forced Labor After Slavery. Lexington, Ky.: University Press of
            Kentucky.
Oliphant, Albert D.
    1916   The Evolution of the Penal System of South Carolina from 1866 to 1916. Columbia, South
            Carolina: State Printer.
Powell, J.C.
    1970   The American Siberia: Or, 14 Years' Experience in a Southern Convict Camp. Montclair, N.J.:
    [1891] Patterson Smith.
Roberts, Derrell C.
    1960   "Joseph E. Brown and the convict lease system". Georgia Historical Quarterly 44 (December):
            399–410.
Rothman, David J.
    1971   The Discovery of the Asylum. Boston: Little, Brown and Co.
Rusche, Georg, and Kirchheimer, Otto
    1968   Punishment and Social Structure. New York: Russell and Russell.
    [1939]
Scull, Andrew T.
    1977   Decarceration. Englewood Cliffs, N.J.: Prentice Hall.
Sellin, Thorsten
    1976   Slavery and the Penal System. New York: Elsevier.
Sneed, William C.
    1860   A Report on the History and Mode of Management of the Kentucky Penitentiary. Frankfort, Ky.:
            J.B. Major, State Printer.

Spitzer, Steven
    1975   Toward a Marxian Theory of Deviance. Social Problems 22(June):638–651.
Stampp, Kenneth A.
    1956   The Peculiar Institution: Slavery in the Antebellum South. New York: Alfred A. Knopf.
    1965   The Era of Reconstruction, 1865–1877. New York: Alfred A. Knopf.
Starobin, Robert S.
    1970   Industrial Slavery in the Old South. New York: Oxford University Press.
Stout, Leon
    1934   "Origins and history of the Louisiana penitentiary." Master's thesis, Louisiana State University, Baton Rouge.
Taylor, Alrutheus A.
    1924   The Negro in South Carolina During the Reconstruction. Washington, D.C.: Association for the Study of Negro Life and History, Inc.
Taylor, A. Elizabeth
    1942   "The origin and development of the convict lease system in Georgia." Georgia Historical Quarterly 26 (March):113–128.
Tannenbaum, Frank
    1924   Darker Phases of the South. New York: G.P. Putnam's Sons.
Teeters, Negley K., and Shearer, John D.
    1957   The Prison at Philadelphia, Cherry Hill. New York: Columbia University Press.
Wade, Richard C.
    1964   Slavery in the Cities. New York: Oxford University Press.
Wagstaff, Thomas
    1970   "Call your old master — 'Master': Southern Political Leaders and Negro Labor during Reconstruction" Pp. 1–23 in M. Cantor (ed.), Black Labor in America. Westport, Conn.: Negro University Press.
Wharton, Vernon L.
    1965   The Negro in Mississippi, 1865–1890. New York: Harper Torchbooks.
    [1947]
Woodward, C. Vann
    1971   Origins of the New South, 1877–1913. Baton Rouge: Louisiana State University Press.
Zimmerman, Hilda J.
    1947   "Penal systems and penal reforms in the South since the Civil War." Unpublished Ph.D. dissertation, University of North Carolina, Chapel Hill.

[23]

Race, Labor, and Punishment in Postbellum Georgia*

MARTHA A. MYERS, *University of Georgia*

JAMES L. MASSEY, *Northern Illinois University*

This paper examines the relationship between the political economy and the organization of punishment in the state of Georgia between 1868 and 1936. Punishment at this time was well-suited to an agricultural mode of production, characterized by chronic labor shortages. Punishment was decentralized, involved forced labor under harsh conditions, and reflected the existence of a labor market grounded in racist assumptions about the nature of black and white labor. Despite extended State control over convicts and expiration of the convict lease in 1909, punishment retained its decentralized and exploitative character. Nevertheless, the demand for convict labor shifted from the private to the public sector. This shift entailed significant changes in the type of labor performed by convicts, thereby broadening demand to encompass the labor of both white and black convicts. Time series analysis suggests that these race differences in labor demand and changes in demand over time found clear expression in the frequency with which blacks and whites were incarcerated.

Criminologists have long contended that the political economy of a society profoundly shapes its system of punishment (Adamson 1983; Rusche [1933] 1978; Rusche and Kirchheimer 1939; Spitzer 1975, 1979). Feudal, mercantile, and capitalist modes of production each develop a system of punishment that reflects the productive activities of labor, its value, and the conditions under which it works (Michalowski 1985:225). Studies have used this perspective to explain both the rise of centralized penal institutions and the checkered history of labor within them. Primary interest has centered on systems of punishment in England, Europe, and the Northeastern United States (Adamson 1984; Dobash 1983; Gardner 1987; Hogg 1979; Miller 1980; Petchesky 1981).

Though its distinctive features are well known, punishment in the nineteenth-century American South has yet to receive similar attention. We know, for example, that the lynching and execution of Southern blacks reached extraordinary levels after the Civil War (Beck, Massey, and Tolnay 1988; Corzine, Huff-Corzine, and Creech 1988; Phillips 1986; Tolnay, Beck, and Massey 1989), with nonlethal punishment taking the brutal form of forced labor for private contractors (Ayers 1984; Carter 1964; Zimmerman 1947). To account for this form of punishment, researchers emphasize the use of the convict lease as a tool specifically designed to subordinate freedmen and exploit their labor for capital accumulation (Adamson 1983, 1984; Ayers 1984; Mancini 1978; Shelden 1981). The relationship between the convict lease and Southern labor market conditions awaits more complete explication, however. Prison populations grew larger under the lease system, but research has yet to examine, much less explain, trends in the use of incarceration under either the convict lease or its replacements. In particular, few studies have explicitly linked changes in punishment over time with changes in general labor market conditions (for example, see Hawkins 1984, 1985).

Studies of Southern punishment have also invariably focused on black punishment because to the extent that systems of punishment reflected the demand for convict labor, they presumably reflected a demand for the labor of black not white convicts. When not ignored

---

* This article is a revision of a paper presented at the annual meetings of the American Society of Criminology, November 9-12, 1988, Chicago, Illinois. Correspondence to: Myers, Department of Sociology, University of Georgia, Athens, GA 30602.

entirely, the incarceration of whites achieves relevance only in comparison with the differential and harsher punishment of blacks. This neglect, while anomalous in itself, becomes especially glaring when we focus on early twentieth century punishment. Although whites continued to be incarcerated at a lower rate than blacks, their risk of being punished increased sharply after the turn of the century (Hawkins 1985; Myers and Sabol 1986).

This paper explores the relationship between the demand for labor and nonlethal punishment in one Southern state, Georgia. The first section examines the extent to which the form of punishment reflected the race-specific demand for labor and changes in that demand over time. In the second section, we develop the implications of the historical narrative and examine the relationship between labor demand and the frequency with which punishment was imposed on both white and black males.

Labor Demands and the Form of Punishment

Forms of Punishment, 1868 to 1936

In antebellum Georgia, criminal punishment took one form for blacks and another for whites (Adamson 1983; Ayers 1984). The punishment of deviant slaves was decentralized, based on plantations, and crafted so as not to impede their value as laborers. In contrast, white convicts worked on industrial crafts in a small penal institution. Originally built in 1816, the prison, often criticized and operated at a deficit, was ultimately destroyed by Sherman's troops in 1864 (Walden 1974; Zimmerman 1947).

With its destruction, Georgia's system of punishment operated without a central penal institution for nearly three-quarters of a century. As a result, convicts were "farmed out" in an unregulated fashion until 1868 when formal leasing of convicts to a private contractor began (Taylor 1942b). For the next forty years, a series of contracts were negotiated, dispersing inmates throughout the state. With the creation of the Georgia Prison Commission in 1897, the state bore the costs of supervising convicts. Nevertheless, private contractors continued to rent the labor of convicts, increasing state revenues (Prison Commission 1907-8).

Among the last states to end their partnership with the private sector, Georgia, unlike other states, did not replace the lease system with large plantation farms (Taylor 1942a). Instead, after 1909 all able-bodied convicts were dispersed to county chain gangs for road construction and maintenance. While hailed as a progressive victory for more humane punishment, the end of the lease system changed little. Punishment was still decentralized, and the state still acted as a "distributing agent, a disciplinarian, and a caretaker of convicts" (McCallie 1911:157). The form of punishment—forced labor under brutal and inhumane working conditions—remained unchanged (Zimmerman 1947:424-9). Not until 1937 did Georgia join mainstream penal developments when it accepted title to a federally funded prison to house most inmates (Prison Industries Reorganization Administration 1937; Zimmerman 1947).

Labor Scarcity and Private Convict Leasing

An understanding of punishment during this period requires consideration of two economic consequences of the Civil War and Emancipation. Economically prostrate, postbellum Georgia lacked the investment capital to rebuild and extend the state's economic infrastructure as well as the tax revenue to support the operation of a central prison (Woodward 1971). For decades after the war, Georgia faced a shortage of unskilled labor previously performed by slaves (Ransom and Sutch 1977:46). This "shortage" resulted more from whites' insistence that freed blacks return to a master-slave form of labor relations than from a dearth in the *number* of actual workers (Flynn 1983:72). To be productive, black labor needed to be reliable and disciplined, and whites thought that neither could be achieved without coercion (Higgs 1977; McMillen 1989; Ransom and Sutch 1977).

Though subject to short-term fluctuations, the demand for black agrarian labor was high, even during depressions (Baron 1971; Flynn 1983; Hart 1910). Seldom curbed successfully (Schlomowitz 1984), the fierce competition among white landowners, came, in part, from the presumption that black labor was more tractable and less expensive than its white counterpart (Higgs 1977; Woodward 1971). This high demand enabled blacks to resist antebellum forms of labor (e.g., gang labor) and to insist on more equitable sharecropping arrangements (Flynn 1983:73). Nevertheless, white Southerners devised ways of exploiting black labor more effectively, in part by restricting mobility. Though never entirely successful, legislation in Georgia sought to stabilize labor supply by prohibiting the enticement of labor, criminalizing failure to provide contracted services, and broadening the definition of vagrancy (Cohen 1976; Novak 1978).

As the predominant form of punishment, the convict lease system helped solve the dual problems of labor and capital scarcity. The leasing of convicts to private entrepreneurs anchored the larger system of involuntary black servitude, and it was the ultimate response to those who resisted other forms of labor exploitation (Adamson 1983). At minimal expense to the state, the lease not only controlled the least cooperative element of the black population, but also converted this element into a cheap labor pool, readily available from sunrise until nightfall for nearly seven days a week.

Employers maintained a consistently high demand for black coerced labor, and prospective lessees faced stiff competition (Principal Keeper of the Penitentiary 1874; Prison Commission 1897-98). Considered less expensive (Carter 1964:80) and "more constant and reliable" (Prison Commission 1901-2:18), convict labor was at times preferred to that of free labor.[1] Moreover, nineteenth century industrialists, lacking the legal mechanisms that planters could use to ensure a constant labor supply, found few workers willing to tolerate the low wages and arduous working conditions they offered (Ayers 1984).

The Good Roads Movement and Public Convict Leasing

In addition to demands for convict labor by private entrepreneurs, a vigorous demand arose in the public sector during the last decades of the nineteenth century. As early as 1889, the Georgia Road Congress supported the use of felons to build roads, and eagerly awaited expiration of the convict lease when it could undertake "another assault upon the legislature" to "get possession" of felony inmates (U.S. Department of Agriculture 1895:16). The lack of alternative sources of reliable inexpensive labor helps explain the "tidal wave of public opinion" favoring convict labor on public roads (Sheffield 1894:26). Since colonial times, road work was traditionally, and inefficiently, performed by male citizens (whites), conscripted by law to work several days a year (Sheffield 1894:25). Allowed to generate revenues for hiring wage labor after 1891, counties found this kind of labor more expensive and less reliable than the conscript system (Holmes 1901:325; Sheffield 1894). Misdemeanor convicts had been used earlier, but they too were considered unsuitable, "owing to the time it required to train the men to do effective work" (McCallie 1911:157).

Much like their private sector counterparts, county authorities considered the labor of convicted felons disciplined, inexpensive, productive, and compatible with free labor in

---

1. As noted earlier, coercive elements characterized the agrarian labor market in Georgia. Along with the lien system, vagrancy and contract enforcement statutes restricted black and, to a lesser extent, white mobility (Cohen 1976). By contemporary standards, black labor was hardly free. Nevertheless, black tenants could and did leave farms (McMillen 1989), an important right not shared by their convicted counterparts. In comparison with convict labor, then, unconvicted blacks were free, and it is from this vantage point that we use the term free labor.

skilled enterprises (Pennybacker, Fairbank, and Draper 1916), and the state gradually accommodated and encouraged this demand. In 1895, the legislature enlarged the pool from which counties could obtain road laborers by allowing judges to sentence many nonviolent felons as misdemeanants who then became eligible for county roadwork. Two years later, the legislature further enlarged the labor pool by permitting counties to obtain felons sentenced to two years or less for road work. Counties, however, seldom used this labor pool since they were required to pay $36 a year for each convict, for which in return they would receive a portion of the school fund. Within six years, the legislature removed this economic disincentive, again enlarging the labor pool to include felons whose sentences were up to five years long. The shift from private to public access to convict labor was completed dramatically in September 1908 when the legislature gave county authorities access to all convicted felons after the convict lease expired in April 1909. Initially, the demand for convict labor exceeded available supply (McCallie 1911), and two years after the lease ended, three quarters of Georgia's 146 counties worked felons on public roads. A quarter of a century later, the demand had not diminished, and nearly 80 percent of all counties used convicted felons on their roads (Prison Industries Reorganization Administration 1937:25).

While policies at the state level increased the available supply of convict labor, federal government policies and programs stimulated public demand for it. The Office of Public Road Inquiries, established in 1893, actively encouraged the Good Roads Movement; it published technical bulletins, sponsored road conferences, and built short "object-lesson" roads throughout the South (U.S. Department of Agriculture 1902). Incentives to use convict labor on roads escalated dramatically in 1916 with the passage of the Federal Aid Road Act which, along with subsequent amendments, provided federal funds to build rural post roads in eligible states. A single provision of the new law ultimately placed an enormous premium on convict labor. To receive federal funds, states were required to pay half the estimated costs of a construction project. Since Georgia's constitution prohibited appropriations of state funds for "internal improvements," the Road Act permitted counties to match federal funds. Significantly, Georgia counties were allowed to meet their share of costs by supplying convict labor rather than money. By the end of fiscal year 1932, Georgia had received nearly $34 million dollars in federal aid, consistently leading the South in the number of miles completed with federal assistance (State Highway Board of Georgia 1932, 1934).

Race and Convict Labor Demand

The arduous working conditions of convicts under the lease system were perceived as appropriate methods for expropriating the labor of *black* convicts (Adamson 1983; Hawkins 1985; Logan 1964:211; Powell [1891] 1969:332; Tindall 1952: 260-76; Wharton 1947:235). "Destitute of pride of character," blacks were considered unintelligent, incapable of reform, and inherently able to perform only the "simplest and roughest" tasks (Principal Keeper of the Penitentiary 1873, 1876). As was the case in other Southern states, there appeared to be little demand for the labor of white convicts, and courts were reluctant to sentence whites to work for lessees.

The race-specific nature of the demand for convict labor became less clear after the lease expired, however. The Prison Commission (1908-9:7) initially preferred a permanent penitentiary farm for white inmates after 1909, perhaps because of the difficulties of ensuring that chain gangs were segregated (Wright 1897:11). While never countenanced, integration became intolerable as the public grew fearful of a "new" black that was "regressing rapidly toward his natural state of savagery and bestiality" (Williamson 1984:6). Consistent with this ideology were the disenfranchisement of blacks and legislation mandating segregated public facilities (Bartley 1983:148; Kousser 1974), including convict labor camps.

However, when the governor disapproved expenditures for a farm, the commission gave up its insistence on a penitentiary for whites and went on record as favoring the use of all convicts on roads "as far as necessity or demand" dictate (Prison Commission 1907-8:8). The lack of opposition to using white inmates on roads could well have been due to the traditional conscript system of road construction, which involved white males. Thus, as long as segregation was maintained, road work was considered appropriate for both black and white convicts (Hawkins 1985). If this is the case, then the demand for convict labor changed fundamentally after the lease expired: it became generic rather than race-specific. In the next section, we will explore the implications of this change on the rate at which whites and blacks were incarcerated.

Convict and Free Labor

The shortage of unskilled industrial labor ensured a sporadic and limited competition between convict and free labor (Principal Keeper of the Penitentiary 1884-6). Importantly, however, the nature of work performed by convicts had the same effect. Many felons were leased by extractive and manufacturing enterprises, like coal and iron ore mining, brick-making, and sawmills, that were related, if not essential, to agrarian pursuits. Railroad construction, for example, was crucial to the growth of "rural cotton centers" that distributed northern goods, marketed cotton, milled cottonseed oil, and, later, manufactured cotton goods (Ransom and Sutch 1977:116-7; Wright 1986:42).

The mutually supportive activities performed by free and convict labor suggest a complementary rather than antagonistic relationship between the two labor markets. Indeed, it is possible that the demand for black agrarian labor stimulated demand for the labor of black convicts (Cohen 1976; McMillen 1989). According to Wright (1986:59), "for most of the region [cotton] defined the opportunities and dictated the pace of economic life." A contemporary observer described the relationship more graphically: "When cotton prices advance, every industry throbs with new vigor" (Poe 1904:5488). It is likely, then, that this growth would be particularly strong for industries that used convict labor to facilitate cotton production and marketing. The next section considers this possibility in depth by exploring the relationship between the demand for free labor and the frequency with which blacks and whites were incarcerated.

Labor Demands and the Use of Incarceration

Hypotheses

The preceding narrative which linked the *form* of punishment with race-specific demands for labor has several implications for the *frequency* with which blacks and whites were incarcerated. First, the narrative suggests that levels of punishment in Georgia should respond, at least in part, to changes in labor demands. The possibility that incarceration will increase (or decrease) contrasts sharply with the stability of punishment hypothesis. Originally derived from Durkheim's ([1938] 1966) insight that the level of deviance is relatively stable within a given society, this hypothesis was developed and refined by Blumstein and his colleagues (Blumstein and Cohen 1973; Blumstein, Cohen, and Nagin 1977; Blumstein and Moitra 1979). It contends that incarceration levels may change in the short run, but these are little more than fluctuations around a level that is basically unchanging. Like previous research (e.g., Berk et al. 1981, 1982, 1983; Myers and Sabol 1986; Rauma 1981), the narrative suggests otherwise. Rather than being a self-regulating mechanism, punishment should expand with growth in the demand for convict and free labor.

The second implication of the narrative is that incarceration rates should reflect the race-specific nature of the demand for convict labor. In essence, there should be *two* patterns of punishment. The incarceration rate for black males should be consistently higher than the rate for white males. This difference should be particularly pronounced before the lease expired when the demand for convict labor was essentially a demand for the labor of black males. The black male incarceration rate should also reflect growth in the profitability of convict labor and rise throughout the period. As early as 1872, the governor suggested that "more rigid and proper enforcement of the laws" was the mechanism for such increases (Georgia General Assembly 1872:139). Thirty years later, A. B. Hart (1910:200) identified another: overt discrimination when the demand for convict labor exceeded supply. We also expect incarceration rates to increase after the lease expired (1909) and after the Federal Aid Road Act was passed (1916). Both events, we argue, stimulated demand for convict labor in the public sector. Neither event should have singular effects on black male incarceration, however. As noted earlier, the nature of convict labor after the lease—work on roads—increased the likelihood that demand could be met by either whites or blacks. Further, the state might have reached a limit on exploitation of blacks but still might have been able to meet labor demands through increased imprisonment of whites (Hawkins 1985).

Different expectations inform our analysis of white punishment. The narrative suggests that the demand for the labor of white convicts was comparatively low under the convict lease system. As a result, we expect the rate at which white males were incarcerated to fluctuate little until the lease expired in 1909. If the Good Roads Movement did indeed broaden the demand for convict labor to include whites, then the white male incarceration rate should increase after 1909, when the State made all convicts available for road work. White incarceration rates should increase even more dramatically after 1916, when the Federal Aid Road Act provided strong financial incentives for using convict labor on public works.

The final implication of the narrative centers on the relationship between free and coerced labor markets. Research on contemporary punishment suggests that labor scarcity, reflected in declining unemployment rates, fosters *declines* in the use of incarceration (Inverarity and McCarthy 1988; Parker and Horwitz 1986). Underlying this hypothesis is the assumption that incarceration serves to control a permanent feature of capitalist political economies, namely, its labor *surplus*. Incarceration becomes less necessary, then, as that surplus becomes smaller. The narrative describes a quite different political economy with different labor market conditions: an agrarian mode of production characterized by a chronic shortage of unskilled labor. In this context, incarceration was instrumental not in controlling a surplus labor pool but in marshalling a relatively scarce resource for the accumulation of capital.

To the extent that the markets for free and coerced labor reinforced each other, then increased demand for black agrarian labor should accompany if not generate increased demand for black convict labor. By extension, the rate at which black males were incarcerated should increase. The same reinforcing relationship between free and convict labor could be true for white males after the lease expired. While the demand for white labor, particularly in the twentieth century, was cotton-centered, it was not primarily or exclusively a demand for agrarian labor, but for workers in the rapidly growing industry of cotton textiles (Wright 1986). Thus, we expect increased demand for the labor of free whites to accompany if not simulate demand for white convicts after the expiration of the lease and, by extension, the rate at which white males were incarcerated.

Data

Published state documents provided information about felony convicts (Principal Keeper of the Georgia Penitentiary 1868-1896; Prison Commission 1897-1936). Black male incarceration rates were derived by dividing annual figures by the population of black males and multiplying by 10,000. The white male incarceration rate used the population of white males as the base. The decennial Census provided population figures. Within each decade, population figures were estimates derived by linear interpolation, which assumes a linear increase (or decrease) in population during that decade.

The absence of direct information about labor demand dictated the use of proxy measures. Two events indicated shifts in the demand for convict labor: expiration of the lease (1909) and passage of the Federal Aid Road Act (1916). To measure the demand for black agrarian labor, we assumed that growth in cotton production generated growth in the demand for black field hands (Baron 1971:14). Cotton production was measured by the size of the annual cotton harvest in thousands of acres (U.S. Department of Agriculture 1951-2).[2] Measuring the demand for white labor also required a simplifying assumption, namely, that as cotton textiles became increasingly profitable, the demand for textile workers increased (Baron 1971; Woodward 1971:222; Wright 1986:179-80). The proxy measure of demand, obtained from Censuses of Manufactures, was Value Added by Cotton Goods Manufacture in constant 1900 dollars.

Analytic Strategy

In the first stage of analysis, we identified the relationship between measures of labor demand and each incarceration rate; in the second stage, we estimated these relationships. To identify the relationship between incarceration and the two events of interest (lease expiration and passage of the Federal Aid Road Act), we inspected the differenced incarceration rates. Of central interest were three pieces of evidence: noticeable changes in levels of incarceration, delay in the onset of any changes, and returns to previous levels (implying a temporary effect rather than permanently altered levels). Taken together, this evidence was used to specify the appropriate transfer functions to be estimated.

To identify relationships involving the two time series measures, Cotton Harvest and Value Added by Cotton Goods Manufacture, we estimated a crosscorrelation function. This diagnostic, whose range lies between -1 and $+1$, indicates the direction, strength, and duration of the relationship between an input series and the past, present, and future values of the output time series (Makridakis, Wheelwright, and McGee 1983).[3] Crosscorrelation functions were computed using the ARIMA procedure in Statistical Analysis Systems (SAS). Each function was inspected for evidence of a dynamic relationship between the two series.

Once transfer functions were specified (Box and Tiao 1975; Harvey 1981), maximum likelihood estimates of their parameters were derived. Analysis used ARIMA procedures to fit a model with two major components.[4] The first component was the set of transfer functions representing the effects of labor demand proxies on incarceration. The second component

2. Analysis explored the effect of an alternative measure of demand, annual bales of cotton produced. This indicator proved to be more tenuously linked with incarceration. Most notably, its crosscorrelations with black male incarceration were identical in direction, but weaker in magnitude (CCF+3=.18; CCF+4=.16; CCF+5=.21).

3. To estimate crosscorrelation functions accurately, input and output series must be stable in level and variance (McCleary and Hay 1980). Otherwise, common patterns of drift or trend generate spurious correlations. If the variance of the original series is nonstationary, the natural logarithm of the series can be taken and the log-transformed series analyzed. If the mean of the series is nonstationary, a new series can be created by taking the differences of successive periods ($X_t - X_{t-1}$, $X_{t-1} - X_{t-2}$. . . .). All time series in this analysis were log-transformed then differenced before estimation. To estimate crosscorrelation functions accurately, the input series must be a white noise process (Montgomery and Weatherby 1980). Otherwise, significant within-series autocorrelations can distort correlations between two series (Haugh and Box 1977; Montgomery and Weatherby 1980). Autocorrelations are removed by modeling the underlying process that generated the series as a moving average, autoregressive, or mixed process (Makridakis, Wheelwright, and McGee 1983:487-92). The input series is "prewhitened" by inverting its ARIMA model, and this prewhitening transformation is applied to the output series. A crosscorrelation function between the series is then estimated. This procedure was followed for Value Added by Cotton Goods Manufacture, which was adequately modeled as a first-order moving average process [$\theta = -.59(SE = .10)$].

4. Autoregression procedures were less appropriate than ARIMA modeling because they assume the output series is an autoregressive process of order p. The white male incarceration series violates this assumption. Autoregression

was an estimate of the effect that previous values of incarceration, previous random error, or both had on incarceration in any given year. Models were accepted if parameter estimates were statistically significant (p < .05); the residual sum of squares was reduced in comparison with a model of the noise component; and the residuals of the model contained no significant autocorrelation (i.e., were white noise).

Incarceration Trends

Figures 1 and 2 present the black and white incarceration rates between 1868 and 1936. As expected on the basis of the narrative, neither rate was stable.[5] Also as expected, the pattern of incarceration for black males differed dramatically from that of white males, continuing at a consistently higher rate than for white males. The incarceration rate of black males increased significantly after the signing of the first lease in 1868 and continued a modest upward trajectory until 1926, after which it rose again sharply. In contrast, the incarceration rate for white males remained relatively stable until 1910, after which it began a nearly linear increase. Between 1909 and 1932, for example, the rate at which white males were incarcerated nearly tripled, from 3.6 to 12.4 per 10,000. Other fundamental differences between the two incarceration rates will become apparent later, when each series is modeled.

Identifying Impacts

Inspection of the incarceration series suggested that expiraton of the lease and passage of the Federal Road Aid Act had different effects on the incarceration of white and black males. Each event appeared to have a temporary effect, lagged by one year, on the black male incarceration rate. To capture these effects, we created two binary "pulse" variables. Lease Expiration was coded 1 for 1909 and 0 the remaining years. Federal Aid Road Act was coded 1 for 1916 and 0 the remaining years. Each event appeared to have a gradual permanent effect, after a lag of two years, on white male incarceration. To estimate these effects, we created two binary "step" variables, which indicated the absence of a state prior to the event and the presence of the state during and after the event. The first variable, Lease Expiration, was coded 0 in years prior to 1909 and 1 thereafter. The second binary variable, Federal Aid Road Act, was coded 0 for years before 1916 and 1 thereafter. For each event, we estimated a first-order transfer function.

Table 1 presents the crosscorrelation functions between incarceration rates and the two measures of free labor demand, Cotton Harvest and Value Added by Cotton Goods Manufacture. The decay in crosscorrelations suggests the need for a first-order transfer function to estimate the effect Cotton Harvest had on black male incarceration. In this function, denoted $[\omega/(1-\delta B)]X_{t-2}$, ω measures change in level, δ the rate at which change was realized, and B refers to the backward shift operator ($B^n X_t = X_{t-n}$). The parameter, δ, must lie between -1 and 1, and as it approaches unity, the impact is realized slowly. A single significant crosscorrelation between Cotton Harvest and white male incarceration (CCF+0 = $-.335$) suggests a contemporaneous permanent change in incarceration. To estimate this kind of impact, the model includes a zero-order transfer function, ωX_t, where ω indicates the magnitude and direction of impact. Though in the expected direction (CCF+2 = .196), no crosscorrelation between Value Added by Cotton Goods Manufacture and white incarceration reached statistical

---

procedures also cannot estimate dynamic effects that decay over time—namely distributed lags—nor do they provide an obvious way to remove autocorrelation within the input series.

5. To obtain a clearer picture of instability, we estimated an autocorrelation function for each incarceration series. This function describes the association between values of the same time series at different time periods (Makridakis, Wheelwright, and McGee 1983:891). The persistence of large autocorrelations at long lags indicated that each series had a nonstationary mean. Further evidence of instability was indicated by small but significant constant increments over time in the differenced series ($\mu = .023[SE = .008]$ for whites; $\mu = .031[SE = .015]$ for blacks).

Black Male Incarceration

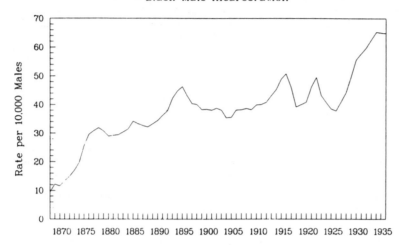

Figure 1 • *Black Male Incarceration*

White Male Incarceration

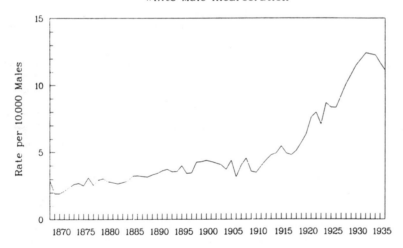

Figure 2   White Male Incarceration

276   MYERS/MASSEY

Table 1 • *Crosscorrelations between Labor Demand and Incarceration*[a]

Input Series	Cotton Harvest		Valued Added by Cotton Goods Manufacture	
Incarceration	Black Male	White Male	White Male	
			1868-1936	1900-1936
Crosscorrelations at Lag				
0	.018	−.335*	.060	−.007
1	.049	.095	−.069	−.018
2	.251*	.098	.196	.237
3	.247*	−.108	−.176	−.260
4	.231*	.137	.049	.180
5	.196	−.036	.108	−.018
6	.073	.048	−.129	−.064

Notes:

a. Each series was log-transformed and differenced to achieve stationarity. Value Added by Cotton Goods Manufacture was also prewhitened as a first-order moving average process.

* $p < .05$

significance. Crosscorrelations based on the post-1900 series suggest stronger impacts, but these too were statistically insignificant.[6] Nevertheless, the presence of single spikes suggests the appropriateness of zero-order transfer functions, and subsequent analysis therefore tests for abrupt permanent impacts.

Estimating Impacts

Table 2 presents the results of analyses focussing on the black male incarceration rate. As expected on the basis of the narrative, neither measure of the demand for convict labor (lease expiration and federal legislation) significantly affected the rate at which black males were incarcerated. The demand for black agrarian labor, as indicated by the Cotton Harvest, had the expected positive effect. An increase in acres of harvested cotton generated a gradual and permanent increase in incarceration, and this impact decayed slowly with time. Model II presents the results after insignificant estimates were dropped. Note the slight decline in the magnitude of Cotton Harvest's effect. This decline, along with an intensified correlation between estimated parameters of the transfer function ($r = −.86$), accounts for the statistical insignificance of the *omega* estimate. In both models, the rate at which black males were incarcerated was also a function of the incarceration rate the previous year. Figure 3 graphs the predicted values obtained from this model, along with the original series. It provides strong evidence of the extent to which the model fits the data.

Table 3 reports the results for the white male incarceration rate. The models in the upper half of the table are based on the entire time series (1868-1936). Contrary to expectation, expiration of the lease had no impact on white male incarceration. The Federal Aid Road Act, though, significantly increased the rate at which white males were incarcerated; its effect, delayed by two years, decayed slowed with time. The narrative also led us to expect that the demand for agrarian and industrial labor would increase white male incarceration rates. This did not appear to be the case. Neither Cotton Harvest or Value Added by Cotton Goods Manufacture had significant effects.[7] The models presented in the second half of Table 2 are based

6. Analysis begins with 1900, rather than with lease abolition in 1909, to ensure a series long enough to yield reliable estimates.

7. Though Cotton Harvest and Value Added by Cotton Goods Manufacture were not significantly crosscorrelated,

Table 2 • *Estimated Effects of Labor Demand on Black Male Incarceration*[a]

Input Series	Function	Parameter	Model I Estimate (SE)[b]	Model II Estimate (SE)
Lease Expiration	$[\omega/(1-\delta B)]X_{t-1}$	ω	.026 (.044)	
		δ	.298(1.976)	
Federal Aid Road Act	$[\omega/(1-\delta B)]X_{t-1}$	ω	.040 (.024)	
		δ	−.553 (.327)	
Cotton Harvest	$[\omega/(1-\delta B)]X_{t-2}$	ω	.146 (.075)*	.115 (.071)
		δ	.763 (.109)*	.801 (.103)*
Noise	ϕY_{t-1}	ϕ	.540 (.111)*	.505 (.109)*
RSS			.173	.188
RSS (Noise Model)			.324	.324
Residual autocorrelations $\chi^2(p)$			5.4 (.4)	5.5 (.4)

Notes:
a. Series were log-transformed and differenced before estimation.
b. Standard error of estimates.
* $p < .05$.

Table 3 • *Estimated Effects of Labor Demand on White Male Incarceration*[a]

Input Series	Function	Parameter	Model I Estimate (SE)[b]	Model II Estimate (SE)
1868-1936				
Lease Expiration	$[\omega/(1-\delta B)]X_{t-2}$	ω	.102 (.076)	
		δ	.582 (.372)	
Federal Aid Road Act	$[\omega/(1-\delta B)]X_{t-2}$	ω	.087 (.041)*	.109 (.043)*
		δ	.875 (.086)*	.894 (.065)*
Cotton Harvest	ωX_t	ω		(c)
Value Added by Cotton Goods Manufacture	ωX_{t-2}	ω	.001 (.001)	
Noise	$-\theta e_{t-1}$	θ	.500 (.126)*	.366 (.120)*
RSS			.539	.610
RSS (Noise Model)			.878	.878
Residual autocorrelations	$\chi^2(p)$		2.7 (.7)	2.5 (.8)
1900-1936				
Lease Expiration	$[\omega/(1-\delta B)]X_{t-2}$	ω	.184 (.084)*	.147 (.082)
		δ	.674 (.220)*	.616 (.285)*
Federal Aid Road Act	$[\omega/(1-\delta B)]X_{t-2}$	ω	.121 (.054)*	.107 (.051)*
		δ	.928 (.067)*	.893 (.077)*
Cotton Harvest	ωX_t	ω	−.166 (.171)	
Value Added by Cotton Goods Manufacture	ωX_{t-3}	ω	−.003 (.003)	
Noise	ϕY_{t-1}	ϕ	−.406 (.180)*	−.425 (.171)*
RSS			.298	.319
RSS (Noise Model)			.486	.486
Residual autocorrelations	$\chi^2(p)$		5.7 (.3)	5.7 (.3)

Notes:
a. Series were log-transformed and differenced before estimation.
b. Standard error of estimates.
c. Estimates failed to converge when Cotton Harvest was included in the analysis (see *supra*, Footnote 7).
* $p < .05$.

on incarceration rates after 1900. Note, first, that measures of free labor demand continue to have no effect. Both measures of convict labor demand, Lease Expiration and the Federal Aid Road Act, significantly increased the rate at which whites were incarcerated. Reestimation (Model II) slightly attenuates the effect of the former. The parameter estimate for change in level (ω) loses significance, in part because of its substantive decline and because the correlation between estimated parameters of the transfer function (ω and δ) is stronger in the reestimated model than in the original ($r = -.64$). The predicted and actual values of the entire series, presented in Figure 4, indicate a close fit between the model and the series.

Discussion

This examination of punishment in Georgia after the Civil War began from the premise of a close correspondence between the organization of labor and systems of punishment within a society. A decentralized form of punishment involving coerced labor was consistent with a predominantly agrarian mode of production experiencing chronic shortages of labor. The nature of work and the harsh conditions under which convicts labored were but one step removed from the nature of free black labor and its laboring conditions.

The frequency of incarceration reflected differences as well as changes over time in the relative demand for black and white labor. The consistently higher rates of incarceration among blacks reflected the greater demand for black convict labor. The increased profitability of convict labor found expression in the general tendency for the black incarceration rates to rise throughout the period. Neither expiration of the lease nor federal legislation dramatically increased the rate at which black males were incarcerated. As noted earlier, the state may have reached the limit of black exploitation and found it necessary to meet labor demands through increased imprisonment of whites. The shift from arduous manual labor for private profit to work on public roads and projects was instrumental in rendering this necessity more palatable (Hawkins 1985).

The contrastingly low demand for white forced labor in the nineteenth century was reflected in a much lower and more stable rate of incarceration. In the early twentieth century, however, the locus of the demand for convict labor shifted from the private to the public sector, but with little effect in the form of punishment and the conditions under which convicts labored. Instead, public sector involvement altered the type of labor performed by convicts and generated a generic rather than race-specific demand for convict labor. The rate at which whites were incarcerated increased dramatically, particularly after 1916, when the Federal Aid Road Act escalated the demand for the types of labor suited to both whites and blacks.

Finally, time series analysis reinforced our narrative argument that a high demand for the labor of free blacks reinforced the demand for black convict labor. The general demand for black labor in the agrarian sector, as indicated by the size of the cotton harvest, stimulated the rate of black incarceration. This complementary demand arose from the shortage of unskilled agrarian and industrial labor and from the mutually reinforcing nature of productive activities in both sectors. In contrast, neither the demand for agrarian labor nor the demand for white labor in the textile industry had implications for the rate of white incarceration. For reasons that merit further attention, these findings suggest a looser coupling between the markets for free and coerced white labor.

---

estimates failed to converge when both series were included in the model together. Cotton Harvest was dropped and the model reestimated. An alternative model that included Cotton Harvest and excluded Value Added yielded similar estimates. Lease expiration had no significant effect ($\omega = .13[SE = .08]$; $\delta = .62$ [SE = .28]), while the effect of the Federal Aid Road Act was significant ($\omega = .10[SE = .04]$; $\delta = .90[SE = .07]$). Cotton Harvest had no significant effect ($\omega = -.03[SE = .12]$).

Black Male Incarceration

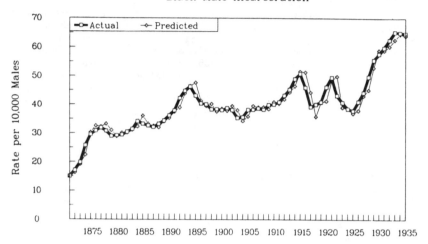

Figure 3 • *Black Male Incarceration*

White Male Incarceration

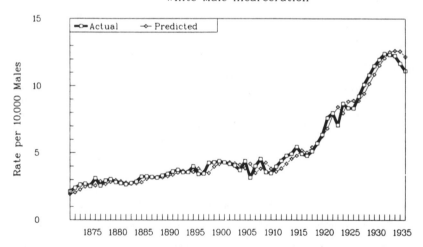

Figure 4 • *White Male Incarceration*

Alternative Explanations

Though we confined our attention to the demand for labor, we are not arguing that it alone shaped the form and use of punishment. The volume of crime and race differences in criminal involvement undoubtedly played a role. Regrettably, we cannot determine with any precision the extent to which race differences in incarceration reflected race differences in criminal activity. Data on persons formally accused of crime have been recovered from the often incomplete court records of a few counties, but not all identify defendants by race or age (e.g., Ayers 1984; Department of Public Welfare 1925; Engerrand 1981; Fuller 1929; Smith 1982). These indictments imperfectly measure actual criminality, as they too may have been driven by the same demand for labor that fueled subsequent incarceration. On the basis of additional analysis, however, we do know that our results are unaffected by changes in the size of the population that ran the greatest risk of being incarcerated (males between 20-29 years old).[8]

Georgia experienced dramatic demographic changes during this period, some of which profoundly affected the *supply* of black labor. After the turn of the century, thousands of blacks, primarily from depressed rural areas, left the state (Fligstein 1981; Johnson and Campbell 1981). Indeed, Georgia lost approximately 9 percent of its black population between 1910 and 1930. It is possible that these losses contributed to short-lived declines in the rate at which black males were incarcerated and to more sustained increases in the rate at which white males were incarcerated. At the state level, though, there is no evidence this was the case. Neither percent black nor percent black male noticeably affected the rate at which blacks *or* whites were incarcerated.[9] It is possible that erosion in the black population base affected incarceration at the county level. Thus, a clearer understanding of the relationship between punishment and the labor market awaits an analysis of transformations in labor supply at this level.

In addition to population shifts outside the state, Georgia experienced major shifts within the state. Though still predominantly rural, the percentage of the population residing in urban areas quadrupled between 1870 and 1940 (from 8 percent to 33 percent). Again, additional analysis indicated that the profound social changes wrought by urbanization found no expression in the rate at which either black or white males were incarcerated.[10] Southern agriculture did, however, lose momentum after 1915, eroding the economic position of white farmers (Fligstein 1981). Increasing numbers lost their land in the next two decades through cotton overproduction and inability to pay debts. By 1930, the majority of white farmers were tenants. Their position worsened during the 1930s, when reduced cotton acreage, subsidy payments to large landowners, and mechanization reduced further the need for tenants and stimulated their replacement by wage laborers. When coupled with the high demand for convict labor, this "proletarianization" of whites could well have increased their vulnerability to criminal punishment.

The foregoing discussion by no means exhausts possible determinants of black and white

8. Neither percent young in the white male population nor its black equivalent was significantly crosscorrelated with white male incarceration ($\chi^2 = 2.3$ [p = .9] and 6.6 [p = .3], respectively). Percent young black male, once purged of the effect of Cotton Harvest, was insignificantly crosscorrelated with black male incarceration (CCF+1 = .16). When included with the harvest series, its net effect was insignificant ($\omega = .02$[SE = .14]), and the effect of Cotton Harvest unchanged ($\omega = .11$[SE = .07]; $\delta = .80$[SE = .11]).

9. Percent black was not significantly crosscorrelated with black or white male incarceration ($\chi^2 = 3.6$ [p = .7] and 2.0 [p = .9], respectively). In contrast, percent black male, once purged of harvest's effects, was inversely crosscorrelated with black incarceration (CCF+4 = −.24). Its effect persisted when included with the harvest series ($\omega = .35$[SE = .17]). Nevertheless, percent black male neither altered the effects of Cotton Harvest ($\omega = .12$[SE = .07]; $\delta = .80$[SE = .11]), nor noticeably reduced residual sum of squares (RSS = .180).

10. The crosscorrelation function between percent urban and black male incarceration was statistically insignificant ($\chi^2 = 4.5$[p = .6]) and no crosscorrelation was significant. An identical situation characterized the crosscorrelation function between percent urban and white male incarceration ($\chi^2 = .9$[p = .9]).

incarceration during this period. Taken together, supplemental analysis underscores the significance of the results presented earlier and enables us to place greater confidence in them. At the same time, our discussion demonstrates a clear need for research that determines whether changes in crime levels, labor supply, and urban concentration were more keenly felt at the county level.

Implications and Conclusion

In one sense, this historical account of punishment contrasts sharply with its contemporary counterparts. Recent research has discovered that trends in incarceration do not simply mirror levels of criminal activity. They are influenced as well by exogenous factors such as the size of the surplus labor supply and by internal factors such as the capacity of existing institutions (e.g., Berk et al. 1981, 1982, 1983; Inverarity and McCarthy 1988). Neither factor helps us understand punishment in a context that lacked both a "reserve army of unemployed" and central penal institutions. Yet *both* factors may be relevant to our understanding of more contemporary punishment in Georgia. We noted earlier that by 1937 Georgia had joined the mainstream in its treatment of convicted felons. Thereafter, facilities at the local and state level grew rapidly, and crowding became a perennial concern. These changes in the organization of punishment raise the dual prospect of discontinuity with past practice in Georgia and continuity with penal developments elsewhere. More generally, the fundamental shift in punishment after 1937 cautions us against assuming that any single factor has implications for punishment that transcend time.

In another sense, our findings identify two fundamental continuities between historical and contemporary punishment. The first is the importance of region to our understanding of criminal punishment. The system of punishment that developed in Georgia and in the South more generally was strikingly different from punishment in the Northeast (e.g., Petchesky 1981; Gardner 1987; Gildemeister 1987). Northern convicts worked for the private sector, but they did so within centralized institutions. Their labor took different forms, was more consistently and vigorously opposed, and ultimately was shorter-lived. These regional differences reflect in part the coexistence of very different modes of production within a single political unit. Such differences persist today and take the form of different levels of punishment (Myers and Sabol 1986) and in the greater sensitivity of Southern rates to changes in agricultural rather than manufacturing output (Myers and Sabol 1987). Regional differences make it imperative that regardless of the time period under consideration, we firmly ground studies of punishment in regional political economies.

Though broadly similar to punishment elsewhere in the South, this account also reveals intra-regional differences in punishment. Opposition to the lease by free labor was both more vehement and successful in other Southern states (Ayers 1984; Carter 1964; Shelden 1981). Similarly, the cooperation among federal, state, and local authorities in Georgia found no parallel in neighboring North Carolina, where state and county officials competed for the labor of convicts (Hawkins 1984). These differences underscore the difficulty of specifying in advance the contours of punishment, even in political units that share a similar mode of production. Thus, while a consideration of the political economy may help researchers specify a "space for penal relations," it can only be used as a starting point for more concrete analyses of punishment bounded by both time and space (Hogg 1979: 58).

The second continuity between nineteenth century and contemporary punishment is the centrality of race. Patterns in the incarceration of black males during the period considered here bore little resemblance to trends in the incarceration of whites. Time series analysis indicated that different processes generated each incarceration series, and each was influenced by different factors. To a certain extent, the same situation prevails today. For example, the rate at which blacks were incarcerated in the North between 1890 and 1980 declined as manufacturing output grew and increased as the unemployed black population grew. The incarceration of whites, in contrast, responded poorly, if at all, to manufacturing output or white unemployment (Myers and Sabol 1987). The existence of dual systems of punishment in both the North and South provides strong grounds for incorporating race into research that seeks to evaluate general theories of punishment.

Finally, the work reported here has implications for theoretical perspectives linking political economy and punishment. Rusche ([1933] 1978), for example, clearly specified the implications of labor scarcity for both the form and conditions of punishment. Because scarce labor is valuable labor, corporal punishment should decline and forms of punishment that exploit the labor of convicts should arise. Left unspecified was the effect of labor scarcity on the *frequency* with which punishment is used. Our results suggest that a strong demand for free labor does not necessarily reduce the invocation of punishment that uses forced labor. Said differently, the demand for free labor and the demand for convict labor do not necessarily stand in opposition to one another. Further elaboration of the political economy-punishment relationship requires comparative research specifically designed to determine whether the patterns found here represent legacies of Southern slavery and racism or whether they are valid across a variety of contexts.

References

Adamson, Christopher R.
   1983   "Punishment after slavery: Southern state penal systems, 1865-1890." Social Problems 30:555-69.
   1984   "Toward a Marxian penology: Captive criminal populations as economic threats and resources." Social Problems 31:435-58.
Ayers, Edward L.
   1984   Vengeance and Justice: Crime and Punishment in the 19th-Century South. New York: Oxford University Press.
Baron, Harold M.
   1971   "The demand for black labor: Historical notes on the political economy of racism." Radical America 5:1-46.
Bartley, Numan V.
   1983   The Creation of Modern Georgia. Athens: University of Georgia Press.
Beck, E.M., James L. Massey, and Stewart E. Tolnay
   1988   "The gallows, the mob, and the vote: Sanctioning of blacks in North Carolina and Georgia, 1882 to 1930." Law and Society Review 23:317-31.
Berk, Richard A., David Rauma, Sheldon L. Messinger, and Thomas F. Cooley
   1981   "A test of the stability of punishment hypothesis: The case of California, 1851-1970." American Sociological Review 46:805-29.
Berk, Richard A., David Rauma, and Sheldon L. Messinger
   1982   "A further test of the stability of punishment hypothesis." In Quantitative Criminology: Innovations and Applications, ed. John Hagan, 39-64. Beverly Hills, Calif.: Sage.
Berk, Richard A., Sheldon L. Messinger, David Rauma, and John E. Berecochea
   1983   "Prisons as self-regulating systems: A comparison of historical patterns in California for male and female offenders." Law and Society Review 17:547-86.
Blumstein, Alfred and Jacqueline Cohen
   1973   "A theory of the stability of punishment." Journal of Criminal Law and Criminology 64:198-207.

Blumstein, Alfred, Jacqueline Cohen, and Daniel Nagin
   1977   "The dynamics of a homeostatic punishment process." Journal of Criminal Law and
           Criminology 67:317-34.
Blumstein, Alfred, and Soumyo Moitra
   1979   "An analysis of the time series of the imprisonment rate in the states of the United
           States: A further test of the stability of punishment hypothesis." Journal of Criminal Law
           and Criminology 70:376-90.
Box, G.E.P, and G.C. Tiao
   1975   "Intervention analysis with applications to economic and environmental problems."
           Journal of the American Statistical Association 70:70-9.
Carter, Dan T.
   1964   Prisons, Politics and Business: The Lease System in the Post-Civil War South. Masters
           Thesis, University of Wisconsin.
Cohen, William
   1976   "Negro involuntary servitude, 1865-1940: A preliminary analysis." The Journal of
           Southern History 42:31-60.
Corzine, Jay, Lin Huff-Corzine, and James C. Creech
   1988   "The tenant labor market and lynching in the South: A test of split labor market theory."
           Sociological Inquiry 58:261-78.
Department of Public Welfare
   1925   "Crime and the Georgia courts: A statistical analysis." Journal of the American Institute
           of Criminal Law and Criminology 16:1-52.
Dobash, Russell P.
   1983   "Labor and discipline in Scottish and English prisons: Moral correction, punishment and
           useful toil." Sociology 17:1-27.
Durkheim, Emile
   [1938]   The Rules of Sociological Method. New York: Free Press.
   1966
Engerrand, Steven W.
   1981   "Now Scratch or Die": The Genesis of Capitalistic Agricultural Labor in Georgia, 1865-
           1880. Ph.D. Diss., University of Georgia.
Fligstein, Neil
   1981   Going North: Migration of Blacks and Whites from the South, 1900-1950. New York:
           Academic Press.
Flynn, Charles L., Jr.
   1983   White Land, Black Labor: Caste and Class in Late Nineteenth Century Georgia. Baton
           Rouge: Louisiana State University Press.
Fuller, Hugh N.
   1929   Criminal Court Statistics, Studies #2-#7. Atlanta: Department of Public Welfare.
Gardner, Gil
   1987   "The emergence of the New York State prison system: A critique of the Rusche-
           Kirchheimer model." Crime and Social Justice 29:88-109.
Georgia General Assembly
   1872   Journal of the Senate of the State of Georgia. Atlanta: Franklin Printing Company.
Gildemeister, Glen A.
   1987   Prison Labor and Convict Competition with Free Workers in Industrializing America,
           1840-1890. New York: Garland.
Hart, Albert Bushnell
   1910   The Southern South. New York: D. Appleton Company.
Harvey, A.C.
   1981   The Econometric Analysis of Time Series. Oxford, Eng.: Philip Allan Publishers.
Haugh, Larry D., and G.E.P. Box
   1977   "Identification of dynamic regression (distributed lag) models connecting two time series."
           Journal of the American Statistical Association 72:121-30.
Hawkins, Darnell
   1984   "State versus county: prison policy and conflicts of interest in North Carolina." Criminal
           Justice History 5:91-128.

284   MYERS/MASSEY

1985   "Trends in black-white imprisonment: Changing conceptions of race or changing patterns of social control?" Crime and Social Justice 24:187-209.

Higgs, Robert
1977   Competition and Coercion: Blacks in the American Economy, 1865-1914. Cambridge: Cambridge University Press.

Hogg, Russell
1979   "Imprisonment and society under early British capitalism." Crime and Social Justice 12:4-17.

Holmes, J.A.
1901   "Road building with convict labor in the Southern states." In U.S. Department of Agriculture, Yearbook of Agriculture, 320-325. Washington, D.C.: Government Printing Office.

Inverarity, James, and Daniel McCarthy
1988   "Punishment and social structure revisited: Unemployment and imprisonment in the United States, 1948-1984." The Sociological Quarterly 29:263-79.

Johnson, Daniel M., and Rex R. Campbell
1981   Black Migration in America: A Social Demographic History. Durham, N.C.: Duke University Press.

Kousser, J. Morgan
1974   The Shaping of Southern Politics: Suffrage Restriction and the Establishment of the One-Party South, 1880-1910. New Haven, Conn.: Yale University Press.

Logan, Frenise A.
1964   The Negro in North Carolina, 1876-1894. Chapel Hill, N.C.: University of North Carolina Press.

Makridakis, Spyros, Steven C. Wheelwright, and Victor E. McGee
1983   Forecasting: Methods and Applications. New York: John Wiley and Sons.

Mancini, Matthew J.
1978   "Race, economics, and the abandonment of convict leasing." Journal of Negro History 63:339-52.

McCallie, S. W.
1911   "Use of convicts on the public roads of Georgia." Engineering Record 64:157-8.

McCleary, Richard, and Richard A. Hay, Jr.
1980   Applied Time Series Analysis for the Social Sciences. Beverly Hills, Calif.: Sage.

McMillen, Neil R.
1989   Dark Journey: Black Mississippians in the Age of Jim Crow. Urbana: University of Illinois Press.

Michalowski, Raymond J.
1985   Order, Law, and Crime: An Introduction to Criminology. New York: Random House.

Miller, Martin B.
1980   "Sinking gradually into the proletariat: The emergence of the penitentiary in the United States." Crime and Social Justice 14: 37-43.

Montgomery, Douglas C., and Ginner Weatherby
1980   "Modeling and forecasting time series using transfer function and intervention models." AIIE Transactions 12:289-306.

Myers, Samuel L., and William J. Sabol
1986   "The stability of punishment hypothesis: Regional differences in racially disproportionate prison populations and incarcerations, 1850-1950." Paper given at the annual meeting of the Law and Society Association, Chicago, Ill.

1987   "Unemployment and racial differences in imprisonment." The Review of Black Political Economy 16:189-209.

Novak, Daniel A.
1978   The Wheel of Servitude: Black Forced Labor after Slavery. Lexington: The University Press of Kentucky.

Parker, Robert Nash, and Allan V. Horwitz
1986   "Unemployment, crime and imprisonment: A panel approach." Criminology 24:751-73.

Pennybacker, J.E., H.S. Fairbank, and W.F. Draper
    1916   Convict Labor for Road Work. U.S. Department of Agriculture, Bulletin 414.
            Washington, D.C.: Government Printing Office.
Petchesky, Rosalind P.
    1981   "At hard labor: Penal confinement and production in nineteenth century America." In
            Crime and Capitalism: Readings in Marxist Criminology, ed. David F. Greenberg, 341-57.
            Palo Alto, Calif.: Mayfield Publishing Company.
Phillips, Charles David
    1986   "Social structure and social control: Modeling the discriminatory execution of blacks in
            Georgia and North Carolina, 1925-1935." Social Forces 65:458-75.
Poe, Clarence H.
    1904   "Rich kingdom of cotton." World's Work 9:5488-98.
Powell, J.C.
    [1891] The American Siberia. New York: Arno Press/The New York Times.
    1969
Principal Keeper of the Penitentiary
    1868-96 Reports to the Governor of the State of Georgia. Atlanta, Georgia: Department of
            Archives and History.
Prison Commission
    1897-   Reports to the Governor of the State of Georgia. Atlanta, Georgia: Department of
    1936   Archives and History.
Prison Industries Reorganization Administration
    1937   The Prison Labor Problem in Georgia. Unpubl. manuscript, University of Georgia Law
            Library.
Ransom, Roger L., and Richard Sutch
    1977   One Kind of Freedom: The Economic Consequences of Emancipation. Cambridge:
            Cambridge University Press.
Rauma, David
    1981   "Crime and punishment reconsidered: Some comments on Blumstein's stability of
            punishment hypothesis." Journal of Criminal Law and Criminology 72:1772-98.
Rusche, Georg
    [1933] "Labor markets and penal sanction: Thoughts on the sociology of criminal justice."
    1978   Trans. Gerda Dinwiddie. Crime and Social Justice 10:2-8.
Rusche, Georg, and Otto Kirchheimer
    1939   Punishment and Social Structure. New York: Columbia University Press.
Schlomowitz, Ralph
    1984   " 'Bound' or 'free'? black labor in cotton and sugarcane farming, 1865-1880." Journal of
            Southern History 50:569-96.
Sheffield, O.H.
    1894   Improvement in the Road System of Georgia. U.S. Department of Agriculture, Office of
            Public Road Inquiries, Bulletin 3. Washington, D.C.: Government Printing Office.
Shelden, Randall G.
    1981   "Convict leasing: An application of the Rusche-Kirchheimer thesis to penal changes in
            Tennessee, 1830-1915." In Crime and Capitalism: Readings in Marxist Criminology, ed.
            David F. Greenberg, 358-68. Palo Alto, Calif.: Mayfield Publishing Company.
Smith, Albert Colbey
    1982   Down Freedom's Road: The Contours of Race, Class and Crime in Black-belt Georgia,
            1866-1910. Ph.D. Diss., University of Georgia.
Spitzer, Steven
    1975   "Toward a Marxian theory of deviance." Social Problems 22:638-51.
    1979   "The rationalization of crime control in capitalist society." Contemporary Crises 3:187-206.
State Highway Board of Georgia
    1932   Fourteenth Report. Atlanta, Ga.
    1934   Fifteenth Report. Atlanta, Ga.
Taylor, A. Elizabeth
    1942a   "The abolition of the convict lease system in Georgia." Georgia Historical Quarterly
            26:273-87.

286   MYERS/MASSEY

    1942b   "The origin and development of the convict lease system in Georgia." Georgia Historical Quarterly 26:113-23.

Tindall, George Brown
    1952   South Carolina Negroes, 1877-1900. Columbia, S.C.: University of South Carolina Press.

Tolnay, Stewart E., E.M. Beck, and James L. Massey
    1989   "Black lynchings: The power threat hypothesis revisited." Social Forces 67:605-23.

U.S. Department of Agriculture
    1895   Progress of Road Construction in the United States. Office of Road Inquiry Bulletin 19. Washington, D.C.: Government Printing Office.
    1902   Road Conventions in the Southern States. Public Road Inquiries Bulletin 23. Washington, D.C.: Government Printing Office.
    1951-2 Statistical Bulletin 99. Bureau of Agricultural Economics. Washington, D.C.: Government Printing Office.

Walden, Mary
    1974   History of the Georgia Penitentiary at Milledgeville, 1817-1868. Masters Thesis, Georgia State University.

Wharton, Vernon Lane
    1947   "The Negro in Mississippi, 1865-1890." The James Sprunt Studies in History and Political Science, Vol. 28. Chapel Hill: University of North Carolina Press.

Williamson, Joel
    1984   The Crucible of Race: Black-White Relations in the South since Emancipation. New York: Oxford University Press.

Woodward, C. Vann.
    1971   Origins of the New South, 1877-1913. Baton Rouge: Louisiana State University Press.

Wright, Gavin
    1986   Old South, New South: Revolutions in the Southern Economy since the Civil War. New York: Basic Books.

Wright, R.F.
    1897   Report of Special Inspector of Misdemeanor Convict Camps of Georgia. Atlanta: Franklin Printing and Publishing Company.

Zimmerman, Hilda Jane
    1947   Penal Systems and Penal Reform in the South since the Civil War. Ph.D. Diss., University of North Carolina.

[24]

THE KILLING FIELDS OF THE DEEP SOUTH: THE MARKET FOR COTTON AND THE LYNCHING OF BLACKS, 1882-1930*

E. M. BECK
University of Georgia

STEWART E. TOLNAY
State University of New York at Albany

We reconsider the relationship between economic conditions and the lynching of blacks in the Deep South from 1882 to 1930 using time series analysis. Net of other factors, lynchings were more frequent in years when the "constant dollar" price of cotton was declining and inflationary pressure was increasing. Relative size of the black population was also positively related to lynching. We conclude that mob violence against southern blacks responded to economic conditions affecting the financial fortunes of southern whites — especially marginal white farmers. These effects were significantly more important in the decades before 1900, possibly because of the declining importance of agriculture, the "Jim Crow" disenfranchisement of blacks, and the increasing out-migration of blacks and whites from the Deep South.

B etween Emancipation and the Great Depression, about 3,000 blacks were lynched in the American south. Despite extensive commentary by contemporary observers of the lynching era (e.g., Ames 1942; Cutler 1905; Raper 1933; White [1929] 1969; Young 1927-28), and recent attention by social scientists, we still know little about the underlying causes of mob violence during this period. Some consensus has emerged that lynching was a response by white southerners to perceived *threats* from the black population. Recent empirical investigations have referred to: (1) the *political threats* of a large black population (Beck, Massey, and Tolnay 1989; Corzine, Creech, and Corzine 1983; Reed 1972; Tolnay, Beck, and Massey 1989); (2) *economic competition* between southern white and black laborers (e.g., Corzine, Corzine, and Creech 1988); or (3) maintenance of the *caste boundary* that assured whites superior social status, despite the often minuscule difference between the economic well-being of blacks and whites (e.g., Inverarity 1976). While this research has produced fragmentary evidence to support a "threat model" of black lynchings, that model largely remains a working hypothesis. A somewhat

different emphasis is found in the perennial suspicion that mob violence responds to temporal swings in economic conditions, particularly cotton production, with lynchings increasing during times of sparse cotton revenues, and declining with increasing cotton profits. This hypothesis has an interesting history.

In the 1933 classic The *Tragedy of Lynching*, Arthur Raper presents graphic evidence apparently linking the incidence of lethal mob violence against southern blacks to variation in the value of southern cotton crops. Raper concludes " . . . periods of relative prosperity bring reductions in lynching and periods of depression cause an increase. Mathematically, this relationship is shown by the correlation of -0.532" (1933, p. 30). According to Raper (1933, p. 31), economic competition between marginal black and white laborers accounts for the association between economic conditions and lynching. The economic hardship caused by a poor profit from the cotton crop leads to an effort by whites to replace black workers with unemployed white laborers. Mob violence was a form of intimidation to facilitate this labor substitution.

Seven years later, Hovland and Sears (1940) used similar data to again demonstrate an association between swings in the southern economic cycle and lynching. They report impressive evidence that lethal mob violence against blacks became more acute during years of economic stagnation when the value of cotton was depressed. Unlike Raper, however, Hovland and Sears interpret the association as support for a

* This research was partially funded by grants from the National Science Foundation [SES-8618123], and the University of Georgia Research Foundation to Stewart E. Tolnay, E.M. Beck, and James L. Massey. The suggestions and criticisms of Pat Horan, Martha Myers, and Peggy Hargis, the editor and three anonymous reviewers, greatly improved our manuscript.

goal-frustration model of aggression. When low cotton prices frustrated southern whites in their quest for economic security, they lashed out violently at the subordinate black population. They buttress their "goal-frustration" interpretation by noting, "By no conceivable stretch of the imagination could the victims of lynchings, either Negro or white, be considered responsible for the value of cotton or the general level of business activity" (Hovland and Sears 1940, p. 348). Clearly, Hovland and Sears had rather limited imaginations, since southern whites had a well-documented history of blaming blacks for social and economic problems for which they were not responsible. It was the empirical evidence offered by Hovland and Sears, however, that was challenged.

Mintz (1946) found Hovland and Sears' study methodologically wanting. By re-analyzing the lynching data using a different measure of association and allowing for nonlinearities and other methodological complexities, Mintz found that the relationship between the value of southern cotton and black lynchings was still negative, but substantially weaker than reported by Hovland and Sears. He concludes that the evidence does not support a linkage between the value of the southern cotton crop and lynching.

Despite the serious questions raised by Mintz, the assumption that black lynchings were partially a function of swings in the southern economic cycle (primarily the fortunes of cotton) persists in the social science literature. Reed and colleagues surveyed this literature and found the cotton price lynching association cited routinely and uncritically as an example of the frustration-aggression process (Reed, Doss, and Hulbert 1987). They dubbed this presumed relationship as "too good to be false." Still, a definitive assessment of the form or strength of association between southern cotton production and black lynchings has yet to be offered.

In this paper, we reconsider the relationship between lynching and economic conditions by examining annual trends between 1882 and 1930. We build upon earlier work by: (1) employing more accurate lynching data; (2) specifying more precisely the relationship between mob violence and the price of cotton by decomposing price changes into changes in the constant dollar price of cotton and changes due to inflation; (3) differentiating between the effects of cotton price changes and cotton productivity; and lastly, (4) exploiting analytical techniques unavailable to Hovland and Sears.

WHITE CLASS STRUCTURE AND ECONOMIC EXPLANATIONS FOR LYNCHINGS

The hypothesized link between temporal swings in the price of cotton and black lynchings assumes that southern whites responded to economic stress by resorting to racial violence. Their motives may have been "instrumental," as suggested by Raper (1933), or "emotional" as described by Hovland and Sears' (1940) frustration-aggression model. Is it naive, however, to believe that southern whites were unanimous in their economic interests and responses? Bonacich (1972, 1975) argues that rural southern white society was divided into two major classes — the dominating planters and employers, and a class of day laborers, sharecroppers, and tenants. Planters and employers were *dependent* on the cheap labor provided by blacks. But, white laborers were *threatened* by the competition from a cheaper black labor force. While the economic interests of these two white classes diverged in many important respects, periods of economic distress may have created a potential for convergence — at least with respect to racial violence. When cotton profits were down, both the white elite and the white poor may have perceived certain advantages to heightened racial hostility and mob violence.

The late 19th and early 20th centuries were years of shrinking fortunes for many southern rural whites. The rate of white farm tenancy increased throughout the period (U.S. Bureau of the Census 1975), and black and white labor was thrown into direct competition on a significant scale for the first time (Jaynes 1986). This was an undesirable situation for marginal whites during the best of times; when the cotton economy was slack it was virtually intolerable. Poor whites, suffering from reduced incomes, perceived neighboring blacks to be competitors for a shrunken economic "pie," as well as a challenge to their superior social station that was "guaranteed" by the caste system.

In some cases, the response of poor whites to financial stress was clearly instrumental, driven by a desire to reduce competition from blacks. Williamson (1984, pp. 441-42) notes,

> . . . the history of bust and boom [in the cotton economy] had something to do with the history of Radicalism. Heated anti-black sentiment in the early nineties was related to the fact that black men sought places that white men felt they needed

in order to live and support their wives and children.

Violence was used by marginal whites to force black tenant farmers off desirable land (Williamson 1984), or to drive away successful black businessmen or landowners (e.g., White 1969, pp. 11-2).

Worsening economic conditions for poor rural whites also emphasized the relatively small difference between their level of financial well-being and that of nearby blacks. This made more salient the superior social status that even desperately poor whites took for granted as members of the dominant southern caste. As White (1969, pp. 11-2) observed, "It is not difficult to imagine the inner thoughts of the poor white as he sees members of a race he has been taught by tradition, and by practically every force of public opinion with which he comes into contact, to believe inferior making greater progress than his own." Thus, violence in response to economic distress sometimes took on an "expressive" nature as well. In some cases, poor whites reacted out of frustration to the contradiction between their objective economic status and the expected benefits of white supremacy. In other cases, lynchings were intended as a message to the black community — reminding them of their inferior position in white society.

The white elite also benefitted from a heightened sense of racial antagonism and the violence that accompanied it. Most important was their perennial fear of a coalition between black and white labor. Such a coalition was perhaps the greatest threat to the social, economic, and political hegemony enjoyed by the southern white elite. It was in the interest of the white elite, therefore, to perpetuate hostility between black and white laborers. Raper (1933, p. 47) noted this function of lynching when he wrote, "Lynchings tend to minimize social and class distinctions between white plantation owners and white tenants . . . ." Shapiro (1988, p. 219) put it more directly, "When those committed to racial subordination saw the possibility of blacks and whites coming together for common purposes, their response most often was to reach for the gun and the rope." The threat of a coalition between black and white laborers likely increased when the poor of both races suffered from reduced cotton prices.

In sum, the economy of the Deep South was dependent upon the fortunes of the cotton crop. As "King Cotton" went, so went the region.

Declining prices had serious consequences for *all* groups involved in the production of cotton. Rural blacks were the most vulnerable in a society stratified by class *and* caste. There is reason to believe that racial hatred and the violence it spawned served the interests of poor whites *and* the white elite during periods of economic stress. Of course, the motives and objectives of the two classes were not necessarily the same. For poor whites, violence was a response to fear of black competition for economic and social position. For the white elite, violence prevented a coalition between black and white laborers. Thus, the relationship between swings in the cotton economy and black lynchings does not assume participation by a single *class* of southern whites. Nor does it assume a coordinated response by all whites.

KING COTTON AND MOB VIOLENCE: GENERAL PATTERNS

The broad historical sequence is uncontested: the peak of black lynchings in the early 1890s coincided with a softening demand for southern cotton, the rise of populism and agrarian protest, and the birth of radical racism (Gaither 1977; Hahn 1983; Shapiro 1988; White 1969; Williamson 1984; Wright 1986). The bloody 1890s were followed by several years of ballooning cotton prices and an apparent decline in violence against southern blacks. Following World War I, however, there was a significant reversal of this trend, when an alarming bottoming of the cotton market was accompanied by another wave of radical racism, signalled by the dramatic re-birth of the Ku Klux Klan and the popular acclaim lavished on D.W. Griffith's epic film, *Birth of A Nation*.

To examine this apparent relation, we employ newly available data on lynchings in the Deep South to trace trends in the annual number of black victims of lynch mobs and the price per pound of cotton during the years 1882 to 1930. The basic data are displayed in Figure 1.[1] Between the early 1890s and mid-1910s,

---

[1] Both time series have been twice-smoothed statistically using three-year moving averages in order to visually simplify the underlying trends. The Deep South is defined as the six states of Alabama, Arkansas, Georgia, Louisiana, Mississippi, and South Carolina. The cotton price data refer to December 1 average prices for years prior to 1909 and seasonal averages thereafter (U.S. Bureau of the Census 1975, Series K 555). Texas was also a major producer of

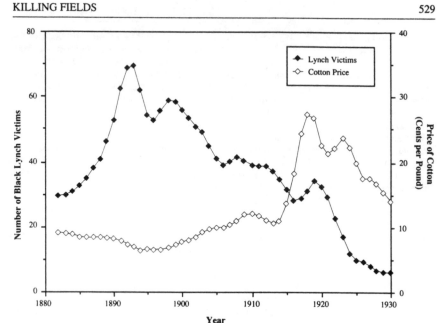

Figure 1. Number of Black Lynch Victims and the Price of Cotton in the Deep South, 1882-1930 *

* Both trends twice-smoothed statistically using three-year moving averages. Cotton prices per pound are unadjusted for inflation.

there was a broad downward trend in the number of black lynch victims, concurrent with a general upward swing in the market price of cotton. These two smoothed trends are linearly correlated -.67 over the entire 48-year period. Using the raw, unsmoothed series, the correlation is still a respectable -.52. Raper (1933) and Hovland and Sears (1940) based their conclusions on similar evidence.

It must be demonstrated, however, that this general historical correspondence between mob violence and the vagaries of the cotton market is something more than coincidence. Several problems must be considered before concluding that swings in the price of cotton actually drove corresponding swings in the level of mob violence against blacks. First, a correlation between any two time series is insufficient to establish a functional relationship. To reach conclusions about the covariation of two time trends, their dependence on time must be re-

cotton and could have been included in the time series. However, because of difficulties in locating suitable local newspapers, we have not been able to confirm a sufficient number of Texas lynchings to justify its inclusion in our analysis.

moved by "detrending" both time series.

Second, the overall negative correlation suggests that as prices rose, the likelihood of a black lynching diminished. But increasing cotton prices may reflect *inflationary* trends as well as changes in the *constant dollar* price of cotton. Would black lynchings decline if cotton prices increased solely as a result of inflation? Between 1917 and 1918, the average market price for cotton *increased* almost 1.8¢ per pound, but the deflated price actually *fell* close to 1.6¢ per pound. Thus an apparent increase in market price masked what was in reality a worsening condition for cotton producers and others whose livelihoods depended on a healthy King Cotton.

To the degree that advances in cotton prices were matched by inflation in the cost of staples, marginal whites experienced no net gain, and thus there would be no softening of racial antagonism. In fact, if inflation were sufficiently high, the plight of many agrarian whites would harden, and their tenuous position become even more precarious. Under these conditions, the frustration-aggression model predicts that increased hostility would be directed toward blacks, even though the apparent price of cotton was increasing. Thus, increases in the constant dollar price of cotton should be *negatively* correlated with lethal violence against blacks, while increases due to inflation should have the opposite effect. To adequately consider the cotton price lynching hypothesis, "price" data must be decomposed into two parts: the deflated price and an inflationary component, and each component related separately to the frequency of lynching.

The third problem is the lack of any considerations of the concentration of black population living in the Deep South. Although there is no logically necessary relationship between black population concentration and the frequency of black lynchings, dwindling black population might produce some lessening of black white competition (see e.g., Blalock 1967; Tolnay and Beck, forthcoming), as well as offer fewer targets for white aggression, resulting in fewer blacks killed by mob action.

Fourth, Figure 1 ignores the effects of changes in agricultural productivity that are not translated into price shifts. Changes in cotton productivity may affect lynchings net of their impact on prices. During the 1882-1930 period the amount of cotton harvested in the Deep South varied from a high near 9,000,000 bales in 1914 to less than 4,000,000 bales in 1923. The *total income* derived from the cultivation of cotton is determined by both the price per pound paid to farmers *and* the number of pounds produced. The potential economic hardship implied by declining cotton prices could be offset by higher yields — resulting in relatively stable *total* income.

Finally, while previous interpretations of the link between cotton prices and lynching assume a process of "black victimization" (either expressive or instrumental) at the hands of southern whites, alternative interpretations are possible. An increase in the number of lynchings during periods of economic distress could be a white reaction to an increasing incident of crime committed by blacks during these periods. If so, we would expect a significant attenuation in the association between cotton prices and lynching after controlling for the level of black crime. If the relationship persists, then the "black victimization" theory cannot be dismissed. (It is possible that both processes were operating.)

In sum, the apparently straightforward evidence demonstrating a linkage between the value of cotton and lynching, presented in Figure 1, is far from conclusive. In light of the issues discussed above, we have formulated an analytical model of black lynchings that incorporates: (1) a distinction between the deflated price of cotton and it's inflationary component; (2) a control for changes in the size of the black population; (3) a measure of cotton productivity; and (4) a proxy measure of the level of crime committed by blacks.

DATA AND METHOD OF ANALYSIS

Our dependent variable is the number of black lynchings each year between 1882 and 1930. We focus on the 1882-1930 period because: (1) there were no reasonable data on lynchings prior to 1882, and (2) 1930 marked the end of widespread lynchings in the South. For our purposes, a lynching is defined as the killing of one or more blacks at the hands of an extra-legal mob of three or more individuals. This definition is generally consistent with the definition adopted by the NAACP [1919] (1969), and does not include casualties of race riots, racially-motivated murders committed by fewer than three conspirators, or mob violence that did not end in the death of a victim.

It is debatable whether the most appropriate measurement of the dependent variable is the number of *incidents* in which at least one black was killed by collective action, or the number of blacks killed at the hands of a mob. In most instances the two are identical since most lynchings involved only one victim. Preliminary analysis using both variables demonstrated that it did not matter which dependent variable was used. We report the results using the number of black lynching victims as the dependent variable.

There are three public sources of data on lynchings. The best known is the inventory distributed by the NAACP (1969) covering the years 1889 to 1918, and the annual supplements thereafter. From 1882 through 1918, the Chicago *Tribune* newspaper published a list of lynchings in their year-end summaries. Finally, there is an inventory compiled by Daniel Williams (unpublished) of Tuskegee University. Initially we planned to use these three files as cross-checks for accuracy, but quickly learned that the sources were not independent. Williams's list utilized data from both the Chicago *Tribune* and NAACP, as well as from newspaper clipping files at Tuskegee. It also appears that the NAACP relied upon the *Trib-*

une with some frequency.

Starting with these three sources, we compiled a master list of reported lynchings, noting discrepancies in details. Next, we verified every lynching on our master list using local and regional newspapers of the period. During this process, we found that the three sources contained many factual errors. We also discovered lynchings that had been overlooked by all three sources. The analysis presented here includes only those black lynchings we were able to confirm. Our inventory consists of 2,041 victims killed by lynch mobs in the Deep South between 1882 and 1930 of whom 1,844 were black. While these data are subject to revision in light of new information, we believe they are now the most reliable and accurate data on southern lynchings.

The independent variables in our analysis were chosen in consideration of the issues discussed above. The overall price of cotton was decomposed into the constant dollar (deflated) price per pound and the inflationary component of the price per pound. The inflationary component is the simple difference between the unadjusted market price and the deflated price. Information to determine the inflationary component of cotton prices was drawn from annual consumer price deflators for the relevant years (U.S. Bureau of the Census 1975, p. 210).

Two measures of the size of the black population are included — the absolute size of the black population and the percent of the population that is black. Statistics on the size of the black population were obtained from decennial census data (U.S. Bureau of the Census 1975, pp. 23-37). Black population for inter censal years was estimated by linear interpolation.

Total annual production of cotton is measured by the number of bales of cotton (in 1000s) ginned in the Deep South. These data are from *Statistics on Cotton and Related Data* (U.S. Department of Agriculture 1951-52).

Our measure of the annual level of black crime is necessarily less precise than the other explanatory variables. Annual statistics on crimes committed by blacks in all six states are not available for this historical period. We constructed a somewhat imperfect proxy based on the number of blacks legally executed annually in the Deep South:[2]

---

[2] The numerator of this ratio uses the number of black executions in year (t+1) to reflect black crime in year (t). Considering the lag between the commission of a crime and the executions, executions in

Black crime rate$_t$ =
	10,000 (black executions$_{t+1}$ /
	black population$_t$)

This proxy has two weaknesses: (1) by using executions we capture only the *most serious* crimes and thus underestimate the actual amount of crime committed by blacks; and (2) blacks were executed for crimes against blacks as well as crimes against whites so that using black executions overestimates the rate of black against white crime. This variable must be interpreted with caution.

We estimated a time-series model that could have both auto-regressive and moving-average components:

$$Y_t = \phi_0 + \Sigma\phi_k(X_{kt}) + \alpha_1 u_{t-1} + \alpha_2 u_{t-2} \ldots + \\ \alpha_p \mu_{t-p} + e_t - \beta_1 e_{t-1} - \beta_2 e_{t-2} \ldots - \beta_q e_{t-q} \quad (1)$$

where t is a given year from 1882 to 1930, Y_t is the number of black victims of lynch mobs in year t, ϕ_0 is a constant, ϕ_k are effect parameters, X_{kt} are the exogenous factors (size of black population$_t$, percent black$_t$, deflated price of cotton$_t$, inflation in cotton price$_t$, cotton bales produced$_t$, and the black crime rate$_t$), u_{t-p} are auto-regressive disturbances, α_p are the pth-order auto-regressive coefficients, e_t is random noise, and the β_q are the qth-order moving-average coefficients that permit the random components to be serially related. We examined a variety of auto-regressive and moving-average specifications before settling on the differenced, first-order moving-average models presented in Table 1.[3] These models produced the most parsimonious and conceptually meaningful results.

---

period (t+1) reflect criminality in year (t). The execution data are from Watt Espy's Capital Punishment Research Project. Espy conducted a detailed examination of local records and archival collections in an attempt to identify every legal, non-military execution conducted in the United States. His inventory is considered the most complete enumeration of executions currently available (Bowers 1984).

[3] Taking first differences removes trends that could lead to spurious conclusions (see Gottman 1981, and McCleary and Hay 1980). We used iterative nonlinear least squares to estimate the auto-regressive and moving-average models, using the Box Jenkins routine in the R.A.T.S. (Regression Analysis of Times Series) software produced by VAR Econometrics, Inc. We also explored various lags for the exogenous variables, but none of these models proved superior to the ones reported here.

RESULTS

The results of the time-series analysis of the effects of cotton prices, cotton productivity, and demographic factors on the frequency of lynchings for the 1883-1930 period are presented in Table 1.[4] All variables have been differenced to produce stationarity and then lynchings modeled as a first-order moving-average process, as described above.

Model A includes the main effects of the exogenous variables, ignoring any interactions between changes in the real price of cotton and changes in productivity. In this model, the coefficients for the constant dollar price of cotton, the inflationary component of cotton price, and the quantity of cotton harvested are in the expected direction, although the effect for cotton production is not significant. The interpretation of the coefficients for the black population measures in Model A is muddled because of a strong correlation between change in the absolute and relative size of the black population over this historical period. This collinearity introduces undesirable redundancy into the analysis. Model B re-estimates the equation omitting the absolute population size variable. The t-ratio for percent black increases from 1.01 in Model A to 2.31 in Model B, and the t-ratios for the remaining variables increase as well. Model C includes an interaction term between constant dollar cotton price and cotton production to allow the effect of cotton price on lynchings to vary depending on the amount of cotton harvested.

Several findings are noteworthy. First, changes in the constant dollar price of cotton have the expected negative effect on black lynchings, while inflationary changes in cotton price have the anticipated positive relationship. This indicates that when the constant price was climbing the likelihood of black lynchings declined. During hard times when the price of cotton stagnated, or when inflation was a significant problem, black lynchings in the Deep South were more frequent.[5] Furthermore, the

Table 1. Regression of Number of Black Lynching Victims on Cotton Price and Production, and Related Variables: 1883-1930[a]

Variable	Model A	Model B	Model C	Model D
Constant	3.499 (0.56)	2.794 (1.66)	2.851 (1.74)	2.797 (1.94)
Size of black population	-0.00001 (-0.12)	----	----	----
Percent black	17.945 (1.01)	16.056 (2.31)	16.194 (2.39)	15.453 (2.57)
Market price for cotton:				
Constant dollar price	-2.130 (-2.22)	-2.148 (-2.31)	-4.699 (-1.57)	-5.353 (-1.81)
Inflationary component	2.371 (2.42)	2.374 (2.46)	2.420 (2.52)	2.327 (2.55)
Cotton bales produced	-0.002 (-1.05)	-0.002 (-1.08)	-0.005 (-1.21)	-0.007 (-1.54)
Constant dollar price × cotton bales	----	----	0.0004 (0.90)	0.001 (1.24)
Black crime rate proxy	----	----	----	113.665 (1.87)
Moving-average coefficient	-0.463 (-3.21)	-0.465 (-3.26)	-0.483 (-3.37)	-0.541 (-3.89)
R^2	0.738	0.738	0.743	0.763
Adjusted R^2	0.699	0.706	0.705	0.721
Ljung-Box Q Coefficient	20.04	19.82	18.23	19.65
Durbin-Watson Statistic	1.78	1.78	1.77	1.89

[a] First-order moving-average models, all variables differenced once; t-ratios in parentheses; N = 48.

coefficients for Model C indicate that a one-cent advance in the constant dollar price of cotton had a larger effect in reducing lynching victims (-4.70) than a one-cent rise in the inflationary component for increasing mob violence (+2.42).[6]

ship between change in the *unadjusted* price of cotton and black lynchings, suggesting that if cotton price had not been decomposed into constant dollar changes and inflationary changes, we would have missed the significant relationship between the market for cotton and mob violence against blacks.

[6] While the coefficient for the deflated price of cotton in Model C is not twice its standard error, this is due to its collinearity with the interaction term. If the interaction term is omitted from Model C (as in Model B), the coefficient for the deflated price of cotton has a t-ratio of -2.31.

---

[4] Since the variables in the empirical models in Table 1 have been differenced once, the actual time period covered is 1883 to 1930, rather than 1882-1930.

[5] To examine the effect of decomposing cotton prices, we replaced the two components (deflated price and the inflationary component) with the unadjusted price of cotton and re-estimated each of the models in Table 1. The results show little relation-

Second, changes in the racial composition of the population influenced the likelihood of lethal mob action. Net of price factors, increases in percent black are associated with more frequent black lynchings. This finding is consistent with the conflict perspective of social control that suggests that a high proportion of blacks in the population represents a "threat" to white hegemony and leads to stern measures of social control, such as lynching (e.g., Blalock 1967). Naturally, we cannot decipher from these results the social or economic processes represented by the strong impact of percent black on lynchings.

Third, net of price shifts, cotton productivity had a negative relationship with lynchings, but this effect is not large relative to the amount of variation in the time series, as shown by the coefficient's small size relative to its standard error. We also found a positive interaction, albeit small, between cotton productivity and constant dollar price indicating that during years of enhanced production, the inhibiting effect of the deflated price of cotton on lynchings weakened. In other words, the link between the deflated price of cotton and the frequency of black lynchings was strongest during periods of slowed cotton production. Thus, it appears that higher levels of production were able to "blunt" the sensitivity of agrarian whites to the farm price of a pound of cotton.

These findings are consistent with an interpretation of lynching behavior that stresses the victimization of blacks at the hands of whites. Sour market prices threatened the life chances of many southern whites, especially those on the margins of society. Economic distress also raised the possibility of a coalition between black and white labor, which threatened the social, economic and political advantages held by the white elite. The combination of these forces, which cut across class lines, generated aggressive and hostile behavior directed at the most vulnerable and powerless targets — southern blacks. The most radical form of this aggression was lethal mob violence, lynching.

The Role of Crimes Committed by Blacks. While these findings are consistent with the "black victimization" model of lynchings, they are also consistent with a radically different perspective that rests on the victimization of whites at the hands of black criminals. This interpretation rests on a different presumption, one that permeated the mentality of many whites in the Deep South (see e.g., DuBois 1969; Wil-

liamson 1984). Contemporary newspaper accounts and editorials often refer to crime committed by blacks, and to fears within the white community of the black "brute" criminal. In the popular mind of the times, lynching was a morally justified solution to virtually all crimes perpetrated by blacks against whites, ranging from insolence and petty theft to murder and rape. If worsening economic conditions produced more crime by blacks against whites and if there was little confidence in the criminal justice system, then increases in the frequency of lynching could be a logical although radically reactionary consequence. In this scenario, the role of commodity market factors is indirect.

Model D in Table 1, includes the proxy for the crime rate among blacks as an additional predictor of lynchings. If the "black crime" hypothesis is correct, inclusion of this factor should diminish or eliminate the net effect of cotton prices on black lynchings. This is not the case. In fact, including the crime rate proxy *increases* the coefficient for the constant dollar price of cotton, and reduces or has no effect on the standard errors of the remaining variables.[7]

Even if our indicator of black crime, however flawed, is only partially reflective of crime by blacks against whites, these findings suggest that black lynchings were not a simple reflection of criminal activity by blacks and that economic factors played an important and independent role in affecting mob violence.[8]

---

[7] There is considerable collinearity between the deflated price of cotton and the interaction term. Reestimating Model D without the interaction term, the t-value for the deflated price coefficient is -2.05 (detailed results not reported here but available from first author).

[8] The black crime explanation suffers from two other weaknesses. First, the southern criminal justice system was not lax in punishing blacks convicted of crime. Blacks received the same discriminatory treatment in southern courts that they received in the rest of society, including disproportionate imposition of the death penalty. Thus, it is unlikely that lynching was necessary to control crime. Second, if lynching was used to combat increasing crime, why was lynching used almost exclusively against blacks after 1900? Surely, criminal activity by whites should also have peaked during periods of economic stagnation or recession. A definitive investigation of the role of criminal behavior by blacks — either real or imagined — in mob violence against blacks awaits better measures.

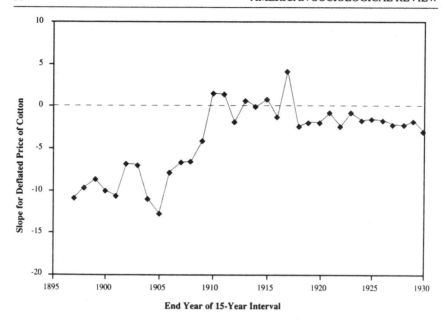

Figure 2. Effect of Deflated Price of Cotton on Number of Black Lynch Victims, 1883-1930 [a]

[a] The x-axis represents the end year of 15-year intervals, e.g., 1900 for the 1886-1900 interval, etc.

Historical Effects. Table 1 provides evidence that between the early 1880s and 1930, the frequency of black lynchings was influenced by the market for cotton. If this relationship was stable over this period, the results are informative. But if there were significant historical episodes that altered that basic relationship, our conclusions may be in error. This uncertainty is caused by the ahistorical nature of traditional time-series analysis.

The time-series model portrayed by equation (1) is "ahistorical" in the sense that there is no provision for changes in the functional relationship between black lynchings and the market for cotton. In other words, it precludes any interaction between "time" and the explanatory variables and implies that the relationship between mob violence against blacks and the southern cotton economy was the same during the 1920s as it was during the 1880s. This is a very restrictive assumption for a historical process.

One method for coping with this problem is to follow a "moving" time-series strategy that estimates the model parameters using successively incremented and overlapping time points over a fixed-length time interval. This proce-

dure is the same as the "diagonal" model discussed by Isaac and Griffin (1989, p. 879) in their timely discussion of the ahistorical properties of traditional time-series analysis. We first estimated the parameters for Model B for the 15-year interval 1883-1897. We then computed a second set of parameter estimates using the incremented 15-year interval 1884-1898, a third set for the interval 1885-1899, and so forth until the parameters of the last 15-year interval (1916-1930) had been estimated.[9] Using 15-year intervals and following this incremental procedure, we obtained 34 sets of coefficients. These coefficients were then plotted chronologically to show the longitudinal consistency of the relationship between lynchings and the explanatory variables.

---

[9] Model B was chosen to conserve degrees of freedom. Like the times-series findings reported in Table 1, the variables in the moving-regressions were differenced once, and the model estimated assuming a first-order moving-average specification. We also investigated alternative moving-regression specifications. Instead of a moving-regression with a fixed-length interval (e.g., 15 years) and floating beginning and end points, we also estimated models with a fixed starting point in 1883 but with variable inter-

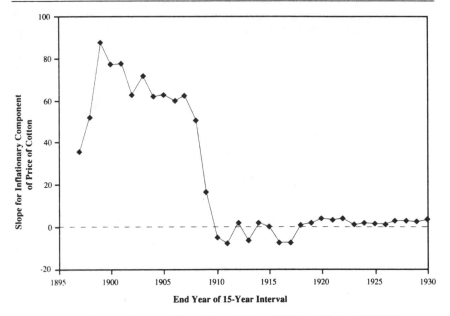

Figure 3. Effect of Inflationary Component of Cotton Price on Number of Black Lynch Victims, 1883-1930 *

* The x-axis represents the end year of 15-year intervals, e.g., 1900 for the 1886-1900 interval, etc.

In Figure 2, we plot the moving time-series for the effect of the deflated price of cotton on black lynchings, based on Model B. This graph clearly shows that the negative effect of the constant dollar price of cotton on mob violence was much stronger in the 1880s and 1890s than in the years following 1905. For example, for the fifteen years between 1891-1905, the effect of the deflated price of cotton on the number of black lynching victims was -12.72, while for the fifteen years ending in 1920, the effect was much weaker at -1.93.

In Figure 3, we graph the moving time-series effect of the inflationary component of cotton price on black lynching victims. This coefficient was not longitudinally stable either — it follows the same general declining trend as

val lengths ranging from 13 years (1883-1895) to 48 years (1883-1930). The results revealed the same patterns as shown in Figures 2 and 3. We also explored a "backwards" specification in which the end point was anchored at 1930, but the interval varied backwards (e.g., 1883-1930, 1884-1930, etc.). The results of these regressions suggested much less change over time in the model's parameters. Results of the moving-regressions are available from the first author.

Figure 2, i.e., inflation's positive effect on lynchings is considerably stronger in the 1880s and 1890s than in the later decades.

In sum, although gains in the constant dollar price of cotton were associated with declines in the annual toll of blacks lynched between 1882 and 1930, the effect was greatest during the last two decades of the nineteenth century. Similarly, inflation in cotton prices was associated with heightened lynching activity, but the link was stronger in the 1880s and 1890s than afterwards. These plots indicate that lethal mob violence against blacks was more tightly linked to the market for southern cotton before 1900 than later.

What social and economic trends might account for the weakening effect over time of the deflated price of cotton *and* inflation on black lynchings? While a definitive answer is beyond the scope of this paper, we advance some possible explanations that might be pursued in subsequent research. First, by the end of the first decade of the 20th century, these states had enacted measures that effectively disenfranchised blacks (Kousser 1974).[10] The politi-

[10] For some southern states, the "official" dates of

Table 2.   Selected Characteristics of the Deep South Economy, 1880 to 1930

Characteristic	1880	1890	1900	1910	1920	1930
Percent of workers in agriculture [a]	80.2	71.8	70.6	65.8	56.8	49.5
Percent of improved land in cotton [b]	34.1	36.1	33.2	35.1	31.6	34.2
Wage earners in manufacturing (1000s) [c]	66.1	136.5	268.7	397.2	478.5	541.5
Net migration of native whites (1000s) [d]	-19.1	-99.3	-187.5	-132.5	-243.2	-452.5
Net migration of blacks (1000s) [d]	1.0	22.7	-134.4	-134.8	-401.8	-685.6

[a] Source: Lee, Miller, Brainerd, and Easterlin (1957), Volume 1, Table L-4.

[b] Source: Census Office (1883, 1895, 1902); U.S. Bureau of the Census (1913, 1922, 1931, 1932).

[c] Source: Lee et al. (1957), Volume 1, Tables L-4 and M-2.

[d] Source: U.S. Bureau of the Census (1975). Net migration estimates for blacks and whites apply to the decade *preceding* the year shown. For example, net migration for 1900 refers to the decade 1890 to 1900.

cal neutralization of blacks may have allayed fears among the white elite about a political coalition between white and black labor.

A second possible explanation for the reduced influence of the cotton economy on black lynchings centers around the changing character of the southern economy during the late 19th and early 20th centuries. If the grip of King Cotton on the economy relaxed, its salience for lynchings would decline. Table 2 presents trends in selected characteristics of the southern economy from 1880 to 1930. In general, the evidence in Table 2 is consistent with this perspective. Although the percent of improved land planted in cotton remained relatively stable during this period, greater numbers of southern workers engaged in non-agricultural occupations. The percent of all workers employed in agriculture dropped from 80.2 percent in 1880 to 49.5 percent in 1930. The number of wage earners in manufacturing grew from 66,100 in 1880 to over 541,500 in 1930 — far outstripping the overall growth in the southern labor force.

A final potential explanation lies in the history of migration from the South during this period. Table 2 reveals increasing net *out-migration* for blacks and whites after 1890, with the pace of out-migration accelerating sharply after 1900. The out-migration of both races may have altered the association between swings in the cotton economy and black lynchings. White

voter disenfranchisement post date actual measures to reduce black political participation. For example, 1908 is generally considered the date of disenfranchisement for Georgia, since several restrictive voting statutes were approved in that year. In fact, blacks had been voting in very small numbers in Georgia long before 1908 (Kousser 1974).

migration may have acted as a "safety valve" of escape for marginal whites, while black migration reduced competition between blacks and agrarian whites.[11]

CONCLUSION

Using annual time-series data for the period 1882-1930 for six Deep South states, we find evidence that advances in the constant dollar price of cotton are associated with *fewer* black lynchings, while inflationary shifts in the price of cotton are associated with *increased* mob violence against blacks. After removing price fluctuations, changes in cotton production had little direct effect on lynchings, but there was a modest interaction effect between the deflated price of cotton and cotton production on black lynchings. In other words, increases in deflated cotton prices per pound had a deleterious effect on black lynchings, but the strength of this relationship was mediated somewhat by cotton crop productivity: as productivity grew, the salience of cotton price for mob violence declined. Finally, racial composition was also found to have an effect on lynching, with relatively large concentrations of black population accompanied by more lynchings.

We also examined an interpretation that lynchings were a white response to a perceived increase in crimes by blacks against whites. Controlling for a measure of crimes by blacks did not diminish the net importance of cotton prices or other predictor variables suggesting that powerful economic factors influence lethal

[11] See Tolnay and Beck (forthcoming) for a discussion of the effect of black out-migration on the southern economy and lethal violence against blacks.

mob behavior that cannot be reduced to simple issues of crime by blacks against whites.[12]

These findings are consistent with the view stressing the victimization of blacks in southern society. Economic downturns negatively impact all cotton producers, but the small farmer, sharecropper, or tenant suffers disproportionately because of a lack of capital resources. This economic squeeze not only threatens current standards of living, but jeopardizes the future as well. In Hovland and Sears' (1940) view, this represents "goal-frustration" and produces aggressive behavior. Although Hovland and Sears impute no "rational" motive to such aggressive behavior, Raper (1933) suggests it was related to attempts by white laborers to reduce competition from black laborers, and to replace blacks with unemployed whites. While this "marginal" class of southern agrarians contained both blacks and whites, blacks were relatively powerless to protest their plight or externalize their aggression. Whites, on the other hand, had options.

Marginal whites could direct their rage toward the powerful class of whites — large land owners, merchants, and bankers — but the costs of such hostility were clear.[13] Given the Deep South's racial caste structure, whites could

---

[12] Based on accounts of lynchings, it is clear that whites didn't congregate at the gin to lament the soft price of cotton, then decide to murder a black to relieve their psychological stress. Lynch mobs reacted to some supposed infraction of the norms governing caste relations, whether it be a minor act of racial imprudence or the major crime of murdering a white man. In this sense, it can be argued that black lynchings were a function of crimes committed by blacks. This perspective, however, goes on to argue that the prime reason for lynching was the inability of the existing system of criminal justice to cope with crime, and the motivation of lynch mobs was deeply rooted in a desire to maintain law and order. In the alternative "black victimization" view, such "crimes" were only specific triggering incidents that focused and justified outbreaks of violence toward blacks. The powerful dynamics driving these repressive forces originated in the southern economic system.

[13] This is not to argue, however, that there was no hostility between marginal whites and local elites. As early as the 1870s, there was growing conflict between these groups, and yeoman farmers began to organize for collective action. The swelling membership of the Southern Farmer's Alliance during the 1870s and 1880s is testimony to this conflict (Hahn 1983; Wright 1986). The point is that hostile actions toward the white elite risked retribution, while penalties for hostility against blacks were minimal.

harass and assault blacks with virtual impunity. Blacks were considered legitimate, and even deserving, objects for white wrath. White workers were in more direct economic competition with black laborers than with the white elite [see Bloom (1987) for a competing view]. Not only were black laborers a more immediate economic threat, but as the financial fortunes of poor whites and blacks converged, the superior status of whites was endangered.

According to the black victimization interpretation, the white elite also benefitted from increased racial hatred and violence during hard times. A coalition of poor whites and blacks threatened the privileged social, economic, and political position of the white elite. Such a coalition seemed most likely during the early stages of the Populist movement when poor whites and blacks in the south temporarily focused on a common antagonist. This racial alignment was quickly scuttled, however, as the southern Populist movement turned radically racist (Gaither 1977). During this same period — the early 1890s — black lynchings reached new highs.

Finally, our analysis suggests that the association between lynchings and cotton prices was not invariant throughout the time period examined here. The response of black lynchings to shifts in the deflated and inflationary components of the price of cotton weakened considerably after 1900. While this is not inconsistent with a linkage between the southern cotton economy and racial violence, it introduces a need for more exhaustive exploration into the precise nature of the linkage. We suggest several possible explanations, based on the changing character of the Deep South economy and the history of out-migration from the Deep South.

In future research we shall investigate the motivations underlying the relationships found in this analysis, especially the significance of the "cotton culture" for black lynchings. In the frustration-aggression hypothesis, cotton is a convenient indicator of economic conditions in the rural South. Yet Daniel (1985) advances a compelling argument that cotton had its own distinctive culture and historical legacy — that while sharing some features with the tobacco and sugar cultures in the South, it remained somehow "different." This raises an interesting question: Did lethal mob violence vary among the three agrarian "cultures" independent of shifts in the market price of southern crops? If so, cotton in the Deep South may have a dual role in the dynamics leading to mob violence: first, as an indicator of general economic conditions, and second, as representing a unique set of social relations and cultural values. Investigation of these "economic" and "cultural" roles await a time-series, cross-sectional analysis using disaggregated county-level data for the 1882-1930 period.

Our demonstration of a longitudinal association between cotton production and black lynchings resurrects an interesting relationship that had been prematurely laid to rest (Reed et al. 1987). Perhaps the relationship between "King Cotton" and black lynchings really is "too good to be false."

E. M. Beck is Associate Professor of Sociology at the University of Georgia. His current research focuses on the political economy of racial violence, in particular the relationship between economic changes in the status of the white lower class and violence against blacks. Beck and Tolnay are currently working on a book based on their recent research into southern lynchings.

Stewart E. Tolnay is Associate Professor of Sociology at the State University of New York at Albany. His research has been concentrated in two primary areas: (1) the causes and consequences of racial violence in the American South, and (2) fertility transitions in historical populations.

REFERENCES

Ames, Jesse. 1942. *The Changing Character of Lynching.* Atlanta, GA: Commission on Interracial Cooperation.

Beck, E.M, James L. Massey, and Stewart E. Tolnay. 1989. "The Gallows, The Mob, The Vote: Lethal Sanctioning of Blacks in North Carolina and Georgia, 1882 to 1930." *Law & Society Review* 23:317-31.

Blalock, Hubert M. 1967. *Toward a Theory of Minority-Group Relations.* New York: John Wiley.

Bloom, Jack M. 1987. *Class, Race, and the Civil Rights Movement.* Bloomington: Indiana University Press.

Bonacich, Edna. 1972. "A Theory of Ethnic Antagonism: The Split Labor Market." *American Sociological Review* 37:547-59.

Bonacich, Edna. 1975. "Abolition, the Extension of Slavery, and the Position of Free Blacks: A Study of Split Labor Markets in the United States, 1830-1863." *American Journal of Sociology* 81:601-28.

Bowers, William. 1984. *Legal Homicide: Death as Punishment in America, 1864-1982.* Boston: Northeastern University Press.

Corzine, Jay, James Creech, and Lin Corzine. 1983. "Black Concentration and Lynchings in the South: Testing Blalock's Power-Threat Hypothesis." *Social Forces* 61:774-96.

Corzine, Jay, Lin Corzine, and James Creech. 1988. "The Tenant Labor Market and Lynching in the South: A Test of Split Labor Market Theory." *Sociological Inquiry* 58:261-78.

Cutler, James Elbert. 1905. *Lynch-Law: An Investigation into the History of Lynchings in the United States.* New York: Longsman, Green.

Daniel, Pete. 1985. *Breaking the Land: The Transformation of Cotton, Tobacco, and Rice Cultures Since 1880.* Urbana: University of Illinois Press.

DuBois, W.E.B. [1903] 1969. *The Souls of Black Folk.* New York: The New American Library.

Gaither, Gerald H. 1977. *Blacks and the Populist Revolt: Ballots and Bigotry in the "New South."* Tuscaloosa: University of Alabama Press.

Gottman, John M. 1981. *Time-Series Analysis: A Comprehensive Introduction for Social Scientists.* Cambridge: Cambridge University Press.

Hahn, Steven. 1983. *The Roots of Southern Populism: Yeoman Farmers and the Transformation of the Georgia Upcountry, 1850-1890.* New York: Oxford University Press.

Hovland, Carl I. and Robert R. Sears. 1940. "Minor Studies of Aggression: Correlations of Economic Indices With Lynchings." *Journal of Psychology* 9:301-10.

Inverarity, James M. 1976. "Populism and Lynching in Louisiana, 1889-1896: A Test of Erikson's Theory of the Relationship Between Boundary Crises and Repressive Justice." *American Sociological Review* 41:262-80.

Issac, Larry and Larry Griffin. 1989. "Ahistoricism in Time-Series Analyses of Historical Process: Critique, Redirection, and Illustrations from U.S. Labor History." *American Sociological Review* 54:873-90.

Jaynes, Gerald David. 1986. *Branches Without Roots: Genesis of the Black Working Class in the American South, 1862-1882.* New York: Oxford University Press.

Kousser, J. Morgan. 1974. *The Shaping of Southern Politics: Suffrage Restriction and the Establishment of the One-Party South.* New Haven: Yale University Press.

Lee, Everett S., Ann R. Miller, Carol P. Brainerd, and Richard A. Easterlin. 1957. *Population Redistribution and Economic Growth, United States, 1870-1950.* Volume 1. Philadelphia: The American Philosophical Society.

McCleary, Richard and Richard A. Hay Jr. 1980. *Applied Time Series Analysis for the Social Sciences.* Beverly Hills: Sage Publications.

Mintz, Alexander. 1946. "A Re-examination of Correlations Between Lynchings and Economic Indices." *Journal of Abnormal Social Psychology* 41: 154-60.

National Association for the Advancement of Colored People. [1919] 1969. *Thirty Years of Lynching in the United States, 1889-1918.* New York: NAACP.

Raper, Arthur. 1933. *The Tragedy of Lynching.* Chapel Hill: University of North Carolina Press.

Reed, John Shelton. 1972. "Percent Black and Lynching: A Test of Blalock's Theory." *Social Forces* 50:356-60.

Reed, John Shelton, Gail E. Doss, and Jeanne S. Hulbert. 1987. "Too Good to be False: An Essay in the Folklore of Social Science." *Sociological Inquiry* 57:1-11.

Shapiro, Herbert. 1988. *White Violence and Black Response: From Reconstruction to Montgomery.* Amherst: The University of Massachusetts Press.

Tolnay, Stewart E. and E. M. Beck. Forthcoming. "Lethal Violence and the Great Migration, 1900 to 1930." *Social Science History.*

Tolnay, Stewart E., E. M. Beck, and James L. Massey. 1989. "Black Lynchings: The Power Threat Hypothesis Revisited." *Social Forces* 67:605-23.

U. S. Bureau of the Census. 1913. *Thirteenth Census, 1910. Volume V. Agriculture. 1909 and 1910. General Report and Analysis.* Washington, D.C.: Government Printing Office.

_____. 1922. *Fourteenth Census, 1920. Volume V. Agriculture. General Report and Analytical Tables.* Washington, D.C.: Government Printing Office.

_____. 1931. *Fifteenth Census, 1930. Agriculture. Volume I. Farm Acreage and Farm Values by Townships or Other Minor Civil Divisions.* Washington, D.C.: Government Printing Office.

_____. 1932. *Fifteenth Census, 1930. Agriculture, Vol. II, Part 2. The Southern States, Reports by State with Statistics for Counties and a Summary for the United States.* Washington, D.C.: Government Printing Office.

_____. 1975. *Historical Statistics of the United States: Colonial Times to 1970.* Washington, D.C.: Government Printing Office.

U. S. Census Office. 1883. *Tenth Census, 1880. Report on the Production of Agriculture. General Statistics.* Washington D.C.: Government Printing Office.

_____. 1895. *Eleventh Census, 1890. Report on the Statistics of Agriculture in the United States.* Washington, D.C.: Government Printing Office.

_____. 1902. *Twelfth Census, 1900. Agriculture. Part 1. Farms, Live Stock, and Animal Products.* Washington, D.C.: Government Printing Office.

U.S. Department of Agriculture. 1951-52. *Statistics on Cotton and Related Data.* Bureau of Agricultural Economics, Statistical Bulletin No. 99. Washington, D.C.: Government Printing Office.

White, Walter. [1929] 1969. *Rope and Faggot.* New York: Arno Press.

Williams, Daniel T. Unpublished. *Amid the Gathering Multitude: The Story of Lynching in America. A Classified Listing.* Tuskegee University.

Williamson, Joel. 1984. *The Crucible of Race: Black-White Relations in the American South Since Emancipation.* New York: Oxford University Press.

Wright, Gavin. 1986. *Old South, New South: Revolutions in the Southern Economy Since the Civil War.* New York: Basic Books.

Young, Earle F. 1927-28. "The Relation of Lynching to the Size of Political Areas." *Sociology and Social Research* 12:348-53.

[25]

Prologue to a History of Women's Imprisonment: In Search of a Feminist Perspective

Adrian Howe

The question for feminists has always been: Where do we start? The answer cannot be other than: where we are and with the condition and problems which history presents to us.

— Mary O'Brian (1986)

I WOULD LIKE TO WRITE A HISTORY OF WOMEN'S IMPRISONMENT IN Australia. It would be written from a feminist and socialist perspective and would focus on penal policies which affected women in states, such as Victoria, that did not originate as penal colonies. The aim would be to shed light on dimensions of penality that have been ignored by the plethora of masculinist studies of "our" convicts (read: male convicts) in that premier penal colony, New South Wales — studies which purport to be general histories. A feminist intervention in this field is long overdue: mine has been delayed by denial of access to historical records pertaining to women's imprisonment in my home state, Victoria.[1]

This article is a search for an appropriate framework in which to situate a history of women's imprisonment in Australia: it is a necessary prolegomenon to that history. The range of possibilities includes the "new" scholarships in neo-Marxist theories of crime, social control histories and penology, feminist criminology, feminist social histories, feminist epistemologies as well as the crucial, though still androcentric, processes of theorization that have taken us from penology to "the social analysis of penality" (Garland and Young, 1983: 2). Of particular interest are recent feminist challenges to the hegemony of

ADRIAN HOWE is a lecturer in criminology, Legal Studies, La Trobe University, Bundoora, Victoria, Australia 3083. She is currently writing *Beyond Penology* for the book series entitled *The Sociology of Law and Crime: Feminist and Socialist Perspectives*, edited by Carol Smart and Maureen Cain.

patriarchal forms of "knowledge" — challenges which have empowered me not only to dismiss criminology, but also to dip irreverently into recent "social" histories of crime and punishment; to raid and pilfer ideas from them; to trample across the freshly painted discursive boundaries of "penality" and "social control." My aim here is to disrupt the newly formulated discourse on "penality" — to "use it, to deform it, to make it groan and protest" — and if the new grand masters, i.e., the revisionist plotters of "master patterns" of penal history (and their apologists), wish to protest that I have been "unfaithful," may I say with Foucault that "that is of absolutely no interest" (Foucault, 1980: 53–54).

II

Where to start? This is a difficult decision as it may commit me to a position which I may wish to abandon, or modify, or even soundly condemn. It seemed logical, however, that a history of women's imprisonment — a history, that is, of the criminalization of women — would start with criminology or, at least, with its sub-branch, penology. This proved to be an inauspicious start. Let feminist analysts explain why. Inasmuch as "theoretical criminology was constructed by men, about men," it is "simply not up to the analytical task" of explaining women's crime (Leonard, 1982: *xi*). Furthermore, when traditional criminologists did, on occasion, deign to consider women, they were obsessed with "violations of gender prescriptions" and their explanations of "female criminality" were consequently "steeped in gender assumptions." This silence, broken occasionally by an obsession with the two dominant images of female criminals — that of the "evil woman" and the bad (or "fallen") little girl (Rafter and Stanko, 1982: 5–10) — proved to be a fatal combination: it led criminologists to overlook the historical realities of women's crime and punishment and, thus, to contribute to a process by which criminology and penology came to "distort their own subject matter" (Rafter, 1982: 256). The first, belated, feminist interventions into these heavily male-dominated fields of "knowledge" were predictable enough: they criticized the almost exclusive focus on the male subject within criminological and penological discourse and called for more studies of female offenders. The goal was to redress the balance and also to correct false stereotypes about female lawbreakers. However, problems attached to the idea of developing a feminist criminology became apparent. First, there was a tendency to get caught up in old etiological questions — questions which had already been discarded by the "new" criminologies. Second, there was a tendency to reduce the whole question of women and crime to that of the impact of women's liberation on patterns of female lawbreaking (Smart, C., 1977). Third, the idea of subjecting women to criminologically based research was highly problematic in that it assumed that such research, "emptied of sexism" would be valid. The problem with this was not merely that criminological theorizing is "riddled with false stereotypes of men" (Gelsthorpe, 1986: 143). More crucially, a feminist criminology would only "repeat the same criminology" it had berated for leaving women out. That is, by taking "female criminality" as its object, a feminist criminology would repeat the most traditional, most unquestioned, concept of criminology — "criminality" (Cousins, 1980: 111).

Now, a critical examination of "criminality" — in particular, a close analysis of how the penal system is implicated in the gendering of males, could lead to a new feminist criminological agenda. Certainly, it *is* "astounding that the most significant feature of 'criminality' — its profound gendering — has been ignored for so long" (Cain, 1986b: 21). But while theorizing about why most criminals are men would help move feminist criminologists beyond critique, and while this theorizing is bound to have implications for a study of the "notsaid" of women prisoners, it is doubtful whether what we would be doing could validly be called "criminology." Carol Smart was one of the first to explain why. As early as 1976 she claimed that although it "might appear desirable" to formulate a feminist criminology to supplement the "new" criminologies which had failed to address the question of women (in this respect they were not so "new"), it was "perhaps more appropriate" to develop a feminist sociology of crime in that criminology had "invested so much of its interest in social policy and control" (Smart, C., 1976: 182). In this, Smart anticipated the major source of disenchantment with the project of creating a more plausible criminology, for that discipline, as historical analysis shows, is hopelessly compromised by its past and continuous collusion with governmental power and policy — that is, by its long-established association with the social control apparatus of the state.

This is not the place to explore the historical origins of that collusion. We need only note in passing that David Garland's (1985b) account of the formation of positivistic criminology ("the criminal's science") at the end of the 19th century shows convincingly that criminology was the product of the prison; of an ideology which individuated and differentiated the criminal; and of the "social desire to do so in a thorough and rigorous manner." We would divert too far from the trail of a framework for a history of women's imprisonment to pause to consider Garland's account of how criminology, in the formulation of its arguments during the period of penal crisis in late-19th-century Europe, colluded with government policy to control criminals (Garland, 1985c). There is no space here to examine his examples of "external factors," such as social policy requirements and penal politics, finding a discursive place within criminology's discourse without "theoretical warranty." Nor is there time to check the points at which "political desire" disrupted "theoretical logic." We can merely note his conclusion that criminology's "will to truth, such as it is, has been continually compromised by the will to power" (Garland, 1985a: 3–4). And as for penology, traditional or empirical penology, it is merely "technicist" — it deals only with the technical efficacy of specific practices, it narrows the field of inquiry, and it denies the connections of penal practices to "other social practices" (Garland and Young, 1983: 10–14).

Penology then, like criminology, is beyond reclamation: a Stanley-Cohen-style "cognitive remapping" (Cohen, 1985: 1) of the whole field is neither possible nor desirable. Moreover, as I have argued elsewhere, a "sense of history" — once thought to hold the key to revitalizing criminology — will not save it (Howe, 1986b). Not even a dramaturgical sense of history — one informed by an analysis utilizing a "theater model" — can redeem criminology (Howe, 1988). Consequently, we need to search for other discursive sites on which to construct a feminist history of women's imprisonment in Australia.

III

Two alternatives look promising. First, the sociology of social control — as developed by feminist scholars — provides valuable insights and methodological directives for a study of women's imprisonment. Most important, it reminds us that the social control of women takes many forms. As Carol Smart points out, it may be "internal or external, implicit or explicit, private or public, ideological or repressive." Indeed, the "primary sources" of such control are "outside or even beyond, judicial influence" — they are located within "seemingly innocuous social processes" (Smart and Smart, 1978: 1–2). From this perspective, a "model for the study of the structural coercion of women" must be built outside traditional criminological approaches to the question of women, crime, and punishment. The point of departure must be "women's material conditions" and the first issue is to "find a language in which women's experiences can be communicated and understood." Once we have a language, we can develop an analysis which shifts the focus from an etiological concern with female offenders to an understanding of "the coercion of privacy" — a coercion that restrains women to the point where we can speak of them "living their lives in a private prison" (Dahl and Snare, 1978).

The concept of the "private prison" is an important one for understanding the restraints placed on women's lives all along the "freedom" — imprisonment continuum. It suggests that an historical analysis of the social control of women should shift away from the formal custodial institutions to informal sites of social control. Yet although *Joann is you, Joann is me/Our prison is the whole society* (Freedman, 1981: 1), we must avoid the absurdity of infinite relativism: we must not forget that incarcerated women are more coerced than those outside the walls. We need to remember, too, that the history of women's imprisonment in Australia is still waiting to be written. It is, however, crucial to realize that the history of incarcerated women could (and should) incorporate feminist sociological conceptions of the social control of women. Pat Carlen's analysis of a Scottish women's prison is a case in point. When she came to write her definitive sociological study of the "meaning and moment" of women's imprisonment in Scotland, she strayed way outside the walls of the prison and the field of criminology. As she states, the meanings of women's imprisonment in Scotland

> are to be found within discursive forms and practices which, conventionally, are considered to be quite unrelated to penology — within, for example, the conventions of the family and the *kirk*; within traditional forms of public conviviality and ethics of domesticity and masculinity; within some peculiar absences in Scottish social work practices; within the ideological practices of contemporary psychiatry; and within some over-determined presences (e.g., alcohol, unemployment, poverty) within Scottish culture and society (Carlen, 1983: 5).

Although her approach is not historical, Carlen thus provides many points of departure for a study of the history of women's imprisonment in Australia.

Carlen's directives for a more broadly gauged analysis of criminalized women are echoed by Frances Heidensohn. In her book, *Women and Crime* (1985: 162–200), she claims that we have to "step outside the confines of criminological theories altogether" if we want to understand women and crime from a feminist perspective. Where once she argued for a reintegrated study of male and female crime within a new critical criminology, Heidensohn now advocates an "autonomous" approach along the lines taken by Pat Carlen. But rather than explore what this "autonomous" approach might look like, let us take note of the other inviting conceptual terrain for a history of women's imprisonment — the "revisionist" histories of social control, and of crime and punishment in particular.

Social Control

This article is not the place to review the impact of the convergence of social history and the sociology of crime which resulted in what Cohen and Scull have described as a "quantum leap" in the quality and quantity of work done in the field of social control by the new "revisionist" histories of the 1970s (Cohen and Scull, 1983: 1). It is important to note, however, that several of these innovative "revisionist" histories focused on the development of the prison system — notably those of Michel Foucault, Michael Ignatieff, and David Rothman. But we would divert too far away from our search for a theoretical framework for a study of women's imprisonment if we were to assess these different stories, each with their own "master theory" of how correctional changes occur (Cohen, 1985: 15). Neither do we have time to situate *them* historically. We should, however, briefly acknowledge that these stories were instrumental in transforming the study of punishment into a more sophisticated analysis of penality; that they demonstrated the contingency not only of criminology and penology but also of crime and punishment; and that they reconnected the study of crime to the state and its apparatus of social control. More broadly, these revisionist stories provided a general conception of the overall pattern of the penal complex in the 19th century. We should be grateful, too, that they paved the way for criminologists to rediscover *some* of their imagination about crime (Carson and Ditton, 1978:14).

Before we get too excited about the prospect of situating my proposed history of women's imprisonment on the edge of the revisionists' discursive site, two caveats must be placed on enthusiasm for their "new" social histories of crime and punishment. The first caveat was placed by some of the revisionist historians themselves, notably Ignatieff, who upon reconsideration of the revisionist work of the 1970s and his own *A Just Measure of Pain* (1978), asserted that the new social history of law and punishment had exaggerated the "centrality" of the state, the police, and the prison. His revised view — one which does not appear to be informed by highly relevant feminist analysis of social control — urges us to look more at informal control of rituals and practices, at the "whole invisible framework" of sanctions and regulation (Ignatieff, 1983: 97–100). The second, and related, caveat that must be placed on waxing enthusiastic about these new social histories is that they ignore women and, in this significant respect, are not so "new."

This formidable silence about the historical realities of women's imprisonment raises important historiographical questions about the best way to analyze the evolution of the prison system. First, we need to ask how broadly we should apply the findings of revisionist histories of male prisons — histories which have passed themselves off as general histories of crime and punishment (Rafter, 1985: 179–180). The answer is not self-evident. For in the process of theorization, the "master" theorists of penality ignored part of the object of analysis — namely women — while other aspects (namely male prisons) were "seized upon, expanded, and given pride of place in the theoretical analysis." In other words, they ignore the "overall configuration" of "*the* penal system" while according a privileged place to "particular sanctions" — namely, those applied to men (Garland and Young, 1983: 9–10). By assuming the "penal realm" to be a coherent unit, they have presented a "monolithic portrait" of "the" prison system which overlooks the crucial importance of "internal differentiation" of that "system" (*Ibid.*: 15; Rafter, 1985: 180). A second and related question, then, is: How will looking at difference — at "differentiation by gender" — challenge the findings of these male-focused histories, histories in which (as their apologists concede) gender remains "a neglected concept compared with class and power" (Cohen and Scull, 1983: 11)?

IV

Estelle Freedman and Nicole Hahn Rafter are among the few historians who have sought to find out. Their work has done much to reconstruct the historical realities of women's imprisonment in the United States. More generally, they have demonstrated how women's prisons reflected the "different contours of women's historical experience" and how their "unique origins and functions" raise important questions about the received history of "the" prison system. For Freedman (1981: 2), women prison reformers (their Sisters' Keepers) provide the focus; and women's history, rather than the history of prisons, provides the "central context." In contrast, Rafter's main concern was to correct the "skewed picture of the evolution of incarceration" that emerges from "even recent" male-focused prison histories — histories which "limit our access to a significant chapter" in women's history (Rafter, 1985: *xiii*).

In view of the paucity of historical studies of women's imprisonment, a list of her major findings is in order:

(1) Although the reformatories established between 1870 and 1930 played a crucial role in the development of the American women's prison system, this was only a partial picture; (2) the "custodial" model (which was more "masculine" because it resembled maximum security prisons for men) was the first of the two styles of women's prisons to develop and was more widely adopted than the reformatory across 19th-century America; (3) the almost exclusive focus on reformatories has therefore produced a picture of the women's prison system that is distorted and has obscured our understanding of the origins of the problems faced by that system today. Most importantly, this focus has blinded us to the development of a "bifurcated" women's prison system — with reformatory institutions for misdemeanants and custodial institutions for felons (Rafter, 1982: 261–256). At the same time, however, she shows that the establishment of the women's reformatory after 1870 was a "major development in prison history" because the new model "broke radically with male-orientated prison traditions, creating a set of feminized penal practices and extending state control over a population of young, working-class women convicted of minor sex-related offences" (Rafter, 1983: 288–290). (4) Finally, Rafter situates her study of the women's reformatory movement in the context of a variety of late-19th and early-20th-century social changes associated with immigration, urbanization, and the development of capitalism; with the broader institutionalization movement; with the evolution of the juvenile justice system (which provided a model for the new women's prison); with the growth of the social feminist and social purity movements (which were "just as influential as institutional developments") and, more

broadly, with changes in gender roles and the widening of class divisions (*Ibid.*: 305–306).

Rafter has contributed in significant ways to the process of producing the histories of women's imprisonment that she predicted would be written over the decade spanning 1980 to 1990. In 1980, she anticipated that scholarship would establish "an empirical foundation for theory about the punishment of women"; would "clarify the role played by female institutions" in the development of the whole prison system; and would "force us to rethink some of our assumptions about the incarceration process" (Rafter, 1980: 261–267).

Several observations are salient here. On the positive side, Rafter does provide some of these goods. She forces us to revise the revisionist historians' picture. For while she concedes to them that the emergence of the penitentiary was "one of the most dramatic innovations in this history of punishment," she reminds us that it was inhabited by women as well as men (Rafter, 1985: 3). She also forces us to rethink periodization. For example, the 1870s — when the penal treatment of women began to undergo a "revolutionary change" by breaking with custodialism to produce a unique model of prison (the women's reformatory) — must now loom large in any history of women's imprisonment (*Ibid.*: 23). And, the year 1933 — when the two types of women's prison merged on one site (at least in New York) — provides us with a date for the end of the bifurcated system and the beginning of the process that produced the "mixed code of custodialism and nurturance" which is the women's prison today (Rafter, 1983: 255–256). Thus, Rafter's ideas about the American system provide some obvious points for comparison. These have already been taken up by a recent history of women's imprisonment in Great Britain, which makes a favorable comparison of conditions for women in British prisons in the mid-19th century but which claims that in Britain, unlike America, penal arrangements for women changed very little in the last decades of that century (Dobash, Dobash, and Gutteridge, 1986: 60–61).

On the negative side, we should note the shortcomings of these recent histories, which have been designed to show how class and gender assumptions shaped the imprisonment of women over time (*Ibid.*: 10–11). First, they fail to provide methodological directives beyond a comparative analysis which privileges men and male institutions. Rafter's *modus operandi* is to compare historical differences between the incarceration of men and women — a comparative project that for her "*necessarily* starts with prisons that mainly held men" (Rafter, 1985: *xix*, emphasis added). If this is so, then men and male prisons necessarily remain the norms from which women and women's prisons deviate. Second, the "theory" about the punishment of women that was supposed to materialize from her study also leaves something to be desired. Her theoretical conclusions appear to be that changes in gender roles and class relationships influenced the women's reformatory movement which, interestingly, is presented as a struggle between two groups of women: middle-class women, who needed to maintain a cheap pool of domestic labor, and working-class women, who needed to be taught "a new concept of womanhood" (*Ibid.*: 175). Strangely, neither working-class women nor middle-class men have agency here — a double falsification of women's relative power. Rafter's only other theoretical conclusion appears to be that we should pay attention to "variations" within the prison system — variations such as "period, region, and inmates' sex, race, and age" (*Ibid.*: 180). Thus, women finally emerge from this history as a "variation." They are not a subject in their own right.

There are, then, clear limits to the transformative power of this kind of feminist prison history. Rafter has revised the revisionist picture of the evolution of the prison system by including women, but adding women to revisionist prison history (women, moreover, who are struggling against each other) does not challenge the androcentric nature of the revisionists' theoretical framework. It does not disturb the newly discovered "master patterns" of 19th-century penality in Western Europe. Nor does it accomplish a paradigm shift such as that achieved by the revisionists when they exposed traditional prison history as hopelessly teleologically biased and thus, effectively, "ahistorical history" (Cohen and Scull, 1983; Mayer, 1983: 22). Ultimately, Rafter's women's prison history remains auxiliary history — a "variation" of a male-focused historiography. It does not move us beyond a revision of the revisionists. Consequently, following her model can only lead to an application of a revised ("add-in-women") revisionist framework to the historical records in relation to women's imprisonment in Australia. This would amount to little more than a progression from the "repetitive discourse of criminology" (Foucault, 1977: 18) to the repetitive discourse of gender-revised prison history revisionism.

Where, then, can we turn to now? New developments in feminist epistemology provide some important clues. Indeed, recent feminist challenges to hegemonic discourses have ensured that a feminist history of women's imprisonment will now have to take a wholly different form from those written without benefit of their insights.

V

Feminist theorizing has come a long way since the 1970s. Previously, feminist scholars were preoccupied with the inclusion of women, that is, with redressing their omission and placing them "on an equal theoretical footing with men in existing theory." Now, disenchantment with such a "domesticated feminism," one which failed to raise questions not already asked, has sounded the death-knell of "sexually particular theory that masquerades as universalism" (Pateman, 1986: 2–10). Feminist researchers are now challenging the whole research enterprise as it has been defined by "male-stream" theory. This new challenge was born of the realization that what counts as knowledge must be grounded in experience and that women's experience "systematically differs from the male experience on which knowledge claims have been based" (Harding and Hintikka, 1983: *ix–x*). The subsequent interrogation of patriarchal "knowledge" — the profound questioning of what actually counts as knowledge — has been characterized as "one of the most subversive challenges to patriarchal theory" (Gross, 1986: 194). More modestly, it has been described as a shift from research on women to research for women — a shift that entails a "breaking out" of existing conceptualizations (Stanley and Wise, 1983: 29–30) and a developing of strategies for social change which, among other things, will "bring feminists into positions of power inside academia" (Duelli Klein, 1983: 97).

In the 1980s we have been confronted by a more "fundamental project" than that of merely including women: the goal now is nothing less than the rooting out of "sexist distortions and perversions" in epistemology, metaphysics, methodology, and the philosophy of science. This "fundamental" project actually breaks down into two complementary projects: the "anti-sexist" or "deconstructive" project (which identifies and deconstructs male perspectives on "human" experiences) and the "reconstructive project" (which identifies "distinctive aspects of women's experience" that will provide resources for "the construction of more representatively human understanding") (Harding and Hintikka, 1983: *x*). This is tantamount to a call for a "revolution in epistemology" — a new theory of knowledge — in which women will become the subjects and producers of knowledge and not mere revisionists of patriarchal theory. Put simply, it amounts to a demand for autonomy: "We need to be able to see what there is for us rather than what we have been told there is" (Sutherland, 1986: 155).

Today, feminist theory still appears to be "provisionally located at the interface of the negative, anti-sexist project and a more positive speculative, project" (Gross, 1986: 198). In its search for a new discursive place, this theory has inevitably had to confront the question of method. Although this is not the place to join in the controversy over whether the emergent rules of feminist method — for example, the rule that those investigated should remain active subjects of the research process — constitute a distinctive feminist method (Cain, 1986a: 5), it is pertinent to note here that these questions of methodology are bound up with the development of the concept of "standpoint" from which it is hoped an adequate feminist social theory will emerge. The concept of "standpoint" — variously described as a "politically activated perspective" (Harding, 1983: 321), as "an epistemological tool for understanding and opposing all forms of domination," as an "engaged vision" which "carries a historically liberatory role" (Hartsock, 1983: 283–285), and as a theoretically conscious site in the sex/gender or class structure (Cain

1986b: 4–5) — is seen to be the key concept for the development of a distinctive feminist epistemology that will be grounded in women's experiences and labor. The concept of "standpoint" — the standpoint specificity of knowledge — is today providing feminist researchers with an empowering sense of the potentiality of a new feminist epistemology to offer "a transformative knowledge of the social" (Rose, 1986: 171).

Feminist philosophers have put these transforming epistemological questions on the Australian research agenda. They argue, convincingly, that for feminists working in *any* academic discipline, "the most pressing difficulty in relation to affirming the presence of women is the theoretical exclusions" implicit in prevailing discourses: the task ahead is therefore to create "other modes of conceptualizing human culture" that do not render women passive or invisible (Gatens, 1988: 69). A crucial first step in the development of a new theory based on women's experiences is that of effecting "radical ruptures and displacements in socially dominant knowledges" — that is, challenging the phallocentrism of those knowledges. The "foundational reliance" of those knowledges on phallocentric norms, which conflate the two sexes into a single universal model, one which is "congruent only with the masculine," and in which women are "construed on the model of masculine," must be exposed. More specifically, the "inherent masculinity" of universal models must be deconstructed by an analysis which shows "how concepts, values, and methods have been insidiously related to masculinity" and their "excluded negative counterparts" connected to "a devalorised femininity" (Grosz, 1988: 92–96). In short, this deconstruction process must demonstrate that "patriarchal discourses are not neutral, universal, or unquestionable models," but rather, "one of the effects of the specific position occupied by men" (Gross, 1986: 198).

Today, in 1990, this process is well under way. We are in the midst of a movement — a transition from the anti-sexist equality feminism of the 1970s to an autonomous feminism that specifies the masculinity of theoretical phallocentrism. It is "a movement from a sixties to an eighties political consciousness" — a movement transforming women from objects into subjects of knowledge (Grosz, 1988: 96–97). This new, "autonomous" feminist theory is profoundly unsettling to masculinist theory because it challenges its purported "objectivism" by openly avowing the masculinity of its assumptions and methods. Equally disturbing, it openly admits its own "perspectivism." Autonomous feminist researchers openly admit their own partial and invested position in the production of knowledges: they openly admit their own position is "context- and observer-dependent" — that is, "historically, politically and sexually motivated." Indeed, autonomous feminist "in(ter)ventions aim at establishing an openly sexualized body of knowledges" (Grosz, 1988: 100–103). One final point: this new feminist theory is neither relativist nor absolutist. Rather it is "relational": it recognizes power relations and "the necessity of occupying a position, particularly a changeable one, with regard to the socio-political context of theory production." From all this Grosz concludes:

> for men to take back what they have produced and for us to see that this is only half of the productive possibilities of knowledge, perception, or practice is itself one of the most dramatic revolutions to have occurred in Western knowledges (*Ibid.*: 103).

VI

I remain perplexed as to what all this means for writing a history of women's imprisonment in Australia. Certainly it will not mean writing a history of convicts *and* convict women — a history in which it could be said that "one person in seven" transported to the penal colonies were women and that "doubtless some were" (whores) (Hughes, 1986: 71). What I have in mind is something more along the lines of Paula-Jane Byrne's (1986) insightful and challenging study of women and the criminal law in early-19th century New South Wales in which she shows that women were punished differently from men. While men were corporally punished and minimally incarcerated because of the value of their labour, women, whose labour was devalued, were imprisoned. The female factory at Parramatta was, she says emphatically, a place of incarceration for women. Clearly, this research is of profound historiographical significance because it demonstrates that the emphasis placed on imprisoning women "placed them close to the development of the prison." Women, Byrne concludes, "were closer to the development of incarceration in the sentences they received and were thus closer to the development of the prison as an institution" than men (*Ibid.*).

Feminist historians apprised of the "revolution" in feminist theorization provide further guidance. They advise that we write history which:

> looks first at women, not in relation to men, but as autonomous shapers and creators of meaning, makers of our own history, within the bounds of our physical, psychological, and social circumstances (Matthews, 1984: 19).

We should also attempt to "account for the silence of those who have not registered themselves in historical discourses" — the silence of women, of the institutionalized, of all those who are "effectively the non-discursive" (Allen, 1986: 184). Surely women prisoners are eminently qualified for such research. But without access to their records, I cannot even know whether the evidence is available for such a project. Still less can I ascertain whether I share their standpoint and whether, consequently, they are "entitled" to be active subjects in the research project (Cain, 1986a: 16).

Ultimately though, I will have to take a position on the status of my researched population, on my methodology and, crucially, on androcentric histories. Without wishing to commit myself to a position on the continuum of feminist research positions — from accommodation to outright rejection of the male-focused tradition (Sutherland, 1986: 147) — I will say here that a disdainful rejection of Foucault as simply phallocentric, would be counterproductive. And I say this despite the fact that he is, indisputably, "a profoundly androcentric writer" (Morris, 1979: 152) and also despite the fact that (and certainly not because) a male critic asserts that: "to write today about punishment and classification without Foucault is like talking about the unconscious without Freud" (Cohen, 1985: 10). This is not the place to create a usable Foucault for feminist historians. It suffices to say that he does provide a smorgasbord of possibilities. One of the most crucial is his mode of historical analysis — his "genealogy" — which concerns itself with phenomena (women prisoners?) lacking a history, and which aims to "disrupt common conceptions about events and practices," but "provides no place for 'speaking for' the people" (Smart, 1983a: 82). Also crucially relevant are his "methodological precautions" inviting us to study "power at its extremities" and in its more "regional and local forms" where it becomes "less legal"; to concern ourselves not with conscious intention but with "the point of application of power"; to ask "how things work at the level of ongoing subjugation, at the level of those continuous and uninterrupted processes which subject our bodies..."; to see power as a "network"; and to attempt an "ascending analysis of power" starting with its "infinitesimal mechanisms" — "mechanisms of exclusion" that include "the apparatuses of surveillance, the medicalization of sexuality, of madness, of delinquency, all the micro-mechanisms of power..." (Foucault, 1980: 96–102; Smart, 1983b).

In short, Foucault's methodological directive to turn away from the "juridical edifice" and state institutions (1980: 102) — to dispense with the "juridico-discursive" concept of power (1984: 82) — is obviously relevant to an analysis of the punishment of women which, historically, has been inflicted outside the criminal justice and penal systems. So, too, is his analysis of "the fundamental implications of power-knowledge and their historical transformations" — an analysis which provides a more productive approach to "the articulation of the struggles of those resistant objects of knowledge, 'women'" (Morris, 1979: 159). Finally, his analysis of the formation of the disciplinary society and the establishment of a "carceral network," understood as "an extension of surveillance" and the "power of normalization" throughout society (Foucault, 1977: 300–308), connects in self-evident ways to feminist sociologies of the social control of women.

More specifically, a feminist interrogation of Foucault relevant to the writing of a history of women's imprisonment must include the following

Foucauldian issues: the role of the prison in the disciplining of women; the question of the diffusion of "discipline" itself; and the concept of "bio-power" (Foucault, 1984: 140–143), particularly its manifestation in the "hysterization" of women's bodies (*Ibid.*: 104). Such an interrogation would benefit from his directive to analyze institutions from the standpoint of power relations, rather than vice versa and the reminder that "the fundamental point of anchorage" of power relationships, "even if they are embodied and crystallized in an institution, is to be found outside the institution" (Foucault, 1982: 222). But at the same time, feminist analysis would have to question Foucault's already questioned periodization — how relevant is it to women's lives? Moreover, if the role played by the prison in the larger story of the disciplining of men's lives has already been questioned (Donnelly, 1986: 24), we will need to determine whether it is indeed the prison that should play the central role in our account of the disciplining of women. We might well chose another institution as the "exemplary instance of 'discipline'" (*Ibid.*) — perhaps psychiatric hospitals or, especially, heterosexuality.

Ultimately, I will have to take a position on the politics of history. Having cowered so long behind disclaimers and uncertainty, let me conclude by coming out as an historian committed to politicizing history. We have been warned, from a masculinist perspective, of the dangers of overpoliticizing history: the "veritable anarchy" of "usable pasts" allegedly commits us to an infinite relativism (Tomlins, 1985: 145–146). Alternatively, we have been warned, from a feminist perspective, that feminist research which re-examines the evidence with a view to locating "the silences or non-discursive domain against which such evidence is framed" does not produce the kind of history which professional historians regard as valid (Allen, 1986: 188). I have three connecting responses to this. First, the "revolution" which is transforming history's project is mischaracterized as an "anti-relativist" (read, presumably, absolutist), "anti-scholastic" (read, presumably, subjective and biased) revolution (Tomlins, 1985: 145). Rather, it is a feminist epistemological revolution which openly admits that it occupies a position — that of the sexed subject (Grosz, 1988: 100). Second, it is the task of a new kind of history to discover ways of giving voice to the "not-said" and of privileging that non-discursive domain where women prisoners, among other, are out of hearing. Moreover, just such a new kind of history — one written "from the bottom up" in order to give voice to the historically "inarticulate" — has been written for the last 20 years and has come to be recognized as valid. Third, prison history is irredeemably interventionist. Just as the desire to transform the study of punishment into the social analysis of penality has, and should be, "characterized by a healthy appreciation of the need to discuss policy" and to "intervene in the practical," so the desire to write theoretically informed prison history must be "irrevocably tied to practice" (Garland and Young, 1983: 5; Howe, 1986b:

20–23). That is, in the final analysis, we have to take sides. After all, history either is, or is not, "primarily the story of whom and how" (Genovese and Genovese, 1976: 219).

NOTES

1. The Office of Corrections, the Public Record Office, and, now, the Attorney-General of Victoria have denied me access to the historical records relating to women's imprisonment in this state. The stated reason for thus closing off the possibility of a history of Victoria's women prisoners — the "private and personal" nature of the documents — provides yet another instance of the coercive implications for women of the private/public dichotomy.

REFERENCES

Allen, J.
1986   "Evidence and Silence: Feminism and the Limits of History." C. Pateman and
                E. Gross, (eds.), Feminist Challenges: Social and Political Theory. Sydney:
                Allen and Unwin.
Byrne, P.
1986   "Women and the Criminal Law in New South Wales, 1810–1821." D. Kirkby
                (ed.), Law and History in Australia, Vol. 2.
Cain, M.
1986a   "Realism, Feminism, Methodology and Law." International Journal of the So-
                ciology of Law 14.
1986b   "Socio-legal Studies and Social Justice for Women: Some Working Notes on
                a Method." Paper presented at the Australian Law and Society Conference,
                Brisbane.
Carlen, P.
1983   Women's Imprisonment. London: Routledge and Kegan Paul.
Carson, W.G. and J. Ditton
1978   "The Tyranny of the Present: Post-War British Criminology and the Redis-
                covery to the Past, and the 'Dinosaur' Theory of History." Unpublished paper.
Cohen, S.
1985   Visions of Social Control: Crime, Punishment and Classification: Oxford
                Polity Press.
Cohen, S. and A. Scull (eds.)
1983   Social Control and the State. Oxford: Martin Robinson.
Cousins, M.
1980   "*Men's rea*: A Note on Sexual Differences, Criminology, and the Law." P.
                Carlen and M. Collinson (eds.), Radical Issues in Criminology. Oxford: Mar-
                tin Robinson.
Dahl, T.V. and A. Snare
1978   "The Coercion of Privacy: A Feminist Perspective." C. Smart and B. Smart
                (eds.), Women, Sexuality and Social Control. London: Routledge and Kegan
                Paul.
Dobash, R.P., R.E. Dobash, and S. Gutteridge
1986   The Imprisonment of Women. London: Basil Blackwell.

Donnelly, M.
  1986   "Foucault's Genealogy of the Human Sciences." M. Gane (ed.), Towards a
                  Critique of Foucault. London: Routledge and Kegan Paul.
Duelli Klein, R.
  1983   "How to Do What We Want to Do: Thoughts about Feminist Methodology."
                  Bowles and Duelli Klein (eds.), Theories of Women's Studies. London:
                  Routledge and Kegan Paul.
Foucault, M.
  1984   The History of Sexuality, Vol. 1. Harmondsworth, Middlesex: Peregrine
                  Press.
  1982   The Subject and Power. H.L. Dreyfus and P. Rabinow, Michel Foucault: Be-
                  yond Stucturalism and Hermenentics. Chicago: University of Chicago Press.
  1980   Power/Knowledge: Selected Interviews and Other Writings, 1972–1977. C.
                  Gordon (ed.), Brighton, Sussex: Harvester.
  1977   Discipline and Punish. London: Penguin.
Freedman, E.
  1981   Their Sisters' Keepers: Women's Prison Reform in America, 1830–1930. Ann
                  Arbor: University of Michigan Press.
Garland, D.
  1985a   "Politics and Policy in Criminological Discourse: A Study of Tendentious
                  Reasoning and Rhetoric." International Journal of the Sociology of Law 1.
  1985b   "The Criminal and His Science." The British Journal of Criminology 109.
  1985c   Punishment and Welfare: A History of Penal Strategies. Aldershot, Hants:
                  Gower.
Garland, D. and P. Young
  1983   The Power to Punish. London: Heinemann.
Gatens, M.
  1988   "Towards a Feminist Philosophy of the Body." B. Caine, E. Grosz, and M.
                  Lepervanche (eds.), Crossing Boundaries: Feminisms and the Critique of
                  Knowledges. Sydney: Allen and Unwin.
Gelsthorpe, L.
  1986   "Towards a Sceptical Look at Sexism." International Journal of the Sociology
                  of Law 14.
Genovese, E.D. and E. Fox-Genovese
  1976   "The Political Crisis of Social History: A Marxist Perspective." Journal of So-
                  cial History 9,2 (Fall): 205–220.
Gross, E.
  1986   "What Is Feminist Theory?" C. Pateman and E. Gross (eds.), Feminist Chal-
                  lenges: Social and Political Theory. Sydney: Allen and Unwin.
Grosz, E.A.
  1988   "The In(ter)vention of Feminist Knowledges." B. Caine, E. Grosz, and M.
                  Lepervanche (eds.), Crossing Boundaries: Feminisms and the Critique of
                  Knowledges. Sydney: Allen and Unwin.
Harding, S.
  1983   "Why Has the Sex/Gender System Become Visible Only Now?" S. Harding
                  and M.B. Hintikka (eds.), Discovering Reality: Feminist Perspectives on
                  Epistemology, Metaphysics, Methodology, and Philosophy of Science. Lon-
                  don: D. Reidel Publishing.
Harding, S. and M.B. Hintikka (eds.)
  1983   Discovering Reality: Feminist Perspectives on Epistemology, Metaphysics,
                  Methodology, and Philosophy of Science. London: D. Reidel Publishing.
Hartsock, N.C.M.
  1983   "The Feminist Standpoint: Developing Ground for a Specifically Feminist
                  Historical Materialism." S. Harding and M.B. Hintikka (eds.), Discovering
                  Reality. London: D. Reidel Publishing.

Heidenshohn, F.
    1985   Women and Crime. London: Macmillan.
Howe, A.
    1988   "Toward Critical Criminology and Beyond." Law in Context 6,2.
    1986a   "Equal Justice for Women Prisoners: Why Settle for Less." Refractory Girl
                     29.
    1986b   "Politicising Social History: The Bayard Treason Trial, a Case Study." D.
                     Kirkby (ed.), Law and History in Australia, Vol. 3.
Hughes, R.
    1986   The Fatal Shore. New York: Alfred A. Knopf.
Ignatieff, M.
    1983   "State, Civil Society and Total Institutions: A Critique of Recent Social Histo-
                     ries of Punishment." In S. Cohen and A. Scull, Social Control and the State.
                     Oxford: Martin Robinson.
    1978   A Just Measure of Pain. London: Macmillan.
Leonard, E.B.
    1982   Women, Crime and Society: A Critique of Criminological Theory. New York:
                     Longman.
Matthews, J.J.
    1984   Good and Mad Women. Sydney: George Allen and Unwin.
Mayer, J.A.
    1983   "Notes Toward a Working Definition of Social Control in Historical Analy-
                     sis." S. Cohen and A. Scull (eds.), Social Control and the State. Oxford:
                     Robinson.
Morris, M.
    1979   "The Pirate's Fiancée." Morris, M. and Patton (eds.), P. Michel Foucault:
                     Power, Truth, Strategy. Sydney: Peral Publications.
O'Brien, M.
    1986   "Hegemony and Superstructure: A Feminist Critique of Neo-Marxism." R.
                     Hamilton and M. Barrett (eds.), The Politics of Diversity. London: Verso.
Pateman, C.
    1986   "Introduction: The Theoretical Subversiveness of Feminism." C. Pateman and
                     E. Gross (eds.), Feminist Challenges: Social and Political Theory. Sydney:
                     Allen and Unwin.
Rafter, N. Hahn
    1985   Partial Justice: Women in State Prisons, 1800–1935. Boston: Northeastern
                     University Press.
    1983   "Chastizing the Unchaste: Social Control Functions of a Women's Reforma-
                     tory, 1894–1931." Cohen and Scull (eds.), Social Control and the State. Ox-
                     ford: Martin Robinson.
    1982   Hard Times: Custodial Prisons for Women. N. Rafter and E. Stanko (eds.),
                     Judge, Lawyer, Victim, Thief. Boston: Northeastern University Press.
    1980   "Matrons and Molls: The Study of Women's Prison History." J.A. Inciaridi
                     and C.E. Faupel (eds.), History and Crime: Implications for Criminal Justice
                     Policy. Beverly Hills: Sage.
Rafter, N. and E.A. Stanko
    1982   Judge, Lawyer, Victim, Thief: Women Gender Roles, and Criminal Justice.
                     Boston: Northeastern University Press.
Rose, H.
    1986   "Women's Work: Women's Knowledge." J. Mitchell and A. Oakley (eds.),
                     What Is Feminism: A Re-examination. New York: Pantheon.
Rothman, D.
    1980   Conscience and Convenience: The Asylum and Its Alternatives in Progressive
                     America. Boston: Little, Brown.
Sheridan, A.
    1980   Michel Foucault: The Will to Truth. London: Tavistock.

Smart, B.
    1983a   Foucault, Marxism and Critique. London: Routledge and Kegan Paul.
    1983b   "A Review of Foucault's Geneological Analysis." D. Garland and P. Young
                (eds.), The Power to Punish. London: Heinemann.
Smart, C.
    1977   "The New Female Criminal: Reality or Myth?" British Journal of Criminology
                19.
    1976   Women, Crime and Criminology. London: Routledge and Kegan Paul.
Smart, C. and B. Smart
    1978   Women, Sexuality and Social Control. London: Routledge.
Stanley, L. and S. Wise
    1983   Breaking Out: Feminist Consciousness and Feminist Research. London:
                Routledge.
Sutherland, C.
    1986   "Feminist Research: A Voice of Our Own." B. Marchant and B. Wearing
                (eds.), Gender Reclaimed: Women in Social Work. Sydney: Hale and
                Ironmonger.
Tomlins, C.L.
    1985   "Whose Law? What Order? Historicist Interventions in the 'War Against
                Crime.'" Law in Context 3.

Name Index